The Printer Bible

Scott Foerster

The Printer Bible

Copyright © 1990 by Que® Corporation

All rights reserved. Printed in the United States of America. No part of this book may be used or reproduced in any form or by any means, or stored in a database or retrieval system, without prior written permission of the publisher except in the case of brief quotations embodied in critical articles and reviews. Making copies of any part of this book for any purpose other than your own personal use is a violation of United States copyright laws. For information, address Que Corporation, 11711 N. College Ave., Carmel, IN 46032.

Library of Congress Catalog No.: 89-63570

ISBN 0-88022-512-2

This book is sold *as is*, without warranty of any kind, either express or implied, respecting the contents of this book, including but not limited to implied warranties for the book's quality, performance, merchantability, or fitness for any particular purpose. Neither Que Corporation nor its dealers or distributors shall be liable to the purchaser or any other person or entity with respect to any liability, loss, or damage caused or alleged to be caused directly or indirectly by this book.

92 91   8 7 6 5 4 3

Interpretation of the printing code: the rightmost double-digit number is the year of the book's printing; the rightmost single-digit number, the number of the book's printing. For example, a printing code of 90-1 shows that the first printing of the book occurred in 1990.

DEDICATION

To water polo, for giving me the successful experiences I needed in life to build an ego. In particular, I dedicate this book to Harold (Hal) Hevener and Page Remillard, my coaches.

Publishing Director

Lloyd J. Short

Acquisitions Editor

Karen A. Bluestein

Product Director

Karen A. Bluestein

Book Design and Production

Dan Armstrong
Bill Basham
Brad Chinn
Don Clemons
Sally Copenhaver
Tom Emrick
Dennis Hager
Corinne Harmon
Bill Hurley
Becky Imel
Jodi Jensen
Kathy Keehn
David Kline
Larry Lynch
Lori A. Lyons
Jennifer Matthews
Cindy Phipps
Joe Ramon
Dennis Sheehan
Louise Shinault
Bruce Steed
Mary Beth Wakefield
Jenny Watson

Developmental Editor

Shelley O'Hara

Production Editor

Kelly D. Dobbs

Editors

Jo Anna Arnott
Fran Blauw
Kelly Currie
Jeannine Freudenberger
Daniel Schnake

Technical Editor

James T. Karney

Editorial Assistant

Renée Ackermann

Indexer

Joelynn Gifford

Composed in Garamond and Excellent #47 by Que Corporation.

ABOUT THE AUTHOR

Scott Foerster

Scott Foerster received a masters degree in engineering from Harvey Mudd College and Claremont Graduate School. He has written a word processing program and managed the service center of a ComputerLand retail store. He taught electronics at Howard Community College for five years. Currently, he is a consultant and lecturer on microcomputers, data communications, and local area networks. He is married, has four children, and lives in the Washington, D.C., area.

Contents at a Glance

Introduction 1

Part I   The Basics

Chapter 1	The Information Process: from Keyboard to Printer	13
Chapter 2	The Information Process: from Printer to Paper................	39
Chapter 3	How the Printer Interprets Data	81
Chapter 4	Font Basics................................	125
Chapter 5	Printer Hardware Features	161
Chapter 6	Printer Software Features	237

Part II   Printer Setup and Management

Chapter 7	Making a Purchase Decision...................	287
Chapter 8	Installing and Testing Printers	317
Chapter 9	Configuring PC Applications...................	363

Part III   The Publishing Challenge

Chapter 10	Typesetting	433
Chapter 11	PostScript Printers	471

Part IV   Maintenance and Troubleshooting

Chapter 12	Isolating Problems and Finding Solutions.........	503
Chapter 13	Solving Serial and Parallel Interface Problems.................................	529
Chapter 14	Troubleshooting	553
Appendix A	Programming Command Language Reference	589
Appendix B	Printer Vendor List........................	613
Appendix C	Font Vendor List..........................	617
Appendix D	Symbol Names of Characters	623
Glossary	....	653
Index	....	665

TABLE OF CONTENTS

Introduction 1
   This Book's Objectives 1
   What Is and What Is Not in This Book 2
   How To Use This Book 4
      Troubleshooting Tips 4
      Cautions 5
      Hints 5
   How This Book Is Organized 5
      Part I 5
      Part II 6
      Part III 7
      Part IV 8
      Appendixes 8

I   The Basics

1   **The Information Process: from Keyboard to Printer** 13
   A Brief History of Printers 13
   Activating Printer Features 17
   Comparing How Programs Use Printers 19
      Software That Provides No Support 21
      Page Setup Software 22
      Software That Displays Printer-Specific Commands 22
      Printing with Generic Printer Commands 23
   Observing Printer File Characteristics 25
   Configuring Applications for Your Printer 29
   Predicting What Printers Do with Arriving Data ... 33
   Chapter Summary 36
   In the Next Chapter 37

2   **The Information Process: from Printer to Paper** 39
   Turning On the Printer 39
      The Power Supply 39
      Test Programs 41
      Switch and Button Positions 42
   Transmitting Data 43

Parallel Interface	43
Serial Interface	45
Video Interface	46
HPIB Interface	47
SCSI Interface	48
Receiving and Processing Data	48
Storing Data in Printer Memory	49
Developing the Image	50
Moving the Paper	52
Tractor Feed	53
Friction Feed	55
Cut-Sheet Feeders	56
Paper Trays	58
Moving the Print Head	60
Using Pulleys or Screws	61
Controlling the Location of the Print Head	63
Using Line Printers	65
Printing the Data	66
Laser Printers	67
LED and LCS Printers	69
Dot-Matrix Printers	72
Inkjet Printers	74
Daisywheel Printers	75
Thermal Printers	76
Dealing with Print-Head Alignment Problems	77
Chapter Summary	79
In the Next Chapter	80

3 How the Printer Interprets Data — 81

Describing Bits and Bytes	82
Using Decimal Notation	84
Using Hexadecimal Notation	85
Using ASCII Notation	86
Understanding Printer Modes	87
Graphics Mode	88
Object Mode	92
Plotter Objects	93
Object Printers	94
Character Mode	95
Using Character Sets	96
Character Set Introduction	97
Character Set Standards	97
Line-Draw Characters	102

  Dingbat Characters. 105
  Symbol Character Set 106
  Characters of Other Languages 106
  Scientific and Mathematic Symbols. 111
  Character Set Problems. 111
 Generating Printer Bytes from a Keyboard 115
  Using the Keyboard. 116
  Using the Shift, Ctrl, and Alt Keys. 116
  Using Basic, Pascal, and dBASE 117
  Using 1-2-3 118
  Using WordPerfect. 119
   Generating a Symbol Found on the Keyboard. 120
   Generating a Symbol Not Found on the Keyboard. . . 120
   Generating a Symbol in the Videoboard
    Character Set 120
   Generating a Symbol in the Printer Character Set . . . 121
  Using the Macintosh 121
  Solving Problems When Sending Specific Bytes
   to the Printer 122
 Chapter Summary. 123
 In the Next Chapter. 124

4 Font Basics 125

 Defining Fonts, Typefaces, and Typeface Families. 125
  Font Families. 126
  Typeface Characteristics 127
  Font Features 127
 Understanding Font Characteristics 128
  Font Height. 128
   Lines Per Inch 128
   Point Size 130
  Character Width. 131
   Fixed Spacing. 131
   Proportional Spacing. 132
   Lining Up Columns 134
   Centering Lines 135
   Right Justification 136
   Kerning. 137
  Font Attributes 137
   Italic. 138
   Bold. 138
   Underlining. 139
   White Letters 141

   Filled... 142
   Strikeout and Redline........................... 142
   Outline... 142
   Stretched and Curved............................ 143
   Comparing Draft and Letter Quality.............. 143
  Typeface Differences................................ 143
   Serifs.. 143
   Descenders...................................... 144
   Ligatures....................................... 144
   X-Height.. 144
   Regularity...................................... 145
Purchasing Fonts.. 145
  Screen and Printer Fonts............................ 145
  Fixed and Scalable Fonts............................ 146
  Expanded and Compressed Printing.................... 146
  Landscape and Portrait Fonts........................ 147
  Pros and Cons of Fixed Fonts........................ 147
   Dot-Matrix Fonts to Laser Fonts................. 148
   Equal Horizontal and Vertical Resolution........ 150
  Fixed Fonts from Scalable fonts..................... 150
   Font-Generation Software........................ 150
   Applications and Fixed Fonts.................... 151
   Object-Mode Devices............................. 151
  Scalable Font Types................................. 151
   High-Resolution Fonts........................... 152
   Medium-Resolution Fonts......................... 152
   Low-Resolution (Hinted) Fonts................... 152
  Finding Font Sources................................ 152
   Font Creation................................... 153
   Macintosh Fonts................................. 153
   PC Fonts.. 154
Managing Fonts.. 154
  Storing Fonts....................................... 154
  Downloading Fonts................................... 155
   Downloading to Printer Ram...................... 155
   Downloading to a Printer's Hard Disk............ 156
   Downloading Manually............................ 156
   Downloading Using Batch Files................... 156
   Downloading On Demand........................... 157
   Printer-Initiated Downloading................... 157
  Font Numbering...................................... 158
Looking into the Future of Fonts........................ 159
Chapter Summary... 160
In the Next Chapter..................................... 160

5 Printer Hardware Features 161

Reviewing Printer Requirements 161
Reviewing General Features 163
   Specifying Paper Sizes 163
   Printing Mailing Labels 165
   Assessing Font Needs and Upgrades 166
      Upgrading in the PC World..................... 166
      Upgrading in the Macintosh World 167
   Supporting the IBM-Character Set................... 168
   Defining Interface Types.......................... 168
      Interface Characteristics...................... 169
      Printer Interfaces............................ 170
      Serial Interfaces or RS-232.................... 171
      Local Talk or RS-422......................... 172
      Centronics 172
      Epson/IBM................................. 173
      SCSI 174
      The Hewlett-Packard Interface Bus 175
      Video Interfaces............................. 176
      Multiple Interface Options..................... 178
   Investigating Front-Panel Features................... 178
      Ease of Use................................ 180
      Reset Features 180
      Using Built-In Forms and Other Features 182
   Purchasing Computer Furniture 183
   Reviewing Printer Manuals........................ 183
   Checking the Printer Warranty 183
   Calculating the Mean Time between Failure........... 184
Determining the Necessary Printer Resolution 185
   Text Resolution 185
   Scanner Resolution............................. 186
   Resolution and Memory 188
Measuring Speed................................... 189
   Character-Mode Speed.......................... 191
   Graphics-Mode Speed 192
   Object-Mode Speed 194
Reviewing Dot-Matrix Features........................ 195
   Printing Mailing Labels and Other Output Types....... 196
   Reviewing Tractor-Feed Options.................... 197
   Tearing Paper 197
   Switching from Hand-Feed to Tractor-Feed............ 202
   Using the Paper-Out Switch....................... 202
   Using Cut-Sheet Feeders and Paper Trays 204

Cleaning the Printer	205
Changing Ribbons	205
Varying Fonts	206
Locating Ports, Data Cables, and Power Cords	206
Controlling Printer Noise	207
Noting Temperature Ratings	207
Reviewing Inkjet Printers	207
Comparing Paper and Ink Costs	208
Determining the Resolution	208
Warming Up the Printer	208
Considering a Laser Alternative	209
Reviewing Laser Printer Engines	210
Engine Model	210
Engine Type	210
Engine Life	211
Duty Cycle	211
Resolution	212
Speed	212
Stacking Pages in the Right Order	213
Paper Weight, Thickness, and Smoothness	214
Paper Jams	215
Paper Chemistry	216
Paper Trays	216
Envelope Feeder	216
Manual Feed	217
Replacement Supplies	218
Font Cartridge Slots	218
Blacker Blacks	218
Turn-On Time	219
Considering Replacement Supplies	219
Reviewing Features Added to Laser Engines	222
Memory	222
Fonts	223
Font Cartridges	223
Paper Trays	223
Front Panel	224
Weight	224
Dimensions	224
Ports	225
Reviewing Object-Printer Features	226
Fonts	226
PC Slots and Ports	226
Horsepower	226
Microprocessors	227

Clock Speed	227
Character or Graphics Mode	227
Start-Up Page	228
Shades of Gray	229
Reviewing Plotter Features	229
Interface	230
Speed	230
Paper Size	230
Resolution	230
Pen Movement	231
Single versus Multipen	232
Pen Tips	232
Types of Paper	232
Scanner	233
Plotter Emulation	233
Chapter Summary	233
In the Next Chapter	235

6 Printer Software Features 237

Features of Printer ROM Software	237
Solving Font and Memory Problems	238
Assessing Emulation Quality	240
Features of Printer Programming Languages	243
Job Control	244
Indicating Error States	245
Handling Macros	246
Checking Printer Direction	247
Entering Carriage Returns	248
Querying the Printer	248
Page Control	250
Paper Source	250
Paper Orientation	251
New Page and Overlay Concepts	251
Number of Copies	252
Page Layout	252
Controlling Margins	253
Skipping the Perforation	254
Skipping Unprintable Regions	255
Defining Page Length	257
Printing in Landscape and Portrait Orientation	257
Cursor Positioning	257
Spacing	258
Using Tabs	259
Entering Super- and Subscripts	260

Backspacing	260
Supporting General Word Processing Commands	260
Font Manipulation	260
Font Selection	262
Printer Decides Font	262
PC Software Decides Font	265
Graphics	265
Command Syntax	267
Printer Languages	269
Diablo	269
Epson	270
Hewlett-Packard	271
ISO	272
PostScript	272
Output Device Independence	273
Standard File Structure	273
Protocol Converter	274
Output Device Management	274
Scalable Fonts	274
Plotters	274
PC DOS, OS/2, and MAC SYSTEM 7	275
Printer Utilities	279
Chapter Summary	282
In The Next Chapter	283

II Printer Setup and Management

7 Making a Purchase Decision ... 287

Reading Printer Reviews in Magazines	288
Assessing Your Printer Possibilities	289
Money	289
Special Capabilities	289
Paper Size	290
Determining Life-Cycle Costs	290
Determining Your Required Output	293
Printing Internal Reports	294
Printing Letters and Papers	294
Printing Mailing Labels	294
Printing Banners	294
Printing Wide Spreadsheets	295
Printing Forms	295
Printing Newsletters, Brochures, and Handouts	295

Printing Magazines and High-Quality Output	295
Sharing the Printer	295
Recovering from Disaster	296
Considering the Printer Environment	297
Determining the Printer for Your Application Needs......	297
Printing with Spreadsheet Applications	297
Printing with Database Applications...................	298
Printing with Word Processing Applications...........	299
Printing with Desktop Publishing Applications.........	299
Printing with Accounting Applications.................	300
Printing with Graphics and Drawing Programs.........	300
Printing for Programming and Error Logging	300
Printing with Educational Software....................	301
Determining the Hardware Features You Need...........	301
Choosing an Interface	301
Reviewing Front Panel Features	302
Assessing Printer Manuals...........................	302
Checking the Warranty..............................	302
Determining the Resolution..........................	302
Testing for Speed...................................	303
Purchasing a Dot-Matrix Printer	303
Paper Handling.....................................	304
Ribbons	305
Purchasing an Inkjet Printer.........................	305
Purchasing a Laser Printer...............................	306
Life Expectancy	306
Duty Cycle	306
Resolution	307
Memory	307
Fonts..	307
Cartridges	308
Speed	308
Paper Feeding......................................	308
Consumables.......................................	308
Object Mode.......................................	309
Purchasing a Plotter	309
Reviewing Current Printer Categories, Prices, and	
Recommendations....................................	310
Low-Cost 9-Pin Dot-Matrix Printers	310
Low Cost 24-pin Dot-Matrix Printers..................	311
Wide-Carriage Dot-Matrix Printers	311
Inkjet Printers......................................	311
Personal HP-PCL Laser Printers......................	311
Business HP-PCL Laser Printers......................	312

	High-Speed, Shared Laser Printers	312
	PostScript Laser Printers	312
	Other Recommendations	313
	Deciding Where To Purchase Your Printer	313
	A Purchasing Checklist	314
	In the Next Chapter	316
8	**Installing and Testing Printers**	**317**
	Unpacking the Printer	318
	Testing the Printer without the Computer Attached	319
	Installing Ribbons and Toner Cartridges	319
	Inserting Paper into the Printer	319
	Turning On the Printer	320
	Performing Printer Self-Tests	321
	Barber-Pole Test	322
	Vertical-Line Test	323
	Font Test	325
	Configuration Test	325
	Gray-Scale and Registration Test	327
	Preparing To Connect the Printer to the Computer	329
	Locating and Using the Printer's Switches	329
	Understanding Defaults	332
	Controlling the Sounds	332
	Clearing the Buffer	333
	Controlling Line Feeds and Carriage Returns	333
	Controlling Text Wrap	334
	Testing Front-Panel Menus	336
	Choosing a Menu	338
	Scrolling through Menu Options and Parameters	338
	Selecting Menu Option Parameters	339
	Resetting the Printer	339
	Continue	340
	Soft Reset	340
	Cold Boot	341
	Hardware Reset	341
	Testing the Computer's Capability To Print	342
	Testing the Capability of a PC To Print	342
	Testing PC Parallel Ports	342
	Testing PC Serial Ports	343
	Testing the Capability of a PostScript Printer	343
	Testing a Macintosh Printer	344
	Preparing for Printer Trouble	344
	Installing, Testing, and Managing Printers	345

      Determining the End of File 346
      Stopping a Print Job 347
      Finding the Printer Bottleneck 347
      Managing the Buffer 348
      Providing for Two-Way Communication. 349
      Using the DOS Print Command 350
      Using WordPerfect's Spooler. 350
   Sharing Printers. 351
      Using a Variety of Interfaces 353
      Using a Manual Switch Box 353
      Using an Electronic Switch Box 354
         Dumb Electronic Switch Box 355
         Dumb Electronic Switch Box with Buffer. 356
         Smart Electronic Switch Box. 356
         Smart Electronic Switch Box with Buffer 358
      Setting Up a Local Area Network 358
      Testing the Shared Printers 360
      Managing Fonts. 360
   Connecting Multiple Printers to One PC 361
   Chapter Summary 362
   In the Next Chapter. 362

9   Configuring PC Applications 363

   Printer and Font Installation Basics. 364
      Drivers. 364
      Font Files. 365
      Definition/Configuration Files. 367
   Features of Printing 368
      Character Sets. 368
      Document, Font, and Print Driver Relationships 369
      Macintosh Documents. 369
         Windows Documents 369
         Ventura Documents 369
         WordPerfect Documents 370
      Line Spacing Adjustment. 371
      Features of Printing Utilities. 372
      Multiple Form Support 373
      Binding. 375
      Preview 375
      Printing to a File 376
      Application Error Messages 379
   Macintosh Printing 380
      Installing Printer Drivers. 381
      Installing New Screen Fonts. 381

xvii

- Adding Printer Fonts 382
- Using the Printer Dialog Box 383
- Comparing System 7 to Adobe TypeManager 384

PageMaker (Windows) 386
- Installing Printer Drivers 386
  - Copying Printer Drivers to Hard Disk 387
  - Establishing the Printer Port 389
  - Choosing the Default Printer 390
  - Configuring the Printer Driver 391
  - Initializing the Serial Port 395
- Adding Printer Fonts 395
- Installing New Screen Fonts 398

GEM Ventura 399
- Installing Printer Drivers 399
- Adding Printer Fonts 400
  - Copying Fonts to a Ventura Subdirectory 400
  - Creating New Width Files 401
  - Selecting New Width File 401
  - Testing and Cleaning Up Width Files 402
- Downloading Printer Fonts 403
- Installing New Screen Fonts 404
- Knowing Memory Requirements 406

WordPerfect 407
- Reviewing the Printing Menu 407
- Installing Printer Drivers 408
- Changing the Printer Definitions 409
- Adding Printer Fonts 411
- Editing Printer Definition Tables 413

1-2-3 Printing 414
- Installing the Printer 415
- Using Setup Strings 416
- Solving Common Problems 417
  - Page Creep 417
  - Large Spreadsheets 418
  - Extra Blank Rows 418
  - Compressed Print 419
  - PrintGraph Problems 419

DOS Printing 419
- Initializing the Port 420
- Using Typewriter Mode 420
- Printing a Directory 420
- Printing a File 421
- Recording DOS Conversation 421

Spooling a File 421
Using Shift-PrtSc To Print Graphics 421
OS/2 Printing 422
Installing Printer Ports 422
Port Definition 422
Port Initialization 423
Spooler Initialization 425
Installing Printer Drivers (Presentation Manager) 426
DOS Emulation Printing 427
Chapter Summary 427
In the Next Chapter 428

III The Publishing Challenge

10 Typesetting 433
Defining the Typesetting Process 434
Creating Text 434
Creating Drawings 436
Adding Color 437
Color Fundamentals 437
Four-Color or CMYK Color Printing 437
One-, Two-, Three-, and Five-Color Printing 438
Separation 439
Color Adjustment 439
Typesetting 440
Laying Out the Pages 440
Stripping 441
Printing 442
Summarizing the Typesetting Process 442
Desktop Publishing 443
Setting Up Your Desktop Publishing System 444
Using a Low-End Desktop Publishing Program 444
Using a High-End Word Processing Program 445
Using a High-End Desktop Publishing Program 445
Laying Out Your Pages 446
Using Desktop Publishing Software for
  Page Layout 446
Creating Galleys with a Laser Printer 447
Creating and Adding Drawings 448
Types of Drawings 448
Drawing Software 449
Scanned Drawings 450

xix

  Purchased Drawings 450
  Computer Screen Images 451
  Converted Images 451
  Color Drawings 452
 Adding Photographs 456
  Lines Per Inch versus Dots Per Inch 456
  Dot Shapes and Sizes 457
  Angle 458
  The Optimal Scanner Resolution 458
  Optimal Number of Scanner Grays 459
  Scanning Uniform Grays 460
  Print Engine Influence on Grays 460
 Printing in Color 461
 Summarizing Desktop Publishing 462
Improving Your Document's Appearance 463
 Printing Large and Reducing or Printing Small 463
 Renting Time on a PostScript Printer 464
 Sending Files to a TypeSetter 464
  Transferring Files through LAN Cables 465
  Exchanging Floppy Disks 465
  Exchanging Tapes and Removable Hard Disks 465
  Transferring Files through Modems 465
 Avoiding Potential Typesetting and Printing
  Problems 466
  Sending Desktop Publishing Drafts 466
  Sending a Copy of the Fonts Used 467
  Sticking with Standard Font Names 467
  Sticking with Adobe Fonts 467
  Staying Away from Bit-Mapped Fonts 467
  Capturing PostScript Header Files 468
  Standardizing Margins 468
 Critiquing Typesetting and Printing Problems 468
  Moirè Patterns 468
  Dark Photos 469
  Washed-Out Photos 469
 Chapter Summary 470
 In The Next Chapter 470

11   PostScript Printers 471

 History of PostScript Printers 471
  PostScript's Influence on Typesetting 472
  PostScript in the Microcomputer World 473
  PostScript as a Translator 476
  PostScript as the Standard 477

Long-Term Benefits of PostScript Printers 478
    Fonts.. 479
    Character Set.. 481
    Emulation of Other Printers........................ 481
    Printer Independence 482
    Objectivity.. 482
    Standard File Format 483
    Two-Way Communication 484
Basic PostScript Features...................................... 485
    Compatibility, Clones, Upgrades, and Version Differences 485
    Speed 487
    Virtual Memory... 487
    Two-Way Communication 488
    LAN Connection....................................... 488
    Fonts.. 489
HP LaserJet versus PostScript 489
Who Should Use a PostScript Printer?..................... 490
Purchasing or Upgrading to a PostScript Printer......... 491
Adding PostScript to Your Computer System 492
PostScript for Dot-Matrix Printers 492
Purchasing a Printer Controller 493
Adding a PostScript Cartridge................................ 494
Upgrading Laser Printers 495
PostScript Language 495
Future of PostScript Printers.................................. 497
Chapter Summary 497
In the Next Chapter... 498

IV   Maintenance and Troubleshooting

12   Isolating Problems and Finding Solutions...... 503

Developing the Magic 503
    Gaining a Positive Attitude........................... 504
    Learning from Experience 505
    Documenting Your Troubleshooting 506
    Solving Paradoxes..................................... 507
Using Evidence-Gathering Tools............................. 508
    Checking the Simple Things......................... 508
    Isolating the Problem 509
        Operator Experience 509
        Application Software............................ 510

       Operating System 511
       Computer Printer Port............................. 512
       Printer Cables 513
       The Printer 513
   Repeating the Problem 513
   Configuring the Printer to the Minimum............... 514
   Swapping Printers..................................... 515
   Changing One Thing at a Time 516
   Resetting the Printer 517
   Turning the Printer Off and On 518
   Performing Self-Tests................................. 518
   Printing a Test Page.................................. 519
   Moving the Printer to a Different Location............ 519
   Installing Software That Shares the Printer 520
   Resigning Yourself to Wasted Paper................... 520
   Printing to a File 521
   Inserting Paper in Manual Feed....................... 521
  Preventing Problems 521
   Installing the Printer Correctly 522
   Checking the Environment........................... 522
       Checking Wall Outlets 523
       Checking for Shared Circuits.................... 523
       Checking the Grounds 524
       Purchasing Surge and Spike Protectors 525
   Following Proper Operation Procedures 525
   Performing Preventive Maintenance................... 526
  Chapter Summary 528
  In the Next Chapter..................................... 528

13 Solving Serial and Parallel Interface Problems.. 529

  Working with Parallel Interfaces 529
   Optional Wires..................................... 531
   Initialization 531
   Buffer Management 532
  Constructing a Serial Printer Cable 533
   Identifying the Connectors........................... 533
   Purchasing Serial Cable Wire......................... 535
   Drawing a Cable Pinout Diagram 535
  Configuring the Printer's and PC's Serial Interfaces 538
   Configuring the PC Serial Interface................... 538
       Configuring the COM1, COM2, COM3,
       and COM4 Ports 538

Testing the Serial Port Hardware 539
Configuring the Printer's Serial Interface 540
Printing on a Serial Printer through DOS 541
Testing the Serial Printer with an Application 542
Configuring the PC Application Software 543
Understanding Buffer-Management Protocols 543
Making the Computer Slower than the Printer 544
Using Hardware Handshaking 544
Using Software Handshaking 544
Implementing and Testing a Buffer-Management
Protocol 545
Slowing the PC 546
Testing with Hardware 547
Testing with Software 548
Implementing a Software-Management Scheme 548
Letting Each PC Application Talk to the Serial Port 549
Using DOS To Redirect from Parallel to Serial 550
Using Third-Party Software To Redirect Data 551
Chapter Summary 552
In the Next Chapter 552

14 Troubleshooting 553

General Problem Areas 553
Black Lines 554
Boldface Type 554
Centering 555
Columns Are Misaligned 556
Decimals Are Misaligned 556
Dead Printers 556
Devils or Shorts 557
Disappearing/Reappearing Characters 557
Display Does Not Match Printout 557
Divide Overflow, Divide by Zero, and Fatal Stack
Error Messages 558
Double-Height Characters on First Line 558
Downloading Fonts 559
Duplicated Characters 559
Errors Caused by Current Document Version 560
Extra Characters 560
Font Chosen Doesn't Print 561
Front Panel Does Not Work 561
Garbled Characters 561
Ghosts of Previously Printed Characters Appear 562
Initializing 562

Intermittent Operation	563
Justifying Last Line of Paragraph	563
Left Margin	564
Legal-Size Paper	564
Letters Are Not Fully Formed	565
Letters Misaligned	565
Letter Spacing	566
Lost Characters	566
Lost Paragraphs and Lines	566
LPT1/LPT2 Switch	567
Noise Produced when Head Moves	567
Nothing Prints	567
Old Documents Do Not Print Correctly	568
Out of Memory	568
Outbound Paper Feeding into the Inbound	568
Output Is Faint and Uneven	569
Page Creep	569
Paper Advancement	569
Paper Is Spewed	570
Paper Out	570
Parity-Check Error Message	571
Power-Up 901 Error Message	571
Printer Error Messages	571
Print Head	572
Printer-Specific Instructions	573
Printing Stops before the End of the Page	573
Right Margin	574
Rotated Text	574
Setting the Top of the Page	574
Setup Instructions Are Not Remembered	575
Shared Printers	575
Shift-PrtSc Key Combination Does Not Work	575
Single-Spacing	576
Slow Operation under PC DOS	576
Small Fonts	576
Spaces Print instead of Symbols	576
Start-Up Page Prints	576
Underlining	577
White Letters	577
White Lines	578
Wrapping Text	578
Wrinkled or Jammed Paper	578
Laser Printer Error Codes and Symptoms	579
Black Pages	581

	Faint Print	581
	Horizontal Streaks	582
	Right Side of Paper Is Missing or Distorted.	582
	Smeared Print	582
	Repetitive Defects	583
	White Pages.	583
	White Streaks (Vertical)	583
	Other Laser Printer Problems	584
Dot-Matrix Printer Problems.	584
	Excessive Component Lead Length.	584
	Ribbon Problems	585
	Serial Interface Problems	585
	Possible Adjustments.	586
Chapter Summary	587

A Programming Command Language Reference 589

Introducing Printer Programming 589
Revisiting ASCII. 590
Sending Instructions to a Printer 592
    Using BASIC 592
    Using Utility Programs. 593
Generating Codes from the Keyboard. 593
    Keys on the Keyboard. 593
    The Ctrl Key. 594
    The Alt Key. 594
Using Printer Commands. 594
Creating Files of Printer Commands 596
HPCL, Epson, ISO, and Diablo Command Reference 596
    Job Control. 597
        HP Job Control 597
        Epson Job Control. 597
        ISO Job Control. 598
        DIABLO Job Control. 599
    Page Control. 599
        HP Page Control 599
        Epson Page Control 599
        ISO Page Control. 600
        DIABLO Page Control. 600
    Cursor Positioning. 601
        HP Cursor Positioning 601
        Epson Cursor Positioning. 601
        ISO Cursor Positioning. 602
        Diablo Cursor Positioning 603

	Font Manipulation	603
	HP Font Manipulation	603
	Epson Font Manipulation	604
	ISO Font Manipulation	604
	Diablo Font Manipulation	605
	Font Selection	605
	HP Font Selection	605
	Epson Font Selection	606
	ISO Font Selection	606
	Diablo Font Selection	608
	Font Management	608
	HP Font Management	608
	Epson Font Management	608
	ISO Font Management	609
	Diablo Font Management	609
	Word Processing Support	610
	HP and ISO Word Processing Support	610
	Epson Word Processing Support	610
	Diablo Word Processing Support	610
	Graphics	610
	HP Graphics	611
	Epson Graphics	611
	ISO Graphics	612
	Diablo Graphics	612
B	**Printer Vendor List**	**613**
C	**Font Vendor List**	**617**
D	**Symbol Names of Characters**	**623**
	Glossary	**653**
	Index	**665**

ACKNOWLEDGMENTS

I want to thank my wife and extended family for helping me develop the discipline I needed to write this book. In particular, I want to thank my wife, Fawn Foerster, for the editing she did. For motivation, hand-holding, and encouragement, thanks go to Hank Stanton and Paula Longhi. Without them, I probably would not have attempted this writing. I also want to thank Moulton Minasi & Company (Pete Moulton and Mark Minasi) for opportunities and experiences that made this book possible.

Finally, I want to thank the editors at Que. Specifically, thanks go to Shelley O'Hara for asking the questions that kept this book from drifting into techie never-never land. And, thanks to Kelly Dobbs for the amazing job she did of turning what I wrote into English sentences.

TRADEMARK ACKNOWLEDGMENTS

Que Corporation has made every effort to supply trademark information about company names, products, and services mentioned in this book. Trademarks indicated below were derived from various sources. Que Corporation cannot attest to the accuracy of this information.

1-2-3, Lotus, and Freelance are registered trademarks of Lotus Development Corporation.

3Com is a registered trademark of 3Com Corporation.

3+ is a trademark of 3M Company.

Amiga C is a registered trademark of Commodore-Amiga, Inc.

ANSI is a registered trademark of American National Standards Institute.

Apple, Apple II, Apple IIc, Apple IIe, Apple II+, Apple III, Apple Font/DA Mover Utility, Apple daisywheel, AppleWorks, ImageWriter, LaserWriter, LaserWriter Plus, LaserWriter II NT, LaserWriter IISC, Mac, and MacPaint are registered trademarks, and Apple IIGS, ImageWriter 2, Macintosh System, and MultiFinder are trademarks of Apple Computer, Inc.

ARCnet is a registered trademark of Datapoint Corporation.

AST TurboLaser is a registered trademark of AST Research, Inc.

AutoCAD is a registered trademark of Autodesk, Inc.

Bitstream is a registered trademark of Bitstream, Inc.

Canon IX-12 is a registered trademark of Canon, Inc.

Centronics is a registered trademark of Centronics Data Computer Corporation, licensed to Genicom Corporation.

CompuServe Information Service is a registered trademark of CompuServe Incorporated and H&R Block, Inc.

dBASE is a registered trademark of Ashton-Tate Corporation.

Diablo 630 is a registered trademark of Xerox Corporation.

Dr. HALO is a registered trademark of Media Cybernetics, Inc.

Epson is a registered trademark of Epson Corporation.

GEM, GEM Draw, and GEM Paint are trademarks of Digital Research, Inc.

Helvetica is a registered trademark of Allied Corporation.

HP is a registered trademark, and HP DeskJet, LaserJet, and ScanJet are trademarks of Hewlett-Packard Co.

InSet is a registered trademark of INSET Systems Inc.

Intel is a registered trademark of Intel Corporation.

IBM, IBM PC, IBM AT, OS/2, IBM Personal PagePrinter, and Quietwriter are registered trademarks, and IBM PC XT, IBM Personal Editor, IBM ProPrinter, IBM ProPrinter XL, and PS/2 are trademarks of International Business Machines Corporation.

ITC Zapf Dingbats is a registered trademark of International Typeface Corporation.

Micrografx is a registered trademark of Micrografx, Inc.

Microsoft, Microsoft Windows, Microsoft Word, and MS-DOS are registered trademarks of Microsoft Corporation.

Motorola is a registered trademark of Motorola, Inc.

MultiMate is a registered trademark of MultiMate International, an Ashton-Tate Corporation.

NEC and NEC 3550 Spinwriter are registered trademarks of NEC Information Systems Inc.

Norton Utilities is a trademark of Peter Norton Computing.

OKIDATA is a registered trademark of Oki America, Inc.

PageMaker is a registered trademark of Aldus Corporation.

PC Paint is a trademark of Mouse Systems Corporation

PC Paintbrush is a registered trademark of ZSoft Corporation.

PFS is a registered trademark, and First Publisher is a trademark of Software Publishing Corporation.

Phoenix Bios 3.0 is a trademark of Phoenix Technologies Ltd.

PostScript and Encapsulated PostScript are registered trademarks, and Adobe Illustrator is a trademark of Adobe Systems, Inc.

Qume SPRINT 11/55 PLUS is a trademark of ITT Qume.

TANDY is a registered trademark of Radio Shack.

Turbo C is a registered trademark of Borland International, Inc.

UNIX is a trademark of AT&T.

Ventura Publisher is a registered trademark of Ventura Software, Inc.

WordPerfect is a registered trademark of WordPerfect Corporation.

WordStar is a registered trademark of MicroPro International Corporation.

Trademarks of other products mentioned in this book are held by the companies producing them.

Introduction

Anyone who has ever been frustrated by printers needs this book. If the paper jams, the left margin drifts uncontrollably, or legal-size paper battles have driven you crazy, this book is for you. If you have not tried to add fonts to your current system, or if you have not looked at sophisticated printers such as PostScript printers, this book is the place to start.

If you are hesitant about upgrading software because of printer concerns, purchase this book and learn the fundamental concepts behind the operation of all printers. Treat the software upgrade as a challenge that you can win.

This book assumes that you have no background in computers or printers. Terms are defined as they are introduced. For example, *PC* refers to any of the IBM microcomputers and clones, and *Mac* refers to Apple's Macintosh. Unless you are interested in the evolution of technology or sleep with DOS manuals by your side, don't plan on reading this book just for fun. If you are planning on buying or have recently purchased this book, you already should be using a microcomputer and at least planning on buying a printer soon.

This Book's Objectives

The Printer Bible covers everything from printer cable wires to printer-related error messages from the operating system. Everything about printer buttons, switches, and knobs is discussed in detail. The path traveled and problems encountered by keyboard information as it flows toward the printer are examined. The majority of *The Printer Bible* focuses on the microcomputer world created by IBM and Apple. Specific references are made to PCs, XTs, ATs, PS/2s, clones, and Macintoshes.

The Printer Bible starts with basic printer concepts, moves to purchasing issues, guides you through printer management, and introduces the publishing challenge. The last chapters should help solve most of your printing problems.

This book was written to satisfy needs in three major areas. The first area is printer knowledge. *The Printer Bible* provides a generic tutorial about printers. Most printer manuals have a tutorial on their printer's programming language, but this information requires that you already know a computer programming language like BASIC. All examples of printer programming are sent to the printer using a computer programming language like BASIC. Most computer users are not interested in programming printers, nor are they interested in programming computers. You probably just want to read a simple discussion of how to insert paper into the printer.

The Printer Bible also addresses needs in the area of troubleshooting. Scattered throughout this book are troubleshooting trips. In addition to these tips, three chapters are dedicated to printer troubleshooting—Chapters 12, 13, and 14. If you have trouble with your printer, turn to Chapter 13. This chapter contains an alphabetical listing of most printer problems.

The third major area in which *The Printer Bible* addresses a need is printer management. Most users waste sheets of paper, never clean their printers, and fight and curse every time a new version of their favorite software package comes out. Today, users are starting to share printers. By nature, computers encourage creativity and individual activity, without cooperation or sharing, but the minute a printer is shared, cooperation and coordination become necessary. Fundamental problems in the actual design of printers frustrate the sharing of printers. These issues are addressed in Chapter 8. In addition, hints scattered throughout the chapters will help you use your printer more efficiently.

The overall goals of *The Printer Bible* are to cover all the issues relating to operating, purchasing, installing, managing, upgrading, and repairing printers and to document all common printer features and problems.

What Is and What Is Not in This Book

The Printer Bible does not try to teach you proper English, describe the best-looking newsletter design, or tell you the characteristics of a good company logo. *The Printer Bible* describes how to coerce a printer into printing a letter in the place, size, and style you want. *The Printer Bible* also describes the pitfalls of using fonts for purposes other than those intended by the creators (see Chapter 4).

This book does not teach you how to spell, but it describes how you can figure out whether the printer is misspelling, your computer is misspelling, or whether you made a typing error (see Chapter 13).

This book is designed to be more useful than printer manuals, but don't throw your manuals away. The technical details found in your printer manual are only summarized in this book because there are too many different printers. If each model were described in detail, this book would be ten times as large. *The Printer Bible* should help you solve most of your printing problems, but if not, *The Printer Bible* certainly will describe the specific technical information needed.

This book is not a guide to printing with your specific software package. Don't throw away any application program instructions relating to printers. Don't expect this book to list exact keystrokes for a specific feature of your printer from within your favorite software package. For example, don't expect detailed instructions on how to underline or draw a box in WordPerfect. Do expect to learn the general principles behind underlining and drawing a box. Do expect to find specific instructions that cause most software packages to underline and draw boxes. Do expect to see the procedures for installing fonts in the Macintosh, Windows, GEM, and WordPerfect environments. (See Chapter 9 for more information.)

The Printer Bible does not contain a guide to choosing fonts. No attempt is made to give a history of fonts, describe current font selection trends, argue which style is more readable or better for presentations, advertisement, newspapers, magazines, and books. *The Printer Bible* describes the features of fonts so that you know what to look for. You can converse with the font professionals. The goal of *The Printer Bible* is to describe the terminology and characteristics of fonts so that you can purchase, install, test, and print them. For example, the differences between proportional and fixed fonts are described in the context of spacing and column-forming problems. A character set is contrasted with a font, and specific procedures are outlined for printing each symbol of the character set. How you actually use the fonts is not covered.

The Printer Bible defines the most common typesetting terms appearing with more frequency in application software packages. Hopefully, almost all the terms related to printing are reviewed.

This book does not try to describe printer features of specific printer models; the models are changing too fast to make this practical. The goals are to document all the features that may be found in any given printer model and to provide a feature list for use in comparing various printer models.

Because the majority of printer problems occur in the IBM PC, XT, AT, compatibles, and PS/2 world, most examples are from this environment. Just because the IBM PC printer problems are more severe does not mean that Apple IIs, Macintoshes, and other microcomputer systems are ignored. Outside the IBM world, most systems use the same printers and have the same problems. The IBM microcomputer systems have more problems because there are more of them, and each of these systems has printers, software, and a system unit from a different manufacturer.

This book is not just a description of printer technologies. This book does not celebrate the existence of printers and review each with a picture and text describing the printer's interesting and unique details. *The Printer Bible* provides the facts, the concepts, and the procedures to reduce your printer problems. *The Printer Bible* helps you locate, test, and implement those hidden printer features.

How To Use This Book

If you are new to printers, you want to start by reading Chapter 1. If you have specific printing problems, you may want to jump straight to Chapter 13. If you are having trouble operating the front panel of your printer, you may want to read the appropriate section in Chapter 8. In other words, skim this book and locate the section that meets your needs.

The Printer Bible was designed so that terms are defined in earlier chapters and used throughout the book. Occasionally, terms are defined several times. If you are just beginning to learn about printers, the best idea is to read the first six chapters straight through.

If you just want to skim the book, look at the troubleshooting tips, cautions, and hints. They give you a good synopsis of the surrounding paragraphs. Often, nearby paragraphs explain the tip or hint in more detail.

Troubleshooting Tips

Troubleshooting tips briefly describe a problem and its solution. Symptoms and solutions, therefore, are discussed in chapters organized by similar content. Chapter 13 focuses on the symptoms and helps you locate the causes and solutions scattered throughout this book.

Some troubleshooting tips contain the same solution but with different symptoms. Other tips describe the same symptom, but different solutions are scattered throughout *The Printer Bible*. Chapter 14 ties all the troubleshooting tips together, creating a useful troubleshooting tool.

Cautions

Cautions describe situations where you may be hurt, the printer may be damaged, data may be lost, or files may be destroyed. Together, the cautions form the preventive maintenance, safety training, and proper operation procedures. Cautions are placed next to detailed descriptions about these procedures.

Hints

Hints offer suggestions about how to make life easier for yourself. Hints are procedures you can follow to have a better chance of printing right the first time, and they help you manage the different printer and software combinations. Following the advice offered in the hints should make your printing an easier, less frustrating experience.

How This Book Is Organized

The Printer Bible is divided into four parts. Part I presents the basics that everyone who uses a printer should become familiar with. Part II helps you to make a purchase decision and explains how to configure and test your printer. Part III explains how microcomputers and printers are invading areas that in the recent past were inhabited only by typesetters. Part IV helps you to troubleshoot your printing problems and offers some possible solutions.

Part I

Part I, "The Basics," includes Chapters 1–6. Printers are simple. Their job is to place dots on paper. Printers are perceived as complicated because they receive instructions from microcomputers, which receive their instructions from you. Different printers also interpret these instructions in different ways. Some printers may print symbols of foreign languages. Others may print in different fonts. You need to know the speed and resolution differences when comparing printers. You also have to worry about compatibility with your microcomputer's software. These issues are explored in the first six chapters.

Chapter 1, "The Information Process: from Keyboard to Printer," looks at each component in the printing process, exploring the different ways that component can affect the output of a printer. A printer needs a functioning computer. A functioning computer needs functioning software, which requires a functioning user. The role of micro software, and the differences among character-mode, graphics-mode, and object-mode printing are reviewed.

Chapter 2, "The Information Process: from Printer to Paper," explores the generic hardware underneath the hood of most printers. After a printer receives information from the microcomputer, the printer begins processing that information. The printer has to separate instructions from text, compute an image of dots to be printed, and fire the wires of a dot matrix or pulse the beam of a laser. This chapter also reviews the names and functions of the circuit boards and printing mechanisms.

Chapter 3, "How the Printer Interprets Data," describes the problems associated with character sets. The bytes a printer receives in character mode or object mode consist primarily of descriptions of which character to print. Although all printers can print the characters found on keyboards, many printers cannot print all the characters that can be displayed on-screen. And, many of us want to print characters from languages other than English.

Chapter 4, "Font Basics," focuses on the different types of fonts available, and the features of different fonts. Output quality of a printer always has been judged by how crisp and smooth the fonts are produced. Early dot-matrix printers sacrificed font quality for cost and speed. Even fully-formed daisy-wheel printers constantly were being compared with the much better-looking work of a typesetter. However, the gap is narrowing. The features of fonts are influencing printers in significant ways. For example, proportional fonts look better but also create problems.

Chapter 5, "Printer Hardware Features," helps you compare printer types and performance criteria, such as resolution and speed. (Chapter 2 introduces dot-matrix and laser printing mechanisms, but other types of printers exist, such as inkjet.) Chapter 5 also reviews add-on features, such as paper trays, and operation costs accumulated by paper, ribbons, and toner.

Chapter 6, "Printer Software Features," reviews the issue of compatibility and the features of printer languages such as HP LaserJet, Epson, and PostScript. For example, some languages enable you to print white letters on black backgrounds; other languages normally do not enable objects to blend or add together. These features can influence purchasing decisions and printer operation.

Part II

Part II, "Printer Setup and Management," includes Chapters 7–9. These three chapters focus on some practical dos and don'ts when purchasing, installing, configuring, and testing printers. Many people purchase their printer with a new computer system, but really don't start to use the printer until it is almost out of the warranty period. Other users never fully test the printer and stumble over compatibility or expectation problems well after the return period is over. This section is designed to make sure that you install a trouble-free printing system.

Chapter 7, "Making a Purchase Decision," helps you figure out which type of printer you need, depending on what type of documents you are planning on printing and what application software you are using. Suppose that you decide on a laser printer. You need to read the section describing the various differences among laser printers so that you can purchase the most appropriate printer for your needs. Advice on whether to purchase a printer that emulates another and where to purchase the printer is given.

Chapter 8, "Installing and Testing Printers," helps you install and test a printer by explaining the switches, the changes you need to make on the front panel so that the printer listens to you, the reset and self-test options available, and the advantages and disadvantages of sharing printers.

Chapter 9, "Configuring PC Applications," reviews most of the major PC applications available. After the printer is installed and tested, you need to configure the printer for each PC application used on the system and test it again. This chapter contains specific printer and font installation instructions for Windows (Pagemaker), GEM (Ventura), 1-2-3, WordPerfect, and other packages.

Part III

Part III, "The Publishing Challenge," includes Chapters 10 and 11. The output of printers attached to microcomputers is looking more and more like magazine print each day. *Typewriter quality* is no longer a goal, but a feature of all printers sold today. The better printers are producing output that in some cases rivals the work of typesetters. And, typesetters are using microcomputers and printers everyday as tools in the typesetting process. These two chapters explore how printers are expanding and challenging the typesetting world.

Chapter 10, "Typesetting," explores what is possible with a laser printer and microcomputer and how typesetters are using microcomputers to make their job more efficient, more accurate, and more flexible. Typists (those using word processors) are learning typesetting concepts. Typesetters are learning to use microcomputers. A very clear difference, however, still exists between what can be produced with a microcomputer and what can be produced by a typesetter. This chapter discusses methods of combining the best of the microcomputer and typesetting worlds.

Chapter 11, "PostScript Printers," focuses on why IBM, Apple, and Microsoft have made strategic commitments to PostScript. The one printer language that seems to be uniting all output devices, such as phototypesetters and dot-matrix printers, is PostScript. This printer language is explored from a feature and troubleshooting point of view—not a programming point of view.

Part IV

Part IV, "Maintenance and Troubleshooting," includes Chapters 12–14. Printers can cause you almost as much trouble as your microcomputer. Although books have been written about troubleshooting microcomputers, few books address printer problems. Throughout this book are troubleshooting tips. The three chapters in this section give you step-by-step procedures for determining the exact location of a problem.

Chapter 12, "Isolating Problems and Finding Solutions," focuses the troubleshooting process by providing step-by-step procedures for figuring out whether the problem is in the printer, the cable, the hardware, or the software.

Chapter 13, "Solving Serial and Parallel Interface Problems," explains how to install serial printers right the first time and how to test printers after installation. Hooking serial printers up to PCs is difficult. Many things can go wrong, but you can install printers right the first time without any guessing.

Chapter 14, "Troubleshooting," lists unrelated printing problem symptoms alphabetically. You can match your printing problems to this list. Then, you can look up the solution to your problem.

Appendixes

This book contains four appendixes and a glossary. Appendix A, "Programming Command Language Reference," teaches you how to customize or configure a printer and how to access your printer's special features. This appendix reviews graphic and character printer commands.

Appendix B, "Printer Vendor List," provides the names and mailing addresses of more than 50 printer manufacturers. Use this list to write for service, programming help, and technical reference manuals.

Appendix C, "Font Vendor List," provides the names and mailing addresses of more than 75 companies that sell fonts for PC and Macintosh printers. Write to these companies for free samples and literature.

Appendix D, "Symbol Names of Character Sets," lists symbols alphabetically. The printable alphabet is expanding all the time. Today, over 1,500 symbols are in use (compared to the 26-character English alphabet). Scan the symbols in this appendix and start using the additional ones that you need.

I

The Basics

Includes

The Information Process: from Keyboard to Printer
The Information Process: from Printer to Paper
How the Printer Interprets Data
Font Basics
Printer Hardware Features
Printer Software Features

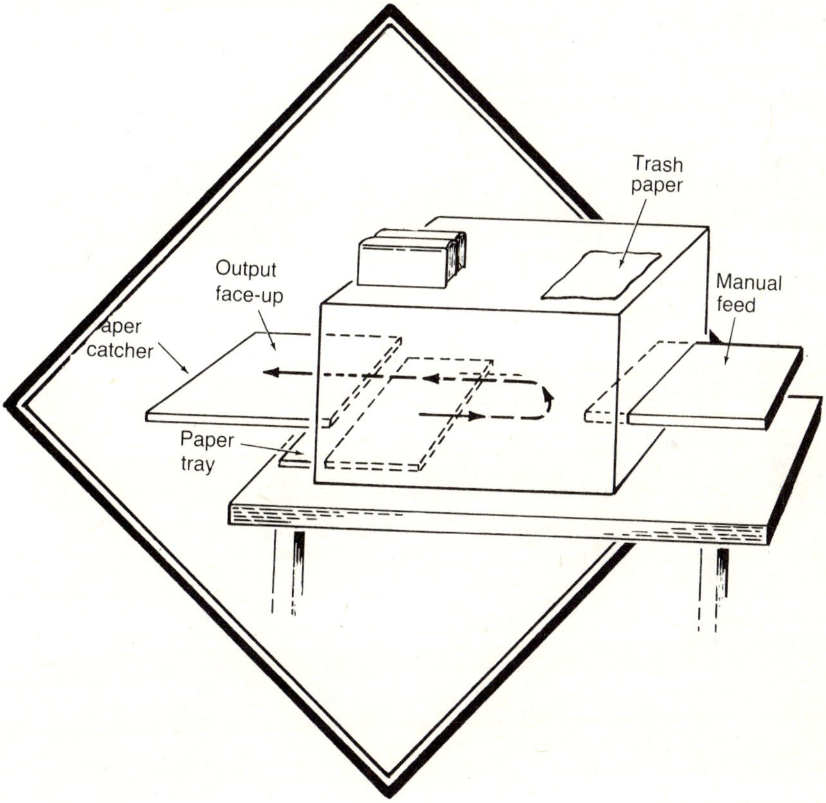
Trash paper
Output face-up
Manual feed
aper catcher
Paper tray

The Information Process: from Keyboard to Printer

This chapter focuses on what happens from the moment a key is pressed to the moment a character appears on paper. This chapter helps you figure out where problems can occur. You need to know how the micro software and printer should be cooperating.

When you press a key, information travels down the keyboard cable into the computer. The keystroke may be stored and eventually printed, or it can be interpreted as an instruction by the computer. After creating and storing information, the computer eventually prepares it for a printer.

What happens to keyboard information, how it appears on-screen, how information is stored on a floppy, and what eventually is sent to the printer are explored in detail.

A Brief History of Printers

Today's printer is the offspring of typewriters and the typesetting industry. The printer has passed through many primitive and frustrating early life forms. In spite of this, printers have populated the earth and evolved many subspecies. Even now, this rapid evolution has not stopped. Daisywheels begot dot matrixes, which begot inkjet printers, which begot laser printers. Daisywheels have died, and laser printers under $1,000 are crowding out dot-matrix and inkjet printers. In circular evolutionary fashion, printers are starting to encroach on one of their ancestral parents' niche—the typesetting industry. Desktop publishing is an up-and-coming reality.

Most of a printer's genes came from the typewriter. Only recently has the typesetting world started to influence printers. *The Printer Bible*, therefore, tells how typewriters turned into printers and discusses the recent influence of typesetting concepts.

Typewriters turned into printers when they were attached to the first mainframe computer. Users punched holes in cards and fed the cards into windows through the wall of the computer room. Inside the computer room, operators manually fed cards into the computer. As the mainframe printer piled up paper, operators ripped the printouts into bundles with the author's name on top, and then pushed the bundles out other windows in the computer room wall. The mainframe printer was an integral part of the whole system's operation. These printers were very expensive, operated at high speeds, and produced poor-quality printouts.

The next evolutionary step was the development of the TeleTYpe (TTY) terminal. Although mostly mechanical, TTY had a built-in printer, and TTY terminals eliminated the pilgrimage to the computer room. As users typed on the keyboard, the characters were sent to the mainframe. The mainframe then sent a copy of the characters back to the TTY terminal. A typist, therefore, could check whether the character made the round trip successfully. The most important aspect of this developmental stage was the removal of the printer from the mainframe site to the TTY terminals. This move eliminated the tedium of operators manually feeding computer cards and babysitting printers. The TTY displayed everything on paper.

The next big change was the development of CRT (Cathode Ray Tube) terminals. CRT terminals are much quicker than the TTY terminals because they have no moving parts. Furthermore, they do not need a printer because all the characters sent and received can be displayed on-screen. The need for paper, therefore, was greatly reduced. The one drawback of a CRT was that printouts still required a trip to a printer or a window in the computer room wall. Initially, TTY terminals were retained as remote mainframe printers.

At the same time that the quality of remote mainframe printers was being improved, microcomputers started to appear. The first true printers hooked directly up to microcomputers and served as remote mainframe printers. The first popular printer, designed exclusively for microcomputers, was manufactured by Centronics. The printer's simplicity and low cost created the first market for a printer dedicated to microcomputers.

Simple printers have their roots in TTYs, which were simple to operate. TTYs had two modes of operation and were attached to a computer or functioned as a typewriter. The button that controlled the terminal's function still is called the on-line/off-line button.

> HINT | Modern typewriters that also function as printers usually are slow and often break down. These machines mainly are designed to be used as typewriters. Do not consider this duality a worthy feature when purchasing a printer or typewriter.

Chapter 1: The Information Process: from Keyboard to Printer

When the TTY terminal was off-line, every character typed went straight to the simple printer inside the terminal, and the printer functioned as an electronic typewriter (see fig. 1.1). When the terminal was on-line, every character typed went to the computer (see fig. 1.2). The computer made a copy of each character and sent it back to the terminal's simple printer. Because each character made a round trip, you could tell whether the computer received the character by examining the printout.

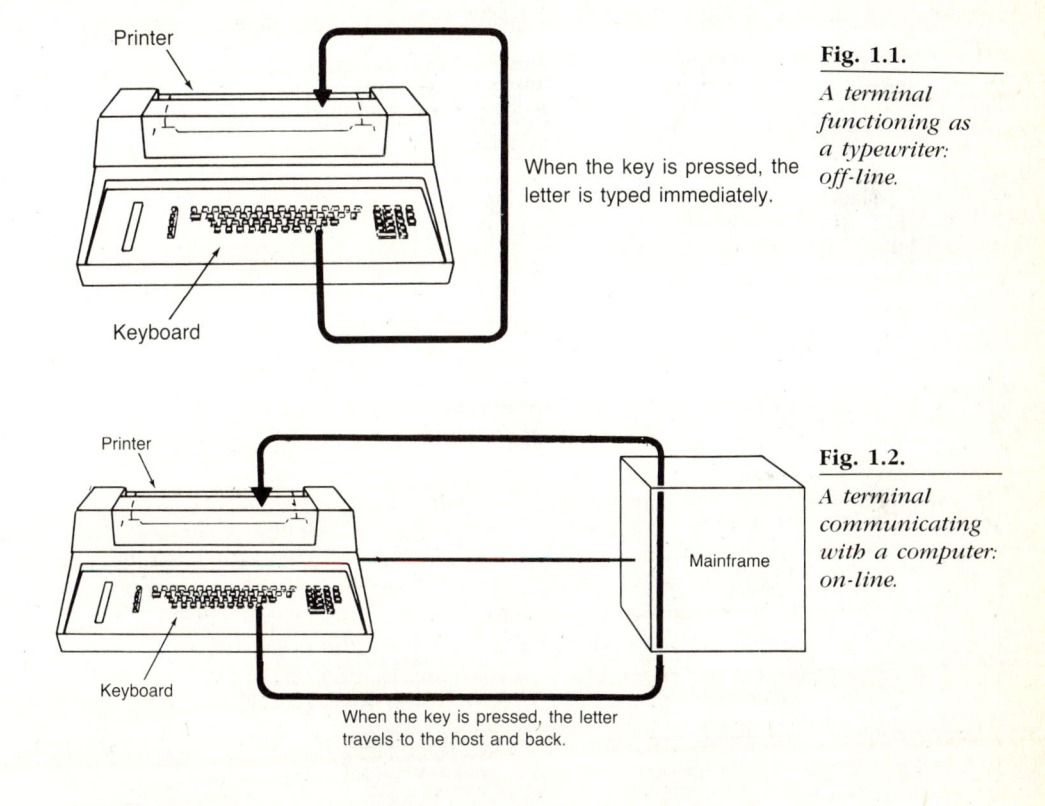

Fig. 1.1.

A terminal functioning as a typewriter: off-line.

When the key is pressed, the letter is typed immediately.

Fig. 1.2.

A terminal communicating with a computer: on-line.

When the key is pressed, the letter travels to the host and back.

Today, dumb terminals operate the same way, except that the simple printer has disappeared. The simple printer originally was replaced with a monitor or CRT. Although the older dumb terminals still were needed to produce hard copy, the keyboards were worthless. Eventually, keyboards disappeared, leaving just a simple printer. The capability to function as a typewriter also disappeared.

To replace the keyboard, printers have been growing buttons in the area called *the front panel* or *menu pad*. Modern simple printers have just three buttons: on-line/off-line, Line Feed or LF (the capability to advance the paper one line at a time), and Form Feed or FF (the capability to eject the current sheet of paper). The LF and FF buttons (and all other buttons on smarter printers) can be activated only when the printer is off-line.

When a simple printer is on-line, it receives information from the computer. A simple printer scans incoming information for text and instructions. These instructions can be buried anywhere in the text. Every character received has to be examined by the printer to see whether it is an instruction or a letter to be printed.

After examining the text, the printer prints the appropriate letter or acts on the instruction received. Simple printers have one font and understand only three *instructions* or *commands*. The font contains all the letters, numbers, and punctuation symbols usually found on a typewriter keyboard. The three instructions a simple printer understands are as follows:

Carriage Return (CR)	Go to the beginning of the current line
Line Feed (LF)	Move to the line below
Form Feed (FF)	Eject current sheet of paper; go to the top of the next sheet

Two of the three instructions are identical to buttons on the simple printer. The LF instruction (sent by the computer) advances the paper when the printer is on-line, and the LF button (pressed by a user) advances the paper when the printer is off-line. The FF instruction (sent by the computer) advances the paper when the printer is on-line, and the FF button (pressed by a user) advances the paper when the printer is off-line. Only the CR instruction is not available to the user.

A CR instruction enables computers to underline and boldface text. The computer underlines by printing the line twice. On the first pass, all the letters are printed. On the second pass, certain letters are underlined. The computer also boldfaces by printing the same line twice. On the second pass, the bold letters are printed a second time. The letters printed twice appear darker. The CR instruction enables the printing of a line twice.

> HINT | The CR command enables any printer to underline and boldface text with any word processing software. If your printer does not work, the word processor is not set up correctly, or a wire is not firing in a dot-matrix print head.

Printers have come a long way since the first simple printer. Today, modern printers that print very respectable letters and mailing labels can be bought for under $190. Top-of-the-line printers with hard disks, optical disks, and

4.5M of random access memory (RAM) can add, subtract, compute trigonometry functions, read credit cards, and hook directly into Local Area Networks (LANs) without the help of a microcomputer.

Activating Printer Features

Understanding the history of printers also provides an introduction into how to use the printer buttons. This section explains how to activate the printer features using the keyboard. You need to read this section because many PC software packages never seem to activate printer features described in the printer manuals, and, at other times, the PC software manuals describe printouts that you can never get the printer to print.

Keystrokes from a keyboard arrive in the computer and become the responsibility of the application program running in the computer. Application software then sends the proper instructions to the printer. If you press a word processor's underline key, the key is translated into an underlining command understood by the printer.

Two application programs rarely underline with the same keystrokes, but the programs send the same underlining instructions to a printer.

The computer industry has specialized into software companies, hardware companies, and printer companies. Software companies shoulder the burden of implementing printer hardware features. Many software companies approach this problem by surveying printer features and making a list of what is most common among all printers; then, they write software that uses just those features.

A software company can designate Alt-U as the underlining command and translate Alt-U to underlining instructions for any printer attached. The software company then can provide a database describing how to translate all generic printer commands to specific printer models. These databases are called *printer drivers* or *printer definition tables* (see Chapter 9).

HINT | If you change printer models, don't expect your old documents to print the same on the new printer. You may have to reformat the entire document.

Because printer manufacturers want to sell printers, new features always are being added. Most software companies do not revise their software to take advantage of new printer features, but the new feature is there.

This process leads to the *hidden treasure* syndrome in which some techie figures out how to activate the new feature. The techie then writes a letter to a magazine describing the new feature. Everyone in the office soon starts clamoring for the feature. Consultants, help desks, and micro managers begin tearing their hair out while trying to figure out what the techie did. The time spent to implement the new feature is wasted, however, as soon as the printer or software is upgraded.

> HINT | Avoid modifying printer drivers or printer definition tables. This time is wasted as soon as the printer or software is upgraded.

Any software company that tries to implement diverse printer features has a difficult job. In 1983, Okidata began selling printers (among other products) that single and double underlined. WordPerfect modified the word processor package to implement the double underlining of the Okidata printer. If an Okidata printer was not attached, however, WordPerfect's double underlining did not work.

Today, many other printers can double underline, and WordPerfect can make the printer double underline, even if the printer does not have the built-in feature.

History, however, repeats itself. The problem of some software feature not working persists. When something does not work, the software or the attached printer looks bad. Sometimes the problem is not solvable—especially when new software versions are combined with old printers. If the software is old and the printer is new, wait for a new software version. Then, the printer's unusual feature will be exploited.

A danger also exists when a software company tries to support too many printers. Today, WordPerfect the company and WordPerfect the software product are successful. WordPerfect can use more printer features than most other software packages. The *hidden treasure syndrome* is not as prevalent. WordPerfect, however, has so many features that all of them will never work on any one printer. Suppose that WordPerfect tells a printer to redline when it cannot. How is the user supposed to know that the printer cannot redline? How is the user supposed to determine whether he is doing something wrong, WordPerfect is not set up properly, or the printer does not have the capability?

> HINT | Don't expect all the printer features available with an application program to be implemented. The printer you have may not support the feature. The better software companies have a test page that exposes the limits of the printer's capabilities.

Comparing How Programs Use Printers

Now that you know some PC programs never use all of the printer's capabilities and some PC programs imply the printer has features that it really doesn't have, the next step is to examine more closely what goes on between programs and printers. Some software packages want to control each dot a printer puts on paper; other software packages let the printer determine the shape and location of the symbol to be printed. You need to know how the software is using the printer to figure out where the characters are coming from.

Novices expect to print what they see on-screen. Unfortunately, monitor (and video board) technology is completely different from printer technology. Application software sends one set of commands to present a diagram on the monitor and another set of commands to present a diagram on paper. Application software has the difficult task of translating between all combinations of monitors and printers. This task is so difficult that a special term has entered the language: **W**hat **Y**ou **S**ee **I**s **W**hat **Y**ou **G**et. The acronym for this phrase is WYSIWYG—pronounced *Wizz ee wig*.

Applications that attempt WYSIWYG are called graphics, drawing, or desktop publishing packages. Apple's Macintosh has been the leader in making WYSIWYG available to the masses. These packages send dots to the screen and printer. Most other applications do not attempt WYSIWYG. Instead, they send letters to the screen and printer. When applications send letters, the screen and printer decide how to draw the letters.

If printing the screen is so desirable, why aren't more companies writing WYSIWYG programs? First, WYSIWYG programs are harder to write. Second, you need a Macintosh, IBM AT, PS/2 models 55sx, 50Z, 60, 70, 80, or a clone 80386 computer. These computers are expensive, but they can house enough memory to run the software. The more the computer costs, the faster it is going to draw the screen and compute the dots sent to the printer. The amount of information that needs to be computed and transmitted is much larger in a WYSIWYG application.

For example, to send a capital A, a unique pattern of 8 bits is required. The computation of the individual dots making up the letter A requires more time and transferred information (see fig. 1.3). If the device is a monitor, the letter A usually is drawn in a 9-by-18-bit box. This means that $9 \times 18 = 162$ bits are computed and transmitted. If the device is a laser printer, the number is 900 bits.

Fig. 1.3.

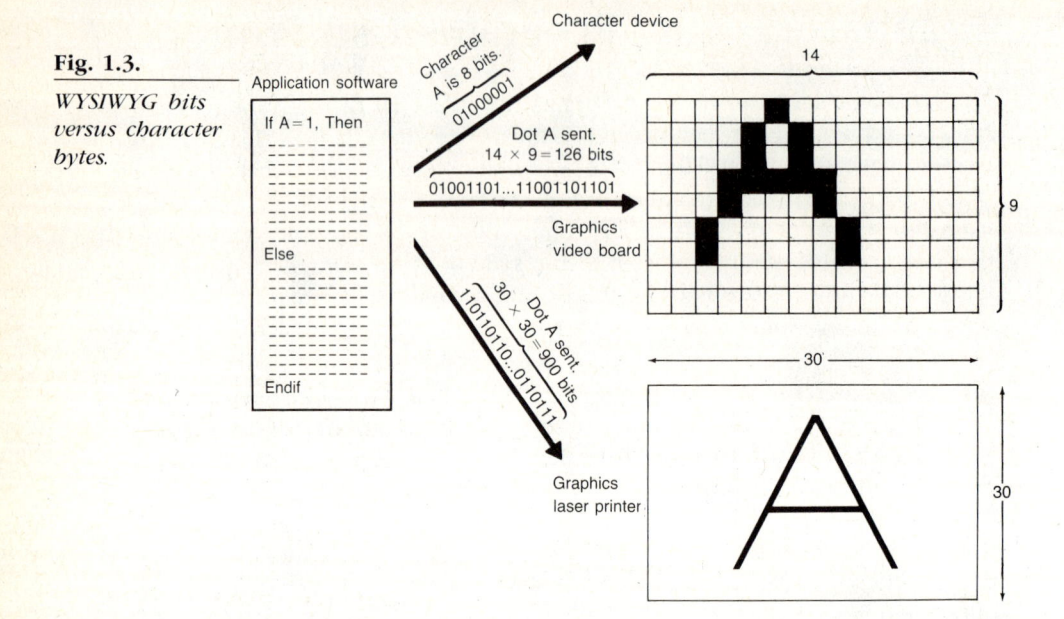

WYSIWYG bits versus character bytes.

> HINT | Printing with WYSIWYG programs, such as those found in Macintosh, Windows, and GEM environments, usually is very slow. You need to identify whether the printer or computer is slowing everything down. Almost every printer has a light that blinks as the printer receives data. (The Caminton TurboLaser/PS-Plus 3 is one of the rare printers without this feature.) If the light is blinking constantly, the printer is the bottleneck. If the light stops blinking in the middle of printing a page, the computer is the bottleneck.

Printers and monitors with WSYIWYG features are called graphics printers or graphics videoboards. Original printers and monitors could receive only characters and were called character printers and character videoboards. Most software today, such as WordPerfect, Lotus, and dBASE, is character-oriented. You can tell by changing fonts. If fonts cannot be changed or the font on-screen does not change, then the software has put the screen in character mode. The WSYIWYG features of graphic printers and graphic videoboards are not used by character-oriented software.

Character-oriented software changes fonts, underlines, and boldfaces text by sending instructions to printers. Early character-oriented software forced you to read the printer manuals and to enter the proper printer command. If the printer changed, you had to learn new printer commands. Today, when configuring your system, you tell the software which printer is attached and enter generic printer instructions. If the printer changes, you reconfigure the software.

> HINT | Never change printers and software versions at the same time. Changing more than one component at a time increases the possibility of failure.

> HINT | Develop your own *test page* to test all the features of the software you use. When changing software versions or printers, use this *test page* to make sure that the system is working.

The big mystery is how printer instructions appear on-screen before being printed. If the screen cannot underline, how can you see that certain characters need to be underlined? If a screen can display only one size of letters, how can the monitor show changes among letter sizes? Different character-oriented software vendors solve the problem by offering a variety of software packages:

❏ Software that provides no support
❏ Page setup software
❏ Software that displays printer-specific commands
❏ Software that displays generic printer commands

Software That Provides No Support

Some application programs create boring outputs in which underlining, font changes, and so on are not important. Applications in this category include most databases, mailing list programs, and accounting packages. As information is typed, it is examined carefully. Because underlining or boldfacing a general ledger entry is inappropriate, elaborate printer commands are not supported. If special effects are needed, they are built into the application program. In these cases, the application program may ask for a printer name during configuration, but no special effects are available during data entry.

Often, the printer can be told to use a smaller font prior to execution. This can be done by using the printer's front panel or by using another software package. After a print command is executed, the printer remembers the earlier instructions and can continue to print with the smaller font.

Page Setup Software

Page setup programs send printer commands at the beginning of the page. If the printer command is to begin underlining, the whole page is underlined. More often, a font change is made, and the entire page is printed in a smaller font. The most famous program in this category is 1-2-3. All local area networks and most other printer-sharing software programs are in this category. DOS's MODE command falls into this category. Applications of this type often require you to enter printer-specific commands that you need to look up in printer manuals.

Like the applications without printer support, page setup applications often can be told to use a smaller font prior to execution.

Software That Displays Printer-Specific Commands

Some programs insert funny-looking symbols on-screen to represent printer-specific commands. Reading the screens is an exercise in imagination. Some printer commands use regular letters and can be confused with text. The printer commands also may look like multiplication signs, dots, or tiny arrows (see fig. 1.4). Modern programs in this category most often are called editors and essentially are word processors without generic printer support (for example, IBM's Personal Editor program).

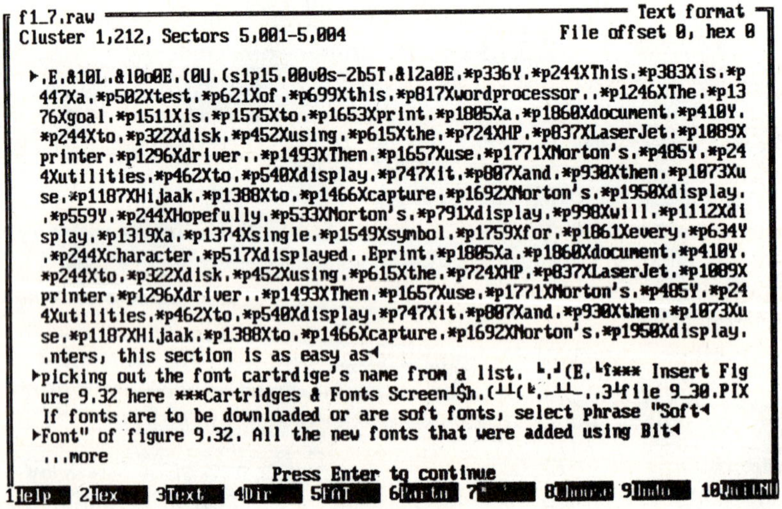

Fig. 1.4.

Printer-specific commands in a document.

Modifying printer-specific commands is possible. You can use the typical search-and-replace commands found in most editors to search for these commands. When you want to convert old documents for the new printer, you have to write a program.

> HINT: Stay away from programs that instruct you to enter printer codes that you must look up in a printer manual. The most notable among these programs are editors (usually used by programmers) such as DOS's EDLIN program or IBM's Personal Editor. When you change printers, you may need to change the printer codes in all the macros, documents, database reports, and spreadsheets.

Printing with Generic Printer Commands

Some programs mix text and generic printer commands on-screen. Most word processors fit into this category.

Some programs display symbols for each of the generic printer commands (see fig. 1.5). For example, generic symbols representing font changes and underlining may be displayed. At first, the screen appears cluttered with funny-looking, unprintable characters. Because the symbols are the same for all printers, your eye soon learns to skip over them, and documents become more readable.

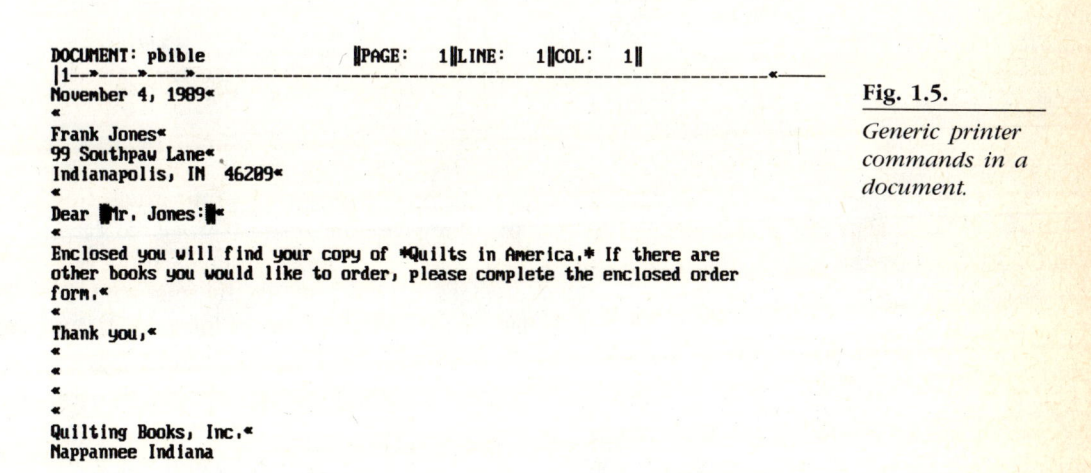

```
DOCUMENT: pbible            ‖PAGE:   1‖LINE:   1‖COL:   1‖
 |1-->----->----->--------------------------------------<-----
November 4, 1989«
«
Frank Jones«
99 Southpaw Lane«
Indianapolis, IN  46209«
«
Dear ▌r. Jones:▌«
Enclosed you will find your copy of *Quilts in America.* If there are
other books you would like to order, please complete the enclosed order
form.«
«
Thank you,«
«
«
«
Quilting Books, Inc.«
Nappannee Indiana
```

Fig. 1.5.

Generic printer commands in a document.

As printers have evolved, a large number of generic printer commands have been created. There are not enough strange, funny-looking symbols to represent all the possible generic commands. The generic printer commands are spelled out, or a symbol is created to represent a group of printer commands.

Programs such as WordStar spell out generic printer commands. The WordStar designers figure that nothing ever written with Wordstar will contain a line that begins with a period. Every line that begins with a period in WordStar, therefore, is treated as a printing or formatting instruction. The problem is that word processing turns into a programming language (see fig. 1.6). Separating commands from the text takes a trained eye. Because the learning curve is high, the popularity of these types of programs is declining.

Fig. 1.6.

Generic printer programming language.

```
          C:FIG0106           P00 L01 C01 Insert Align
         L----!----!----!----!----!----!----!----!----!--------R
         .he Printer Bible
         .rm65
         .pl66
         .pn
         .fo 11/4/89

         This chapter focuses on what happens between the moment a key is
         pressed and the moment a character appears on paper. To start
         with, a "simple printer" is defined. Then various software
         components are introduced that modify printer information. What
         happens to keyboard information, how it appears on the screen,
         how it is stored on a floppy, and what is eventually sent to the
         printer are explored in detail.

         (c)A Brief History Of Printers

         Today's printer is the offspring of typewriters and the
         typesetting industry. The printer has passed through many
         primitive and frustrating early life forms. In spite of this,
         printers have populated the earth and evolved many subspecies.
         Even now this rapid evolution has not stopped. Daisy wheels begat
         dot matrixes which begat inkjets which begat laser. Daisy wheels
         have died, and laser printers under $1000 are crowding out dot
```

Programs such as MultiMate lump generic printer commands into categories and display a symbol representing the category. The result is easier to read because it is less cluttered with printer commands. Specific details, however, are hidden. For example, all font changes are represented by one symbol. You cannot determine exactly what the font change is by looking at the symbol.

Another approach spells out every generic printer command, but displays them one at a time in the corner of the screen. Locating these commands then becomes a major problem. The commands are hidden behind the characters on-screen. When you are scrolling, the cursor will stop on a character hiding the printout command. You must press the cursor movement key twice to move to the next character. Ventura displays some information about the printer commands in the bottom left corner of the screen as you pass over them. Because Ventura is WYSIWYG, the generic printer command usually is ignored. When you need to find the hidden printer commands, you have to move the cursor over every letter in the document.

A method with no drawbacks creates two screens—one screen for the text and another for printer commands embedded in the text. Use the text screen for writing. Use the text and printer commands screen for formatting a document (see fig. 1.7). Although you may not be able to see both on the same monitor, you can switch between different views or screens of the same document in many software packages. WordPerfect has implemented this approach and has added a third screen that shows what the page looks like —called a *preview screen* or *graphics screen*.

```
WE, THE COMMUNITIES OF LARK BROWN ROAD, HEATHERWOOD ESTATES,
ANNETTA GARDENS, DEEP RUN PARK, MAYFIELD AVENUE, KENDALL RIDGE AND
OTHER INTERESTED CITIZENS OF HOWARD COUNTY OPPOSE THE APPROVAL OF
BENSON BUSINESS CENTER, CASE #242--FDP #202, S-89-29.

Signature            Name            Address            Phone Number


E:\SCOTT\BBCPETIT                              Doc 1 Pg 1 Ln 5.27i Pos 1i
[                ▲    ▲    ▲    ▲    ▲    ▲    ▲    ▲    ▲    }    ▲
[HRt]
[SM CAP][BOLD]WE, THE COMMUNITIES OF LARK BROWN ROAD, HEATHERWOOD ESTATES,[SRt]
ANNETTA GARDENS, DEEP RUN PARK, MAYFIELD AVENUE, KENDALL RIDGE AND[SRt]
OTHER INTERESTED CITIZENS OF HOWARD COUNTY [DBL UND]OPPOSE THE APPROVAL [dbl und
]OF[SRt]
BENSON BUSINESS CENTER, CASE #242[-][-]FDP #202, S[-]89[-]29.[bold][HRt]
[HRt]
[SMALL]Signature [small] [sm cap]                [SMALL]Name [small]            [SM
ALL]Address [small]                [SMALL]Phone [small][SMALL]Number [small][HRt]
[HRt]

Press Reveal Codes to restore screen
```

Fig. 1.7.

A split WordPerfect screen showing text and text containing generic printer commands.

Observing Printer File Characteristics

Different software packages structure files stored on disks and in printers in different ways. Some file format structures are very simple, and almost any program can print the file. Other file structures are very complicated, and only the program that created the file originally can print it. Still other files have printer-specific information in them and cannot be printed on another printer without a lot of work. You need to know how to identify the different file types, not only to clean up your hard disk, but also to understand the problems associated with printing the same file on different printers.

Whether a program or application saves a file, posts a journal entry, closes a database, or updates a record, it saves information that eventually is printed. The saved files are designed to optimize data processing, not printing. Because the file information is related to the software that created the file, you need the software that created the file to print the file. Most files are in this category. Some files are printable without the application software. You can use the operating system to print this type of file.

The two basic printable files are text files (often called ASCII files) and binary files. Text files contain the letters and symbols found on a keyboard plus the printer commands that a simple printer understands: LF, CR, and FF (see fig. 1.8). Text files are created using an editor or the operating system. Word processors can create text files through special procedures, which are different for each word processor. The biggest use of text files probably is for configuring the operating system: writing batch files and configuration files.

Fig. 1.8.

A text file.

```
C:\> type config.sys
files = 20
buffers = 30
device = c:\pstyler\psept.sys -P2 -L2 -I7
DEVICE = DMDRVR.BIN
DEVICE = SPC.COM
DEVICE = D:\EVEREX\EMM.SYS /C
DEVICE = C:\bat\mouse.sys
FCBS = 32,16
device = himem.sys
device = smartdrv.sys /320

C:\> type autoexec.bat
COMMAND /C C:\PSTYLER\PSSTART.BAT -C
PATH C:\pm;C:\AI;d:\pctools;d:\wp;d:\basic;C:\;c:\bat;C:\PSTYLER
mirror c: /tr
prompt $p$g
cd\spc
spcbio
c:
SET temp=C:\PM
CD\BAT
TYPE HELP

C:\>
```

TROUBLE-SHOOTING TIP	If your printer prints a few characters, ejects a sheet, prints a few more characters, and ejects another sheet in a repetitious pattern, you probably are trying to print a file with the wrong software or with software configured for a different printer. To solve the problem, use the software program used to create the file or reconfigure your software to match the attached printer.

Programs that print to disk normally create text files when transferring data from one program to another in the IBM PC, PC-DOS, and MS-DOS world. Most software can import and create text files. Printing to a disk or printing to a file is similar to putting text on a Macintosh clipboard. Programs that print to a disk strip all elaborate printer instructions and create output for a simple printer. On-disk text files, however, can be pulled into a word processor and enhanced.

Any file containing more than just text and the three basic printer instructions is called a *binary file*. Binary files can contain text and additional printer instructions. The printer instructions can consist of any random pattern of 1s and 0s (see fig. 1.9). You can create binary files with editors without printer support. Editors enable binary printer instructions to be entered for special effects such as underlining. You also can create binary files using application software, but this process usually is very complicated.

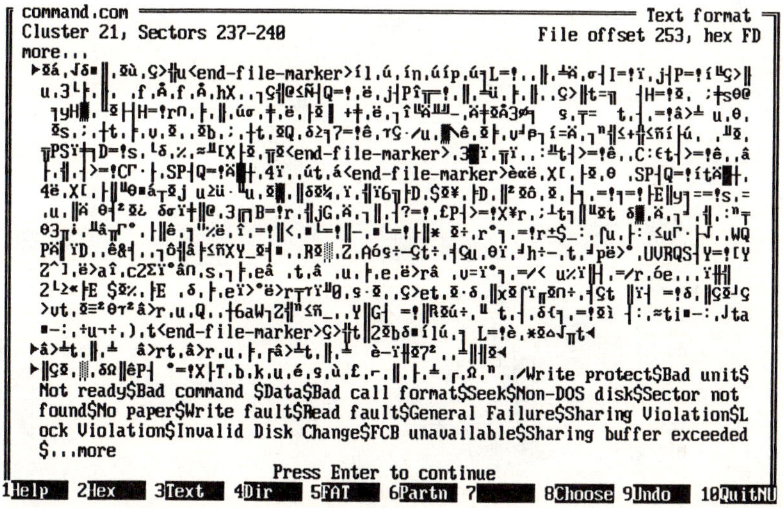

Fig. 1.9.

A binary file.

Binary files also are created by software that sends dots to printers. The individual dot information sent to a printer can contain all possible bit patterns. Because a binary file is often 10 times larger than a text file, if something goes wrong, the paper mess is 10 times larger.

Most application software that creates binary files uses *device redirection*. Device redirection prints software normally, but at the last moment, sends the output to a file rather than the printer. Many application software packages cannot create binary files.

In most cases, creating a binary file requires that you have a memory resident program or that you make a second computer pretend it is a serial printer. Binary files are useful for debugging the instructions a program is sending to the printer. The only people who read binary printer files are techies and programmers trying to troubleshoot a printer problem.

Binary files most often are created by software to temporarily hold printer information until the printer is ready. This information usually is stored in temporary files on a disk. Software that temporarily creates printer files is included with all the leading word processors and local area network software packages and is called *printer spoolers*, *print queue*, or *buffering* software (see fig. 1.10). Occasionally, print spoolers leave a mess on the hard disk. This mess may contain files with binary printer information. Normally, the print spooler should delete binary files when the files are printed.

Fig. 1.10.

A printer spooler, queue, or buffer software.

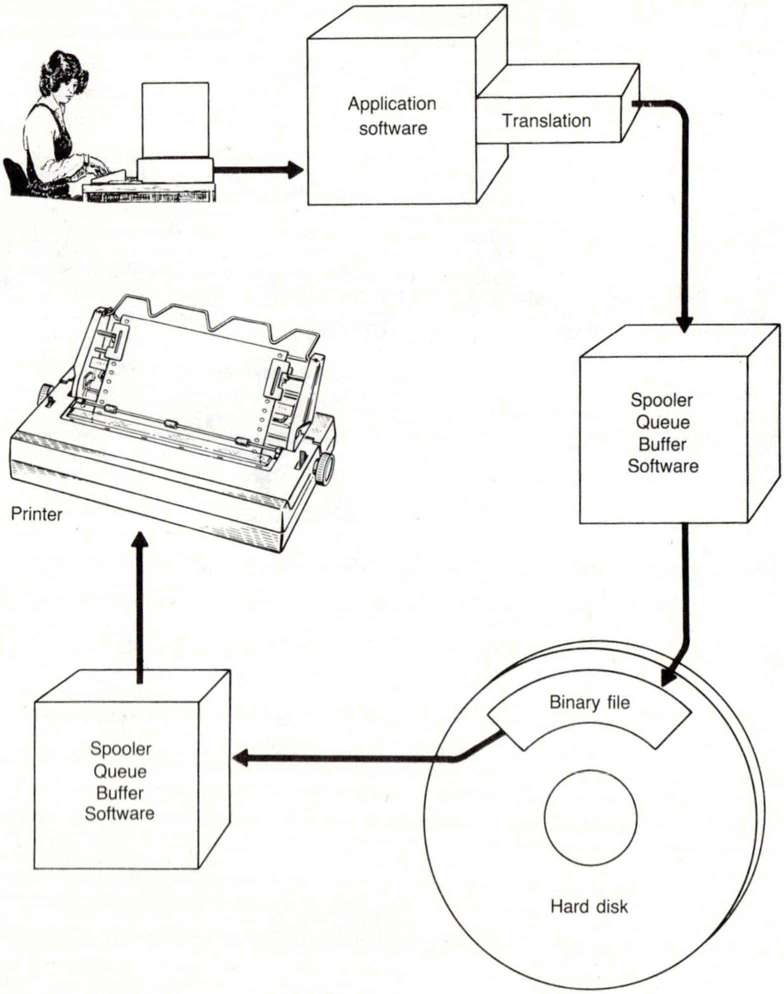

HINT | Figure out where the spool, queue, or print buffer files are created on your hard disk. Turn the computer off while printing and look and see which files are created. Periodically, check this area of the hard disk for pieces of files and delete them. Beware of software that scatters pieces of files all over your hard disk.

Configuring Applications for Your Printer

Most microcomputer programs store data in different file formats. In addition, there is a tremendous variety of printers on the market. Software vendors have a hard time making sure that their files can be translated to all the different printers. You need to know how software vendors organize themselves to support the thousands of printers so that you can properly install new software packages to work with your printer.

Some programs don't need to know any information about a printer. Some programs create boring printouts or rely on another program to edit the output before printing. Today, during installation, you tell most programs which printer is attached. When installed, the printer is reconfigured if the printer type is changed. Configurable programs can create exciting printouts, depending on the printer's features.

If a program asks for the printer's name during installation, a list is presented from which you can pick (see fig. 1.11). The more specific names support more features. For example, if the installable printers consist of Epsons, Okidatas, Hewlett-Packards, and Diablos, don't expect much. If the list of installable printers consists of Epson MX, Epson FX, Epson LQ, HP LaserJet +, and HP LaserJet II, you can expect more. If exact printer model numbers are mentioned, expect the most support possible.

What if the name of your printer, the *Gorilla Banana*, is not on the list? Read the printer's manual. The manual usually mentions whether the printer is compatible with an Epson or Diablo printer. Unfortunately, 41 different Epsons are mentioned on the install screen. Which Epson? You have two choices. Choose `Simple printer`, `DOS printer` or start guessing which of the Epsons. Try using a prefix and model number closest to yours. For example, if your printer is an LQ 850, try using LQ1000 Epson. Guessing does not risk hardware damage. If you guess incorrectly, the worst case scenario consists of the lights flashing, the speaker sounding like a fire alarm, and paper spilling onto the floor.

In the worst case scenario of printer configuration, you choose a simple printer. The naming of the printer, however, does not end. When a new ver-

Fig. 1.11.

A sample list of printers displayed during configuration.

```
        Select Printer: Additional Printers
        Apple Laserwriter Plus
        AST TurboLaser/PS
        Canon LBP-8II/LBP-8IIT
        Cordata LP300X
        Dataproducts LZR-1230
        Epson GQ-3500
        HP LaserJet
        HP LaserJet 2000
        HP LaserJet Series II
        HP LaserJet+, 500+
        IBM Personal Pageprinter 4216
        LaserImage 1000
        NEC Silentwriter LC-860+
        NEC Silentwriter LC-890
        Okidata LaserLine 6
        Olympia Laserstar 6
        QMS Kiss Plus (Personality Card 30)
        QMS PS Jet Plus /800 II/810
        Quadram Quadlaser
        Ricoh PC Laser 6000
        Silver-Reed EXP 800

   1 Select; 2 Other Disk; 3 Help; 4 List Printer Files; N Name Search: 1
```

sion of the software arrives, all the names change. You have to guess all over again. If you purchase a new software package, you must configure it, selecting another printer name. Every time software is added or upgraded, repeat this procedure. If guessing was required the first time, count on more guessing the second time.

> **HINT** Purchase only name-brand printers or clones of name-brand printers. These printers always are supported. Otherwise, expect support for your nonstandard printer to disappear in the next software version.

The name of a printer identifies a database that holds information necessary to translate between the generic printer instructions and specific instructions sent to a printer. The database also may contain font files, character width tables, and sheet feeder tables. Some vendors have separate databases for over 300 different printers, and the amount of information can be stored in several megabytes of memory. Transferring the entire database to a hard disk usually is not necessary. Often, the database is copied to the hard disk anyway. If each installed application brings with it 2M of printer information, the hard disk fills up. Managing different printer configuration files turns into a hassle.

> **HINT** After you have installed the printer correctly, delete all other printer names to save space on the hard disk.

Ideally, you should install a printer just once—when you install the operating system or the printer. Mainframes and the Apple Macintosh work this way. Application software can translate generic printer commands to another generic format understood by the operating system. The operating system then can translate to the specific printer commands (see fig. 1.12). The IBM PC World is moving in this direction with products called GEM, Windows, and Presentation Manager. Applications written in the GEM, Windows, or Presentation Manager environments are not configured. GEM and Windows are configured for a printer.

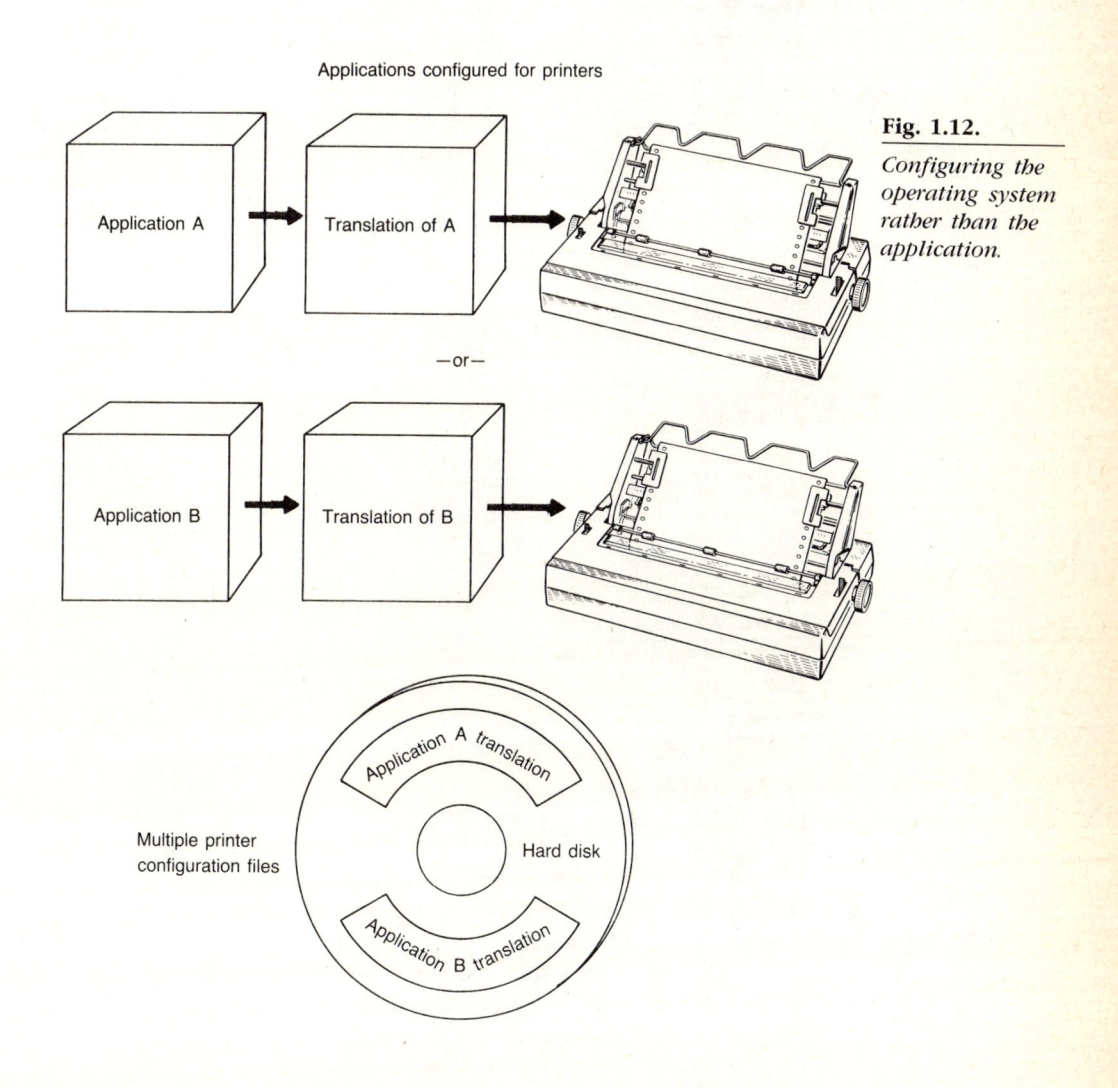

Fig. 1.12.
Configuring the operating system rather than the application.

Fig. 1.12—continued

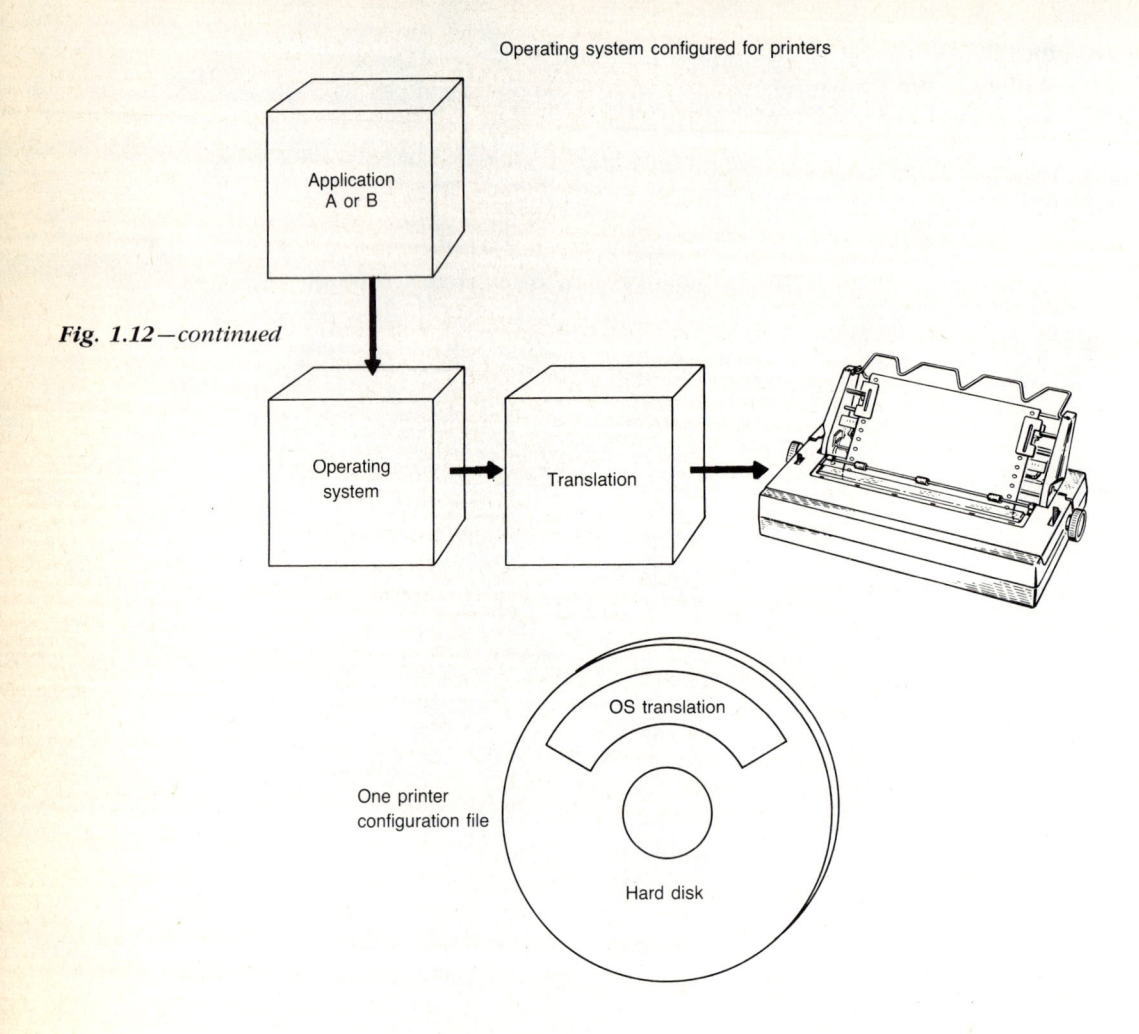

Configuring your printer at the operating system level enables you to change, update, and add to the application program version, without requiring you to reconfigure the printer. If you have only one printer configuration file, you do not have any management headaches, nor does your hard disk fill up with configuration information. When this type of configuration works, you save tremendously in configuration time and have fewer printer problems. When you do have a problem, however, you do not have any diagnostic tools or procedures to work with, and fewer trained people are available. Those people who are available have less information to troubleshoot with. Despite this, the advantages outweigh the disadvantages by a large margin.

Predicting What Printers Do with Arriving Data

So far, the discussion has been focused on what can happen to keyboard information as it travels to the printer. This section focuses on what happens to the data once it arrives in the printer. In essence, this section introduces the rest of the book. It reviews the concepts of printer operational modes (character and graphic), printer buffers (character, line, and page), and printer responses to problems (too many characters on a line, running out of memory, troubles distinguishing text, and instructions). You need to read this section because these concepts are introduced and repeated throughout the book.

Printers have two basic modes of operation: graphics mode in which they receive dots and text mode in which they receive characters. When a printer receives data, it does not print the data all at once. Instead, the printer stores the data in a buffer while it is examined. Printer buffers range in size from around 512K in a fully formed, impact printer to over 4M in a laser printer.

> **HINT** Large printer buffers are not always better. These buffers have a harder time stopping the printer from printing, take longer loading the extra memory with data, have more RAM that can go bad, and have almost no way of checking the memory.

Printers start processing data character by character, line by line, or page by page. In a character-by-character printer, a character is printed the minute it is received. This feature was important in early simple printers. With character-by-character printers, you could check whether a letter made the round trip to a host properly. These printers mechanically moved to the beginning of the next line when a line became full. The software packages run on these early printers did not notice whether printing started at the top or at the bottom of a page because these programs were not that sophisticated. The software did not even try to keep track of where the top of a page was. Because the early printers printed on a roll of paper, printing on the crease between sheets of computer paper was not a problem.

> **CAUTION** Do not let a dot-matrix printer, especially a 24-pin-head model, print on the crease between fanfold sheets of paper. Printing on the crease can bend and eventually prevent a wire from firing.

Most printers today buffer a whole line before printing. Try this process yourself. Put an IBM PC in BASIC. Then, type the following command:

   LPRINT "This is a test";

Be sure to put the semicolon at the end. The semicolon indicates that a new line should not begin. The printer does nothing. Next, type the following command:

   LPRINT "This is the end of the test"

Now, the printer should display "This is a test" and "This is the end of the test" on the same line. A line seldom is left unprinted in a dot-matrix printer by application software. Almost all software ends the last line with a CR or LF.

The printers print a line on receiving a CR or LF command, or they print a line when it is full of characters. The big question is what to do with the extra characters that do not fit on a line. The extra characters can be ignored, or they can be *wrapped* to the next line. If the characters are ignored, everything sent is not printed. If the extra characters are placed on the next line, the page length changes. If the page length changes, software ends up wasting a page; the print head may end up printing on the platen or the crease between sheets of fan fold paper. Neither results are good for a printer. Switches inside most printers tell the printer whether to ignore the extra characters or put them on a new line.

TROUBLE-SHOOTING TIP	If a printer is double spacing randomly, spaces may have been sent at the end of each line. When more spaces are sent than the line has room for, a new line is created. The extra spaces are put on the new line, which remains blank. Try removing spaces at the end of the lines near where the double-spacing occurs.

TROUBLE-SHOOTING TIP	If a printer is loosing characters at the end of a line, you may be instructing the printer to put too many characters on a line. Try making the line shorter, adjusting the margins, and so on.

Page printers, such as laser printers, store a whole page before printing it. As each line is received, these printers figure out where to put the line on a page. When a page is full, the page is printed. Laser printers encounter the same problem of having too many characters on a line, but they also encounter the additional problem of having too many characters or pages in memory.

> HINT | If you accidentally press PrtSc (print screen) on a character laser printer, press the Reset button to erase the page without wasting a sheet of paper.

Many application programs do not worry about page formatting; the page printer has to assume responsibility. Chaos occurs if the page printer and application software are paging at the same time. For example, 1-2-3 skips lines in the middle of the page, and the laser does not print data at the top and bottom. Learning to use the Lotus Align command and adjusting the Lotus page length usually solves the problem.

> HINT | When using 1-2-3, press the Align command when beginning to print. Avoid selecting the Page command unless you have proven that the Page command ejects a page rather than adds spaces to the next page.

If an application does not fill up a page, the laser printer does not print the page. A light may come on in the printer indicating that data is to be printed, but the page does not print until the laser is put off-line and you press the form feed (FF) button.

Another issue concerns how the printer separates the data into characters and instructions (see fig. 1.13). This task is not easy. There is a fine line between characters and instructions to the printer. If the printer turns characters into instructions, wild things can happen, including the printer spitting out paper. Characters changed into instructions also can disappear.

> TROUBLE-SHOOTING TIP | If a printer is losing characters randomly, try printing a few screens with PrtSc (print screen). If the characters still disappear, the problem is in the interface or printer. Try reconfiguring the software for a different printer.

If the printer changes instructions into characters, extra characters appear within the document. Most of the extra characters are strange looking, but some can be disguised as spelling mistakes. If the wrong instructions are sent, the printer also prints strange characters and wastes paper. A one-page drawing sent to the wrong printer can waste 400 sheets of paper.

Fig. 1.13.

Separating instructions from characters.

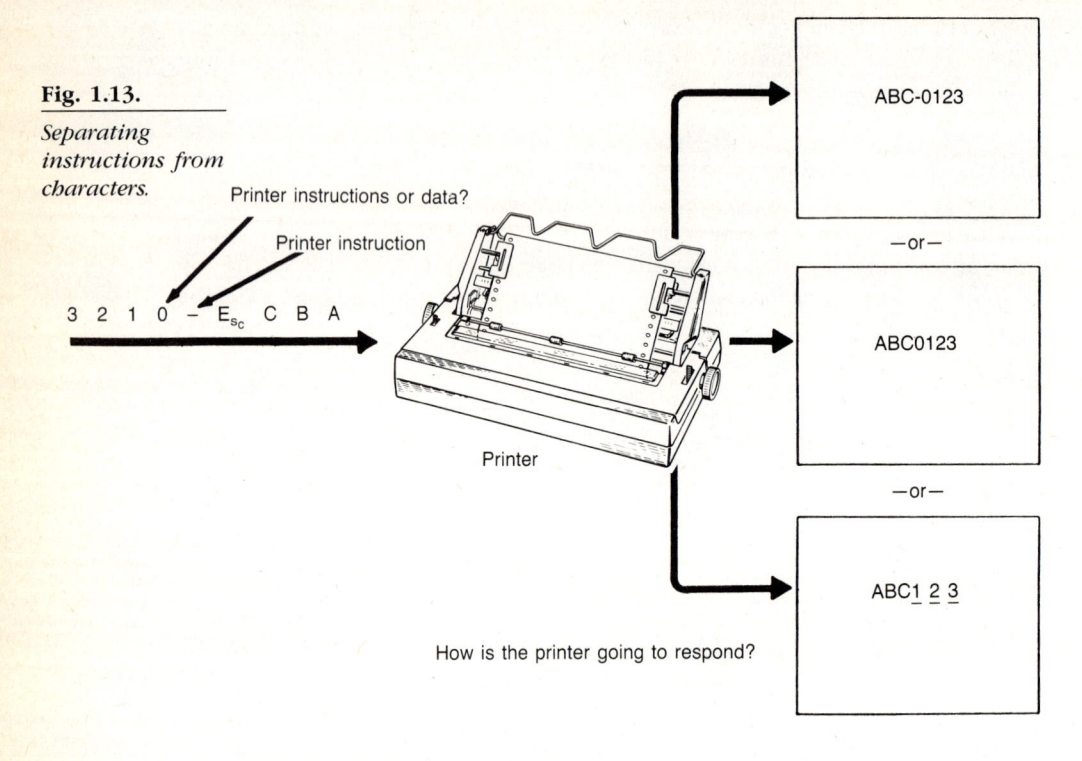

| TROUBLE-SHOOTING TIP | If a printer is adding odd characters, usually in the upper left corner, check the printer setup strings or the printer configuration. Reconfigure or reinstall the software. Commands sent to the printer are being printed rather than acted upon. |

Chapter Summary

Printers have typewriters and terminals as ancestors. The on-line and off-line buttons are used to select between these two heritages, except that the typewriter keyboard has been replaced by additional buttons on the front panel of the printer.

PC application program manuals describe printouts that may be impossible on your printer because your printer lacks features that it expects. Conversely, your printer manual may describe features that you can never get your software to exercise. Ideally, what is described in all manuals and what is displayed on-screen can be printed. This ideal is called WYSIWYG, What You See Is What You Get.

PC programs have to be told which printer is attached. If your printer is not mentioned on the list, guess. Some PC programs control each dot printed (graphics mode) and other PC programs tell the printer which character to print and let the printer determine where the character is located and what style it is (character mode).

The concept of a printer buffer was introduced in this chapter, and the different problems of character, line, and page buffering printers were discussed.

In the Next Chapter

This chapter took a global approach to printers and explored how they cooperated with the different components of the microcomputer system. Most of the topics raised in this chapter, such as performance and the configuration of application software, are covered in more detail later.

The next chapter focuses entirely on how the printer processes the information received and changes this information into characters on paper. The components common to all printers are named and each component's function is described. The general features of different printing mechanisms also are reviewed.

The Information Process: from Printer to Paper

The first chapter explored information flow through a computer system. This chapter explains information flow through a printer. The chapter starts with a description of what happens when a printer is turned on. Next is a brief survey of the various ways data can be transmitted to a printer. The printer receives data into memory, where the data is processed. Finally, this chapter explains what happens when the printer starts moving the paper and print head and printing occurs.

Turning On the Printer

What happens when a printer is first turned on indicates a great deal about the printer's health and current configuration. This section explores the printer power-on process.

The Power Supply

Finding the power supply switch is always fun on a new printer. Don't look at the manual. Don't examine the printer with a flashlight. The power switch is usually in the back in a corner where you will never see it. Feel the printer; run your hands over every surface. Discover the power-on switch as if you were blindfolded.

The purpose of any power supply is to change the alternating current (AC) coming out of a wall socket, into direct current (DC). DC is the type of power that batteries deliver, and the type of power that components in a printer need.

The power supply in most printers today is not in a box and is not marked with a warning sticker. As a result, a printer is much more dangerous than a personal computer.

When a printer's lid is removed, the printer's power supply is exposed. Turning on the printer without its lid is risking death. Touching certain parts of the printer while it is turned on is the equivalent of sticking your fingers into a wall outlet to see whether it is working. Most printers have a switch that detects the presence of the lid. An interlock switch prevents the printer from working when the lid is off. Although this switch is easy to find and disable, do not disable the safety switch unless you are trained in electronics.

> **TROUBLE-SHOOTING TIP** If the printer seems dead, you usually can check for a blown fuse. Replacing the fuse will not solve the problem until the interlock switch is disabled or the lid is replaced.

Two basic types of power supplies are used in electronic equipment today. One power supply, called a *linear power supply*, has been around for years. A newer power supply, which first became popular in the middle 1970s, is the *switching power supply*. Switching power supplies are more efficient, do not heat up much, are lighter and smaller, and protect against normal electrical problems. Switching power supplies use the same technology found in modern dimmer switches that do not heat the wall. Old-fashioned dimmer switches are warm to touch. These power supplies are found in boxes with warning stickers.

The old-fashioned linear power supply is not usually in a box. Linear power supplies are much more sensitive to surges and spikes, are heavy, and generate more heat. Most printers today have linear power supplies. Parts of the power supply can be found on or near the main logic board. This location is what makes linear power supplies so dangerous. The raw AC from wall outlets is exposed where you may accidentally touch it.

The important points to remember about printer power supplies are the following:

❏ Printer power supplies are much more dangerous than PC power supplies.

❏ Printer power supplies need more protection from surges and spikes.

❏ Printer power supplies generate more heat.

Test Programs

When the power switch is turned on in a printer, the power supply starts building up its voltages. When the voltages are high enough, the power supply signals the printer to start executing the Power-On Self-Test (POST) program. POST programs are essentially a quick diagnostic executed when a printer is first turned on. The program itself is permanently burned into a special chip in the printer; this chip is called a read-only memory (ROM) chip. Different printers have different POST programs. Some programs move the print head back and forth. Others may flash lights or display messages like Warming up. When the test is finished, a light may turn on, or Ready may be displayed.

TROUBLE-SHOOTING TIP	If the print head moves when the printer is turned on but the printer does not print, the logic board in the printer is working and the motors are working. The problem is the print-head driver circuitry or the print head itself. Swap print heads to isolate the problem. Don't leave a known good print head in the broken printer for more than a couple of seconds when the printer doesn't work. The print-head driver circuitry can destroy print heads in some failure modes. This danger is present whether all the wires or just one wire of the print head fails.

ROM also may contain user-initiated self-test programs. Some printers have several different self-tests. You initiate these self-tests by holding down a button(s) while you turn on the printer or by pressing special buttons after you turn on the printer. How these different self-tests are executed and what they can tell you about the printer and general features of printer self-test programs are explored in Chapter 8. The important point is that the printer self-test programs are stored in ROM chips.

The first program executed when you turn on a PC or printer does a quick diagnostic test, which includes checking RAM. If a PC detects a problem during the power-on diagnostic, the computer displays an error code on-screen. If a printer detects a memory problem, the printer flashes a light or error code or may print an error code.

As more memory has been added to PCs and printers, the power-on memory diagnostic test takes longer, and some tests have been redesigned to do a less thorough job. Consumers prefer PCs and printers that turn on quickly. Because of this preference, manufacturers are under pressure to design PCs and printers that check their memory less and less thoroughly. As a result, you cannot trust memory tests executed when a PC or printer is turned on.

If a memory problem goes undetected during the power-on diagnostic, several problems can arise. When a PC memory chip goes bad, the cursor doesn't move, an error message appears, and often hours of work disappear instantly. When a printer memory chip goes bad, however, often nothing happens. Most likely the printer will garble a letter every now and then. On other occasions, the printer may seem to be incompatible with a software package. The bad news is that you may not even notice or think that you have a printer memory problem. Instead, you may think you have a cable or interface problem.

In the PC world, some available software can check PC RAM. Unfortunately, like the diagnostics executed when power is applied, RAM diagnostic software is becoming less and less reliable. The reason is simple. RAM is cheap, so you have more of it, and more RAM takes a long time to test properly. Testing RAM is not cost effective. Professionals are now replacing groups of PC RAM chips whenever the user finds a failure symptom.

A mechanism to load RAM test software into the printer, execute the test, and then report the results does not exist. The good news, however, is that engineers today can design RAM that tests itself and can correct most problems. Self-diagnostic and self-healing PC hard disk drives and modems exist. Even CPU chips can heal themselves today. Self-healing RAM chips, however, are not readily available. Manufacturers implement healing algorithms only when the implementation increases profits. Adding the self-correcting feature to RAM increases costs approximately 10 percent. The debate is whether the larger up-front cost is worth the long-term benefits received.

Switch and Button Positions

After the POST or self-tests have been completed, the printer starts configuring itself by looking at switch and button positions. Just after passing the POST, printers quickly scan their manual switches and other memory locations that may have configuration information. Printers read switches and configuration information only once during the power-on process. Afterwards, the printer ignores any changes made to physical switches and any configuration changes.

A printer is constantly scanning the front panel for buttons pushed after the printer is turned on. For example, the printer is constantly scanning the on-line/off-line button. An interesting experiment is to press the off-line button while the printer is printing. How quickly does the printer stop? Can fonts be changed by using the front panel while the printer is printing? These types of features are explored in Chapter 8. Usually, the on-line/off-line button halts printer operation and activates all the other keys and buttons.

Transmitting Data

Microcomputers transmit data to printers. Circuitry inside the printer must be capable of determining when information is being transferred. Sometimes the printer has to acknowledge that data was transferred successfully. The printer circuitry that listens to data coming from the computer comes in five different varieties. Two of the five are common: parallel and serial. Video and HPIB are significant minorities. The last, SCSI, is a future possibility. In Chapter 5, these interfaces are discussed again from the feature, reliability, cabling, testing, and installing points of view. Here, a general historical introduction to these interfaces is presented.

Parallel Interface

With a parallel interface, each bit that represents a character or instruction has its own wire. For example, the bit pattern representing a capital letter A is 01000001. To transmit the letter A all at once (transmit parallel), at least eight wires are needed: one wire for each of the 8 bits representing the letter A (see fig. 2.1).

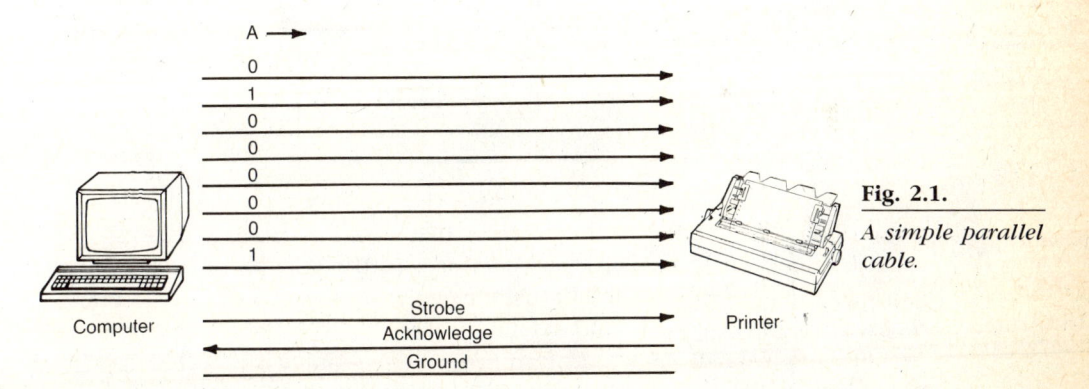

Fig. 2.1.

A simple parallel cable.

Two more wires are needed to tell the printer when to look for data and to enable the printer to acknowledge receipt of the data. These wires are named *strobe* and *acknowledge*, respectively. The company that made this parallel interface popular is Centronics. Although no standards organization blessed this particular standard, the parallel interface has become the standard way of hooking a printer to IBM PCs. (Only Apple has not adopted this standard.) The reason for the parallel port's success is its simplicity.

Centronics released the technical details of its simple parallel port to the public with the objective of selling more printers. Centronics figured that its printer was so simple to use that more engineers would decide to use Centronics printers when designing computer systems. Centronics did sell more printers until Epson came out with its *Centronics-compatible* printer.

Epson improved the Centronics parallel port. First, and most important, Epson changed the connector used on the printer end. The Centronics connector attaching the cable to the printer was an *edge connector*. An edge connector was essentially a part of the logic board that stuck out of the printer (see fig. 2.2). The cable that attached to this edge connector had no way of being screwed on tight like modern cables and therefore fell off easily. When the cable fell off, it had a tendency to twist and short the logic board, causing the logic board to smoke.

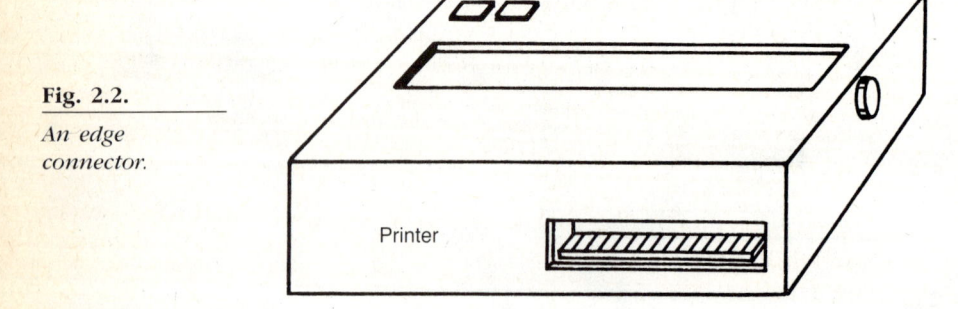

Fig. 2.2.

An edge connector.

Epson popularized a different connector that clips into place and never falls out. This connector is similar to that used by the telephone company for wiring a phone with several buttons. If exactly the same connector had been chosen for parallel ports, old telephone cables and connectors could be rebuilt into parallel cables. Unfortunately, this printer connector had 36 wires rather than the 50 wires the phone company usually used. Today, this connector has a different name in every parts catalog. The connector is sometimes called a Centronics connector, even though Centronics was not the company that made this connector popular (see fig. 2.3).

The final chapter of parallel interface history started in August 1981 with the introduction of the IBM PC. At that time, IBM did not make a low-end, inexpensive printer. IBM purchased the leading dot-matrix printer at that time, the Epson printer, and put the IBM name on the printer. IBM sold the printer as if IBM had manufactured it, changing the printer's ROM software slightly. Basically, the original IBM parallel printer was a pure Epson printer. This fact

Fig. 2.3.

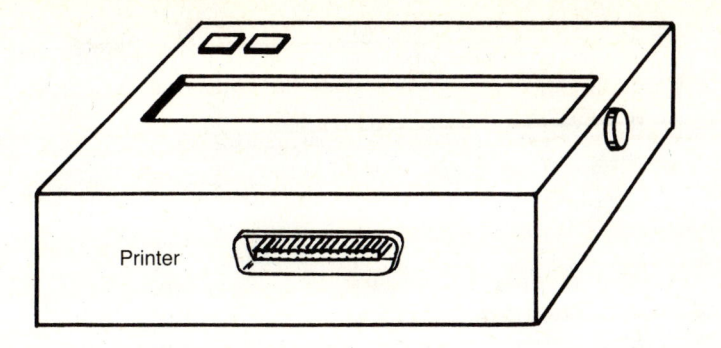

A Centronics line printer connector.

is significant because Epson—not Centronics—became IBM's standard. And, as most of us know, IBM's standards have become the world's standards. Thus, the Epson standard became the world's standard.

Even though Epson printers were compatible with Centronics printers, the two printers were not identical. Any other printer company, therefore, had the choice of designing its printer to Centronics' specifications or to Epson's. The situation for a third printer company was a no-win situation. The other companies could not come up with a third standard and sell any printers. If the company chose the Centronics parallel, the company lost the Epson-compatible market. Companies that chose the Epson parallel lost the Centronics-compatible market.

As a result, 1982 was the year of parallel port problems because of the confusion between Epson and Centronics standards. Some printers occasionally doubled the characters received. For example, a third-party printer may double the first character of a line or the first cell of a spreadsheet. The parallel port problems disappeared when the Epson parallel port version was adopted by the industry. Today, all parallel printers are Epson compatible although "Epson compatibility" is not advertised. Parallel printers are so reliable that they can be advertised simply as parallel. Epson parallel or Centronics parallel is no longer necessary.

Serial Interface

The most simple serial interface consists of two wires—like old wall outlets. One wire is for data, the other for ground. The data wire is similar to a one-lane road. Bits follow each other down the wire one at a time (see fig. 2.4). All Macintosh printers attach to the Mac through a serial port.

Compared to parallel cables, serial cables contain fewer wires, are not as thick, and can be much longer. Serial interfaces are not used just by printers. Because the serial interface is so simple, it has become the universal mecha-

Fig. 2.4.

A simple serial cable.

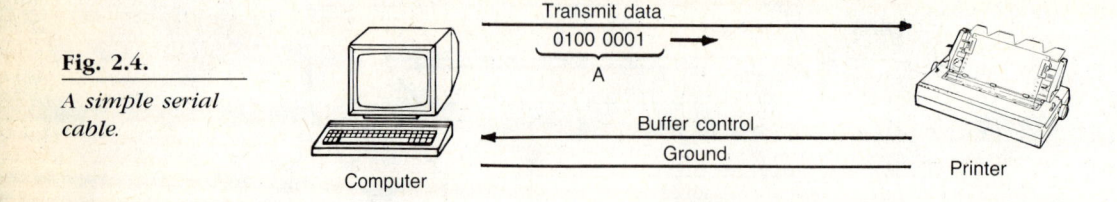

nism for hooking anything to anything. Plotters, scanners, mice, digitizers, cars, sewing machines, voice-recognition units, and speech-synthesizing units all attach to the PC through a serial port. The official connector of the serial port found on printers and most other devices is called a DB-25 female connector. This connector is shaped like the letter D and contains 25 little holes (see fig. 2.5).

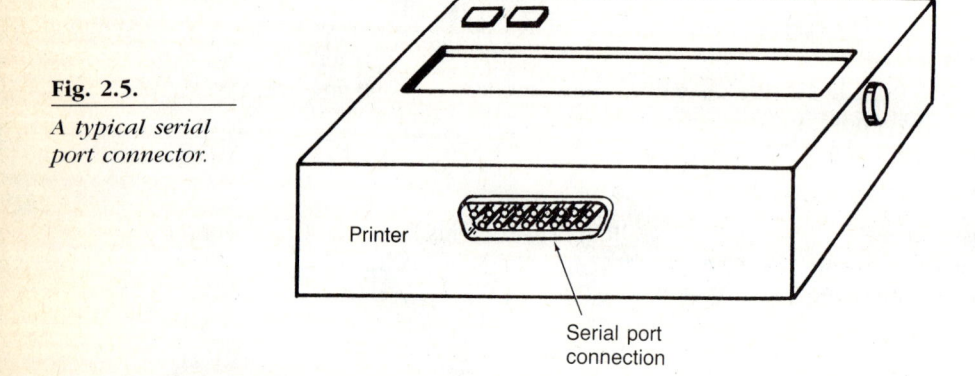

Fig. 2.5.

A typical serial port connector.

Serial ports first were used to hook terminals and printers to mainframe computers. A standard, now called EIA-232D, guides the design and manufacture of serial ports. Early printers hooked up only through the serial port. Of course, serial ports could be added to Epson printers, but then the Epson printer lost many of its features. All printer manufacturers, therefore, had an incentive to migrate to a parallel port. Even today, most new printer technologies hook up through the serial port first and then the parallel port.

Video Interface

A video interface is a parallel transfer system found only in laser printers. The video interface is the fastest method of transferring data into a printer. The data rate in a video interface cable is approximately 2 megabits per second (M bps). Serial cables usually transfer data at approximately 0.1M bps. Epson parallel cables are usually slower than serial cables.

A video interface has nothing to do with TV signals or signals coming from the circuit board to which a monitor is attached. A video interface was designed to transfer the image data created by image-drawing software. This design means that the image-drawing software must be in the computer and that the printer's CPU and RAM must be housed on a circuit board in one of the PC's slots. From this board, the video interface cable transfers image data to the device-driver software in the printer. After the image data arrives in the printer, the device-driver software uses the image data to turn solenoids off and on, move mirrors, and pull paper.

Most printers don't have a video-interface cable. Instead, the image data is transferred from one chip to another on the printer's logic board. It is possible that 2M bps in the video interface cable may slow a printer. The following analysis, however, shows that in most laser printers this interface will not slow the printer.

Information that device-driver software receives is graphical in form. The letters are transmitted as dots. If the page is 8 1/2 by 11 inches and the resolution is 300 dots per inch, approximately 1M of data is transmitted. If the video cable is transmitting at 2M bps, it will take $1M \times 8/2M = 4$ seconds to transmit the entire page. Because the paper moves at only 8 pages per minute, or 7.5 seconds per page, the video cable is not slowing the printer.

HPIB Interface

HPIB stands for Hewlett-Packard Interface Bus. Other names for this bidirectional parallel interface include IEEE 488 and GPIB. These different names came about because a standards organization, the Institute for Electronic and Electrical Engineers (IEEE), accepted HPIB. The IEEE standard was named General Purpose Interface Bus (GPIB). The standards number was IEEE 488.

The only company that actively supplies HPIB printers is Hewlett-Packard. These printers work only with old HP personal computers and other HP test equipment. Because HP test equipment is popular only among engineers, the market for these printers is limited. Avoid HPIB printers unless your company has a large number of HP minicomputers and HP personal computers.

The advantage of HPIB is that theoretically two personal computers can share one printer by using the HPIB, or one PC can switch between two printers attached to the same cable. The HPIB interface can mediate between the PCs. According to the HPIB standard, two PCs can share a printer and a hard disk through the same HPIB cable. The HPIB standard theoretically can perform the functions of a LAN. Therefore, HPIB interfaces should benefit from LAN popularity. But, this benefit has not happened. The SCSI interface, described next, suffers for the same reason.

SCSI Interface

The Small Computer Systems Interface (SCSI, pronounced "scuzzy") could become the interface of the future. SCSI is a two-way parallel interface that multiple devices can share. This interface has the same features as the HPIB; the only difference is that SCSI has more PC support. Right now, most external hard disk drives, fast tape backup systems, and scanners use some kind of modified SCSI interface. The trouble is that these interfaces are not compatible—none can share the same cable.

Specifically, three things have to happen before SCSI or HPIB can become a standard. Currently, SCSI and HPIB are used to create proprietary interfaces that lock users into one company. To become standards, SCSI and HPIB need to do the following:

1. Develop a standard software interface.
2. Be implemented uniformly in hardware.
3. Be mass produced.

The most important factor holding back SCSI and HPIB technology is the development of LANs. SCSI, HPIB, and LANs are competing technologies. Even though LANs are serial, they are just as fast as the other two cables. LANs are simpler and cheaper than SCSI and HPIB. The only advantage SCSI and HPIB have in the war against LANs is the increase in hard disk performance that SCSI and HPIB can provide. Right now, most LANs share hard disks through PCs. The PC is slowing access to the hard disk. By removing the PC and attaching the hard disk directly to the LAN, the user can achieve a vast speed improvement. SCSI hard disk drives exist right now. Directly attached LAN hard disk drives don't. The outcome of the battle is not clear. Printers will tag along with the winner.

Receiving and Processing Data

The data arriving on printer cables has to be put somewhere. Then, the data has to be processed and eventually sent to the moving parts of a printer where actual printing occurs. This section discusses the receipt and processing of data.

Storing Data in Printer Memory

Arriving data is stored in printer memory chips called random-access memory (RAM) chips. (Printer RAM can be as small as 2K or larger than 5M.) Although arriving data is most often text, the data also can include the following:

- ❑ Image of what is to be printed
- ❑ Programs
- ❑ Fonts
- ❑ Setup information

Information not yet processed is put into part of the printer's RAM called a *buffer*. RAM also is used to store instructions on how to draw letters or objects. Some printers can have macros or programs sent to them. When a printer program is executed, an image is created in printer RAM. The image can be of just a line or band, or the image can represent an entire sheet of paper or even several sheets of paper. Multiple images can sometimes be merged into one image in the printer RAM. The more page images required, the more printer RAM is needed.

> **TROUBLE-SHOOTING TIP** If a printer flashes an out-of-memory error message, try pressing the Reset or Continue button on the printer. If that action doesn't correct the problem, try editing the document being printed. Reduce the complexity of the document. If you are printing a drawing, remove some objects from the drawing. If you are printing a document, turn off all the graphics being printed or reduce the number of font changes. If the printer works with the less complex document, find the printer manual and try to reconfigure the memory. Otherwise, purchase more memory for the printer.

Printer RAM also is used to store printer configuration information. Configuration information can include, for example, which font to print first or whether to listen for data arriving from the serial or parallel port.

If the printer is turned off, RAM chips usually instantly forget what they were told. This information is sometimes kept alive by a battery or capacitor when the power is off. Printers with batteries have the advantage of making printer installation and operation easier, but batteries create the need for occasional reinstallation and make troubleshooting more difficult. (Printer setup is discussed in Chapter 8.)

HINT | If you have a problem with a printer with batteries and turning the printer off and on does not solve the problem, turn off the printer and remove the battery. An hour later, put the battery back in and try again.

Developing the Image

The heart of a printer is its *imaging software*. This software, built into the ROM chips on the logic board of a printer, creates the image data and distinguishes between instructions and characters to be printed. Imaging software keeps track of the font last used and the printer's mode. The software then searches through all the fonts scattered throughout the printer for the proper character.

The imaging software finds the instructions for drawing the letter A and formulates the dots that make up the letter. The dots that describe the letter A are then placed in printer memory. A specific range of printer memory is used for drawing an electronic version of a page or fraction of a page. For the purposes of this discussion, the electronic image of a page is called the *image data* (see fig. 2.6).

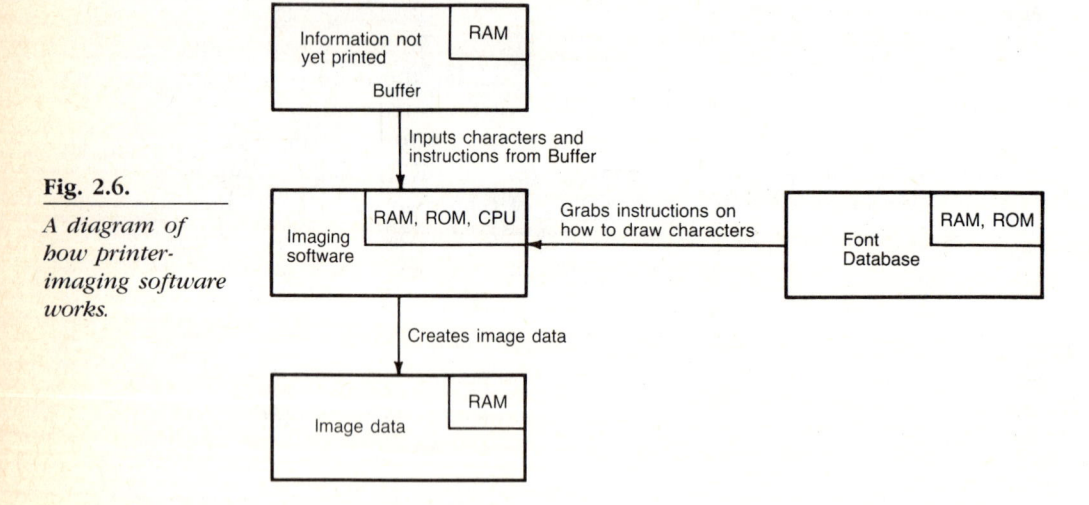

Fig. 2.6.

A diagram of how printer-imaging software works.

After the image data has been created, the image software turns control over to the print-engine software. This software turns on the motors that move the paper and move the print head or mirrors off of which a laser printer bounces laser beams. Print-engine software turns the laser on and off or causes wires to fire out of a print head (see fig. 2.7). In a dot-matrix printer, the imaging software controls the behavior of a *solenoid*. A solenoid is the device that moves the wires of a print head. A solenoid is essentially a circuit breaker that resets automatically.

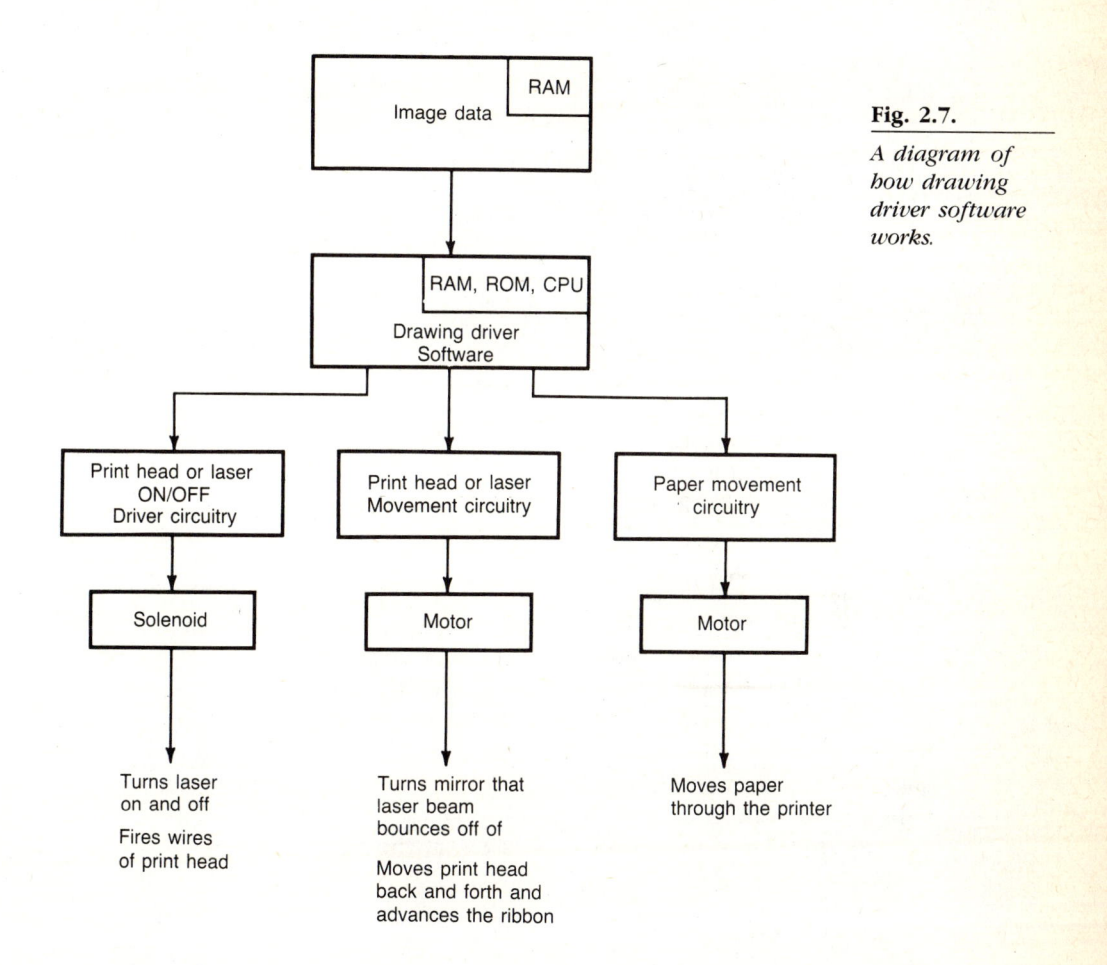

Fig. 2.7.

A diagram of how drawing driver software works.

```
                    ┌─────────────────┐
                    │         RAM     │
                    │  Image data     │
                    └────────┬────────┘
                             │
                             ▼
                    ┌─────────────────┐
                    │ RAM, ROM, CPU   │
                    │ Drawing driver  │
                    │    Software     │
                    └────┬────┬───┬───┘
                         │    │   │
          ┌──────────────┘    │   └──────────────┐
          ▼                   ▼                  ▼
 ┌─────────────────┐ ┌─────────────────┐ ┌─────────────────┐
 │ Print head or   │ │ Print head or   │ │ Paper movement  │
 │ laser ON/OFF    │ │ laser Movement  │ │    circuitry    │
 │ Driver circuitry│ │   circuitry     │ │                 │
 └────────┬────────┘ └────────┬────────┘ └────────┬────────┘
          ▼                   ▼                   ▼
    ┌──────────┐        ┌──────────┐        ┌──────────┐
    │ Solenoid │        │  Motor   │        │  Motor   │
    └────┬─────┘        └────┬─────┘        └────┬─────┘
         ▼                   ▼                   ▼
    Turns laser         Turns mirror that    Moves paper
    on and off          laser beam           through the printer
                        bounces off of
    Fires wires
    of print head       Moves print head
                        back and forth and
                        advances the ribbon
```

> **HINT** Most laser printers have a self-test of the print-engine software and associated hardware. You initiate this self-test by pushing a button on the back or side of the printer. Sometimes you have to push a pen into a hole in the printer to initiate the test.

Moving the Paper

Paper is moved through printers by motors. These motors are attached to the paper-movement circuitry, which is fed instructions by the print-engine software (see fig. 2.7). The motors used are called stepping motors because they don't spin. Stepping motors move a precise distance and then hold their position. The printer has one stepper motor whose sole job is to hold the knobs still. Trying to turn them causes stress to the plastic of the knobs, the gears connecting the stepper motor to the knobs, and ultimately the stepper motor itself. Some earlier printer knobs had a clutch that disengaged the knobs from the stepper motor. But most of these printers have disappeared. Even if the knobs can be turned, the printer loses track of where the top of a page is. This loss usually means that the printer must be turned off and on again. Turning off the printer before touching the knobs will extend the printer's life.

> CAUTION Don't touch printer knobs while the printer is on. You will damage the printer if you do. Remove and hide printer knobs or be sure to use the on-line, form feed, and line-feed buttons correctly.

One characteristic of all PC and printer motors is that they commit suicide when they cannot do their job. If a motor cannot spin or hold its position, it heats up, and the insulating paint separating the windings starts to burn. After the paint melts or burns, the wires touch, and the motor is not as strong as it used to be. To check for this condition, disconnect the motor from the paper-movement circuitry. Then, measure the winding resistance. The resistance is usually around 50 ohms, but find a known working motor and compare the two just in case. Motors in the process of committing suicide are very hot—be careful. Finding replacement motors is practically impossible because too many models exist. The best source for a replacement motor is from an old printer saved for spare parts.

One of the biggest problem areas with printers is the paper. Feeding paper so that it does not jam, crinkle, or tear is difficult. The objective of this section is to introduce the printer paper-movement mechanisms.

> CAUTION If a motor cannot turn something, turn off the printer or any other electronic device immediately. Otherwise, the motor will slowly commit suicide. Before death, the motor also may kill some other parts of the printer.

Chapter 2: The Information Process: from Printer to Paper

TROUBLE-SHOOTING TIP | If a motor cannot do its job, isolate the problem by removing the motor from the broken printer and a motor from a functioning printer. Compare the winding resistance. If the winding resistances are not within 10 percent of each other, one motor is bad. Otherwise, the motor's drive circuitry or logic board is bad.

Printers pull paper in a variety of different ways. The most popular method for dot-matrix and daisywheel printers is called *tractor feed*. For single sheets of paper, most printers today have *friction feed*. *Paper trays*, like those found in copy machines, also are becoming popular. *Cut-sheet feeders* should be extinct. The following sections discuss these methods in detail.

Tractor Feed

Tractor feeds are found on most dot-matrix and daisywheel printers. A tractor feed consists of spokes that stick out of two wheels. The wheels, or sprockets, turn, and the spokes poke into holes along the edges of the paper (see fig. 2.8).

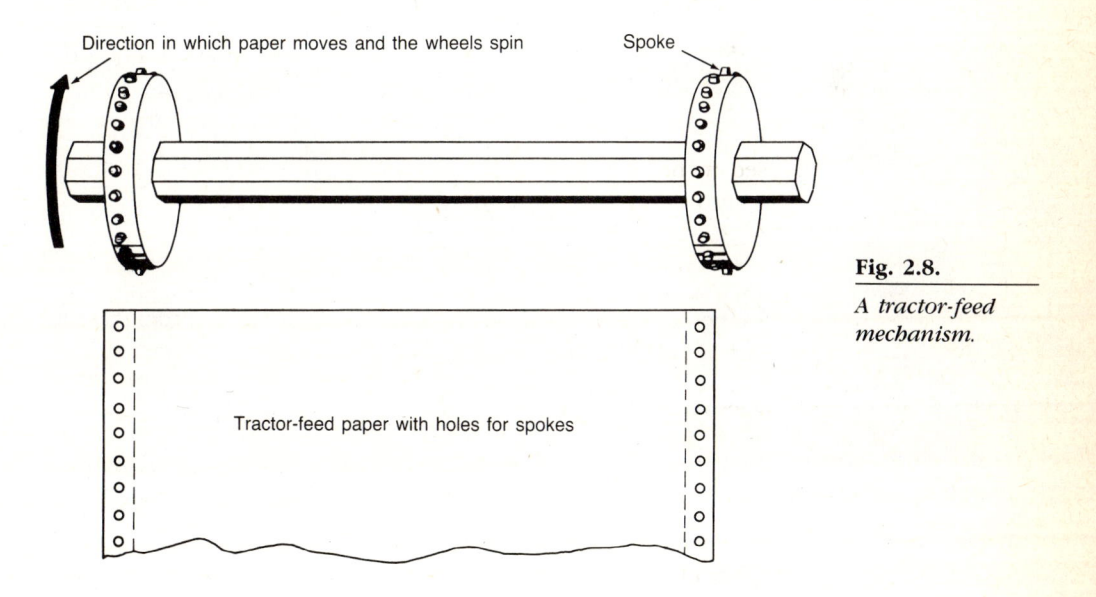

Fig. 2.8.

A tractor-feed mechanism.

Almost all tractor feed mechanisms pull paper out of the printer. As the sprockets turn, paper is pulled out by the spokes. A cover on the sprocket holds the paper in place on the spokes. But, even with the cover down, paper still shifts. If the spokes shred paper, look for one of these possible causes:

- Paper installed crookedly
- Friction feed on
- Paper inserted into the printer incorrectly
- Paper binding against the cables coming out the back of the printer
- The outbound paper piling on top of the inbound
- The outbound paper not stacking neatly so that one edge has more tension than the other
- The sprockets not the right distance apart

You can push the sprockets closer together for narrow mailing labels or farther apart for wide computer paper. Or, the sprockets can be exactly 8 1/2 inches apart for normal paper. When the sprockets are in position, you can move them simultaneously to adjust the left margin. Clamps are used to lock the sprockets into place. When clamped into place, the sprockets can still cause problems. The paper can mound up in the middle and crinkle or can stretch too tight and tear. This problem can happen in the middle of a print job after you have adjusted everything perfectly. The solution is to clip one of the sprockets in position and let the other one drift. Then, the tractor works fine.

> **HINT** When you use tractor feed, leave the right margin sprocket loose. Clip paper to the right margin sprocket, but don't anchor the right margin sprocket to the bar the sprocket slides on. This practice prevents many paper feed problems.

Normally, paper moves in only one direction through a printer. But, most printers have the capability to move the paper in a reverse direction. When activated, this feature causes nothing but problems. Stay away from software that tries to reverse the path of the paper flow. If reversing the paper direction is a requirement, the best solution is to purchase a special tractor called a *bidirectional tractor*. A bidirectional tractor pulls paper through the printer in two directions. Bidirectional tractors are used primarily in applications that fill out multipart forms. These tractors are hard to find and are not available for most printers today.

Friction Feed

The friction-feed method of pulling paper relies on two devices' functioning perfectly. One device, the platen, is a rubber cylinder that sits in a cup. At the bottom of the cup is a curved plate that presses paper up against the platen. The paper then curls around the platen and pops out under the print head. This method of pulling paper is called *friction feed* (see fig. 2.9).

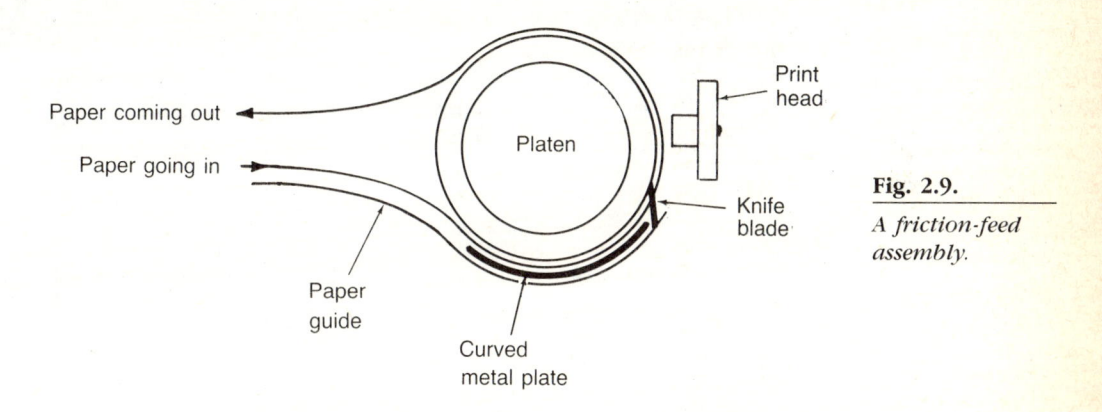

Fig. 2.9.

A friction-feed assembly.

> HINT | In dot-matrix and letter-quality printers, underneath the print head is a sharp piece of metal that pushes against the platen and holds the paper against the platen. This piece also will cut your fingers easily. Do not bend it. If you do, your printout will not look as nice as it does with the metal not bent.

As paper goes underneath the platen, a plastic or metal blade is used to hold paper against the platen underneath the print head. Above the print head are rollers that hold the paper against the print head. Together, the blade and roller bars provide a paper-platen surface to push the ribbon against. Otherwise, the print head has to push the paper against the platen before making an imprint.

> CAUTION | Do not allow the printer to work without paper. Printing without paper damages the print head wires because the wires travel farther than they are supposed to. The wires can bend and not retract properly. This practice also damages the platen by making it less pliable and smears ink on the platen, which may soil the back side of future pages.

> **HINT** Do not remove the platen when cleaning it. Putting the platen back in the printer is easy, but if done incorrectly can cause many problems. Clean the platen only when paper is getting dirty. Leave the printer alone otherwise.

All sorts of things can go wrong and cause the friction-feed assembly to pull paper unequally so that it drifts to one side or another. For a few pages, the drift may not be noticeable. New printers may last until the tenth page before the left margin changes noticeably. Older friction-feed assemblies can print barely one page without shifting. The trouble is that the curved metal plate and platen are not parallel to each other, or perhaps the knife blade has been bent or damaged so that the blade is pressing paper against the platen on only one side.

> **HINT** Do not try to print more than a few pages in a row with friction feed. Otherwise, the margins will drift. This defect is found in all printers.

Cut-Sheet Feeders

Cut-sheet feeders send sheets of paper one at a time into the printer. Although cut-sheet feeders occasionally work unattended, if you walk away, the feeder starts grabbing large chunks of paper and jams the printer. Most cut-sheet feeders have been, and always will be, a disaster waiting to happen. You can never leave these feeders alone. Plan on their failing during the critical moment a report is needed.

Cut-sheet feeders are found on older daisywheel and dot-matrix printers. To install a cut-sheet feeder, you have to remove the tractor. The cut-sheet feeder then has to hand paper to the friction feed, and the friction feed has to hand the paper back to the cut-sheet feeder. Too many things can go wrong.

First, remember that friction feed is not a reliable mechanism in the first place. Second, the cut-sheet feeder has a tendency to send several sheets of paper through the printer at once. This problem occurs because the cut-sheet feeder sits up almost vertically and uses gravity to pull paper into the friction feed. Some cut-sheet feeders come with elaborate cork-covered clamps that try to feed only one sheet. But in the end, gravity wins and pulls a wad of paper into the friction feed (see fig. 2.10).

Fig. 2.10.

Cut-sheet feeder operation.

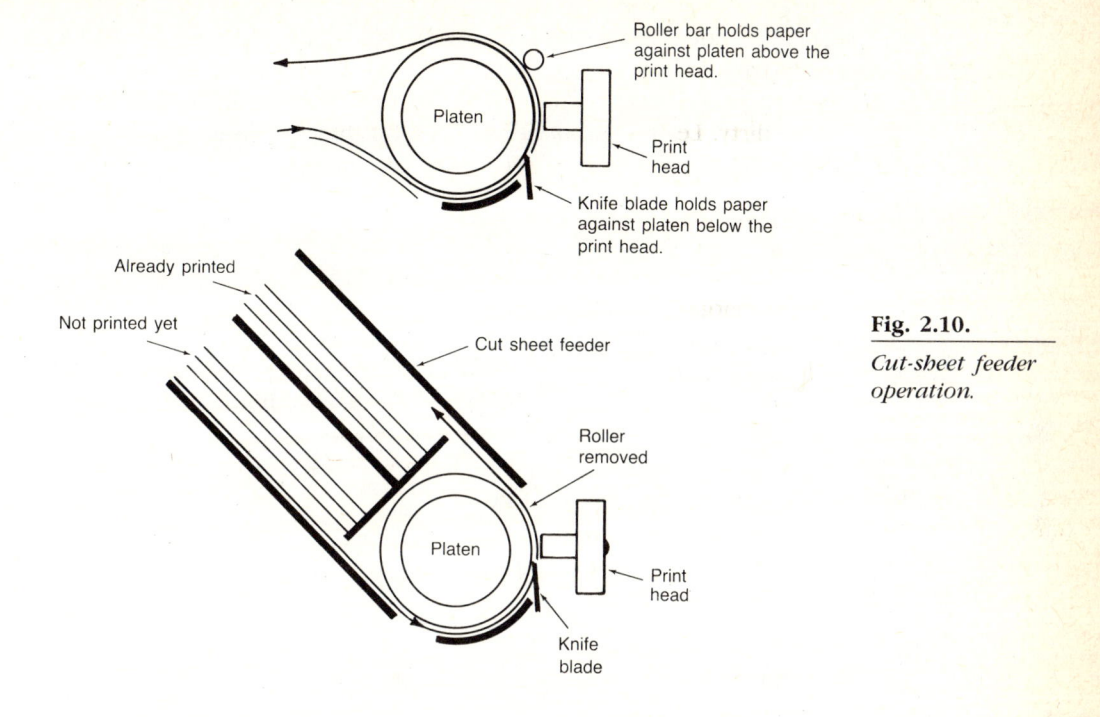

As the friction feed takes the wad of paper, the elaborate cork-covered clamps in the cut-sheet feeder move out of alignment. This movement makes pulling several sheets of paper more likely next time. The mass of paper can kick the platen and blade out of alignment. Then, the friction feed cannot hand paper to the cut-sheet feeder so that it can pull paper out of the printer. Or, the sheet of paper is not held as tightly against the platen, and the output quality deteriorates.

When the mass of paper reaches the print head, the wires or hammers encounter resistance too soon and cannot travel their full range of motion, and the solenoids start to overheat. This overheating makes the print head age rapidly. Motors that try to pull the print head back and forth work harder when the print head is rubbing against several sheets of paper. If the print head moves off the paper and then tries to move back on to it, the print head usually starts to rip the paper. In any case, the motor moving the print head and the motor rotating the platen are subject to stress.

> CAUTION Don't permit wads of paper to move through a printer. Wads of paper are a sign of trouble. They will become more frequent, and more printer damage will result. Solve the problem.

Most cut-sheet feeders require the removal of the top roller bar that holds paper against the platen above the print head. (Remember that the knife blade holds the paper against the platen below the print head.) After this roller bar is removed, the print head is responsible for holding the paper against the platen until the cut-sheet feeder can grasp the paper and pull it out of the printer.

The fundamental design problem of cut-sheet feeders is the coordination of responsibility for keeping the print head on the paper. PC software assumes that the printer does what it is told. But, some printers are designed to ignore PC software's instructions. Some manufactures have designed "smart" cut-sheet feeders that take over the printer and ignore the PC's software to make sure that the print head stays over the paper. If the PC software "thinks" that the print head is off the paper, however, the printer or cut-sheet feeder does not tell the PC of the problem. Then, the PC software gets lost, and the printer's left margin drifts.

Paper Trays

Paper trays are the best invention yet. They work like the paper trays in copy machines. Unfortunately, paper trays have not yet been attached to dot-matrix printers—only to laser printers. The incredible thing is that paper trays work, day in and day out. They work with paper that does not have holes punched in the side. Paper trays enable your printer to put characters on the pages in the same spot each time. Hold two pages up to the light to prove this statement.

Paper-tray feeders are much more sensitive to paper length than other kinds of feeders. These feeders are designed to measure the length of every page. If the page is too long, the paper-tray feeder assumes that more than one sheet of paper has come through; the feeder stops and flashes an error message. Legal-size paper causes this error message. Problems of this type are discussed in Chapter 14.

The feeder takes each sheet of paper and guides it through the printer. At the top and bottom where paper is grasped, nothing can ever be printed. Where the paper is guided along the edges, nothing can be printed. In laser printers, therefore, you find on each sheet an "unprintable" border about .18 inch deep, in which nothing can be printed. If text is sent to this region of the paper, it simply disappears.

> **TROUBLE-SHOOTING TIP** — If lines disappear at the top or bottom of a page or if letters disappear in a column on the left or right edge of a page, try turning the printer off and then on. If this solution doesn't work, try increasing the margins. If neither solution works, you have an application software problem. Try modifying the printer configuration of the PC software program.

> **TROUBLE-SHOOTING TIP** — If blank lines appear in the middle of a page, try resetting the top of the form. Turn off the printer, place the perforation line just above the print head, and turn the printer back on. If this strategy doesn't work, look in the application software manual or operating system manual for instructions on how to empty application software buffers or spoolers. Look for ways to reset the application printer driver. 1-2-3 uses the Align command for this purpose, for example. Another solution is to turn off the perforation skip on a 24-pin dot-matrix printer with a switch inside the printer or an instruction to the printer.

Laser printers will move text out of the unprintable region into the printable area of the page. This movement shrinks the paper size to 10 inches by 8 inches. The capability of laser printers to move text out of the unprintable region can be turned off by the computer's software. In this case, the software becomes responsible for keeping text out of the unprintable region. Word processors are pretty good at not sending text to the unprintable region, but spreadsheets usually expect the laser printer to move text out of the unprintable region. If the word processor is executed first, the printer stops moving text. If the spreadsheet is used next, text goes into the unprintable region and disappears. Furthermore, because the page is longer, the laser printer does not page correctly. If the printer is turned off and back on, the spreadsheet software prints properly.

> **TROUBLE-SHOOTING TIP** — If the text creeps up or down the paper, look for page length adjustments in the application software printer configuration and in the printer. You adjust the printer's page length by using switches or knobs or by sending instructions to the printer.

Moving the Print Head

Daisywheel and dot-matrix printers have two ways of moving the print head back and forth: a pulley or a screw. The comparable mechanism in a laser printer uses mirrors to aim a laser. All these methods are trustworthy, and all have advantages and disadvantages. The motors that move the print heads and mirrors are driven by print-head or laser-movement circuitry.

Print-engine software can optimize the print head's movement to speed the printing of a document. One decision that print-engine software can make is not to print spaces at the end of a line. Print-engine software can translate spaces used to center text or position columns into absolute head-movement commands, which are much quicker. Rather than move to each place and "print" a space, the print head zooms to the position of the next character to be printed.

If print-engine software can print in both directions, you save a tremendous amount of time. The time saved is the time required for the print head to go to the beginning of the line each time. Rather than retrace steps, the print head turns around and starts printing the next line backwards.

Because most printers can print bidirectionally, print-engine software has the opportunity to compute the most efficient direction to print the next line. This computation of the shortest possible path necessary to print the next line is called *optimization* (see fig. 2.11).

Some printers have no moving parts and therefore no motors. If the printer has no moving parts, the optimization techniques described in the preceding text are not applicable.

HINT | If the print head is old, letters are not looking nice, letters are not lining up underneath each other, or graphics look terrible, look in the printer manual for a way to turn off bidirectional printing. This solution often makes your materials look better.

TROUBLE-SHOOTING TIP | If letters occasionally appear on paper in reverse order, the printer and the application software are trying to optimize printer head movement. In this case, you have to modify the application software printer configuration or send an instruction to the printer.

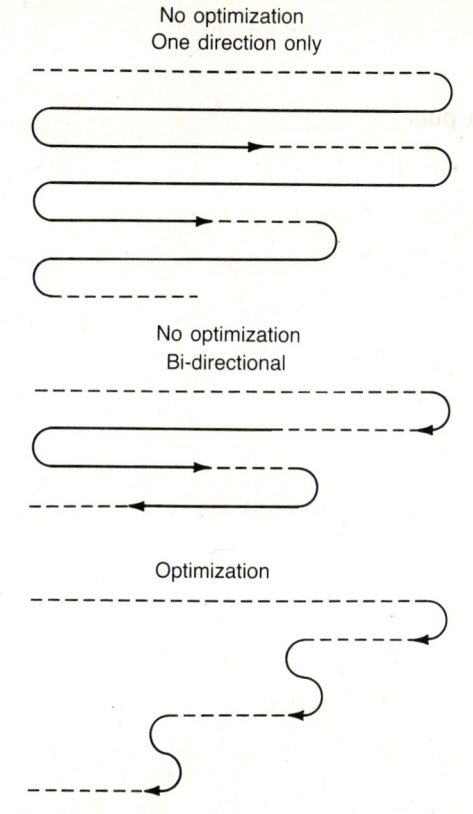

Fig. 2.11.

Driver software head-movement optimization.

No optimization
One direction only

No optimization
Bi-directional

Optimization

Arrow lengths represent the time that the print head spent moving while not printing.

Using Pulleys or Screws

A pulley print-head movement system is the most common in dot-matrix and daisywheel printers. The system consists of a pulley, belt, and motor. The print head is clipped to the belt. As the motor turns, the belt moves, and the print head moves (see fig. 2.12).

Like any pulley or belt system, if the belt is too tight, the motor works harder and wears out sooner. Usually, the belt is corrugated so that it cannot slip. If the belt is too loose, the print head develops play. Try gently to move a print head. If the print head moves even a fraction of an inch, the amount is usually too much. The letters in consecutive rows may not line up underneath each other. A solid vertical line may become fragmented.

Fig. 2.12.

The pulley mechanism to move a print head.

Motor spins counterclockwise; print head moves left.

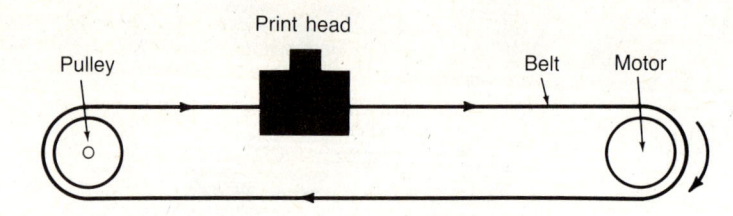

Motor spins clockwise, print head moves right.

To solve the print head play problem, loosen the pulley-mount screw and push the pulley farther away from the motor. Then, tighten the pulley-mount screw. Test the play by squeezing opposite sides of the belt together. The total combined distance both sides move should be half an inch—no more or less (see fig. 2.13).

Fig. 2.13.

A diagram of how to adjust the play in a pulley system.

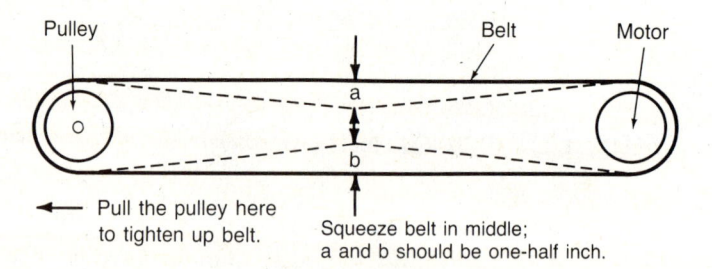

Pull the pulley here to tighten up belt.

Squeeze belt in middle; a and b should be one-half inch.

An alternative to the pulley system is the screw method of moving the print heads. The print head in this case is like a nut on a long bolt. If the bolt is turned in one direction, the nut unscrews. If the bolt is turned in the other direction, the nut screws tighter (see fig. 2.14). The drawback of this system is that when the print head develops play, the threads of the screw are worn. No cost-effective method of repairing worn threads exists; you must replace the print head and screw. IBM has made this technology popular again in the ProPrinter line of printers.

Chapter 2: The Information Process: from Printer to Paper 63

Fig. 2.14.

The screw method of moving a print head.

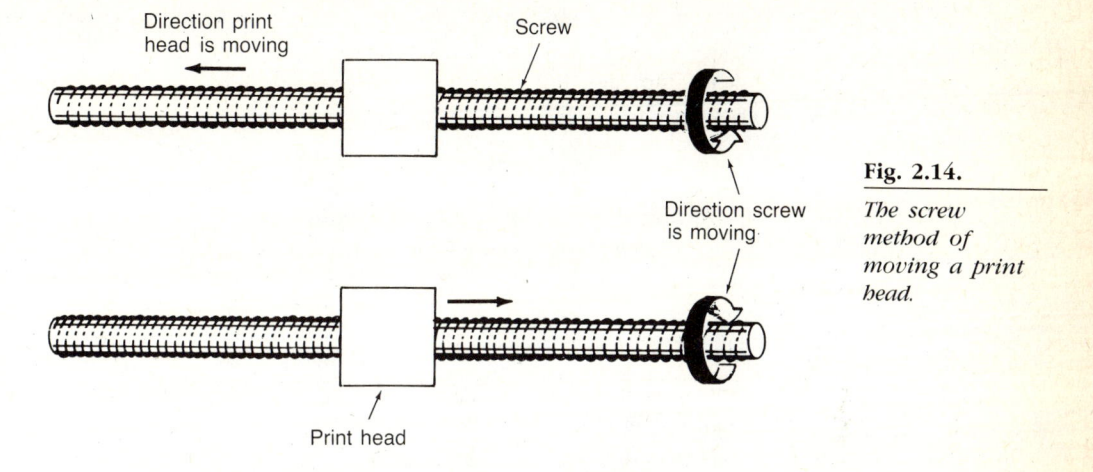

Controlling the Location of the Print Head

Both the pulley and screw technologies depend on motors turning to move the print heads. In some printers, the print-engine software tells the motors to turn a specific distance and then "prays" that the motor does its job. Other printers tell their motors to turn and then "spy on" the motor. These printers keep sending commands to the motor until the print head arrives at the right spot. Keep in mind that some printers can send their print heads to 360 different locations per inch.

The capability to check the motor's performance is an important feature. The only way to tell the difference between these two types of printers is by the symptoms when the printer has a problem. Printers with the capability of checking head position lose the left margin by jumping randomly to a new one. Printers without the capability to check let their margins drift randomly—even though the paper is in the same place.

The print-engine software keeps track of the position of the print head. When a printer is first turned on, the print-engine software does not know where the print head is located. The print-engine software, therefore, drags the print head to the left side of the printer. Here, the print head trips a left margin switch. At this point, the print-engine software knows where the print head is. Now, the print-engine software can ask the motor to move the print head to a specific position.

TROUBLE-SHOOTING TIP | If a print head bangs against the left side of the printer repeatedly, try cleaning the left-margin microswitch or removing the rubber inserts used to hold the print head in place during shipment.

CAUTION | Do not spray any chemicals inside a printer. Many plastic pieces can be ruined by the chemicals in some cleaners. Clean with damp rags. Put the chemicals on the rag.

HINT | Try cleaning before lubricating. Try adjusting physical position before lubricating. Lubrication in printers usually does not solve problems and sometimes creates them.

To determine where the print head is located, the printer has a round piece of metal with tiny slots drilled in a single circle. A light shines through the holes and illuminates a light sensor. If the circular piece of metal is attached to a spinning motor, the light sensor experiences a strobe effect. By counting shadows or flashes of light, the driver software can accurately determine how far the motor has turned and exactly where the print head is, unless dust and dirt inhibit the strobe effect (see fig. 2.15).

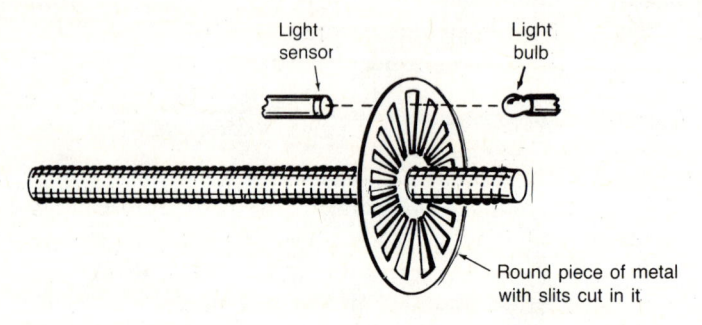

Fig. 2.15.

A diagram of how the printer checks the position of the print head.

Light sensor

Light bulb

Round piece of metal with slits cut in it

As the shaft spins, the light sensor counts strobe pulses. Then you accurately can determine where the print head is located.

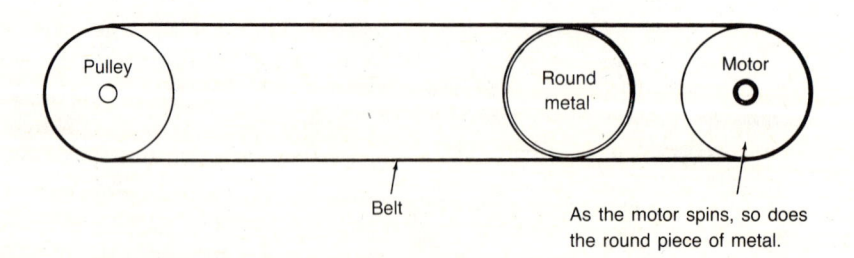

Pulley

Round metal

Motor

Belt

As the motor spins, so does the round piece of metal.

TROUBLE-SHOOTING TIP | If the left margin floats, try cleaning the left-margin microswitch or LED and sensor. If this solution doesn't work, look for the circular piece of metal under a metal hood near the motor moving the pulley or the screw. Clean the circular piece of metal. If you have a cut-sheet feeder, you need to try a different printer driver.

Using Line Printers

The term *line printer* refers to a fast printer. A line printer's performance is not measured in characters per second, but lines per minute. A slow line printer may be rated at 200 lines per minute. This rate translates to a page every 3/10 second, or 440 characters per second (cps). A typical inexpensive dot-matrix printer with one print head can print at 200 cps. By adding a second print head, many dot-matrix printers can out-perform low-end line printers for less money (see fig. 2.16).

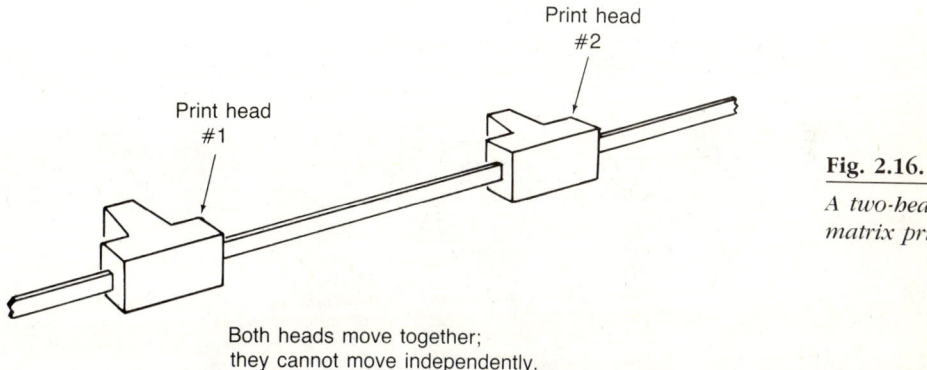

Fig. 2.16.

A two-head dot-matrix printer.

Most line printers today are called *band printers* because a metal band with letters on it spins around inside the printer (see fig. 2.17). Band printers achieve their speed by positioning a hammer at each print position. Usually, 132 hammers aim at the letters on the band flying around in front of the hammers. Each hammer reaches out and hits its assigned letter as it flies by. In many ways, the band printer is like the LED laser printer. Both have multiple print heads that don't move.

The market for high-speed printers is tiny but growing. The market is so small that high-speed printers cost more than twice as much as a dot-matrix printers. Manufacturers of the very fast dot-matrix printers cannot afford much advertising, so these printers are difficult to find in magazine ads. The main application of high-speed printers is to back up a database on paper. This backup is usually part of a disaster recovery plan. Companies plan on using the paper backup while the computer is being fixed.

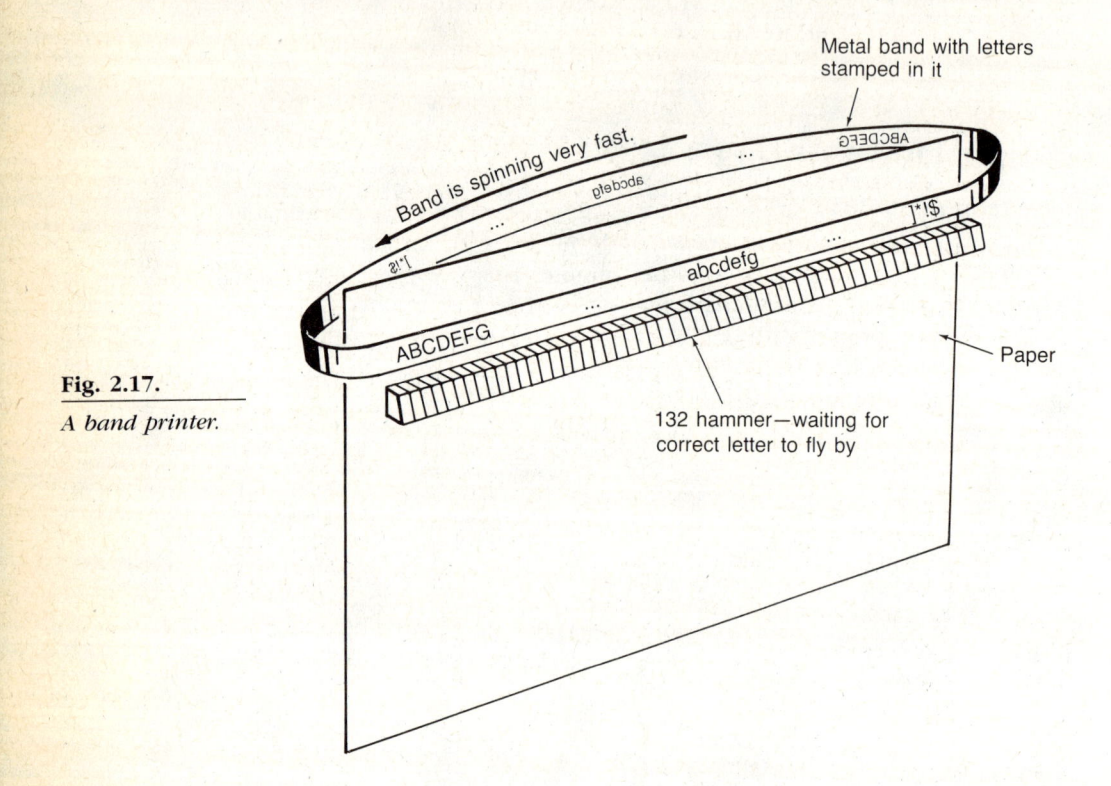

Fig. 2.17.

A band printer.

Printing the Data

How printers actually deposit ink or toner on paper is the interesting part of a printer. The various methods of depositing ink or toner are collectively referred to as *printing mechanisms*. The remainder of this chapter reviews the printing mechanisms of most printers: laser, LED and LCS, dot-matrix, inkjet, daisywheel, and thermal printers. Plotters are usually put in a different category, but really they are just a unique type of printer. Plotters are reviewed in Chapter 7 along with the other printers from a purchasing/feature point of view. This section explains how the various printer technologies put images on paper.

Laser Printers

Laser printers are becoming the most popular printers. The laser printing mechanism is simple. A laser is turned off and on. The laser beam bounces off of mirrors and exposes a photosensitive drum, the equivalent of the platen on other printers. The equivalent of a print head in a laser printer is the laser beam, a special form of light. In a laser printer, the beam travels through a fiber-optical cable, emerges from the fiber, and bounces off a mirror into the toner cartridge. A flap in the lid hides the mirror when you lift the laser printer's lid. Sometimes, this fiber-optic cable becomes disconnected, or the power supply of the laser goes bad.

The platen, or drum, is covered with a light-sensitive material similar to film. The laser beam exposes this film. How this film is used to produce an image is described in the LED laser printer discussion.

> TROUBLE-SHOOTING TIP | Sharp vertical white streaks may result when the mirror is dirty. The mirror is in the lid of the laser printer, above where the toner cartridge slides in. A flap protects the mirror. The flap has to be opened gently and then cleaned. Try cleaning the corona wire and fuse bar and replacing the toner cartridge first.

Photosensitive drums cannot be manufactured so that they are exactly alike in their degree of light sensitivity. The drums are sorted into three categories during the manufacturing process and put into different kinds of plastic toner cartridges. Drum sensitivity is indicated by means of plastic tabs on the cartridge. These plastic tabs are detected by microswitches in the lid of the laser printer.

The laser and the mirrors are housed in the hood, or lid, of the laser printer. The photosensitive drum is housed in the toner cartridge. The mirrors and the green photosensitive material are hidden by flaps (see fig. 2.18).

> HINT | In a laser printer, many flaps open and close to the toner cartridge. The flaps are in the toner cartridge itself and in the lid. Do not force a toner cartridge into position. Guide the cartridge gently; otherwise, you may break a flap or the mechanism that opens or closes the cartridge. Or, you may break off from the toner cartridge the tabs that indicate drum sensitivity. Also, make sure that you use the proper toner cartridge.

TROUBLE-SHOOTING TIP | If nothing is printed, check the toner cartridge first. You must pull the sealing tape out of the cartridge. The electrical connections all have to be made. The drum has to rotate. The mirror may not be spinning. In the base of the printer, the corona wire may be broken.

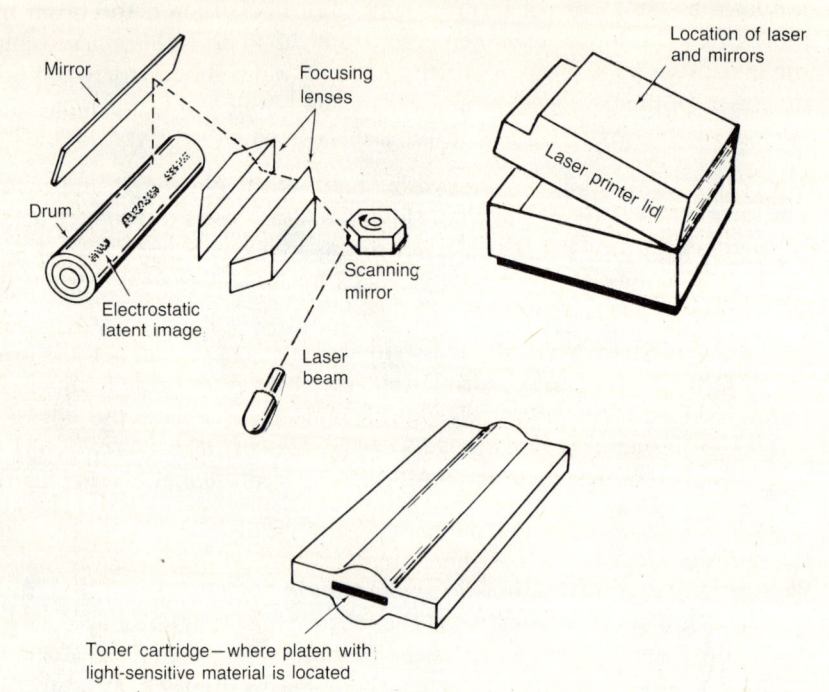

Fig. 2.18.

Laser-beam movement inside a laser printer.

TROUBLE-SHOOTING TIP | If dark black horizontal lines appear through letters or the entire page is black with a few white horizontal lines, the problem is that the laser beam is turned on constantly. This problem is caused by a malfunction of the circuitry in the lid of the laser printer.

TROUBLE-SHOOTING TIP | If a background of black snow appears over the text, the laser is turning off and on randomly. This problem is caused by a malfunction of the circuitry in the lid of the laser.

LED and LCS Printers

Light-emitting diode (LED) and liquid-crystal shutter (LCS) printers are competing with laser printers on all fronts. For about 10 to 15 percent less money, the LED and LCS printers can deliver at higher speeds the same resolution and print quality as laser printers. LED and LCS printers are essentially laser printers with 2,400 tiny lasers (300 dots per inch $\times$ 8 inches). In an LCS printer, one light source stays on and off while a liquid crystal shutter array (like the screen of a laptop computer) blocks or allows the light to pass (see fig. 2.19). In the LED printer, however, the individual LEDs are turned off and on. Thus, the head-drive circuitry selects different LEDs, or crystal grid points, to turn off and on, rather than instructing motors to rotate mirrors. Because LEDs, or crystal grid points, can be turned on or off simultaneously, speed is improved. Reliability also is increased because the printer has fewer moving parts, and you have fewer problems with blurred characters on the edges.

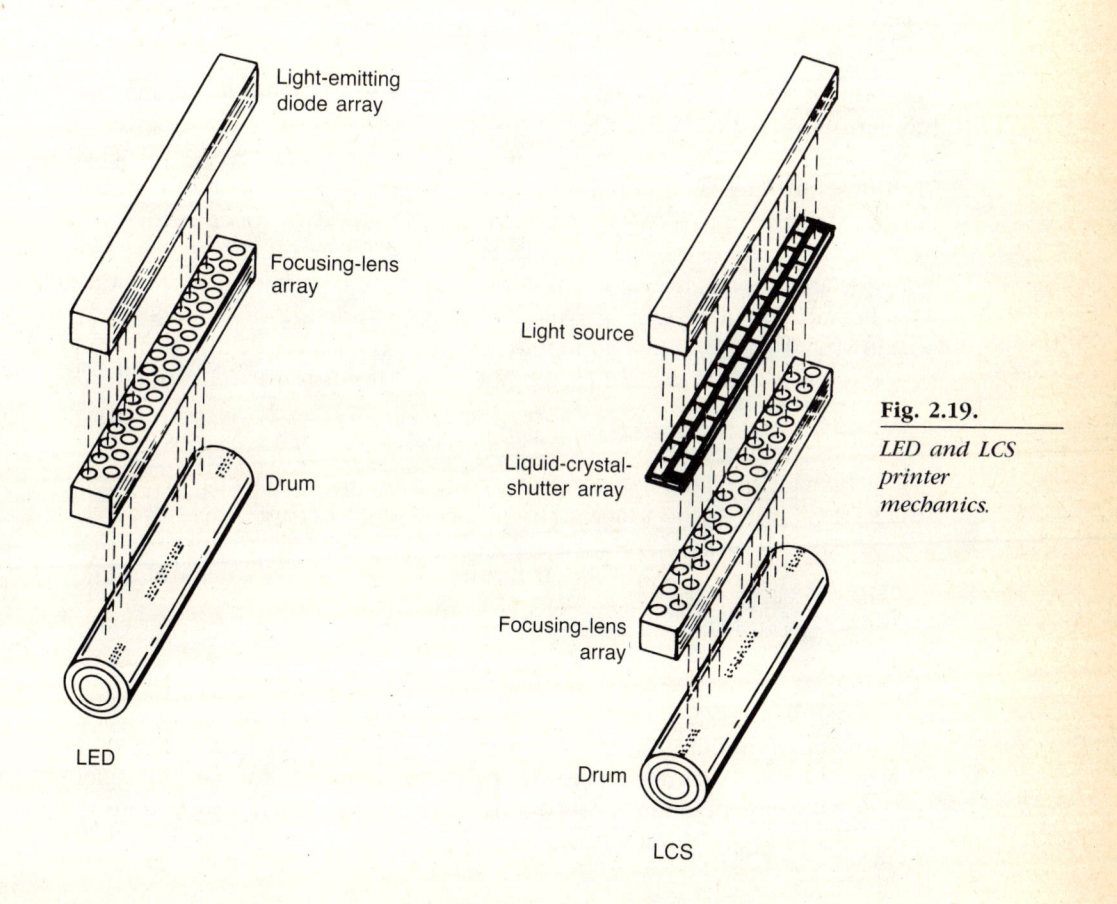

Fig. 2.19.

LED and LCS printer mechanics.

LED and LCS printers are being sold as laser printers because little difference exists between them. In fact, even a true laser printer has a row of cheap LEDs used to erase the photosensitive drum. LED printers use more expensive LEDs to write and erase the photosensitive drum. Laser printers are so popular that salespeople don't risk making the distinction—customers may think LCS or LED is an untried technology.

> **TROUBLESHOOTING TIP** If ghosts of characters already printed appear (something like the burn-in problem with monitors), perhaps the characters are not being erased properly by the erase LEDs in a laser printer. Because these LEDs usually don't break, try swapping them. They are in the laser printer's lid. Perhaps the erase circuitry in the laser is not working properly. Another solution involves cleaning or repairing microswitches in the printer's lid; these switches detect the degree of sensitivity of the photosensitive drum in the cartridge.

LED printers, laser printers, and copy machines use the same techniques for transferring the image from the photosensitive drum to paper. As the drum spins, it passes through a cloud of toner dust. Toner dust consists of magnetized dust particles. Because the drum is charged up by laser beams, toner dust particles are attracted to the drum. If the cloud of toner particles is evenly distributed, a thin, uniform layer of dust forms on the drum. (This magnetic attraction is the same attraction by which dust is attracted to monitors. Behind the glass tube of your monitor is a charge of approximately 30,000 volts—30K V. When a monitor is turned on, all the dust in the room feels the electric field created by the 30K V and heads toward the monitor.)

> **TROUBLESHOOTING TIP** If speckled areas appear on the printout, the electrical connection to the toner cartridge necessary to charge the drum may be bad. Try removing, rocking back and forth, and reinserting the toner cartridge. If this solution doesn't work, try cleaning the exposed metal pieces of the toner cartridge.

> **TROUBLESHOOTING TIP** If output is faint and uneven, the problem may be that the electrical connection to the cartridge necessary to turn the toner into a cloud is not working. Clean the electrical connections to the toner cartridge.

Chapter 2: The Information Process: from Printer to Paper **71**

> HINT | Toner dust is so light that it floats around the room and so fine that it kills normal vacuum cleaners. Spend the extra money for a special computer vacuum cleaner. Use it when doing preventive maintenance on a laser printer.

The thin layer of toner dust forms a picture on the photosensitive drum. As the drum rotates out of the toner cloud, toner stays attached to the drum in the shape of the picture. Next, the drum and its toner come in contact with a piece of paper. Underneath the paper, a wire, called the corona wire, also is charged to a high voltage. The electric field of this wire pulls the toner off the drum on to the paper. The corona wire must be cleaned regularly; otherwise, the voltage is not uniform.

> TROUBLE-SHOOTING TIP | If output is faint or has sharp vertical streaks, the corona wire may be dirty. Clean this wire regularly.

At this point, the toner is just lying on the paper. The next step is to melt the toner into the paper. This melting is done by passing the paper over a hot roller. Heat from underneath the paper melts the toner deeper into the paper. The hot roller is the central component of what is called the *fusion assembly*.

> TROUBLE-SHOOTING TIP | Smeared print occurs if the fusion assembly is not heating to the proper temperature. Clean or replace the fusion assembly.

Laser printers and copy machines have one major difference. The laser beam in a laser printer outlines the letters to be printed. The laser beam in a copy machine bounces off the white part of paper but is absorbed by the black letters. Thus, a copy machine's laser draws the background of what is to be printed, not the letters. Because of this difference, laser printers and copy machines cannot use the same toner (see fig. 2.20). An LED printer can be designed to use either type of toner at the flick of a switch. If the switch is in the wrong position, a negative image is printed, wasting toner.

Fig. 2.20.

The difference between a copy machine and laser printer.

Black indicates path or area illuminated by laser.

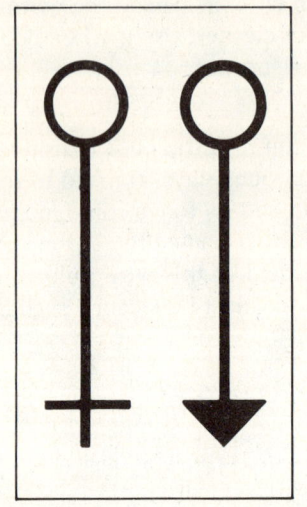

Path laser travels in laser printer

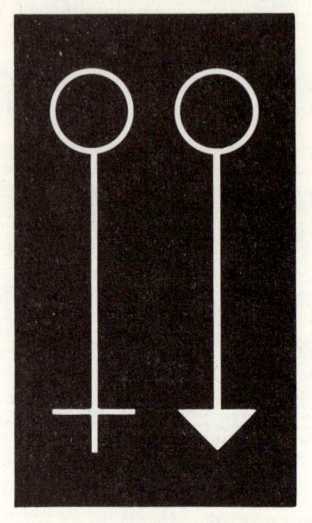

Area illuminated by laser in copy machine

White indicates what toner has to be attracted to. Two types of toner are required.

Dot-Matrix Printers

All dot-matrix printers operate on the same basic principle of firing wires at a ribbon. Each wire prints a dot. By firing the wires in different patterns, the printer makes letters or pictures. Dot-matrix printers use the same technology found in any speaker. All speakers work by pushing and pulling on a circular piece of cardboard. Dot-matrix print heads push and pull a wire. The components needed to accomplish this movement consist of a magnet and coil of wire. When current is pumped through the coil of wire, the current sets up a magnetic field that repels the magnetic field of the permanent magnet. This repelling forces the permanent magnet to move. The wire attached to the permanent magnet moves out, hits the ribbon, and pushes it against the paper (see fig. 2.21). A spring pulls the permanent magnet and wire back.

Most dot-matrix printers use 9 wires (or pins) spaced over 1/6 inch. Thus, the wires are 1/54 inch apart. A 24-pin print head has become popular because the wires are 1/144 inch apart. Most 9-pin printers can produce higher resolutions by printing a line several times with each pass offset slightly.

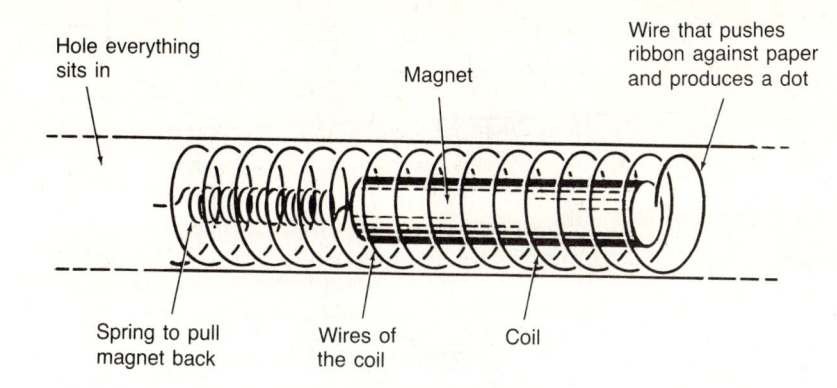

Fig. 2.21.

A dot-matrix printer solenoid.

Early American-made dot-matrix print heads were huge, heavy, and expensive, but repairable. The magnets, the wires, the coils—everything—could be taken apart and put back together again. Although the pieces were small, the assembly was easier than working on a mechanical watch.

The first cheap dot-matrix print head was made by Seiko. This printer was designed to print the winning times of races in the 1964 Tokyo Olympics. The design proved so successful that Seiko formed a division to manufacture the print heads. These print heads ended up in Epson printers. (Epson is a Seiko company.) Epson printers were first sold in the U.S. in 1978. Within a year, one company in Japan had 80 to 90 percent of the world-wide print-head market.

All the early dot-matrix print heads had problems when heating up. When they overheated, they usually died. The printing speed and the font were carefully engineered to provide the optimum blend of readability and speed without overheating. Dot-matrix printers were easy to sell because they were cheap and much faster than daisywheel printers. Dot-matrix printing, however, did not look as nice as other printing. Bidirectional and optimized printing were not attempted because those procedures force the print head to heat up more. With one-direction printing, the print head could rest and cool off when being moved into position for printing the next line.

Problems first surfaced when the dot-matrix printers started supporting more fonts. Early dot-matrix printers either had just one font or allowed that font to be stretched across the page. Even though the font was stretched horizontally, the number of dots that made up a letter stayed the same. To create a marketing edge, new fonts were created. Actually new fonts were not designed and stored in the printer; the print-engine software modified the current font within the printer. This software could double the firing of the 9 wires to create a wider, darker font (*expanded print*). To create *com-*

pressed print, print-engine software changed the distance the print head moved before firing the 9 wires again. Both these techniques caused more dots to be printed on the same line.

The new fonts caused the print head to heat up more. To stop overheating when printing the new fonts, the printer company modified the image software to turn off compressed or expanded printing at the end of each line. This way, the print head could cool while printing the next line. This modification prevented someone from turning on compressed print and leaving it on for the whole page.

> HINT | Print heads never die immediately. As in any motor or device that has a coil of wire, the insulation separating the wires starts melting, thinning, or cracking as the wire heats up. The damage is gradual. Print a massive number of documents during the warranty period to make sure that this problem does not exist in the printer you have just purchased.

Because the warnings about printing a whole page in compressed print were all hidden inside printer manuals, programmers could ignore the warnings. Programmers would command the printer to go into compressed print and then discover that the compressed print was turned off at the end of the line. So the programmer would modify the program to turn the compressed print back on at the beginning of each line. Then, the print heads died an early death.

As technology has improved, the overheating problem has gone away. Dot-matrix printers can print many fonts and probably make a page black without overheating. Because this technique had been working so well, dot-matrix manufacturers decided to increase the number of wires from 9 to 24. Then, history repeated itself. Some 24-pin Toshiba dot-matrix printers purchased in 1987 had a terrible problem with overheating. The problem has been fixed since.

Inkjet Printers

The concept of spraying drops of ink on paper has been around for a long time. The technology has been plagued with design problems that only recently have been worked out economically. The design problems have never been with the technology to propel or aim the ink. Instead, the problem has been with the chemistry of the ink. The ink has to stay in liquid form for long periods of time, yet instantly melt into the paper and dry.

To solve the first problem, pumps circulated the ink constantly. When turned on, the inkjet printers had to be primed. If the ink dried up in any of the plumbing, the printer had to be cleaned. If the nozzle clogged up, it had to be cleaned. If the plumbing leaked, the mess was incredible.

Hewlett-Packard was the first company to come up with an economical solution. Hewlett-Packard solved the problem by eliminating pumps and plumbing. Instead, ink is sold in a bladder. The bladder is attached to a print head that moves back and forth like a dot-matrix print head. HP's first inkjet printer worked fine when in constant use. But, if allowed to sit, the ink sometimes dried up, and when the printer was turned on, it did not print anything. Furthermore, the bladder stopped working before all the ink was emptied out. To clear out the dried up ink, the best approach was to massage the bladder (like milking a cow). Using a pin to clean out the nozzle succeeded only in pushing dried bits of ink back into the bladder. The dried bits came out later and clogged everything again. Modern inkjet printers don't normally have this problem.

Creating an ink to melt into the paper and dry quickly has proved difficult. Special paper produces the best results. The output of an inkjet printer on ordinary paper is faint but readable; the result looks like someone has been painting with water colors that were too thin. In summary, inkjet printers work best when under constant use with special paper.

Daisywheel Printers

Daisywheel printers cannot produce drawings, change fonts easily, or underline or print boldface acceptably. Daisywheel printers are slow (30 cps average), noisy, and violent. They put a dent in paper that reminds people of the output of typewriters. If you are impressed with the quality of typewriter output, you will be impressed by the quality of daisywheel printers. Because they were the first printer technology for the masses, any book on printers should contain a section about daisywheels. Diablo popularized daisywheels. Many other companies are cloning the Diablo printer. NEC made a successful variation called a thimble printer.

Daisywheel printers are simple. They consist of a hammer and a wheel. The wheel looks like a person's hand with more than one hundred fingers and a letter at the end of each finger. The hammer stays still, but the hand waves. Suppose that the hammer is given the assignment of hitting the finger with the letter A on it. If the hammer times everything just perfectly, it hits the moving finger with the letter A on it (see fig. 2.22). The finger pushes into the ribbon and paper just like an old manual typewriter key. If the hammer misses, it can break the plastic fingers off and throw them out of the printer. If the fingers are made of metal, expect terrible noises. Either way, this failure is spectacular.

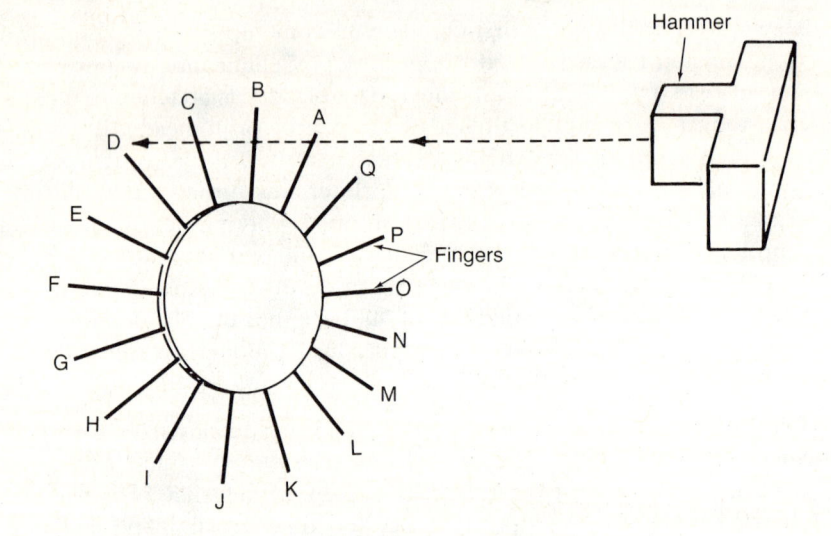

Fig. 2.22.

Daisywheel printer operation.

NEC's thimble printer worked in a similar fashion, except that the print head sat in a cup with fingers on its lip. The fingers spun horizontally rather than vertically like a daisywheel. Most typewriters that can be converted to printers fall into the daisywheel category. The ball printers have the letters stamped on a round hammer. The hammer is rotated to the right letter before hitting the ribbon—another form of a daisywheel printer.

Daisywheel printers are used today in applications where multipart forms or stencils are required and dot-matrix quality is not acceptable. But, even this market segment is being crowded out by the newer dot-matrix printers that can make the stencil look better than a daisywheel because the ink does not bleed through the stencil holes as much.

Thermal Printers

All thermal printers work just like dot-matrix printers, but rather than having 9 wires fly out at a ribbon, the tips of the 9 wires heat up and cool down rapidly. Early thermal printers required special paper. These thermal printers are still used in portable printers, hand-held calculators, adding machines, and some cash registers. Where light weight and simplicity are important, these printers are good printers. The reason they are not popular is that they require a special paper.

IBM tried a variant on this printer called a thermal-transfer printer or the Quietwriter. This thermal printer can print on normal paper, using a special ribbon that has a wax-like coating. The ribbons cost about three times as much as dot-matrix printer ribbons and don't last as long. The idea is that the heat from the print head melts the wax off the ribbon and onto the paper. This printer is quiet (accept when buzzing to indicate a problem, which this printer usually has). The wax melted on the paper has the raised ink feel that expensive business cards have. The trouble is that if the paper is left in the sun and heats up, the wax melts out of the paper into a little ball. When the paper is picked up all the balls roll off! This technology has basically lost the war with inkjet and laser printers.

Dealing with Print-Head Alignment Problems

All printers with heads that move back and forth have alignment problems. The more violent the technology, the more problems. Daisywheel printers are the most violent; therefore, they have the most problems. In daisywheel printers, every joint between pieces of metal would break if welded into place; therefore, daisywheel printers have the most adjustments. Most printers have some adjustments. How often a printer needs adjusting depends on its use. Many printers never need adjusting. Daisywheels need adjusting all the time. These adjustments take patience and practice, both of which are expensive.

The adjustments are worth going over because most dot-matrix and inkjet printers occasionally have the same problems. Dot-matrix and inkjet printer adjustment problems should never appear during normal use. Most problems arise after a paper jam or mailing label problem. Not all the printers have all the adjustments. Symptoms you can correct through adjustment include the following:

- ❏ Poorly aligned characters
- ❏ Letters on the right side of the page fine but those on the left light
- ❏ The top of each letter black but the bottom light
- ❏ The left of each letter black but the right light

The six adjustments listed in the following paragraphs are illustrated in figure 2.23.

Fig. 2.23.

Print-head adjustments.

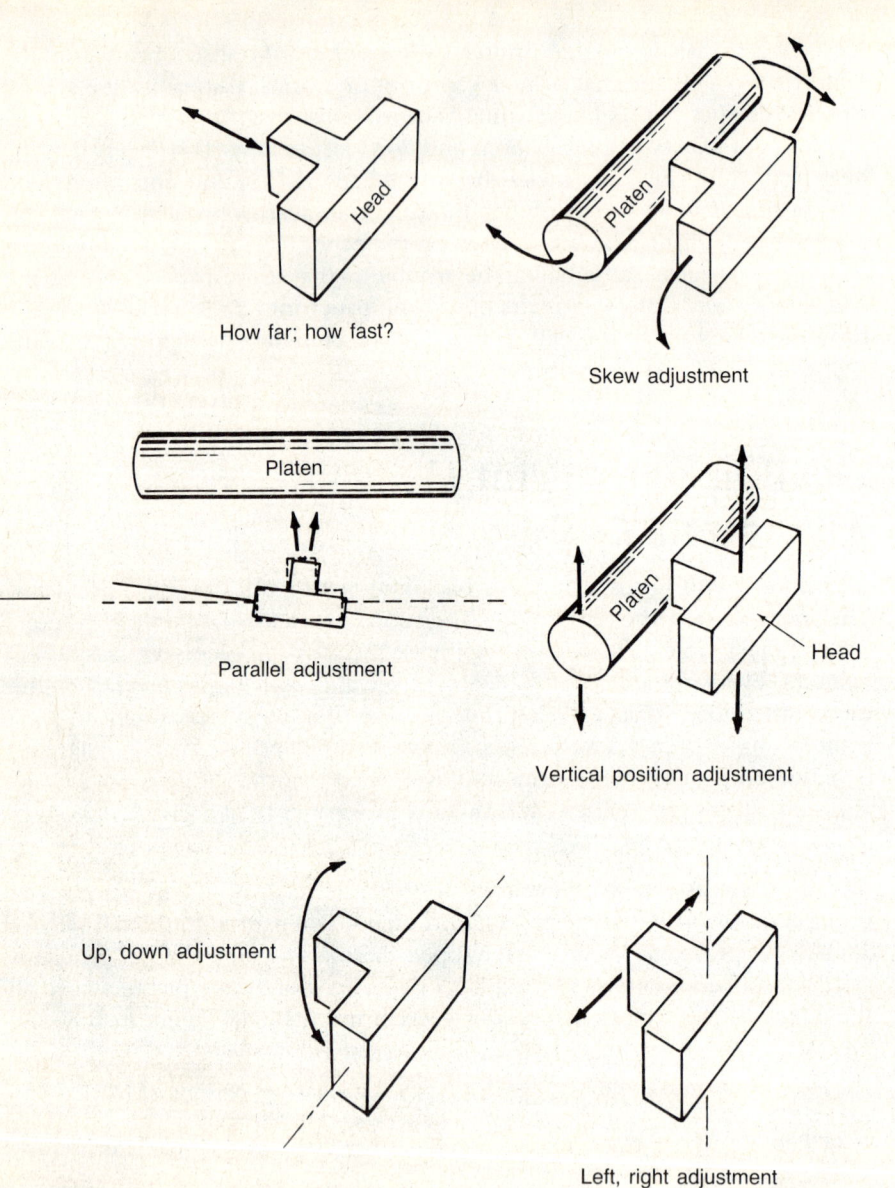

How far; how fast?

Skew adjustment

Parallel adjustment

Vertical position adjustment

Up, down adjustment

Left, right adjustment

The first problem is how far and how fast the hammer is thrown. Dot-matrix printers can bend wires if this distance and rate are not adjusted for multi-part forms. When wires are bent, the letters do not look as nice, and the only solution is to replace the print head.

The second adjustment is for skew problems. Imagine two pencils that do not touch, yet are not parallel. By rotating one of the pencils, you can make them parallel. One pencil is the platen and the other is the path that the print head travels.

The third adjustment deals with the issue of two pencils intersecting. An adjustment is again necessary to make them parallel. Again, one pencil is the platen and the other is the path the print head travels.

The fourth adjustment moves the platen and the print head up and down with respect to each other so that the hammer has a nice flat surface to hammer against.

The fifth adjustment rotates the head up and down on a horizontal axis, and the sixth rotates the head on a vertical axis. These last two adjustments are usually found on daisywheel printers.

The service manuals that show you how to perform these adjustments must be special-ordered from the printer manufacturer.

Chapter Summary

Printers contain microcomputers similar to PCs. The printer's CPU, RAM, and ROM have the same characteristics as the same elements in a PC. The printer's ROM contains imaging software that scans incoming data for characters and instructions. The imaging software then builds in RAM an image of what is to be printed. Print-engine software receives the image data and sends commands to print-head movement circuitry and paper-movement circuitry. These circuits turn motors on and off. The print-engine software also sends commands to head-drive circuitry. Head-drive circuitry turns lasers on and off and causes wires to fly out of a print head and push a ribbon against paper.

For the printer to work, it must have power. This chapter discussed power supply issues. For example, power supplies in printers are more dangerous than power supplies in PCs. The lid on a printer trips an interlock switch that prevents the printer from working when the printer is on.

In addition to describing the printer's computer, the various methods of hooking a printer and PC together were described in this chapter. The connectors, basic features, history, and future of printer cables were reviewed. The methods surveyed included parallel, serial, HPIB, SCSI, video, and LAN.

Paper-movement mechanisms include tractors, friction feed, paper trays, and cut-sheet feeders. This chapter discussed how each mechanism works and the advantages and disadvantages of each. Tractors are the most popular among dot-matrix printers. Paper trays are standard in laser printers. Cut-sheet feeders never work consistently.

The technology of how print heads are moved in dot-matrix printers as well as the details of how laser printers and copy machines work were reviewed. Fast line printers, or band printers, were compared with dual-head dot-matrix printers.

The actual mechanisms of placing ink or toner on paper in all the major printer categories were examined.

In the Next Chapter

Chapter 3 examines the information flowing into a printer, the information printers listen to. Merely talking about this information is confusing—people use several different languages simultaneously to describe what computers are listening to. Chapter 3 reviews the methods used to describe computer and printer information.

The most important goal of Chapter 3 is to separate the description of data from the printer reaction to data. Often, users describe a byte as the letter A, because the printer sometimes prints the letter A. But, printers do not always print the letter A when it is received. Typical printer reactions to data are reviewed.

After descriptions of data and printer reactions to data are reviewed, the problems with foreign language, math, and scientific symbols are studied.

This chapter laid the groundwork for troubleshooting printer software problems, customizing software, and installing software. Chapter 3 lays the groundwork for making an intelligent purchase decision, reading printer manuals (or not reading them), and programming printers.

3

How the Printer Interprets Data

If you just want to print the characters found on your keyboard, skip this chapter knowing that keys like Esc, Ctrl, and Alt will continue to intimidate you; special bullets, symbols, and foreign characters will continue to elude you. If your goal is to develop a fundamental grasp of printers, to have enough knowledge to be independent of techie gurus, you need to read this chapter for the following reasons:

❏ To learn the general principles behind a printer's interpretation of data so that you can isolate printing problems

❏ To develop a foundation to help you understand all printer manuals

❏ To learn how to print symbols and foreign languages

Printers listen to bits and bytes in a manner similar to computers. To understand bits and bytes, you must develop a language to describe them. Computers and printers communicate with pulses. Computer users typically represent pulses by drawing a pattern of 1s and 0s: for example, 01000001. The first part of this chapter explains how these patterns are described.

The second part of this chapter reviews the meaning printers attach to different patterns of 1s and 0s. The goal here is not to turn you into a printer programmer, but to describe three different computer-printer relationships (modes). One pattern of 1s and 0s is interpreted differently by each mode. Knowledge of each mode's characteristics is necessary for troubleshooting and configuring PC systems.

The third part of this chapter describes the different symbols that can be printed and the problems associated with supporting different character sets.

The fourth part of this chapter reviews how to print any character in the printer's character set. This section reviews typical uses for the Alternate (Alt) and Control (Ctrl) keys in DOS applications.

Describing Bits and Bytes

Within computers and printers, chips talk to each other. Understanding this complicated world is not what *The Printer Bible* is all about. The secret to understanding all printing problems lies in the cable running between the computer and printer. To feel in absolute control of a printer, you must know what goes on in this cable.

Computers and printers communicate through the cable using pulses of voltage, or current, (see fig. 3.1). The pulses can be thought of as ocean waves. To describe these pulses, translate the waves or pulses into 1s and 0s (bits).

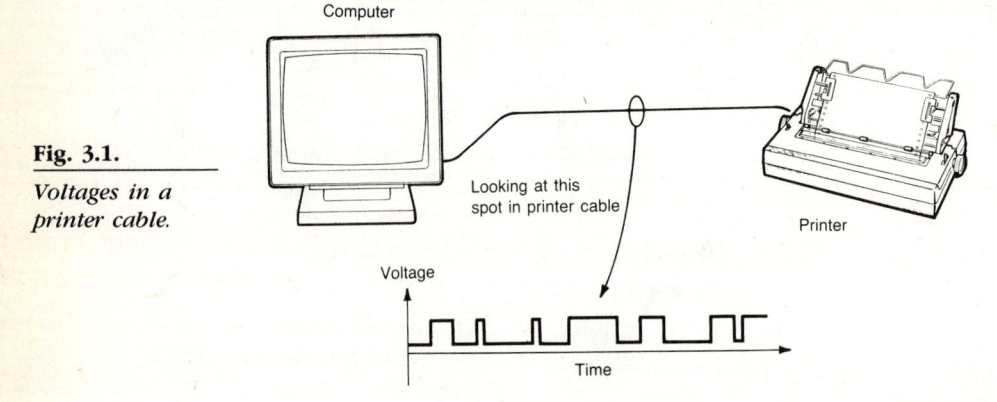

Fig. 3.1.

Voltages in a printer cable.

At the most fundamental level, printer data looks like an endless stream of 1s and 0s (see fig. 3.2). To function, the printer groups the 1s and 0s into manageable chunks. Eight bits has become the uniform size of each chunk throughout the printer world. There are 256 unique combinations of eight bits. Eight bits form a byte. Think of each byte as representing a key pressed on the keyboard, a letter displayed, and a symbol printed.

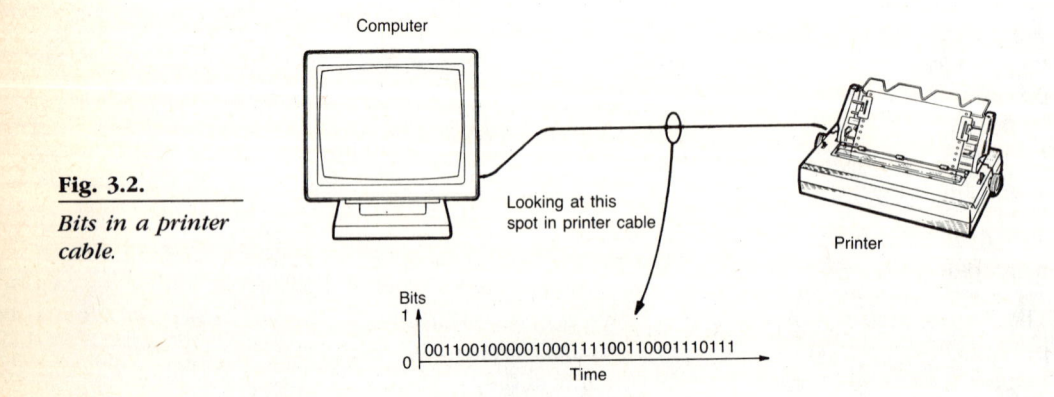

Fig. 3.2.

Bits in a printer cable.

After a printer has grouped bits into bytes, the printer begins to interpret the bytes. Bits and bytes are simple and what they mean to a printer is simple. Problems arise when users try to describe the byte. Often, a person mixes up describing bytes with describing how the printer responds to them. For example, a printer manual may require that the printer be sent the letter "A." The printer may not print the letter "A." Instead the printer may think the letter is part of a command. The following section concentrates on describing bytes. When you understand this information, you can understand what the printer does with the information.

> **TROUBLE-SHOOTING TIP** If the printer prints spaces rather than what is on-screen, the printer thinks that the symbol is an instruction or graphics data, or the printer does not know how to print the symbol. The solution is to change the printer's font or configure the software to translate from one character set to another.

Computers and printers communicate with only one language, the language of 1s and 0s. For example, a computer may say to a printer "01000001." This language is called binary.

Binary is hard to communicate verbally, and it takes up too much space on paper. Because remembering binary bit patterns is hopeless, other means of describing binary were developed.

Popular methods of describing binary include decimal, hexadecimal (Hex), and ASCII. For example, the binary pattern 01000001 is translated in decimal notation to a 65, a Hex value of 41, and an ASCII symbol "A." Understanding these notation differences is a prerequisite of being able to read printer manuals. This information is important when writing a dBASE report-generating program or printing a 1-2-3 spreadsheet in bold or compressed print. You will have to tell Lotus and dBASE which bytes to send to the printer to change fonts. The exact bytes the printer needs to change fonts are found in printer manuals.

> **HINT** When reading a printer manual, beware of numbers; they can be decimal or ASCII. If the manual is not clear about which it uses, try both ways.

> **HINT** Be careful when entering a decimal 26, Hex 1A, or ASCII SUB for any reason. This code is PC DOS's end-of-file marker and can cause a document or file to end prematurely.

Using Decimal Notation

Decimal notation is a simple way of describing bytes; just count them. Table 3.1 shows decimal numbers and their binary descriptions. Decimal notation is easy to remember, and has made decimal the preferred way of describing bytes in the world of printer manuals.

Table 3.1
Decimal Byte Descriptions

Binary	Decimal Description	Binary	Decimal Description
0000 0000	0	0001 0000	16
0000 0001	1	0001 0001	17
0000 0010	2	0001 0010	18
0000 0011	3	0001 0011	19
0000 0100	4	0001 0100	20
0000 0101	5	0001 0101	21
0000 0110	6	0001 0110	22
0000 0111	7	0001 0111	23
0000 1000	8	0001 1000	24
0000 1001	9	0001 1001	25
0000 1010	10	0001 1010	26
0000 1011	11	0001 1011	27
0000 1100	12	0001 1100	28
0000 1101	13	0001 1101	29
0000 1110	14	0001 1110	30
0000 1111	15	0001 1111	31

Decimal has one significant drawback. Decimal is similar to a TV set with a numeric keypad for selecting stations. The TV does not know whether you want a one-digit or two-digit channel. When a *3* is pressed, you can be asking the TV for channel 3 or you can be entering the first digit of channel 30. To make TV channel selection easier, you are required to enter *03* when selecting channel 3. Decimal values range from 0 to 10 to 255, from 1 to 3 digits. When entering decimal values, always enter all three digits. For example, when entering a decimal value of 1, enter *001*.

> **HINT** Adding leading zeros when entering or documenting in decimal notation always makes reading and understanding the values easier.

Using Hexadecimal Notation

Hex notation is a more compact notation for describing binary bit patterns. Instead of requiring three digits like ASCII, only two digits are needed (see table 3.2). Hex is a slightly different way of counting that uses letters along with numbers.

Table 3.2
Hexadecimal Notation

Binary	Hex
0000 0001	01
0000 0010	02
0000 0011	03
0000 0100	04
0000 0101	05
0000 0110	06
0000 0111	07
0000 1000	08
0000 1001	09
0000 1010	0A
0000 1011	0B
0000 1100	0C
0000 1101	0D
0000 1110	0E
0000 1111	0F
0001 0000	10
0001 0001	11
.. ..	
.. ..	
1111 1111	FF

The main advantage of Hex is that converting from Hex to binary and back can become almost second nature. Technical personnel can learn to look at Hex and convert to binary instantly. Learning how to convert between the two is not necessary for the casual user; however, charts and tables are in the back of most books. To develop this skill yourself, notice how the eight bits are split into two groups of four. Each group of four bits represents a Hex digit. Each of the four bits needs to be multiplied separately by 8, 4, 2, or 1 as follows:

1. Write down the binary value: 0 1 1 0
2. Write down the multipliers: 8 4 2 1

3. Multiply 0 × 8 = 0, 1 × 4 = 4, 1 × 2 = 2, 0 × 1 = 0

4. Add the Results 0 + 4 + 2 + 0 = 6

5. Translate to Hex 6

The last step of translation to Hex is easy. Just remember that in Hex, A = 10, B = 11, C = 12, D = 13, E = 14, and F = 15. Consider the following steps:

1. Write down binary value: 1 0 1 1

2. Write down multipliers: 8 4 2 1

3. Multiple 1 × 8 = 8, 0 × 4 = 0, 1 × 2 = 2, 1 × 1 = 1

4. Add the Results 8 + 0 + 2 + 1 = 11

5. Translate to Hex B

The binary pattern 1011 0110 is represented in Hex as B6. Understanding Hex is important for entering data into many printer definition tables associated with word processors (see Chapter 9). However, only true techies love Hex, because the notation looks like gibberish.

Using ASCII Notation

ASCII stands for American Standard Codes for Information Interchange. ASCII became a standard in 1969, with the primary objective of transmitting typewriter and keyboard symbols to printers and host computers. Because ASCII assigns a letter or punctuation symbol to bit patterns, it can serve as an alternative to decimal and Hex.

ASCII's advantage over decimal and Hex is compactness; only one letter is needed to describe all 8 bits. For example, 0100 0001 represents an A; 0100 0010 represents a B, and so on. However, this may not mean the letter will print when sent to the printer. The letter can be part of an instruction. The relationship between binary bit patterns and ASCII is explained in the Character Set Standards section of this chapter.

A problem with using ASCII as a notation for describing bit patterns is that the first bit from the left has to be a 0. Furthermore, bit 6 or bit 5 has to be a one. In the following example, bit 7 is a zero, bit 6 is a 1, and bit 5 is a zero. Therefore, the example can be defined as the "A" symbol on a typewriter keyboard.

Binary pattern: 0100 0001
Bit number: 7654 3210

Also, ASCII does not cover all the possible bit patterns, so mixtures of decimal and ASCII notations are used to describe printer codes. When you are reading printer documentation, the mixing of notations causes problems when numbers are mentioned. For example, which parts of the following command are in ASCII notation, and which are in decimal? Is 027 decimal notation for a single byte, or is it ASCII notation for three bytes? Is 174 decimal notation for a single byte, or is it ASCII notation for three bytes?

/027)s174W

All printer manuals do not answer these questions the same way; each printer manual has its own style. You must figure out this style before the printer codes can be split up into ASCII notation parts and decimal notation parts. Look for tables in the back of the printer manuals.

The ideal ASCII method would create 256 symbols representing the 256 possible bytes. IBM has done this in the PC-8 character set. Most other companies, however, have symbols for only some of the bytes. Because printer manufacturers have to support many different computer environments, they play it safe by sticking with the standards: ASCII and decimal.

In summary, learn decimal and ASCII if you plan on programming or reading printer manual tutorials. Learn Hex if you plan to repair, troubleshoot, or dive deeper into computers and printers. The engineers that design printers and the techies that make them work all speak Hex. The next section explores how and when symbols are sent to the printer, and the following section describes the symbols in detail.

Understanding Printer Modes

Approximately 90 percent of all printers print the capital letter A when receiving the binary bit pattern of 01000001 (Hex 41, decimal 65, symbol "A"). Five percent of all printers print something else because they are designed for mainframes. The other 5 percent do not print anything. These printers may seem broken when really they don't know what to do. The 01000001 sent to these printers is ignored, unless the printer is prepared for the byte beforehand.

Printers have three characteristic modes that govern how they respond to the arrival of binary bytes. Two of these modes—character and graphics—are discussed in Chapter 1. In character mode, a printer prints an A in response to 01000001. A printer in graphics mode fires two wires in a dot-matrix print head, creating two dots for the two 1s in the byte 01000001.

A third mode, called object mode, is emerging. The most popular example of object mode printers are those containing PostScript software. In this mode, the printer behaves more like a plotter, and a printer initially thinks all bytes are instructions. The letter A is not printed because the printer thinks the letter A is part of an instruction.

Most printers support the first two modes. PC software can tell the printer to switch from character to graphic mode. Before switching to graphics mode, a printer is told how many bytes of graphics data are coming. Once in graphics mode, the printer counts the bytes of graphics data received. When all have been received, the printer switches back to character mode automatically. PCs cannot force a printer back into character mode from graphics mode. Because object mode is so new, most object printers cannot function as character or graphics printers. Many people, therefore, think that an object-mode printer cannot print graphics, which is almost correct. An object printer cannot print regular graphics, but if an object printer is told to print graphics data, and if the data is formatted correctly by software, an object mode printer can print graphics data.

> HINT | Object-mode printers never work with the PrtSc key. Also, object-mode printers do not print standard text files using the PC DOS Copy or Print command.

Graphics Mode

Many micro applications put printers in graphics mode. When in graphics mode, the printer's performance changes, sometimes dramatically. You need to understand these changes in order to purchase the best printer and software combinations, and not waste your time, ribbons, and toner.

Most printers have a graphics mode. Individual dots are drawn using the period symbol, wires, or laser beams. When graphics information is sent to the printer, it is sent in 8-bit chunks. In most printers, the 8 bits represent 8 vertical dots. Before going into graphics mode, the printer has to be told the following:

1. How close the dots are to be placed vertically
2. How close the dots are to be placed horizontally
3. How many bytes are going to be sent
4. The coordinates of where to start printing

A band of 8 bits is sent horizontally across the page. You can see this band in dot-matrix printers, and most laser printers also work this way. Some printers have special graphics-like commands to print horizontal lines quickly so that the same 8-bit pattern does not have to be sent over and over again.

In graphics mode, software in the computer controls each dot placed on the paper. Even daisywheel printers print graphics using the period symbol, over and over again. Very little software supports printing graphics on daisywheel printers because the process requires an incredible amount of time. Equally ridiculous is graphics printing on plotters. Imagine the pen of a plotter hitting the paper rather than drawing a smooth line. Even though a graphic printing mode can be found in all printers and plotters, using the feature is not always practical.

Graphics mode printing is difficult for all printers and computers. In Chapter 1, the tremendous amount of information involved is described. The following difficulties are encountered with graphics mode printing:

1. Computer computational capability is the bottleneck, not the printer. All buffers, spoolers, and queues are useless.

2. Computers slow down to a crawl in multiuser, multitasking environments.

3. LANs slow down because of all the information being transferred through the LAN cables.

4. Expensive printers spend most of their time being told what to do rather than printing. This method is an inefficient use of the print engine. Individual productivity may decrease.

5. Sharing printers becomes much more difficult because of the time spent sending data rather than printing data.

Software that puts the printer in graphics mode is completely responsible for what is printed. The fonts can have jagged or smooth edges, depending on the quality of the application software. In other printing modes, however, the printer is responsible for what is printed. If one software package can produce fantastic output, consumers naturally feel that all software running on the same computer with the same printer should be able to produce the same output quality. Unfortunately, this is not always true. In the IBM PC MS-DOS world, each application software has its own font. The fonts cannot be shared. The Macintosh world, on the other hand, has a common pool of fonts that all Mac software can use for drawing on-screen and printing.

> **TROUBLE-SHOOTING TIP** If one software package prints attractive output and another prints unattractive output, try doing a self-test that lists all the fonts inside the printer. If the attractive printout uses a font not present in the printer, the first software package places the printer in graphics mode, and the second application cannot do the same.

HINT | If a PC software package prints using a font you have never seen your printer display before, chances are that the printer was put into graphics mode. In these cases, software is responsible for how smooth the curves are in graphics mode.

HINT | Just because one software package can print an attractive character, don't expect all software running on that machine to print a character that looks the same. Often, software comes with its own fonts and does not share them, or the software cannot take advantage of the pool of shareable fonts the operating system maintains.

Graphics mode is great for printing digitalized photographs. Only this mode can produce attractive shadows and shading. The drawbacks are that the digitalized photographs cannot be enlarged or reduced without degrading. An originally smooth curve looks jagged when enlarged or reduced.

HINT | Scanning a photograph is good only for enlargement, cropping, and text layout purposes. The quality of most scanned photos is not good enough for most professional documents.

A printer in graphics mode has a unique problem that other printer modes don't have. A printer in graphics mode cannot receive instructions, only data. A printer in graphics mode is like an out of control car sliding down a hill from the PC's point of view. In the middle of printing a graph, the PC cannot say to the printer, "Stop. Listen to me." The PC has to continue feeding bytes to the printer until the printer ends graphics mode. Then, software can send instructions to the printer.

HINT | When printing in graphics mode, don't ask the software to stop. Don't turn the PC off and on. To stop printing, turn off the printer and exit out of your software, back to the operating system. Reset everything. Otherwise, the software will lose track of when the printer is going to pop out of graphics mode. If the printer pops out too early or too late, garbage is printed.

Normally, graphics mode printing is reliable. Suppose that you are in the middle of printing a document in graphics mode. You change your mind and stop printing. You push the right buttons to stop printing, but the printer keeps on printing. You turn the printer on and off. The printer finally stops, but the software does not know that the printer was turned off and back on. You signal the PC to resume printing. The printer is not in graphics mode, but the PC thinks that the printer is in graphics mode. The printer interprets the graphics data to be printed as text and prints random symbols including happy faces, sex symbols and other unusual things that you did not even know the printer was capable of.

> TROUBLE-SHOOTING TIP: If the printer starts spewing paper, try turning off the printer and rebooting the PC. Perhaps the PC is in graphics mode, and the printer has somehow dropped into character mode. Always save your graphic before printing. Many programs force you to do this.

Suppose that a strong electromagnetic wave, from the ballast of a fluorescent lamp or the dimmer switch in the ceiling, hits the printer cable. This wave can produce what the printer thinks is graphics data. The PC does not know what has happened. The printer prints some garbage and finishes printing graphics data before the PC expects it to. The PC sends the same graphics data to the printer. The printer interprets the PC's graphics data as instructions and again prints happy faces and sex symbols and then ejects many sheets of paper.

> TROUBLE-SHOOTING TIP: If the printer starts acting up during the afternoon when the room and ceiling are warm, certain devices like the ballast of a fluorescent lamp or a dimmer switch may act like a broadcast radio station. The printer cable acts like a receiving antenna and prints garbage. Perhaps the printer will just sit and listen to the music. Shielded printer cables do exist, but are so expensive that most people never purchase them.

Endless scenarios exist for the printer and PC getting out of sync in graphics mode. All of these scenarios involve the software losing track of the printer and causing the printer to do crazy things. From the user's point of view, no solutions exist other than preventing the problem. Never turn a printer off while the PC thinks it is in graphics mode. Design engineers and programmers have tackled this problem by moving the computation of the dots function into the printer. This reduces the risk of printer problems by encouraging more cooperation between software and printer.

> HINT: When you print something, never try to interrupt the process. Instead, let the printer continue and waste paper. If you interrupt the process, you could lose your file if you have not saved it; you also can cause characters or even paragraphs to disappear inside the printer and end up needing to print the whole document over because the paging is distorted. In the long run, you waste less paper and are more productive.

Object Mode

Object printing is the process of software asking the printer to compute the dots of a circle or bar chart. The object, whether a circle, square, or letter, has to be described by software to be printed. If the object already is known by the printer, only the object's name and what to do with the object have to be transmitted. If the printer has not heard of the object, the printer has to be told how to draw the object.

Object definitions originate at the hand of an artist. The artist defines objects by describing paths, formulas, or vectors rather than dots. Sometimes the objects are drawn directly on PCs. Objects can be converted from paper to electronic form using auto-tracing software. Auto-traced objects usually need to be touched up with a drawing package.

Objects have a shape, but no defined size. To print, the printer needs to know the object's size, position, fill colors, line thickness, and so on. From this information, the printer can compute dot positions. Objects can be any shape and any combination of lines.

Fonts are built so that each letter is a separate object. These fonts are called *object fonts* throughout this book. Each character in an object printer has a name (see Appendix D).

Designing the formulas for any object takes much more time than a graphics or dot version. A curve cannot be drawn in a normal fashion. To draw a curve, first draw a straight line to connect the points. Then, the line is "bent" into the curve desired. The best software creates what are called Bezier curves in a manner similar to drawing French curves manually.

> HINT: Smooth curves are impossible unless object printers are used or the PC application software supports the bending of lines. Graphics mode smooth curves are created connecting dots at a microscopic level, which is both time-consuming and frustrating. Most people find this impractical.

In object mode, a dot is really a short line. Short lines disappear when the object is shrunk and look gross when the object is enlarged. To solve this problem, the object boundaries are filled in with a color or shade. If highlighting or shading is desired, object mode gets complicated. A formula must describe the dot density changes and the direction the changes must take place. If this process sounds impossibly complex, it is. Do not expect to see much more than line drawings and wire drawings in object mode.

Plotter Objects

The first object printer available was a plotter. A plotter prints by imitating the human hand. Normally, the pen is down on the paper. The pen draws smooth lines as it moves. The letters drawn contain circles and straight lines and are usually primitive looking. Lines with French curves are impossible for a plotter because the formulas describing the letters have to be so simple. In fact, plotters essentially have developed a new font.

> HINT | Don't get excited about using a laser printer to emulate a plotter, unless the software can print on only a plotter. The drawing may look nice, but the fonts still look like plotter fonts.

When drawing a line, the software must tell the plotter the starting and ending points. The plotter moves the pen from one point to another, in contrast to a graphics printer, which simulates the line with dots. Even an object-oriented laser printer has to simulate the line with dots. The difference is that an object-oriented laser printer is told the starting and ending points. A graphics laser printer is told the coordinates of a bunch of dots (see fig. 3.3). The line they draw is exactly the same. The differences are where the computation is done and how much information flows through the printer cable. In summary, an object laser is only transferring object information between the computer and printer. Ultimately, an object laser still prints dots. A plotter requires that object information comes in and tells the pen what to do in an object sort of way—a plotter does not print dots.

Plotters are a special class of printer that for a few years enjoyed limited popularity. Plotters can draw in different colors by grabbing different pens. By drawing lines instead of a string of dots, a plotter can draw better-looking bar and pie charts than dot-matrix printers. Furthermore, a plotter can draw charts on clear acetate for presentations. However, the market quickly dried up when the laser printer became popular. A laser can produce better-looking charts, can produce the charts much faster, and is more flexible. Plotters are slow and cannot draw many objects. Plotters cannot be taught new object descriptions. Plotters can just draw straight lines, circles, and ellipses. Plotters have drifted back to their primary market of creating blue prints.

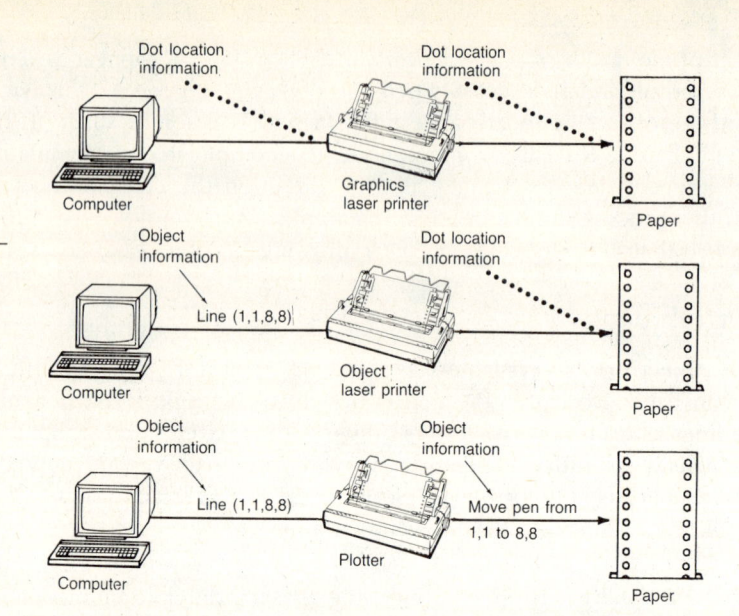

Fig. 3.3.

Differences between graphic laser printers, object laser printers, and plotters.

> HINT | Plotters always are going to be a specialty item in the PC marketplace. Don't invest much time with a software package that uses plotters unless you are interested in printing very large drawings.

Object Printers

Suppose that you are drawing a circle using a mouse. When the program is told to print the circle, it translates that circle into an object command that an object printer can understand. Object commands are an English-type of language that usually consist entirely of characters found on keyboards. Little need exists for Hex or decimal notation. For example, suppose that the PC's software wants to draw a circle. The command sent to the object printer would be something like CIRCLE (12,8,6). The object printer would receive this and draw a circle centered on 12,8 with a radius of 6. The object printer would not print the text "CIRCLE (12,8,6)". The default mode of an object device is to receive instructions, not text. If a sentence is sent, the object printer looks for instructions; finding none, the printer does nothing (see fig. 3.4).

> HINT | Don't expect object printers to print screens or print using DOS commands.

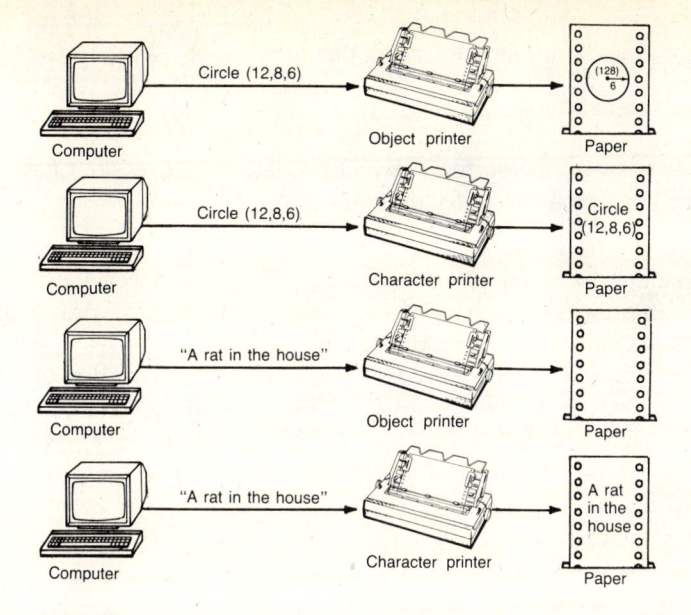

Fig. 3.4.

Object printers versus character printers.

Because object or PostScript printers must be told what to do in an English-type language, object printers are much harder to test and troubleshoot. Traditional printers are character-oriented or graphics-oriented, so they do something when a byte is sent. An object printer sometimes sits there, capable of working, but doing nothing. Object printers also require a much more expensive CPU and lots of RAM. These printers cost more and usually need a series of object descriptions before working. Therefore, they take much longer to begin functioning. When you have a problem, the power off and on solution takes longer.

> HINT | Object-only printers hooked up to the PC DOS world are difficult to install. They work only with the more expensive software packages, because most IBM software works in character mode only.

Character Mode

Ninety percent of all printers are character-mode printers. All IBM PC computer software expects character-mode printers. These printers have hard fonts (resident fonts or internal fonts). Hard fonts are not object fonts because hard fonts are described by dot patterns, and object fonts are described by formulas. Hard fonts cannot be enlarged or reduced and still look nice. Dots representing each letter have to be manipulated. To expand a hard font, the dots are doubled horizontally, doubling the width of the font, but not the height.

Character printers have a mind of their own. Before receiving a letter, the printer already has decided on the letter's font, size, and location. Character-mode printing and installation are therefore easy.

The drawback of character printing is that software has to assume much about what the printer is doing. software cannot ask the printer questions to verify any assumptions. For example, software cannot ask the printer how wide the letter A is. Instead of asking the printer, the software resets the printer and selects a font all over again. The software must know a lot of technically accurate information about the printer for character-mode operation. Most PC manuals are dedicated to a discussion of character-mode operation.

> HINT | Character-mode printers cannot talk back. PC software has no idea which font will be printed. Sometimes, software resets the printer so that it has a better chance of predicting which font to use. Other software enables the printer to print whichever font the printer wants to.

Using Character Sets

So far, you have developed a notation for describing the bytes sent to a printer. You learned that a printer can respond to the bytes in three ways. The printer can print up to 8 dots (graphics mode). The printer can print a character defined as a dot sequence within the printer (character mode), or it can trace lines stored within the printer (object mode).

In graphics mode, the dot patterns that make up a letter can be computed by the software. In character mode, the bytes sent indicate a predrawn dot pattern in the printer's memory that forms a character. In object mode, the name of the object can refer to a sequence of lines that represent a character. Groups of characters form character sets. Character sets exist on keyboards, in videoboards, in software, and in printers. Character sets assume different roles depending on which mode the printer is in.

The following section explores the character set concept, character set standardization efforts, specific character sets common in the PC world, and the problems of coordinating character sets in different locations.

Character Set Introduction

A different character can be designed for each of the 256 8-bit patterns of a byte. Each character in the character set also can have a long English-type of name, which makes the number of characters almost unlimited. The printer's response to each of the bytes or names is called a *printer character set*. Most printers today have more than one character set. The character set usually is changed by a dip switch inside the printer or an instruction sent to the printer. When a character set changes, not all the characters change. Usually, just a few are redefined. You will want to change character sets to print the new symbols defined.

The character set concept differs from the font concept. Up until now, the word font has been used rather loosely. Almost everyone has some idea of what a font is. Printer advertisements even announce how many fonts they contain. Although this is a good advertising strategy, it does confuse the market. Font used to have a very specific meaning in the typesetting world. Today, the word font can mean anything. Advertisements count different sizes of the same character style as different fonts. Advertised font specifications tend to mislead typesetters and confuse the rest of us. Chapter 4 is dedicated to describing what a font is.

Fonts are artistic. The shape of the letter A differs between fonts. Character sets are mechanistic. Most character sets include the letter A. Different character sets contain different foreign language symbols or math symbols. For example, one character set may contain the English pound sign, and another may contain the U.S. dollar sign. Still another character set can contain both. All three of these character sets can be represented in the same font.

Character sets are discussed at international standard organization meetings. Every country, company, and discipline needs their own special characters. Many different character sets are available. When a character set is designed, someone discovers some important symbol that is missing. Character sets are designed through the democratic process of compromise. Because of character set chaos, many character set problems occur. Before the character set problems can be discussed, a history of printer/computer character sets is needed.

Character Set Standards

Character sets often are called codes or symbol sets. They meet all the requirements of a secret code. Most of us learned some sort of secret code in grade school. With this secret code, you learned when to throw spit wads and who to throw them at. Boy Scouts and amateur radio enthusiasts learn Morse code, which can be considered the first international standard character set. When in distress, you are taught to send SOS: S = dit, dit, dit; O = da, da, da; S = dit, dit, dit. This can even be translated into binary that a computer and printer can understand: S = 111, O = 000. The problem with Morse code is that some letters are represented by one bit; other letters are represented by six bits. In the 1940s, Captain Midnight had a radio show that he would end by reading off a series of numbers. Kids with the magic decoder ring could change the numbers into letters. Computers also work this way; Captain Midnight's possible letters are a character set.

Computer character sets can contain symbols, device instructions, and undefined symbols. Undefined symbols are assigned meaning by printers and other equipment for their private communication. Character sets also differ in the number of different symbols and instructions they define. Because a maximum of 256 symbols are represented by a byte, 256 is the maximum number of symbols and instructions simultaneously available for printer communication. Character set standards exist that use 16, 32, 64, 128, and 256 of the possible 256 bytes.

The first primitive character set of computers was simple. This set contained no letters, just numbers, and was called *binary coded decimal* (BCD). Because the early computers were used for number crunching, letters were not important. Only number symbols had to be represented, as follows:

Binary	Symbol
0001	1
0010	2
0011	3
0100	4
0101	5
0110	6
0111	7
1000	8
1001	9
1010	0
1011	not defined
..	not defined
1111	not defined

Baudot was designed in 1870 by Emile Baudot. This set uses a 5-bit code with 32 different possible patterns. With an alphabet of 26 letters, you have only 6 extra patterns. To support the alphabet, numbers, and punctuation, one 5-bit pattern is reserved to switch between two character sets: an alphabet character set and a punctuation/numbers character set. Because Baudot was the first character set that could be automated, it was the set chosen when the first printers were attached to phones to enable two deaf people to communicate. These Baudot printers were still available in the U.S. as late as 1979.

In the late 1950s, binary coded decimal was extended to include the alphabet. This new character set was called binary coded decimal interchange code. This 6-bit code allowed 64 different combinations, enough to represent the alphabet, numbers, and some punctuation in one character set. This standard was used in the early TTYs or Teletype and governed the holes punched in paper tape machines in the 1960s and early 1970s.

In the late 1960s, ASCII was developed. ASCII was designed by the American National Standards Institute (ANSI). ANSI is charted by the U.S. Congress to represent U.S. interests at all international standard organization meetings. Also, ANSI is chartered to be the clearing house for all the standards organizations located in the U.S. ASCII is a 7-bit standard, defining the symbols of 128 bytes.

Table 3.3
The ASCII Table

	0	1/16	2/32	3/48	4/64	5/80	6/96	7/112
0	NUL	DLE	Space	0	@	P	`	p
1	SOH	DC1	!	1	A	Q	a	q
2	STX	DC2	"	2	B	R	b	r
3	ETX	DC3	#	3	C	S	c	s
4	EOT	DC4	$	4	D	T	d	t
5	ENQ	NAK	%	5	E	U	e	u
6	ACK	SYN	&	6	F	V	f	v
7	BEL	ETB	'	7	G	W	g	w
8	BS	CAN	(	8	H	X	h	x
9	HT	EM	)	9	I	Y	i	y
A/10	LF	SUB	*	:	J	Z	j	z
B/11	VT	ESC	+	;	K	[	k	{
C/12	FF	FS	,	<	L	\	l	|
D/13	CR	GS	-	=	M	]	m	}
E/14	SO	RS	.	>	N	^	n	~
F/15	SI	VS	/	?	O	_	o	DEL

ASCII represents the symbols commonly found on a U.S. typewriter. ASCII was the first standard to support upper- and lowercase. Of the 128 symbols possible, 95 are symbols and 33 are instructions. No bytes are undefined. Therefore, ASCII avoids problems caused by manufacturers using the undefined bytes differently.

The ASCII table in table 3.3 is organized in a traditional way. You need to learn to use the ASCII table. ASCII symbols have to be translated to Hex and decimal in the process of troubleshooting, configuring, and even using printers. Hex values can be found for any symbol or instruction by writing down the row value in table 3.3 and then the column value. Use the smaller column numbers and the row letters when appropriate. For example, a Z would be a HEX 5A. To compute the decimal values using table 3.3, add the larger column number to the row numbers. The decimal value of A is 65 (64+1). Another way of organizing the ASCII table is shown in table 3.4. Some software and printer manuals use this table. This helps compute the decimal values by again adding the larger column and row numbers. For example, a Z is 90 (90+0). Table 3.4 makes the addition a little easier, but makes the table look much more complex, so it is rarely used.

Table 3.4
The ASCII Table
Arranged for Decimal Computation

	0	1	2	3	4	5	6	7	8	9
0	NUL	SOH	STX	ETX	EOT	ENQ	ACK	BEL	BS	HT
10	LF	VT	FF	CR	SO	SI	DLE	DC1	DC2	DC3
20	DC4	NAK	SYN	ETB	CAN	EM	SUB	ESC	FS	GS
30	RS	US	Space	!	"	#	$	%	&	'
40	(	)	*	+	,	-	.	/	0	1
50	2	3	4	5	6	7	8	9	:	;
60	<	=	>	?	@	A	B	C	D	E
70	F	G	H	I	J	K	L	M	N	O
80	P	Q	R	S	T	U	V	W	X	Y
90	Z	[	\	]	^	_	`	a	b	c
100	d	e	f	g	h	i	j	k	l	m
110	n	o	p	q	r	s	t	u	v	w
120	x	y	z	{			}	~	DEL		

Table 3.3 contains two general categories of symbols. The first two columns are printer control codes. The last six columns are typewriter symbols, with the exception of the DEL instruction.

Control codes are used to program printers. Several control codes are discussed in Chapter 1 along with a description of a simple printer (CR, LF, and FF). Many other commands have important roles in programming printers. Unfortunately, most other codes or commands are not used consistently. For example, SI (shift in) means *compress current font* to an Epson printer but means *select current primary font* to a Hewlett-Packard printer. The purpose of this book is not to document these programming differences. Instead, printer features are discussed.

ASCII is now an international standard. Unfortunately, American symbols are not the same as those of other countries. The international 7-bit version of ASCII replaces the screened symbols in table 3.3 with characters specific to different countries.

ASCII also has been extended to an 8-bit standard, covering all 256 bytes. All the 8-bit standards use the original ASCII for the first 128 bytes. Unfortunately, many 8-bit ASCII variations exist, but no standard. The most dominant 8-bit versions are the ROMAN-8 symbol set, the ECMA-94 Latin 1 symbol set, the IBM-US (PC-8) symbol set, and the IBM-Denmark/Norway (PC-8D/N) symbol set.

The ROMAN-8 set is the default character set of HP printers. The ROMAN-8 character set was designed to be flexible when supporting foreign languages, having many accents, tildes, and so on that are separate characters (see fig. 3.5). These symbols can be added to American letters to create foreign characters.

The ECMA-94 Latin 1 symbol set has the copyright (©), registered trademark (®), 3/4's, and divide (÷) symbols. This set has less foreign language support and contains some of the Dingbat symbols.

The PC-8 character set has something for everybody, but not enough to keep anybody happy. The strength of the IBM PC-8 character set is that it has good line-draw or character graphic symbols. These symbols are discussed in more detail in the section that examines line-draw characters.

The only uniformly implemented 8-bit standard in wide use has nothing to do with ASCII. This character set is EBDIC, an extension of BCDIC. EBDIC was developed by IBM and is used by IBM and other mainframe manufacturers. Their printers use the EBCDIC character standard. Several translators are available to convert from EBCDIC to ASCII so that an ASCII printer can be hooked to the mainframe. EBCDIC is an evolutionary character set; whereas ASCII was designed from scratch. EBCDIC is fading from the printer

a Acute	á
A Acute	Á
a Breve	ă
A Breve	Ă
a Circumflex	â
A Circumflex	Â
a Diaeresis (Umlaut)	ä
A Diaeresis (Umlaut)	Ä
a grave	à

Fig. 3.5.

The Roman-8 symbol set adds many foreign accents and symbols to American letters.

world because it has no foreign language support and many undefined bytes. EBCDIC includes all the instructions of ASCII plus many more.

Character set discussions normally focus on the symbols contained, not the bytes necessary to generate them. The following sections discuss the extra symbols added to ASCII.

Line-Draw Characters

Line-draw or character graphic symbols are the building blocks of drawings. These symbols always are added to the ASCII character set. Typical applications are organizational charts, stick figures, pull-down menus, boxes, and so on (see fig. 3.6). Line-draw figures look nice as long as the object represented is characterized by vertical and horizontal lines with sharp corners. Circles and diagonal lines look jagged. Even big line draw fonts can be created. Line-drawing operations are supported by editors and some word processors. Converting line-draw characters to graphic or object drawing packages is impossible.

Line-draw symbols first became popular in early Radio Shack PCs. Because Radio Shack made the computer and printer, the character set of the video-board was identical to the character set of the printer. If a line-draw figure was designed on-screen, therefore, it could be printed on a Radio Shack printer.

```
                      TERMINAL SUBSYSTEMS
                          _____           _____
                         |           |         |                   |
                         |  PRINTER  |         |     DISPLAY       |
                         |_____|         |_____|
                                |                       |
                                |                       |
         _____            |_____|
        |           |                    |
        |           |            _____|_____          _____
        |           |_____|                 |_____|           |
        | Auxiliary             |    CONTROL      |        | KEYBOARD  |
        | Memory                |_____|        |_____|
        |_____|                    |
                                         |
                                         |
                                 _____|_____
                                |                 |
                                |  COMMUNICATION  |
                                |_____|
                                         |
                                        /|
        INTELLIGENT WORKSTATION  ====== PERSONAL / DESKTOP COMPUTER
```

Fig. 3.6.
Line-drawing examples.

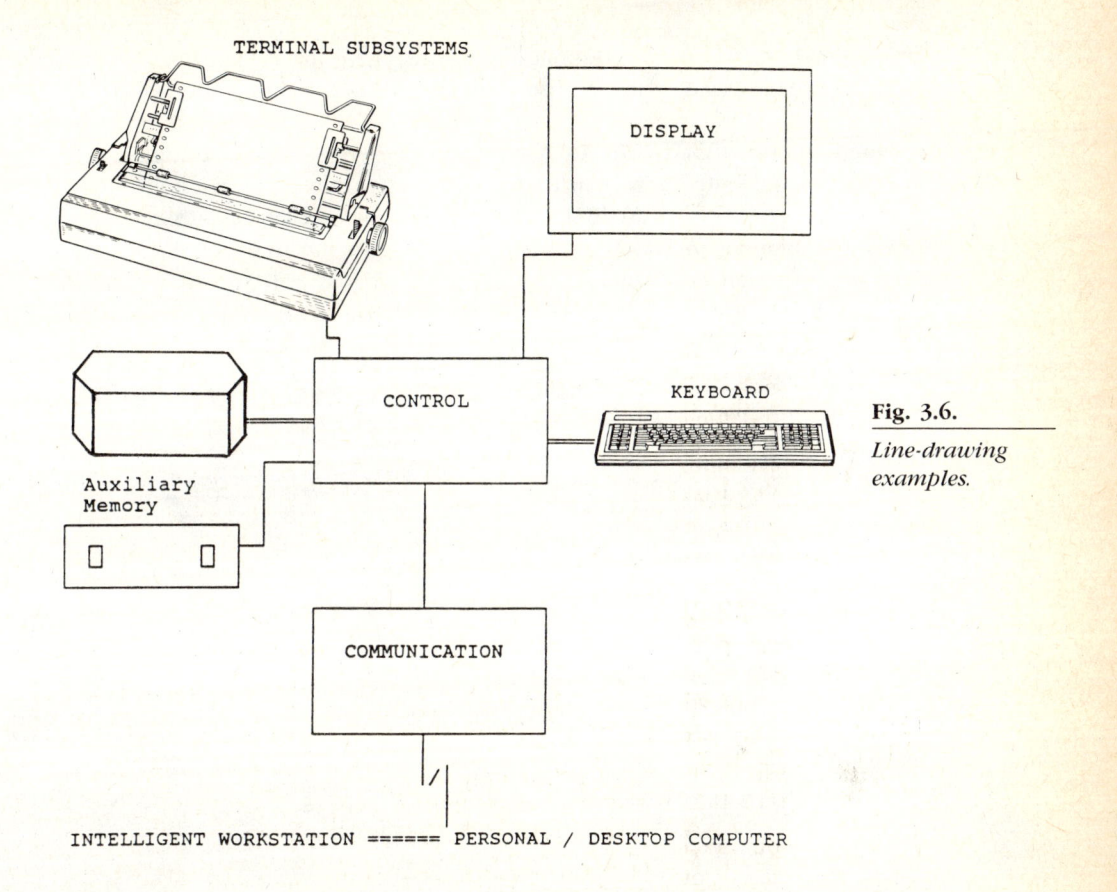

IBM designed the PC-8 character set by improving on Radio Shack's character set. When IBM released their first PC, the PC-8 character set was present in the videoboards. Unfortunately, IBM could not make a PC printer in the early days. Instead, IBM purchased Epson printers with IBM logos. The Epsons that IBM bought had Radio Shack's character set in them. With one character set in the videoboard and a different one in the printer, Shift-PrtSc could not print all of the display. The standard ASCII characters printed fine, but the box would be replaced with italics or some foreign language.

TROUBLE- | If what is printed is not what is on-screen, yet there is a funny
SHOOTING | symbol consistently replacing the symbol expected, try chang-
TIP | ing the character set.

Slowly, Radio Shack's character set disappeared, and IBM's videoboard character set is now available in most printers. The IBM character set standard has evolved into U.S. and Denmark versions, with little difference. Most printers support either one because the differences are minor. Today, printing every line-draw symbol shown on-screen is easy, as long as printers designed for the IBM world are used (see fig. 3.7). Printers designed for other computer systems will fail to print IBM line draw symbols. If an Apple printer is hooked up to an IBM PC, the Apple printer does nothing when sent a line-draw character. Most companies support the IBM line-draw character set. Although the original HP LaserJet supported only the HP's character set, the HP LaserJet II supports IBM's line-draw character set.

Fig. 3.7.

Line-draw characters available with the PC-8 symbol set.

Box [left TOP bottom]	┨
Box [left top bottom]	┯
Box [LEFT top bottom]	┯
Box [LEFT top BOTTOM]	┦
Box [LEFT TOP bottom]	┥
Box [left top BOTTOM]	┰
Box [LEFT TOP BOTTOM]	┰
Box [left TOP BOTTOM]	┰
Box [LEFT TOP right BOTTOM]	┿
Box [left top right BOTTOM]	┻
Box [left top RIGHT BOTTOM]	╀
Box [LEFT TOP right bottom]	╈
Box [left top right bottom]	┴
Box [LEFT top RIGHT bottom]	╫
Box [LEFT TOP RIGHT bottom]	╉
Box [LEFT top right BOTTOM]	┼

HINT | The default mode of early dot-matrix printers and character laser printers is not the line draw character set of IBM. Even IBM printers don't default to the line-draw character set. Look for ways of switching to this character set or purchasing the character set for IBM PCs, so that pressing Shift-PrtSc creates a printout containing the boxes and borders on-screen as well as the characters.

TROUBLE-SHOOTING TIP | If the boxes and borders are not printing properly, try changing the character set in the printer and the character set used by the software. Selecting different fonts changes character sets. The line-draw character set is usually within printers sold in the IBM PC market today, but it may not be the default character set.

IBM's line-draw character set also contains some support of foreign languages and the scientific and mathematics applications. The most unusual feature is that this set defines symbols for each of the bytes normally reserved for instructions in the ASCII character set. The major use of the IBM character set is for line-drawing applications; therefore, it has been called the line-draw character set in this book. Different printer and application manuals have different names for the IBM character set (PC-8, for example).

Dingbat Characters

In the printer world, dingbat is the name of a character set. The Zapf dingbat character set from ITC is the most common. Dingbat symbols consist of decorative circles, snowflakes, and squares used to point out important text (see fig. 3.8).

Fig. 3.8.

Examples of dingbat characters.

Right Pointing Index	☞
Solid Lozenge	◆
Solid Square	■
Solid Star	★
Spade	♠

The dingbat character set is designed to use the same bytes as ASCII and to replace ASCII momentarily. The dingbat character set does not extend ASCII like the 8-bit character sets. Character mode support requires ASCII and dingbat symbols in the memory of the printer and the videoboard. There must be instructions to switch between the character set modes. Many printers can store two character sets and switch between them, but videoboards cannot.

The dingbat symbols normally are found only in object-mode printers. Because most printers do not have an object mode, printing dingbats will require graphics mode operation. Videoboard support of dingbats also has to be in graphics mode.

When using a character videoboard, you can print a dingbat symbol on an object-mode printer. First, issue an instruction to ask the printer to switch from an ASCII character set to the dingbat character set. How this process is done depends on the application software (see the last section of this chapter for ideas). Second, choose the ASCII letter that generates a bit pattern identical to the dingbat symbol's bit pattern. What appears on the character mode screen is an ASCII letter. What prints is a dingbat symbol.

Symbol Character Set

The symbol character set functions like the dingbat character set. The symbol character set holds most of the math symbols and the trademark, copyright, and registered trademark symbols. This set even includes the Apple logo, although implementations for the IBM PC and compatible world do not print this symbol (see table 3.5).

Characters of Other Languages

Every language has its own symbols. Most of the European languages have symbol sets close to the ASCII symbol set. Most of the Asian languages have a special symbol for each word. Thousands of symbols, therefore, are necessary for rudimentary Asian language support. The only practical character sets that can be supported by PCs and printers are those similar to ASCII. For this reason, Europeans use a modified ASCII.

> **TROUBLE-SHOOTING TIP** If the printer starts printing in Japanese, it has a built-in Japanese Katakana character set. A dip switch in most dot-matrix printers controls the default character set. First try turning the printer off and on. If this does not work, try reading the manual to figure out which switch controls the default character set.

Table 3.5
Symbol Character Set

Alt-	Int'l	Symbol	Alt-	Int'l	Symbol	Alt-	Int'l	Symbol
1–31	not used		63	?	?	95	_	_
32	space	space	64	@	≅	96	`	―
33	!	!	65	A	Α	97	a	α
34	"	∀	66	B	Β	98	b	β
35	#	#	67	C	Χ	99	c	χ
36	$	∃	68	D	Δ	100	d	δ
37	%	%	69	E	Ε	101	e	ε
38	&	&	70	F	Φ	102	f	φ
39	'	∋	71	G	Γ	103	g	γ
40	(	(	72	H	Η	104	h	η
41	)	)	73	I	Ι	105	i	ι
42	*	∗	74	J	ϑ	106	j	φ
43	+	+	75	K	Κ	107	k	κ
44	,	,	76	L	Λ	108	l	λ
45	-	−	77	M	Μ	109	m	μ
46	.	.	78	N	Ν	110	n	ν
47	/	/	79	O	Ο	111	o	o
48	0	0	80	P	Π	112	p	π
49	1	1	81	Q	Θ	113	q	θ
50	2	2	82	R	Ρ	114	r	ρ
51	3	3	83	S	Σ	115	s	σ
52	4	4	84	T	Τ	116	t	τ
53	5	5	85	U	Υ	117	u	υ
54	6	6	86	V	ς	118	v	ϖ
55	7	7	87	W	Ω	119	w	ω
56	8	8	88	X	Ξ	120	x	ξ
57	9	9	89	Y	Ψ	121	y	ψ
58	:	:	90	Z	Ζ	122	z	ζ
59	;	;	91	[	[	123	{	{
60	<	<	92	\	∴	124				
61	=	=	93	]	]	125	}	}
62	>	>	94	^	⊥	126	~	~

Table 3.5 — *Continued*
Symbol Character Set

Alt-	Int'l	Symbol	Alt-	Int'l	Symbol	Alt-	Int'l	Symbol
127			159	ƒ	⏎	191	™	⇓
128	Ç		160	á	ℵ	192	„	◊
129	ü	ϒ	161	í	ℑ	193	…	⟨
130	é	′	162	ó	ℜ	194	‰	®
131	â	≤	163	ú	℘	195	•	©
132	ä	⁄	164	ñ	⊗	196	–	™
133	à	∞	165	Ñ	⊕	197	—	∑
134	å	ƒ	166	ª	∅	198	˙	⎛
135	ç	♣	167	º	∩	199	Á	⎜
136	ê	♦	168	¿	∪	200	Â	⎝
137	ë	♥	169	"	⊃	201	È	⎡
138	è	♠	170	"	⊇	202	Ê	⎢
139	ï	↔	171	‹	⊄	203	Ë	⎣
140	î	←	172	›	⊂	204	Ì	⎧
141	ì	↑	173	¡	⊆	205	Í	⎨
142	Ä	→	174	«	∈	206	Î	⎩
143	Å	↓	175	»	∉	207	Ï	⎪
144	É	°	176	ã	∠	208	Ò	
145	æ	±	177	õ	∇	209	Ó	⎞
146	Æ	″	178	Ø	®	210	Ô	⎟
147	ô	≥	179	ø	©	211	Š	⎤
148	ö	×	180	œ	™	212	š	⎥
149	ò	∝	181	Œ	∏	213	Ù	⎦
150	û	∂	182	À	√	214	Ú	⎫
151	ù	•	183	Ã		215	Û	⎬
152	ÿ	÷	184	Õ	¬	216	Ÿ	⎭
153	Ö	≠	185	Š	∧	217	ß	⎪
154	Ü	≡	186	‡	∨	218	⎟	⎟
155	¢	≈	187	†	⇔	219	⎟	⎟
156	£	…	188	¶	⇐	220	⎞	⎞
157	¥	⎜	189	©	⇑	221	}	}
158	¤	—	190	®	⇒	222	⎠	⎠

With 7-bit ASCII foreign-language support, certain American symbols are replaced with symbols of different languages. The American symbols being replaced are screened in table 3.3. This standard is supposed to apply to all ASCII devices. In reality, the standard applies only to the few printers manufactured by companies that follow the international standards. The good news is that more and more companies are starting to support the international standards. The bad news is that videoboard symbol sets have not yet supported the ASCII foreign-language extension.

The international ASCII standard is not popular because switching between symbol sets is hard to implement in application software. The most common application of the ISO substitution characters is in redefining keyboards. Also, many printers only partially implement the international ASCII character set standards. Either you have to be aware of what is happening, or the foreign character has to appear on-screen. Current videoboards can display only limited foreign characters, so users have to consciously switch between ASCII American and another ASCII version. As a result, you see an increase in complexity, training, and support costs.

Rather than switching character sets, most U.S. firms add symbols to the ASCII set by increasing it to 8 bits. The problem is that each company picks a different set of foreign language symbols to add. For example, the HP ROMAN-8 character set supports 62 foreign language symbols; the IBM PC-8 character set supports 31. Because the character sets do not assign the same symbol to the same byte, supporting the 8-bit character sets is difficult.

In addition to creating a special foreign-language symbol, character set designers often depend on software adding two symbols together when printing. Accents, dots, and tildes can be added to ASCII characters by using the Backspace instruction. Backspace is abbreviated BS in table 3.3. When the Backspace key on a PC keyboard is pressed, the cursor usually backs up one space and deletes the preceding character typed (see fig. 3.9). When the backspace bit pattern is sent to a printer, the printer's cursor backs up underneath the preceding character printed, but the preceding character is not deleted. At this point, another symbol can be printed on top of the previ-

	What appears on-screen from video board		What prints out on paper
Before	_		_
A sent	A _		A _
BS sent	_		A
^ sent	^		Â _

Fig. 3.9.

Using the instruction BS to create a foreign-language character.

ously printed symbol. For example, the additional symbol can be an accent symbol.

The Macintosh officially supports the Backspace method by using the Option key. The Option key functions like the Shift or Alt key on an IBM keyboard. This key is held down while another key is pressed. In fact, on some third-party boards for the Macintosh, this key is called the Alt key. The Macintosh has Shift, Control, Option, or Alt keys and a key that started off being called the Apple key, and since has been renamed the Command key. The Command key has symbols on it and is used as an alternative to the mouse to provide shortcuts through the menu system. The Macintosh Option key defaults to BackSpace mode whenever diacritical marks are used. The following are diacritical marks:

Keystroke	Symbol	Symbol Name
Option `	`	grave
Option e	´	acute
Option i	^	circumflex
Option u	..	umlaut
Option n	~	tilde

If you press Option-e, nothing appears on-screen. The next character pressed will have the ´ appearing above it when printed (the ´ may even be on-screen). If the tilde is desired all by itself (not above a character), press Option-n twice. This feature of the Macintosh System 6 operating system is used by all Mac software. IBM does not have similar support at the operating system level.

> HINT | Even if nothing is displayed when you press some keys within an application, something still may have happened. Try pressing a normal letter next and see whether the letter prints differently.

The difficulty with the Backspace method is that the application software or the operating system has to be intelligent. Application software has to be able to tell the difference between a Backspace code sent to it, and a Backspace code that the software is supposed to store and send to the printer. As an alternative, the application software may provide another keystroke that it translates to a Backspace when sending information to the printer. Another problem is that this process cannot be displayed on-screen. The accent or the letter can be displayed, but not both in the same space. Therefore, this mode of supporting foreign languages has not been very successful.

The only successful character-mode support of foreign languages requires that the videoboard be able to display the symbol or a generic substitute character, indicating that the symbol is not in the character set. In this case, some of the better character-mode software packages will enable a translation of the foreign-language symbol into character and Backspace commands necessary to construct it on the printer. The better software packages support foreign language symbols by sending the videoboard and printer into graphics mode.

Scientific and Mathematic Symbols

The notation of scientific documents and math equations is probably the most difficult to support with character mode. The vertical and horizontal positions of characters within a formula are critical. Character size changes are demanded along with the Greek alphabet. Any number of dots potentially can be put over any letter. Scientific and mathematic symbol support has all the problems of the foreign languages. In addition, printing these symbols has the positioning and font change problems.

Most software never attempts to support the creation of mathematical formulas on-screen. Software that does support on-screen viewing is difficult to use. Trying to look at a screen and predict what the formula will look like on paper is difficult. The most popular way of dealing with formulas is to draw them in a graphics program, then print them with a program that can mix text and graphics.

Several programs now have equations on-screen as interactive options. Ventura Publisher, WordPerfect 5.1, and TeX on the Mac use a version of EQN (a math language).

Character Set Problems

The languages of the world can be split into two categories: those that spell out words and those that have a unique symbol for each word. Counting all the symbols used in Greek, Hebrew, Russian, European, Japanese Kana, Math, Scientific, Iconic, Typographic, and Box, around 1,500 different symbols exist. Almost all printers, video boards, keyboards, and software choose a group of between 95 and 256 characters to support. Problems arise when the printer videoboard, keyboard, and software do not choose the same character set.

If software is running the printer and videoboard in graphics mode, you encounter fewer problems. Whenever the printer or videoboard is run in graphics mode, the software is responsible for the character set. Most keyboards are configured once at the operating system level; therefore, only installation problems with keyboards arise. Most problems arise when either the videoboard or printer contain printer sets. Object and character printers contain character sets, and object and character videoboards contain character sets. When the character sets do not match, strange characters can appear on-screen and can be printed.

> **TROUBLE-SHOOTING TIP** If the same strange character appears in place of some other character consistently, you have a character set problem. Even if the same strange character replaces multiple characters, you may have a character set problem, especially if most of the other characters are printing fine.

Ideally, all character sets are identical; every symbol is stenciled onto a key cap, and each of these symbols can be displayed and printed. Unfortunately, the keyboard does not have enough keys to generate all the characters possible. Videoboards have a limited character set that seldom matches the printer's character set. Everyone wants to print a character not found on the keyboard, in the video character set, or the printer character set. Use the following process to solve the problem.

Probably the easiest solution is to use a graphics package. Graphics packages can print every character that can be displayed. Unfortunately, this solution is not usually practical because of the time required to create a lot of the symbols and to accurately position them. Long scientific or foreign language documents are impractical to create in a graphics package.

> **HINT** Don't try to draw a curve or do word processing within a graphics package. Instead, use object-oriented drawing software. You will waste much time trying to draw a curve or do word processing with a graphics package.

> **HINT** When the application requires strange-looking symbols, make sure that the printer can print the symbols through a self-test, font test, or salesperson's demonstration before purchasing the printer. If the printer can print the symbols, software exists to use that feature of that printer.

If a character-mode solution is required, the first step is to make sure that the printer can print the character desired; otherwise, add a character set to the printer. Character sets are the easiest to add to daisywheel printers. You just need to find a print wheel with the characters desired. Cartridges can be added to laser printers. You can use software in the PC to send character sets to lasers and some dot-matrix printers.

Most printer manuals are full of instructions on how to design and send a character set to the printer. Only programmers ever do this. If a program sends new symbols to a printer, the program is unique, and usually works only with that printer. Programs that run on only one particular model of a printer are not very popular. Not much incentive exists to write such a printer-specific program, unless the printer is popular. HP laser printers are popular enough that such programs are starting to appear for them.

> **HINT** Avoid developing or purchasing software that works with only one type of printer. Eventually, you will want to run the software on another printer and will have to go through emulation hassles.

When the character or group of characters are present within a printer, the next step is to figure out how to generate them using the keyboard. You need to do this for testing purposes during installation as well as for educational purposes, so users are aware of what is possible using the keyboard. Exactly which combination of keys are pressed depends on the application software. When looking through the software manuals, don't look for the specific symbol desired. Instead, look in the manual for keyboard techniques that will allow symbols not found on keycaps to be entered. The last section of this chapter reviews some options if the application software is not clear on how you generate printer characters.

Next, develop a test document that prints all 255 bytes, skipping the first 32. The first 32 are instructions to the printer. These bytes cause most printers to eject sheets of paper. Don't worry if the desired symbol cannot be displayed. The symbol still may appear when printed. Try printing the document. If the symbol appears, correlate the symbol with what appears on-screen and which keys were pressed. Write a note describing which keys are pressed, what symbol appears on-screen, and which symbol is printed.

> **CAUTION** When entering all 255 bytes into an application, prepare for the worst case—the cursor locking up. Save everything frequently. Application software often abuses you by locking up while entering, saving, or printing the 255 bytes because most programmers do not test software to this extent.

If the symbol exists in the printer, yet cannot be printed, the problem is in the software. Software can be divided into two categories. Software with no character set information just passes bytes through itself, leaving the translation for the printer. The previous steps should work with this type of software. When the steps do not work, the software is smart.

Smart software contains its own character set. When a key is pressed, the smart software maps that key into its own internal character set. When the character is displayed, the smart software translates from its internal character set to the video board's character set. When the character is printed, the software translates or maps from its internal character set to the printer's character set.

Smart software tries to translate bytes so that the same character typed is displayed and printed, but the software can make mistakes. To ask the printer which character set it is using is almost impossible for software. For a few object-mode printers, software can ask the printer which character set it is currently using and get a reply. Usually, the user is responsible for telling the software which printer character set is being used.

If the user does not tell the software that the character set has been changed, the smart software translates the best it can and fails. Some software cannot be told that the printer character set has been changed and thus the problem cannot be solved. In these cases, you have no alternative but to change software packages.

> HINT | Try to purchase software that supports the same character set. This action will reduce troubles and headaches caused by managing the different printers. In the IBM PC world, stick with the PC-8 character set. In the Mac world, the Adobe character set is best.

Many laser and some dot-matrix printers contain two or more character sets. Early daisywheel printers required that the print wheel be changed to change character sets. Dot-matrix printers require that switches underneath the lid be changed. Laser printers can contain multiple character sets like dot-matrix printers. Laser printers also can have character sets added. The details of adding fonts are explained in the next chapter.

Some software can support switching character sets. Daisywheel printers with two print heads enable software to switch from one print head to the other. If the daisywheel has just one print head, some software can be set up to stop printing, buzz either the printer or the PC speaker, and wait for the daisywheel to be changed. After you press a key, the software assumes that the new daisywheel has a new symbol set. Now that laser printers have multiple character sets present, you do not have to pause to change daisywheels. Software supports laser printers by asking which character set to use first, which to search through second, which to search through third, and so on.

Printers that respond to only 7 bits can have a maximum character set of 128 bytes. Of those 128 bytes, only 95 can be used for symbols, because the other 33 are reserved for instructions in the ASCII standard format. Printers that respond to 8 bits can have a maximum of 223 (256-33) symbols in their character set. Some object printers get around the 223 symbol limitation problem by giving each symbol in the character set a name. Appendix D lists over 1,000 symbols and their names. If multiple bytes now have to be sent for each letter printed, however, the time to transmit a document to the printer and the time to process the document within the printer increases. To cut down on this time, some object-mode printers and some software can negotiate a 256 character set before printing a document.

Apple always has sold dot-matrix printers with only 95 symbols in their character set. Because Apple usually runs the dot-matrix printers in graphics mode, this limitation is not a problem, but Apple does use the character-mode feature of dot-matrix printers in draft mode. Expect to lose some symbols when printing in draft mode. Most Apple laser printers are object printers with the exception of the least expensive model, which essentially emulates a dot-matrix printer, the LaserWriter SC. IBM PC printers traditionally have been run in character mode with a full 256 character set. Apple had about a two-year head start supporting object-mode printers.

In summary, character set problems arise because the keyboard, videoboard, software, and printer can all have different character sets. When a key is pressed, a byte is generated. Software receives the byte and then sends the byte to the videoboard and to the printer. Software can instruct the printer to switch character sets or negotiate new character sets with the printer.

Generating Printer Bytes from a Keyboard

You now know that your printer supposedly can display many marvelous symbols. How do you tell your application software to print them? This section explores the generic keystrokes common to many software packages that can access all the characters in a printer.

In a byte, 256 possible combinations of the eight 1s and 0s exist. Generating all 256 from the keyboard and then sending them to the printer never has been easy. The first part of this section reviews the bytes that can be generated from a generic terminal or PC keyboard. Then, the bytes that can be generated using the Ctrl and Alt keys are covered.

This section then reviews several programming languages and application software packages with specific instructions on how to generate all the possible byte patterns. Finally, the problems encountered by random bytes are reviewed.

Using the Keyboard

Most PC keyboards can be divided into four sections. The most often used section contains traditional typewriter keys with 95 symbols stenciled on them. The symbols represent the character set of ASCII, which contains 26 uppercase letters, 26 lowercase letters, 10 numeric symbols, 32 punctuation symbols, and the space character.

Other sections include the function keys, the numeric keypad, and the cursor control keys. These keys do one of the following:

1. Duplicate the traditional typewriter symbols
2. Modify the meaning of the typewriter keys
3. Issue instructions to the application software or device to which the application software forwards the instructions

Certain non-typewriter keys issue ASCII instructions that are among the 33 instructions of the ASCII standard. These instructions include Tab (HT for horizontal Tab), Backspace (BS), Escape (Esc), and Enter (CR for carriage return).

Using the Shift, Ctrl, and Alt Keys

Most PC keyboards have Shift, Ctrl, and Alt keys. These keys can be used to generate any byte. The Shift key is used to create capitals and the symbols above the number keys. To create a capital or symbol, hold down the Shift key and press the other. The Ctrl key and the Alt key operate in the same way.

Because the first two columns of the ASCII table are reserved for instructions to devices, most do not have a keyboard key dedicated to them. Only a few instructions have their own key: Esc, BS, Tab, and Enter. The Ctrl key is a method of generating instructions to devices. In fact, the first two columns are called *control codes*. In table 3.3, if Q or q is pressed, the bit pattern represented by the ASCII instruction DC1 is created. If Q is pressed, move over 4 columns. If q is pressed, move over 6 columns. From the computer or binary point of view, the Ctrl key forces bits 6 and 7 to be zero.

The Alt key can function like the Shift or Ctrl key. Most application software makes the key function in this way. The Alt key changes the meaning of keys that are pressed. But columns are not shifted, and bits are not forced to be zero as with the Shift and Ctrl keys. Although the Shift and Ctrl keys are found on terminal keyboards, the Alt key is unique to PCs.

To understand the Alt key, some fundamental concepts of PC keyboard operation are needed. When any key is pressed on a PC keyboard, the row and column coordinates or scan codes of the key are sent to the PC. When the key is released, the scan codes are sent again. The operating system inside the PC changes the X,Y coordinates into bytes. The column shifting associated with the Shift and Ctrl keys is performed by the operating system, not the PC keyboard.

The Alt key is used in two different ways. The most common way changes the meaning of the next key pressed, but this change was not intended when IBM designed their PC keyboard. The Alt key was originally designed to provide a uniform mechanism of generating any byte from the keyboard. In the terminal world and the world of companies that restrict printer data to 7 bits, this use of the Alt key is not necessary. The keyboard, Shift, and Ctrl keys can be used to generate all the possible 128 byte patterns. In the IBM PC world where 8 bits and 256 different bytes can be sent to the printer, the Alt key is necessary.

Another Alt key use generates bytes on most IBM or IBM clone keyboards. (Some laptop Alt keys may not do this.) Using the Alt key for generating any byte requires knowing the decimal value of the byte. After you calculate the decimal value, follow these steps:

1. Press and hold down the Alt key.
2. Type the decimal value on the keypad (the numbers on the typewriter keyboard do not work).
3. Release the Alt key.

Releasing the Alt key is the unusual step. You hold the Alt key down, type up to three numbers, then release. Do not let the Alt key up simultaneously with the last number typed. The byte is available to the PC application software.

Using Basic, Pascal, and dBASE

Most languages use a common syntax to send bytes to printers. Basic, Pascal, and dBASE examples are in this section. Most printer manuals show how to exploit the features of their printer using the BASIC language, but most users don't want to program printers. Instead, they thumb through the manual, see fancy sample printouts, and wonder why they cannot make their printouts look as nice. Even programmers don't want to program printers. Printer-specific programs run only on one type of printer. If the printer changes, the program may not work. The purpose of this section is to quickly review how most programming languages send bytes to printers.

Most popular programming languages require that you look up the decimal value of the byte to be sent to the printer. When you know the decimal value, use the CHR( ) function to send the byte to the printer. Suppose that you want to send the Esc instruction to the printer. According to table 3.3, Esc = 16×11 = 27. The following command lines show how to send Esc to the printer in BASIC, Pascal, and dBASE:

BASIC: LPRINT CHR$(27)
Pascal: WRITE (PRINTER, CHR(27))
dBASE: @ 3,4 SAY CHR(27)

Using 1-2-3

1-2-3 is a popular spreadsheet program. This discussion assumes that you have used 1-2-3 or a similar spreadsheet, know how to enter a function into a cell, and can find the printer setup string. Chapter 9 has a section on 1-2-3 printer installation if you need more background.

The first version of 1-2-3 used the IBM PC-8 videoboard character set and assumed that the printer had the same character set. The second version changed everything. 1-2-3 does not use the character set that typically comes on a PC videoboard. Instead of using the standard PC-8 character set, Lotus switched to the ASCII/LICS character set, better known as the ECMA-94 Latin 1 character set. Furthermore, when printing, 1-2-3 translates from the ECMA-94 character set to the printer's character set. When displaying, 1-2-3 translates to the videoboard's character set. As a result, printing anything but the symbols on the keyboard can be very confusing.

Rather than going through a messy explanation of how 1-2-3 translates, the following discussion describes how to design a test spreadsheet of 16 rows and 16 columns. Divide the 16 columns into 8 pairs. At the top of each column, alternate placing the words Decimal Value and Character so that you have 8 of each column. Then, fill the columns sequentially, going down the rows, starting at 128 and ending with 255. In each cell next to a number, place the following formula:

@CHAR(xx)

XX is the coordinate of the cell containing a number. The characters displayed are not printed.

Using WordPerfect

WordPerfect 5.0 leads the industry in character-mode printer support. A study of WordPerfect prepares one for any other character-mode software support and for most object software. Before Version 5.0, WordPerfect's support of printers was relatively simple. Version 5.1 probably has the best support of character-mode printers available. The examples in this section refer to Versions 5.0 and 5.1. Earlier versions are similar, but not as complex.

WordPerfect 5.0 has a character set of 1,500 characters. The program maps the keyboard, screen, and printer into this character set. The advantage is that a WordPerfect document is independent of keyboards, videoboards, and printers (see fig. 3.10). If any device is changed, WordPerfect still has a chance of displaying and printing all the symbols of the document unchanged.

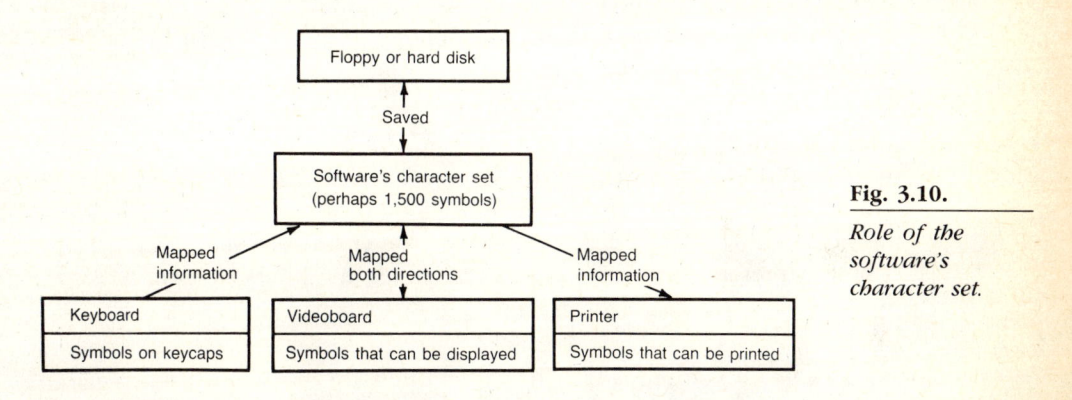

Fig. 3.10.

Role of the software's character set.

WordPerfect has four basic methods of entering printer information into the document:

1. Symbol found on the keyboard
2. Symbol not on the keyboard
3. Symbol in the videoboard character set
4. Symbol in the printer character set

The Alt key works as expected, although WordPerfect maps the videoboard's symbol to the same symbol in the printer character's set. The Alt key does not create a byte that is sent to the printer.

The Ctrl key does not work as described previously. The Ctrl key is used to send instructions to WordPerfect, not the printer. WordPerfect intercepts the control codes, responds to them, and discards them. The codes never reach the printer.

Generating a Symbol Found on the Keyboard

If the symbol desired is on the keyboard, try pressing the key. PCs are designed with specific keyboards in mind; therefore, every symbol on the keyboard should be available in the videoboard character set. Pressing the key should cause the PC to display that symbol. Even if the symbol is displayed, however, it is not necessarily printed. The symbol must be present in the printer's character set to be printed.

Generating a Symbol Not Found on the Keyboard

If the desired symbol is not present on the keyboard, look at the appendixes of the WordPerfect manual to find the group number and character numbers within the group of the symbol you are interested in. For example, a Chi symbol is character 47 in group 8. Although there are 1,500 symbols to choose from, this method is the simplest. WordPerfect cannot display all 1,500 symbols on-screen because it is limited by the videoboard's character set. The list of 1,500 symbols, therefore, is not available through WordPerfect's help.

After the symbol's group and character numbers are known, you can enter the symbol by pressing Ctrl-V, the group number, a comma, the character number, and Enter. A small square appears on-screen if the symbol is not in the videoboard's character set. Otherwise, the character itself appears. If the symbol is present in the printer's character set, the symbol is printed.

> HINT: If you use a certain symbol often, create a WordPerfect macro to run the keystrokes.

Generating a Symbol in the Videoboard Character Set

If the videoboard's character set contains a desired character, figure out the decimal value of the byte that the videoboard needs to display the character (IBM videoboards use the PC-8 character set). WordPerfect enables all 256 possible bytes to be present in a document except the decimal value 240. For some reason, this value causes WordPerfect to lock up; turn the PC off and on to reset. Sometimes pressing Ctrl-C or Ctrl-Break resurrects WordPerfect, but not always.

Enter the decimal value of the videoboard's character set by using the Alt key. Press and hold down the Alt key. Then, enter the decimal value on the keypad. Finally, release the Alt key. The videoboard's symbol should display. WordPerfect looks up this symbol in the videoboard character set and traces back to its own character set of 1,500. WordPerfect then translates the decimal value into its group and character numbers just as if the symbol had been entered using Compose (Ctrl-V). If the video character set is changed, the document does not have to be. WordPerfect should be able to find the same symbol in the new character set and display it.

If the symbol is not present in the printer's character set, WordPerfect doesn't attempt to print the symbol. A space appears in the printout.

Generating a Symbol in the Printer Character Set

If the symbol exists in the printer's character set, you may figure out its decimal value and send it to the printer by using WordPerfect's Print command. This mechanism is not recommended for the following reasons:

1. The symbol is printed properly on the current printer—only with the current default font's character set. If the font cartridge changes, the default font changes, or the printer is replaced, the document does not print correctly. The document has to be modified for the new printer.

2. Nothing is displayed on-screen, only in WordPerfect's Reveal codes.

3. The printer can become so messed up that the rest of the document prints incorrectly or not at all.

This method requires using the greater-than and less-than brackets to enclose decimal values rather than the square brackets that the rest of Word-Perfect currently uses. This method, hard to find beneath a pile of menus, is included to maintain compatibility with older WordPerfect document versions. If you want to send a decimal value to the printer by using the Print command, use the following keystrokes:

Format	Shift-F8
Other	4
Print Functions	6
Print Command	2
Command	1

At this point, holding the Alt key down does not work. Enter the symbols to be printed in ASCII or decimal. A maximum of 16 symbols is possible. Enclose the decimal value in <> brackets. When finished, press Enter. (Expect all the problems mentioned previously.)

Using the Macintosh

Apple has the best method of generating symbols from the keyboard. This method is straightforward and does not require knowledge or even the existence of Hex or decimal notation. By the time the System 6 operating system for the Macintosh appeared, the desk accessories contained a button called Key Caps. While in the middle of running any program, you can use this button. When you click on this button, the screen clears, and a map of the keyboard appears. The symbols generated when each particular key is pressed are displayed. If you press the Shift key, all the symbols on-screen instantly change to uppercase. If you press the Options key, all the symbols change depending on the character set in use. If you press the Shift and Option keys simultaneously, still other symbols appear. Furthermore, a little window appears in which you can type text while looking at the keyboard on-screen. When the screen is closed, the characters are copied into the current application.

The Macintosh typically uses the Adobe character set. The dingbat character set and symbol set also are present. The latter two have to be selected as if they are fonts. The Macintosh keys produce symbols that are not part of the alphabet.

Solving Problems When Sending Specific Bytes to the Printer

The programming language of most applications typically supports printers by providing commands like those reviewed in the Basic, Pascal, and dBASE languages. The data going to the printer first has to flow through the programming language's interpreter or library. Then, the data has to flow through the operating system, the BIOS or PC ROM software, and into the cable. Along the way, many programs and many devices can translate, delete, corrupt, add, or stop the data flow. Following are some of the problems that can develop:

- ❏ ESC is often treated as an instruction by software in the PC; therefore the instruction never reaches the printer.

- ❏ BS is treated as an instruction by software in the PC; therefore, the instruction never reaches the printer.

- ❏ LF is added to all CR instructions by software before reaching the printer. The effect is random double-spacing or lines printing on top of each other.

- ❏ NULs are treated as nothing by PC software and never reach the printer.

- ❏ CR and LF instructions are added by software before data reaches the printer. The software thinks that the data is too long to fit on a line of the printer. Software that does this defaults to 80 characters, then 132, then 256, and then 32K.

❏ SUB and ETX instructions may be treated as the end of a file by software; therefore, the printing is prematurely stopped.

❏ Tab keystrokes are translated into spaces by software before the TAB instruction reaches the printer.

❏ Print-sharing devices, LAN printer servers, and so on can think that instructions or text intended for the printer are instructions for themselves. Some instructions (and text), therefore, may not reach the printer.

The preceding problems have no solutions. They are listed here because isolating them is difficult. Avoid problem packages; write nasty letters to the programmers who wrote them.

Chapter Summary

Computer users and printer manuals use three different methods of describing bytes that flow down printer cables: Decimal, Hex, and ASCII. When the bytes arrive at the printer, they are interpreted as graphics data, instructions, or a pointer to a bit-mapped character stored in the printer's ROM.

Videoboards function much like printers and play a large role in helping you predict what is going to be printed. Printers and videoboards can be in character, graphics, or object modes. In graphics mode, the individual dots displayed or printed are controlled by software. In object mode, software sends the names of objects to be displayed along with position, size, line type, and coloring or fill information. In character mode, the PC just sends bytes representing letters and the printer or videoboard decides which font is used, how thick or bold the font is going to be, and where the character is displayed. Because printers cannot talk back, character mode is the most difficult for software to support. Most printer manuals are dedicated to describing character-mode operation. Videoboards in the PC DOS world are usually used in character mode. Macintosh video is always in graphics mode.

PC software places the printer and videoboard in the same mode, so that what is displayed is close to what is printed. Supporting object-mode printers is harder because they usually don't print anything unless set up properly first.

Over 1,500 different characters are used in alphabets around the world. Most printers and videoboards choose 95 to 256 of these characters to support.

Keyboards, software, printers, and videoboards all can have their own character sets. If the character sets don't match, the symbol typed may not be displayed, and a third symbol may be printed. Object printers supply the best support because each symbol is named rather than using a byte to point to the symbol. A large number of potential symbol names are listed in Appendix D.

Generating all the possible characters from an IBM PC keyboard using Basic, Pascal, dBASE, Lotus, and WordPerfect was reviewed in this chapter. Because Macintosh supports this feature through the operating system, the Macintosh provides much more consistent and simpler methods of generating foreign-language symbols.

In the Next Chapter

This chapter drew a distinction between a character set and a font. Even today, however, changing one letter in a character set is often called a new font rather than a new character set. The word font is abused. Chapter 4 reviews what the word font used to mean and why the typesetting industry has disowned the word. In Chapter 4, terms like typeface, point sizes, bit-mapped or character fonts, outline or object fonts are defined. The physical differences between typefaces and general families of typefaces are surveyed. Where fonts are added, where they are managed, and the problems associated with fonts are also discussed.

Font Basics

Chapter 3 described character sets; this chapter focuses on fonts—defining a font and describing different font characteristics.

This chapter defines a font and typeface so that you can purchase printers and software with more confidence. The various types of fonts and font families are reviewed, enabling you to purchase the right fonts. After reading this chapter, you should be able to make better-looking documents by using fonts appropriately, and you should be able to spot font problems by glancing at a page.

Defining Fonts, Typefaces, and Typeface Families

Currently, the word font has a variety of meanings. For the purposes of this book, a *font* is any change in appearance of characters—other than size or underlining. If you change a font's slant or stress, or you add shadow, bold-facing, or italics, you create a new font. If you simply underline or change the size of the font, the font is still the same one. Occasionally, advertisers distort the definition for their own purposes.

You must understand the definition of a font because some manufacturers advertise printers with dozens of fonts. But, after you print a page in each font, perhaps only 7 fonts look different. In this case, the printer manufacturer is counting fonts differently than the definition in this book (perhaps counting 9 sizes of 7 fonts as 63 fonts). Furthermore, the printer manufacturer falsely raises your expectations concerning the printer's capabilities.

In this book, the term *typeface* describes a group of fonts designed to work together. A typeface contains a stable of fonts necessary to project a certain style. Helvetica Bold and Helvetica Italic are two fonts within the same typeface. These different fonts share a common style or theme. Together, the group of fonts is called a typeface.

Four basic *typeface families* exist: Roman, sans serif, script, and black letter. Most typefaces belong to one of these families.

Unfortunately, much of the world is confused about definitions of families, typefaces, and fonts. Early printers had one font, but as competition grew, printers developed more fonts. Manufacturers know that ads listing the quantity of fonts sell printers, not descriptions of how attractive the fonts are. Consider these two advertisements:

OVER 50 PRECISION FONTS IN ANY SIZE

- Top quality typefaces (including 35 for object printers) are included for screen and printer...
- Easy typeface selection with font shapes visible during font selection

25-IN-1 FONT CARTRIDGE

- Fonts from all 25 HP Cartridges
- 88 fonts in 11 sizes
- 20 symbol sets

In these examples, the manufacturers clearly advertise font quantity, but they do not mention typefaces or how the fonts support the typefaces. Suppose that you need an italic font in each typeface—you cannot tell if these products are satisfactory. After reading the next section, you can call the font vendor and ask the necessary questions.

Font Families

The font families differ in obvious ways. The most common family by far is the Roman. The Roman family has hooks, blocks, wedges, lips, lids, bases, and blobs on the ends of the lines that form the letters. These frills that finish each unattached line of a character are called *serifs*. The Roman family contains more typefaces than any other family.

The sans serif family has no serifs (sans means without). Each line of a sans serif character finishes in a point. This family is almost as popular as the Roman family. Most people categorize the sans serif family typefaces as modern; whereas, the Roman family typefaces are considered more traditional.

Script typefaces try to connect each letter together as if the text is cursive handwriting. An all-capital letters headline in a script font looks strange because the capital letters don't connect. script typefaces are rarely included in printing software because they are seldom used except for decorative or formal documents, like wedding invitations. None of the fonts that come with an Apple LaserWriter printer are part of a script typeface family.

Black letter typefaces have ornate serifs and reinforcement lines supporting most vertical sections of the letters. Many people look at black letter typefaces and describe them as old-fashioned or gothic. Black letter typefaces are rarely used.

Typeface Characteristics

Within a family, typefaces differ in many ways, sometimes obviously, sometimes not. Typeface consultants look for the following characteristics when they try to match a font with the image the client wants. The characteristics also describe typeface features that some software programs keep track of to sort, classify, substitute, and manage fonts within an organization. You can find all the following characteristics in WordPerfect 5.0's printer definition tables.

Serifs: cupped, exaggerated, hairline, slab, slanted, transitional, triangular, ball

Shape: curved, bowed, nonconnecting enclosures, round, square

Stress: angular, exaggerated, uniform

Proportions: capital height, descender height, lowercase x-height, lowercase t-height, slant adjust, fixed spacing, proportional spacing

This list is not exhaustive; the following sections describe these characteristics and others in more detail. The purpose is to clearly define the differences between typeface families, typefaces, and fonts.

Not all of these characteristics apply to each typeface family. For example, because the sans serif family does not have serifs, the serif characteristics don't apply. For the sans serif family, the shape characteristics are most important.

Font Features

Fonts differ in weight and attributes. Some examples in both categories are shown below:

Weight: extra light, light, normal, demi, bold, extra bold

Attributes: italic (oblique), outline, shadow, small caps

Typefaces may be selected from within a publishing package, but then font details still need to be specified before a font can be chosen. A printer may support 60 fonts, but only 4 typefaces from 1 typeface family.

Understanding Font Characteristics

Much remains to be said about design concepts, but such information is outside the scope of a book on printers.

The objective of this section is to review font appearance characteristics and to explain how software handles fonts. This section illustrates the pitfalls of trying to use the wrong font when printing a spreadsheet and the joys of using the correct font in a word processing document. This section also examines font characteristics in-depth.

Font Height

Font height has two definitions: one from the typesetting world, the other from the typewriter world. Typesetters discuss font height in terms of *points*. On typewriters, however, font height gave way to indirect terms like *lines per inch*. This section reviews these concepts and the problems associated with them.

Lines Per Inch

In the non-typesetting world, font height was not an issue. During the typewriter era, the issue was the number of lines on an 8 1/2-by-11-inch page. You chose 6 or 8 lines per inch. Today, most character-mode printers and software assume 6 lines per inch. Changing to 8 lines per inch does not change the font height; the lines just become more crowded (see fig. 4.1). Dot-matrix printers are starting to offer double-height and half-height font options.

> HINT Remember that 11-inch pages have a maximum of 66 lines because most printers and software space lines at 6 per inch. Remembering this fact saves time when you must figure what page length should be.

> TROUBLE-SHOOTING TIP When you change to double-height mode from the front panel of the printer, the line spacing remains the same. To make the document look correct, you must also change the line spacing.

When dot-matrix printers change the height of letters, the dots of a character font are doubled, or every other dot is printed. During the height change, the printer is in character mode, and software is responsible for changing the

Chapter 4: Font Basics 129

```
As early as December 18, 1917,     As early as December 18, 1917,
the keeping of the civil status   the keeping of the civil status
records was handed over to the    records was handed over to the
Soviet authorities. In the        Soviet authorities. In the
Commissariat for Justice, a       Commissariat for Justice, a
liquidation department was        liquidation department was
established, which began with the established, which began with the
liquidation of church             liquidation of church
possessions. ... The anti-        possessions. ... The anti-
religious propaganda began with   religious propaganda began with
the exposure of the clerical      the exposure of the clerical
hierarchy's direct deception of   hierarchy's direct deception of
the people. The holy fountain of  the people. The holy fountain of
the Sergius Church turned out to  the Sergius Church turned out to
be a simple pump. The brow of     be a simple pump. The brow of
many a saint proved to be nothing many a saint proved to be nothing
other than a cleverly arranged    other than a cleverly arranged
piece of leather.                 piece of leather.
```

Fig. 4.1.

Lines per inch.

line spacing. The resulting characters have the same width—the taller characters look skinny, and the shorter characters look fat. Either method calls attention to the fact that you are using a dot-matrix printer (see fig. 4.2).

```
This is regular text
This is double high
This is double wide
This is double high, double wide
```

Fig. 4.2.

Manipulating dots to change a character's height.

TROUBLE-SHOOTING TIP	On a dot-matrix printer, if you attempt double height on the first line, the printer refuses to print double height. The rest of the lines, however, switch to double-height mode. Adding a blank line or top margin solves this problem.
HINT	Some application software forces you to adjust line spacing if the font height is changed. Other software scans each line for the tallest character and adjusts the spacing. This automatic adjustment means less work for you, but you may not like the way the software adjusts the spacing. With either method, the printer is not at fault if the spacing is incorrect.

Double-height characters and changes in line spacing are impossible to display with most character-mode videoboards. Don't expect to print either correctly the first time.

Point Size

Character laser printers are much more sophisticated than dot-matrix printers. Instead of manipulating character fonts to change the height, character lasers simply require the creation of another character font. If you have the character laser emulating a dot-matrix printer, however, the output may actually look worse than it would on a dot-matrix printer. Object laser printers can generate a large range of fonts in different sizes that look nice.

Character font height is measured in points. A point is related to an inch—72 points equal one inch. The reason an inch is chopped up into 72 points is that 1/2, 1/3, 1/4, 1/6, 1/8, 1/9, 1/12 increments are easy to see on a ruler if inches are chopped into 72 pieces. Before the days of calculators, this measurement made typesetting math better than any other system.

> **HINT** Tall Adjusted is an option in some Macintosh Page Setup dialog boxes supporting LaserWriter printers. When this option is activated, the printable region of the 300-dpi paper is reduced 4 percent so that the dots per inch are an exact multiple of 72. If you print the screen font with this option activated, the printer output is nearly identical to the screen font.

Character fonts are specified by their point height. The most common point heights relate directly to the 4, 6, and 8 lines per inch used since the days of a typewriter. The following list shows common point sizes and corresponding lines per inch:

```
 7.5 points = 8 lines per inch
10   points = 6 lines per inch
12   points = 5 lines per inch
15   points = 4 lines per inch
```

> **TROUBLE-SHOOTING TIP** If the printout on a 9-pin dot-matrix printer in graphics mode has 1-dot-tall horizontal strips on it, the software is sending carriage returns to move to the next line, yet the printer is advancing the paper as if it is in character mode (the 10th dot is skipped to space between lines). Reconfigure the software for another printer.

> HINT: To convert from lines per inch to point size, divide 72 by the lines per inch. Then, divide that number by 1.2. For example, suppose that you want to convert 6 lines per inch to points:
>
> Step 1: 72 ÷ 6 = 12
>
> Step 2: 12 ÷ 1.2 = 10
>
> Therefore, 6 lines per inch is 10 points.

Character Width

One of the major differences between typeset documents and typewriters is the letter width. When typewriters were designed, the mechanical assembly required that the carriage move the same distance after each letter was typed. Typeset documents, on the other hand, can have variable character widths. Because printers evolved from typewriters, the major difference between printer output and typeset documents is fixed vs. variable character widths. This section explores the advantages and problems associated with each method.

Fixed Spacing

Because the typewriter moved the exact same distance for each letter typed, a new typeface had to be designed to fill up the space. The lowercase i was stretched to fill up the cell, and the uppercase W was compressed to fit into the cell. These new typefaces are known as *fixed-space* fonts.

Fixed-space fonts may have different widths. But instead of describing how wide the characters are, the usual measurement is done by counting the number of characters per inch. The most popular fixed-space width is 10 characters per inch (cpi). Characters per inch has been translated to the word pitch. If a font is described as 12 pitch, the font is a fixed-space font printing at 12 characters per inch.

The typewriter world has stolen the term *pica* from the typesetting world. A typewriter pica refers to a 10-pitch font. Pica in the typesetting world, however, means 1/6th of an inch—the term has no relationship to the typewriter's pica font.

The world of typewriters is ignored by typesetters because typesetters rarely work with fixed-spaced fonts. But, fixed-spaced fonts do have their advantages. All character-mode screens are fixed-spaced. The cursor is a block or horizontal line that indicates how much space letters occupy. The cursor moves in a predictable manner. Columns on the screen create columns on the printer. Application software does not have to be told how wide each character is, but rather how many characters per inch. If a 10-pitch font was told to print at 12 pitch, the characters look crowded, but the text is still readable (see fig. 4.3).

Fig. 4.3.

Fixed-spaced font printed at the wrong pitch.

```
As early as December 18, 1917,
the keeping of the civil status
records was handed over to the
Soviet authorities. In the
Commissariat for Justice, a
liquidation department was
established, which began with the
liquidation of church
possessions. ... The anti-
religious propaganda began with
the exposure of the clerical
hierarchy's direct deception of
the people. The holy fountain of
the Sergius Church turned out to
be a simple pump. The brow of
many a saint proved to be nothing
other than a cleverly arranged
piece of leather.
```

```
As early as December 18, 1917,
the keeping of the civil status
records was handed over to the
Soviet authorities. In the
Commissariat for Justice, a
liquidation department was
established, which began with the
liquidation of church
possessions. ... The anti-
religious propaganda began with
the exposure of the clerical
hierarchy's direct deception of
the people. The holy fountain of
the Sergius Church turned out to
be a simple pump. The brow of
many a saint proved to be nothing
other than a cleverly arranged
piece of leather.
```

10-pitch font printed at 10 pitch   10-pitch font printed at 12 pitch

Proportional Spacing

Typesetters work with characters of different widths—fonts that contain such characters are called *proportional fonts*. The characters must be measured independently for the best results, even though uppercase W is usually one of the widest letters and the lowercase i is one of the narrowest. Today, most printers still line up letters in columns like typewriters. But, the fancier printers support proportional spacing (see fig. 4.4).

Fig. 4.4.

Proportional versus fixed-spaced printing.

ABCDEFGHIJKLMNOPQRSTUVWXYZ
ABCDEFGHIJKLMNOPQRSTUVWXYZ

abcdefghijklmnopqrstuvwxyz
abcdefghijklmnopqrstuvwxyz

The first proportional font support appeared in printers around 1982. Early proportional font support consisted of including a character-width table in the printer's ROM.

After printing the character, the printer ROM moves the print head a variable distance. If a nonproportional font is used with the proportional spacing capability of the printer turned on, the output looks terrible (see fig. 4.5).

> As early as December 18, 1917,
> the keeping of the civil status
> records was handed over to the
> Soviet authorities. In the
> Commissariat for Justice, a
> liquidation department was
> established, which began with the
> liquidation of church possessions.
> ... The anti-religious propaganda
> began with the exposure of the
> clerical hierarchy's direct
> deception of the people. The holy
> fountain of the Sergius Church
> turned out to be a simple pump.
> The brow of many a saint proved
> to be nothing other than a
> cleverly arranged piece of leather.

Fig. 4.5.

Fixed-spaced font printed proportionally.

If the proportional characters are placed at regular intervals across the page, the result is characters too close or too far away from each other (see fig. 4.6). The advent of proportional spacing brought along many possible problems.

```
As early as December 1
the keeping of the civ
records was handed ove
Soviet authorities. In
Commissariat for Justi
liquidation department
established, which beg
liquidation of church
possessions. ... The
religious propaganda b
the exposure of the cl
hierarchy's direct dec
the people. The holy f
the Sergius Church tur
be a simple pump. The
many a saint proved to
other than a cleverly
```

Fig. 4.6.

Proportional font printed with fixed spacing.

Even if the printer has the correct proportional print wheel and the proportional printer feature activated, the output can still look terrible. Spreadsheet columns can be jagged. If the right margin is unjustified, the output consists of long lines followed by short lines, even though the lines contain the same number of characters (see fig. 4.7). Because of these problems, the proportional spacing capability of printers is seldom used.

TROUBLE-SHOOTING TIP | If vertical columns of text do not line up, try printing with a fixed-spaced font.

Fig. 4.7.

Problems lining up columns.

```
      Fixed-space              Same document printed
       printout              with proportional-spaced font

     dogs      1                 dogs     1
     cats      0                 cats     0
     phones    2                 phones   2
     mice      5                 mice     5
     fish      2                 fish     2
     children  4                 children 4
```

Most PC software does not use the proportional spacing feature of a printer's ROM. Instead, the software sends the exact coordinates of each character's position just before each character. Some character printers do not like this method. For example, some printers are designed to use the print head to hold paper against the platen (this topic is discussed in detail in Chapter 2). If told to move off the paper by PC software, the printer refuses, and the software loses track of the print head. The result is often letters on top of each other or ragged left margins.

> **TROUBLE-SHOOTING TIP** If the left margin is drifting around, try turning off the proportional printing feature of the printer. Also, try removing the cut-sheet feeder.

Software that supports proportional printing has to know the width of each symbol. You tell the software the widths during installation. Most software comes with a long list of supported printers, and most software developers have included character-width information about their printers on installation disks.

Lining Up Columns

From the consumer's point of view, proportional printing software is a big headache. The application software seems mysterious. If spaces are used to line up columns on-screen, the columns do not line up when printed (see fig. 4.7). If the Tab key is mixed up with spaces to add a left margin, the left margin does not line up. Traditional typewriter methods simply do not work.

Instead, you have to learn the concept of absolute horizontal position. The Tab key is important—you cannot hit the space bar five times to substitute. Disciplining yourself to use the Tab key and learning how to reset the tab stops within a document is necessary. Most software doing proportional spacing has the capability to display tabs on-screen. This feature is useful when trying to get proportional columns to line up.

> HINT When the left margin of a column does not line up, look for a feature of your software that reveals tab symbols and spaces—then eliminate the spaces.

For a column of dollar values, you often want to line up the decimal places and allow the left and right margins of the column to be ragged. With character-mode printers, aligning numbers is easy. With proportional fonts, aligning numbers is almost impossible. To solve this problem, the *decimal tab* (also called tab align or just plain align) was created. To include a decimal tab, consult your software manual for the command. If the cursor is left of the decimal tab, any characters you type scoot to the left while the decimal tab align character stays in the same place. Most software supports decimal tabs.

> HINT If the decimal place of a column of numbers does not line up, explore your software package to see whether it supports the concept of decimal tabs.

Centering Lines

Today, software *micro centers* instead of centering by character. Micro centering shifts letters so that they are exactly centered, unlike character centering, which is off-center on lines with an even number of characters (see fig. 4.8).

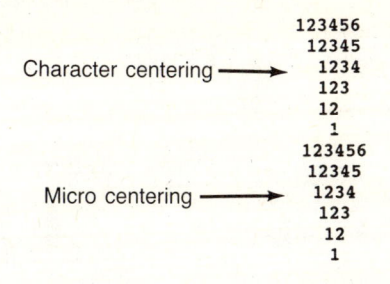

```
                                    123456
                                    12345
              Character centering ──▶ 1234
                                     123
                                     12
                                      1
                                    123456
                                    12345
              Micro centering ────▶  1234
                                     123
                                     12
                                      1
```

Fig. 4.8.

Micro and character centering.

Micro centering requires a change in how you tell PCs to center. Instead of using the space bar to move characters until they look centered on-screen, now, you press a special centering key. If you use the space bar to make characters look centered on-screen, proportionally spaced fonts are not centered when printed.

If the output looks like figure 4.8, first figure out which mode (graphics, character, or object) your printer is in. If the printer is in character mode, the printer may be causing the problem, but software is a likelier culprit. Try deleting the line and reconstructing it. If this step fails, print to a file and look through the file for unnecessary printer commands. If in graphics mode, the software is responsible for centering and, if in object mode, the printer is responsible.

> TROUBLE-SHOOTING TIP
>
> Centering problems are usually caused by leading or trailing spaces or tabs in the text to be centered. Characters can be printed on top of each other if non-centered text and centered text overlap on the same line. You can solve this problem by reducing the size of the noncentered text and centered text so that they can live on the same line or by splitting the line's contents into two lines.

Right Justification

A space used for positioning characters is called a *hard space* or micro space by application software. A space used to separate words is called a *soft space*. Normally, soft spaces are generated when the space bar is pressed, and hard spaces require some special keystroke. Application software can adjust the width of a soft space. The print head moves a predictable distance whenever a hard space is encountered. Soft spaces are often shown on-screen as a faint dot appearing right in the middle of the space.

> TROUBLE-SHOOTING TIP
>
> If space widths look irregular, look for hard and soft spaces within the document.

Soft space widths are often adjusted when right margin justification is turned on. Right margin justification produces columns of text that have ragged left margins and smooth right margins. Problems with right margin justification almost always occur on the last line of a paragraph because the line may not have enough characters to warrant justification. If the last line is justified without enough characters, letters may have huge gaps between them (see fig. 4.9).

In the following line, hard spaces and soft spaces are alternated. The hard spaces are a fixed width, the soft spaces can be wider. The wordprocessor can add spaces to the line to fill out the letters to the right margin. The last
l i n e   c a n   b e   i m p r o p e r l y   s p a c e d .
— Last line of paragraph should not be justified.

Fig. 4.9.
Justification problems.

| TROUBLE-SHOOTING TIP | If the last line of a paragraph has the letters and words stretched far apart, try turning justification off on the next-to-last line. |

Kerning

Despite how nice proportional spaced fonts look, they also create a difficult problem. Proportional fonts look better when certain letter combinations are closer than others. For example, when a lowercase i is printed next to a capital W, the lowercase i only looks good if it crawls underneath the capital W (see fig. 4.10). The solution to this problem is another spacing table called a *kerning table*. Problems with this table and the concept of kerning are explored in more detail in Chapter 10.

WiWiWiWiWiWiWiWiWiWiWiWi

WiWiWiWiWiWiWiWiWiWiWiWi

Fig. 4.10.
Kerning.

| TROUBLE-SHOOTING TIP | If letters look too far apart or too close together, this problem is due to software. Check to see if the software supports manual kerning. |

Font Attributes

Font attributes include italics, bold, shadow, inverse video, draft, letter quality, red lining, outlining, and so on. Each of these concepts is reviewed.

The base font (most frequently used font) of a document is usually designed to be attractive and easy to read. In contrast, some fonts are designed to draw attention to something in the text. Such fonts may be harder to read, but they get noticed in a sea of normal text. Usually, you choose a different font in the same typeface—bold or italic, or you can simply underline the base font. This section describes these methods.

Italic

Printers support italic fonts in the following three ways:

Slanting the dot-matrix. Some dot-matrix printers modify the original bit map using a simple algorithm while printing. In italic mode, the dot-matrix printer just slants the dots. Some printers actually need to be told the angle for the slant.

Changing a screen font. Graphics-oriented software can create italic fonts using screen fonts. Then, the italicized screen fonts are sent to a graphics-mode printer.

A new font. Ideally, italic should be treated as a separate font. This font is loaded, and software tells the printer to switch fonts. Because the font has been designed from scratch, it almost always looks better than a slanted font.

Bold

Italic enables you to add emphasis to text, but you can also focus attention on a font in other ways. Because italic is difficult to read, you may want to try boldfacing. This section discusses the ways printers can add emphasis to a font.

Bold fonts receive more attention because their lines are blacker and wider—in other words, they have more *weight*. In the typesetting world, you have a range of weights to choose from. In the PC character printer world, typefaces are either bold, or they are not bold. Only two weights are usually supported.

PC printers can boldface letters in many ways:

Double strike. Simple printers can boldface letters if the application software prints the line twice. A similar method of boldfacing uses the backspace character—the letter to be boldfaced is printed, followed by a backspace, then the same character is printed again. Both methods, sometimes described as *double strike*, work only when the ribbon is almost worn out. If the ribbon is brand new, the double strike looks no darker than normal print. Double strike on a laser printer does not produce any noticeable changes.

> **TROUBLE-SHOOTING TIP**
>
> If double strike is turned off and on again frequently on the same line, the line may stair-step down the page. This stair-stepping occurs because most dot-matrix printers advance the paper in only one direction. The printers cannot move the paper back up after double striking. The same thing happens if dot-matrix subscript and superscript characters are used over and over again on the same line. The only solution is to avoid using these features too often on the same line.

Shadow printing. The second way PC printers create bold letters is by shifting a tiny amount horizontally and printing the character again, known as shadow or emphasized printing. To combat the new-ribbon problem, 9-pin dot-matrix printers double strike by shifting down half a dot and printing the line twice. The characters created are ugly; they have the same height, but not the same width. Often boldfacing upsets the character spacing and causes vertical column problems.

> **TROUBLE-SHOOTING TIP**
>
> If a Backspace (BS) space character is sent to the printer, it may not back up properly and place its cursor directly underneath a shadow or emphasized character. Many backspaces can cause problems.

A new font. As with italic, the best way to use boldface is to purchase a bold typeface designed to be bold. Bold character widths are all different; only parts of the characters become wider. A new character or object font is needed to truly appear boldface (see fig. 4.11).

> **HINT**
>
> If you are boldfacing on a laser printer, try turning down the intensity if everything looks uniformly dark.

Fig. 4.11. *Boldface fonts.*

Laser-produced boldface:
- Normal
- Redesigned boldface
- A type of shadow

Dot-matrix boldface:
- Normal
- Double-strike
- Emphasized or shadow

> HINT Bold fonts on a laser printer usually have different character widths. Therefore, if you use micro spaces or spaces to line characters up on a page, boldfacing these characters may mess up column alignment.

Underlining

Underlining is a tradition that arose from the typewriter world. If you look through books, magazines, and other professional documents, underlining is not often used. In the PC world, however, underlining has almost evolved into an art form. You can underline just the words and not the spaces, or you can underline with different characters. The underline itself can be solid or dashed.

To underline, you can send an underline command to the printer, send the line twice, or use the backspace command. None of these methods have anything to do with a font—they are something the printer does to a font. However, some recent PC fonts have underlining instructions built into their font definition database that place the underline and determine its thickness.

Specifically, a character font contains information about the largest character's cell dimensions, the location and thickness of the underline, and the font name. Each character of the font has to include the byte that activates the underline, its width, and a list of which dots need to be drawn (see table 4.1). Some public-domain utilities aid in the designing of your own special character symbols or fonts.

Table 4.1
Features Common to All Symbols of a Font

Byte Number	Description
0-1	Font descriptor size
2	Reserved
3	Font type
4-5	Reserved
6-7	Baseline distance
8-9	Cell width
10-11	Cell height
12	Orientation
13	Spacing
14-15	Symbol set
16-17	Pitch (default HMI)

Table 4.1—*Continued*
Features Common to All Symbols of a Font

Byte Number	Description
18-19	Height
20-21	x-Height
22	Width type
23	Style
24	Stroke weight
25	Typeface
26	Reserved
27	Serif style
28-29	Reserved
30	Underline distance
31	Underline height
32-33	Text height
34-35	Text width
36-39	Reserved
40	Pitch extended
41	Height extended
42-47	Reserved
48-63	Font name

Table 4.1 describes the font structure as defined in the HP LaserJet Technical Reference manual. This font structure has become the default standard font file structure for many programs. These files even have a fairly standard extension of SFP (Soft Font Portrait) and SFL (Soft Font Landscape) in the PC world.

White Letters

You can create special effects two ways: redesign the font or crank an old version of the font through some formula. This section describes what the formulas or redesigners of fonts can do to make them look unusual.

Printing a white character on a black background is possible (see fig. 4.12). Few character-mode printers support this feature. Normally, only software that puts the printer in graphics mode can accomplish this. This feature goes by a variety of names:

- ❏ Inverse printing
- ❏ White letter printing
- ❏ Reverse printing
- ❏ Drop out
- ❏ Light bulb effect

Fig. 4.12.

Inverse video.

THIS WILL BE INVERSE VIDEO

Filled

Object fonts may be filled with patterns or colors. Sometimes this feature is called *shadow printing*, but do not confuse it with the type of bold printing that goes by the same name. Character fonts cannot have a filled effect (see fig. 4.13).

Fig. 4.13.

Filled special effects.

Filled normal ⟶ FILLED EFFECT
Filled boldface ⟶ **FILLED EFFECT**

Strikeout and Redline

Redline developed back in the days of manual typewriters as a more obvious bold. Typewriter ribbons had two colors and a Shift key or lever that could switch between the colors. Today, most printers don't print in color. Redline means do something to the font to make it different from the normal text. Sometimes this means print the line twice and on the second pass, print some character on top of the characters printed on the first pass.

Strikeout was used in law firms to indicate deleted or revised text by placing lines through the text. Strikeout was easy to do on a typewriter—just put minus signs through each character. The text was still readable.

Both strikeout and redline are sometimes supported within printers, or the word processor provides them by printing the line twice. On the first pass, the characters are printed; on the second pass, the characters are struck out or redlined. No difference exists between strikeout, redline, and underline—except for the character that is typed on the second pass.

Outline

Outline fonts look like someone traced the outside edges of each letter. Outline fonts could be used as coloring books so kids could color the inside of each letter. The thickness or patterns of the lines that outline a symbol can be varied to create some interesting effects (see fig. 4.14).

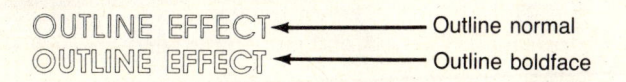

OUTLINE EFFECT ◄——— Outline normal
OUTLINE EFFECT ◄——— Outline boldface

Fig. 4.14.

Outline special effects.

Outline is a characteristic of object or scalable fonts only. Software may be able to create outline fonts and put the printer in graphics mode. Character printers usually cannot print an outline font.

Stretched and Curved

Because each character in an object font is composed of formulas, the characters can be warped in weird, eye-catching ways (see fig. 4.15).

POST SCRIPT *Curves*

Fig. 4.15.

Stretched and curved effects.

Comparing Draft and Letter Quality

To print good-looking characters, dot-matrix printers have to reprint each line several times, which slows them down. Letter-quality printing usually takes two to four times as long as draft printing. Furthermore, letter-quality printing increases wear and tear on the dot-matrix print head, increases ribbon use, and gives the printer a shorter life span. Laser printers do not have a similar letter-quality font concept.

Typeface Differences

Most typefaces differ in some obvious way. One line is thicker than another; the diameter of the holes in Os and Ps varies. This section explores features that are similar across fonts in each typeface family.

Serifs

Serif differences account for the subtle variations between typefaces. Serifs are hooks, wedges, blocks, lips, lids, bases, and blobs on letters that can be cupped, exaggerated, hairline, slab, slanted, transitional, triangular, and ball.

Character-mode screens rarely display serifs because the screens lack the necessary resolution. Serifs help readers distinguish between 1, l, and i. Serifs are found where the emphasis is on encouraging readers to read the entire document.

> HINT: When you examine a 24-pin dot-matrix printer, print its fonts and compare them with those shown in the printer's manual. A common problem is the top or bottom wire not firing. Because most letters do not need the top or bottom wire, you may not notice the problem in everyday use.

Descenders

Descenders are the tails of lowercase letters like y, p, and q. The lengths of these tails vary among typefaces (see fig. 4.16).

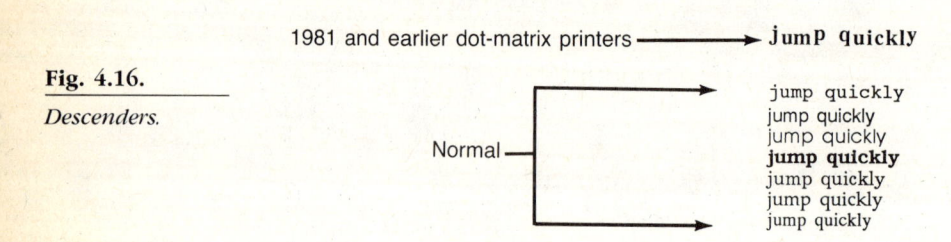

Fig. 4.16.

Descenders.

1981 and earlier dot-matrix printers ⟶ jump quickly

Normal ⟶
jump quickly
jump quickly
jump quickly
jump quickly
jump quickly
jump quickly
jump quickly

Ligatures

Ligatures are letter pairs that are tied together. For example, lowercase f followed by an i looks strange if the i is dotted. Rather than dotting the i, the cross bar of the lower case f is extended over the i. Actually, each ligature is an additional character in the set instead of a character combination. Unfortunately, ligatures confuse spelling checkers and hyphenation programs.

X-Height

A lowercase letter's height (without ascenders or descenders) is the x-height. Different fonts of the same point size can have different x-heights.

Regularity

The older, manual typefaces are slightly irregular, meaning that irregular gaps occasionally appear within words. Modern electronic fonts can eliminate irregularity, but for some applications, irregularity is desirable.

Purchasing Fonts

Purchasing fonts is difficult. Macintosh owners purchase screen fonts and occasionally fonts for the LaserWriter. PC owners purchase printer fonts and occasionally screen fonts. PC owners sometimes send the screen fonts to the videoboard and put the videoboard in character mode. Other times, the PC owners must send the screen fonts to RAM, crowd out application software, and slow the system down. This section describes the different types of fonts available, simplifying your purchasing decisions.

Screen and Printer Fonts

One of the first PCs to display proportional characters on-screen was the Macintosh. The Mac screen is always in graphics mode. The trouble is that tremendous processing power is needed to manipulate the screen. Unfortunately, the original Mac did not have much horsepower, and the screen was slow.

To display proportional characters, the Mac changed the cursor. Instead of indicating how much space the character was going to take up, an I-beam (vertical line) indicates where the next character appears.

Most screen fonts are designed for the typical resolution of a PC screen: 70 to 80 dpi. To look good on-screen, the font must be redesigned. A much better-looking character can be designed for a 300 dpi laser printer. Because of the resolution differences, printers and screens have always had separate fonts.

Printer font data is usually sent to the printer for storage, unless the printer is in graphics mode, when printer font data stays out on disk until printing time. Screen font data is different. Because most PCs run their videoboards in graphics mode, the fonts have to be in memory at all times, so applications and their data files have less room. For this reason, programs like Ventura and PageMaker suffer when too many screen fonts are loaded into memory (see Chapter 9). The same is true on a Mac.

> HINT | If your PC seems slow, try reconfiguring the application so that fewer screen fonts are in memory.

In summary, screen fonts are purchased for the purpose of displaying on-screen a more accurate picture of what is to be printed. The closer the screen font is to the printer font, the better the chance you will have of printing a document correctly the first time, saving time and money.

Fixed and Scalable Fonts

The traditional typesetter's definition of a font included size as a distinction. In other words, 9 pt. Helvetica and 12 pt. Helvetica were different fonts to a typesetter. This distinction no longer holds—Helvetica is one font, no matter what the size is. Also, two new categories exist for fonts: fixed and scalable. Fixed fonts are designed to be printed at a certain point size. Scalable fonts are designed to print in a large variety of sizes. Fixed fonts are always found in character-mode printers. Scalable fonts were born in object printers, but are making their way into character-mode printers.

This section explores the differences between fixed fonts and scalable fonts, and the advantages and uses of each.

Expanded and Compressed Printing

By modifying the software in a dot-matrix printer, each dot of a character can be printed twice, which creates a wider font. This process is called *expanded printing*. By moving 60 percent of the normal distance between dots, a narrower font also can be created—this is *compressed* or *condensed print*. By combining the shorter movement and the dot doubling, you get *letter-quality print*. The original font is called *draft*. As a result, dot-matrix printers were once advertised as containing four fonts: draft, expanded, compressed, and letter quality (see fig. 4.17).

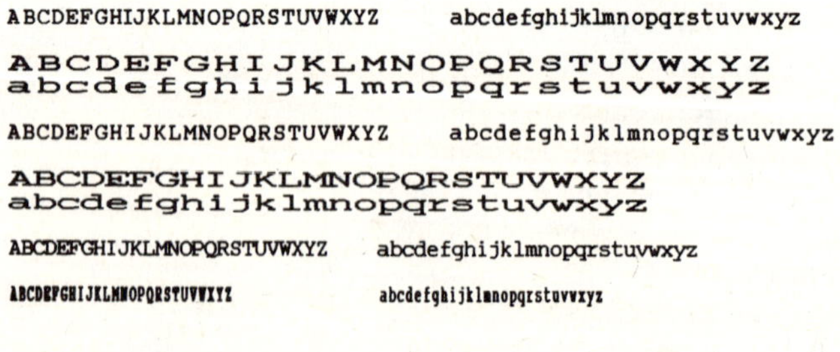

Fig. 4.17.

Expanded, compressed, letter-quality, and draft print.

```
A B C D E F G H I J K L M N O P Q R S T U V W X Y Z      abcdefghijklmnopqrstuvwxyz
A B C D E F G H I J K L M N O P Q R S T U V W X Y Z
a b c d e f g h i j k l m n o p q r s t u v w x y z
ABCDEFGHIJKLMNOPQRSTUVWXYZ      abcdefghijklmnopqrstuvwxyz
ABCDEFGHIJKLMNOPQRSTUVWXYZ
abcdefghijklmnopqrstuvwxyz
ABCDEFGHIJKLMNOPQRSTUVWXYZ      abcdefghijklmnopqrstuvwxyz
ABCDEFGHIJKLMNOPQRSTUVWXYZ      abcdefghijklmnopqrstuvwxyz
```

Expanded, compressed, draft, and letter-quality printing are concepts associated with the fixed fonts of dot-matrix printers. Only one dot pattern is stored in printers that have expanded, compressed, draft, and letter quality printing modes. The dots of this single font are used to generate different sizes and qualities of the one font—not four, as the advertisers suggested.

Landscape and Portrait Fonts

Laser printers added another characteristic to fonts. Because 8 1/2-by-11-inch paper can be fed only one direction through a laser printer, fonts can only be displayed only across the 8 1/2 inch width. These fonts are portrait (horizontal) fonts. To print across the 11-inch dimension, new fonts were created—landscape (sideways) fonts. Of course, if the printer can rotate the fonts, some manufacturers double the number of fonts advertised. With the advent of fonts that can be rotated, expect the landscape and portrait distinction to disappear.

Pros and Cons of Fixed Fonts

Fixed fonts contain a list of dots that need to be drawn for each symbol. Fixed fonts can produce characters just as good as those of a scalable font. At tiny point sizes, fixed fonts may look even better because they are designed to be printed at that point size.

The trouble with fixed fonts is that they cannot be enlarged or reduced without altering their true form. The problems that apply to enlarged and compressed dot-matrix printing also apply to changing the size of fixed fonts. The Macintosh is responsible for elevating these techniques to higher levels, and the Windows and GEM environments are doing the same things.

The manipulation of dots has its limits. Consider figure 4.18. The letter S is displayed four different times. The first time, it is displayed in the size it was designed to be displayed. The second and third time it was printed, an expanded size was chosen. By doubling dots, the features of the S are still recognizable, but less attractive. The letter S on the extreme right was *smoothed* using a special dot manipulation algorithm, but it still does not look as good as the original. This smoothing function is available in printer dialogue boxes in the Macintosh and Windows worlds.

> HINT | A circle on-screen may print as an oval or vice-versa. This warping occurs because the resolutions on the screen and printer are different.

Fig. 4.18.

Bit-mapped font enlargement/ reduction limitations.

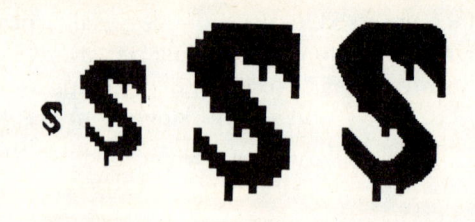

$SSS

THIS IS A LASER WRITER....

> HINT | Even if the fonts look jagged on-screen, they may print smooth. Try printing them to see.

Object printers can distort scalable fonts in so many ways that they all haven't been explored, but despite this, scalable fonts never have the squarish edges displayed in figure 4.18.

Dot-Matrix Fonts to Laser Fonts

Most dot-matrix fonts are stored on a disk and sent to the printer in graphics mode, meaning that the printers can be potentially turned into laser fonts. But, most laser printers have trouble printing dot-matrix fonts. Figure 4.19 shows a dot-matrix printout and figure 4.20 shows the laser emulation. Fancy fonts purchased for dot-matrix printers cannot be transferred to the laser printer without distortion. Most videoboards have the same problem. This causes programmers to design two completely different fixed fonts; one for the printer, one for the videoboard. The videoboard's resolution is usually inferior to the printer's.

> HINT | You can set the Shift-PrtSc key on the IBM PC keyboard to print a graphics screen, but the printout cannot look like the screen. Letters designed to look nice on-screen look terrible when printed. Use Shift-PrtSc only when the quality of the output is unimportant.

> HINT | Don't waste your time purchasing software for the purpose of printing dot-matrix fixed fonts on a laser printer. The results always look worse on the laser because of the resolution problem. If you need the fonts, purchase a $200 dot matrix—the cost is only slightly more than the cost of the emulation software.

Chapter 4: Font Basics **149**

Fig. 4.19.

A dot-matrix *printout*

Fig. 4.20.

Laser emulation of dot-matrix distortion.

Scalable fonts are independent of the screen and printer resolution. This means that the same font can be used for the screen and the printer. While the scalable fonts are harder to design, only one has to be designed compared to the two required for the screen and printer.

Equal Horizontal and Vertical Resolution

When the number of dots horizontally equals the number of dots vertically, the dots are called *square dots*. If all printers and videoboards were designed with square dots, font creation would be much easier. When devices use square dots, one fixed font can be used for printers and screens.

Fonts will proliferate once all screens and printers have square resolution. One of the reasons the Macintosh is so popular is that its screen resolution is square, like most laser printers. The next generation of videoboards in the IBM world will be square, or else scalable fonts will take over completely.

Fixed Fonts from Scalable fonts

Scalable fonts also are known as object, outline, and PostScript fonts. In *The Printer Bible*, they are called scalable fonts, because they are composed of formulas rather than dots. From these formulas, fonts of any size can be created with equal smoothness.

You can use scalable fonts to generate fixed fonts from three sources: font-generation software, applications, and object-mode devices. The following sections explain these methods.

Font-Generation Software

Font-generation software is simple. All it needs is the typeface name and size. After this, the software usually estimates the time the process takes and gives you a chance to stop it. The hard part is telling the application software about the new font. Good font-generation software tries to communicate the necessary information to the application software directly, but not all applications are supported. In the IBM world, the leading font-generation software company is BitStream.

BitStream scalable and fixed-font generation software is bundled with every major application in the PC world, including WordPerfect, Ventura, GEM, Windows, and PageMaker. BitStream creates screen and printer font files that follow each application's naming and file formats. BitStream updates the necessary character width tables and available font lists of the appropriate software packages. Supporting these different formats, however, means that these applications cannot share common character width tables and kerning information.

> HINT | Because of font encryption, fonts that come with software and clone PostScript printers cannot be transferred to other software packages.

The reason BitStream has created a minor mess in the IBM PC world is because BitStream encrypts their fonts. While not exactly the same as copy protection, encryption limits use and flexibility just like copy protection.

Font-generation software has a number of drawbacks. You have to learn another application. You have to configure the PC DOS batch files so that they download the fonts during power up, when a menu item is chosen, or from within the software. You must make font size decisions before the creation of a document. After the fixed fonts have been created, the freedom to try different sizes is unavailable. If a different size is needed, you have to exit the application software and create another font with the font-generation software.

Applications and Fixed Fonts

A fixed font is a type of character font generated from a scalable font. Either printers, videoboards, or software can generate many fixed fonts in different sizes from one scalable font.

Today, most scalable fonts are found in object (PostScript) printers. Soon, software will be able to generate fixed fonts for graphics mode videoboards and perhaps graphic printers from scalable fonts that are installed in the operating systems. In the IBM PC world, Presentation Manager is supposed to do the same.

The next step would be to send scalable font instructions to videoboards. This concept has not been purchased by any company.

Object-Mode Devices

Object-mode devices can decide when to change data or settings themselves, without the computer's assistance. The reason object-mode printers have not become the dominant species is their cost. These printers require a faster CPU and more RAM than most personal computers! Object-mode videoboards are the next logical development. The computer closest to approaching the ideal—supporting object-mode printers and videoboards—is the Next. The operating characteristics and advantages of object-mode printers are contrasted with normal printers in Chapter 11.

Scalable Font Types

Most companies sell fonts in scalable form. These fonts are usually encrypted. Under certain circumstances, fonts from different companies cannot be used in the same application with the same printer. Also, most companies have different versions of the same scalable font: high resolution for typesetters, medium resolution for most users, and low resolution for users requiring small fonts.

High-Resolution Fonts

Scalable fonts consist of formulas. High-resolution fonts have many formulas, which makes their files longer, and the PC must take more time to compute such fonts. These fonts create ugly bit-mapped characters at the medium resolutions (300 dpi) of typical PC laser and dot-matrix printers, but these fonts are not designed for 300 dpi printers. High-resolution fonts work best on high-resolution phototypesetters (1200 dpi or more). These fonts, therefore, are not normally advertised in PC magazines.

Medium-Resolution Fonts

Font companies have designed special scalable fonts for PCs. Medium-resolution fonts are designed to look nice on 300 dpi lasers, calculate quickly, and not take up much space. Ideally, if documents designed with medium-resolution fonts are sent to a phototypesetter using high-resolution fonts, the output will look identical to the 300 dpi laser printout using the low-resolution fonts.

The trouble with most PC scalable fonts is that they are ugly-looking at small point sizes. If you need small fonts, read the following section on hinted fonts.

Low-Resolution (Hinted) Fonts

Rounding errors are a problem with object fonts at small point sizes. Suppose that each leg of the letter M is 1.2 dots wide on a particular printer. The printer cannot print fractions of a dot. If you print the M and one leg happens to be located halfway between dots 45 and 46 on the page, both dots are filled because each dot is more than half-full. The other leg of the M is mostly in dot 52 and a little in dot 53, but only dot 52 is filled because the font's formula rounds down. All of a sudden, one leg of the letter M is two dots wide, and the other is one dot wide.

Hinted fonts have formulas that avoid rounding errors, so hinted fonts print perfectly at small sizes.

Finding Font Sources

Fonts come in all sorts of formats and storage locations. Because fonts have been around for so long, they are not protected by patents, copyrights, or trademarks. To make money, font companies have encrypted their fonts and developed proprietary software necessary to install them in various application programs. This software is sold to application developers who incorporate it into their PC programs. This strategy makes money for the PC developer and the font company. But the software can only understand the fonts from one company. This does not encourage a wide selection of inexpensive fonts.

On the other hand, many individuals have developed fonts and released them into the public domain. Sometimes fonts are released with a notice to send money to the author or designer if you like them; these are known as *shareware fonts*. CD laser disks are available with over 300 shareware and public-domain fonts for less than $200. Shareware and public-domain fonts are usually character fonts, although object fonts are starting to appear.

This section explores the different issues surrounding the purchase and creation of fonts.

Font Creation

An incredible amount of information is required for a 96-character font. The time it takes to gather all this information and enter it properly makes this impractical for most people. Even converting an old dot-matrix font to a character laser font is difficult. The following steps describe the process:

1. Convert the dot-matrix pixel patterns to laser pixel patterns. Change the aspect ratio and smooth out the rough edges of the dot-matrix font.

2. Make a table of the character widths and then figure out an automated way of sending this information through the PTR program and into the printer definition file.

3. Print out every possible pair of characters in the character set (order makes a difference), identify the obvious spacing problems, and build a kerning table.

In other words, this process is impractical; you may as well purchase new laser fonts. However, some users have gone to all this trouble and released their efforts to the public domain. Public domain fonts are inexpensive and respectable in the Macintosh world. They should be in the PC world, but for more on that subject, read on.

Macintosh Fonts

Macintosh computers ship with four fixed screen fonts: New York, Geneva, Monaco, and Seattle. Most of the fonts sold for the Macintosh are fixed screen fonts that have been designed to look good on a 72 dpi screen. No printer fonts are included because the printer is run in graphics mode. Laser-Writer printers are usually sent an outlining program that converts the largest screen font available to a scalable font for printing.

However, scalable laser printer fonts for the LaserWriter printer are available. Associated fixed screen fonts in various sizes have to be installed to access the scalable printer font after it is sent to the printer. Laser fonts are always going to look better than the screen fonts. *Note:* The fonts that are chosen from pull-down menus are screen fonts, not printer fonts.

PC Fonts

The PC world is driven by printer fonts. After selecting a printer font, the best matching screen font is located. Programs that use a single font videoboard in character mode have only one screen font to choose from. Few programs can use multiple screen font character videoboards in the PC world. One example is WordPerfect, which can select the fonts available on a Hercules board.

Manufacturers have traditionally supplied fonts in cartridges that are inserted into a slot in the printer. Unfortunately, cartridge printer fonts are expensive; selection is poor; they are not scalable, and screen font versions are nonexistent.

Because of the printer font cartridges in the PC world, public domain and shareware fonts are unheard of. This situation may change. Many PC users are starting to shy away from printer font cartridges. Instead, PC users are turning to fonts that are shipped on disks. But this creates a font-management problem. How are all the fonts transferred to the various software programs? How are the printer fonts sent to the printer? The next section tackles these issues.

Managing Fonts

Fonts are needed for videoboards and printers. Fonts fill up hard disks, computer memory, and printer memory. Most attempts to use many fonts create font-management problems. These problems often surface when you attempt to print a document on a different computer than the document was created on. This section provides some advice on how to manage your fonts.

Storing Fonts

Fonts can be added directly to the printer or indirectly to the computer. If the computer puts the printer into graphics mode, practically any font can be printed.

The most common method of adding fonts is to purchase them on disk. The fonts are then copied off the disk and into the computer's hard disk. CDs also contain fonts. CDs have the advantage of storing tremendous quantities of fonts. Disks and CDs share the advantage of being easy to back up—a luxury cartridges and cards do not have. In addition, disk fonts are usually designed to supply the videoboard and the printer with matching fonts, enabling the screen to match the output as closely as possible.

Some printer manufacturers install a credit card reader on their printers and supply fonts on credit cards, but this method is not popular. Purchasing fonts on a credit card is more expensive and available from fewer sources. You can purchase devices that create the credit cards from floppy fonts, but these devices just add expense and complexity.

Some laser printers come with the circuitry and software to store and retrieve files from a hard disk. You can purchase printer hard disks with fonts already on them. Although printer hard disks are convenient, they make font backups harder. Printer hard disks are explored more in the next few sections.

Downloading Fonts

Downloaded fonts are often called *soft fonts*. Temporary soft fonts are sent for only the current print job. Permanent soft fonts are remembered by the printer for future documents.

Downloaded fonts can be scalable or fixed. Fixed fonts take more time to download, but less time to print. Scalable fonts take less time to download, but more time to print the first page. Subsequent pages usually print as quickly as printing with fixed fonts.

The rest of this section describes how to download fonts.

Downloading to Printer Ram

Laser printers are designed with 512K to 4M of memory for graphics-mode operation. Because the most complicated character-mode operation of laser printers takes less than 128K, the extra memory is available for downloaded fonts. A problem occurs if the printer is full of downloaded fonts and put into graphics mode—the printer runs out of memory. In this event, you get error messages from the printer and the software. Sometimes, the printer prints half of a graphics page, and then the other half on a second sheet of paper. This is because the printer is running out of memory.

> **TROUBLE-SHOOTING TIP**
>
> Clearing downloaded fonts from the printer's memory is not always easy. Some laser printers have different reset methods. The reset button is usually used for clearing paper jam error messages, not clearing downloaded fonts.
>
> If the laser printer starts flashing an out-of-memory error message, try reset buttons and whatever else the printer manual suggests. The last resort is turning the printer off and on to clear out any downloaded fonts.

Downloading to a Printer's Hard Disk

The most elegant solution is to purchase a printer that manages its own memory by storing downloaded fonts on its hard disk. If the printer senses that it is running out of memory, the printer may try to dump the downloaded fonts to its hard disk, clearing space in its memory. Printer hard disks may have the following capabilities:

- ❏ Store downloaded fonts so that you don't have to download them from the PC
- ❏ Store bit-mapped character sets so that the printer prints faster because it does not have to recompute character sets
- ❏ Temporarily hold a copy of the printer's RAM, so the printer can print complicated documents

Downloading Manually

Manual downloading requires you to choose a certain menu option in the font software (typically called Download Fonts or Initialize the Printer). After the fonts are downloaded, you are responsible for managing the fonts within the printer: if a paper jam occurs; the printer's lid is lifted, or the printer loses power, you may have to download the fonts again.

> **HINT**
>
> Always try to resolve paper jams and printer error messages without turning the printer off and on. Otherwise, the printer may have to be initialized again.

Downloading Using Batch Files

The second method of downloading fonts—using a batch file—does not improve on the manual method much. Using a batch file downloads the printer fonts whenever the PC is turned on. Batch-file downloading requires that the printer be on first, but makes the time required less of a burden. It is not a desirable method when more than one PC is attached to the printer.

Downloading On Demand

On-demand downloading solves most downloading problems. On-demand downloading requires that software download only the fonts needed prior to sending the document. Because the software does not know the printer's font situation, the software resets the printer to clear its memory, making room for the fonts. On-demand downloading creates temporary soft fonts, so that after the document is printed, the fonts disappear from the printer's memory.

On-demand downloading solves the shared printer problem by encouraging every PC to send its fonts to the printer before printing a document. Unfortunately, this process also slows the printing process. Also, on-demand downloading is inefficient—the printer is constantly resetting and receiving the same font information.

Printer-Initiated Downloading

Printer-initiated downloading is a difficult concept if you usually think of printers as "brainless" devices. Printer-initiated downloading is currently happening only in the Mac world. The LaserWriter can ask the Mac questions. If a printer can do this, it can manage the fonts. Users and software are free to work on other matters.

The Mac software sends the document to the LaserWriter; then, the software listens to the printer for status messages. If the printer reports that all is well, the Mac sends another document. If the printer discovers that the document requires a font not present in the printer's RAM or hard disk, the printer tells the Mac. The Mac responds by sending the printer a copy of the screen font (which sometimes doesn't look so good on a printer), by downloading a printer font, or by aborting the print job. If the Mac sends the printer a font, the printer has the option of storing that font on its hard disk, leaving it in memory, or deleting it from memory after printing the document.

The type of printer that can assume responsibility for the fonts is called an *object-mode printer*. Besides asking the Mac for fonts, an object-mode printer also assumes responsibility for generating fixed fonts from scalable fonts and for managing the fixed fonts it generates.

An object printer creates a fixed font only once; thereafter, it re-uses the same font. A new fixed font is stored in a *font cache* that exists in the printer's RAM. As additional sizes of different typefaces are asked for, an object-mode printer computes the bit-mapped information necessary and adds it to the font cache. If a new font is asked for and the cache memory is full, the object printer throws out the least-used font to make room for the new one.

If the printer has a hard disk, instead of throwing the least used font away, the printer stores the font on its hard disk. (If the printer's hard disk becomes full, the printer throws away the font.) A printer's hard disk keeps copies of the most active fonts on the hard disk in case the printer is turned off. When the printer is turned back on, it can copy the cache off the hard disk into its memory, a much faster process than recomputing the fixed fonts.

If the printer does not have a hard disk, some manufacturers of object printers encourage the use of the PC's hard disk for the same purpose. Using PC hard disks this way has the following limitations:

- ❏ The printer cable must enable the object printer to talk back, and the cable must transmit data quickly.
- ❏ You must run a program that asks the printer to send the printer's font cache to the PC.

These limitations are not that bad. Fortunately, most documents contain just a few fonts in a few point sizes, and different documents often use the same fonts. Therefore, the contents of the font cache remain relatively the same, and the PC hard disk can speed up printing.

Font Numbering

The advantages and disadvantages of font numbering are explored in Chapter 3. Numbering automatically presorts information, reduces the details that need to be stored, and makes finding this information easy (if the number is known). Numbering can make managing information easy.

But, numbering only works when a strong central authority controls the numbering process. In a chaotic world of PCs, numbering systems for symbols and fonts often fall apart. Moreover, numbering symbols has the following drawbacks:

- ❏ Limits the total number of symbols
- ❏ Develops multiple symbol numbering schemes
- ❏ Causes selection, management, and configuration problems for symbols

You see a good example of proper use of internal font numbers in the HP LaserJet. Fonts are numbered during the Print Font self-test. You can enter these font numbers to select the default font from the front panel, but a PC cannot use these numbers to select fonts in the printer. Instead, the naming scheme explained in Chapter 6 has to be used.

The Macintosh uses a poor internal font numbering scheme. The Mac was designed to support multiple fonts. Like HP LaserJet printers, Apple chose to assign a unique ID number to each font. This ID number serves as the font's name. Unfortunately, Apple encouraged programmers to save this font number in documents instead of saving the number in the font description. Apple only planned on everyone purchasing their fonts from Apple.

When the Mac market started to flood with fonts, all sorts of problems resulted. In some cases, five different fonts with the same number are available from different font vendors. The same document, printed on different Macs containing this font number, produces five different fonts.

The Mac's original font numbering scheme (plus a bug in the original Mac ROMs) limited the total number of fonts to 256. Furthermore, of the 256 fonts, 93 were reserved by Apple, so only 163 unique font numbers were available to non-Apple companies.

> HINT | When printing a Macintosh document on a different Mac than the document was originally designed on, make sure that the same fonts are installed and numbered in the same way.

Because many more than 163 fonts are available on the open market, Apple decided to solve this problem by changing the font numbering scheme. Starting with Version 6.0 of the system and Version 3.8 of the Font/DA mover, the Mac has a font numbering scheme with a limit of 32,768. Now, all Mac software must support both numbering schemes. Furthermore, Apple has not set up some standards body (or hired an accounting firm) to control font number assignments. The possibility of two vendors using the same font number still exists!

Right now, fonts are not numbered in the PC world. Ideally, they will never be, and Microsoft will design Windows 3.0 and Presentation Manager so that fonts are named rather than numbered. Internally, of course, programmers should be free to number fonts for housekeeping purposes. But, allowing programmers to present these numbers to users is detrimental.

Looking into the Future of Fonts

Ideally, fonts should be downloadable using any software package, or by including the DOS COPY command in a batch file. Printer and screen fonts could be generated from the same fixed font and scalable font file formats. The standard fixed font format should be that described in the HP LaserJet series II Printer Technical Reference manual. The standard scalable font file format should be unencrypted PostScript code following standard PostScript programming procedures.

Unfortunately, the font world is blighted by encrypted fonts. Font file formats are protected like trade secrets. In the PC world, application vendors deliberately encode their fonts so that they cannot be transferred to other applications.

The Mac world is currently in a transition between fixed screen fonts and scalable screen fonts. Adobe Systems is shipping a product called Adobe Type Manager that provides scalable screen fonts (and additional features described in Chapter 9). Unfortunately, these scalable screen fonts cannot be built from the generic laser fonts currently available.

Apple is upset at Adobe's success. Apple has sold off its Adobe stock and created a scalable font standard called Royal for Microsoft's PostScript clone software. For more on this battle, see Chapter 9.

Chapter Summary

The word font can mean anything. Usually, if the look of a character set changes, you have a new font of that character set. In this chapter, you find definitions of typeface, family, point, pitch, bold, and proportional.

Important problems described in this chapter are those dealing with columns lining up and character spacing. In addition, procedures on how to install new fonts and discover fonts already in existence were explored.

Fonts are the most important method of making your documents different. How to manage fonts, where they are stored, and how they are sent to the printer were reviewed in this chapter. The role of a printer's hard disk in font management was described.

In the Next Chapter

Chapter 5 is a buyer's guide that also contains a list of printer features. Chapter 5 provides printer purchasing hints.

5

Printer Hardware Features

Printers differ much more than PCs. Daisywheel printers are popular one year and out the next. Previously, 24-pin dot-matrix printers were the hot item; now, laser printers costing $1,000 or less are hot. Because printer technology is changing so rapidly, a complete chapter dedicated to printer hardware is needed.

The goal of this chapter is to help those people who want to purchase a printer. This chapter sets up guidelines for you so that you can put together a shopping list for printers. You should be able to determine what you need, rather than letting a salesperson or consultant make the decision for you. If you are developing the rationale for a corporate printing technology strategy, this chapter contains the information to build your justifications.

If you already own a printer, you need to know how it works in order to operate it properly and handle any minor problems that arise. Information about how your printer works is lacking in most printer manuals; this chapter provides these details.

Dot-matrix, laser, and inkjet printers are covered in detail in this chapter. Fully formed daisywheel and thimble printers are not covered, because printer manufacturers are not designing new ones and have sold off their inventory. The combination of 24-pin printers and lasers has completely destroyed the niche that these printers had in the market.

Reviewing Printer Requirements

You must know the complete list of parts required to assemble a fully functional printer. Unfortunately, not all salesmen are qualified for this task. For example, you need a PC, software, a cable, and paper. Often, the printer will be cheap, but the package deal will not. When pricing printers, make sure to include *everything* that you will need. Keep in mind that it is impossible for most stores to stock all the pieces and even more difficult to make sure that you walk out the door with them. The following is a list of all the items that you need:

- printer
- ribbon
- print head
- paper
- cable
- power cord
- manuals
- shipping box
- toner cartridges
- font cartridges
- paper trays
- PC interface
- plastic covers
- paper rack
- wire paper guide
- printer interface
- tractors
- tear bar
- printer software

Ideally, the advertised price of a printer includes all of the preceding items. Salesmen may hesitate about throwing in a box of paper, but it never hurts to ask. There should not be any expensive additions that the salesperson describes as absolutely necessary to use the printer. All the interfaces, tractors, tear bars, and printer software necessary should be included in the price of the printer. A *tear bar* is simply a bar that you use to tear the paper. Sometimes these bars can cost more than $150 each. Yet, the printer costs only $175. Prices for the additional options should never be more than $100. All dot-matrix printers should come with a printer interface, tractor, tear bar, and ribbon for the advertised price. Advertising a printer that does not come with all these necessary items is like advertising a car without tires.

Even more infuriating than paying more money than expected is the tension caused by walking away without everything that you paid for or everything necessary to use the printer. In fact, some people prefer to buy from mail-order businesses because the printer arrives from the manufacturer untouched. Everything that was there originally is still there. Often, paying full price for a printer that has been tested is simply paying for someone to lose a piece.

> HINT | Print the test page on a laser printer and check the number of pages printed to see whether the laser has been used.

This chapter begins by discussing general printer features. Within this chapter, you will find more information about each of the required printer parts.

Reviewing General Features

All printers have certain features in common. For example, they all print at a certain number of dots per inch (dpi), and they all print at certain speeds. This section introduces these features in order of importance (although everyone places a different emphasis on specific features). This chapter covers the following topics:

- Paper
- Font quality and symbols
- PC interface
- Ease of use, modification, and repair

The first section covers these topics in general.

Specifying Paper Sizes

If you require many paper sizes, a dot-matrix printer is the most flexible. Paper sizes in the U.S. are dramatically different than in Europe or Japan. Because printers are designed for the world—not specifically the U.S.—most printers support a variety of paper sizes. But, laser printers cannot support larger sizes of paper. The paper width must be smaller than 8 1/2 inches to fit most laser printers. Paper widths larger than this require a dot-matrix or inkjet printer. Table 5.1 describes some of the page sizes typically supported.

Laser printers typically require that you manually feed individual sheets, or that you purchase special paper trays to hold the different sizes. Most lasers come with at least one tray; additional trays cost about $100 each. If you use special trays with laser printers, you can select the page size automatically (just like a copier machine). The trays have a size stamped on them that the laser printer can read after you have slid the tray into place. If you use the laser printer in manual mode, the printer still needs to know how long the page is for the paper jam circuitry to function properly. You can tell the laser printer the paper size by using the front panel or PC software that sends the proper commands.

Table 5.1
Paper Sizes

Name	Size
Executive	7.25-by-10.5 inches
Letter	8.5-by-11 inches
Legal	8.5-by-14 inches
A4	210-by-297mm*
Monarch	3.875-by-7.5 inches
Business	4.125-by-9.5 inches
DL	110-by-220mm*
C5	162-by-229mm*
Computer	11-by-14 inches

* To convert from mm to inches, divide by 25.4.

> HINT: When you use the front panel of the laser printer to change paper sizes, the PC software does not know that the change has taken place. There is no way for the PC and the printer to coordinate their activity unless the printer is an object printer. Use the front panel for paper size adjustment only if you are not worried about page formatting.

When dot-matrix printers were created, people had to enter the paper length using the units of lines. The problem with this method was that the lines could be spaced differently. Also, if printing in graphics mode, the "lines" unit of measurement does not make any sense. For this reason, most dot-matrix printers can now accept the page length in millimeters or lines, and assume that the current line spacing is correct. This is usually done through the software, although some models have paper-length adjustments on the front panel. Most dot-matrix printers have adjustable widths, depending on the model. The wide carriage models can expand to 16.25 inches; the smaller models can expand up to 10.25 inches.

> HINT: With PC character-mode printers, 90 percent of the time there are 66 lines per page or 6 lines per inch. This fact is helpful when determining top and bottom margins and other page-formatting instructions while inside PC software.

Printing Mailing Labels

Addressing envelopes is one of the few office chores that has defied automation. The easiest and most cost effective way to address envelopes is to purchase envelopes with windows. Then print the letter or form and fold the paper so that the address shows in the window.

Another method of addressing envelopes is to print the mailing labels and then paste them on the envelope. Sticking labels on the wrong envelope is a constant hazard. Printing the labels is difficult also. Labels have a tendency to peel off inside dot-matrix and laser printers; then, you have to clean the printer. Also, the printer may not work right after you clean it.

When installing and removing the mailing labels from dot-matrix printers, always pull the labels through the normal paper path in the normal direction of operation. Do not try to pull the extra labels out the back of the dot-matrix printer, or they may peel off.

Mailing labels come in all sizes and shapes. They come in sheets, rolls, or fan-folded. A page can have one, two, three, or four labels across the paper. The sheets of labels can have borders. These factors make it difficult for software to print in the proper places. Different organizations may want the labels sorted horizontally across the page or vertically up and down the page. All these potential problems have created special market programs that manage labels. Most good label-printing software packages list the types of labels they support—for example, PostWare from Postalsoft, Inc.

The best solution probably is to never put mailing labels in the printer. Instead, print the labels in the proper place on paper. Then, use the copier machine to transfer the addresses to mailing labels. Feed the labels through the copier machine rather than the PC printer. Most copier machines are designed for copier labels. Use the paper version printed by the PC as a master and make the actual labels using a copier machine. Print updates to the master as the list changes. This way, the printer does not have to print duplicate mailing labels over and over, which reduces PC wear and tear as well mailing label waste.

The final solution is to try to print the addresses directly on the envelopes. Unfortunately, it is a lot of work typing the address, sticking the envelope in the printer, and printing the envelope. Many people find it easier and quicker to use a typewriter. In fact, the only reason many typewriters are still around is to address envelopes. You can buy envelope feeders for laser and dot-matrix printers for about $100. However, these feeders hold only 10 envelopes. Envelope feeders that hold 200 envelopes cost $1,000 and have a tendency to jam.

Assessing Font Needs and Upgrades

The sample fonts displayed in magazine printer reviews are always the character fonts stored within the printer. If these fonts satisfy your requirements, an IBM-type PC with character-mode software, a character-mode videoboard, and a character-mode printer will be the most cost-effective system. If you need other fonts, you must upgrade. The ease of upgrading depends on your system type. In an IBM system, the following is true:

- ❏ The applications program is responsible for knowing the features of the each printer.
- ❏ Printer companies don't provide any PC software.
- ❏ Each application may cause the printer to behave differently.
- ❏ You cannot add features to all application programs.

In a Macintosh system, the following is true:

- ❏ The applications program is responsible for knowing the features of the Macintosh operating system.
- ❏ The printer companies are responsible for supporting features of the Macintosh operating system.
- ❏ Features added to the operating system are added to the applications.

The following sections discuss these ideas in more detail.

Upgrading in the PC World

You always can upgrade a system to display better-looking fonts, but only with pain and suffering in the IBM PC world (see Chapter 9). Each PC application has different installation methods and different font file formats. If you require the flexibility of object fonts, purchase a Macintosh. Many other personal computers such as the NeXT, Amiga, and Atari are good alternatives to the Macintosh, but are not as popular.

The problem with the IBM PC world is that most printing is character-oriented. The MS-DOS, PC DOS operating system provides no font management or character-set management support. Every IBM PC application struggles to provide the features; the font and character-set management is uneven and inconsistent. Installing every application and printer is a separate battle. Even upgrading software versions is a tremendous battle. However, if you need only the fonts available on the printer, an IBM PC system can be cost-effective.

The prospects for meaningful change in the IBM world at the time of this writing are bleak. Ideally, the PC world will develop printer support at the operating system level. Ideally, fonts would be installed into the PC operating system and then would be instantly available to all programs—making the PC more like the Macintosh.

The marketplace is pushing DOS in the Macintosh direction by making Windows programs popular—including PageMaker, Word, Adobe Illustrator, and Excel. Unfortunately, the printer support for Windows is not generic, nor are fonts supported or managed easily. Standard font formats do not exist; individual printer drivers support printer fonts rather than Windows (see Chapter 9).

In the spring of 1988, Microsoft announced a generic printer driver for Windows and the printer driver that matches OS/2's Presentation Manager screen. But, this generic printer driver still has not been released. Microsoft is continually changing its mind on what exact printer features the final products will have. Microsoft now may add Apple's Royal font technology for scalable screen and printer fonts to Windows and Presentation Manager.

Upgrading in the Macintosh World

The Macintosh upgrade path is clear and consistent; all Macintosh software is pretty much the same. Screen object fonts are going to be a feature of the System 7 Mac operating system. An object printer upgrades all Macintosh software instantly. The operating system handles all font and character set management. The only drawback of the Macintosh world is that Apple has a choke hold on the environment's development. Market forces are slowly starting to influence Apple. But, only until IBM and Microsoft get their act together and challenge Apple will fonts be freely available, compatible, and easy to incorporate into every application and operating system.

The Macintosh operating system is designed to support two basic types of printers; a dot-matrix printer operating in graphics mode, and an object-oriented laser printer. Character printers are supported in one unique circumstance that is rarely used. The majority of printers hooked up to Macintosh's are made by Apple, but this does not have to be the case. Good clones of both types of printers exist. PC printers, such as HP LaserJets, can be used as a higher resolution version of the Apple dot-matrix printer, the ImageWriter. The lower-priced PostScript printers from QMS are about $1,000 less than an ImageWriter.

Clone Macintosh printers come with software that enables the printers to be compatible with the Macintosh. In the IBM world, each application program has to be compatible with all printers. Apple forces printer companies to write Macintosh software. Printers for the Macintosh come with floppy disks—for example, Epson 24-pin LQ printers for the Macintosh come with two 3 1/2-inch, 800K disks. These disks contain 1.6M of files loaded onto the Macintosh hard disk. The software included is a chooser, installer, and screen bit-mapped fonts that match the character fonts in the printer. By forcing printer companies to provide software that attaches to the Macintosh operating system, Apple is insulating application programs from the printer, relieving application programmers from the burden of having to support 1,000 different printers. But, an even bigger advantage is that different application programs make the printer behave the same way. Consistency minimizes problems and makes identification of problems easier.

The only drawback of the Macintosh system is that Apple has complete control over the operating system. For example, Apple can change the operating system so that it disables the Epson Macintosh print driver software, but this usually disables the software Apple provides for the printers. Mac owners will make sure that Apple upgrades software for their printers if it changes its operating system. However, Apple is not responsible for forcing Epson to upgrade its printer software. Nor are there many Mac owners printing on Epson printers, even though Epson printer drivers will eventually appear. They may take six months to develop, but they will eventually be available. Manufacturers of Mac-compatible printers will compete to see who can come out with drivers first.

Supporting the IBM-Character Set

Every IBM PC keyboard made has a PrtSc key, which means "print the screen." After you press the PrtSc key, a copy of the 25 lines and 80 columns on-screen is sent to the printer. This key works because the screen and the printer are usually in character mode. The trouble is that the IBM PC videoboard has a unique character set developed by IBM. When you display lines, boxes, or character graphics, pressing Shift-PrtSc may print some other characters.

The PrtSc key on an IBM keyboard is an important management and troubleshooting tool as explained Chapter 8. When foreign letters are displayed instead of the lines representing a box, the utility of the PrtSc key is questionable. Don't purchase a printer and attach it to the IBM PC unless it can display the IBM character set. Sometimes, this character set is referred to as the graphics character set, higher order ASCII, or upper ASCII character set.

Defining Interface Types

In Chapter 1, you learn about the concept of printers listening to data arriving on cables from PCs. That chapter describes the historical development of the first two interfaces (serial and parallel), as well as the more recent interfaces. Interfaces differ in speed, price, sharing capabilities, availability, cabling hassles, and cable lengths. This section explores these interface features in general and then reviews specific interfaces. The final interface, including cable building problems, is covered in Chapter 13.

Interface Characteristics

Interface speed does not become important until the printer and the PC can work faster than data can be transmitted over the cable. The printer or the PC has always been slower than the interface; thus, the speed of an interface is not nearly as important as the speed with which a printer can image data or a PC can transmit pixel information in graphics mode. Only in the case of a serial interface can the interface slow down the PC and printer. In this particular case, serial port speed is measured in bits per second (bps). Most modern serial interfaces are set at 9,600 bps for laser printers and 2,400 bps for dot-matrix printers. These speeds can be translated into the characters per second (cps) at which a printer would have to print to keep up with data coming through the cable by dividing by 10. For example, 9,600 bps is equal to 960 cps, and 2,400 bps is equal to 240 cps. At these speeds, the cable transmits data faster than the printer can print characters.

However, font downloading is not limited by the printing activity of the printer. Instead, font downloading is limited by how fast the printer can receive information and transfer it into memory. This occurs at speeds of more than 2,000,000 bps. The newer interfaces (Video and SCSI) can operate at these speeds. However, these interfaces are not needed for normal, character-mode printing.

Serial, RS-232 interfaces are the lowest in cost. A ranking of interfaces in terms of cost from lowest to highest includes the RS-232, parallel, video, HPIB, LAN, and SCSI. All the interfaces mentioned can share a cable with multiple printers and computers attached.

Although the printers of the world can have many different interfaces, most individual printers come with only one. The matching interface for the PC is most often built into the PC or Macintosh. If not, you must add a board. The most widely available interfaces are the serial (Macintosh) and parallel (PC).

The interface with the most cabling problems (see Chapter 13) is definitely RS-232—the cheapest interface. All the other interfaces use standard cables that make them much easier to install and maintain. These interfaces usually come in standard fixed lengths 15 feet or less.

Printer Interfaces

It is always important to purchase standard equipment. Purchasing strange printer interfaces will cause all sorts of compatibility and portability problems. For example, consider the Osborn computer's old printer interface. It consisted of an edge connector sticking out of the plastic case near the monitor. The edge connector was essentially an HPIB interface that was redesigned to be compatible with the Centronics interface that was emerging at the time. Finding the proper printer cable was almost impossible and there were many compatibility problems. If the Osborn printer interface had been more standard, perhaps the company would still be in business today. It should be your goal to purchase printers and computer interface cards that are the most common in the industry.

This section tries to define what is normal in the PC and Macintosh worlds. Table 5.2 describes where these interfaces are most often used. Hewlett-Packard is an important vendor of printers. Just as Epson dominates the dot-matrix market, HP dominates the laser and inkjet market. HP also sells PCs, as does Epson. HP also has its own printer interface called HPIB but is abandoning it. Most HP printers come with standard parallel and serial interfaces, since the release of the original HP LaserJet.

Table 5.2
Interfaces

Printers	IBM	*Macintosh*
RS-232 Serial	x	x
Local Talk		x
Centronics		
Epson/IBM	x	
SCSI		x
HPIB		
Video	x	

Most printer manufacturers have developed optional boards that will enable you to insert a variety of interfaces without much hassle. The x in Table 5.2 marks interfaces officially supported by IBM or Apple. Most RS-232, Local Talk, and Epson/IBM parallel interfaces are built into modern PCs. Many times they are sitting around inactive—waiting for a printer. The SCSI port is built into Macintoshes that have hard disks. You must add a new interface card to the PC for Local Talk, HPIB, and video interfaces.

Printers usually come with one or two interfaces. Some printers come with none. Instead, you must add a *personality module* to make the printer functional. Sometimes, the personality module is the hardware interface; other times, it is a ROM chip that contains printer software. Personality modules are not popular. Their advantages are supposed to be modularity for the dealer, flexibility for the customer, and capability to advertise lower base prices. In reality, these modules cause more connection problems and inventory problems; they also frustrate customers with the confusing options and prices.

> HINT | Avoid printers with personality modules. The modularity does nothing but cause problems.

> HINT | Always try to add an interface card to the PC to match the printer's interface. Add an RS-232 serial interface only to the printer to match the PC's interface. Most printers do not support any other interface.

Serial Interfaces or RS-232

The most universal (and cheapest) interface is the RS-232 serial interface. Most printers and personal computers come with serial ports. But, serial ports also can be found in cars, sewing machines, modems, mice, plotters, and scanners—practically any peripheral. The only place a serial interface is not standard is in the IBM PC dot-matrix printer world. Dot-matrix printers in the IBM world usually come only with an Epson/IBM parallel port.

Serial interfaces for PC dot-matrix printers are an option—typically at a cost of $15 to $120. If you buy the proper serial port board and Macintosh software, you can attach the dot-matrix printer to the Macintosh. Because the Macintosh puts the dot-matrix in graphics mode, the character-mode features of the printer are worthless. Almost all other computers cannot use character-mode features if they just print in graphics mode. Thus, dot-matrix printer manufacturers often save themselves money and time by not supporting advertised character-mode features when the serial port is added.

> HINT | Adding a serial interface to a dot-matrix printer and attaching the printer to an IBM PC may cause the dot-matrix printer to lose some character-mode features.

One advantage of a RS-232 serial interface is that the cable can be long. Using regular wire, a distance of 50 feet is possible. Using special wire (shielded, large diameter, stranded), distances of more than 300 feet are possible.

In the Macintosh world, all ImageWriters hook up to the RS-232 serial port. This interface originally looked like a letter D with nine holes—technically called a DB-9 female connector. Somewhere during the introduction of the Fat Mac or the Macintosh+, Apple changed the connector to a round shape with five holes. The typical data transfer rate through this cable is 2,400 bps or 240 cps.

In the IBM world, the daisywheel printers were the only printers hooked up serially. Today, the printers hooked up serially include plotters, old laser printers that came just with a serial port, and new laser printers that don't work well with the faster parallel ports found in some lasers.

Local Talk or RS-422

The RS-422 cable is a revised version of the RS-232 cable. RS-422 is popular in Europe where it is more commonly known as X.27. The RS-422 cable deals with how bits are changed into electrical energy, how the electrical energy is transported through wires, and how that energy is received. Every Macintosh built has an RS-422 port. RS-422 cables can be longer and the data can travel faster than in RS-232 cables. 240K bps is possible with RS-232 rather than the 50K bps or 110K bps possible with PC RS-232 ports.

Apple calls the RS-422 port the Local Talk port. The important feature Apple implemented with this port was the capability to share a printer. This feature is the equivalent of an instant LAN dedicated to sharing a printer. Because the Apple operating system funnels all printer information through itself, some amazing (from the IBM PC point of view) local area network font management utilities are available. The only problem is that not all Apple printers can use Local Talk. You can hook up only object printers through Local Talk. Apple's object printer is the LaserWriter II. Other companies produce object printers called PostScript printers. Chapter 11 explores the features of these LAN network font-management utilities. Chapter 8 explores other printer-sharing alternatives.

You also can reconfigure most printers that support RS-422 so that they will support RS-232. This flexibility enables you to attach the printer to different computer interfaces in case you need to move the printer. You use the same interface connector for the RS-232 as you do for the RS-422. Most RS-232 ports in PCs however, cannot be switched to RS-422.

Centronics

Centronics parallel ports do not exist anymore. Most parallel interfaces called Centronics-compatible today are really Epson/IBM-compatible parallel ports. When purchasing a printer, ask the salesperson whether the company supports the two types of parallel ports. If one type is Centronics and the other has some other name—IBM, Epson, industry standard, or generic, for example—choose the other name. Don't buy a Centronics interface if another IBM or Epson interface is offered. Get the IBM or Epson parallel interfaces.

Centronics parallel ports cause all sorts of problems. The only time true Centronics parallel ports were popular was in the middle 1970s. At that time, Centronics ports were found in Apple IIs and Ataris. Epson modified the parallel port, and called the modification a Centronics parallel port, which caused confusion that persists to this day. Today, if just one parallel port is available, it is the Epson modified parallel port.

Epson/IBM

The Epson/IBM parallel port is almost universally available in the IBM PC world. Parallel ports are sprinkled everywhere. All printers sold into the IBM PC market today have a parallel port. The cable is standard, and the PC DOS operating system defaults to it. The Shift-PrtSc key is designed to send a copy of the characters currently displayed on-screen out the parallel port of the PC. For ease of use, a printer in the IBM PC world must use the parallel port.

One drawback of the parallel port is that most other computing systems are not using it. The reasons are significant. First of all, the parallel port is slow; most 9,600-bps serial ports are faster. Hewlett-Packard speeded up the printer side of the parallel data transfer in the parallel port of the LaserJet II line of printers. Sometimes, this works; other times, nothing is printed. Sometimes, making the parallel printer cable longer, shorter, cheaper, or more expensive solves the problem. Try doing all the preceding and see what works if you have parallel port troubles.

> **TROUBLE-SHOOTING TIP** If you have trouble with a PC talking to an HP LaserJet II through the parallel port, try the serial port. If the serial port works, try activating the parallel port with shorter or longer cables. The shorter or longer cables are acting like a delay line—delaying or speeding up the electrical energy representing bits.

The future of the parallel port looks bleak. The cable has to be less than 15 feet. Hooking a manual AB switch box in the middle of this cable (which enables two computers to share one printer using a manual switch) can kill more sensitive circuitry in the printer interface, especially in the HP LaserJet II. In fact, the HP LaserJet II parallel port will not be repaired under warranty if you used it with a manual AB switch box.

The most significant drawback is that the parallel port is fundamentally a one-way communication device. Information flows from the computer to the printer. The computer cannot ask the printer questions: "Are you at the top of the page? How wide are the letters on a line? What size of paper is in use? Have the fonts already been downloaded, or do I have to do it?" Similarly, the printer cannot ask the computer "Do you have the fonts?"

In the parallel port, there is a tiny bit of information that trickles back from the printer; therefore, some two-way communication is possible. But, the hardware design philosophy and software implementation of most parallel ports is fundamentally one directional.

Successful two-way use of parallel ports is possible. Most laptop IBM PC clones have a parallel port that can talk one way to a printer or two ways with a floppy disk drive. When designing the IBM portable PC, IBM built a parallel port that temporarily disabled all slots (and circuit boards in them) when transforming the two-way bus into a parallel port. IBM also released a data migration kit to move data from old PC, XT, and AT parallel ports to parallel ports in PS/2s. The data migration kit consisted of a cable hooking up parallel ports to software. You can use parallel ports on some machines for bi-directional communication. But, none of these applications has featured a printer talking back. Instead, floppy disk drives, circuit boards, and file transfer software has talked back through parallel ports. And, the two-way communication is just between two devices—not multiple devices. No company is going to design a printer that talks back and shares a cable that has a maximum distance limitation of 15 feet.

SCSI

SCSI, which stands for Small Computer System Interface, is a standard, two-way parallel data transfer system originally developed by Shugart for floppy disk, hard disk, and tape drives. SCSI became an official standard of the American National Standards Institute with the number X3.131 in 1986. The standard was designed to go six meters (extendible to 25 meters) at 4M per second—that is 4,000,000 cps or 32,000,000 bps. Because the standard supports eight devices, SCSI can be used to support a fast, tiny, LAN. The cable contains 50 wires.

Apple chose the SCSI standard when designing a hard disk for the Macintosh, because among the alternatives Apple had at the time, SCSI was the best and, for all purposes, still is the best. The IBM PC world has been struggling to catch up. Because the SCSI standard was so complicated and required such a "smart" disk drive, the prices of Macintosh drives at first were two to three times more expensive than IBM PC drives. Now that the prices are about the same, the IBM PC drives seem slow in comparison.

Because multiple devices can hook to the same SCSI cable, Apple designed a printer that works off the same port as the hard disk. Apple chose this cabling system for its low-end graphics-mode laser printer called the LaserWriter SC. Apple wanted the fastest cable possible in order to transmit tremendous quantities of graphics data as quickly as possible. This means that Apple's cheapest laser printer shares the same interface as the hard disk. Unfortunately, the SCSI standard Apple implemented has not enabled Macintoshes to share a SCSI cable. For now, just one Macintosh, multiple hard disk drives, and printers can share a SCSI cable. In the future, perhaps a PC, Macintosh, printer, and hard disk drive will share the same cable without LAN software.

There is one important point that needs to be made about SCSI cables. The same point is true about the cables to floppies and hard disk drives in the IBM PC world. Each of these cables functions best with a T-resistor plugged into the device at the end of the cable. A *T-resistor* (terminating resistor) absorbs electrical energy in the wires and turns it into heat. Without the T-resistor, each of the 50 wires in the SCSI cable acts like an antenna picking up TV and radio stations. Music may sound like data to a Macintosh, printer, or hard disk attached to the same cable. Garbage files may be created that overwrite good data. The printer may start ejecting pages, start printing funny things, or just go off into never-never land. The same sort of thing happens if the T-resistor is pulled off the device at the end of the cable rather than in the middle. T-resistors come with most devices because they may be the first on the cable. SCSI T-resistors are pressed into a socket on the top of a SCSI connector.

Most printers and drives come with T-resistors, so the problem is usually having too many, not too few. With two T-resistors, a circuit component has to work twice as hard to use the wire; it also heats up twice as much and lives half its designed life. In other words, if a SCSI printer is added to the SCSI hard disk drive, pull the terminating resistor off the device in the middle of the cable. Otherwise, hard disk damage will occur.

HINT | Check SCSI cables that have multiple devices on them for terminating resistors. To prevent software or hardware damage, make sure that only one T-resistor is installed in the device at the end of the cable.

The Hewlett-Packard Interface Bus

HPIB is known also by its standard number IEEE 488 and GPIB—its official name. These four-letter acronyms mean the following:

HPIB	Hewlett-Packard Interface Bus
IEEE 488	Institute of Electrical and Electronic Engineers
GPIB	General Purpose Interface Bus

GPIB became a standard in April, 1975 when the IEEE published it as standard 488. This interface was revised in 1978 and 1980. The revisions were just clarification. GPIB is essentially an earlier version of SCSI. The cables can go 20 meters at 1M per second (8,000,000 bps) and up to 15 devices can be attached. More than 2,000 different GPIB devices have been made by more than 200 companies. But, most companies today are moving on to other, higher speed standards. The market for GPIB products is stable. GPIB is most commonly found in research labs where engineers use it to collect data.

In the computer world, GPIB was primarily used by Hewlett-Packard in its minicomputers and early personal computers. Now, even Hewlett-Packard computer equipment no longer uses GPIB. Instead, most Hewlett-Packard printers come with standard parallel and serial interfaces. Early Hewlett-Packard printers, and especially Hewlett-Packard's first inkjet printer—the little DeskJet—were designed with GPIB interfaces. Many marvelous plotters exist with GPIB interfaces. You can purchase GPIB boards for IBM PCs that make them function as a parallel port to MS-DOS software.

Video Interfaces

Video interfaces are a feature of laser printers. Laser printers grew out of copier machine technology. Early on, the copier machine manufacturers needed a partner to help turn them into printers. So, they turned to computer manufacturers. The computer companies had to write some software, design a front panel, and get the entire system to work with computers. Today, the copier machine part of the laser printer is called the *engine*. The computer part is called the *engine interface*.

The interface between the printer logic board and the engine is called the *video interface*. An external video interface is really a method of bypassing the printer logic board (see fig. 5.1). The external video interface is a data pipe directly into the engine. The cable has to be extremely well-built and short. The data transfer rate is at bus speeds—supposedly around 2.5M per second or 20,000,000 bps. When the video interface is active, the printer's logic board is disabled.

The first video interfaces appeared for the Hewlett-Packard LaserJet II. The LaserJet II was the first laser printer with an actual video interface available out the back, along with the RS-232/RS-422 and parallel interfaces. The Hewlett-Packard manuals do not consistently call this interface the video interface. Stenciled on the face plate covering the video interface are the words *Optional I/O*. In the manuals it is called the *Expansion Interface Slot*,

Fig. 5.1.

A video interface.

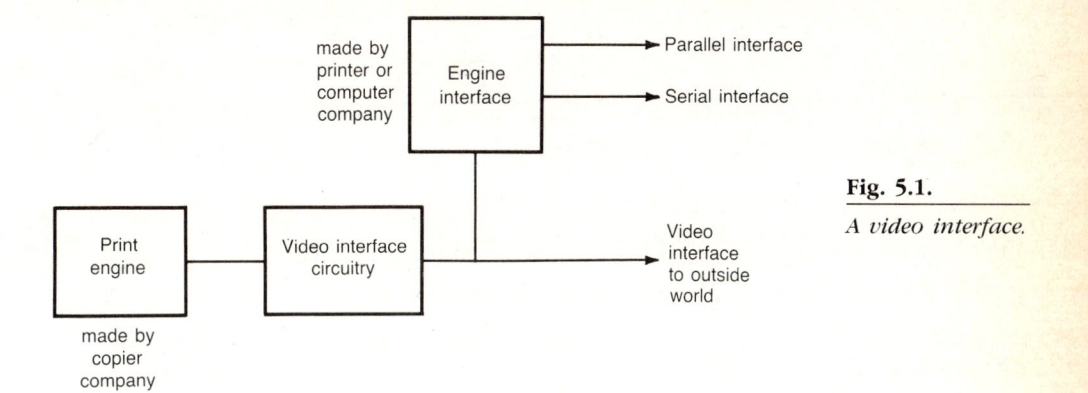

which is different from the *Expansion Memory Slot*. Today, it is most often called the *video interface slot*.

To connect to the video interface, you need a completely new engine interface for the print engine. Because there is not room in the printer for another circuit board, you have to place the new engine interface inside the personal computer and take up a slot. The special video interface cable attaches to the external video interface on one end and to a connector mounted on the new engine interface board in the PC (again, see fig. 5.1). The video interface is really not an interface at all in the sense of GPIB, SCSI, parallel, or serial. In reality, a video interface is more like an umbilical cord. The printer is actually part of the PC!

There are advantages and disadvantages to this type of system. Advantages are that the transfer of data to the printer imaging system is performed through the PC bus rather than a serial or parallel cable. Unloading fonts and downloading font caches are much faster. The bottleneck is how fast the new engine interface can do its job.

The disadvantages arise when you attempt to share the printer. Because part of the printer is now inside the PC, there is no way to share the printer. Normal switch boxes do not work. The PC has to be shared if the printer is shared. This is the function of a LAN. In fact, because all PC printers are "dumb," they need a "smart" PC to manage all the users that want to print. Because PC LANs have to negotiate the sharing of a printer, you need software to share this non-standard engine interface board with those on the LAN. Unfortunately, it is not the responsibility of the LAN software vendors to write this software, because the engine interface board is a non-standard interface, meaning that the manufacturer of the engine interface board in the PC would have to write special drivers for all types of LANs.

Multiple Interface Options

Some printers come with multiple interfaces. Look around the edge of the printer for places that cables plug into. Most of the connectors (besides power) represent the different interfaces a printer supports. All types have distinctive features that are illustrated in Chapter 1.

If a printer comes with multiple interfaces, the next question is how are they used. For example, suppose that a printer comes with three different interfaces: serial, parallel, and video. The first question is, "Does the printer listen to all three interfaces simultaneously, or does it listen to one at a time?" Most printers listen to only one interface at a time. These printers are configured using switches or jumpers usually hidden in the back of the printer or underneath the lid. It may not be easy to flick a switch to change from one interface to another. Recently, manufacturers are starting to put the interface selection option on the front panel. This option performs the same effect as a manual switch box. Suppose that a printer has a serial port and a parallel port. Hook PC number 1 to the serial and PC number 2 to the parallel. When PC 1 wants to print, walk over to the printer and configure it to pay attention to the serial port. When PC 2 wants to print, configure the printer to pay attention to the parallel port.

> HINT | If a printer has more than one interface, figure out how easy it is to switch between them. If the switch is on the front panel within easy reach, you will not need a manual switch box.

Some printers have the capability to scan multiple ports on a first-come, first-serve basis. The busy printer can behave as though it is out of paper or off-line to the second computer. In addition, some printers can enable the operating system to control scanning through commands sent to the printer.

Investigating Front-Panel Features

The original printers had just three buttons on the front, labeled ON LINE, LF, and FF. The operation of these buttons was simple. The ON LINE button had a light near it. When this light was on, the printer was ready to receive information from the computer. When the light was on, the LF and FF buttons would do nothing. When you pushed the ON LINE button, the light would go out, and the other two buttons, LF and FF, would work. LF advanced the paper one line at a time. FF ejected a sheet of paper. These buttons were provided so that a user would not try to move the paper by hand and ruin the stepper motor that moved the paper electronically while printing.

As printers started to develop more features (fonts), access to these features became important. Accessing these features through software has always been a problem, but accessing the fonts through switches on the front of the printer is easy to understand. If you want to print in a compressed font so that you can print an entire spreadsheet, mailing labels, or use some other PC program, the buttons on the front of the printer work great. Some printers have one font button and an LED that displays a font number. Pressing the button causes the font number to cycle from 0 through 9 before starting over again at 0. You can figure out exactly what is printed for each font number by trial and error, by using the font self-test, or by reading the manual.

> HINT Font buttons on the front of a dot-matrix printer will always be a worthless, unused feature in the Macintosh world because the Macintosh can adequately simulate the printer's front panel on-screen. Why get up and walk over to a printer when you can access the front panel from the desktop computer?

Laser printers have much more in the way of options than just fonts. To provide access to all these options, it looked as though the front panel would end up with as many keys as a keyboard. Fortunately, there has been a revolution in user interfaces. Instead of 60 buttons that each do something different, there are just a few buttons and a computer-like screen to display menus. Not only are laser printers beginning to come with menus, but fancy technical equipment like oscilloscopes, network analyzers, remote controls, and telephones also are developing menus.

The real question is why not pretend the laser printer is a mainframe and have the PC display the laser printer menus on-screen? The answer is that most printers cannot talk back. However, object printers can talk back, and the evolution of front panels on the PC screen is occurring. For example, the Apple object printer, LaserWriter II, has just four lights on its front panel and no buttons. Software is available, however, that asks the printer to display on the PC's screen how much memory is available, which fonts have been downloaded, and so on.

Chapter 8 explores front panel features in more detail. The front panel is really a window into the software features of the printer. Here, these hardware-related features of a front panel need to be discussed: ease of use, reset features, dip switch location, font support, and form concepts.

Ease of Use

How easy is it to use the front panel of a printer? How do the buttons feel; how many characters are displayed; how many LED lights are there? How confusing is it? These questions can be answered fairly quickly. Learning how to push the buttons should be instinctive.

You can push the buttons on the front panel of a printer to perform four basic functions:

- Toggling
- Scrolling through menus
- Scrolling through menu line items
- Selecting menu line items

A toggle switch is similar to a light switch. A light can be on or off. Toggle buttons switch between the two printer modes or features. For example, you can switch between on-line and off-line, serial port or parallel port, and bold face and shadow.

Most front panels of printers become active when you switch to off-line. You use certain buttons to call up menus. You use other buttons to scroll through the menu items—for example, the up and down arrows on a keyboard. Other buttons select the line items—for example, the Enter key on a PC keyboard.

> HINT | Play with a printer menu before purchasing it. If it is easy to understand without the manual, you can save much time.

Reset Features

The biggest problem with front panels and dip switches is getting them to do something. Sometimes, this process is referred to as getting the changes to "stick." You push the buttons and select the menu options, but the printer does not change its behavior. To understand the problem, you must understand the evolution of dip switches into front-panel features.

Switches and front panels exist so that they can provide the flexibility required of a printer in today's market. From the quality control and the technical support point of view, most companies would like to keep the flexibility to a minimum. The more options there are, the more printer confusion is possible.

Early printers had physical switches. The printer looked at these switches while powering on. If the switches were changes, the printer had to be turned on and off to read the switch changes. Changing the switch positions when the printer was on did nothing. If the printer constantly scanned the switches to see whether any had changed position, the printer would be much slower. Originally, the requirement to turn off and on the printer to read the switches was not unreasonable. Today, however, laser printers have downloaded fonts that are cleared when the printer is turned off, and turning off the printer is unreasonable.

To solve this problem, a new concept had to be developed that enabled the user to tell the printer to look at the menu changes (menus have replaced switches). Most people assume that pressing on-line tells the printer to look at the changes, but this is not so. Traditionally, the on-line/off-line button merely has switched the printer's attention from data arriving from the PC to the keyboard or front panel. Today, many printers use the reset button to indicate that the printer should look at the new menu settings. This concept is explored in more detail in Chapter 8.

When menus replaced switches, the question of what to do when the printer was turned off arose. The options are to remember the menu changes you made while the printer was on or to revert to the factory default positions. Obviously, the best solution is for the printer to remember your changes so that you don't have to modify the menu each time you turn on the printer.

PC software always has had the capability to override any switches and menu selections. If PC software told the printer to do something, the printer did it. Furthermore, the printer remembered the PC's last instructions unless it was specifically told to forget them. When laser printers were created, their high-resolution and page buffering caused problems. The big question was how to recover from memory overflows and paper jams without loosing the downloaded fonts—without turning off and on the printer. In a dot-matrix printer, fonts are usually not downloaded. Thus, turning the printer off and on to set the top of form or switch to the default font does not cause any information to be lost. But, turning a laser off can lose downloaded font information.

Instead, when the laser printer detects a problem, it stops and flashes warning messages just like a copier machine. The user is supposed to clear the warning message. Clear or Continue buttons on the front panel instruct the laser printer to remember the last PC software instructions.

Suppose that a laser has a partial page in memory when some changes are made using the front panel. The laser does not know whether to apply the changes made using the front panel to the data already in memory or when to apply the changes to future text received.

Various manufacturers handle the situation differently. Some printers eject the partial page and do what the user asked. Other printers refuse to do anything; they will not even look at the new menu selections unless there is no data to print. Keep in mind that even if a laser printer has printed a page, it still holds a copy of that page in memory until it is sure that the page was ejected properly. This way it can reprint the entire page if the paper jams.

> HINT │ If the changes for the menu selections aren't implemented, eject a blank sheet of paper and press any button labeled reset, continue, or clear. Press the buttons while the printer is on-line and off-line. Keep pressing the buttons, and watch which type of reset implements your menu selections.

Using Built-In Forms and Other Features

In their search for an edge, certain printer manufacturers have violated the historical patterns that this chapter has described. For example, one manufacturer's printer scans the font buttons of the front panel while on-line. If you push one of the buttons, the font changes immediately without the printer going off-line, without the PC's permission or control, and perhaps just because someone leaned on the printer or brushed it with his arm. To experienced printer users, this would look like a hardware problem with the printer—not a feature.

Other printer manufacturers are extending the font selection concept to whether the PC or printer is in ultimate control of the fonts used. Currently, the front panel buttons are submissive to the PC software. If the PC software tells the printer to change fonts, it does so even if the front panel font selection is different. In perhaps a vain attempt at equality, certain manufacturers are starting to allow fonts to be set two ways: permanently or temporarily. *Temporarily* means that PC software can override the printer. *Permanently* means that the printer will ignore all PC software font-changing instructions. To the experienced printer user, this would look like a PC software configuration problem at first—not a feature.

Finally, some printer manufacturers are including built-in forms. You can select different forms from the front panel. The idea behind this feature is to reduce the need for a second paper tray. Instead of using PC software to select letterhead from the second paper tray, select a form that is in the printer—a form that has your company's letterhead on it. Then, the letterhead graphics data does not need to be transmitted each time, and you can print the rest of the letter at traditional character-mode speeds.

Purchasing Computer Furniture

Printers are the most awkward part of a computer system. Paper is draped everywhere. Good computer furniture hides this mess. Yet, the paper should be easy to get to in case it jams. Power cords and data cables should be neatly tucked out of the way. The printer should be in good light in order to see what is happening. Some people may need to place the printer at standing level if they have back problems.

Probably the biggest mistake made is to put the printer in a closet or cupboard low to the floor, turn everything on with a single power-on switch, and keep the door shut so that nobody can see the printer. Dot-matrix printers count on the weight of hanging paper to feed paper properly in the input path. Bending over is not good for your back. Shutting the door while the printer is on essentially creates an oven—the heat generated is trapped. This heat can destroy the printer's electronics.

The best printer furniture places the printer at about desk level. Paper is fed from the floor and piles up on the floor. The weight of hanging paper helps the printer to feed paper properly. A stand or shelf with a slot cut in the back for the paper and power cables is ideal.

Reviewing Printer Manuals

Printer manuals are often a good indication of how many problems there will be with the printer. The following is a series of informational items that should be in a printer manual. If these items are not in the manual, don't purchase the printer. Otherwise, there may be many problems down the road that even experts cannot solve.

- ❏ A page that lists all the characters the printer can print.
- ❏ A sample page describing all the fonts the printer can print.
- ❏ A section describing the programming language of the printer. You don't have to understand it, just find it.
- ❏ A description of every printer emulation that the printer supports.

    For example, if the printer supports Epson LQ emulation, look for a list of Epson LQ software commands. Many companies offer emulation with no documentation.

Checking the Printer Warranty

Most electronic devices die at an early age—within 90 days—or work for a long time. Therefore, the support offered during the early part of the warranty period is critical. Warranties run from 90 days to a year or more. At the beginning of the warranty period, some companies include a 90-day on-site warranty. This warranty is meaningless, however, unless the company guarantees to arrive at your site within a certain amount of time. This is referred to as the *response time*. Sometimes, it is more cost-effective to have a cab or courier drive the broken printer to a repair facility. The time spent to fix the printer—called the *turnaround time*—is also an issue. Good on-site service contracts state specifically the response time and turnaround time. Because on-site service contracts rarely specify response time or turn-around guarantees and are a big source of frustration to consumers, some printer companies offer a return period during which you can return the printer and receive a refund. Other printer companies offer an exchange period during which time you can exchange the printer for another model.

> HINT | Do not purchase a printer until you really need it. Then, put stress on it by printing a great deal during the warranty period. Spend the entire warranty period trying to "kill" the printer.

The biggest warranty problem is identifying who is responsible for fixing the printer if a problem occurs. The company, consultant, or the person who sold you the printer many times does not know who is responsible. The printer manufacturer can advertise a fantastic warranty policy. But, if that company does not provide the incentive, training, parts, and support necessary for a printer to be repaired, the warranty is useless. Be sure to identify and interview the person and organization responsible for warranty repair before you purchase a printer. If the printer is really cheap, start by calling the manufacturer, rather than asking the salesperson. The cheaper the printer, the more likely it is that the salesperson will not know what you are talking about.

> HINT | If a problem occurs during warranty, do not waste any time initiating the warranty repair process. Document the process thoroughly. It is beneficial for the printer companies to stall so that your printer goes out of warranty while they fix it—or claim to fix it.

Calculating the Mean Time between Failure

Judging the life span of any physical or biological device is difficult. One of the most scientific methods related to electrical components is called the *mean time between failure*. Suppose that a printer has a mean time between failure of 18,000 hours. What this means exactly is that half the printers will break before the 18,000-hour mark, and the other half will break after the 18,000 hour-mark.

Looking at mean time between failure ratings of printers is not useful if your goal is to determine how long your printer is going to live. Mean times between failures are not the results of statistical measurements in the field, but rather a design parameter computed from the components with which a computer is built. Mean time between failures governs the quality of every component put into the printer. The higher the number, the higher the quality and the longer in general the printer will last. But, after the printer is purchased, nobody knows how long the printer will live. The life span depends on where the printer is housed, how often it is greased, and other events that the printer manufacturer cannot control.

The mean time between failure is measured in hours of operation. Examples include 8,000 hours, 18,000 hours, or 32,000 hours. Most electrical parts also are limited in the number of times they can be turned off and on. This number is not as widely reported.

Determining the Necessary Printer Resolution

The resolution question can be complex or simple. If you are printing text, the resolution issue is simple. If you are printing bit-mapped graphics, scanning a photo, or filling objects with different shades of gray, the resolution issue becomes complex. Using scanners to capture these grays can be frustrating. When talking about resolution, the amount of memory required always needs to be discussed.

Text Resolution

When the intensity or size of black dots does not vary, the resolution issue is simple. Resolution is specified in terms of dots per inch. For dot-matrix printers, this resolution always has been a function of how far apart the dots are in the print head and how precise the head and paper movement can be controlled by motors. In all dot-matrix printers, the vertical and horizontal resolution is different.

In the 9-pin dot-matrix world, 216 dpi is a multiple of 72 (1/3 of a point). This is evidence that the world of typewriters influenced the design of the first 9-pin dot-matrix print head. All other numbers are multiples of 60. This is evidence of design engineers allowing *stepper motor* (the motor that moves the paper and the print head) features to determine the resulting dpi.

The increments in which motors turn are measured in degrees, with 360 degrees in a circle.

When you print graphs in the 9-pin world, the vertical resolution defaults to 72 dpi; thus, achieving 216 dpi is a struggle. Not all printers can achieve 216 dpi all the time. Therefore, dot-matrix printers have many graphics-mode dpi-densities available. As a result, dot-matrix graphics printing can be different, even if you use the same printer.

The technology to manufacture 600-dpi laser printers is here. If all manufacturers upgraded their production lines to 600 dpi overnight, the costs of laser printers would not be any different than 300-dpi machines. Eventually, this will happen, but because perceived quality will not improve noticeably, the marketplace probably will not change from 300-dpi to 600-dpi lasers for quite some time. Also, the 600-dpi printers must have four times the amount of memory in order to use this increased resolution. Thus, the change to 600-dpi printers will be gradual.

Only typesetters are willing to spend $10,000 on a printer that cannot produce newspaper- or book-quality camera-ready output. Typesetters spend $10,000 to proof the output of $300,000-scanners before sending the document to a $400,000 printer that prints on film. These typesetters need high resolutions for color printing and color proofing. 300 dpi is sufficient for black-and-white proofing.

The density of black and white dots that make up characters in newspapers and magazines is around 1270 dpi. Books are usually printed at 2540 dpi. If an 8 1/2-by-11-inch page is printed at 300 dpi and then reduced to a quarter of its size (2 1/4-by-2 3/4 inches), then the print quality could be 1200 dpi. Unfortunately, this is not practical because PC laser printers are limited to 8 1/2-by-11 inches. However, you can purchase some 300-dpi inkjet printers that work with larger sheets of paper; then, the reduction technique is feasible.

Scanner Resolution

Scanners are used many ways in today's world. The majority of scanners are used for sorting checks and mail. These scanners look at dot patterns and attach ZIP code or bank code meanings to the dot patterns. Probably, the next most common use of scanners is for reading surveys, forms, and multiple-choice tests. How many times have you filled in a dot with a pencil? Scanners have long promised to be able to read handwriting, magazine ads, and other printed matter to save people from typing. It usually takes people more time to teach the scanner how to read, feed the paper in, and then check the scanner's grammar and spelling than it does to retype it. Scanners can read text for the blind by combining text recognition with speech synthesis. A more popular use of scanners is to scan-in graphics data (bit-mapped data) and then have outlining programs change the graphics data into object data. None of these uses for the scanner involves a printer, so they are not explored any further in *The Printer Bible*.

There are three major uses of scanners today that involve printers:

- *Scanners used with fax boards or modems inside the PCs.* The receiver can then print the scanned documents remotely. The issues here revolve around the type of fax board and how well-configured the fax software is for the printer attached. Usually, functionality, not quality, is the issue. Most faxes look terrible compared to a 300-dpi laser printer. Therefore, a discussion of scanner grays is still not important.

- *Scanners used during desktop publishing.* You can use a scanner to scan a photo and then paste it into a document. After you are in the document, you can position text around the photo, enlarge the photo, and put a box on top of the photo showing exactly which parts of the real photo are to appear in the final document. In this case, you use the scanner as an aid to make the desktop publishing process more efficient. You use printed versions of a scanned photo only to communicate enlarging and cutting instructions to the person who pastes the photo onto the typeset sheets. Here, again, the quality of the scanned document and its relationship to the printer is not an issue.

- *Scanners used to prepare electronically colored photographs for color printing.* Big typesetting shops use scanners to scan at more than 2000 dpi and accumulate 24 to 32 bits of color information about each dot. These scanners cost between $10,000 and $20,000 dollars and can be attached to PCs. But, this is a specialized application. Most users are not doing this yet. (See Chapter 10 for more information.)

The only time the scanner-printer relationship is important is when you are trying to produce camera-ready copy from a PC desktop publishing system. Scanners are available with 400 dots per inch and an 8-bit gray scale behind each bit. Because most laser printers can print at only 300 dpi with no gray scale, a 400-dpi, 8-bit gray-scale scanner will not improve the laser printout quality. In fact, a 300-dpi no-gray-scale scanner would be sufficient if just printed on a 300 dpi laser printer.

The only way to get the most out of the 400-dpi, 8-bit scanners is to send the bitmap to a typesetter. Then, however, the files are large and there is no way to proof the image. Therefore, there really is no need for this scanner until a 400-dpi, 64-gray scale printer comes along. None of these are on the horizon.

> HINT When working on drafts, scan at a low resolution. This will speed draft printing and drawing the document on the PC screen. It also will take up less space on the hard disk. Save the high-resolution scan for the final print output.

Resolution and Memory

Whether scanning or printing at high resolutions, much more data is involved. Table 5.3 illustrates the amount of data and memory involved to print an 8-by-11-inch graphic.

Table 5.3
Memory Requirements To Print a Graphic

Printer	Megabytes required
9-pin dot-matrix	0.18
150-dpi laser	0.24
24-pin dot-matrix	0.68
300-dpi laser	0.94
400-dpi laser	1.67
600-dpi laser	3.78
1270-dpi laser	16.92
1690-dpi laser	29.96
2540-dpi laser	67.68

The first interesting fact that you can observe from this table is that the 300-dpi laser needs 1M of memory. Most lasers come with 512K. These printers cannot print a full-page 300-dpi graphic unless more memory is added. Only a half-page 300-dpi graphic can be printed. Because the memory in a printer is used for things other than just the graphic image, a small amount of additional memory is needed. If fonts are downloaded, the memory available for printing graphics decreases. The standard 512K, 300-dpi laser can print at only 150 dpi. This is less than the resolution of a 24-pin dot-matrix printer. The reason dot-matrix printers can print a 180-by-360-dpi graphic with so little memory is that they print an 8- or 24-bit-wide strip across the page, and thus have to image only that strip rather than the whole page. Inkjet printer models can image the whole page like a laser printer or image part of a page like a dot-matrix printer. If object capabilities are in the printer, add 2M to the numbers in table 5.3.

> HINT Some lasers that run out of memory when printing a graphic print half the page, eject the paper, and then print the other half. You can combine these halves to form a full-page 300 dpi graphic.

Most people complain how slow object printers are when printing text compared to character-mode printers. If the same fonts are available for both, character-mode printers will print the document quicker. But, object printers print faster when flexibility and creativity are required. Object printers also print faster than graphics printers. It can take more than 17 minutes just to transmit the graphic data to a 300-dpi graphics-mode printer at 9,600 bps. Much less data has to be transmitted to an object-mode printer. Of course, after the data arrives, the object-mode printer has to think about it. The amount of time an object printer spends thinking about an object depends on the object, how much memory, and how fast the object printer is.

Look at the 2,540-dpi laser printer. Consider how long it would take to transmit 67.68M at 9600 baud—more than 20 hours. If an electronic form of a graphics page is going to be transmitted over telephone wires to a publishing house, this seems almost impossible. However, an object page can be transmitted easily.

To speed the transfer of graphics data to its printers, Hewlett-Packard modified the parallel port of its LaserJet II to work much faster than the parallel port ever has worked before. This causes intermittent compatibility problems with many PC printer interfaces; the printer acts "dead." If the parallel interface works, data can be transmitted up to 10 times quicker—1.7 minutes for a 300-dpi page rather than 17 minutes.

Measuring Speed

Before you examine printing speed, ask yourself how fast do you need the printer to go. Many factors can influence the speed you need. One person may use a printer very infrequently. Another person may print a great deal, yet both people may be doing the same job. The fundamental question is: "When will a faster printer enable you to do your job more efficiently and productively?" But, an equally important question is: "When does a faster printer encourage waste?" In fact, a faster printer may make you more inefficient. For example, with a slower printer you are encouraged to find something else to do while waiting for the printout. Yet, with a faster printer you may be inclined to watch the process. If the printer is too fast, people tend to turn the printer into an expensive duplicating machine.

Certain applications will always require a high-speed printer. Suppose that you need the printer to make a paper copy of a massive inventory to be used only if the computer stops working. This would require a fast printer and tractor-feed paper. Font quality would be a secondary issue. Printing speed may be very important in this case, because it could mean the difference between finishing the job at 10 p.m. and finishing the job at 2 a.m.

What good is a special high-speed printer if it needs a babysitter because the paper tray does not hold many sheets or because the paper always jams? What good is a fast expensive printer if the output is so unreadable that it will never be used? How often is draft mode ever used anyway? How many people always print in letter-quality mode (the slowest mode), hoping that the printout will be correct the first time? Is a LAN always best served by the fastest, highest quality printer around? When are the employees better off with two slow-speed printers (one for documents and one for mailing labels) than one high-speed printer?

The point of the preceding speed discussion was to show you that faster is not always better. You can find the optimal speed best by looking at the users involved, the job requirements, and the turnaround time required with the appropriate failure recover margins built in. But, suppose that the time required to print a specific document has been calculated. For example, suppose that the page has to appear in the amount of time it takes to shove a chair away from a desk, stand up and lean over the printer—three seconds. How fast does the printer have to be in order to produce a page in three seconds?

A printer's speed in the past has been measured in characters per second, lines per minute, or pages per minute. But, often these measures of speed have little relationship to how fast paper comes out of the printer. Before you develop a speed rating of a printer, you must identify the slowest part of the printing system. This is usually called the *bottleneck*. Often, this has nothing to do with characters per second, lines per minute, or pages per minute. For example, suppose that the printer is 300 feet away from the computer. This means that the data transfer rate has to be lowered. And perhaps the cable may turn into the bottleneck.

The various modes in which you operate a printer can have a big effect on printer speed and the location of the bottleneck. In character mode, some feature of the printer is usually the bottleneck. In graphics mode, the printer or even the PC is the bottleneck. In object mode, the printer's CPU is the bottleneck, rather than something mechanical. The following paragraphs explore these issues in more detail.

Character-Mode Speed

The first character printers were daisywheel printers and were very slow. The bottleneck was created by the speed at which the print head rotates a pin, placing the correct letter in front of the hammer and then firing the hammer. An effective method of measuring this speed was characters per second (cps). It took time to move the print head over to the next character position and to rotate the paper. But, these events required little time compared to the time spent to print a character. Early daisywheel printers printed at about as fast as the fastest typists—10 characters per second (10 cps). This meant that it took eight seconds to print a line or about seven minutes for a page. A vast majority of the time was spent actually printing characters. A small minority of the time was spent moving the head and paper.

The fastest daisywheel printers reached speeds of more than 55 cps, but these were specialized, expensive daisywheel printers. The most cost-effective speed for daisywheel printers was around 30 cps before those printers became extinct.

Dot-matrix printers always have been able to print much faster than daisywheels, and they are much cheaper. Because of this, daisywheel printers competed with dot-matrix printers. Today, dot-matrix printers that print at 240 cps are not unusual, and speeds of up to 800 cps are possible.

Back in the days of daisywheel printers, characters per second was a good measure of a printer's speed. This was because the daisywheel was the bottleneck. Today, it is inappropriate to rate a printer's speed in characters per second. Printer speeds are so fast that the time to get to the beginning of the next line, advance the paper, dry the paper, or melt toner is significant. Today, most dot-matrix printers can print the line at 240 cps. This means it takes one third of a second to print a line of 80 characters. The time spent moving the print head into position for the next line and advancing the paper suddenly becomes significant. The slower the printer, the more accurate the cps value is going to be. Average throughput of a printer rated at 200 cps is really only 100 cps once the movement of the print head and paper is taken into account. Character-mode speed is like the miles-per-gallon rating of a new car; the printer never seems to perform at the rated speed.

Laser printers operating in character mode could be advertised as having a speed of millions of characters per second. Because everyone would know this was a ridiculous speed rating, laser printers are often rated in pages per second. In character mode, the speed at which the printer can push paper through is the bottleneck. To translate pages per minute to characters per second, an assumption has to be made concerning the average number of characters per page. If a page has 55 lines and an average of 60 characters per line, then each page has 3,300 characters. Usually, the more accurate average is around 2,000 characters per page because some lines are skipped, lines are not usually 60 characters long, and so on. If 2,000 characters are assumed to be on the average page, here is the math:

$$\frac{8 \text{ pages}}{\text{minute}} \times \frac{2{,}000 \text{ characters}}{\text{page}} \times \frac{1 \text{ minute}}{60 \text{ seconds}} = 267 \text{ cps}$$

$$\frac{8 \text{ pages}}{\text{minute}} \times \frac{3{,}300 \text{ characters}}{\text{page}} \times \frac{1 \text{ minute}}{60 \text{ seconds}} = 440 \text{ cps}$$

Although inkjet printers are fast, you need to let the paper dry for about three seconds before you stack it. This reduces throughput to between 40 cps to 60 cps. Still, this is fast, considering the letter-quality speed of most dot-matrix printers. Most inkjet and dot-matrix printers print at between one to three pages per minute.

The speed of printers attached to mainframes and minicomputers is measured in lines per minute. When people move a massive database off a mainframe or minicomputer to a PC, often they must print the entire inventory or accounting journal. Obviously, they would need a fast printer for this task. Usually, these printers are printing 132 characters per line; the math converting to effective characters per second throughput follows:

$$\frac{500 \text{ lines}}{\text{minutes}} \times \frac{132 \text{ characters}}{\text{lines}} \times \frac{1 \text{ minute}}{60 \text{ seconds}} = 1{,}100 \text{ cps}$$

$$\frac{100 \text{ lines}}{\text{minutes}} \times \frac{132 \text{ characters}}{\text{lines}} \times \frac{1 \text{ minute}}{60 \text{ seconds}} = 220 \text{ cps}$$

Dot-matrix printers that are achieving speeds of more than 400 cps effective throughput are available (best is 800 cps). These speeds are obtained by using 18-pin print heads. The 18 pins are divided into two groups of nine. These two groups alternate; one group cools off while the other is working.

Graphics-Mode Speed

Character-mode printers are rapidly disappearing. Macintosh PCs rarely put printers in character mode. PC DOS and Microsoft Windows are merging, and OS/2 and UNIX are developing graphics interfaces. This means that future printers will spend more of their lives in graphics mode. Unfortunately, the graphics-mode bottleneck could be the PC software, printer, or cable. Furthermore, different PC software packages may cause the bottleneck to change. This makes the bottleneck identification in graphics mode much more difficult.

The printer cable may be the bottleneck when you are working in graphics mode. Suppose that a laser or inkjet printer is printing in 300-by-300 dots-per-inch resolution. A full page of graphic information would equal 8,415,000 bits (300 $\times$ 300 $\times$ 8.5 $\times$ 11). If these bits are transmitted at 9,600 bps, it will take 877 seconds or 15 minutes to send just the data. Most of the time, the page is smaller than 8 1/2-by-11 inches, and just certain dots—not all dots—are sent. Therefore, the amount of data is much smaller.

A dot-matrix printer's graphics mode speed is computed in a different way. For a 9-pin dot-matrix printer, assume that the cell size is 9-by-9 bits. If the printer is printing at 100 cps, this means that the printer could theoretically print at 8,100 bps (9 $\times$ 9 $\times$ 100). If the cable is not the bottleneck, there is a good chance that the printer is the bottleneck. Following the same logic, a 24-pin dot-matrix printer could print at 57,600 bps (24 $\times$ 24 $\times$ 100). But, a 24-pin printer has to print seven times as much data—24 $\times$ 24/(9 $\times$ 9) as a 9-pin printer. This means that graphics printing speed (if the cable is not the bottleneck) should be the same for 24-pin printers as for 9-pin printers. Unfortunately, experiments show that 24-pin dot-matrix printers in graphics mode print at about half the speed of 9-pin printers. The manufacturer has had to slow down the 24-pin printers in order to keep the heads from heating up.

Laser and inkjet printers can print dots so fast in graphics mode that the paper movement is still the bottleneck within the printer. More often, however, the cable is the bottleneck. Recall that at 300 dpi, it would take 15 minutes to send a full page in graphics mode at 9,600 bps. The laser or the inkjet printer is rarely the bottleneck in graphics mode. To relieve the cable bottleneck, the parallel port has been redesigned to transmit data up to 10 times faster than the serial port. This means that the entire page can be transmitted in 1.5 minutes compared to 15 minutes. Because lasers can print eight pages per minute, the cable is still the bottleneck. Inkjet printers, however, can print an effective page-per-minute rate of only 1.2 pages per minute, so they can turn into the bottleneck.

Besides the cable and the printer bottlenecks, a common bottleneck is the PC software. Because the PC software has to compute the dots to be sent to the printer, the time it takes to do this can be the bottleneck. In fact, in most applications, PCs and XTs are almost certainly the bottleneck. In other words, when printing in graphics mode with an IBM PC or IBM XT, it really doesn't matter how fast the printer or the cable is. The PC will slow down the whole process. Most PCs are fast enough today that graphics-mode printing is a toss-up. Sometimes it is the PC software; sometimes it is the cable, and sometimes it is the printer.

You can determine easily whether the software is the bottleneck by looking at the on-line or ready lights on the printer. These lights usually flash when the printer is receiving data. If the lights are flashing constantly, the printer is the bottleneck. If the lights flash with pauses, the cable or the PC is the bottleneck.

Object-Mode Speed

Object-mode printers require that objects be sent to them. Object descriptions consist of character descriptions, so just characters are usually sent. If the formulas describing the object need to be sent, they consist of characters also. The quantity of formula information is usually less than a typical 12-point bit-mapped version. After you send the object description, you can refer to the object only by name. This means that the PC software usually has little work to do, and the printer cable does not have much information sent through it. Unfortunately, sometimes PC software's native mode of operation is not object-oriented. In order to print, PC software has to ask the object printer to simulate a graphics printer or reformat its data into object format. Either method takes time. As a result, PC software or the cable can be the bottleneck with object printers, but usually, this is not the case.

Usually, object printers are the bottlenecks. The object printer is responsible for changing the formulas into dots before printing, and this process is slow. For this reason, object printers have developed font caches and hard disks. Object printers usually have between 2M and 4M of memory with fast CPUs. Depending on the object sent, object printers can spend seconds or hours computing the dots. Depending on the resolution asked for, up to 70M of data may be created for a page. This is when it is necessary to have a hard disk attached to the printer.

You can use the object laser printers attached to PCs for the final, camera-ready output for low-quality publications. Often, people use these printers to proof a document before they send it to high-resolution laser printers owned by print shops. In the PC object-laser world, the time required for printing is an important factor. Usually, people are willing to sacrifice time for higher resolution only in the final camera-ready printout. If the object printer has color capability, the time can go from minutes to days easily. Most object laser printers are being developed with the latest and fastest processor and memory technology available.

Factors influencing the speed in object printers include the fonts, memory available, presence of a printer hard disk, and the version of object-imaging software in the printer. Fonts stored in the ROMs of object printers always print faster than those downloaded. Thus, the more fonts a printer comes with, the faster it will print. Certain company's fonts are faster than others, whether they are stored in ROMs or downloaded.

Small amounts of memory slow down the imaging process. As long as memory is large enough to hold an image, more memory does not speed the process. A printer hard disk can speed the printing process noticeably if there is too little memory. Printer hard disks are a little slower than memory. But, if a hard disk isn't present and if there is not enough memory available, a document can take eight times longer to print.

If the Apple LaserWriter IINT is used as a bench mark (its speed is 1.00), the top-of-the-line Apple LaserWriter IINTX is between 1.23 and 2.16 times faster, depending on the file it is printing. Alternative top-of-the-line printers are between 1.8 and 2.34 times faster. Clones of the Apple LaserWriter are between 1.09 and 2.48 times faster. Older versions of the Apple LaserWriter are between .45 and 1.00 times slower. There does not seem to be a price/speed correlation. When changing from 300-dpi to 400-dpi and 600-dpi laser printers, the times stay the same, even though much more data is being manipulated. This means that the 400-dpi and 600-dpi laser printers must be operating with faster processors, more memory, and hard disks, just to keep up with their lower resolution cousins.

When you are printing massive documents or many small documents, the number of sheets that the paper tray holds can limit speed. While you change the paper, the printer gets a rest. If you have to change the paper frequently, not as much work can be done. For more details on this, see the discussion on paper trays later in this chapter.

Reviewing Dot-Matrix Features

Dot-matrix printers come in all sorts of shapes, sizes, and speeds. The print heads are 9, 18, or 24 pins. The 9-pin print heads are the slower, bottom-of-the-line printers and are discounted to less than $200. The 24-print heads enter the market at about $400 and extend all the way up into the laser printer price range. The 18-pin print heads are all specialty printers, usually designed to go fast—as fast as 800 cps. This is twice as fast as a dot-matrix printer. Dot-matrix printers can use up to 12/1000 inch, or one millimeter. Twelve millimeters are equal to the thickness of approximately three sheets of paper and two carbons.

Printing Mailing Labels and Other Output Types

One of the biggest problems with mailing labels is that they gum up the paper path. This happens to all dot-matrix printers. The damage is done after printing labels. Many people try to save as many of the mailing labels as possible by reversing the direction that the labels flow through the printer. These people grab the labels on the inbound path and pull them out of the printer. Unfortunately, no labels come out. The labels peel off inside the printer, gumming up everything. Often, you can use a cloth rag to clean the platen without removing the platen. If you cannot feed the paper through the path anymore, find a thin, flexible, plastic ruler. Force the ruler through the paper path and push out the mailing label. If this does not work, you must remove the platen. The process of removing the platen, cleaning, and reassembling it can take up to four hours. The best solution to this problem is to buy a second printer to use only for mailing labels.

> **TROUBLE-SHOOTING TIP** Teach people to waste mailing labels. If the mailing labels get stuck, teach people to clean the printer before the labels dry. Use a flexible plastic ruler to push the labels out and clean the platen with a rag; then you will not have to take the printer apart.

In addition to printing mailing labels, you may want to use your printer to make stencils. The 24-pin dot-matrix printer can make excellent stencils—even better than typewriters. The little holes created can deposit more precise quantities of ink, making the mimeographed documents look much better. Many people remove the printer's ribbon to more accurately control the holes created. The drawback of printing stencils is that they can gum up the dot-matrix print head.

> **HINT** When you print with certain mimeograph stencil brands, wax from the stencil can gum up the dot-matrix printer pins. Try leaving a thin, faint, old fabric ribbon in to shield the print head. Also, purchase stencils made especially for computer printers.

> **HINT** When making drawings, underlining, or drawing rules, try using dotted lines rather than solids when printing on stencils. Solid lines tear the stencil and make reproduction hard and sometimes impossible. The same is true for printing solid black; instead, try to print using gray fill patterns.

Reviewing Tractor-Feed Options

Tractor feed is the most popular method of pulling paper through dot-matrix and daisywheel printers. When printing in massive quantities, tractor feed is the only way to get paper into the printer. Tractor feeds are usually pull-only. The tractor is above the print head and pulls the paper out of a box below. The next most common tractor is a bi-directional or push-pull tractor. The idea here is for the tractor to be able to back the paper up to print subscripts and superscripts correctly. Some printers come with two tractor feeds. These printers are usually high-speed and designed to support two forms in one printer—an airline ticket operation may use two tractor feeds, for example. The problem with printers that use two tractor feeds is that it takes a minute to switch between the two tractors.

Dot-matrix printers vary widely with regard to how paper is fed into the tractor and out of the printer. In many printers there are two options for pulling paper: back-to-top and bottom-to-top. Each method has its advantages.

Back-to-top is the traditional paper path of dot-matrix printers. This method has several problems, however. The data and power cables interfere with the paper path. The paper is fed crooked; the cables pinch the paper against a wall, or the cables catch paper edges. Paper coming out the top stacks on top of the paper coming in, causing problems. The paper coming out the top joins the paper coming in and wraps around the platen creating a big mess (see fig. 5.2).

The *bottom-to-top* paper path is an alternative method. Many printers have the capability to pull up paper stacked directly beneath the printer. One advantage of this method is that gravity helps guide the paper. Another advantage is that the printer and its paper do not take up as much space as the back-to-top method (see fig. 5.3). Disadvantages are that special furniture is required and that paper-loading requires two people. One person has to push the paper up from the bottom while another person catches it as it comes up through the print head. Because of these disadvantages, bottom-to-top paper-feeding is most often used only when the printer is dedicated to a certain task. A typical application is printing sales receipts or mailing labels.

> HINT | When shopping for a printer, always try to insert paper into the printer to see how easy this task is.

Tearing Paper

Many people hate to waste paper. If a document does not fill up a page, don't try to save the rest of the page to print the next document. Tearing in the

Fig. 5.2.

Paper wrapping around the platen.

Fig. 5.3.

A printer pulling paper up from the bottom.

Paper coming out the top of the printer

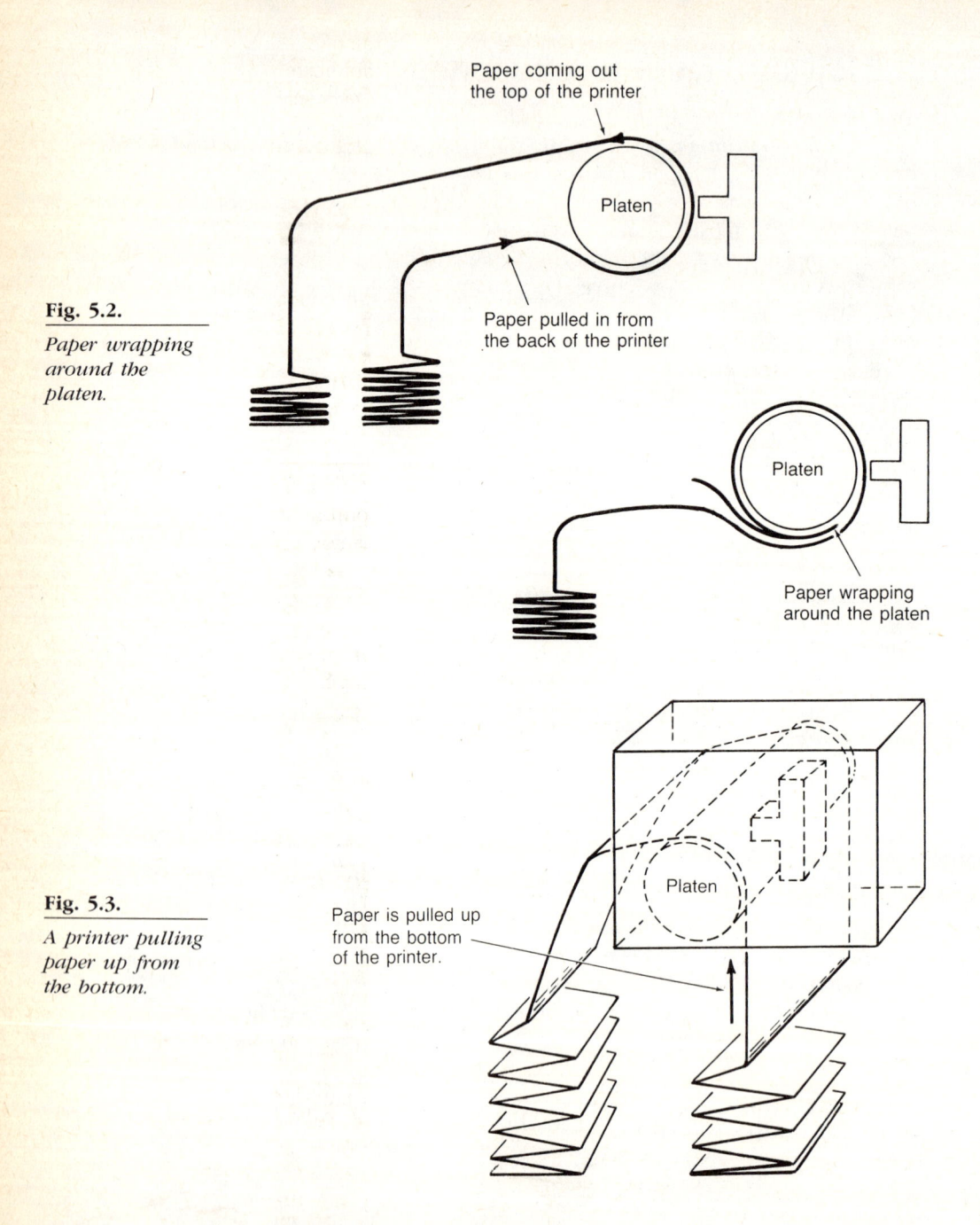

Paper pulled in from the back of the printer

Paper wrapping around the platen

Paper is pulled up from the bottom of the printer.

middle of a sheet of paper, instead of the perforations, stresses all the printer components in the paper path. Eventually, these components will not pull paper right.

To avoid tearing in the middle of a sheet of paper, you often have to eject a blank page so that tearing on the perforation is possible. This is because the tractor is usually about an inch or two above the platen. Because the tractor needs to grab paper in order to pull paper, there has to be some wasted paper between the top of the print head and the tractor feed. This area is called the tear-off or dead zone (see fig. 5.4).

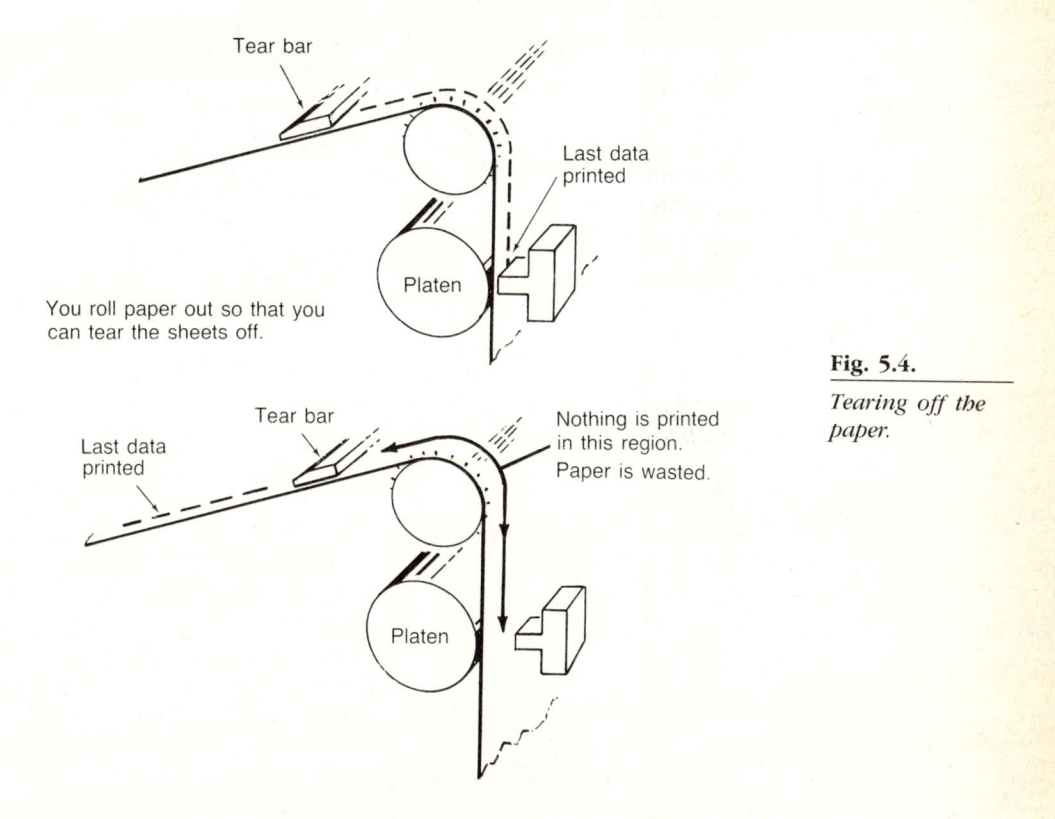

Fig. 5.4.

Tearing off the paper.

Actually, only two or three inches need to be wasted each time. But, then the page perforations do not match up any more. Following is a summary of the attempts that have been made to solve this problem:

❏ *Removing the platen and replacing it with a tractor.*
Unfortunately, it was impossible to make this process easy and accurate enough to be worthwhile. Usually, the tractor and platen were not put in correctly, and the quality of the output suffered. Users stopped buying these printers because they wanted the convenience of being able to use tractor-feed and friction-feed paper.

❑ *Mounting the tractor on the same bar as the platen.* This method proved to be an elegant solution. Not as much paper was wasted, and the tractor and friction feed did not fight each other. The paper did not crinkle as much, and the holes did not strip out as much. Many people still love these types of printers. The problem was that the tractor's sprockets could not slide to accommodate different form widths (see fig. 5.5).

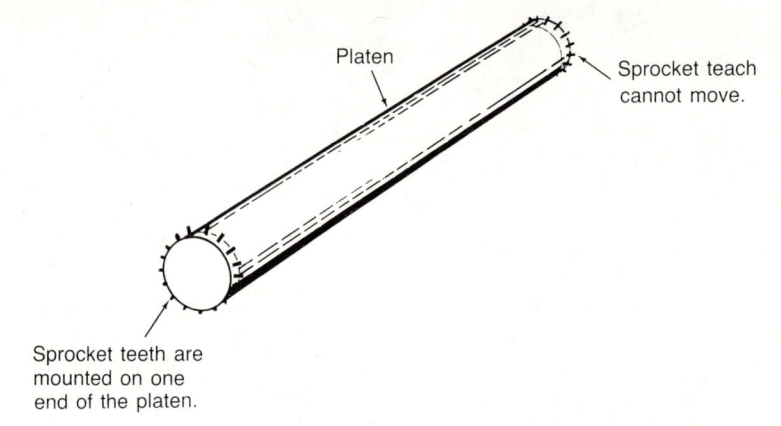

Fig. 5.5.

Sprocket teeth mounted on ends of the platen.

Platen

Sprocket teach cannot move.

Sprocket teeth are mounted on one end of the platen.

❑ *Using the tractor to push paper up to the print head rather than pull it.* The problem with this system is that you still need a roller bar to hold paper against the platen above the print head. This roller bar can be lifted automatically, but when it breaks you are forced to lift the roller bar by hand and insert the paper. Then, all the advantages of the push tractor are gone (see fig. 5.6).

❑ *Pressing the tear button.* This is a feature on some of the more modern printers. When you push this button, the printer temporarily pushes a piece of paper out of the printer so that you can tear it off; then it pulls the paper back into the printer so that it can print on the first line. This feature is similar to automatic windows in a car; it is marvelous when it works.

HINT | During the sample printout demonstration of a printer, watch how much paper is wasted during the tear-off process.

The most successful attempt to stop wasting so much tractor feed paper has been to try to make the paper path straight and flat through the printer. Rather than curling around a platen, the paper moves over the platen (see

Chapter 5: Printer Hardware Features **201**

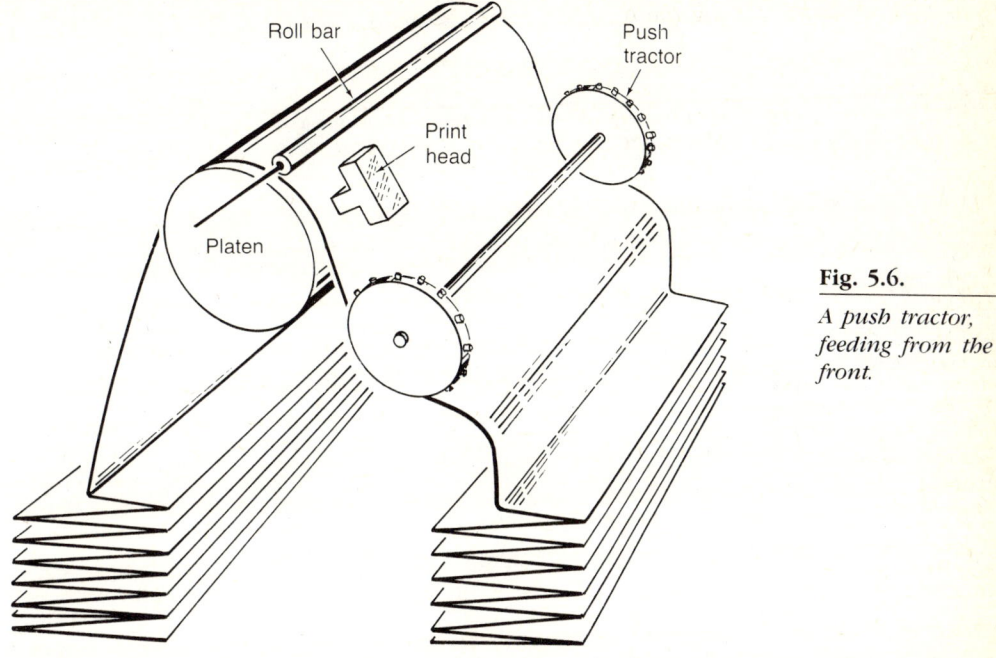

Fig. 5.6.

A push tractor, feeding from the front.

fig. 5.7). With the straight-line paper path, there are fewer problems with stencils and multipart forms. However, the printer is unable to absorb the printing noise. These printers are the noisiest ones on the market. The other drawback is that the paper feeds in the front and out the back, which tends to look messy.

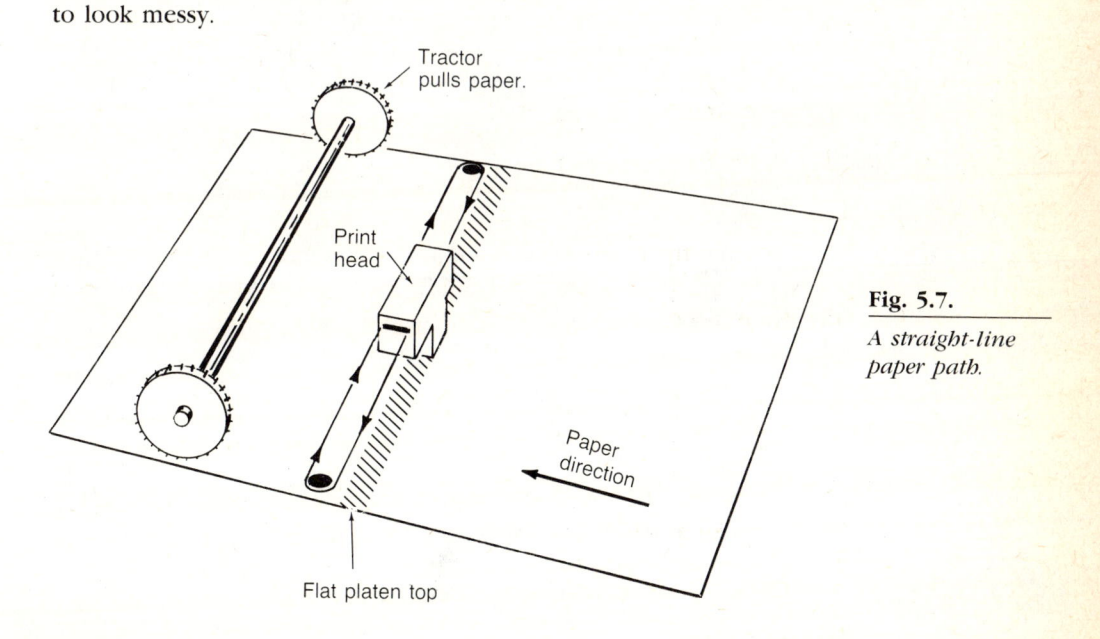

Fig. 5.7.

A straight-line paper path.

Switching from Hand-Feed to Tractor-Feed

Many times you may want to insert single sheets of paper or envelopes into your dot-matrix printer. You can do this in one of three ways:

❑ *Remove the fanfold paper.* Removing the tractor paper from the printer is the old-fashioned solution. This takes time, and occasionally when you replace the fanfold paper, you may forget to turn off the friction feed. This can cause the paper to crinkle or cause the holes on the side of the fanfold paper to strip, leaving paper shreds everywhere.

❑ *Park the fanfold paper.* A feature that has become popular is a button on the front of the dot-matrix that "parks" the fanfold paper out of the way. Then, hand-fed sheets can be printed. Later, you simply "unpark" the fanfold paper.

❑ *Lay the envelope or sheet on top of the fanfold.* Some printer companies have decided that people are perfectly willing to waste fanfold paper and allow a hand-fed envelope or paper to ride through the printer on top of the fanfold. The envelope is printed on, yet the fanfold piece of paper underneath it is blank.

In many printers, the hand-fed sheets are grabbed by the printer. You do not have time to make decisions about left margins and paper alignment. The paper is usually positioned exactly above the print head.

What is sacrificed to obtain the automatic paper feature is the capability to line up hand-fed sheets of paper using an old typewriter trick. Insert the paper around the platen and then grab all four corners. Line the corners up perfectly. Then, clamp down on the friction feed. The paper should be perfectly square with the platen.

Using the Paper-Out Switch

In the early history of dot-matrix printers, there were several wires in the Centronics parallel port that were supposed to indicate different fault conditions to the PC. The PC software usually messed up and translated all these fault conditions into one condition called "paper out." Even today, when PC DOS detects a problem with the printer, it assumes that you have run out of paper. This topic is explored more thoroughly in Chapter 14, "Troubleshooting."

There also is a paper-out switch in the printer. Early dot-matrix printer manufacturers wanted to make certain that the print head did not print without paper, and therefore, ruin the platen. Unfortunately, the paper-out switch is located early in the paper path—perhaps three inches before the print head.

This means that the printer will think it is out of paper while the print head is printing a line three inches from the bottom of the page. In effect, there is no way to print in the bottom three inches of the last page to go through the printer (see fig. 5.8). The only solution is to disable the paper-out switch.

TROUBLE-SHOOTING TIP | If you manually insert a page, chances are the printer will think that it is out of paper prematurely, because it cannot print on the bottom three inches of a page. Try disabling the paper-out switch.

HINT | Printing on the platen causes the rubber of the platen to harden. This reduces the capability to make good-looking characters and to grab paper. In addition, it makes the platen dirty, smearing ink on the backs of papers. Later, when the paper is stacked, the ink comes off the back and smudges the front.

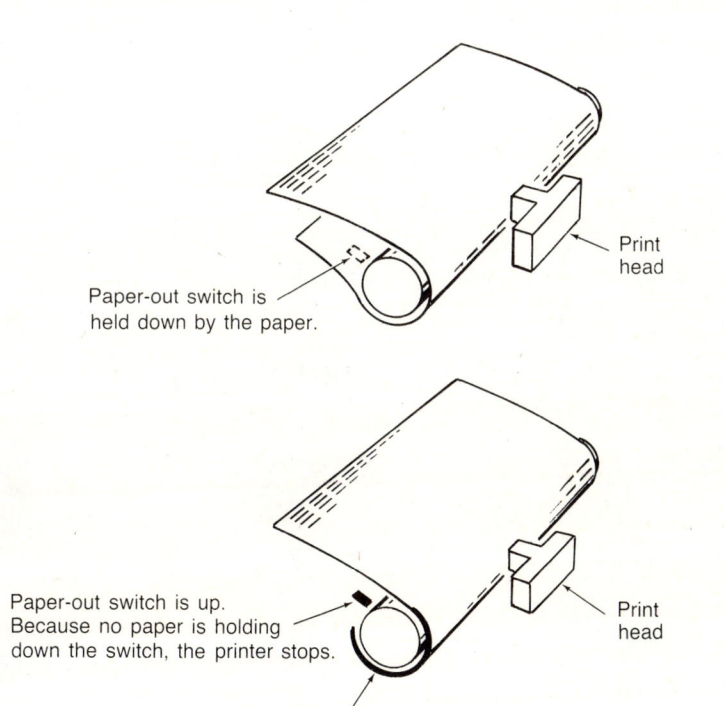

Fig. 5.8.

A poorly located paper-out switch.

You can disable the paper-out switch by doing one of four things:

- *Adjusting the software.* This is the preferable method. Some printers can ignore their paper-out switches if the proper command is sent to them by PC software.

- *Adjusting the dip switch inside the printer.* See your printer's manual.

- *Adjusting the paper-out switch.* Locate the paper-out switch by pulling strips of paper through the paper feed path. Then, try to put a piece of tape over the switch. Paper-out switches are usually mechanical types of switches that can be held down with a piece of tape.

- *Electronically shorting the switch together.* Take the printer apart, cut the switch out of the circuit, strip the ends of two wires, and twist together the ends of the wires (recommended only for techies).

The first option temporarily disables the paper-out switch through software; then it turns the paper-out switch back on. The second, third, and fourth options disable the paper-out switch and are dangerous. If the printer continues printing with no paper, the platen gets dirty and can become pitted and harden. The print head can become damaged. Most print heads today are made out of pot metal; the pot metal holding the individual print head wires wears out before the wires bend, break, or stop firing. Printing without paper will cause the pot metal to wear out.

Using Cut-Sheet Feeders and Paper Trays

Cut-sheet feeders use gravity to pull wads of paper into the printer. These feeders stick up out of the printer and make it much taller than it needs to be. Avoid these feeders. Luckily, they are disappearing slowly from the market. Laser printers have been so successful with the copier machine-like paper trays that paper trays are starting to appear in dot-matrix printers.

Paper trays will eventually be the method of choice for any dot-matrix work. The temporary paper-ejection feature that advances the paper so that you can tear it off, and then retracts the paper to the first line will not be needed. You will not need to park the tractor feed paper. You will not need to disable the paper-out switch. The big question really is when does tractor-feed and fanfold paper die? It does not look as though wide-carriage paper (approximately 11-by-17 inches) will ever be supported by paper trays. However, demand for wide-carriage printing has decreased tremendously with the advent of compressed laser fonts.

A choice must be made between using the tractor-feed method and using paper trays. Even if both methods are possible in a printer, they usually cannot be installed at the same time. Only the very high speed, 18-pin dot-matrix printers (costing approximately $3,000) support tractor feed and a couple of paper trays at the same time, with software selecting where the paper comes from.

Cleaning the Printer

Dot-matrix printers accumulate more dust and dirt than almost any other electrical device. Dust and dirt act a like a blanket and trap the heat chips that are trying to be released into the air. The chips heat up, but the case does not become hot to the touch.

To clean the printer, unplug the printer cable and the power cable. Just turning off the printer will not protect you from electric shock. There is no warning sticker on the lids of most printers, despite the fact that they are much more dangerous than the insides of a PC. There are usually only a few screws holding the lid on the printer. After you remove the lid, vacuum or blow out all the dust. Don't blow dust all over the room.

Changing Ribbons

Changing dot-matrix printer ribbons can be an easy process of just snapping one ribbon out and putting in another ribbon. In some dot-matrix printers, it is more difficult. For example, the light may have to be just perfect. Some printer companies actually ship clear plastic gloves to use while changing the ribbon so that your fingers don't get dirty.

Ribbons have been a major problem with printers for a long time. OKIDATA made big waves by trying to use the ribbon that became more or less the standard for manual typewriters. The OKIDATA ribbon changed direction. Other ribbons are in cartridges that essentially contain a large continuous loop. Some of these loops actually have a half twist in them. The half twist causes the ribbon to be used more efficiently. Both sides are used and both the top and bottom halves will be used equally.

You should keep some things in mind when using unofficial replacement ribbons:

- ❏ Damage can occur if the ribbon-drive gears and carriage-drive motor do not line up with the cartridge-drive opening.
- ❏ Re-inking devices cause damage to print head wires and other metal and plastic parts due to chemicals used in the ink. Some inks

contain acid and caustic chemicals that can pit metal parts and deteriorate completely the plastic parts. Other inks (especially old typewriter re-inking kits) gum up the print head, clogging the firing mechanism and destroying the print head.

- ❏ Some print heads require the use of a specific ribbon. The wrong thickness or the wrong ink can damage the print head.

Varying Fonts

Dot-matrix fonts still vary. Laser fonts all look the same, but dot-matrix printers are still putting out different-looking fonts. Because the dot-matrix fonts usually cannot be upgraded with downloadable fonts or font cartridges, study the sample printouts in the magazines. You will have to live with these fonts in the IBM-PC world. In the Macintosh world, don't bother looking at the fonts; you will rarely use them. In the Macintosh world, the screen fonts will be sent in graphics mode to the dot-matrix printer.

Locating Ports, Data Cables, and Power Cords

In dot-matrix printers, the location of the power and printer cables is important. Traditionally, the power and data cables come out the back of the printer. The fanfold tractor paper has to be pulled around and through these cables to get into the printer. It is a constant battle to arrange the cables and paper so that they don't fight each other.

Some printer companies actually mount the power and data cables on the side of the printer. This is almost always good if the cables are on the side closest to the PC and power outlet. If the PC is on the other side, it is in some cases worse. Again, another no-win situation.

Many companies make wire or plastic stands for the printer to sit in that are attractive and effective at keeping the paper and cables separate. Some printer companies are starting to include fold-out legs on the bottom of the printer that serve the same purpose and save you the $40 cost of one of these stands.

Dot-matrix printers also have dip switches. The most common place for them today is underneath the print head. The print head needs to be moved to one side. Sometimes a metal lid or plastic lid covers the switches, but usually these switches are easy to get to.

Controlling Printer Noise

Dot-matrix printers make the most noise of all printers being sold today. The following table enables you to compare how much noise they make.

Sound	Decibels
Gun Muzzle Blast	140
Rock Concert	120
Auto Horn	115
Chain Saw	100
Truck Traffic	90
Average Dot-Matrix	72
Dot-Matrix Variation	50-80
Typewriter	60
Average Office	50
Rustling Leaves	20

Printers use speakers to indicate running out of paper and other error conditions. Some printers do not use speakers anymore. By vibrating the pins in the dot-matrix printer head, different noises can be made to serve the same purpose.

Noting Temperature Ratings

If a printer has to be operating in a dirty, hazardous, hot environment, the only candidate today is the dot-matrix printer. Certain 18-pin varieties are specifically designed for stressful environments.

Reviewing Inkjet Printers

Inkjet printers have a long history, but only recently have they become popular. Inkjets struggle for identity, yet they remain popular in diverse niche markets. They have the resolution of a laser, but often the features of a dot-matrix printer. If you need large sheets of paper (16 inches wide) at 300 dpi, your only choice is an inkjet printer.

The speed of inkjet printers places them in the dot-matrix category. Sometimes, inkjets are sold like a dot-matrix printer with an inkjet head; sometimes, they are sold with a great deal of memory like a laser printer. Inkjet printers range in cost from $200 to $3,000. The inkjet is probably the lightest, smallest, portable printer. One of the fanciest printers on the market is an inkjet—it produces raised ink—the kind of ink that mounds up on the paper. Because of the past failures of inkjets, much of society has a bad impression of these printers. This reputation prevents inkjets from directly competing with dot-matrix printers.

Comparing Paper and Ink Costs

Because the inkjet printer is still a specialty item, it is important to consider the cost of the consumables—ink and special paper stock. Usually, you must buy ink from the manufacturer, and there is no price competition. The ink cartridges last for about 500 pages, compared to 1,000 pages for most dot-matrix ribbons. And inkjet cartridges cost twice as much. Although most inkjet cartridges do not require special paper, many are sensitive to different paper types. The best printouts from inkjet printers are still obtained on special paper.

Inkjets have higher operating costs—even higher than that of laser printers—even when limiting analysis to ink and toner. The overall life-cycle costs of an inkjet printer can approach that of a laser, even if the capital investment in the laser is twice as much.

Determining the Resolution

The inkjet print head is similar to that of a dot-matrix. Instead of having pens, though, it has nozzles. Some inkjets have 12 nozzles, but 32 nozzles is more common. The print quality of inkjets varies from worse than dot-matrix printers to better than laser printers. Most fall somewhere between the best dot-matrix and laser printers. The best inkjet printers can print at the same resolution (300 dpi) as a laser.

The combination of ink chemistry and paper type determines print quality. Some inkjet printers offer different types of ink for different types of paper. When the ink does not match, the printout quality suffers. In fact, copier machine paper has two sides. One side causes the correct ink to bleed all over the paper. When printed on the other side, the ink looks fine. Some inks are water-soluble, so a drop of water can ruin the page. Other inks come in pellets; the pellets melt inside the printer. This is how the raised-ink printer works.

> HINT | When print quality does not look good with an inkjet printer, try turning the paper over. If this does not work, try changing to more expensive paper.

Warming Up the Printer

Because the raised-ink printer takes 10 minutes to warm up, it does not have an on/off switch; you just plug the printer into the outlet and it remains on permanently. Although this is an extreme, all inkjet printers have the same symptom to a degree. Inkjet printers work best when in continual use. This is because ink is a fluid. When a fluid sits still, it tends to clog up. To combat this, some inkjet printers circulate and filter their ink when it is not in use. This is called a *self-cleaning* feature.

Considering a Laser Alternative

Most inkjet printers sold are targeted for those interested in laser-printer quality at a cheaper price. For the cheaper capital investment, the inkjet printer is much slower. It prints at about 1.5 pages per minute, versus six pages a minute for most lasers. You must replace the inkjet cartridge every 500 pages, versus every 3,000 pages for lasers. The inkjet printer is designed to print about 1,000 pages a month, versus 3,000 pages for the average laser.

The popular inkjet printer is sold with 128K of memory and fewer fonts than the laser. Because most lasers come with 512K minimum, 128K is much smaller. Fewer fonts can be downloaded.

Inkjet design engineers have two choices for implementing graphics mode. The first choice is to print the graphics in *band mode* (printing a horizontal band of graphics), like dot-matrix printers. The second choice is to buffer the whole page and print it all at once like a laser. Because the inkjet performs at dot-matrix-type speeds, the band technique is more popular.

Most laser printers buffer a whole page in graphics modes. Although the benefits of whole-page buffering are great—for example, reprinting the page if the paper jams—these benefits also could be implemented in the PC software. Currently, however, most printers cannot tell the PC that the paper has jammed. Thus, printers are responsible for reprinting after a paper jam. Only laser printers currently are capable of doing this, because they are the only printers that can buffer a whole page.

Inkjet printers should really be compared to dot-matrix printers. They should be treated as high-resolution, dot-matrix printers with more font flexibility. Inkjets' big advantage over dot-matrix printers is the capability to accept downloaded fonts. There is no reason, however, that 24-pin dot-matrix printers could not develop this capability. In fact, dot-matrix printers technically have this capability; they just do not have the massive quantity of memory required. Furthermore, if copier machine prices are any indication of the bottom-line laser-printer prices, there is still room for low-end laser prices to drop below even that of the Hewlett-Packard LaserJet IIp (four pages per minute) street price of $900.

Reviewing Laser Printer Engines

Few laser printers are sold by the company whose name is on the printer. Most lasers can be divided into two parts: the engine and the computer. The engine usually is made by companies in the copier-machine market. The computer is added by a company in the printer market. Probably, the first popular laser printer was sold by Hewlett-Packard. The engine of the Hewlett-Packard LaserJet, for example, was made by Canon.

The engine part of a laser printer dictates most of the laser-printer features. When comparing the laser printers of companies that use the same engine, certain things are the same. Because of this, the features of laser printers are split into three sections: laser engines, features that manufacturers add to the laser engines, and object printers (see later sections in this chapter).

Engine Model

A laser printer's engine model is important for several reasons. First, many manufacturers use the same engine. This means that the engines share similar features (toner cartridges, for example), as well as similar problems. For example, Ricoh engines use a *white-writer* technology like copier machines and fax machines. This technology moves the laser over the area that is to remain white. Most other laser printers use their laser to draw where it wants toner to be placed. Because laser beams are not square, the *black-writer* lasers draw different-shaped dots than white-writer lasers. Black-writer laser dots tend to bloom, while white-writer lasers tend to pinch out the black areas. This means that lines will be narrower when printed on white-writer lasers, and fonts have to be redesigned. Obviously, picking a minority engine where everything is slightly different is not a good idea. Picking an engine is the first important step when purchasing a printer. The Cannon SX is the most popular model at the moment and also is the best.

These are some example model numbers of laser engines: Canon LBP-SX, Toshiba A-739, Casio LCS 130, Canon SX, Ricoh 4081, Fujitsu, Ricoh LP-1060, NEC LC 800, Canon TX, Minolta SP 140. Some of these companies are coming out with laser printers of their own. You would think that the laser engine company would know the engine so well that it would be able to design the computer part to take advantage of some "secret features" that were not revealed to other companies. Sadly, there are no "secret features."

Engine Type

In Chapter 2, these types of laser printers were reviewed: laser, liquid crystal shutter (LCS), and light emitting diode (LED). Laser printers are the most common. LCS printers are being positioned as low-priced alternatives. LED printers are often the highest priced. The LCS and LED printers have the advantages of fewer moving parts and less problems with text blurring or curving near the margins.

Engine Life

Like cars, printers have a lifetime. Rather than counting miles, they count pages printed, just like copier machines. After a certain number of pages, the copier falls apart. Laser printers are no exception. Dot-matrix and inkjet printers have no comparable statistic. A similar statistic does not exist because the alternative measure of component life, *mean time between failure* is used (see "Calculating the Mean Time between Failures," earlier in this chapter).

To convert mean time between failure to pages for comparison purposes, assume that mean time between failure is 18,000 hours, and that the dot-matrix printer is printing at 1.5 pages per minute. The page lifetime would be roughly 27,000 pages. Fanfold paper comes in boxes of 2,500 sheets, so this would equal about 11 boxes of paper.

In contrast, the most popular laser printer engine—found in the Canon SX and Canon LBP-SX—has a lifetime of 300,000 pages. The liquid crystal shutter printers have lifetimes of about 180,000 pages, and the lifetime of LEDs is about 600,000 pages. Laser printers are designed to print 10 times more pages in their lifetime. When using a laser printer, however, you probably print each page 10 times more often before printing the page correctly. You will waste 10 times more paper than you will with a dot-matrix. This does not mean that the laser printer will live longer than a dot-matrix. Use these numbers for comparison purposes before purchase. After purchase, these numbers have little value in predicting a specific, individual printer's life.

Duty Cycle

Duty cycle is usually measured in terms of working time versus total time. The duty cycle of printers working eight hours a day is 8 hrs./24 hrs. or 33 percent. When a printer is built, the motors and heating elements chosen usually need a rest. Of course, motors can be built that are intended to work continuously. Faster motors can be built for the same amount of money, however, if they are guaranteed a rest.

For example, automobile engines get a rest at every stop sign. These engines are designed to take advantage of traffic jams. If you put an automobile engine in an airplane, however, and ran it at a constant, reasonable number of revolutions per minute, the engine would fall apart quickly. This is because airplanes cannot rest. Similarly, a car driven on the highway only or in the city only may not have a good engine. Only the car that is driven with the blend of highway and city miles that the engineer planned on is going to live the longest.

Engineers of printers take this fact into consideration just as much as engineers of cars do. Engineers discovered a clever method of forcing laser printers to take a rest by making sure that they run out of paper frequently. This means there is a direct relationship between the paper tray size and the duty cycle.

A laser printer's duty cycle is measured in pages per month. The average laser printer is rated at 3,000 pages per moth. Normal dot-matrix printers and inkjet printers have a duty cycle of approximately 1,000 pages per month. To get a better picture of this rate, assume that your printer could possibly be working 40 hours per week, four weeks per month. This equals 9,600 possible minutes a month (40 $\times$ 4 $\times$ 60). You would have to average 1/3 of a page per minute every working minute of the day to have a chance at exceeding the duty cycle. The range of laser printers is 1,500 to 25,000 pages per month—or from 1/6 to 2.6 pages per minute. For this reason, you should not use your laser printer as a copier device. Go to a print shop or use a copier rather than print 30 copies of that 200-page proposal.

Resolution

Laser printer resolution is almost universally 300 dpi. Some 400-dpi lasers are available, and 600 dpi exists. It looks like 600 dpi is the maximum possible out of a toner/copier-machine type of technology. Higher resolutions are going to require film technologies. What is limiting the increase from 300 dpi to 600 dpi is the printer memory required to take advantage of the resolution when in graphics mode. For example, 300 dpi would require about 1M of RAM for a full 8-by-11-inch page. 600 dpi would require about 4M. Add another .5M for software and another 1M to 2M for fonts, and the memory requirements quickly become expensive.

Speed

Speed is measured in pages per minute for laser printers. Typical ratings are eight pages per minute, and the range is 6 to 12 pages per minute. There is a wide variation in the models available. When operating in character mode, this speed difference is noticeable. When operating in graphics mode or object mode, the speed differences are not very noticeable.

Stacking Pages in the Right Order

Paper can come out face-up or face-down. When paper comes out face-up, page one ends up at the bottom. Putting the pages in the proper order takes time. Because early lasers pushed paper out the front, many people learned just to let it fall on the floor. During the printing process, the paper was stacked in the proper order. Plastic trays then were developed to catch the paper (see fig. 5.9).

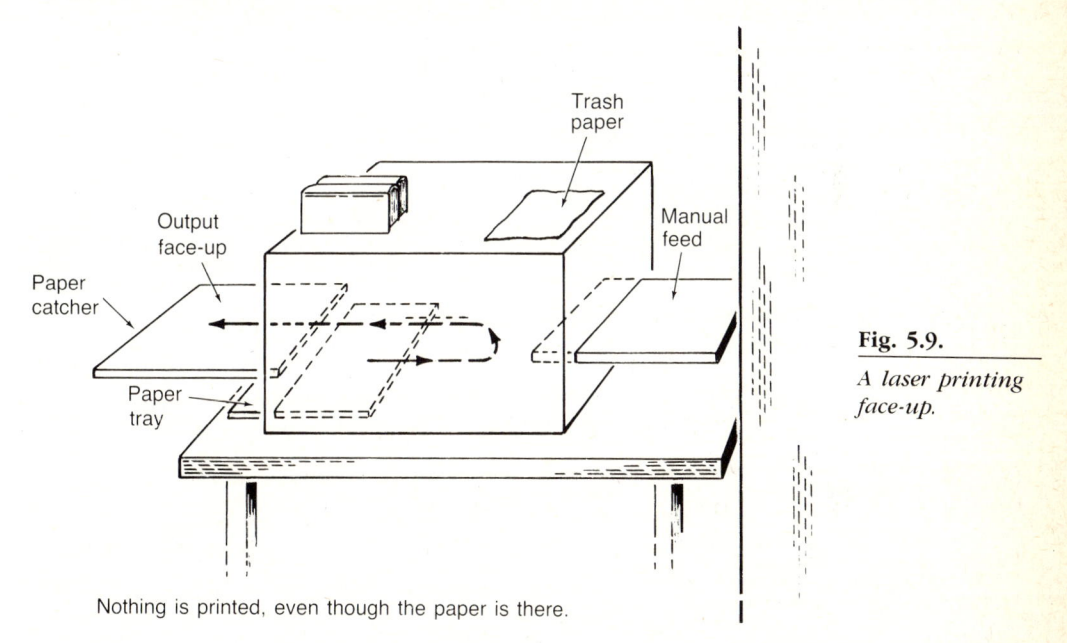

Fig. 5.9.

A laser printing face-up.

Nothing is printed, even though the paper is there.

There were other problems with the early laser printers. The plastic paper-catcher stuck out of the printer. Because most people placed the printer on a table for convenient access, the paper tray usually ended up sticking out into an aisle. This caused people who were walking by to accidentally break the paper tray off, or to hurt themselves. Another problem occurred with the printer when people tried to feed legal paper manually. They had to insert the paper on the side opposite of the paper tray. Usually, this was the side of the printer that was jammed next to the wall. To use it, you had to rotate the printer so that both sides were accessible. The neat thing about this early laser was that the top was completely flat; you could stack books on top of it.

> HINT: If the laser printer pushes pages out the front upside-down and you are tired of sorting them, let them fall on the floor. They will stack in the proper order.

The next generation of lasers defaults to stacking the pages face-down (see fig. 5.10). This method stacks the pages in the proper order. Some laser printers can move bins up and down to collate multiple copies of the same document, much like a copier machine. The manual feed slot is above the new paper tray, so it is much easier to use. For normal operation, the front and top of the printer is used. This means that you cannot stack books on top of it. The other drawback is that the paper has to move around more corners. Straight paper paths are better for thick paper, and have less paper jam potential.

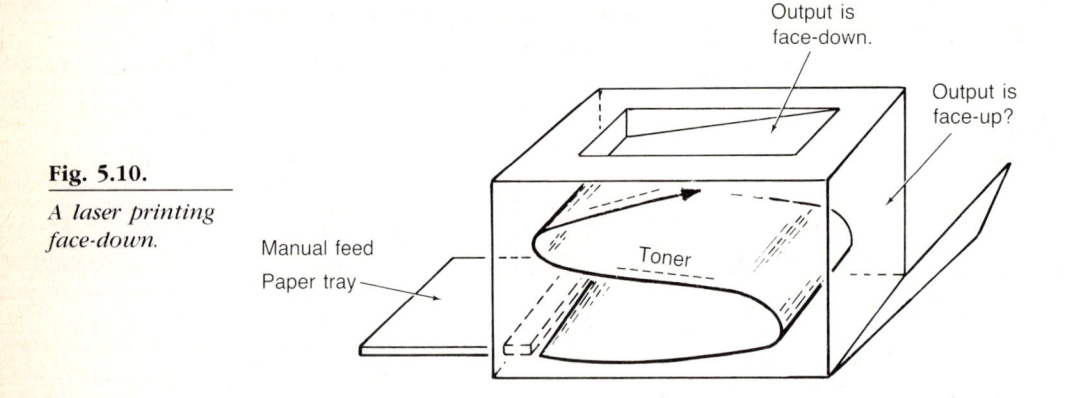

Fig. 5.10.

A laser printing face-down.

Paper Weight, Thickness, and Smoothness

Paper weight refers to how heavy or stiff the paper is. Weight is measured in pounds. A typical laser engine can accept 16 lbs. to 24 lbs. of paper. The range is 16 lbs. or 17 lbs. to 36 lbs. Paper weight is measured according to how much it actually weighs on a scale due to gravity. The international measurement of paper weight is grams per square meter. 16 lbs. is equal to 60 grams per square meter.

The thickness of paper is technically called the *caliper* of paper. The thickness is measured in thousandths of an inch or millimeters. Most engines can use paper between 3.7mm and 7.5mm.

Paper can be too smooth or too rough. Most of the expensive bond paper or water-stamped paper is too rough. Smoothness is measured on a Sheffield scale. Typical laser printers support paper between 100 and 300 on the Sheffield scale.

HINT | Laser printers will print on the cheapest copy machine paper available. But, when the humidity is high, pieces of paper stick together. To prevent this, paper manufacturers put powder between the sheets. The heavier the paper (and therefore more expensive), the more dust accumulates. The more dust there is, the more uneven the paper surface becomes, because the dust tends to stick and create ridges. The more uneven the paper, the poorer the image. Cheap paper costs between $2 and $4 per bundle of 500 sheets. A bundle of 500 sheets is called a *ream*. Ideally, the ream is packaged in polylaminated moisture-proof wrap. A ream of special laser paper, Hammermill laser stock, is discounted to about $5 a ream.

Paper also has *wax pick* measurements that determine the strength of the paper's surface. Cheap paper can leave lint inside your printer, ruining print quality and shortening the engine's life.

Paper Jams

Certain print engines jam up easier than others. If the paper is fed at an angle rather than lying flat in a paper tray, the print engine seems to have more trouble. The printer uses gravity to pull a wad of paper if the tray is at an angle. If the paper tray is flat, the printer uses gravity to separate the pieces of paper. In some print engines, it is hard to reach the places in which paper jams. In some printer engines, the drum or OPC (optical photoconductor) is exposed to room light during the process of clearing out the jammed paper.

HINT | If the paper jams, try a new ream of paper. Fan the paper to make sure that the dust added to keep the sheets from sticking is working. If paper from the new ream works, put the remaining paper in the ream in a moisture-proof container. This keeps the paper from absorbing water from the air and sticking to other sheets of paper.

HINT | If you want to save money spent on paper, you can turn pages over and print on the other side. But, consider this first: you will probably pay $5 to $24 per ream for toner, versus $2 to $6 for a ream of paper. If you want to save money, turn the print density knob all the way down. Printing on both sides of the paper is liable to cause more paper jams in the future.

Paper Chemistry

Do not use paper that contains too much acid. The pH should be 5.5 at a minimum. The paper most not scorch, melt, offset material, or release hazardous chemicals as it goes over the fuse bar. The fuse bar melts toner into the page at 200 degrees Celsius. Horizontal lines across the page are this hot for only 0.1 seconds; still, the paper can be hot. The fuse assembly normally is kept at a temperature of around 110 degrees Celsius. It jumps to 200 degrees when paper is inserted.

> HINT | Be careful when you run letterhead through the laser printer. Sometimes the ink used in the creation of the letterhead melts or is destroyed in the laser. In the worst case, it could gum up your fusing rollers.
>
> Like inkjet paper, laser and copier machine paper prints on one side better than another. The text looks better and the paper jams less. Look for some mark on the packaging material that indicates which side should be printed on.

Paper Trays

The engine determines how many pages can be put in a paper tray. Ideally, the faster the printer is, the higher its duty cycle will be; the longer the engine is supposed to live, and the deeper the paper tray is. Usually, this is true, but not always. Don't assume that the paper tray reflects the engine design.

Usually, paper trays are undersized, forcing you to change the paper more often. The engine rests while you are changing the paper. Paper trays hold between 100 sheets on the slow printers to 250 sheets on the fast printers. Typically, paper trays hold 200 sheets.

Envelope Feeder

Public expectations of an envelop feeder have never been met. The goal of printing addresses directly on envelopes as easily as printing mailing labels has never been achieved at a reasonable cost. You can hand feed envelopes easily one at a time. The $100-envelope feeders hold 10 envelopes. Functional envelope feeders cost $1,000 or more. Some print engines do not support envelope feeders. If the humidity is high, most lasers actually seal the envelopes while printing on them.

HINT | Practice manually feeding the envelope through the printer first. Watch the path it takes. Then switch to landscape printing mode and adjust the margins until the addresses are in the right place while printing on a piece of paper. Hold the paper and envelope up to a light. The light shining through should indicate where the addresses will appear on the envelope. When feeding the envelope through, open the flap, and smooth out the natural curl of the flap. Certain types of envelopes will not feed well, particularly those made of parchment paper.

TROUBLE-SHOOTING TIP | Sometimes, lasers will not print within a quarter of an inch of the edge of the envelope. Try attaching Post-It notes to the edge of the envelope. This fools the printer into thinking that the envelope is larger. The Post-It notes do not seem to get stuck in the laser printer. (Try this at your own risk).

HINT | Envelopes made out of paper with texture are going to jam. Choose smooth paper envelopes. Envelopes with diagonal seams and standard gummed flaps work the best. Also, make certain that the leading edge of the envelope has a sharp crease. This prevents the envelopes from jamming as much.

Manual Feed

Some laser engines sense when paper is in the manual feed slot and grab paper from that location. Other laser engines have to be told to look for a piece of paper in the manual feed location using the front panel or software in the PC. Still more engines force removal of paper trays in order to activate the manual feed feature. If you are planning to manually feed paper, you should investigate this last feature of the printer before you buy it.

HINT | The manual feed button in the Print dialogue box of a Macintosh application is there for the purpose of pausing between pages so that you can insert pages manually into the ImageWriter. If you are printing just one sheet on a LaserWriter, the manual feed button does nothing. Just stick the piece of paper in the manual feed slot and print.

Replacement Supplies

Like copier machines, laser engines have certain supplies and preventative maintenance procedures. How easy it is to perform the maintenance and how expensive the supplies are can drastically influence the cost of the printer. The cost issue is explored in Chapter 7. The replacement supplies are discussed in the following section.

Font Cartridge Slots

Different laser engines come with the capability to insert one, two, or three font cartridges. Because the size of these cartridges varies, it really does not matter how many cartridge slots there are. Fonts that fit on one cartridge range from 4 to 300 fonts. Probably more important is how much the font cartridges cost and the availability of these cartridges. Because the printer manufacturers control the contents of the font cartridges, it is possible for them to develop a monopoly by controlling the design of the cartridges. Therefore, it is important to purchase a laser printer that is popular enough that other companies are selling cartridges for the same printer. Competition lowers prices.

Blacker Blacks

Most laser printers print documents with black lines or objects on white paper. The casual observer usually judges a printout by the contrast between light and dark. More contrast, and even blacks, may seem better. Unfortunately, the trained observer has a different perspective. From the readability point of view, a print engine can be too black. If the printer is too black, the circles in letters fill up, and the letters look jammed together. The difference between bold and regular printing is not distinguishable. Printed versions of scanned photographs look too dark. Scanning the photo over and over again does not solve the problem.

> HINT | Avoid trying to print any page that has solid black objects. They never look good—even out of the best laser printers.

> HINT | Most laser printers have a print density dial. If the difference between bold and regular printing is hard to see, try changing the position of the knob. You could be wasting toner as well as producing ugly documents. Also, toner costs more per page than the paper.

Turn-On Time

Most laser printers warm up within a minute. The colder the room is, the longer it takes. The fusing assembly has to heat up so that toner can melt into the paper. This is what takes so long.

Considering Replacement Supplies

Laser printers are like gasoline engines. They need constant attention and are a source of tension. These are the disposable devices you need to keep laser printers running:

- Toner
- Light-sensitive drum or optical photo conductor (OPC)
- Developer
- Fuser
- Ozone filters
- Cleaning devices

Not all laser printers need all of these items. Some laser printers combine everything into one cartridge, typically called a toner cartridge. Most magazines assume that the convenience of everything in one cartridge costs more. After studying the manufacturer's maintenance specifications and list prices, this proves to be false. Print engines that use disposable cartridges are cheaper.

The costs of laser replacement supplies were computed for each ream (500 sheets) of paper. The costs ranged from $13 per ream to $24 per ream. There were no differences per ream price between laser, LED, and LCS printer engines. The pricing of these replacement supplies could be studied because different manufacturers used the same printer engines. Prices varied from $14 to $21 per ream for the same engine. Obviously, shopping around for laser replacement supplies is worthwhile.

Another factor that should influence your purchasing decision is how popular the print engine is. At the time of this printing, the most popular print engine is the Canon SX. Versions of it were used in the Hewlett-Packard LaserJet II and the Apple LaserWriter II series. Because of its popularity, the list price of the cartridge is $129. Third-party vendors discount the same new Cannon SX engine cartridge to $79. Used cartridges are available for $49. This engine has one of the best-looking outputs, as well as the most convenient and cheapest replaceable supplies. The total replacement supply costs drop from $13 per ream at list price, to $8 if discounted originals are used, to $5 for refilled/rebuilt cartridges.

> HINT: Because a ream of paper costs $2 and the disposables cost from $5 to $24 per ream, your time is better spent saving toner—not paper. Most laser printers have a print density dial. Keep the dial on low until you print the final draft.

Re-usable toner cartridges can save thousands of dollars. The trick to using them is to find a reputable manufacturer. It takes little money to set up a mail-order business refilling toner cartridges for laser printers. Some companies are saving money by doing this in-house. The simplest method of squeezing more life out of the toner cartridge is called "drill and fill." Drill a hole, empty out the spent toner, and fill the cartridge with new toner.

The market has matured enough that most refillers are doing much more than this simple cartridge-refilling procedure today. A good cartridge remanufacturer completely disassembles the cartridge, inspects each part for wear, performs any necessary repairs, cleans all parts and inner surfaces, lubricates the pieces, and recoats the photosensitive drum. Good used cartridges can produce better-looking documents than the original. Good refill companies can extend the cartridge life almost indefinitely.

> HINT: You can tell when a used toner cartridge comes from a fly-by-night company: occasional black streaks may appear on your paper, printing may be extremely light or extremely dark, and toner may leak inside the printer. If any of these things occur, you should find another company that reconditions used cartridges.

Rumors have been floating around about toner cartridges that may actually damage the printer or self-destruct after the first use. Not many people worry about this anymore. Certain companies wanted to prevent rebuilt cartridges. Whether these rumors were started by engineers to protect their print engines or by MBAs to control the market and make more money is uncertain. The rumors all mention an abrasive particle or corrosive chemical that is released when the toner is almost gone. The chemical or particle is supposed to destroy the cartridge and possibly leak out and damage the print engine. To combat these rumors, the more reputable toner rebuilders offer a type of service deal similar to the following example:

Send us a brand new cartridge. Let us check it out to remove the abrasives and corrosive chemicals. Then, let us track your toner cartridge's history and determine when it is too old to be rebuilt any more.

HINT | Rumors are circulating that envelopes damage cartridges and therefore the cartridges should not be rebuilt if they were used to print envelopes. Note which cartridges you use when you print envelopes. Find out for yourself whether this rumor is true.

HINT | Let your toner cartridge cool down before you throw it away. Otherwise, it may melt holes in your plastic trash cans.

If a printer does not use a cartridge that includes all of the replaceable supplies, you must learn more procedures, figure out more containers, and possibly break more things. The human mind is capable of comprehending only a certain number of buttons and gadgets. Don't make things harder than they have to be by purchasing a printer with a complicated toner system.

Also, there are practical reasons for discouraging the purchase of laser printers without cartridges. Most lasers with separate toner bins and OPCs have the problem of accidental toner spills. Toner spills are a mess; you will need a special vacuum cleaner to pick up this fine dust. Even worse than the spill problem is that the OPC is often exposed to light; this may happen if you tear off the front panel to change the toner or to clear a paper jam. The OPC then stops attracting toner, and white spots appear. Trained service personnel usually must adjust laser printers without toner cartridges. This means an additional cost of unavoidable on-site service. The best copier machines are heading toward the use of cartridges.

HINT | Dim the lights in the room and pull the curtains when working on a laser printer. Sunlight can damage the OPC drum.

TROUBLE-SHOOTING TIP | If successive cartridges print too light or too dark and the knob that adjusts how much toner is dispensed does not seem to have any effect, try this tip. Each toner cartridge has plastic holes or knobs that trip some microswitches in the lid of the laser printer. These switches communicate to the laser engine how sensitive the OPC drum is. Usually, you must order spare parts and replace these switches if they become jammed, dirty, or broken. Occasionally, the bristles of a comb, super glue, and a dab of duct tape will put the printer back together.

Trained service personnel means someone with a great deal of manual dexterity, patience, and practice. It also is helpful if they know proprietary secret procedures. In any case, it is always worthwhile to hover about two inches over the shoulders of these trained service professionals. Be sure to ask them many pesky questions while they are working—you may learn something and save your company money.

Reviewing Features Added to Laser Engines

Companies like Hewlett-Packard, Apple, and IBM purchase laser printer engines from companies like Ricoh and Canon. The engines they purchase have all the necessary parts in place. The laser manufacturer designs the computer and software that goes into the laser printer. Because different printer manufacturers often use the same type of printer engine, the features that they add to those engines determine the differences among laser printers.

Memory

Dot-matrix printers don't normally have enough memory for downloaded fonts. In graphics mode, they print a band or strip at a time, so they need just enough memory to hold the graphics data representing the strip. Normally, a dot-matrix printer has around 32K of memory. This is enough to hold a few downloaded symbols but not downloaded fonts.

In a standard laser printer, the amount of memory is 512K—expandable to 4.5M. Typically, character laser printers do not need more memory unless you need many character fonts downloaded at one time. Object-mode laser printers typically come with 2M of memory, although the maximum can be 12M. The typical maximum is 4M, however. More memory increases the number of fonts available and usually speeds up the printing process.

Fonts

Manufacturers put fonts in ROMs of the printer. These fonts are the fastest, so they should be the ones primarily used for optimal performance of the object printer. These fonts may be unique to the printer manufacturer, forcing you to buy all future fonts from that company. This encourages the company to charge a premium and makes availability poor.

Font Cartridges

Font cartridge design is controlled by the manufacturer. Purchase only laser printers that have font cartridges available from other sources. Otherwise, you will be stuck with paying too much money for poor quality and a limited selection of fonts from the same company that made the printer.

> **TROUBLE-SHOOTING TIP** If the font cartridges don't seem to be working, try asking the printer to print all internal fonts. If the cartridge fonts are not mentioned, yet the font cartridges are in place, try pushing them harder (while the printer is off, of course). There may be a connection problem.

Paper Trays

The manufacturer of an engine determines how many paper trays are available. One paper tray is the normal amount. Some laser printer manufacturers add a second tray. You could use one paper tray for letterhead and the other for plain sheets of paper. You can select which paper tray you want to use by sending certain commands to the printer or pushing buttons on the front of the printer. In some cases, you can replace a single paper tray with a dual paper tray; each tray holds half the paper. Other alternatives include sending the letterhead in graphics mode to the printer. Some laser printers use *forms* capability and will substitute paper-tray commands for form-changing commands. The need for multiple paper trays is most prevalent in IBM PCs operating in character mode.

Legal-size paper trays are available for approximately $100. Other paper tray sizes supporting European and Japanese sizes that are 8.5 inches or narrower are available also.

Front Panel

Front panel controls and lights are often a bit cryptic, but this should not influence a purchasing decision. Usually, only a few people ever learn what the buttons and lights mean. Apple LaserWriters have the simplest front panel, with just four LED indicator lights. Below the lights are icons that indicate what the lights do. The meanings of these icons are not clear. Laser printers can blink their lights in the following cases: when warming up, when receiving a document, when thinking about the document, when ready, when paper is moving, when paper is jammed, or when a partial page is present but not enough data is there to warrant printing a full page.

> HINT | When the Macintosh is printing, a box appears on-screen with a message that says the current status is "Processing Job." The screen flickers about every five seconds. Do not panic; nothing is wrong. You will see a small clock or some symbol on-screen that indicates all is alive and well.

Weight

Laser printers can weigh from 38 lbs. to 174 lbs. Even the 38-lb. printer is heavy enough to require two people to move it. Shipping something so heavy and so fragile long distances should be done with care. Always save the original carton that the printer came in. When moving, put the printer on a car seat—not the floor or the bed of a pickup (the floor vibrates too much). Treat it gently—like a hard disk.

Dimensions

The case the print engine comes in is usually not modified much by the printer manufacturer. Features such as the number of buttons and lights on the front panel are different, but the size and dimensions of the printer are the same. Some manufacturers add modules on the bottom to accommodate multiple paper trays.

Laser printers take a lot of space. The laser's cable is 15 ft., so the printer can be only this far away from the computer. Many people have unreasonable expectations about where they can put the printer. You can achieve longer distances using serial cables, but the data transfer rate slows down graphics-mode and font-downloading operations.

You can find printer cables that go underneath carpets and withstand people walking on them. These types of cables are expensive, however. You can hide regular cables in a plastic mound, but this is unattractive to some people.

Ports

Serial, parallel, SCSI, and Local Talk are all ports that the printer manufacturer adds to the laser engine. The video port is already present. Some printer manufacturers do not present this video interface to the outside world; some do. If the video interface is activated by a circuit board inside the PC, but outside the laser printer, this device can disable temporarily the computer developed by the printer manufacturer. The printer manufacturer's serial and parallel ports are essentially put off-line while the video interface is controlled by the device external to the printer.

Suppose that a Hewlett-Packard LaserJet II is hooked to a serial PC, parallel PC, and video PC printer controller. These three PCs are going to share the one laser printer without any added software or a LAN. Suppose that the video-connected PC is not printing anything. Then, the parallel or serial PC will have control over the printer. You can switch the parallel and serial PCs by using the front panel of the PC. The video PC printer controller is actually connected to the laser engine. When the video-connected PC starts to print, it disables the Hewlett-Packard serial or parallel port until it is done. In other words, the video PC printer controller will share with the parallel PC or serial PC automatically. You must switch manually the parallel and serial PCs.

Unfortunately, the video PC printer controller cannot take advantage of any of the features of the Hewlett-Packard. The video PC printer controller uses only the engine of the Hewlett-Packard. The video PC can send instructions only to the Hewlett-Packard part of the laser printer.

TROUBLE-SHOOTING TIP	SCSI cables have terminators similar to the floppy and hard disk drives inside IBM PCs. You should have one T-resistor plugged into the SCSI device at the end of the cable. If you plug in two T-resistors, premature hardware death will occur. If you do not plug in any T-resistors, many soft errors and data damage will occur.
HINT	The official Apple cables for hooking a LaserWriter to a Macintosh are very expensive. As a result, many people purchase the cables from a company called Farallon. Farallon uses regular telephone cables.

Reviewing Object-Printer Features

This section limits its discussion to object-mode printer hardware and implementation features. Object-mode software features are discussed in the chapter on challenging the desktop publishing world. Object mode can be supported in a variety of ways. At the low end of the price scale, you can obtain object-mode features by adding translation software to a PC. At the other end of the price scale, you can purchase true object-mode printers running at 16 MHz on a 68020 with 12M of RAM.

Fonts

The first object printer, the LaserWriter, was created by Apple. This printer set the standard for object printers in the IBM-PC world. Although early versions of this printer had 13 fonts, all versions today have 35 fonts. Because each PC application program must know all the details of the printer, many IBM PC programs are configurable for the Apple LaserWriter. If you purchase a clone of the Apple LaserWriter for the IBM PC, you must have 35 clone fonts that are identical to the LaserWriter.

If you purchase an alternative object printer for the Macintosh, it may come with a different set of fonts. Screen versions of the new printer's fonts should come with the alternative object printer. After you load new screen fonts into the Macintosh, all Macintosh software is capable of using them instantly. It is ironic that Apple is setting an object-printer definition standard for the IBM-PC world, but cannot exercise the same control over its own market. The important point is that there are no Apple secrets or priority software inside a LaserWriter. This is what makes alternative object printers a viable alternative.

PC Slots and Ports

Most printers use traditional parallel or serial ports built into the PC or Macintosh. However, PC object printers often require a video interface, which takes up a slot. The number of slots available in IBM PCs varies from two to eight. There are usually free slots in these machines. However, most of IBM's new PS/2s have only two or three slots free. Filling one slot for the object printer can be a big decision.

Horsepower

When an object printer receives a page, it has to translate the page from formulas into dots. The time that is required to do this depends on the microprocessor and memory available in the printer. The processor used, the clock speed the processor runs at, and the amount of memory, are variables that influence the thinking speed. Many object printers are more powerful than those inside the computers that feed them data.

Microprocessors

The processors most frequently used in object printers are Motorola 68000s, 68020s, and Weitek RISC (reduced instruction set computer) chip sets. Most object-mode printer software uses the Motorola technology. Other companies are beginning to use the Weitek RISC technology because it is much faster.

Clock Speed

Clock speed has nothing to do with date or time. Clock speed is similar to the conductor of an orchestra, a metronome, or a drill sergeant. Inside ever printer and computer is a chip that tells all the others how fast to do their job; this speed is called the *clock speed*. Speeds in object printers run from 16.7 MHz with the Motorola CPU's, to 4 MHz with Weitek RISC chips. RISC chips are simple CPUs optimized for certain specific operations. Although RISC chips are run at a slower speed, they are up to twice as fast as the Motorola CPUs. This is possible because they are simpler; they do their jobs more quickly.

Character or Graphics Mode

Printers always have had the capability to switch between character and graphics mode. The capability to switch between object and character or graphics mode, however, is not easy. This is not important in the Macintosh world because all software can switch over immediately and start using the marvelous capabilities of object printers. In the IBM-PC world, not all application software knows how to use object-mode printers. In order to continue using the old character-oriented software, the capability to support character/graphics and object printer modes at the same time will be important. There are four ways that all three modes can be made available:

- ❑ *Purchase a printer with all three modes.* The difficult part is switching between the modes. The most obvious way would be for PC software to send instructions to the printer to switch modes—just like switching between character and graphics mode. However, the object to character/graphics mode switch is not that easy. PC application software is not programmed to send these types of instructions. Usually, you must make this switch manually.

You must type the name of the switching program, choose a menu option, or walk to the printer and choose an option on the front panel.

❏ *Purchase a PC software program that can support multiple printers attached to one PC.* This is the only completely automatic method of switching between object and character/graphics modes. Use this feature to run two printer cables to an object/character/graphics printer. You then can set up the printer to listen on one port for character/graphics instructions and on the other port for object instructions. By selecting different printers within PC software, you can select different printer modes.

Many PC application programs do not directly generate object-mode printer instructions. Instead, the PC application program sends emulation software to the printer and enables the object-mode printer to translate from character/graphics into object mode. This emulation software is typically called a header file. It is possible to write a generic header file and send it to the object printer so that it can understand character graphics data.

❏ *Purchase a character-mode printer.* This is the cheapest method. Then, purchase PC software that grabs the object-mode instructions before they get to the printer port and translates them to character-graphics software. The drawback of this technique is that it puts all the burden of translating from formulas into dots on the PC rather than the printer. This slows down the PC drastically. A page that normally takes two minutes for a decent object printer to print may take 45 minutes for the translation software to print.

> HINT │ If you use an object printer with the Macintosh, you need to use a utility program that can reset the printer. When used with IBM PCs and Macintoshes, object printers tend to get lost and confused regularly. If the utility program's reset does not work, try using the front panel (if there is one). Otherwise, turn off and on the printer. If that doesn't work, then turn off and on the PC and printer again.

Start-Up Page

Object printers indicate that they are ready or have recovered from a problem by printing a start-up page. The start-up page is like the banner page that old line printers used to print to separate one print job from another on continuous tractor-feed paper.

When working with an object printer, eventually you will be able to tell when it is ready or has recovered. At this point, you no longer need the start-up page; you should be able to disable the start-up page and stop wasting paper and toner (two to three cents per page). Sometimes you can disable the page by using the front panel of the laser printer. Otherwise, you must reconfigure your software in the PC, or run a special program to disable the start-up page. When you are troubleshooting an object printer, it is useful to activate the start-up page again. Reconfiguring the software while you are troubleshooting makes the troubleshooting process more complex and time-consuming. It is easier to activate and deactivate the start-up page from the front panel.

Shades of Gray

300-dpi object printers should be able to print 33 shades of gray without much trouble. The ideal object printer will produce 33 shades that are clearly distinguishable from their neighbors. The distribution should be even. The change between each of the 33 should be gradual. Various printer engines perform differently in this category.

Reviewing Plotter Features

You should consider a plotter for two reasons: if you are interested in making excellent color view graphs for presentations, or if you want to make blueprints.

There are two basic types of plotters: *analog* and *digital*. Strip charts used in lie detectors, earthquake-monitoring stations, and hospitals are types of plotter. The paper is pulled while a pen goes back and forth. Analog plotters exist that look exactly like digital plotters, but analog plotters can never be hooked directly to a computer.

From the personal computer point of view, there is one type of plotter: a digital plotter. Bits and data are not sent to analog plotters. Instead, wiggly, wavy lines are sent to analog plotters to cause the pens to move. Analog plotters don't have a computer, memory, or a programming language— only digital plotters have these elements. The following sections are concerned with the features of digital plotters. From now on, the word plotter refers to digital plotters.

Plotters were the first object-printing devices. Hewlett-Packard makes approximately 80 percent of the plotters sold. The Hewlett-Packard GL plotter language is supported by approximately 90 percent of the plotter market. Plotters are used primarily to print drawings.

Interface

All plotters have a serial interface; a few have a parallel interface or a Hewlett-Packard IB interface.

Speed

Plotter speed is measured by how many inches per second the pen can be moved. The slower plotters are around eight inches per second, and the fastest plotters are around 32 inches per second. The common plotter is around 15 to 20 inches per second. There is a direct relationship between price and plotter speed. Pure pen movement speed is not the only factor to consider when trying to determine the overall speed of a plotter. Because there are various pen types, the plotter must slow down so that the pen line thickness does not vary. In fact, most plotters have the capability to slow the drawing speed down until the drawing looks as good as possible. You can slow down the drawing speed by using the front panel. The time spent grabbing pens of different colors also can slow down a plotter tremendously.

Paper Size

Plotter paper sizes have been standardized and designated with the letters A, B, C, D, and E. The letter A is 8.5-by-11 inches, and E is 36-by-48 inches. The rest of the letters represent sizes somewhere between A and E. Plotters that handle the larger sizes also can be adjusted to handle the smaller. The most common size is D, and there are a few B and E sizes.

Resolution

Suppose that a plotter is moving its pen on a diagonal line. A stepper motor is moving the pen, so the question is how many stair-steps will be on that diagonal line. One thousand steps is typical. A 300-dpi printer can deliver 300 steps. Thus, there is a relationship between steps per inch and dots per inch. Unfortunately, the actual measurement is inches per step. For example, if the smallest distance the plotter can move the pen is in increments of .001 inches, then $1 \div .001 = 1000$ dpi. Plotters vary from .05-inch to .001-inch steps.

Plotters also are rated on how accurate they are at finding the same place on the paper over and over again. The accuracy range is from .4 percent (worse) to .1 percent (best). This is important when drawing multiple objects that have to line up with each other. Most plotted objects have a reference coordinate point that is used while plotting. If these reference points cannot be located accurately, however, the entire object can be off with respect to a previously drawn object. Repeatability is more important in plotters than step inches or dots per inch.

Pen Movement

Plotters come in three basic styles:

- *Drum Plotters.* These are older plotters. When using drum plotters, you must strap the paper into place. The drum spins, and the pens go back and forth in a straight line. Drum plotters are not popular anymore.

- *Flatbed plotters.* These plotters are also old and have almost phased out. A flatbed plotter takes up as much space as a sheet of paper. The paper lays flat on the plotter table while a pin is pulled in x and y directions over the page. Sometimes, you can lean flatbed plotters at an angle, but still they are clumsy.

> HINT | Do not be afraid to move the print head or plotter head when the plotter or printer is off. Grab the print head and move it out of the way to make paper insertion or ribbon/pen insertion easier. Nothing can be damaged by moving the print head or plotter by hand while it is turned off. Be gentle, however. Remember: If you move the print head when on, you will damage the motors that move the head and cause poorer-looking output.

- *Rollerbed plotters.* This is the most popular type of plotter. You feed sheets of paper by hand into the rollerbed plotter. The plotter rolls the paper back and forth, measuring its exact dimensions, and then prints. These plotters are fascinating to watch. It is amazing that they can be so accurate, yet so violent. The paper-insertion process is much easier with rollerbeds. In fact, you can purchase paper trays for this type of plotter so that insertion is automatic. Sometimes, rollerbed plotters are called saddlebed plotters, because they look like a horse saddle.

Single versus Multipen

Some plotters have a head that holds just one pen. In order to change colors with this type of plotter, the PC software has to be able to stop, beep the screen or the plotter speaker, and tell the user to change colors. This feature of software is not unusual. To support multiple fonts or character sets on a daisywheel printer, the software had to be able to stop and ask for the print wheel (or thimble) to be changed. The user then had to tell the PC that the operation was complete after changing the wheel. Now, most plotters have the capability to reach into a cup or special storage place to grab another pen color or pen type. Other plotters have a head that holds multiple pens. There is no performance difference or operational difference between these two types of mechanisms. You may think that multipen plotter heads are faster because they do not have to travel to the cup, but this is not the case. When you are printing a multicolor document, pen-changing can slow down plotting drastically.

Pen Tips

These are the major plotter pen types: fiber-tip, roller-ball (metal and plastic), liquid-ink, and ceramic. Fiber-tip pens wear down, but provide bright colors and operate at moderate speeds. Those fiber-tip pens designed for paper use water-based ink. Those designed for transparencies use oil-based ink. Ball-point pens can plot at high speeds, but often need to be pressurized to ensure an even ink flow. Ball-point pens do not produce the vividness of fiber pens. Liquid-ink pens are probably the best but are messy and clog up often. Some plotters can hold pencil lead. Although most architectural drawings are done in pencil, most final drawings are done in ink. Replacing a pen with a pencil may seem to be counter-productive, but with the proper lead, the output can be better-looking and produced at much higher speeds than with ink. Different pen types require different degrees of pressure and different acceleration speeds.

A major feature of plotters is whether they cap the pens automatically. Some plotters park the pens in an environmentally-controlled chamber when not in use to avoid the time spent capping and uncapping. Some plotters force the user to cap the pens when not in use.

Types of Paper

One of the advantages of plotters is that different pen types can be found that write well on different types of paper. With traditional printers, the paper has to match the print head or the laser engine. You have to purchase special laser-proof mailing labels or dot-matrix-proof stencils. Plotters can write on anything you can write on.

Some of the more common types of paper put in plotters include Vellum, transparency film, and matte-finished polyester film. Vellum is the preferred paper of most draftsmen and plotters. It is specifically coded for maximum smoothness and chemically treated to produce a strong piece of paper that is translucent. The translucent feature enables you to put the vellum on top of another drawing and then trace the lines drawn on the original. Vellum is an aid for manually copying big drawings that don't fit in a normal copier machine. Most pen and pencil types of plotters work with vellum.

Transparencies or acetate sheets need a special oil-based ink; otherwise, the lines smear. The special ink usually requires that you slow the plotter down.

Scanner

By placing a drawing in the plotter, you can grab the pen-holding head and trace the drawing. While tracing, the plotter can send coordinate position changes to the PC where software can store this information. Thus, you can use the plotter head like a mouse as a semiautomatic tracing aid.

Plotter Emulation

Because plotters have their own object type of language, they normally can print a document like a normal character printer can. But, certain plotters can act like a printer and plot each letter of a document. This a slow process, however, and a waste of the plotter's resources, however.

You can purchase software that can take instructions intended for a plotter and translate them into character instructions for a character plotter. This is a straightforward method and actually is useful in proofing a plot before printing it. Some printers have this emulation capability built into their software. Otherwise, you can purchase PC software that will translate the plotter commands to character-mode printer commands and send them on their way.

Chapter Summary

This chapter reviewed the hardware and operation features of printers. You learned that if you need to print on paper that is wider than 8 1/2 inches, you need a dot-matrix or inkjet printer. You also learned that there are many ways of putting addresses on envelopes, from printing the addresses directly to printing on paper and then using a copier machine to copy them onto envelopes. This chapter also showed you that font upgrades are still a confusing mess in the IBM-PC world, but that they are fairly straightforward in the Macintosh world. The chapter also explained that the IBM character set is a must in the IBM world; printer companies are forced to write Macintosh software to support their printer.

The chapter reviewed seven types of printer cables: serial, Local Talk, Centronics, Epson/IBM, SCSI, Hewlett-Packard IB, and video. The speeds, lengths, and features of each type of cable were explored. You also learned that you can use multiple-printer interface options to share a printer.

The front panel ease of use was explored. The problems associated with making the changes "stick" were also explored. For example, the conceptual design problems associated with resetting the printer, yet not clearing downloaded fonts and partially stored documents were explored.

The issues associated with printer resolution, including gray scale concepts and scanners, were explored. There is little difference between 75-dpi, 300-dpi, and 33 gray-scale printing, except that storing 75 dpi with 33 gray scales is a form of file compression that takes advantage of patterns used to create gray scales. Thus, scanning a document at 300 dpi is going to produce a file five times larger than the same document scanned at 75 dpi with 33 gray-scale possibilities.

In this chapter, you learned that to speed up a printer, you must identify the bottleneck. This bottleneck is not always the printer's burst speed—the speed at which it can print a line. Other factors influencing the speed are the mode in which the printer is operated—character, graphic, object—and the speed at which the PC software can generate printer information.

This chapter introduced you to the wide variety of features found in dot-matrix printers. You learned that 9-pin printers are the inexpensive models, that 24-pin printers have replaced daisywheels, and that 18-pin printers are usually specialized. How much paper is wasted when tearing off fanfold paper was also discussed. You learned that switching from hand-feed to tractor-feed has developed concepts of parking paper temporarily. This chapter also told you that cut-sheet feeders are dead and that paper trays could replace tractor-fed, fanfold paper. Also, you saw that dot-matrix printers are good with multipart forms and stencils.

This chapter proved that inkjet printers are still an unknown. They are expensive to operate. They compete with dot-matrix printers in most features, but have a laser's resolution. Unfortunately, the inkjets don't have the laser's memory. The upper-end inkjets compete with upper-end 24-pin printers in terms of font availability and resolution.

The chapter also told you that laser printers are divided into engines and printer computers, and it reviewed the features of engines.

A separate section was dedicated to laser replacement supplies, because they can cost so much. A ream (500 sheets) of paper costs $2, and the toner and other supplies needed to print that ream cost between $5 and $24.

You learned that features which printer companies add to the engine include memory and fonts. Object printers were reviewed from the hardware and feature point of view.

Finally, plotters were explored. Plotters have the special capability to use different types of pens so that they can write on different types of paper.

In the Next Chapter

The next chapter covers the general features of printer software. A majority of these features are associated with character-mode operation. Graphics mode is simple—the PC does all the work. Object mode is the opposite—the printer does all the work. Character mode requires that the PC software know what the printer is capable of. Again, this section is not designed to turn you into a printer programmer. The goal here is to describe the features of the printer software. The most important benefit of understanding printer software is being able to tell the difference between a PC software problem and a printer software problem.

6

Printer Software Features

Printers have software built into them. Certain chips, called *read only memory* (ROM), store programs like floppy disks and hard disks store programs. Programs in ROM, however, can only be read and not written to. ROM versions can dramatically influence which fonts are purchased and which documents can be printed. The first part of this chapter reviews printer ROM features.

Printers listen to the data arriving from the PC and try to separate this data into instructions and characters to be printed. The instructions arriving from the printer form a programming language. Some printer programming languages can drastically limit the number of software packages that can use the printer. Printer programming languages with future expansion built into them are becoming popular. When considering purchasing, realizing which printer languages to look for is important. The second part of this chapter discusses printer languages.

Some PC software translates instructions being sent to the printer, sets up the printer, and manages the printer fonts. Software packages in this category generally are called *printer utilities*. The final section of this chapter reviews this type of software.

Features of Printer ROM Software

PC software sends instructions to the printer and waits for the printer to understand and respond in an appropriate fashion. More accurately, the PC software actually generates printer source code, and the printer must interpret or compile the instructions. A printer's response to PC instructions is determined by the software in the printer's ROM. The first part of this section describes the font and memory constraint problems typical of printer ROM.

When one printer emulates another, it is trying to understand instructions intended for the other printer. Clone printers sometimes try to respond to the instructions in a manner identical to the original; however, sometimes this type of emulation is not desirable. Ideally, clone printers respond in a more desirable way than the original printer. The second part of this section describes printer emulation features.

Solving Font and Memory Problems

ROM stands for read-only memory. ROM consists of the rectangular-shaped chips found on circuit boards everywhere. These chips usually have a sticker or piece of paper on top of them with a copyright symbol. This is because the chips contain copyrighted software or data just like a hard disk or floppy disk. The only difference between ROM and hard or floppy disks is that you cannot erase the software or data in ROM. Instead, if you need to upgrade the software or data in ROM, you remove the old ROM chips and insert new ROM chips.

Printers and printer cartridges contain ROM chips. Although the printer's ROM chips may hold software, the printer cartridge's ROM chips hold instructions or data describing how to draw different fonts. This chapter focuses on the printer's ROM chips. These chips hold a program that is very similar to BASIC, 1-2-3, or dBASE. The ROM chips in a printer respond to instructions going through the printer cable. BASIC responds to the instructions of a BASIC program; 1-2-3 responds to the instructions of a macro, and dBASE responds to the instructions of a dBASE program file. Each of these programs responds to one instruction at a time. Each finishes the first instruction before examining the next. These types of programs are called *interpretative* programs. All printers are essentially interpreters, just like BASIC, 1-2-3, and dBASE. Printers just receive instructions from a cable. BASIC, 1-2-3, and dBASE receive their instructions from a file.

Like BASIC, 1-2-3, and dBASE, printer programs have similar constraints. For example, suppose that a printer's ROM software is similar to a compiler or interpreter and places similar constraints on the programs sent by the PC. Suppose that subroutines can be nested only 2 deep in one printer versus 16 deep in another and that an on-screen drawing is made of all the flowers, tulips, bulbs, and bushes comprising the landscaping of the front yard. The drawing looks beautiful on-screen but does not print. Instead, an error message flashes on the printer or on the PC screen. The error message is described in the appropriate PC or printer manual as `document too complex`. You need to eliminate the picture of each flower and draw groups of flowers with less detail. This will make the document less complex. The following table lists some PC printer error messages similar to `document too complex`:

```
Limit check error
Memory error
Error 20
Error 21
Printer does nothing
Printer prints startup page instead of document
Splits document in half, prints 1/2 on first page, 2nd half
  on the next so you can paste them together
```

The printer that nests subroutines 16 deep can print the drawing. The printer that nests subroutines only 2 deep does not. Nothing can be done except make the drawing simpler. Printer magazines and testing companies are using the word *macro* to describe the capability to store a program and execute it over and over. Some printers cannot store programs and execute them later, but can pass every other test. Because some PC software never uses macros, this feature may not be important to you. Other PC software, particularly drawing packages, are going to use macros. Purchasing printers that pass the macro test is the best practice.

Graphics-mode printers usually run out of memory to image a document properly. Character-mode printers also can run out of room for imaging the page and storing fonts, as well as many other resources (see the list that follows). The majority of the limitations are due to printer software design decisions—the software in the printer's ROMs.

The following list of items may cause a printer to say that the `document is too complex`.

- Number of downloaded fonts
- Fonts per page
- Font changes on a line
- Number of macros
- Number of objects
- Amount of graphics data
- Number of rules
- Integer number size
- Real number size
- Array length (many different types)
- String length
- Object name length

- Number of open files (printer hard disk)
- Stack overflows
- Number of recursive invocations
- Number of formulas describing an object
- Lack of memory
- Memory management confusion

When you receive one of these error messages, first give the printer a chance at solving the problem. Look for a Continue or Clear button on the Macintosh screen or the printer front panel. Sometimes, the printer ejects a partially printed page and then prints the rest of the page on another sheet. You can manually tape the two sheets together to form one complete document. (You then can photocopy the document.)

Second, try pushing the Reset button on the printer. Try putting the printer in its factory default position before printing.

Third, split the complex document into less complex pieces and print the pieces separately. One page, drawing, or font change may be causing the printer to act up. Usually, the problem page has too many font changes, or perhaps you have asked the PC application to overlay several objects on top of each other. Try simplifying the problem page.

> **TROUBLESHOOTING TIP** When a `document is too complex` error message is received, see how the printer responds when you try to continue printing. Then, turn the printer off and on and try printing again. If this action fails, split the document into less complex pieces and print them separately.

Assessing Emulation Quality

Almost all printers today are clones of one sort or another. Even the companies that produced the original printer model that all the clones are based on have evolved their printer models in different directions. To make good purchase decisions, understanding characteristics of the printer market is important.

To avoid the pricing pressures of a commodity market, printer manufacturers try to distinguish their products from the rest. This distinction sometimes is done by making the paper travel a straighter path or increasing the number of pins in the print head. Most manufacturers have created their own printer language. In 1989, however, only one significantly new printer language (from Canon) surfaced, and this language is not given much of a chance for survival. Printer software always has been more difficult to develop than printer hardware. Although the hardware is necessary, software is what sells the printer. Creating a printer language from scratch is easier than trying to clone and then improve someone else's language. Today, printer companies have to do the latter.

Printer languages have matured just as programming languages, such as Cobol, Fortran, and Pascal, have matured. In fact, printer languages are evolving object features like Pascal and other languages. Now, printer companies have to clone the original, make the program execute more quickly, and add more functions. Adding significant new features to a printer language is almost as difficult as adding features to Cobol, Fortran, or Pascal.

Why shouldn't you purchase the new Canon printer with the fancy programming language? First, like any 1.0 version of software, the printer software probably is going to be buggy. Second, your software may not know how to talk to that printer. Future upgrades of your software may not talk to that printer. The time you and your company invest in an application software program is much more than the cost of a printer. Chances are that you will waste time and be forced into unwise PC application purchases, just to keep the printer working. Stick with HP-PCL, PostScript, Epson, and HPGL, the standard printer languages.

> HINT | When purchasing a printer, ask the salesperson whether the features are available when emulating standard printers. If they are not available, the features may never be available.

The trouble is that Epson and Hewlett-Packard are not standing still. Epson and HP are adding features to their printer languages. For example, HP has eliminated the need for separate landscape and portrait fonts and increased the number of fonts per page and the total number of fonts that can be added. These changes really are not changes in the HP LaserJet language commands or syntax but are changes in the ROM software within the printer. The PC software does not have to change.

Epson and HP versions change with the printer model numbers. Today, most changes are minor. Occasionally, the standard level rises. For example, emulating an HP LaserJet+ is no longer adequate in the character laser printer market. A character laser printer should not be purchased unless it has HP LaserJet II emulation. The next major evolution of the HP LaserJet II emulation does not require changes in commands or syntax. Scalable fonts are the next addition to HP LaserJet II emulation modes. The same font selection commands are sent to the printer by the PC software. The PC software does not care whether the fonts inside the character laser printer are scalable or fixed, the software wants the indicated size printed.

Adobe's PostScript language syntax is not changing. When Adobe sells PostScript to a new printer manufacturer, they get a new version number but the same PostScript language. The version number reflects the PostScript software customization done for that particular printer manufacturer. Higher PostScript version numbers do not indicate more features or better features of that particular PostScript printer. Because PostScript has not changed since 1985 and is still the dominate object printer language, PostScript clone printers can be very compatible. Of course, there are slight differences among PostScript versions, and Adobe does improve the output quality and the document complexity possible. But, the important point is that the PostScript language is a stable, mature product that is easy to clone.

The reason that no one can improve on PostScript is because it is similar to the programming language C. (See Chapter 11 for more details.) PostScript can have libraries or macros added, but these enhancements are programming aids; they make programmers more efficient. Whatever enhancements are added will have to be written in PostScript itself.

Answer the following five questions before purchasing a printer that you primarily plan to use in emulation mode:

1. Which version of the standard printer is being emulated?
2. Who wrote the emulation software—the printer company or a third party?
3. How much memory is left over after emulation?
4. How fast is the emulation?
5. How complex can the document be?

The first question asked about the emulation should be, "Which Epson or HP model is emulated?" The PostScript language stabilized at Version 25. The document complexity and output quality improved significantly with PostScript Version 47. HP LaserJet II emulation means that more fonts can be downloaded—versus HP LaserJet original or HP LaserJet+. If no model number is emulated, assume the worst case scenario—that the most primitive version is emulated. Perhaps, the printer company had the idea that if they emulate the most primitive Epson version, their printer language will look a lot better in contrast and make emulation software easier to write.

The second question is "Who wrote the printer emulation software?" Companies specialize in writing Epson, Diablo, HP, and PostScript emulation software for printers. These companies have the goal of emulating as closely and accurately as possible the products of Epson, HP, and Adobe. (Diablo emulation is not evolving.) If the printer company bought the emulation from a third-party company, the emulation is much better than software developed in-house. Unfortunately, native features, such as the capability to switch between two tractor feeds through PC commands, are not usually available in emulation mode unless the printer company modifies the software.

A similar process has occurred in the IBM PC clone world. Rather than write software that makes a clone look like an IBM PC, clone companies purchase their software from companies like Phoenix and Award. The company that had a large chunk of the printer emulation or printer clone market was Bauer Enterprise of San Jose, California.

The third question is "How much memory is left over for documents after emulation mode is chosen?" A printer may come with 1M of memory, yet only 384K is available for documents. For laser printers, figure 1M for full-page 300-dpi graphics and 32K for each font added. The printer software may take anywhere between 128K and 300K. Obviously, a smaller emulation program uses less printer memory, but it may run slower than printer emulation software that takes up more memory.

The fourth question is "How fast is the emulation?" Some printers are up to 20 times slower during emulation mode than in their native printer language.

The fifth question, the most difficult to answer, is "How complex can the document be?" The only way to be satisfied that a Panasonic laser printer can emulate an HP LaserJet is to stress test the printer, as follows:

1. Download 64 fonts.
2. Print a document with 20 fonts on a page.
3. Send the output of a drawing package with as many little circles on the page as the software can keep track of.
4. See whether the printer gives up.

Too often, the document has to be less complex for the printer emulating Epson, Diablo, HP or PostScript.

Features of Programming Languages

The purpose of this section is two-fold. The first purpose is to survey features of printer languages with the goal of pointing out significant differences that affect daily operation—for example, whether the printer decides to skip perforations. The second purpose is to provide the basis for starting to program printers directly. The best graphic artists, PC trouble-shooters, and desktop publishers are all learning to program printers directly. To troubleshoot printer problems, you must know what the printer software controls and what the micro software controls. This chapter is the starting point.

The commands or features of printer languages can be grouped into the following eight categories:

- Reset features
- Job control (which emulation mode to use?)
- Page control (which paper tray?)
- Page layout
- Cursor positioning
- Font manipulation
- Font selection
- Graphics

This section reviews the features of printer commands in each of these categories. Specific details about the types of printer commands are found in Appendix A. The first category, reset features, is covered in Chapter 5.

Some printers have all of the following types of resets:

- Reprint same page
- Return to last known state of healthy operation
- Return to front panel configuration
- Return to default settings

Other printers have just one or two of these reset types. The number of different resets is a feature of the printer language. These resets may be accessed from the front panel, or special commands may be sent to the printer from PC or Mac software.

Job Control

Before printing anything, a PC must determine whether the printer is on. An IBM PC has a hard time determining this state because PC DOS is capable of saying only that the printer is out of paper. Out of Paper is a generic error message indicating that you have a problem with the printer. PC applications often reword this error message to make it more accurate—for example, Printer Needs Attention.

If the printer is not attached or turned on, sometimes the PC locks up, and the cursor freezes. In the worst-case scenario, an error message `Fatal Stack Error System Halted` appears on-screen. This message also should be renamed to something like, "I'm PC DOS, and I'm lost." The only recourse is to turn your computer off and on again. (Remember to save your document before printing because it cannot be recovered.)

> HINT | Always save a document before attempting to print it.

A Macintosh is much more civilized about the printing process. Macintoshes can detect that the printer is not responding and enable you to cancel the print request.

The issue of whether the printer is on and attached falls under the job control category of printer languages. Other issues are explored in the following sections.

Indicating Error States

Most printers cannot talk back to the PC. Instead, they can indicate a problem only by sending two specific bit patterns or applying a voltage on a special wire dedicated to that error state. Traditionally, graphics-mode and character-mode printers can send the following two bytes to PCs:

Xoff—stop sending data to me

Xon—start sending data to me

Most PCs can be programmed to listen for these two bytes coming from a printer. Neither of these two bytes has anything to do with an error condition. Object-mode printers can send elaborate error messages to the PC. The PC can inquire about the exact nature of the object-mode printer's problem, and a conversation can take place. This type of communication is impossible with graphics and character-mode printers.

> HINT | Object-mode printers are much more resourceful at solving their own problems than character- and graphics-mode printers. (Unfortunately, object-mode printers also have more potential problems.)

Depending on the cable connecting the PC to the printer, different wires have different meanings. For example, wires in the Epson/IBM parallel cable have the following meanings:

Wire	Potential meaning
11	Printer busy, off-line, error
12	Out of paper
13	Printer not selected
32	Out of paper, off-line, error

If any of these wires are not connected on the PC's side, the PC never knows whether the printer is functioning. Most other interfaces have just one wire to indicate the printer's state and perhaps one wire to indicate that the printer's buffer is overflowing with data and to tell the computer to stop sending data for a while.

> **TROUBLE-SHOOTING TIP** If you are installing a printer and it does not seem to work, cut the wires mentioned in the preceding section to fool the PC into thinking that the printer is alive and well. You can isolate the problem by determining how the printer and PC are interpreting the voltages on the wires.

Handling Macros

The use of the word *macro* in the PC world was made popular by Lotus. Other software companies use the word macro instead of *programming language* because macro is less intimidating. However, a printer macro is written in the language of the printer. A printer macro is like a subroutine or an object sent to the printer. You create macros with PC software and send them to the printer.

A macro can be a program that draws a company's letterhead on blank sheets of paper or an emulation program that enables the native printer language to emulate another printer's language. A macro essentially modifies or extends the capabilities of the software within a printer. Macros most commonly are sent to object printers, although most character laser printers can accept macros.

In the object-printer world, macros sometimes are called headers because they are sent when a PC application program starts up. If an application is used throughout the day for printing different documents, the header or macro is sent once at the beginning of the day, not at the beginning of each document. Hopefully, the header is sent the first time an application program attempts to print. Applications that send the header at the beginning of each document slow things down. Some applications can be configured to not send the header at all—placing the burden of sending the header on the system configuration. If the printer is turned off, the header may have to be sent again.

TROUBLE-SHOOTING TIP | If an object printer was working and isn't anymore, perhaps the header file has not been sent. Someone may have modified the PC's configuration (CONFIG.SYS or AUTOEXEC.BAT files) or the Mac's system folder. Check the system configuration and restore to original if necessary.

Macros can cause problems. Suppose that PageMaker is supposed to print a document. Before printing the first document since being activated, PageMaker sends a header to the printer. Microsoft Word is activated. Before printing the first Word document, the header is sent. Does the Microsoft Word header clear out PageMaker's header or add to PageMaker's header? Ideally, Word clears PageMaker's header, but if the application does not, headers or macros can accumulate and fill up printer memory. The headers can fight each other, and the printer can start spitting paper or start-up pages.

HINT | Turning off and on the printer clears the macros that may be accumulating.

TROUBLE-SHOOTING TIP | If using different software programs causes printer problems, and turning the printer off and on when changing the programs solves the problem, call the software companies involved. Ask whether they know about the problem and if any solution exists. In this case, the problem is with the application software, not the printer's ROM software.

Checking Printer Direction

While a dot-matrix printer is on, shake the print head gently. If the head moves at all, there is play in the mechanism that moves the head back and forth. This play causes bidirectional printouts to look terrible compared to unidirectional printouts, especially when in graphics mode. Thus, some PC software automatically places a dot-matrix printer in unidirectional mode before printing. The next software to use the printer may not care. The printer, therefore, stays in the slow unidirectional mode until it is turned off.

HINT | If a dot-matrix printer prints unevenly spaced characters, tighten up the belts that pull the print head back and forth.

Entering Carriage Returns

Every printer understands three basic commands: line feed (LF), form feed (FF), and carriage return (CR). Line feed and carriage return commands are required to begin a new line in the left margin. For historical reasons, PC software sometimes sends only CR commands to the printer and expects the printer to add an LF command.

Unfortunately, many different ways of telling a printer to add an LF command exist for every CR command received. Commands can be sent to the printer. The PC can remove the voltage in the wire leaving pin 14 to the printer. Switches can be set in the printer to ignore the voltage arriving on pin 14. Switches can be set to force the printer to add an LF command to every CR command received. How all these possibilities add and subtract can be different from one printer-PC software combination to another. Getting a printer to constantly single-space and not double-space or print over and over again on the same line can be a real challenge. PC software, through a job control command, can tell a printer to change how it deals with an arriving CR command.

TROUBLE-SHOOTING TIP | If a PC program starts double-spacing or printing over and over again on the same line, turn the printer off and on. Try printing again. If the problem persists, reconfigure the PC software.

Querying the Printer

The capability of a printer to listen to questions or queries and then reply traditionally has been an object-mode feature. Some of the more innovative character-mode printers are developing this feature. Even in the object-printer world, the capability of a PC to query a printer is not fully exploited yet. Many of the features described in this section are not reality yet.

In the Macintosh world, utilities for querying LaserWriters are appearing. For example, CE Software sells a utility called DiskTop ($50) that can ask the printer how many pages it has printed since it rolled off the assembly line. This information is useful for a network manager to figure out exactly how many pages were printed by a cartridge and when to change the cartridge. The following paragraphs describe a few of the questions that can be asked of most object printers and some character laser printers.

A printer can be asked "How are you?" if it appears on, yet is not performing correctly from the micro's point of view. The printer may say that it is waiting for a font or that it is busy printing someone's document. The printer may say that it has a certain amount of memory left, and the PC software can determine whether enough memory is available to transmit.

A local area network can be asked, "Which of you are printers? What are your names?" Then, the PC or user can pick between printers. This communication is possible with printers that can talk back. Dumb character printers can ask PCs to respond on their behalf, but the PC must work harder, and the PC doesn't always know what the printer is doing. Why not hang the printer on the network directly? Why not query the printer directly rather than indirectly through a PC? This method is more efficient, makes troubleshooting easier, and cuts down on the chaos caused by flowing documents through intermediary PCs. Apple has implemented this type of communication in Macintosh LANs.

Some PC software can ask a printer specific questions about its error state. For example, the software may ask whether the printer failed to print because too many fonts were on a page.

Eventually, printers will become part of a computer network that can be queried and report problems to a central location. Diagnostics or self-tests should be able to run remotely and the results reported back to a monitoring station that can service all printers on a local area network.

Users that mess with the shared printer's front panel can be caught in the act. (In fact, writing a program that spies on users fiddling around with the front panel should be possible.) The printer can send a copy of its current setup to the PC, and the PC can store the setup. This way, front panel setups can be restored instantly from a remote PC—another form of reset. PostScript printers today often have passwords.

The printer can be out of paper, or the paper can be jammed. Someday, printers will be able to tell the PC where the paper jam is located. Then, the PC can draw a picture of the printer and describe the procedures to fix the printer. Some copy machines are already this sophisticated.

Object printers and some character printers can send font information to PCs. For example, PCs need to know how wide each character is in a proportional font to determine how many characters can fit on a line. PCs need to know the bit patterns of fonts so that the fonts on-screen accurately reflect what is printed. On a local area network, one object printer should be able to ask another for any font information it may have. In other words, the printers should be able to pass fonts around. For accounting, inventory, and bookkeeping purposes, PCs should be able to ask how many times a font was used, in which sizes, where the font came from, and where copies of the font were mailed to.

Page Control

Job-control parameters can affect all documents printed in the future. These parameters, usually sent by PC applications or Mac printer drives, can be sent only once or sent at the beginning of each document. If they are not sent again, the printer is supposed to remember the parameters until the printer is told to change them.

Every page has certain unique features that need to be transmitted before printing. If the page-control parameters are not changed, the preceding page-control parameters can be used, or the printer can default back to the standard page setup parameters. Ideally, the printer reverts back to standard page setup parameters because the preceding document should not influence the current document being printed. Otherwise, the printer's behavior can seem unpredictable. For this reason, most object printers default to standard conditions when finished printing a page.

Page-control data always is transmitted before the contents of a page. Often, identical page-control data is sent at the beginning of each page. Page-control information consists of the following: paper source, page size, page length, orientation, text area, margins, perforation region, spacing, and paper bin selection.

Paper Source

Before printing a page, the PC has to tell the printer where the paper is coming from. The list of possible options include the following: multiple paper trays, multiple tractors, envelope trays, and manual feed slots. Most printers have only a few of these features.

The manual feed option is aggravating to use. You ask the printer to print a document but nothing happens. You walk to the printer, and the front panel is flashing a message, usually something cryptic like PE FEED, an HP LaserJet message. This error message asks you to do something. Because the printer cannot send a message to the PC, it cannot request the PC to ask you. Instead, the printer has to ask you directly.

> **TROUBLE-SHOOTING TIP** Some printers have two paper output paths. One path is straight through and may deliver paper face up. The other path may be curved and deliver paper face down. If the printer has the capability to select the output path, this information also is part of the page-control header.

Paper Orientation

Paper orientation to feed path is a relatively new concept to laser printers but not photocopiers. Currently, most laser printers can accept only 8 1/2-inch-wide paper. In the future, laser printers will be able to accept paper up to 14 inches wide. Then, telling the laser printer about the paper orientation to the feed path will be important. Paper can be fed with the 8 1/2-inch width or the 11-inch length going into the printer. Some character-mode laser printers already have the capability to understand these commands, even though the current feed path does not allow the possibility.

New Page and Overlay Concepts

You have many different ways to eject the current page and load the next page. Should the printer eject the preceding page? Did the preceding PC program eject the page or is the program planning on printing more on the current page? Should the printer eject the current page or save it as a form or an overlay for the next page? If saved as a form or overlay, what should the name or number of this page be? If ejected, is the next sheet supposed to be loaded, or should the printer wait for a specific command to load in the next sheet?

> HINT | Laser printers adjust a sheet just before printing in a coordinated effort. Dot-matrix printers and daisywheel printers print on the platen without paper. These printers have no way of knowing whether paper is inserted or whether the paper is in the correct position. Laser printers, however, can determine the position of the paper.

Normally, new page and overlay commands do not cause much chaos in laser printers other than filling up their memory with useless forms and overlays. Turning the printer off and on clears this information and keeps it from accumulating by accident. In older daisywheel printers with cut-sheet feeders, the problem was more serious. Cut-sheet feeders could pull paper out of and insert paper into the printer. The paper had to be inserted before printing. The old sheet ejected before the next sheet was inserted. This process was coordinated by the PC software. If the PC software messed up, or the printer became confused, every other sheet might be blank. The printer might start printing, thinking paper was loaded when it was not. With laser printers, a separate *load* event does not have to occur.

Number of Copies

Most printers can be told to make duplicates of the document being sent. Although this feature is nice, PC software does not often exploit it because PC printers are not designed to make mass duplicates. Although the cost of paper and expendable supplies may be the same for a laser printer and a copier, you need to figure in other costs. Most important is the capital cost of the laser printer versus the capital cost of the copier. Copiers are built to make multiple copies quickly. Copier motors are chosen because they are quick and do not need to rest. Most PC laser printers have fast motors that need much rest. Asking a laser printer to make multiple copies can almost instantly start overheating the motors. Most copy machines have some kind of service contract under which they are repaired and maintained on a regular basis. Because most laser printers are not under an on-site service contract, shift the duplication requirements to copiers and mimeograph machines.

If your PC software can make multiple copies of a document, try the test in the following hint to see whether the printer is making the multiple copies or whether the PC software is sending the same document through the cables multiple times. If the PC software is sending the document through the cables multiple times, chances are that the printer's motor gets enough rest. If the printer is buffering and printing the page several times, damage can result due to the motor overheating.

> HINT: Watch the lights flicker on the laser printer. If flickering occurs between each page, the document is being retransmitted. You also can send a multiple-page document. If two copies of page 1 are followed by two copies of page 2, the printer is duplicating the pages. If one copy of pages 1 and 2 is printed, then a second copy of pages 1 and 2 is printed, the PC software is duplicating the pages.

Page Layout

Only job-control information should affect general printer operation. Page-control or setup information should be cleared and default page setup parameters used when new parameters are not specified. Similarly, page layout parameters, the printer's cursor position, and font selection should be reset at the beginning of a new document.

Page-layout parameters affect where characters are placed on a page. Many software packages today do not use the page-layout capabilities of a printer.

PC programs would much rather control these capabilities themselves than rely on the printer or operating system to do the same thing consistently.

Suppose that the left margin position was elevated to job-control status. If the printer's left margin was changed, the new left margin would be set for all future documents printed, no matter which application software package the documents came from. Although this may seem advantageous, what if a PC program adds its left margin to the printer's left margin? In fact, left margins can come from the operating system and paper placement. All these left margins create chaos. Every time a document is printed, you have to guess where the left margin is going to be.

> **TROUBLE-SHOOTING TIP** Left margin reduction problems arise because the user, the application software, the operating system, and the printer can all add left margins. Chase each one down. Consistent left margin operation is possible only if all four are under control. See Chapter 14 for a description of the left margin wars.

Controlling Margins

You have four margins: top, bottom, left, and right. The left margin increases as the PC software, the PC operating system, and the printer add spaces to the beginning of the line.

Left and right printer margins are character-mode concepts. The right margin is necessary to prevent printing off the right edge of the paper and onto the platen. The programming language, the PC DOS operating system, and the printer default to 80 characters in a horizontal line. If more characters can fit on a line, all three should be told. Normally, PC software tells the operating system and the printer whether more characters can fit on the line. Occasionally, PC software messes up and sends more characters than fit on one line. In this case, the printer must make a decision. The printer throws away the extra characters (losing part of the document) or places the extra characters on the next line. Neither solution is good. Printers usually have a switch that enables you to choose the lesser of the two evils.

> **TROUBLE-SHOOTING TIP** If whole characters are disappearing into the right margin, they could be clipped off by the operating system or printer. Print using a number of different programs. If just one application has a problem, then that application should be re-installed. Send a line to the printer with more characters than will fit. How does the printer respond? Isolate the problem by repeating this procedure in different ways.

The concept of top and bottom margins can cause just as much confusion as the left and right margins. Most PC software decides to control the margins and does not tell the printer anything. PC software even attempts to clear the margins just to make sure that some other program didn't use them earlier. Most character-mode printers remember what the last PC software package told them to do. Object-mode printers always reset the margins after printing a page.

Conceptually, top and bottom margins can be set in a variety of ways. The overall page length and the number of printed lines can be specified. Then, the software can center the printed document on the page. The top and bottom margin can be specified separately. If the page length is known, the top and bottom can be combined into one number. This number represents the bottom margin of the first page and the top margin of the second page. The trouble with this concept is that with these printers, the first page is printed without a top margin.

Skipping the Perforation

In addition to controlling margins, you often have to make sure that the printer skips the perforation. Fanfold paper has a crease or perforation separating the sheets of paper. After being printed, the fanfold output can be torn into separate pages by tearing along the crease or perforation lines. Early 9-pin, dot-matrix printers could print letters over the perforation without suffering any damage. Twenty-four-pin dot matrix print heads are stressed by printing on the perforation. Continuously printing on the perforation can damage the 24-pin print head. Built into the 24-pin, dot-matrix printer, therefore, is the capability to skip the perforation by adding a top and bottom margin. This feature sounds like a good idea. The trouble is that because the printer does not know where the perforation skip is located, it has to guess that the perforation is always just above the print head when the printer is first turned on (see fig. 6.1).

Fig. 6.1.

The proper perforation location when turning on a printer.

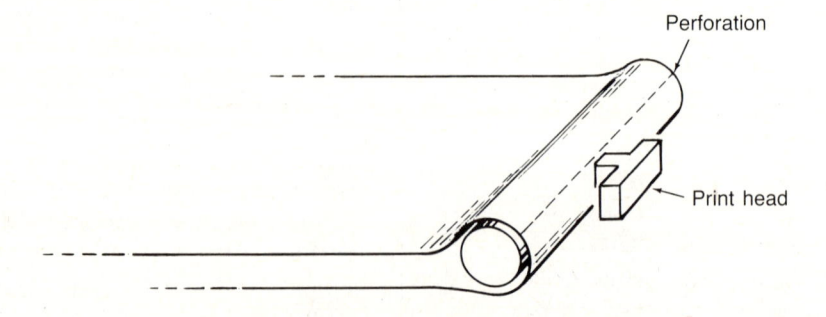

CAUTION | Printing on the perforation with any printer is not good. Twenty-four-pin, dot matrix heads are sensitive to printing on the perforation between fanfold sheets of paper.

If you turn on the printer with the perforation right above the print head, and the printer knows the length of the paper, the printer can skip the perforation correctly. If the printer does not know where the perforation is, however, it skips blank lines in the middle of a page and prints on the perforation.

TROUBLE-SHOOTING TIP | If horizontal blank lines appear in the middle of a document, the software or the printer can be responsible. Both are trying to skip over the perforation area. Write a short BASIC program (LPRINT "this is a test") to send constant lines of text to the printer to see whether the printer is responsible. If the lines appear, the printer is responsible; otherwise, the software is responsible.

The other trouble with the perforation skip feature is that the software cannot ask the printer whether the perforation skip feature is on or off. The PC software, therefore, has to tell the printer to turn this feature on or off at the beginning of each document. Most software turns the perforation skip off and uses its own top and bottom margins (not the printers) to skip over the perforation.

Skipping Unprintable Regions

Like a dot-matrix printer's perforation skip feature, laser printers have an *unprintable region*. Sheets of paper fed through the printer have to travel a specific path. If the paper feeds incorrectly, the image is not deposited in the right spot on the paper. To pull the paper down an accurate path within the printer, you have guides along the paper's edges. These guides brush off any toner left on the edges. The devices that pull or push the paper also brush toner off a strip at the top and the bottom of the sheet. The area outside the window where toner can be deposited is called the *unprintable region*.

Laser printers default to activating the unprintable region skip feature. The default unprintable region skip is 1/2 inch all around the paper. This reduces the printable area from 8 1/2-inches to 7 1/2-inches wide and from 11 to 10 inches long. The number of character-mode text lines at 6 lines per inch is reduced from 66 to 60. Because most software grew up with 66-line pages, many older software programs need to be told to change the number of lines per page to 60. (See your program's manual for instructions.) If not, *page creep* occurs, in which part of the first page spills onto the second, and part of the second page spills onto the third page. Any top or bottom margins that the software adds start appearing in the middle of the page. Today, you have to tell most software to reduce the page length to 60 lines.

> **TROUBLE-SHOOTING TIP** | If characters are missing or partially formed in the left, right, top, or bottom margins, chances are that the software is sending characters into the unprintable region. Adjust the software's margins.

The solution does not stop with reducing the number of lines. Suppose that you use two PC programs. Program A is told that the printer really has 60 lines. Program B seems to work fine without being told anything. Program B disables the unprintable region and uses its own margins to avoid the unprintable regions. When finished, program B leaves the unprintable region skip feature off. Now, the printer thinks that the page has 66 lines. Because program A does not know the unprintable region skip feature is off, it prints 60 lines and then starts the second 60 lines on the first sheet of paper. Because data sent to the unprintable region physically cannot be printed by the laser printer, nothing appears on the paper. The data is lost. A line disappears; page 2 creeps onto page 1, and more of page 3 creeps onto page 2.

To solve this problem, a PC system administrator has to make some clear decisions. Turn the unprintable region or perforation skip feature into a job-control function and turn the feature on or off whenever the printer is on. Configure each application to turn the skip feature off or on at the beginning of each page. Whatever the solution, each user or the person responsible for setting up the system is going to have to deal with this issue.

> **TROUBLE-SHOOTING TIP** | If a document cannot be printed at the exact same place on a page twice in a row, you have a paper creep problem. Print the same document twice, place both pages together, and hold them up to a light. If printed in the same place, the characters seem to glow through the two pages. If not, adjust top and bottom margins, page lengths, perforation skips, unprintable region control, and so on.

Defining Page Length

If the printer is accepting paper from a paper tray, the printer usually knows the length of the paper. If the printer is using tractor-feed paper, it needs to know the form length. Form length usually is specified in inches, fractions of inches, or lines. If form length is specified in lines, the line height is derived from the currently selected font point size. If the length selected is not correct, page creep can occur.

Printers without paper trays learn the proper page length in a variety of ways. Some printers have knobs or switches on the front panel that you set. Other printers expect application software to tell them the page length by using the programming language. Because most software has developed the capability to tell the printer, users usually do not have to get involved in this part of printing, and fewer printers have form-length or page-length switches available on the front panel.

Printing in Landscape and Portrait Orientation

Landscape and portrait orientations are concepts of character laser printers. Character printers need portrait fonts for printing across the 8 1/2-inch dimension and landscape fonts for printing across the 11-inch dimension. Some laser printers eject a page whenever a switch is made from portrait to landscape. Therefore, portrait and landscape can never appear on the same page. Other character laser printers can rotate fonts 90 degrees and do not need landscape fonts, but they can rotate only once per page. Every rotation causes the page to be ejected. Still other character laser printers enable portrait and landscape fonts to be on the same page.

Object printers can rotate a font to any angle, place the rotated character on the page, rotate some more, and still not be forced to eject a sheet of paper. Actually, the object printer is not rotating the character, but rotating the paper underneath the character—not physically, but conceptually. The object printer rotates the paper and then takes a picture of the font's character. The picture bleeds into the rotated paper. The paper is rotated again, and another picture is taken. The paper in an object printer also can be enlarged, reduced, or even temporarily distorted. Because of this capability, letters can be placed on curves, stretched, and distorted in strange ways—all on the same sheet of paper. This manipulation requires lots of memory, lots of CPU horsepower, and can make object printers much slower than character printers.

Cursor Positioning

Most dot-matrix and impact printers have a little window through which the ribbon is punched. The print head is moved to the location where the character is to be printed, and then the character is printed. In a laser printer, a laser is pointed and then fired. In all printers, a location has to be chosen where the printing is to take place. Because this process is similar to moving a cursor around on-screen, it is called *cursor positioning*.

Cursor positioning occurs in one of two ways. The computer enables the printer to choose the next printing position, or the computer decides exactly where to print each character. Character-mode printing traditionally enables the printer to decide where the character is going to go. This process is so unpredictable that many PC word processors actually tell the printer exactly where to place each character. Graphic mode requires that the PC compute each character's location.

Spacing

Before starting this section, you need some background. For character-mode printers, character spacing can be the software's or the printer's responsibility. Object-mode printers must be run by software.

Because character mode was the first printer mode, PC software traditionally has left printers in character mode and enabled them to determine where to place the next character. Like a typewriter determines where the next character is placed, so does a character printer. When the world was simple, PCs and printers cooperated.

The world grew complex, and this relationship suffered when certain typesetting concepts were attempted to improve the quality of PC printouts. First, centering was added; then, right-margin justification was added; then, right margins were aligned, and the left margin remained ragged; then, proportional spacing was added. All of these concepts stressed the PC character-mode printer relationship.

A big decision had to be made. Should the PC software take over the character-mode printers' positioning of characters, or should the character-mode printers learn the new concepts of micro justification and proportional spacing? Character-mode printers lost the battle.

PC software took over character positioning because proportional spacing is difficult. If left up to the printer, gaps appear between certain letter pairs. *Kerning* is the process of adjusting the widths between certain character pairs. Character printers cannot kern, but object printers can. A kerning table that covers all possibilities would require such an incredible amount of information that no printer could hold the table. Assume that the character set just contained the 52 upper- and lowercase letters of the alphabet. The kerning table would contain 1.5×10^{66} bytes—larger than all the world's hard disks added together. A truly good-looking document, therefore, has to be kerned by hand. Maybe, a neural-net type of technology eventually will enable a printer to handle this. For now, the best kerning always is done by hand, inside desktop publishing packages.

Most character-mode printers with built-in proportional fonts know how to place the fonts so that they look nice. The only software that can make use of a proportional-spacing printer is software that expects the printer to be in character mode. This type of software never checks the printer or tells the printer to go into fixed-spaced character mode; the software assumes that the printer is in fixed-spaced character mode because all printers used to be that way.

If a character-mode printer is told from the front panel to go into proportional-spacing mode, the software does not know the difference. The results are usually terrible. Columns don't line up; some lines look short; some lines look long; and some lines are so long that letters are missing at the end. See Chapter 4 for examples of these problems. If you are using software that expects the printer to be in fixed-spaced character mode, place the printer in fixed-spaced character mode and live with the boring output. Don't try to trick the printer.

| TROUBLE-SHOOTING TIP | If the printer is making some lines too short, others too long, and sometimes losing letters at the end of a line, check to see whether the printer is being forced into proportional mode by the front panel. Then, check to see whether the PC software being used expects fixed-spaced fonts. Try putting the printer in a fixed-spaced font and printing again. |

Using Tabs

Like old typewriters, old character-mode printers have tab stops. The idea is the same. PC software has its own tab stops and can translate its tab stops to a character printer's language. Universally positioning each character, however, is much easier. New tab concepts like the decimal tab are all software concepts, not printer commands.

| HINT | If the decimals within a column of numbers don't line up, your printer is not at fault. You or your software is at fault. |

Entering Super- and Subscripts

Subscript and superscript also are character-mode printer commands. Although an object-mode printer can be programmed to emulate a character-mode function, the PC software can change the font size and move the character up or down easier than you can instruct the character-mode printer to. Character-mode printers always have had trouble with the font size change required with super- or subscript. The size usually did not change. Recently, some printers have developed a small character set especially for super- and subscripts. The set contains short, fat, and ugly-looking characters. Most PC software does not take advantage of this printer feature because the characters' appearance makes the software look bad.

Backspacing

The BS or backspace command really is not used much in character-mode printing. At one time, BS helped underline, bold, redline, or overstrike text. Today, those functions are done with special character-mode commands, or the software positions each character and figures out how to perform these functions itself.

Supporting General Word-Processing Commands

Most modern character-mode printers have no word-processing support commands. Older printers have the capability to right justify text for the word processor. Now, however, most word processors control right-margin justification rather than letting the printer take control. Word processors control justification by telling the printers where to place each character using horizontal cursor-positioning commands. In fact, the word processors today do not even let the printer compute where to place characters in fixed-spacing modes.

Font Manipulation

With a typewriter, you can manipulate fonts in different ways to achieve special effects. A word can be retyped to make it bolder, or you can backspace and use the underscore key to achieve underlining. As printers evolved, the first capability they developed was to generate other characters by stretching, doubling, or compressing the dots that made up each character. As these techniques evolved, other manipulations of the dots developed. Most methods are covered in Chapter 4.

Manipulated fonts sometimes are called *enhancements* or *enhanced* fonts. Redesigned fonts are called *cuttings* as in, "Bold italic comes in its own cutting."

Some modern character-mode printers cannot manipulate the fonts (for example, HP LaserJets). The reason probably is a marketing one—to create a market in which to sell fonts. Other modern character-mode printers can manipulate the fonts in many ways (most dot-matrix printers).

The most common font manipulation is underlining. Although never popular with typesetters, underlining became popular with typewriters; therefore, most printers have the capability to underline a font.

PC software can control the underlining or can ask the printer to underline. Each method has advantages and disadvantages. When a font is designed, whether object or character, the exact spot where underlining is to occur is specified. The exact line thickness used to underline also is specified. Unfortunately, the exact same line thickness in the exact same location is not consistent from font to font. If fonts or point sizes are changed in a line and both fonts are underlined, the underline position jumps around with the font.

Two methods of underlining different fonts on the same line look nice. One way is to go back to a more primitive software package that retypes the line using the underline character. Another way is to underline using a straight line called a *rule*. Rules are just starting to become more available in character-mode printers.

> HINT | If different fonts on the same line are underlined, do not expect the underline to be straight. The line changes position underneath the different fonts.

In earlier character-mode printers, asking the printer to underline was dangerous. If the software was using spaces to create a left margin, the printer could not tell the difference between those spaces and the spaces between words. The character-mode printer, therefore, underlined the margins. To not underline spaces, PC software developed the capability to turn off the underlining before a space and turn underlining on just after the space. Software kept track of the difference between left margin spaces and the spaces between words.

> HINT | Printers are not responsible for determining whether a space is part of a left margin or is between words. If told to underline spaces, a printer underlines both. The PC is responsible for turning off the underlining at the end of each line and turning underlining back on at the beginning of the next line. If the document underlines in the margins, you have to be responsible for turning underlining off and on.

Font Selection

Font selection became complicated when laser printers were introduced back in 1986. Before laser printers, usually just one font existed inside the printer. You could change print wheels, balls, or thimbles, but usually only one font was built in the printer. Font selection, therefore, was not an issue before lasers. Dot-matrix printers sometimes claimed that they contained more than one font, but they really just manipulated the one font in their ROMs.

One of the biggest problems of the multifont environment is the response to a requested font that does not exist. All old documents may have to be rewritten or edited to print on the new printer that does not have a font matching the older printer. Suppose that you write a document in 11-point Palatino. The number of characters per line, the placement of graphs and charts, how characters flow around the graphs and charts, the page breaks, and so on depend on the printer having an 11-point Palatino font. If the printer doesn't have the font requested, the printer can react in several ways.

If the font does not exist within the printer, an object-mode printer complains to the PC or Macintosh and uses a version of the screen font that was used to design the document. The output may not look as nice, but the printer at least prints a respectable document. Object-mode printers also can be set up with substitution lists. PC software enables the user to determine which substitutions are made.

> HINT | Printers eventually die; electronic documents do not. Old electronic documents have to print on future printers. Purchase future printers with the same fonts as the older ones to save conversion costs.

Character-mode printers cannot talk back. In a multiple-font environment, this limitation is frustrating. The printer seems to have a mind of its own when deciding which font to use. Adding a font cartridge to the printer can upset old documents that printed fine without the cartridge. Two solutions exist. The printer can choose which font to substitute, or fortune-telling PC application software can substitute font decisions before font changing instructions reach the printer.

Printer Decides Font

All font selection techniques should make selecting a font easy and resolve the `font not available` issue. Object-mode printers name fonts with an English name. Changing fonts is merely a matter of sending the new font name to the object printer. Although this process may take longer, it is more universal and simpler in the long run. The `font not available` issue is resolved by the object-mode printer complaining to the PC; the PC sending a copy of the screen fonts used, or the PC asking the object-mode printer to substitute with a known font.

An unpopular method is to specify the fonts by number. This method may sound simpler and more efficient than sending all the characters of a font's name. This method is simpler—in the beginning, when just a few fonts are in the printer. When many fonts appear in multiple printers throughout the office, the management of font numbers can become a nightmare, especially if the same document needs to be printed on different printers. If the numbering scheme is not the same, the printers never seem to work, which turns into an incredible headache for any person responsible for troubleshooting and maintaining the numbering system. Some printers number the fonts during the font self-test output. This process leads you to believe that the fonts can be numbered and that some relationship exists between how the software is numbering fonts and how the font numbers are coming out of the printer. Remember that numbers are temporary things associated with pieces of hardware. The numbers move and die with the hardware. English names, however, stick around.

> HINT The font ID numbers printed during a laser printer's font self-test have nothing to do with the font numbers inside PC applications. The font ID numbers are useful only when operating the front panel of the laser printer.

A third method of specifying fonts has become popular among character-mode laser printer manufacturers, even though nobody truly understands the method. This method is specifying font features and letting the printer pick the closest-matching font. The reason character-mode printer manufacturers like this font selection method is that the `font not available` problem is solved. An automatic resolution is necessary because character printers cannot talk back to the computer. If asked to print a document, character printers must print something, even if the letter spacing is awful. If a character printer does nothing, the user cannot tell the difference between a broken character laser and a lazy laser.

Character-mode laser printers classify fonts in eight different ways. Each font has eight different characteristics:

1. Orientation (landscape or portrait)

2. Symbol set (character set)

3. Spacing (characters per inch or proportional)
4. Pitch (the number of characters per inch)
5. Height (point size)
6. Style (italics or not)
7. Stroke weight (light, normal, demi, or bold)
8. Typeface (Times, Helvetica, Bookman, and so on)

These characteristics are listed in order as the most important characteristics to match. For example, if the PC wants text to be printed landscape, yet no landscape fonts exist, a portrait font should be selected. If after matching orientation, symbol set, spacing, pitch, height, style, and stroke weight, suppose that the typeface requested does not exist. The printer chooses from the last group of qualified stroke weights using tie-breaker rules. The tie breaker is the font's physical location. The following is a location priority list:

1. Soft fonts (downloaded fonts)
2. Cartridge fonts
3. Internal fonts (come with printer)

Soft fonts are chosen first. If just one soft font or downloaded font is in the group, that font is chosen. If no soft fonts are available, the cartridge fonts are investigated. If just one cartridge font is available, that font is chosen. If no cartridge fonts are available, internal fonts are investigated. If you have multiple qualifying soft fonts, the arbitrary number the printer assigns fonts becomes the tie breaker. The smallest printer-assigned number wins the final tie breaker.

Character laser printers use the preceding priority list no matter what.

Dot-matrix printers are developing a font selection priority list similar to that of the character lasers. Because dot-matrix printers have traditionally manipulated fonts more than selected them, their categories are a little different. Eventually, the dot-matrix and character laser selection processes could merge. The following are the dot-matrix font selection groups in order:

1. Print quality (draft, near-letter quality)
2. Character sets
3. Spacing (proportional, pitch)
4. Enhancements (shadow, outline, bold, italic, and so on)

The dot-matrix categories will eventually mature into those similar to the laser character categories. The important point is that in today's dot-matrix printers, certain combinations are not available. For example, draft outline is usually not possible.

> **HINT** | Choose default fonts from the front panel of the laser printer by using the font ID numbers. Be sure to hold the Reset button down for about five seconds on an HP LaserJet. A quick reset does not change the default font.

> **HINT** | If fonts have to be specified by sending commands to the laser printer, specify all the characteristics of the font, not just enough characteristics to make the printer work. Otherwise, the solution is not universal. The font will not print correctly on someone else's system, and if a cartridge is added to the current printer, the font will stop working. Develop universal solutions.

PC Software Decides Font

Certain PC software tries to learn everything about the attached printer. Instead of leaving the best match decisions up to the printer, certain PC software tries to make the best match decision. The PC software can ask for your input before making a substitution. For example, the software may be able to place a message on-screen saying `The font chosen does not exist in this printer—choose a font from the following list.`

Some software actually has a list of generic font names. When a new font is added to the printer, the software has to be told which of its generic fonts the new font is most similar to. The person installing the printer and software has to make font substitution decisions during software and new font installation.

If a character printer is asked to print an unknown font, the printer makes a best-fit decision. If software has translating or substituting capability, the program can intercept nonexistent printer font commands and substitute existing font switching commands in the data sent to a printer.

Graphics

Dot-matrix printers made graphics printing possible. The Diablo standard, although claiming a graphics mode, really has never supported graphics-mode operation. Even if the printer software supports a graphics version of Diablo, few software packages ever use it. Diablo emulation is basically a nongraphics, primitive character-mode-only emulation.

The first printer language that became popular with graphics software was the Epson dot-matrix printer language. Unfortunately, the graphics modes across Epson's early product line were not standard. At one point, three different Epson printer models had three different graphic mode languages. After IBM picked Epson as their source of PC printers, the Epson graphics language standardized. Today, the only way to switch Shift-PrtSc from character mode to graphics mode is to use the GRAPHICS.COM PC DOS program, and this method still requires an Epson-compatible printer and only works with certain videoboards.

> HINT | Before purchasing a printer, examine the software packages to be used. If the software packages suggest loading the GRAPHICS.COM program, they are going to print only on an Epson-compatible printer. Don't bother purchasing an expensive laser printer if this type of printout is desired. This feature also limits the type of videoboards that you can purchase.

All printers receive graphics-mode information in a horizontal band, usually 8 bits or dots wide. If these printers print the band immediately, they are called *band printers*. These printers may buffer a whole page before printing and, therefore, are called *page printers*, even though they receive the information in band form. The differences between graphics modes are minor. Most differences revolve around how to advance down the paper and begin a new band. Some graphics-mode printers just need a carriage return command to move to a new band. Other printers need special vertical movement information. If the PC graphics-mode software does not match, horizontal strips can appear between the bands (see fig. 6.2). If incorrect graphics-mode commands are sent to a printer, many pages are often ejected per graphics-mode page with a few random characters on them.

> TROUBLE-SHOOTING TIP | Horizontal lines in a graphics-mode printout can be caused by a pin of the dot-matrix print head not firing. This problem would be noticeable during normal printing. For example, the underline function may not work, or the top of a capital T looks funny. If the horizontal line appears during graphics mode and not during character mode, the problem is in the PC software graphics-mode configuration.

Chapter 6: Printer Software Features **267**

Fig. 6.2.
Graphics-mode compatibility problems.

Command Syntax

In Chapter 1, the concept of the PC sending the printer commands is introduced. In Chapter 3, the differences between printer commands and text to be printed became clearer. In the preceding pages of this chapter, the general categories of printer commands are reviewed. This section explains the exact structure of printer commands—how many bytes are involved and how the printer determines when a command stops and text begins.

This section is intended as an introduction for those users interested in programming printers. Printer programming is done mostly by people who write application programs for PCs. Some people also learn to program printers so that they can draw objects that are impossible to draw with a pen, air-brush, and drawing or graphics software. Word processors are essentially generic printer programming languages. If word processors are like Cobol and Fortran, printer programming is like assembly language.

Character and graphic printer commands start with one of 32 special bytes, *control codes*, reserved for sending commands to devices like printers, tape drives, modems, and so on. These special commands are outlined in Chapter 2.

After the first control code, there may be additional command bytes, or the printer command may consist of just one control code. The number of characters that follow the control code depends on the printer instruction. Sometimes, the entire printer command is just one control code. For example, the control code SO or Shift Out is all that is required to send an Epson into an expanded version of the current font. Other printer commands can contain many characters. Printer commands may include two control codes; a control code and number; control code and text; or control codes, numbers, and text. Printer commands can take the following forms.

1. Single control character:

    CR

2. Single control character followed by a fixed length of text, numbers, or combination of text and numbers:

    ESC C 10

3. Single control character followed by a variable length of text, numbers, or combination of text and numbers:

    ESC & l 1 O

Object printer commands look something like the following:

```
/ DefineBar
{    newpath
     38 730 moveto 538 0 rlineto
     0 −23 rlineto −530 0 rlineto
     closepath
```

```
} def
gsave
/Helvetica-Bold findfont
86 scalefont setfont
0 setgray
143.5 696 moveto
(Graphic) Show
```

Object programming languages use characters found on the keyboard, not control characters. All the preceding English-like words are instructions. In the preceding program, lines are being drawn. Regular words are sent to an object printer, but sending a word to a character printer causes the printer to print that word. Character- and graphics-mode printers understand only certain control codes. Object printers understand English. Instructing an object printer to print text, therefore, is difficult.

> HINT | Object printers are not going to work with commands, such as Shift-PrtSc, that expect a character printer.

Printer Languages

Appendix A organizes printer command languages of four different printers (Diablo, Epson, HP, and ISO). This appendix enables you to compare the different printer languages. Specific differences between them are apparent. The rest of this chapter reviews the differences between these printer languages from a feature point of view—what features you can expect from printers emulating these different languages.

Diablo

Diablo began by supplying printers for the dedicated word processors developed during the 1970s. Diablo supplied the printer to the dedicated word processor company, and the dedicated word processor companies built the Diablo printer into the word processing equipment. These printers did not contain a CPU. Instead, the dedicated word processing company supplied all the electronics to hook-up and program the Diablo printers. The cables running to the Diablo printers were nonstandard 12-bit parallel interfaces. These printers are practically impossible to salvage for PC operation.

Companies like Qume competed with Diablo, not only in the word processing market, but also in providing printers for TTYs or teletypes. In the 1970s, the hard-copy terminal market disappeared, and the need for printers attached to terminals appeared. Diablo, Qume, and other companies, therefore, developed serial printers for the terminal market.

The serial printers sold had a standard RS-323C serial interface and a simple printer programming language. These printers were first attached to PCs. Diablos were the most popular and were the first printers widely supported by most PC software. Even today, the effects of this early battle are reflected in laser printers that emulate the early Diablo printers. Unfortunately, the Diablo printer language does not support graphics-mode printing and has primitive font-selection capabilities. The printer can behave like an old daisywheel printer.

Epson

At about the same time that Diablo was becoming the most popular daisywheel printer, Centronics was becoming the most popular dot-matrix printer. In addition to being faster than the Diablo printers, the Centronics printer used a simple, cheap interface, much better than the standard RS-232C serial port. The one-way parallel port helped reduce the cost of a Centronics printer to much less than a Diablo. Centronics created the market for dot-matrix printers. In fact, the first official Atari printer was made by Centronics. Centronics reached their popularity peak around 1980. At about this time, Japanese printers started arriving. Epson printers were cheaper, more reliable, easier to repair, and had better-looking fonts. Similarly, NEC started selling *thimble* printers that looked as good as Diablos, were cheaper, more reliable, and had more features.

IBM also started designing the original IBM PC. IBM needed a printer for this personal computer. Given the time constraints, they could not design their own printer. Therefore, they looked at the dot-matrix printer market and chose to place the IBM logo on an Epson printer. Although the IBM printer was a different color, not much attempt was made to disguise the fact that it was an Epson printer. ComputerLand stores that originally sold IBM PCs had been selling Epson printers for Apple II+s for almost a year before the PC was released. For most people, the decision was to purchase an older Epson model with the IBM logo or purchase the latest Epson model. Either way, Epson won.

Epson rode the coattails of IBM's PC success to become the dot matrix that all other printer manufacturers would have to challenge. In fact, Epson became so popular that NEC produced a letter-quality printer that emulated a dot matrix (Nec SpinWriter model 3550). When IBM eventually developed their own printer, they could not ignore the Epson printer language. Even IBM's printer had to be Epson compatible. Of course, IBM added features to their language. Since then, IBM printers have developed unique features, but the Epson roots are still obvious. As the Epson printer language has evolved, the standard has evolved. Even though Epson no longer dominates the dot-matrix printer market, its evolving printer languages still do.

> HINT When you purchase a printer, ask who made the printer. Ask whether anyone else sells the printer under a different name. Often, companies purchase printers without names so that they can put their own names on them.

Like the Diablo standard, the Epson printer language defaults to character-mode operation. However, Epson provided the first graphics mode that became popular.

Hewlett-Packard

While Diablo leveraged their success in the dedicated word processor and terminal market and Epson succeeded alongside the IBM PC, Hewlett-Packard came out of nowhere. The HP LaserJet printer was the first on the market. The laser printing technology was so revolutionary that the printer language HP included became an instant standard for laser printers. HP's Printer Control Language (HPCL) has remained remarkably stable as font features have evolved. Even more impressive is that all the bigger laser printers HP makes can print any document that a PC LaserJet can. Even the lower priced inkjet printers HP sells today use this language.

HPCL is a character-mode language different from Epson's. The Epson language's strength has been in manipulating fonts (expanding, compressing, and so on) rather than in font variety. HPCL emphasizes the selection of different fonts and the management of fonts. HPCL, therefore, is much more complicated than Epson's printer language.

HPCL has not changed much since it was first released in 1986. This language has evolved by increasing the maximum point size, the number of fonts per page, and the total number of fonts that can be downloaded. Printers that emulate HP laser printers can emulate or reduce these limitations. Whether or not the HP emulation actually does allow more complex documents to be printed can be determined only by experiments. Magazines do not have the time to review this important feature of HP emulation. HP LaserJet and HP LaserJet+ usually have more limitations than HP LaserJet II emulation, but occasionally, HP LaserJet+ emulation has less limitations than another manufacturer's HP LaserJet II emulation.

ISO

The only standard printer language in use was published by the International Standards Organization. The ISO printer language is a character-mode language similar to HPCL. This language adds the font-manipulation features of the Epson language and has some object-mode features, such as being able to respond to a few queries made by PCs. For example, if a PC wants to know how wide all the letters are of a certain proportional font, the PC can ask an ISO printer. Unfortunately, ISO printers cannot initiate conversations with the PCs; they cannot complain that an error condition has arisen or that they need a font.

ISO printers match HPCL and Epson features and then add some. Because ISO printers can rotate fonts, they do not need separate landscape and portrait fonts. However, if landscape and portrait fonts are needed on the same page, separate landscape and portrait fonts are needed. This requirement falls short of an object printer's capability to stretch, distort, enlarge, or reduce any font and place characters anywhere on the paper at any angle.

ISO printers can manipulate fonts in a manner that most Epson printers cannot. ISO printers can invert any font so that the background is black and the letters are white. ISO printers come the closest to supporting all the font features available in word processors such as WordPerfect.

PostScript

PostScript is a printer language developed for the publishing and computerized typesetting world, and this language dominates the market. PostScript exercises a significant influence on PC printers. Yet, PostScript has never been associated with a particular printer manufacturer. This fact is amazing considering that Diablo, Epson, HP, and most other printer languages were created to sell printers. PostScript was developed with the goal of enabling printers to behave uniformly.

The development of PostScript parallels the development of the C programming language in many ways. Both are written to be device independent—C to be independent of the CPU; PostScript to be independent of the output device. Programmers are attracted to C because programs run on more computers with less effort. Programmers are attracted to Postscript because programs print more uniformly on more printers. Although neither has been blessed by a standards organization, both have been turned into de facto standards through books. The PostScript standard is a series of three books written by Adobe and published by Wiley.

Just as developing a C compiler for a particular CPU is difficult, so is developing a PostScript interpreter for a particular printer. The PostScript written for one printer is not usually transferable to another printer; just like a C compiler is not transferable from one CPU to another. Printer developers, however, are purchasing PostScript interpreters for their printers. This way, Adobe, the company that designed PostScript, makes money.

Because PostScript is a language like C, Fortran, Basic, or Cobol, the PostScript commands are not protected by copyrights, patents, or trademarks; however, the name *PostScript* is a trademark of Adobe. Although AT&T (Bell Labs) created the C language, companies like Lattice can name a product *Lattice C*. Because *PostScript* is trademarked, competitors like Destiny Co. cannot create a product called *Destiny PostScript*. Instead of using the word PostScript, Destiny has to make up its own name—*Destiny PageStyler*. The same commands and features of PostScript are supported. Companies like Destiny are supplying excellent object-printer interpreters. These companies can supply object-printer software that behaves and performs exactly like PostScript.

The object-oriented approach pioneered by Adobe's PostScript has the following benefits:

- Output device independence
- Standard file structure
- Protocol converter
- Output device management
- Scalable fonts

Output Device Independence

Object-printer software is designed to be device independent. Actually, it is more like a printer operating system. Application software can issue printer commands, and the printer's operating system translates these commands into ones that the printer understands. Object-printer software always tries to make a document look identical, whether printed on a 300 dpi PC laser printer or on 2640 dpi film.

Standard File Structure

Because Adobe's PostScript has been so good at creating a standard object-printer language, some PC programs are starting to save files in a PostScript format on hard disks and floppies. These PostScript files are sometimes used for failure recovery. They also provide a standard method for different PC software to exchange clip art, graphic, object, and document contents. Public domain and commercial object fonts are delivered or converted to standard PostScript program files before being sent to the printer. However, certain companies are copy-protecting their fonts using encryption techniques. Printer companies actually put encryption software in their printers so that just the fonts they sell work in the printer. Hopefully, this practice will change in the future.

Protocol Converter

Protocol converters in the data communication world convert from one computer language to another. Protocol converters in the printer world convert from PostScript to other languages. PostScript has become the standard transport language. PC software is available that can convert from PostScript to most other printer languages. The PostScript language has enough features that it can be used to clone any other printer's programming language.

Output Device Management

An object-oriented printer language can be asked questions. More importantly, object-printer languages can initiate their own conversations; they can ask PCs questions. This communication enables PCs and object printers to coordinate printer sharing and font management without user involvement. Some object printers can be plugged directly into a local area network. Other object printers can manage their own disk drives.

Scalable Fonts

The capability to create a font of any size inside an object printer was popularized by the PostScript language. Some character printers are developing this capability, but this feature alone does not change a character printer into an object printer.

> HINT: You can see the actual Postscript code if you print to a file. On the Macintosh, press Option-F and print normally. A file with the name PostScript is created. In the IBM PC world, you need a special public domain utility called LPT2DSK.COM.

Plotters

All plotters understand Hewlett-Packard Graphics Language (HPGL) or Digital Microprocessor Plotter Language (DMPL). HPGL is by far the more dominant of the two.

Plotter languages are similar to object-printer languages in that they can talk back. Plotters, when asked, send information to the PC such as the current pen coordinates. A plotter, however, cannot manage fonts or initiate conversations with the PC like object printers can.

PC DOS, OS/2, and Mac System 7

Vendors of PC operating systems currently are struggling to establish printer and video languages of their own. Microsoft has Windows and Presentation Manager; Digital Research has GEM, and Apple has QuickCode. Competing with these products is Adobe's PostScript. The PC operating system vendors have the lead in the video language world, and PostScript is winning in the printer world. This stalemate is stagnating WYSIWYG development. To understand how this situation came about, and where it may lead, a bit of operating system history is necessary.

The original PC operating systems, Apple II DOS (Disk Operating System) and CPM (Control Program Monitor), were just filing systems. All these systems could do was store files and look up pieces of those files on floppy disks. These early microcomputer operating systems were not true operating systems when compared to mainframe operating systems that manage memory, printers, terminals, and disk drives. Each microcomputer application program had to manage the video and printer.

As PC DOS, MS-DOS, and the Macintosh operating systems have evolved, more video support has been added. The capabilities to create windows, move around within a window, open and close windows, manage icons, and so on have been added. These products increase the learning curve of programmers and eventually improve programming productivity through standardization and portability. The major benefit, however, is in lowering each user's initial learning curve. Examples of these products are Windows, Presentation Manager, GEM, AppleWorks, and QuickCode. These products are part of an operating system or add-on extensions of an operating system. Using a mouse and windows, the primary focus of these products is ease-of-use.

Until recently, printer and videoboard support has been of secondary importance. What about font management; what about French-curve support? In these areas is where object-printer languages directly challenge PC operating systems. Object-printer languages are operating systems with programs similar to PC DOS's COMMAND.COM or the Macintosh's System Folder. In essence, a PC can be turned into a terminal, and the printer can be turned into the equivalent of a host minicomputer or mainframe. In the object-printer world, this system is called *interactive mode* rather than COMMAND.COM or System Folder. The prompt is similar to a PC DOS prompt, PS› instead of C›. The commands are different, but the interaction is the same. Object-printer languages look like an operating system and function like an operating system. They directly challenge the evolutionary growth of products like PC DOS, OS/2, and Apple's Macintosh operating system.

Most users will never see the printer operating system just like they never see the PC DOS, Mac System 6, or QuickCode operating system. You may see the details of the Mac system folder or learn a dozen or so PC DOS commands like COPY or DIR, but these commands are not operating system commands. Only programmers—those who write application programs—learn operating system commands, and many programmers use languages like Pascal or Cobol that hide the operating system. Only a few programmers, therefore, are going to know the details of the battle between traditional PC operating system companies and object-printer software.

Programmers cannot choose the ultimate winner because their need to earn money and become productive forces them to pick a side. Consumers have to pick the winner, using the following criteria:

- ❏ Features
- ❏ Cost
- ❏ Device independence

Currently, a Macintosh system has many advantages over the PC in handling printers. The primary advantage being that the Mac operating system is configured for each printer. When this configuration is finished, each Mac application can print on that printer. Each PC application has to be told which printer is attached. Printer companies are responsible for writing Macintosh software. PC application companies are responsible for writing printer drivers.

Apple and Microsoft have the same future in mind (see figs. 6.3 and 6.4). These companies want the application developers to learn only one language and have complete control over the software environment. Both companies face competition from Adobe. If Adobe is successful, Microsoft and Apple probably will be cloning Adobe. The resulting competition will drive prices down. If Apple and Microsoft win, prices will stay high.

Microsoft and Apple are struggling to support scalable screen and printer fonts. In the Macintosh world, Adobe has released a software product called the Type Manager, which competes directly with System 6 or 7 scalable font features. In the DOS world, Adobe has helped develop a PostScript driver and a PostScript Dynamic Link Library for OS/2's Presentation Manager.

An alternative future involves Mac and PC software migrating to the PostScript standard. Many reasons exist for entertaining this possibility:

❏ Application programmers will have less work to do when developing for both environments.

❏ Printer manufacturers will need just one printer model to cover both markets.

❏ Macs and PCs can share printers (not possible in the Apple and Microsoft ideal future worlds).

❏ Printers and monitors can be hooked directly to LAN cables.

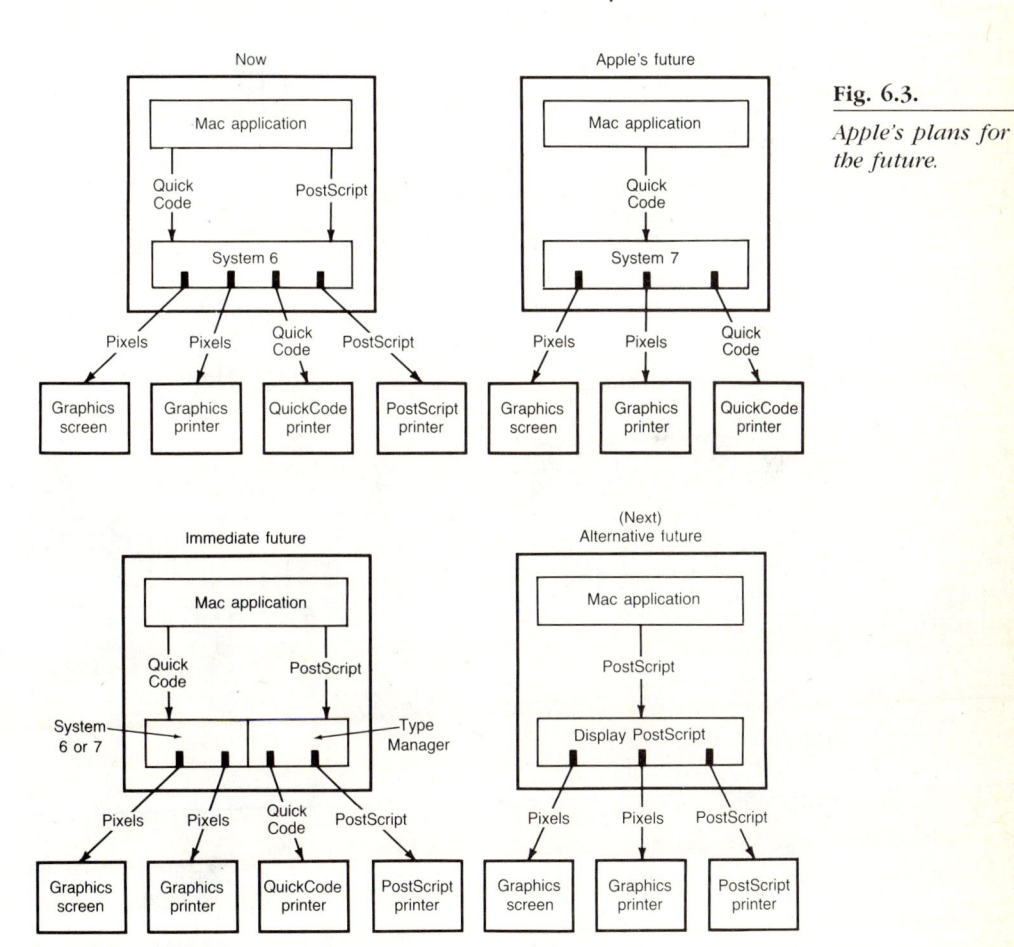

Fig. 6.3.

Apple's plans for the future.

Already, applications involving multiple screens are starting to appear. For example, arrival and departure plane flights, stock quotes, and schedules of daily activities can all be done with LAN PostScript monitors. In the Macin-

Fig. 6.4.

Microsoft's plans for the future.

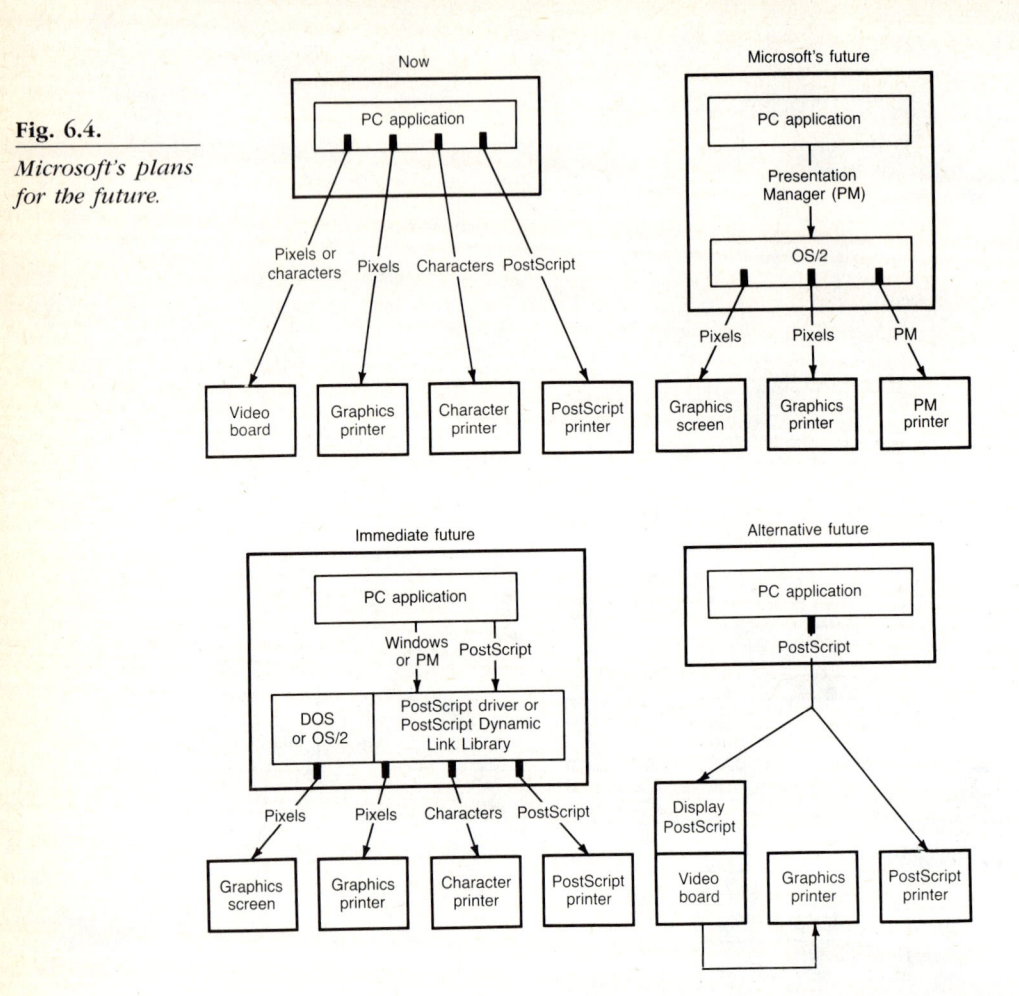

tosh world, multiple screens can be hooked up. A window can be dragged between monitors with a mouse, or the window can be enlarged to fill up multiple monitors.

The biggest reason that Adobe's PostScript has a chance of winning is that its features cannot be improved on—only better PostScript programs can be written. Nothing can be added to Presentation Manager or QuickCode that makes them better than PostScript without making them PostScript clones. Perhaps Presentation Manager or QuickCode can become easier to learn and program in than PostScript, but PostScript has a fantastic head start. PostScript printers have a large font library and a large installed base of hardware and software. PostScript will be around in some form for years to come.

Currently, Macintosh System 7 is supposed to come with a QuickCode that can scale fonts. At the programming level, QuickCode is still primitive. Suppose that three or four pages need to be placed on top of each other; some parts are transparent, and others are not. The figure or graphic of one page is to show through, but white on another page is to block pages below. This design is possible with PostScript. QuickCode pages stacked on top of each other bleed together as if they are transparent. In a QuickCode (or Presentation Manager) environment, the application programmer is responsible for the *block* feature. In the PostScript environment, it is much easier for the application programmer to implement the block by using PostScript.

PostScript has a good chance of bringing the PC and Mac worlds together because PostScript is feature rich, promotes competition (thereby reducing your costs), and is device independent.

Printer Utilities

Printer utilities are programs added to the operating system of the computer that enhance printing features. These utilities normally send commands to the printer that add font-changing and graphic-printing capabilities to software. Generally, these types of utilities are excellent products in the Mac world. In the PC world, most application programs talk to the printer and ignore the utilities and, therefore, are useless. If applications cannot ignore the utilities, they usually lock the keyboard up. Occasionally, printing utilities do work in the PC environment, but they are usually not worth the time you spend testing and the risks you take when installing them. Following is a list of some printer utility programs available:

Ermasoft Laser Envelopes
E.R.M. Association
29015 Garden Oaks Court
Agoura Hills, CA 91301
(800) 288-ERMA
(818) 707-3818

E-Z Set
Orbit Enterprises
P.O. Box 2875
Glen Ellyn, IL 60138
(312) 469-3405

LaserMenu
Micrologic Software
6400 Hollis Street, #9
Emeryville, CA 94608
(800) 888-9078
(415) 652-5464

Laser Ready
Mind Path Technologies
12700 Park Central Drive, #1801
Dallas, TX 75251
(214) 233-9296

Laser Torq, Trading Post
Lasertools Corp.
5900 Hollis Street, Suite G
Emeryville, CA 94608
(800) 346-1353
(415) 420-8777

LaserTwin
Metro Software Inc.
2509 North Campbell Avenue, #214
Tucson, AZ 85719
(800) 621-1137
(602) 299-0313

Lasercount, Typetracker
Lasercount Systems, Inc.
1 Bridge Plaza #110
Fort Lee, NJ 07024
(201) 461-8776

Mac Jet, Mac Kiss
Laser Connection
7852 Schillinger Park W.
Mobile, AL 36608
(800) 233-6687
(205) 633-7223

Mac Print
Insight Development Corp.
1024 Country Club Drive, #140
Moraga, CA 94556
(415) 376-9500

Printer Interface III & IV
Datapak Software Inc.
14011 Ventura Blvd., #507
Sherman Oaks, CA 91423
(800) 327-6703
(818) 905-6419

Because Macintosh utilities are added to the Mac operating system, they are available to all application software. If the utilities are popular, Apple usually tries to incorporate them in the next release of the operating system. Apple purchases the utility company or redesigns the utility. Most Mac utilities deal with the LaserWriter. Some Macintosh utilities include the following:

- Capability to detect whether shared LaserWriter is busy before sending a long print job
- Capability to request detailed information about the printer such as:

    PostScript version
    Page count
    Pages printed since the last toner replacement
    Fonts already downloaded
    Resident fonts

- Capability to download fonts
- Capability to reset the printer if it locks up (or keeps printing start-up pages)
- Capability to capture, modify, and write PostScript programs
- Capability to generate screen fonts from printer fonts
- Capability to list Macs or PCs on a LAN to search for missing fonts

PC print utilities come in several varieties; unfortunately, all have drawbacks.

Enhancements to specific PC application programs have a limited life span. The next version of the PC application program adds the feature, or the old enhancement is incompatible with the new PC software release. Waiting for a new enhancement release is difficult because it often never comes. The market is so small that the enhancement product dies.

The capability to print to a file suffers because the PC application has to be kicked out of memory and the utility program executed before printing can occur. If something is slightly wrong with the printout, the utility program has to be kicked out of memory; the PC program has to be loaded; the file loaded; a print file created; the PC program kicked out of memory, and the print utility loaded again. This process is so time-consuming and tedious that nobody does it. The utility is not used.

The memory-resident utilities are not popular in the PC world because they usually lock up the PC. If these utilities don't freeze the cursor, they translate output to a printer or pop up when a magical key combination is pressed. Usually, the translations or printer commands reach the printer. However, PC application software often sends its own commands that override the utility's commands. The utility's commands, therefore, often are not effective.

Chapter Summary

Printers can become confused. When confused, they eject multiple sheets of paper, print the start-up page, or flash an error message. These printers become confused for a variety of reasons, such as trying to display too many fonts on a page. This chapter discussed what to do when the printer becomes confused.

Emulation of other printers can raise a number of questions, such as: How are unprintable regions and additional features handled during emulation? Who wrote the emulation software? How much memory does it take up?

Printer software concepts that influence printer purchases, operation, and troubleshooting were reviewed. These concepts include:

- ❏ Environment (switch settings)
- ❏ Job control (error states)
- ❏ Page setup (paper tray to be used)
- ❏ Page layout (margins)
- ❏ Cursor positioning (proportional spacing)
- ❏ Font manipulation (expanded, compressed, double height, and so on)
- ❏ Underlining
- ❏ Font selection

These categories form the outline of Appendix A, which shows the commands of the major printer languages and the differences between printer software vendors.

A history of the various standard printer languages was reviewed in this chapter, including Diablo, Epson, HPCL, ISO, and PostScript. A comparison among PostScript, Microsoft, and Apple plans for the future was made. These companies are fighting a war over the control of printer software.

Finally, printer utilities were reviewed.

In The Next Chapter

The next chapter outlines purchase decisions, guiding you to the best purchase possible for yourself or your company. Unfortunately, important considerations like what is in stock, how close is the nearest store, and who will fix it—which can make all the difference in the world—cannot be covered. Many relevant issues remain, however, and they are covered in detail.

II

Printer Setup and Management

Includes

Making a Purchase Decision
Installing and Testing Printers
Configuring PC Applications

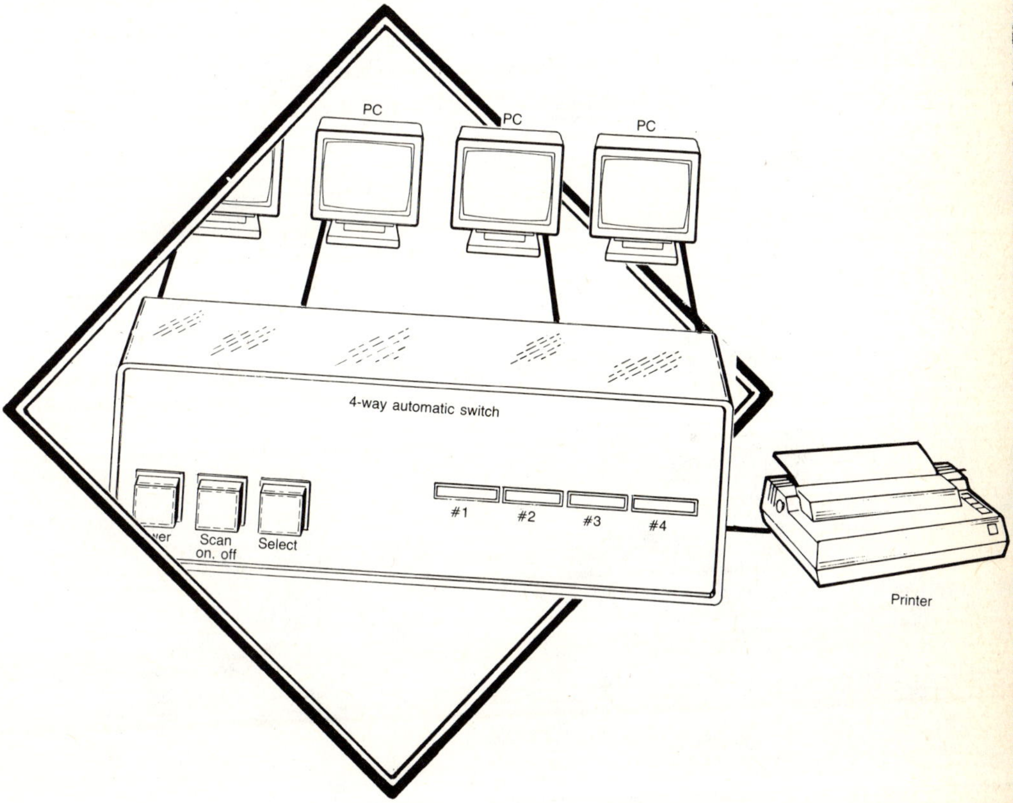
PC
PC
PC
4-way automatic switch
Scan
on, off
Select
#1
#2
#3
#4
Printer

7

Making a Purchase Decision

A mail-order catalog claims that it stocks ribbons for over 7,358 different printers. *PC Magazine* claims that it has reviewed almost 600 different printer models in the past six years. The number of different printers is staggering. Here are some statistics reported in different trade journals during 1989. Over 110 million PC printers have been sold. Currently, approximately 30 million printers are sold yearly. Of these, 20 million are dot matrix. Ninety-eight percent of all PCs are attached to a printer. Of the printers in use, 65 percent are 9-pin dot matrix; 22 percent are 24-pin or 18-pin dot matrix; and 8 percent are lasers, and 5 percent are daisywheels. But, during 1988 and 1989, no daisywheel printers were reviewed. Mail-order catalogs are not even advertising print wheels anymore. No claim is made that these numbers are exact, but the magnitudes reveal how widely printers are being used.

You can ask many questions before purchasing a printer. Salesmen want you to believe that just a few questions exist. In fact, you may consider walking into a computer store and encouraging the salesperson to select a printer for you.

This chapter reviews many possible questions to ask before purchasing a printer. The checklist at the end of this chapter outlines points to consider when purchasing a printer. You can copy this checklist and use it as worksheet when trying to determine which printer to choose. This chapter is also useful when you are deciding on a printer, developing a purchase justification for your boss, bartering prices, or purchasing through the mail.

Reading Printer Reviews in Magazines

The best review of printers is done yearly by *PC Magazine*. The *PC Magazine* "Printer Issue" has been arriving around the beginning of November since 1984. Each year, the reviews cover all the new printer models that companies ship to the magazine's testing labs. Printer companies have learned that they must be included in this review to gain respect and a share of the printer market. *PC Magazine's* printer reviews have an enormous impact on printer purchases. The "Editor's Choice" models become the standard for many people. From these reviews, consultants form their opinions, salesmen decide which models to push, and buyers make purchasing decisions.

Because the magazine review process is a great source of free advertisement for printer companies, the companies have a tremendous incentive to come up with new printer models each year. An average of 100 new printer models are produced each year. This number is starting to decrease as the printer market becomes more stable. Few magazines have the resources to test and compare 100 new printers—even *PC Magazine* cannot compare the current crop with the previous year's models. Before 1985, purchasing last year's printer was crazy—the current year's would be better and cheaper. But today, a printer released the preceding year can still be a better model than any of the current releases. Yet, this fact is usually not mentioned in the current *PC Magazine* review, so the issue is not an encyclopedia of all printers or even the best printer models currently sold.

Older printer models may actually be better. The newer models sometimes contain design flaws that don't show up during the review. In the winter of 1987, *PC Magazine* made the Okidata Laserline 6 an "Editor's Choice," meaning that it was the best in its category. On April 29, 1989, a class action suit was filed in a U.S. District Court, charging that up to 80 percent of the Laserline 6 printers sold produced shadows, blurs, and splotches on printouts. The test of time is not available to magazine reviewers.

Many printers reviewed do not really exist. Companies send preproduction models to the magazine, hoping for a good review. If the review is not positive, the company may not even try to sell the printer.

Most magazines try to come up with a rating scheme for printers. Some use a 1 to 10 scale or even stars, like movie reviews. These rating systems have problems:

- Only a few printers are compared at a time.
- The rating formulas usually do not emphasize your unique needs.
- Printer features are not covered sufficiently to aid your own evaluations.

The other printer-rating technique—the one *PC Magazine* uses—is to write a page or two describing each printer. The readers are free to make up their own minds. The trouble with this technique is that more thorough reviews must be done: readers have to read over 100 pages of a magazine, and then sorting out the reviewers' true feelings requires rereading each review. Because the magazine can lose advertising revenue with an entirely negative review, the reviewers generally try to find something positive to say about every printer. Even so, *PC Magazine* maintains a good perspective, and their reviewers are certainly less biased and more informed than most other sources.

Read the past two special printer issues of *PC Magazine* if you want the facts. Make up your own mind; do not blindly follow the editor's choice. Some other magazines also write fine printer reviews, but they should be used as supplements because they usually are not as detailed.

Assessing Your Printer Possibilities

Certain issues immediately reduce the printer models available. For example, if you have only $500 available or if portability is an issue, laser printers are not an option.

Money

The first question is how much money you have to spend. Around $175 purchases a good 9-pin dot-matrix printer that can print in draft mode or in near-letter quality. At the other extreme, you can use a $5000 PostScript printer for some publishing purposes. In between, many printer models exist to choose from.

Special Capabilities

Most people use their printers to print one copy of a document. Others want a printer that can be carried on the road, or that can print stencils, mimeographs, multipart forms, and transparencies. This section reviews these possibilities.

> *Portability*. Nowadays, many people want a portable printer to go along with their laptop computer. Portable printers must be light, and they run on batteries, so they are more expensive than their desktop counterparts. Older portable printers used a thermal technology. The print head contained dots that heated up. The special paper had to

change color in response to the heat, and the output looked terrible. In some cases, a copy machine could not copy it. Today, most portable printers are using inkjet technology. Canon and Diconixs are the most popular vendors.

Stencils and mimeographs. Some organizations need a printer that can create stencils or mimeographs. A stencil is a paper-like material with holes cut in it. The ink bleeds through the holes. Mimeograph is a paper-like material with special waxy substance attached in a mirror image of what is to appear. The waxy substance picks up ink and then transfers the ink to paper. Stencils look and last better than mimeographs. You can create stencils from typed or printed pieces of paper, but this process is expensive. You can create mimeographs from any document relatively inexpensively. But, if the mimeographs are created by a printer directly, the duplicates look much better. Printing stencils and mimeographs requires an impact printer. The holes a 24-pin dot-matrix printer creates in a stencil are good at limiting the ink flow, thus producing much cleaner looking duplicates. Usually, a wide-carriage printer is needed because landscape printing often is required.

Multipart forms. If you print multipart forms, you need an impact printer. Most dot-matrix printers are specified to print up to five sheets of carbonless forms or three sheets of paper and two carbons. Printing more copies requires a special printer.

Transparencies in more than one color only can be created with plotters. Single-color transparencies for laser printers are available, but they require an expensive special transparency material (a ream costs about $250). Plotter transparencies cost only about $125 per ream, but the output of a plotter is not as nice as a laser printer's.

See the section "Determining Your Required Output" for more information on certain printer capabilities.

Paper Size

Using paper 8 1/2 inches wide or less is easy. Paper wider than 8 1/2 inches requires wide-carriage dot matrix and inkjet printers. Laser printers are normally incapable of printing on anything larger than 8 1/2-by-11-inch paper.

Determining Life-Cycle Costs

The overall cost of owning a printer should influence your purchase decision. For the purposes of the following discussion, the initial and operating costs are combined into one number called the *life-cycle costs*.

Justifying the purchase of a printer is difficult. Internal company politics can make disposable products easy to purchase and capital purchases difficult. Or, capital purchases decisions can be easy, but necessities like paper are hard to come by. Issues like these can determine which printer is purchased. In the ideal world, the life cycle cost should influence a purchase decision. But, different people are going to value different features, so a true cost analysis is hopelessly complex. This section starts the comparison process by comparing the selling price, and the cost of paper, ribbons, ink, toner, and so on. The prices that follow are average mail-order prices. Add 10 to 30 percent for dealer pricing. The following factors are examined:

Paper
Consumable costs including toner, ribbons, ink
Paper and consumable costs combined
Purchase price of printer
Per-ream purchase price
Overall operating cost
Time

Paper costs are surprising. Laser paper is the cheapest. Bundles of copy machine paper must be cheaper to make than either tractor-feed dot-matrix paper or inkjet paper. Different types of paper are available in each category. For example, the smooth-edge tractor-feed paper is compared with the coarser perforations. Because you can use regular paper in an inkjet printer, the special inkjet paper is compared to regular tractor feed paper. Special laser-printer paper is compared to the cheapest copier paper. The high and low prices in each category were developed by reading advertisements in mail-order catalogs from various companies.

Paper Costs Per Ream

Laser (cut sheets)	$2.50 to $ 5.50
Dot-matrix (fanfold)	$3.08 to $ 6.48
Inkjet (special)	$3.08 to $10.00

If you compare costs of toner cartridges, ribbons, and inkjet bladders, dot-matrix printers win because their ribbons are cheap. Inkjet printers lose again. The ink bladders all cost about the same once the cost is normalized to each ream. Representative dot-matrix ribbons that cost $1.50 to $2.50 are chosen, and the ribbons are replaced after printing 1,500 characters. You can leave ribbons in a dot matrix forever, but the output fades past acceptability.

Ribbon, Toner, and Ink Costs per Ream

Dot-matrix	$00.50 to $00.88
Laser	$10.00 to $12.50
Inkjet	$22.10

If paper, toner, ink, and ribbon costs are combined, a pattern starts to emerge. Dot-matrix printers are the most cost-effective way of putting letters on paper. Lasers are the next most efficient, and Inkjet printers are least efficient. If you have finally received a grant or permission to spend money on a printer, but you are positive that you will have little money for paper and supplies, dot-matrix printers are the way to go. If the purse strings are looser, these costs aren't critical.

Paper and Toner/Ink/Ribbon Costs per Ream:

Dot-matrix	$3.58 to $7.36
Laser	$12.50 to $18.00
Inkjet	$25.08 to $32.10

Because magazines advertise the initial cost of printers, the initial costs are obvious. Lasers are the most expensive, and 9-pin dot-matrix printers are the cheapest. The following prices are representative of the most popular models in each category.

Typical Printer Price

9-pin	$175.00
24-pin	$225.00
Inkjet	$675.00
Laser	$1650.00

Each printer is rated according to how many pages it can print before the motors, gears, and so on, start to wear out. If the original printer cost is divided by the total number of pages printed before death, an accurate comparison of printers is possible. Here, laser printers are clearly more efficient because they are designed to print many more pages than a dot matrix.

Purchase Price per Ream

Laser	$2.75
9-pin	$2.92
Inkjet	$3.38
24-pin	$4.16

Remember though, the hardware costs are not on the same order as the expendables. The overall cost of an inkjet is still higher than a 24-pin dot matrix. Dot-matrix printers easily win the overall operation cost of printing.

Overall Cost per Ream

9-pin	$ 6.37 to $ 9.90
24-pin	$ 7.74 to $11.52
Laser	$15.25 to $20.75
Inkjet	$28.55 to $35.48

The cost of owning an inkjet printer is a surprise; most people expect the laser printer to be the most expensive. In fact, laser printers are just over double the cost of a 9-pin dot-matrix printers. Inkjet printers are three to four times the cost 9-pin dot-matrix printers. The bladders and special paper required make the price of operating an inkjet printer so expensive that the initial savings are quickly eroded.

Of all the factors that influence printer costs, your time probably is the most expensive. If the printer prints faster, you're not going to stand around as long and therefore be more efficient. Because the laser printer is the fastest, it wins this category easily. But, remember that even the speed of a printer is a subjective issue. (See Chapter 5 for a discussion of printing speed.) Because the idea that people may be standing around waiting for a printer is not always a valid assumption, the whole analysis quickly becomes unquantifiable. And other factors can affect these calculations. For example, laser printers usually require more management than other types of printers, but laser printers don't have bothersome fanfold paper to tear apart.

Nevertheless, the following chart may give you a rough idea of the "standing around" cost. The assumptions are as follows: While a printer is printing, you don't do other work; the speed is the page per minute (or character per second) rating of the printer; no buffer is used, and your salary is between $20,000 and $40,000.

Expense for Waiting per Ream

Laser	$10.42 to $20.83
Inkjet	$20.83 to $41.67
Dot-matrix	$27.78 to $55.56

What is interesting is not the exact value of these numbers, but the fact that the cost of standing around and waiting for a ream of paper to print is roughly the same as the hardware costs of printing the page. How effectively and efficiently the printers are used is just as important as which printer is purchased.

Determining Your Required Output

When purchasing a printer, you should have a clear idea of the types of documents to be printed and the environment of the printer. For example, you can print banners and wide spreadsheets only on tractor-feed dot-matrix printers. Desktop publishing is crude on dot-matrix printers. Noise is a concern if the printer is going to be in a reception area where visitors are greeted or a place where the telephone is answered. This section explores these types of issues.

Printing Internal Reports

Internal reports are not designed to impress people. Rather, they communicate information clearly and efficiently. Many times, internal reports are printed on tractor-feed paper that is never ripped apart. In fact, the fanfold paper helps keep the pages in order. Usually in these circumstances, speed is important, not text quality. Therefore, a fast dot-matrix printer with tractor feed is the most cost-effective solution.

Printing Letters and Papers

Formal documents designed to impress people are usually bound in a notebook or stapled together. Sometimes a 24-pin printer will produce the required quality. In these cases, you can purchase tractor-feed paper that tears apart, or feed single sheets by hand. For the best quality, however, the only solution is a laser printer.

Printing Mailing Labels

Mailing labels are discussed throughout this book because they are such a problem. Mailing labels reduce a printer's life span by jamming paper, heating motors, and forcing the printer to work harder. In general, try printing label addresses on fanfold paper. Then, copy the addresses on to the labels by using a photocopier. Be sure to purchase special mailing label sheets that can withstand the heat inside a photocopier.

If the photocopier approach is not workable, use the cheapest, 9-pin dot-matrix printer you can find. You do not care about fonts or fancy front panel controls. If possible, use this printer just for mailing labels, leaving them in the printer at all times. This method reduces the problem of mailing labels peeling off inside the printer and jamming things up.

Printing Banners

Banners are pages of fanfold paper that have not been torn apart. Instead, letters are printed sideways (landscape) along the continuous sheet. A sentence can be 12 feet long. Banners are used for signs or for special events like parties. Special software and a dot-matrix printer are required to create the banners, unless you have the $15,000 or so for a laser printer with fanfold paper capability.

Printing Wide Spreadsheets

Wide spreadsheets are similar to banners in that the letters are printed sideways. Laser landscape printing can serve the same purpose if the number of horizontal characters is less than 233 (16.67 pitch, 8.5-point font, 14-inch paper). Otherwise, tractor feed paper is required.

Printing Forms

Filling out forms like checks or purchase orders requires special software. This software almost always is specific to a particular business because each business uses its own special forms, so the software is hard to sell to the general public. To make money, the software has to be expensive, and printer support is limited. Because most forms are fanfolded, they require a tractor. Dot-matrix printers and a few inkjet printers are the only ones that have tractors today. Many forms have second and third copies that require the impact of a dot-matrix printer.

Printing Newsletters, Brochures, and Handouts

Newsletters, brochures, and handouts can all be done with a dot-matrix printer. Unfortunately, the quality suffers. Even though some dot-matrix printers print at 360 dpi, the output still does not look as nice as a 300 dpi laser printer because the dot-matrix dots are not 1/300 inch in diameter. The dot-matrix dots are thick, overlapping, and uneven. Dot-matrix heads heat up and wear out prematurely if used primarily for drawings involving many black areas. If the initial cost of a laser printer is too high, inkjet printers are just about as good. However, the cost of inkjets suffers because their ink and special paper are so expensive.

Printing Magazines and High-Quality Output

Lasers can create camera-ready output for certain types of black-and-white documents like newsletters. But, really good-looking text (like that found in this book) cannot be produced on a laser printer. Instead, this book was printed using film on a typesetting machine rather than ink and a printer. See Chapter 10 for more details on these options.

Sharing the Printer

The different products and methods for sharing a printer are reviewed in Chapter 8. Here, the goal is to decide whether to share a printer. The necessary hardware alone for sharing a printer can climb to over $200 per station.

In other words, the sharing mechanism can cost more than a dot-matrix printer itself.

Sharing a printer has one benefit—fewer printers have to be purchased. But, many disadvantages exist.

Poor Interaction. You tell the PC to print a document. You walk over to the shared printer and discover that somebody else is using it. You walk back to your PC and tell it to try printing again (if the PC has not locked up). You walk back to the printer, and the paper has the wrong letterhead, or the printer has run out of paper. Again, you walk back to the PC. After doing this several times, even the short distance between the shared printer and your PC seems long. The time spent walking is inefficient. Because the printer is shared with another, the time spent coordinating print time, paper, and so on becomes significant.

Printer Glitches. The box that allows the printer to be shared can cause the printer to spit pages when a PC is turned off. Perhaps, the printer flashes an error message when a PC is turned off, or the sharing device must be reset when the PC is turned off. Some print-sharing devices work better than others.

Software Resets. Most PC software expects the printer to be hooked to one PC. The software is always resetting the printer. Fonts that took 15 minutes to download can be wiped out. Different documents rarely appear on the same page because the sharing device usually guesses correctly where the end of a page is. However, the PC software does not know what the print sharing device is doing. The coordination problems just to give each PC a different sheet of paper are not 100 percent solvable, and you may find managing fonts difficult. The best shared printer is a PostScript printer on a LAN.

Recovering from Disaster

Printouts produce the final results of any computer activity. When a report is due or a mailing has to go out, the printer has to work. Electronic offices and electronic mail have come a long way, but paper is still more real than any electronic file. When the payroll checks cannot be printed, you have a disaster bigger than a hard disk crash.

To avoid these hazards, one strategy is to purchase several printers of the same kind. If one printer runs out of toner or paper, or breaks a ribbon, you will have a common resource of spares to draw upon. Before making a purchase decision, look at the other printer models in the office. Multiple identical printers reduce employee training, installation, configuration, and troubleshooting costs.

Considering the Printer Environment

The operating environment of a printer can have a tremendous influence on office procedures. If the printer is loud, nobody will want to talk on the telephone while the printer is operating. If the printer is in a dirty environment, you may need a special printer container. If the printer is in the sun, it may heat up and stop working.

Printers can harm the office environment by making too much noise. Most dot-matrix printers are quiet as long as all the plastic covers are in place, but, your environment may require a soundproof hood.

Printers also can be harmed by the environment. Printers can collect dust, heat up, and suffer from surges and spikes coming through the wall outlet. *Surges* and *spikes* are sudden voltage changes in the power cord into your printer. They can be caused by improperly wired wall outlets or other devices (like space heaters) on the same circuit breaker. In fact, printers are more likely to collect more dust, heat up more, and be more sensitive to surges and spikes than PCs. If the building is old, surges and spikes happen more often. If the room gets really hot, an air conditioner may be needed.

Determining the Printer for Your Application Needs

Different PC programs use printers in different ways. To decide on the type of printer to purchase, consider the printer requirements of your software packages. The following sections break down applications by type.

Printing with Spreadsheet Applications

Spreadsheet programs work with numbers and are designed to talk only to simple printers. Spreadsheets are composed almost entirely of columns of numbers. If the columns are printed in a proportional font, they will not line up. Poor alignment makes the document hard to read. Therefore, the best font for printing a spreadsheet is a simple fixed-spaced font.

Some special spreadsheet fonts have been designed. They are tiny so that many characters can appear horizontally. Usually, however, spreadsheet print quality is not an issue. A good printout should make the rows and columns easy to pick out. Printing speed is not even important. Most spreadsheets are short. Those that are long are printed one page at a time. Printing large spreadsheets usually fails, unless the spreadsheet has been carefully designed.

(This failure occurs because spreadsheets usually print in horizontal columns, and the important summary columns end up all by themselves on another sheet of paper.)

The fanciest feature of 1-2-3 is its capability to translate character sets. Other than this feature, 1-2-3 treats the printer as if it were a dumb, simple printer. 1-2-3 expects the spacing to be fixed, not proportional. If the printer is put in proportional mode, 1-2-3 will not know the difference. 1-2-3 does not send spacing commands to the printer, meaning that none of the columns will line up.

The perfect spreadsheet printer would be a wide-carriage laser printer with a large selection of tiny fixed-spaced fonts. Unfortunately, this printer does not exist. Wide-carriage dot-matrix printers exist, but they do not have the special small fonts. Special spreadsheet font cartridges for laser printers exist, but they cannot print on the wide paper. Therefore, you have to pick one or the other. From an operational point of view, 1-2-3 is designed for a dot-matrix printer. Using a laser with 1-2-3 can be disconcerting because 1-2-3 typically prints partial pages that the laser printer stores until it receives a full page of data. The pause may make you think that something is broken.

Printing with Database Applications

Databases expect simple printers. Databases can send names and addresses to a word processor; then the word processor is responsible for printing the form letter. Many databases have a programming language that enables specific printer commands to be sent to a printer. Unless programmed carefully, the special commands work on just one printer model. To avoid this limitation, most database users do not take advantage of the capability to send printer commands.

Database programs are designed to make sorting, finding, and processing data easy—not to produce beautiful output. For example, a mail-order catalog company does not want to print pretty inventories, just functional ones. When the catalog is produced, the database information is sent to a desktop publishing program and high-resolution printer.

The fanciest printing that database programs do is filling out forms. This printing requires sending printer cursor movement commands to exact horizontal and vertical locations. All printers support these commands, but the program may still have to be modified if the printer model is changed.

Database printing is usually speed sensitive. When a sales receipt is printed, two or more people are standing around waiting. If a large number of records are printed, speed is going to be important. The time to print a big mailing list becomes noticeable for even small speed differences. On the other hand, quality is not that important. Who cares whether a bill, invoice, or receipt contains an unusual font? A fast, wide-carriage, 9-pin dot matrix is the appropriate printer for database printing.

Printing with Word Processing Applications

Word processing programs are rapidly evolving toward desktop publishing programs. Originally, word processors supported single fonts on character printers. The evolution toward proportional spacing and multiple fonts has been painful. Many word processors had trouble computing how many letters should be put on a line when expanded or compressed fonts were chosen. Most of the time, they made the line too short or too long, and the printer lost the extra letters.

Word processors are essentially printer programming languages. Good word processors have generic names for the specific commands your printer understands. Most of the time, a one-to-one correspondence exists between the command you give the word processor and the command the word processor gives the printer.

The printer model is important to a word processor. Word processors have to understand the printer's hardware, software, and behavior. If the word processor does not know the printer, the word processor cannot exercise any of the printer's features. When buying a printer for a word processor, you should stick with mainstream products. Word processors may not support an obscure printer.

Word processors generate documents that someone is going to read. Most people do not read database printouts or all the numbers on a spreadsheet. They are more interested in skimming the document. The uniformity of the columns is important for skimming easily. However, word-processing documents are meant to be read, so quality is important.

When you are printing a letter or short paper, speed is not really an issue. But, if you often print longer documents, speed is crucial. A 24-pin printer is sufficient for most in-house word processing, but if customers read your documents, consider a laser printer.

Printing with Desktop Publishing Applications

Desktop publishing packages, such as Ventura and PageMaker, have all the needs of a word processor, plus graphics, making speed and quality critical issues. Most desktop publishing software really needs a laser printer and preferably an object or PostScript laser printer.

Printing with Accounting Applications

Accounting packages usually print reports for internal use, so the font quality is not important. But, speed is essential. When you are printing checks and pay stubs, specialized forms are necessary. If a firm is big enough to justify printing its own checks with a printer, it is also large enough to dedicate a printer to the task. Because print quality is not an issue, draft font speed is the primary feature of interest—for both the check printer and the reports printer. Therefore, purchase a fast, wide-carriage, 9-pin dot-matrix printer.

Printing with Graphics and Drawing Programs

Popular drawing and graphics programs include PC PaintBrush, GEM Draw, CorelDraw, and Micrografx Designer. Graphics programs, whether object-oriented or paint, usually put printers in graphics mode and control the placement of each dot on the paper. Most graphics programs can output to PostScript printers. In fact, some drawing or graphics programs (like Adobe Illustrator) work only with PostScript printers.

In graphics-mode printing, speed is the issue. If the quality of dot-matrix printers is sufficient, graphics programs can print at better resolutions than lasers. The trouble is that dot-matrix graphics-mode printing requires that the printer be in tip-top shape. If the wires in the print head bend a little or get weak, the print head develops play. If the platen and head are not lined up properly, the output does not look nice at all. Usually, the output looks nice as long as the printer is under warranty.

For reliable, consistent, high-quality printing, you need a laser printer. But, the trouble here is that the laser requires at least 1M of RAM added to the fairly standard 512K of most HP-PCL-compatible lasers.

Printing for Programming and Error Logging

Many PC applications require the PC to listen to some other device, like an uninterruptable power supply (UPS) of a mini or mainframe system. Big, expensive UPSs can send surge, brownout, and spike messages to the PC. Or, a modem conversation may need to be recorded on the printer. For example, DOS is told to echo all COMMAND.COM conversations to the printer. (Press Ctrl-PrtSc to start; press Ctrl-PrtSc again to stop.) Maybe, error messages need to be printed while a programmer is compiling a program.

These types of applications do not send formatted text to the printer. They do not care where page boundaries are. These applications are the most likely to print on the perforations of a 24-pin dot-matrix printer or in the unprintable region of a laser printer. For this reason, 24-pin dot-matrix and laser printers default to skipping the perforations and unprintable regions. Unfortunately, the printer may have had the skipping turned off by a previous PC program. Then, the programming or error-logging program would print in the unprintable region; error messages may not ever be printed. If this type of printing is going to be the primary use of the printer, purchase a 9-pin dot matrix; it can print on the perforation without problems.

If the printer needs to be used with equipment other than a PC, like an uninterruptable power supply, purchase a serial printer. Almost all other equipment that prints status or monitoring information needs a serial printer.

Printing with Educational Software

Most educational software applications only support simple, 9-pin dot-matrix printers. Purchasing a fancy 24-pin or laser printer will not improve the quality of the printout. In fact, the educational software may not even work with the fancier printers.

Determining the Hardware Features You Need

Printer hardware features are detailed in Chapter 5. In this section, hardware features are reviewed from a purchasing perspective.

Choosing an Interface

All Macintoshes come with a serial port. The serial port is used primarily to hook up ImageWriter printers and clones of the ImageWriter. The older Mac and fat Macs came with a DB-9 female serial port connector. Most modern Macs have a round serial port called a *DIN connector* with holes arranged in a semicircle. Older Macs need a converter to turn the DB-9 into a DIN. Also, a Mac can be hooked to a printer through Local Talk cables or by attaching the printer to the cable of the external hard disk drive. The interfaces of the Mac world are all pretty much the same. Let the printer chosen determine the Mac interface used.

In the IBM world, try to purchase parallel interfaces and parallel printers. The only exception should be if a PostScript printer is purchased. In this case, a PC serial interface should be purchased. This is because the best PostScript printer sends information to the PC.

After you choose the PC printer interface, you must get a printer that has the same interface. For example, if the PC has a parallel interface, the printer has to have a parallel interface. Although you may purchase devices that can convert from serial to parallel, they can cause a lot of trouble. Avoid them. Plan ahead and purchase both an interface for the older PC (the PS12's sold by IBM all come with both parallel and serial interfaces), a printer with the same interface, and a cable that hooks them up.

Reviewing Front Panel Features

The front panel of the PC printer has evolved to the point where no switches should be hidden in the back of the printer. The switches should be accessible without removing the paper or taking the printer apart. Most printers today place all the switches on the front panel. Most laser printers have a front panel with a calculator-type LCD screen that can display letters and numbers. Buttons below the LCD screen are used to display different menu options. Other buttons are used to browse and choose menu options. The menus should be easy to understand and easy to use. Ideally, all the printer's features should be available with these menus.

Assessing Printer Manuals

Although you may not need to read your entire printer manual, keep it handy for the technical information to solve problems and customize applications. Many printers do not come with adequate documentation. Look for detailed explanations of all the printer commands. Look for a sample printout of the printer's character set and fonts. All this information is present in a good printer manual.

Checking the Warranty

Some warranties contain on-site service or a money-back guarantee during the first 30 or 90 days. Most printers carry a one-year warranty, but some warranties are longer.

Determining the Resolution

Resolution is not really an issue. All dot-matrix and laser printers have pretty much the same resolution possibilities. Although laser printer resolution may increase from 300 dpi to 600 dpi someday, this change will occur slowly.

Testing for Speed

You find the greatest variety of speeds in dot-matrix printers. In fact, the differences in prices of dot-matrix printers are determined by speed. Character-mode printing is the most speed sensitive. When printing in graphics mode or object mode, the time is taken by the tremendous amount of processing that must be done on the image. How fast the printer can place letters on paper and eject the paper is not as important.

Speed testing printers is a subjective process. To be confident, create your own speed test. Create a typical document and time the printing process yourself. Translating between the pages per minute of a laser and the characters per second of a dot matrix is difficult. But, here is the outline:

Z = number of characters on average page
C = number of characters per second
P = number of pages per second
$C = P \times Z/60$

Laser printers are always the fastest. One of the biggest time savers is that the laser printer stacks paper in the correct order. The fanfold output of a dot-matrix printer unfolds like an accordion. The paper has to be torn apart into sheets and then the perforations torn off the sides. This process takes time. Look at your electric, phone, credit card bills. How are they printed? The old technology uses tractor feed multipart forms. The printed forms are fed into a *splitter* that separates the multipart forms and sometimes rips off the perfetti. Then, the forms are fed into a *folder* that folds and stuffs the envelopes. One laser printer can replace the high-speed printer, splitter, and folder machines with fewer moving parts. The laser prints your bills on paper cut to fit into an envelope.

Purchasing a Dot-Matrix Printer

Dot-matrix printers currently are the workhorses of our country. Object mode versions of a dot-matrix printer do not exist. Dot-matrix printers usually print in only a few fonts, manipulating a few letter styles by expanding, compressing, tilting (italic), outlining, shadowing, and doubling the height. Dot-matrix printers can accept downloaded characters, but they do so only to expand or modify a character set, not to create a font.

Most dot-matrix printers should emulate either the IBM ProPrinter or Epson. They should be able to print the lines and boxes on a PC screen when you use the Shift-PrtSc command. If not, don't purchase the printer. If the printer does not default to printing graphics characters, but can print them if you modify the front panel settings, you will find yourself changing the settings every time the printer is turned on. You will accidentally print something without modifying the front panel, and then have to reprint the document with the graphics character. Purchase a printer that defaults to the character graphic symbol set of IBM PC videoboards (see Chapter 3).

In the Macintosh world, the printer is put into graphics mode 90 percent of the time. Apple sells their printers with software that applications depend upon to print. As a result, manufacturers of ImageWriter clones have to sell their printers with similar software. Don't purchase a printer for the Mac world unless it comes with the proper software. Printers in the PC world depend on each application to have its own printer software code. Therefore, printer software is not an issue in the IBM PC world.

Paper Handling

Good dot-matrix printers should be able to do the following:

- ❏ Organize power and data cables so that they do not interfere with the paper path

- ❏ Pull fanfold paper up through a slot in the bottom of the printer

- ❏ Push fanfold paper up to the print head so that you can tear sheets off immediately after the print head. Many printers force you to print a second document before the first can be torn off. Otherwise, a sheet of paper is wasted.

- ❏ Park fanfold paper out of the way without removing the paper

- ❏ Enable you to manually insert single sheets of paper easily without having to touch any buttons or move any knobs on the printer

- ❏ Provide a straight-through paper path so that you can use thicker, heavier paper, and light paper does not curl during humid weather

- ❏ Have no printer knobs, removable printer knobs, or printer knobs with a clutch to disable the motor that moves the knobs while the printer is on

- ❏ Have a switch that chooses tractor feed or friction feed, and a system of levers that prevents tractor and friction feed from being chosen at the same time

- ❏ Pull at least 10 fanfold sheets of paper using the friction feed without scrolling the paper off the platen

- ❏ Paper trays (not cut-sheet feeders) have proved so successful in the laser printer market that one can hope that dot-matrix printers will develop paper trays. In fact, some models exist already. Paper trays are much easier to use than snaking tractor-feed paper out of a box: paper trays take up much less space; the sheets of paper coming out of the printer can stack in order, saving the time of tearing the fanfold sheets apart; and company letterhead, fancy paper, and stationery is much easier to find in single-sheet form.

Ribbons

Dot-matrix ribbons can cost from $0.30 to $15.00 each, a huge price difference. But, because you can use the ribbons over and over again, the ribbon cost can be mitigated. And, when you compare the ribbon costs to toner, ink, carbon and thermal transfer technologies, the difference is minor. On a tight budget, you may want to compare dot-matrix ribbon costs. Okidata made a few printer models that used the spool-type ribbons of typewriters and teletypes. This is the cheapest ribbon around, yet this factor did not turn out to be a selling point.

A more important problem is how dirty your fingers get when changing the ribbon (typewriter-type ribbons are the worst.) In fact, plastic gloves are shipped with some ribbons. The ink picked up from these ribbons can spread all over the office, creating smudges everywhere.

When you are printing on stencils, mimeographs, and occasionally forms, sometimes removing the ribbon increases the impact and the quality. If the ribbon is easy to remove, you save time. Ribbon changing can require a flashlight held by a second person at just the right angle. Ask to remove and insert the ribbon before you purchase a printer.

Purchasing an Inkjet Printer

Inkjet printers come in all sizes and shapes. These printers have really not found a market niche yet, except in the portable printer market. Because most inkjet printers are either competing with dot-matrix or laser printers, they have the paper handling features of a dot matrix or the paper trays of a laser. Inkjets have the font-manipulation capabilities of a dot matrix or the capability to receive downloaded fonts and behave like a character laser printer. No object inkjet printers exist.

The trouble with the inkjet printer is that the ink bladders are too expensive. The liquid ink has always had plumbing problems— leaking and clogging up. If you are intent on purchasing an inkjet, make sure that it will work after sitting all weekend without you having to fiddle with the ink bladder—inkjets have a tendency to clog when not in use. Hewlett-Packard seems to have solved the problem with the DeskJet inkjet printers, but the bladders are still expensive.

IBM's Quietwriter printer series had the same problem. Although the printout looked great, the ribbons cost $15 each, could only be used once, and did not last very long. The Quietwriter was a very expensive printer to operate.

Purchasing a Laser Printer

PC laser printers first appeared in 1984. The HP LaserJet was an incredible leap forward in technology that directly competed with the expensive and fast daisywheel printers of that era. This section primarily reviews character laser printers and similar features of object or PostScript laser printers. But, PostScript printers are so different that a separate chapter is devoted to their software (see Chapter 11).

Life Expectancy

The fact that laser printer manufacturers advertise the life span of their printers in pages reflects their photocopier origins. This statistic is useful for seeing a major difference between laser printers. Lasers have a life span ranging from 160,000 pages to 600,000 pages. Dot-matrix printers, on the other hand, have a life span of around 30,000 pages. Inkjet printers print perhaps 100,000 pages. Generally, the more expensive laser printers last longer (you get what you pay for).

Duty Cycle

How many pages a printer can print in a row without its motors heating up is unimportant. As explained in Chapter 5, a typical laser printer's duty cycle is 3,000 pages per month. Assuming normal business hours, printing continuously, you would have to average more than 1/3 page per minute to exceed the duty cycle. So, if a printer can print 12 pages per minute, printing at this speed continuously could start overheating the motors, depending on how cold the room is and how long the printer prints. Usually, the time needed to refill a paper tray is all the time that motors need to rest.

Resolution

All laser and inkjet printers print at 300 dpi. This resolution may increase someday, but it is good enough for most purposes. For better quality, you need a professional typesetter.

Memory

The cheaper laser printers come with only 128K of memory. Most laser printers are starting to come with the 1.5M of RAM necessary to print a full 8 1/2-by-11-inch page at 300 dpi.

In addition, there is the issue of how much memory you can eventually add to the laser printer. There is a tremendous incentive to add memory so that you can use better looking or personalized fonts. Some printers allow up to 12M to be added. Others only allow 1.5M.

Fonts

Laser printers differ tremendously in the number and type of fonts they come with. Some fonts are worthless. Some laser printers count one font many times because their software can manipulate that font in different ways. Some printers that come with 65 fonts indeed have 65 fonts, but they are tiny ones that don't take up much memory in the printer. Ask for a sample printout of all the different fonts the printer can produce and then make a decision based on the printout.

Many printer manufacturers are interested in copy protecting their fonts through encryption software built into the printer. Like copy-protected software, this encryption is frustrating. First, the protection limits the number of companies that can supply additional fonts to the printer. Second, the protection limits the capability to create screen fonts from the fonts in the printer.

Object laser printers are starting to develop scalable fonts, which have traditionally been a major selling feature of object printers. This may be a step toward evolving all character printers into object printers. PC operating systems are evolving from character video screens to graphic video screens. This change means that the graphic modes of printers are used more frequently.

Graphics-mode screens will continue to work, but the new high-resolution monitors are going to draw graphic-mode screens so slowly that object videoboards are the next obvious step. Because the IBM PC world has always kept videoboard processors, ROM, and memory separate from the motherboard circuitry, PCs should have faster videoboards than Mac. The Mac still uses system memory for video purposes.

Cartridges

Printer cartridges contain additional fonts in ROM chips. These fonts have the advantage of not needing to be downloaded from the PC. From the manufacturer's point of view, they have the advantage of being considered a hardware add-on that you can purchase from only one source. Only popular laser printers have had cartridges developed by other vendors so that price competition exists.

Speed

Laser printers have their speed measured in pages per minute. A conversion formula from pages per minute to characters per second is developed in the "Testing for Speed" section of this chapter. Most laser printers operate at around 7.5 pages per minute. The slowest models are around 4.5 pages per minute, and the super fast ones are around 10.5 pages per minute. Again, these speeds don't mean much unless the printer is in character mode.

Paper Feeding

Laser printers primarily use paper trays. Some lasers have paper trays that are adjustable; others require separate paper trays for each size of paper. Most companies sell paper trays for different sizes of paper. Envelope trays range from around $100 to $1,000, depending on the number of envelopes they hold.

Hand feeding an envelope may be an important application. The early laser printer had a manual feed slot located at the back or the side of the printer. Modern laser printers have a manual feed slot in the front. Through the manual feed slot, you can feed different sizes of paper. Troubles with this process are always software problems that can require a consultant to solve. You must know which sizes of paper you are going to use; then test the printer.

Consumables

The toner, cartridges, and other consumable supplies of a printer can run between $5 and $24 per ream of paper. Figure out where you can purchase the cartridges and how much they cost. This cost can make a big difference in the overall life cycle cost of a printer. Another consideration is how easily toner is spilled when you add more toner or change cartridges. Toner spills are nasty to clean up.

Object Mode

PostScript printers need a great deal of memory and CPU horsepower. The faster they print the better. Specialized hardware is being developed to make the PostScript printers do their jobs faster. One PostScript printer may take half as long to print a page as another PostScript printer. The technology is advancing rapidly.

You can add PostScript features to certain printer models by purchasing a new printer computer for the laser engine. The new printer computer can be housed inside the PC or can replace the current computer inside the laser printer. If placed inside the PC, the printer computer takes up a slot but can communicate with the PC motherboard at bus speeds. The printer computer placed in a slot inside the PC interfaces with application programs in two different ways. Either the board uses a driver and installs itself as a parallel printer port (to the operating system), or the board comes with software that teaches certain PC programs how to talk to it directly. The latter method may be a faster but less stable platform for your company. Certain PC programs may change versions in such a way that the new board cannot be used any more. Boards that install themselves as parallel printer ports need only a driver update if PC DOS versions change significantly.

Purchasing a Plotter

A plotter's speed is measured in how many inches per second it can move the pen. But, most plotters need to be slowed down, because if the pen is moved too fast, the ink does not have time to flow evenly, and the line looks terrible. Normally, everyone learns to be patient with plotters. Fast plotters move the pen at 32 inches per second; average plotters move the pen at 15 to 20 inches per second.

Plotter resolution is measured by drawing a staircase and measuring the number of stairs to climb the diagonal of an inch by inch square. The more steps, the higher the resolution of the motors moving the paper and pen. The eye perceives a large difference between 200 steps per inch and 1,000 steps per inch. The actual statistic is reported as .05 or .001 inch per step, respectively.

Plotters can draw on many different types of paper, vellum, film, and acetate. Special pens and pencils that can draw on these surfaces are available. The better plotters have a wide assortment of pens. The most popular plotters have pens available from other companies. Look at the plotter pens listed in an INMAC or MOORE catalog—the plotters for these pens are the most popular and have the widest selection of pens at the best prices.

Reviewing Current Printer Categories, Prices, and Recommendations

In this section, printers are lumped into a few categories; then, categories are described, and a recommendation is made. The recommendations can be checked three ways:

- ❏ Compare the following recommendations to printer reviews in magazines.
- ❏ Look at the ads in magazines and see which printer models are most often advertised.
- ❏ Ask your local computer consultant. Choose someone who is impartial (no salesmen).

When you check the following recommendations, you will discover they are conservative—hot-rod printers from unknown companies are not recommended.

The moment a printer model number is written down, it is old. Even the categories of printers are changing fast. The models, categories, and recommendations of a good consultant will change radically as the months pass. Fortunately, the printer market is starting to stabilize. In 1989, no daisywheel printers, significant new features on dot-matrix printers, or LCS or LED lasers were released. This fact means that the following recommendations (written on November 1, 1989) will still be true by the time you read this book.

Low-Cost, 9-Pin Dot-Matrix Printers

The price of a low-end, dot-matrix printer is between $165 and $175 dollars. Printers are not likely to become cheaper than this—though features of the more expensive printers will be moved down to this price level. For the last three years, the printers to recommend in this category have been Panasonic and Epson printers. The current model of the Epson in this category is the LX-810, and the Panasonic is model KX-1180. The Epson is a little faster, but the Panasonic has a proportional font included. Many printers exist at this price level. The Epson and Panasonic have paper parking utilities as well as cut-sheet feeders that can be purchased.

Low-Cost, 24-pin Dot-Matrix Printers

The market leader for low-cost, 24-pin dot-matrix printers is also Epson. The LQ-510 is the current recommendation with a street price of $319. Unfortunately, 24-pin printers are slower and noisier in draft mode than 9-pin printers. However, the letter-quality output is faster and marginally better. In graphics mode, the resolution is higher than a laser printer: 360 dpi both horizontally and vertically. But, the output does not look as nice as that of a 300-dpi laser because of the impact with the paper surface. A 24-pin printer is terribly slow at 360 dpi.

Wide-Carriage Dot-Matrix Printers

This category has always been sort of strange. Initially, manufacturers sold wide-carriage versions of all their printer models, but the low-cost versions never sold well. Usually, people want higher speed if they want a wide-carriage dot matrix. In addition, these users are not as concerned about print quality, so 9-pin print heads are usually just fine. For these reasons, finding a slow, low-cost, wide-carriage printer is difficult. Wide-carriage, 24-pin dot-matrix printers are also rare. Most of low-cost wide-carriages or 24-pin dot-matrix printers are sold by obscure companies. The recommended printer in this category is the Epson FX-1050 (street price is around $419), a 9-pin wide-carriage dot matrix that prints at speeds up to 166 cps.

Inkjet Printers

Inkjet printers may be crowded out of the market. HP completely dominates this market. Most other printer companies have tried to sell inkjet printers, but only Hewlett-Packard has succeeded. The DeskJet models start at a street price of around $675 and can print at 300 dpi, and the output is practically indistinguishable from that of a laser printer. Although the printer can be upgraded like a laser printer—memory can be added, font cartridges are available, soft fonts can be downloaded into memory—all these products are unique to the HP DeskJet. The commodity prices of HP LaserJet laser printer memory and font products are not available. This fact, coupled with the high operation costs and the temptation of a true laser for approximately $250 more, may eventually confine inkjet printers to the portable market.

Personal HP-PCL Laser Printers

The Hewlett-Packard Printer Control Language (HP-PCL) is a character-oriented printer language that a vast majority of lower priced laser printers understand. These printers dominate the PC market and have a significant presence in the Mac market, where they are run in graphics mode.

The Personal HP-PCL laser is the newest category of printer and threatens the top of the inkjet printers by printing faster and producing better output. The entry-level street price also can be as low as $899. The first printer in this category is the HP LaserJet IIp. The paper tray holds only 50 sheets of paper, and it has one font cartridge slot instead of two. But, the IIp has all the fonts of an HP LaserJet IId, plus the capability to rotate the portrait fonts to landscape fonts. The IIp comes with 512K of RAM and the capability to upgrade to 4.5M, just like the more expensive models. The front panel is much easier to use. The IIp's only drawback is speed—it prints 4 pages per minute. The IIp has to be the most exciting printer currently on the market. By the time this book is published, however, competitors will have been released.

Business HP-PCL Laser Printers

The business HP-PCL laser is the standard character laser printer category where printers typically print between 8 ppm and 10 ppm. The current market leader in this category is the HP LaserJet II. This old model is due for revision shortly because both the IIp and IId have better printer ROM software (printer ROM software is described in Chapter 6). Street prices are around $1,600. The major competition recently has been the Panasonic KX-P4450, which prints at around 11 ppm and has a street price of $1,275. Recently, IBM has released a new laser printer (the LaserPrinter) that looks like a winner at $2,695. The LaserPrinter should not be confused with the IBM Personal PagePrinter (not recommended), a PostScript printer.

High-Speed, Shared Laser Printers

Judging by the reviews of these high-speed shared lasers, the speeds don't seem high enough (20 ppm) to justify the price ($19,500). For the same price, 10 HP LaserJet IIs with an aggregate speed of 80 ppm could be purchased.

PostScript Laser Printers

Don't consider a PostScript printer unless it supports the 35 fonts found in the AppleLaser Writer II NT. The PostScript market is in such chaos right now, that only high-end, $2,000 or more products are recommended. For more specific recommendations, see Chapter 11.

Other Recommendations

The printer categories given on the preceding pages are the major market segments where healthy competition exists. Most other printer needs are so unusual that the printer is special ordered, made in limited quantities, has fewer features, and does not work as well. Examples of other categories of printers include high-speed, 24-pin, wide-carriage dot matrixes; very high-speed (but not as high as laser), 18-pin, dot-matrix impact printers; raised-ink printers; portable printers; plotters, and color printers.

Deciding Where To Purchase Your Printer

If you purchase your printer locally, the chances are that you may call the vendor if a problem arises, and damage during shipment is unlikely. Remember that some printers weigh over 80 lbs. But most importantly, printers sold from the local store can be tested before purchase. The demonstrations at the local store should build your confidence in the printer.

Printers have always been the hardest PC system component to purchase by mail order. Versions and models change so frequently that the models advertised are often sold out and have been replaced by newer models, which the magazines have not reviewed. PC clones and Mac accessories are stable enough that they can be purchased through catalogs with confidence. But, printers change so frequently that the stores never try to keep a large inventory.

You can purchase some of the lower end dot-matrix printers through mail order. They are light enough to be shipped without much chance of damage. The heavier printers should not be purchased by mail order. If your destination is a remote area, insist on the original shipping cartons. New printers come in boxes supported by solid foam pieces that cushion the printer from the cardboard on all sides. If the printer does not fit snugly into the box, send the printer back. This condition means that the printer box was opened, and the printer has been used. Look to see whether the box serial numbers and model numbers match your printer. If the printer was shipped with styrofoam beans as the cushion, send the printer back. The beans are good for shipping software and other light products, but not heavy printers. Printers need the solid foam cushions.

In addition, try to purchase computer equipment using credit cards. Many credit card companies offer refunds if your purchase is lost, stolen, or damaged. They also will not pay the company if you make a respectable complaint. In fact, some credit card companies will negotiate the resolution of your problems if any should occur.

To locate good mail-order companies, look through issues of computer magazines. The better mail-order companies have been in business for over a year and have been running full-page ads in most computer magazines. Probably all mail-order companies advertise in *Computer Shopper*, a magazine sold in some supermarkets. To locate local companies selling printers, look in the newspaper. In most towns, all the computer vendors advertise in the a special supplement that comes out weekly. For example, in Washington, D.C., vendors advertise in the Monday's *Washington Post* business section. In New York, vendors advertise in the *New York Times* science section.

A Purchasing Checklist

The following is really a summary of all printer features that have been discussed in the last seven chapters. Copy this page and use it (along with the index) when deciding and reviewing printer demonstrations.

What are the life-cycle costs?

What do you need to print?

> In-house reports?
> Letters?
> Banners?
> Wide spreadsheets?
> Forms?
> Newsletters, brochures, and handouts?
> Magazines and high-quality output?

Do you have to share the printer?

In what environment will you use the printer?

What type of applications do you use?

> Spreadsheets?
> Databases?
> Educational software?
> Word processing?
> Desktop publishing?
> Accounting?
> Graphics and drawing programs?
> Programming, error logging?

What hardware features do you need?

What type of printer interface and port do you need?

What type of power supply—switching or linear?

How easy is the front panel to use?

Do the manuals contain all needed information?

Are technical reference and repair manuals available?

What is the warranty?

What is the resolution?

How fast is the printer? How fast is necessary?

How much noise does the printer make?

Can you attach a keyboard and turn the printer into a typewriter?

How heavy is the printer?

If the printer is a dot matrix, answer these questions:

> Does the printer have a strong motor to pull paper?
> Does the printer have a tractor that has to be adjusted every tenth sheet?
> Does the printer have a tractor that is good at pulling paper slightly off center?
> Can you tear off paper without wasting a sheet?
> Is the paper path straight?
> Can you park the paper for manual feed?
> Where is the paper-out switch?
> Are paper trays available?
> Does the printer use pulley or screw dot-matrix head movement?
> What percent can the black head print at top speed?
> Is the printer good at paper handling?
> What type and how expensive are the ribbons?
> What type of fonts are available?

If the printer is an Inkjet, answer these questions:

> What does the ink bladder cost?
> Does the printer require special paper?
> How long does the printer take to turn on?
> Does the printer have a tendency to clog?

If the printer is a laser printer, answer these questions:

> What type of laser: laser, LED, LCS?
> What is the number of lifetime pages designed to print?

What is the duty cycle, pages per hour, per week, per month?
Does the printer stack paper face up or face down?
How much memory does the printer have?
How much do paper trays cost?
Does the printer print envelopes?
Can you easily feed the printer manually?
How expensive and where can you purchase toner cartridges?
Does the printer have a hard disk?
Does the printer have an object mode?

If the printer is a plotter, answer these questions:

What pen tips are provided?
What paper sizes can you use?
What is the step size?

What software features do you need?

Can the printer print bidirectionally?

How thorough is the self-test program(s)?

What character sets are supported?

What original fonts are supplied?

Can you add font cartridges?

Is there third-party font competition?

Are the fonts copy-protected?

Does the software work with the PC DOS GRAPHICS command?

Can you reset the printer?

Does the printer come with required Macintosh software?

Can the printer print in object mode?

Is it easy to switch from object to character mode?

In the Next Chapter

The next chapter describes how to unpack, install, train, share, and manage printers so that they don't have problems.

8

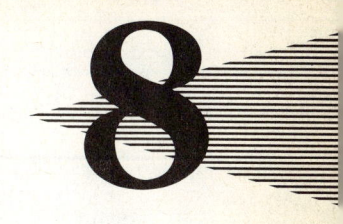

Installing and Testing Printers

Often, people purchase printers and computers at the same time and focus their entire attention on the computers rather than on the printers. Sometimes, days and even months go by before the user installs and tests the printer. In essence, these users are shortening the warranty period of the printer. Instead, they should be printing many documents.

> **TROUBLE-SHOOTING TIP** Purchase the printer when you are sure that you are going to be using it heavily; if possible, do not purchase your printer when you purchase your computer.

This chapter describes how to install and test the printer. In a step-by-step fashion, you are led through these processes:

- ❑ Unpacking the printer
- ❑ Installing ribbons and cartridges
- ❑ Inserting paper
- ❑ Turning on your printer
- ❑ Exercising the printer self-tests
- ❑ Connecting the printer to the computer
- ❑ Setting the printer's internal switches
- ❑ Choosing operational defaults
- ❑ Testing the computer software

In addition, connecting the printer to a printer sharing mechanism, testing the sharing capability, locating the printer in a safe environment, and then managing the different printer models you have accumulated are covered.

Unpacking the Printer

You should unpack your printer as soon as it arrives. The first few months are the critical ones, when you should test and make heavy use of the printer. Most on-site repair or full-refund return policies are in effect only during the first three months. If the printer just sits, these time periods expire before you have tested it. If you are receiving 100 printers for a large company, for example, do not plan shipments that arrive all at once. First, you will have a storage problem. Second, the warranty period may expire, and even the printer model may change before the printers are unpacked. Schedule shipments so that you can receive printers as you can install them.

> HINT | Unless the printer is yours and is being hooked up to your PC, test the printer using a PC and software currently working with another printer.

Unpacking a printer is fun. First, look for a shipping list or packing list describing exactly what was shipped with the printer. Sometimes, this list is on a separate sheet of paper; sometimes the list is in the front of the printer manual. Find each part mentioned. Check each piece or part off this list. Read ahead in the printer manual to find out what the part is for—every piece has a function.

Make sure that you have everything you should have. Carefully inspect each part for damage or previous use. Previous use is not necessarily bad but should be noted in case something goes wrong. After unpacking, do not turn on the printer immediately. Moving parts in printers are usually tied down with wire twisters or tie wraps. Sometimes, the moving parts are wedged into place with plastic spacers. Vibration-absorption pads (equivalent to shock absorbers) are sometimes wedged into place to prevent the parts from falling off during shipment. The vibration-absorption pads are compressed with *shipping screws* (usually found on dot-matrix printers). You need to remove the shipping screws to let the vibration-absorption pads expand and do their job. Otherwise, the machine makes a great deal of noise, and all the pieces and parts vibrate more violently than they were designed for.

You should save the box the printer came in and any special plastic spacers, tie wraps, and shipping screws in case you need to return the printer for repair. If the printer was shipped without the proper packing and without the moving parts tied down, do not purchase any more printers from that vendor.

Testing the Printer without the Computer Attached

After unpacking the printer, the next step is to check the printer as thoroughly as possible before attaching it to the computer. Computer hardware can damage the printer, and software in the computer can make the printer look sick. If so, you will not know the difference between one of these problems and a printer that was dead on arrival. Look for signs that the printer is used—not brand new. Look for obvious pieces of broken plastic. Look for seals that have been broken. Also, check for a packing list and make sure that everything is in the box that should be there. After you have checked the printer as thoroughly as possible, follow the steps in the next sections to convince yourself that the printer is working.

Installing Ribbons and Toner Cartridges

First, insert the dot-matrix printer's ribbon or the laser printer's toner cartridge. The ribbons come in all sorts of shapes and sizes. The hardest part of inserting the ribbon is figuring out how to wrap the ribbon around the front of the print head. The trick is to remember that if the ribbon rubs against the paper, smudges and smear marks will appear on the paper. You always, therefore, should have a metal or plastic barrier between the ribbon and the paper. A window in the metal or plastic barrier should allow the print head to push the ribbon through the window and momentarily touch the paper. This metal or plastic barrier is called a *print shield*. Most printer manuals have good pictures that illustrate how to insert ribbons.

For some laser printers, you need to install toner cartridges. Other laser printers have a bin into which you pour toner, just as you would pour toner into a copier machine. Be sure to first tip or rock the toner cartridge several times at a 45-degree angle to loosen the toner material. Most toner cartridges have a long clear plastic strip that you need to pull out. This clear plastic strip has a black plastic handle that you must break off the toner cartridge. Insert the cartridge and then pull out the strip. The foot-long piece of plastic is sometimes difficult to pull out. Pulling out the plastic piece feels something like starting an old pull-start lawn mower engine.

Inserting Paper into the Printer

You should have some idea of how the paper is going to flow into the printer and where the printed pages are going to stack. Laser printers solve these problems with paper trays and output trays on top of the printer.

Unfortunately, dot-matrix printers require you to manage the paper flow into and out of the printer—the *paper path*. You have to decide where you are going to place the box of paper. You have to make sure that the printer's motors can pull the paper easily from the box. Pull some paper out of the box. If the paper is difficult for you to pull without tearing or creasing, the printer certainly is not going to do any better.

Inserting paper into a printer is becoming more and more of a challenge. Reading the printer's manual and looking at the pictures is important. To learn what the paper path is, leave the printer off. You are not interested in learning all the paper-handling features of the printer at the moment. Instead, you are interested in manually inserting a sheet of paper into the dot-matrix printer while it is off. When you have found what you think is the paper path, push the paper through the path. Move levers and switches on the sides of the printer until the paper can be moved freely by hand. For a laser printer, just put paper in the paper tray and insert it into the printer.

Turning On the Printer

After inserting the paper, plug the printer's power cable into the wall outlet and turn on the printer, even though it is not attached to the computer. You may want to check the wiring in the wall outlet with a circuit tester (available at Radio Shack for $4), check what else is hooked to the same circuit breaker (throw circuit breakers and see what other devices go off; only computer equipment should go off), check the building's ground (hire an expert), and purchase surge and spike protectors. Actually, you should have done this earlier, before setting up the computer.

If you are installing a dot-matrix printer, move the print head gently back and forth with your hand *before* you turn on the printer. Feel how easily the print head moves. If it is easy to move, the motor that moves the print head is going to have a long life. If the print head is hard for you to move by hand, the motor that moves the print head also is going to work harder and have a a shorter life. If you are unsure of how easily a print head should move, go to another dot-matrix printer. Turn it off; move the print head. Develop your own sense of how easily the print head moves. In the future, turn off the power and move the print head back and forth to check whether the metal bars that the print head travels on need to be lubricated. For lubrication instructions, see Chapter 14.

> **HINT** — Moving the head of a dot-matrix or daisywheel printer while the printer is off will not cause any damage. Do this test occasionally to learn how easily the print head should slide. This test enables you to tell when the printer has a problem—before the print head motor burns out.

After moving the print head back and forth by hand, leave the print head in its far right position. Turn on the dot-matrix printer and watch. The print head should move to the left margin and then stop.

Watch what the printer does during the power-on process. The printer may beep, lights may flash, or messages may appear on a front panel. If the printer makes loud noises, turn it off immediately. Go back to the unpacking process. You probably missed a shipping screw, tie wrap, or spacer.

Laser printers act like copier machines when they turn on. They roll their motors, flash their lights, and when ready say so. PostScript printers should print a start-up page just after being turned on, although this feature can be disabled.

Performing Printer Self-Tests

When power is first turned on in a dot-matrix or laser printer, it does a quick self-test. Most printers can do more extensive self-tests. Normally, to get your printer to do these self-tests, you hold down a button (or two) while you turn on the printer. The buttons are different for different printer models. You can usually find the right button faster by trial and error by than reading the manuals. And, no damage is done while guessing, either. In fact, you may find undocumented (hidden treasure) self-tests.

These self-tests are good to run not only when the printer is new but also when it seems to be having problems. Save the results of the first self-tests so that you can compare them with future tests. Remember that the printer is not hooked to the computer, so the printer may be unable to self-test properly. On the other hand, the computer may prevent the printer from running self-tests that it is perfectly capable of running when not attached.

> **TROUBLESHOOTING TIP** — If a printer's self-test fails, try disconnecting the printer from the computer. Sometimes, the computer can prevent the printer from self-testing.

The following self-tests are not found in all printers, although ideally these tests would be. The printer used in the example is the most popular laser printer on the market—the HP LaserJet II.

Barber-Pole Test

The barber-pole self-test is usually a printout of the default character set in the default font (see fig. 8.1). Sometimes, this self-test switches fonts to demonstrate all its features. The barber-pole self-test, named so because all the

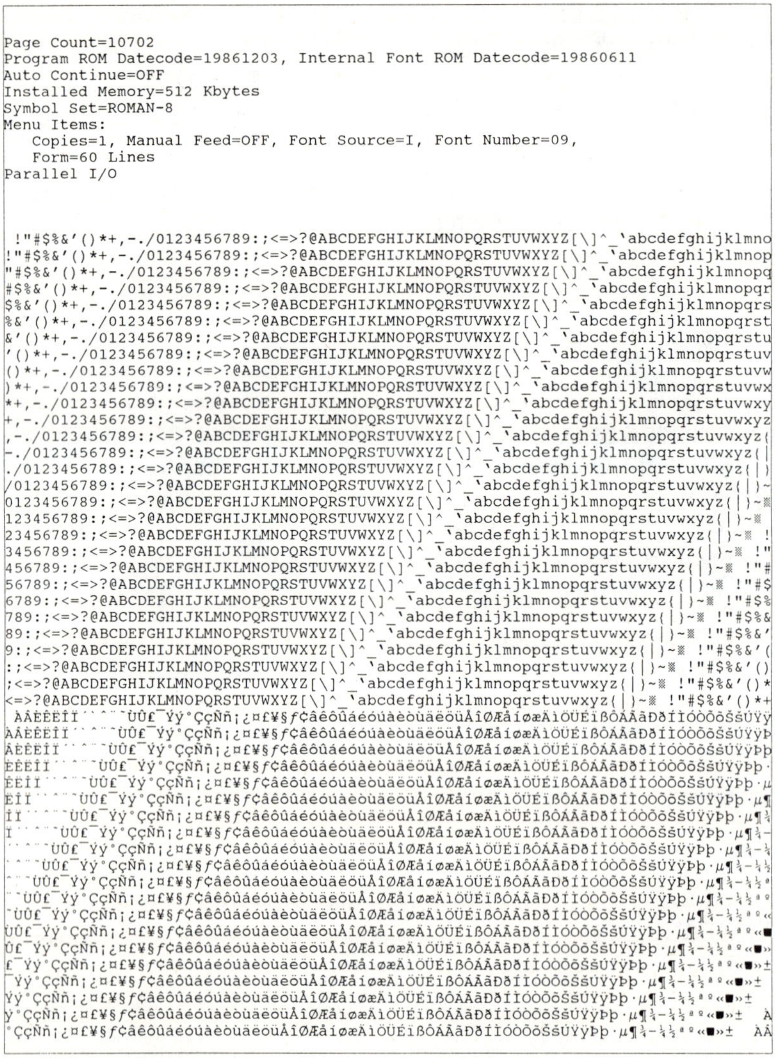

```
Page Count=10702
Program ROM Datecode=19861203, Internal Font ROM Datecode=19860611
Auto Continue=OFF
Installed Memory=512 Kbytes
Symbol Set=ROMAN-8
Menu Items:
   Copies=1, Manual Feed=OFF, Font Source=I, Font Number=09,
   Form=60 Lines
Parallel I/O


 !"#$%&'()*+,-./0123456789:;<=>?@ABCDEFGHIJKLMNOPQRSTUVWXYZ[\]^_`abcdefghijklmno
!"#$%&'()*+,-./0123456789:;<=>?@ABCDEFGHIJKLMNOPQRSTUVWXYZ[\]^_`abcdefghijklmnop
"#$%&'()*+,-./0123456789:;<=>?@ABCDEFGHIJKLMNOPQRSTUVWXYZ[\]^_`abcdefghijklmnopq
#$%&'()*+,-./0123456789:;<=>?@ABCDEFGHIJKLMNOPQRSTUVWXYZ[\]^_`abcdefghijklmnopqr
$%&'()*+,-./0123456789:;<=>?@ABCDEFGHIJKLMNOPQRSTUVWXYZ[\]^_`abcdefghijklmnopqrs
%&'()*+,-./0123456789:;<=>?@ABCDEFGHIJKLMNOPQRSTUVWXYZ[\]^_`abcdefghijklmnopqrst
&'()*+,-./0123456789:;<=>?@ABCDEFGHIJKLMNOPQRSTUVWXYZ[\]^_`abcdefghijklmnopqrstu
'()*+,-./0123456789:;<=>?@ABCDEFGHIJKLMNOPQRSTUVWXYZ[\]^_`abcdefghijklmnopqrstuv
()*+,-./0123456789:;<=>?@ABCDEFGHIJKLMNOPQRSTUVWXYZ[\]^_`abcdefghijklmnopqrstuvw
)*+,-./0123456789:;<=>?@ABCDEFGHIJKLMNOPQRSTUVWXYZ[\]^_`abcdefghijklmnopqrstuvwx
*+,-./0123456789:;<=>?@ABCDEFGHIJKLMNOPQRSTUVWXYZ[\]^_`abcdefghijklmnopqrstuvwxy
+,-./0123456789:;<=>?@ABCDEFGHIJKLMNOPQRSTUVWXYZ[\]^_`abcdefghijklmnopqrstuvwxyz
,-./0123456789:;<=>?@ABCDEFGHIJKLMNOPQRSTUVWXYZ[\]^_`abcdefghijklmnopqrstuvwxyz{
-./0123456789:;<=>?@ABCDEFGHIJKLMNOPQRSTUVWXYZ[\]^_`abcdefghijklmnopqrstuvwxyz{|
./0123456789:;<=>?@ABCDEFGHIJKLMNOPQRSTUVWXYZ[\]^_`abcdefghijklmnopqrstuvwxyz{|}
/0123456789:;<=>?@ABCDEFGHIJKLMNOPQRSTUVWXYZ[\]^_`abcdefghijklmnopqrstuvwxyz{|}~
0123456789:;<=>?@ABCDEFGHIJKLMNOPQRSTUVWXYZ[\]^_`abcdefghijklmnopqrstuvwxyz{|}~▒
123456789:;<=>?@ABCDEFGHIJKLMNOPQRSTUVWXYZ[\]^_`abcdefghijklmnopqrstuvwxyz{|}~▒
23456789:;<=>?@ABCDEFGHIJKLMNOPQRSTUVWXYZ[\]^_`abcdefghijklmnopqrstuvwxyz{|}~▒ !
3456789:;<=>?@ABCDEFGHIJKLMNOPQRSTUVWXYZ[\]^_`abcdefghijklmnopqrstuvwxyz{|}~▒ !"
456789:;<=>?@ABCDEFGHIJKLMNOPQRSTUVWXYZ[\]^_`abcdefghijklmnopqrstuvwxyz{|}~▒ !"#
56789:;<=>?@ABCDEFGHIJKLMNOPQRSTUVWXYZ[\]^_`abcdefghijklmnopqrstuvwxyz{|}~▒ !"#$
6789:;<=>?@ABCDEFGHIJKLMNOPQRSTUVWXYZ[\]^_`abcdefghijklmnopqrstuvwxyz{|}~▒ !"#$%
789:;<=>?@ABCDEFGHIJKLMNOPQRSTUVWXYZ[\]^_`abcdefghijklmnopqrstuvwxyz{|}~▒ !"#$%&
89:;<=>?@ABCDEFGHIJKLMNOPQRSTUVWXYZ[\]^_`abcdefghijklmnopqrstuvwxyz{|}~▒ !"#$%&'
9:;<=>?@ABCDEFGHIJKLMNOPQRSTUVWXYZ[\]^_`abcdefghijklmnopqrstuvwxyz{|}~▒ !"#$%&'(
:;<=>?@ABCDEFGHIJKLMNOPQRSTUVWXYZ[\]^_`abcdefghijklmnopqrstuvwxyz{|}~▒ !"#$%&'()
;<=>?@ABCDEFGHIJKLMNOPQRSTUVWXYZ[\]^_`abcdefghijklmnopqrstuvwxyz{|}~▒ !"#$%&'()*
<=>?@ABCDEFGHIJKLMNOPQRSTUVWXYZ[\]^_`abcdefghijklmnopqrstuvwxyz{|}~▒ !"#$%&'()*+
```

Fig. 8.1.

Configuration self-test.

letters rotate one space to the left on each consecutive line, was the first printer self-test.

The object of the barber-pole self-test is to make sure that all characters are fully formed—no matter where they appear on the page. Examine the printout carefully. For example, check to see whether the bottom part of the letter *A* is dark but the top part is light. Check to see whether the left characters are dark and the right are light. Check to see whether the line curves or angles across the page. All these types of situations can be caused by problems with the mirrors in laser printers and the platen position relative to the print head in dot-matrix printers. Because correcting these problems requires having the proper documentation and practice, solve this type of problem by sending the printer in for repair. If the printer is brand new, it should be returned under warranty.

Follow these steps to generate a barber-pole self-test on an HP LaserJet II printer:

1. Press the ON LINE button until the light goes out.

2. Hold down the PRINT FONTS / TEST button until `04 Self Test` is displayed.

Vertical-Line Test

The barber-pole self-test served its purpose for early printers, but as printers have grown more complex, other self-tests are needed. The vertical-line test draws straight lines down the paper. This test, more common in laser than dot-matrix printers, tests the laser printer's engine rather than the computer added to the engine by the printer company.

On a dot-matrix printer, the reason for printing straight lines down the paper is to check whether the printer can put a character consistently in the same spot on a line when asked to repeat itself. This problem is most obvious when the printer is printing bidirectionally. In graphics mode, the problem is obvious—a straight line down the page is jagged if a problem exists. The problem is caused by slack in the cables pulling the print head back and forth or play in the screw threads that twist the print head.

On a laser printer, the vertical-line test is called an *engine test* because the vertical-line test checks the copier machine part of the laser printer to see whether any mirror problems have developed. Symptoms are vertical lines unevenly spaced or out of focus on the outside edges only. This problem is called a *convergence problem*—many monitors and TVs have convergence problems, where the center is in focus, but the outside vertical edges are not. LCS and LED laser printers do not have this problem.

If the lines gradually spread apart as they go down the page, the problem is still with the mirror positions in the lid of the laser printer.

Again, fixing these problems requires purchasing the technical reference manuals and much trial-and-error practice. Usually, you make the problem worse before you make it better. Unless you are going to repair many printers regularly, repairing this problem yourself is probably not cost effective. Take the printer to a service center if the printer is not under warranty.

On HP LaserJet printers, stick a pen into the hole near the bottom on one side of the printer (look up its location in your printer manual) and wait until 15 Engine Test is displayed. (This hole was a button to be pushed on the side of the earlier laser printers.) Vertical lines should appear, running the entire length of the page (see fig. 8.2).

Fig. 8.2.

Engine self-test.

Font Test

A font test ideally displays all the fonts currently available in the printer. A true font test would display every symbol of every character set in every size of every font. Some printers display a sample of each character set with a written description of the character or symbol set and a description of the point sizes available and the pitch.

Follow these steps to generate a font test on an HP LaserJet II printer:

1. Press ON LINE until the light goes out.
2. Press once and release quickly PRINT FONTS / TEST.

A list of all the fonts is displayed in priority order: soft or downloaded fonts, left cartridge, right cartridge, and resident fonts. These fonts are often numbered in a way that the front panel of the laser printer can understand, unrelated to the way PC software numbers the fonts (see figs. 8.3 and 8.4).

> HINT | The cartridges in printers sometimes do not make an electrical connection inside the laser printer. In this case, the font test does not list any cartridge fonts. Similarly, if fonts were not successfully downloaded, the font test will not display them. Therefore, the font test is useful in determining how well the printer is working, which fonts are available, and whether the font download worked.

Configuration Test

A configuration test should be like the CHKDSK command of PC DOS. The configuration test should tell you the current status of the printer and list all the details concerning the current menu choices, maximum memory, currently free memory, memory each soft font is using, ROM version dates of font cartridges and the laser printer itself, number of pages printed so far (like a counter in a copier machine), and soft fonts by name. Then the test should end with a thorough test of the printer's memory. If the printer is used, you should be able to look at the printer's number of pages printed so far—like the odometer of a car. In figure 8.1, the number of pages printed is 10,702. The rated life of the HP LaserJet is 300,000 pages. Not all printers include such information in a configuration test. The following are the steps to run a configuration test on an HP LaserJet:

1. Press ON LINE until the light goes out.
2. Hold down the PRINT FONTS / TEST button until 05 Self Test is displayed.

Fig. 8.3.

Portrait Fonts.

```
                -------- PORTRAIT FONTS --------

           FONT                      POINT  SYMBOL
           ID    NAME         PITCH  SIZE   SET    PRINT SAMPLE
           ----  ------------ -----  -----  ------ ------------------------

           "PERMANENT" SOFT FONTS

           S16   Dutch BOLD ITALIC    PS     12    0U  ABCDEfghij#$@[\]^`{|}~123

           LEFT FONT CARTRIDGE

           RIGHT FONT CARTRIDGE

           INTERNAL FONTS

           I00   COURIER              10     12    8U  ABCDEfghij#$@[\]^`(|)~123
                                                       ÀÂ°ÇÑ¡¿£§êéàèëöÀØåæÄÜßÁÐÒ
           I01   COURIER              10     12    10U ABCDEfghij#$@[\]¨`(|)~123
                                                       íó|┤┤┐┤┬┴┴┴┴└┌─┐┬╡┤╢█|απΦ
           I02   COURIER              10     12    11U ABCDEfghij#$@[\]¨`(|)~123
                                                       íó|┤┤┐┤┬┴┴┴┴└┌─┐┬╡┤╢█|απΦ
           I03   COURIER              10     12    0N  ABCDEfghij#$@[\]¨`(|)~123
                                                       ¡¢³´¶.¹»½ÁÀÈÉÍÎÐÒÔ×ØÚÞàãè
           I04   COURIER BOLD         10     12    8U  ABCDEfghij#$@[\]^`(|)~123
                                                       ÀÂ°ÇÑ¡¿£§êéàèëöÀØåæÄÜßÁÐÒ
           I05   COURIER BOLD         10     12    10U ABCDEfghij#$@[\]¨`(|)~123
                                                       íó|┤┤┐┤┬┴┴┴┴└┌─┐┬╡┤╢█|απΦ
           I06   COURIER BOLD         10     12    11U ABCDEfghij#$@[\]¨`(|)~123
                                                       íó|┤┤┐┤┬┴┴┴┴└┌─┐┬╡┤╢█|απΦ
           I07   COURIER BOLD         10     12    0N  ABCDEfghij#$@[\]¨`(|)~123
                                                       ¡¢³´¶.¹»½ÁÀÈÉÍÎÐÒÔ×ØÚÞàãè
           I08   LINE_PRINTER         16.6   8.5   8U  ABCDEfghij#$@[\]^`(|)~123
                                                       ÀÂ°ÇÑ¡¿£§êéàèëöÀØåæÄÜßÁÐÒ
           I09   LINE_PRINTER         16.6   8.5   10U ABCDEfghij#$@[\]¨`(|)~123
                                                       íó|┤┤┐┤┬┴┴└┌─┐┤█|απΦ
           I10   LINE_PRINTER         16.6   8.5   11U ABCDEfghij#$@[\]¨`(|)~123
                                                       íó|┤┤┐┤┬┴┴└┌─┐┤█|απΦ
           I11   LINE_PRINTER         16.6   8.5   0N  ABCDEfghij#$@[\]¨`(|)~123
                                                       ¡¢¹´¶.»½ÁÀÈÉÍÎÐÒÔ×ØÚÞàãè

           "PERMANENT" SOFT FONTS

           S01   Swiss BOLD           PS     12    0U  ABCDEfghij#$@[\]^`{|}~123
           S02   Swiss BOLD ITALIC    PS     12    0U  ABCDEfghij#$@[\]^`{|}~123
           S03   Dutch LIGHT          PS     10    0U  ABCDEfghij#$@[\]^`{|}~123
           S04   Dutch LIGHT ITALIC   PS     10    0U  ABCDEfghij#$@[\]^`{|}~123
           S05   Dutch BOLD           PS     10    0U  ABCDEfghij#$@[\]^`{|}~123
           S06   Dutch BOLD ITALIC    PS     10    0U  ABCDEfghij#$@[\]^`{|}~123
           S07   Dutch LIGHT          PS     15    0U  ABCDEfghij#$@[\]^`{|}~123
           S08   Dutch BOLD           PS     15    0U  ABCDEfghij#$@[\]^`{|}~123
           S09   Dutch BOLD ITALIC    PS     15    0U  ABCDEfghij#$@[\]^`{|}~123
           S10   Swiss BOLD           PS     15    0U  ABCDEfghij#$@[\]^`{|}~123

           S11   Dutch BOLD           PS     20    0U  ABCDEfghij#$@[\]^`{|
           S12   Swiss BOLD           PS     20    0U  ABCDEfghij#$@[\]^`{|
           S13   Swiss BOLD ITALIC    PS     20    0U  ABCDEfghij#$@[\]^`{|

           S14   Dutch LIGHT          PS     12    0U  ABCDEfghij#$@[\]^`{|}~123
           S15   Dutch BOLD           PS     12    0U  ABCDEfghij#$@[\]^`{|}~123
```

```
-------- LANDSCAPE FONTS --------

FONT                              POINT  SYMBOL
 ID      NAME         PITCH  SIZE   SET    PRINT SAMPLE
----   ----------     -----  -----  ------ ----------------------

"PERMANENT" SOFT FONTS

 S17   Dutch LIGHT ITALIC     PS    20    0U  ABCDEfghij#$@[\]^`{|}~123

LEFT FONT CARTRIDGE

RIGHT FONT CARTRIDGE

INTERNAL FONTS

 I12   COURIER                10    12    8U   ABCDEfghij#$@[\]^`{|}~123
                                              ÀÂ°ÇÑ¿¡£§èéàeeoÄØåæÀÜßÁÐÒ
 I13   COURIER                10    12    10U  ABCDEfghij#$@[\]``{|}~123
                                              ió|┤┤┐┘└┴┬├─┼╞╧╨╤╥╙╘╒╓╫╪┘┌█▄▌▐▀απ¢
 I14   COURIER                10    12    11U  ABCDEfghij#$@[\]``{|}~123
                                              ió|┤┤┐┘└┴┬├─┼╞╧╨╤╥╙╘╒╓╫╪┘┌█▄▌▐▀απ¢
 I15   COURIER                10    12    0N   ABCDEfghij#$@[\]``{|}~123
                                              ¡¢£¤¥¦§¨©ª«¬®¯°±²³´µ¶·¸¹º»¼½¾
 I16   COURIER BOLD           10    12    8U   ABCDEfghij#$@[\]^`{|}~123
                                              ÀÂ°ÇÑ¿¡£§èéàeeoÄØåæÀÜßÁÐÒ
 I17   COURIER BOLD           10    12    10U  ABCDEfghij#$@[\]``{|}~123
                                              ió|┤┤┐┘└┴┬├─┼╞╧╨╤╥╙╘╒╓╫╪┘┌█▄▌▐▀απ¢
 I18   COURIER BOLD           10    12    11U  ABCDEfghij#$@[\]``{|}~123
                                              ió|┤┤┐┘└┴┬├─┼╞╧╨╤╥╙╘╒╓╫╪┘┌█▄▌▐▀απ¢
 I19   COURIER BOLD           10    12    0N   ABCDEfghij#$@[\]``{|}~123
                                              ¡¢£¤¥¦§¨©ª«¬®¯°±²³´µ¶·¸¹º»¼½¾
 I20   LINE_PRINTER          16.6   8.5   8U   ABCDEfghij#$@[\]^`{|}~123
                                              ÀÂ°ÇÑ¿¡£§èéàeeoÄØåæÀÜßÁÐÒ
 I21   LINE_PRINTER          16.6   8.5   10U  ABCDEfghij#$@[\]``{|}~123
                                              ió|┤┤┐┘└┴┬├─┼╞╧╨╤╥╙╘╒╓╫╪┘┌█▄▌▐▀απ¢
 I22   LINE_PRINTER          16.6   8.5   11U  ABCDEfghij#$@[\]``{|}~123
                                              ió|┤┤┐┘└┴┬├─┼╞╧╨╤╥╙╘╒╓╫╪┘┌█▄▌▐▀απ¢
 I23   LINE_PRINTER          16.6   8.5   0N   ABCDEfghij#$@[\]``{|}~123
                                              ¡¢£¤¥¦§¨©ª«¬®¯°±²³´µ¶·¸¹º»¼½¾
```

Fig. 8.4.
Landscape Fonts.

Gray-Scale and Registration Test

Gray scales are an important feature of a printer if black-and-white scanned photos are to be printed. Printers that have the capability to print gray scales also should have the capability to print a sample gray-scale pattern. The goal is to make sure that the shades of gray change uniformly but are still distinguishable from each other. Factors like the toner cartridge and the position of the intensity knob adjust the gray-scale behavior. This possibility of change is why an easy way of checking the gray scale is good to have.

Registration is the capability to put data in the exact same spot on the paper over and over again. For this reason, the registration test should put the printer into its maximum paper-handling speed and print the same page over and over again. After you decide that the printer has had long enough to make a mistake, you usually have to turn off the printer. Then, put the first and the last pages together evenly and hold them up to a light. If the lines and letters are in exactly the same spots, the printer passed the registration test.

Part II: Printer Setup and Management

The HP LaserJet combines the gray scale and the registration test into one test called the *service test* (see fig. 8.5). This test is activated in a clumsy way (supposedly to keep the test secret). Using only the buttons on the HP LaserJet printer, follow these instructions exactly:

1. Hold down the ON LINE, CONTINUE, and ENTER buttons all at the same time and turn on the printer. The display should come up blank.

Fig. 8.5.
Gray-scale, registration self-test.

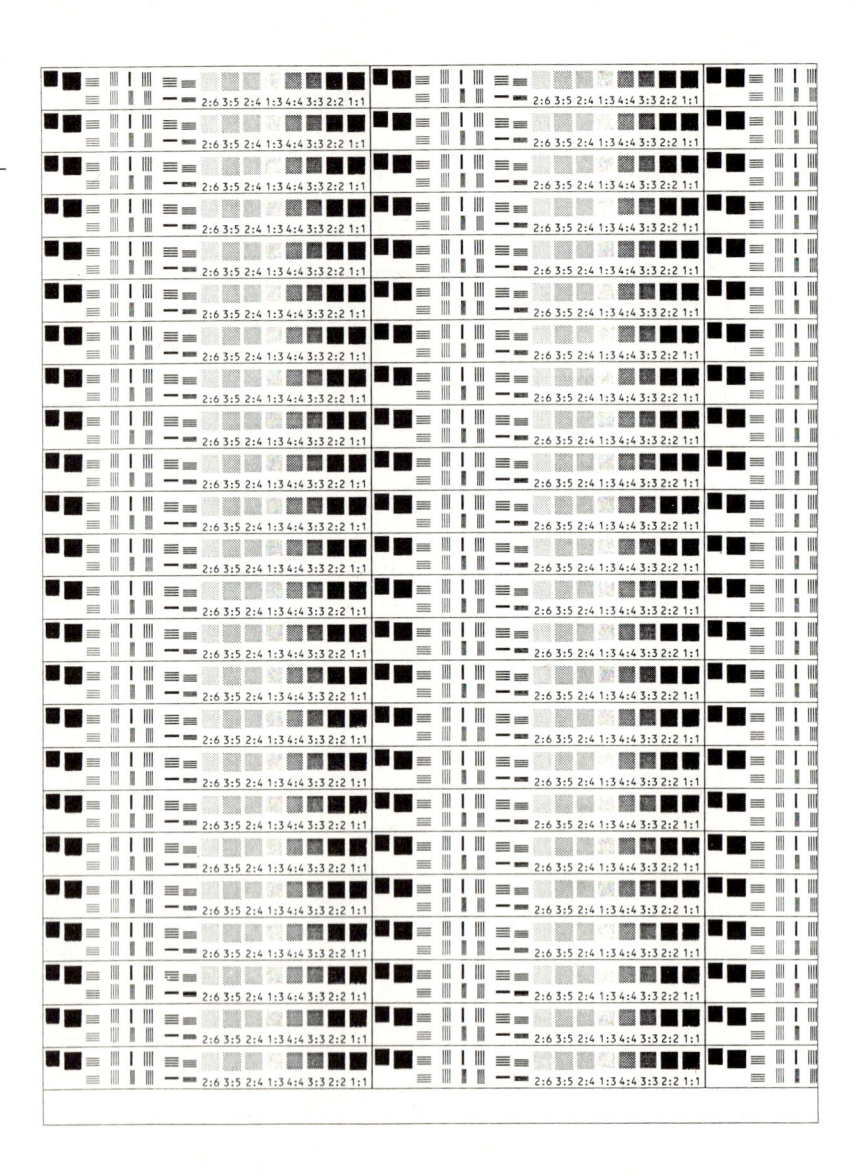

2. Press the CONTINUE button.

3. Press the ENTER button. The display now shows SERVICE MODE. After about 5 seconds, `05 Self Test` is displayed and performed.

4. Press and hold down the TEST button until `04 Self Test` appears.

Preparing To Connect the Printer to the Computer

After you turn on the printer and print a few self-test pages, the next step is to configure the printer so that it will communicate with the computer. Like most personal computers today, printers have to be configured before they will work with the PC. The information a printer needs to know depends on the interface type.

Printers are configured by two different methods: using switches or using the front panel. Older printers were configured entirely by switches. The front panel held only on-line, line-feed, and form-feed buttons. More modern printers have front panels on which you can select fonts. Some printers, especially laser printers, have drastically reduced the number of switches in favor of configuration through the front panel. This same trend can be seen in the computer world as more and more configuration is done through software rather than by switches. Instead of being configured by micro software, character printers are developing their own "little keyboards" and screens on the front panels. True object or PostScript printers do not need the front panel. Instead, they can be configured by software that runs in a PC.

The following sections start off by describing switches and front panels in general. Then, the details of normally configurable features are explored. Sometimes this information is available in the printer manuals. Ultimately, trial and error with your printer's front panel and switches is going to be the best experience.

Locating and Using the Printer's Switches

A printer's switches are located in three possible places. Early printers had the switches hidden underneath the lid of the printer. To gain access to the switches, you had to remove the entire lid. Most early printers had to be turned upside down to get access to the screws holding the lid. Later, screws could be removed from the top. Manufacturers also tried building little windows or removable panels in the back of the printer to allow access to the switches.

Modern dot-matrix printers place their switches underneath the print head when it is parked at the left margin. Turn the printer off, move the print head to the right, and look for a group of switches. Because of the paper dust and dirt, the switches are usually covered by a clear-plastic or metal lid held in place by a single screw. Loosen the screw and rotate the lid out of the way. Then, you can set the switches by using a pencil or pen.

The switches may be slide or rocker switches. You change the position of a *rocker switch* by pushing down one end of a "teeter-totter" (see fig. 8.6). A *slide switch* has a knob that slides back and forth. Near the switches, you see some words or symbols, such as *off* and *on* with an arrow pointing in a certain direction or maybe the words *open* and *closed*. Does the up end of the rocker mean that the switch is open, or does the down end mean that the switch is off? Does the slide over the word *on* mean that it is on, or can the switch be painted wrong or—worse yet— put in back backwards? The whole issue becomes even more foggy when the manuals say put a switch in position 1. Is 1 on or off? Is 1 open or closed?

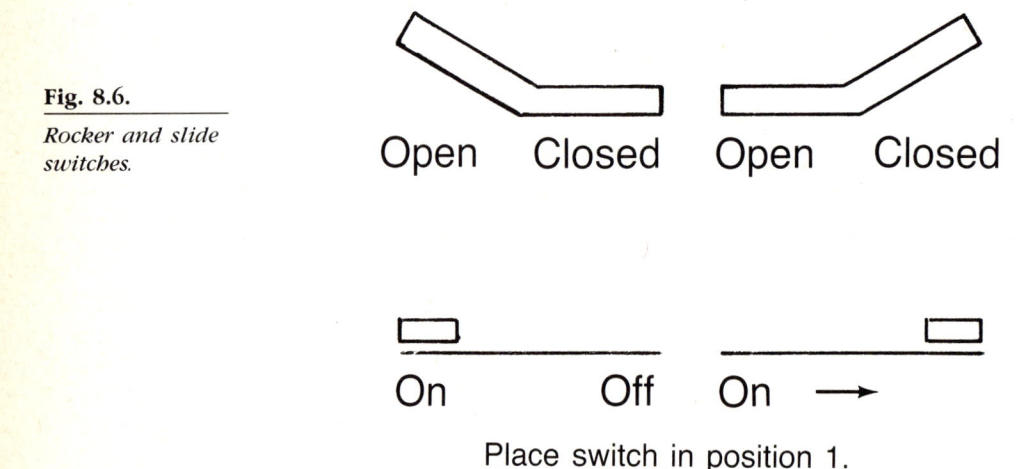

Fig. 8.6.

Rocker and slide switches.

Open   Closed   Open   Closed

On   Off   On →

Place switch in position 1.

Rather than answering these types of questions, remember that if you guess wrong, nothing breaks; instead, the printer just does not work. So try all the combinations. Use the manual as a guide to what each switch controls. Remember that if the switches are changed while the printer is on, nothing changes. The printer looks at the switches only once, when it is turned on. Afterwards, the switch positions do not matter.

> HINT | You can change switch positions while the printer is on, but the changes do not take effect until the printer is turned off and then back on again. Switches are read only during the power-on sequence.

Instead of switches, some printers have jumpers or jumper blocks (see fig. 8.7). *Jumpers* physically connect two posts electrically so that information flows between them. Paper clips can serve as jumpers in a pinch. *Jumper blocks* are rows of hour-glass-shaped pieces of metal. The skinny part between the two parts of the hour glass is supposed to be punctured with a pencil or pen. This is the equivalent of turning a switch off or removing a jumper. The trouble with jumper blocks is that they are hard to reconfigure. And, if they are removed, they usually break. Fortunately, you can use pieces of wire to replace the jumper block. The wire used in staplers is exactly the right size.

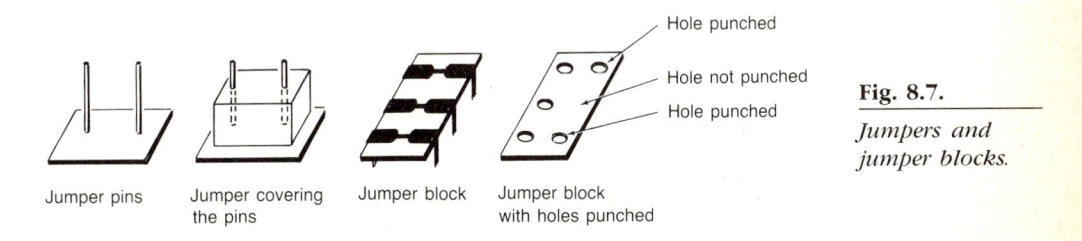

Fig. 8.7. *Jumpers and jumper blocks.*

Jumper pins | Jumper covering the pins | Jumper block | Jumper block with holes punched

Switches are usually underneath hoods in hard-to-reach places. Switches can get dirty; the printer has to be off when they are changed, and usually the printer has to be put back together before it can be turned on. These requirements make guessing long and tedious. Keep notes on the settings you have tried and what happened with each one. For very mysterious reasons, all switches have a tendency to change positions all by themselves.

> HINT | Switches get dirty. Rock or slide them back and forth a few times to clean them.

Because of these problems with switches, most printers are being developed with the capability to remember things without using switches. For example, some printers have a front panel with a Menu button. The Menu button displays a menu on the printer's tiny screen. Using other buttons, you can scroll through menu options, selecting what is appropriate. These types of printers have batteries or special chips that can remember menu settings even if the power is turned off.

Printers that can remember settings have a set of problems different from the problems of printers with switches. Although these problems are not as frequent, they can be more frustrating. These types of printers can forget menu settings.

Understanding Defaults

Now that you know what switches and front panel menus are, you are ready to explore what features these menus activate or deactivate in printers. But, before talking about these features, the concept of *default* needs to be explored.

Defaults are the assumptions that the printer makes when you don't give it enough information to print something. For example, suppose that a character printer is told to print the letter *A*. The printer has to assume that the first letter *A* goes in the upper left corner. The printer has to assume the style, size, and other characteristics, such as whether the letter should be boldface, near-letter quality, or both. Dot-matrix printers usually have switches that govern many different defaults, including the following:

- ❏ Printer cursor position
- ❏ Font
- ❏ Point
- ❏ Pitch
- ❏ Manipulation (bold, expanded, compressed)
- ❏ Character set

These defaults are controlled by the front panel of most dot-matrix and laser printers sold today. Consider, for example, the default font. An easy way of forcing a spreadsheet like 1-2-3 or a database reporting program to print in a compressed font is to use the front panel of the printer to tell the printer that the default pitch is compressed. The interesting characteristic to observe is whether the printer remembers this information when it is turned off and then turned on. Try this experiment on your printers. You will find that most laser printers remember everything and dot-matrix printers forget everything.

Controlling the Sounds

Each printer has a speaker that can emit loud noises, which can be irritating. The noises can be caused by error conditions the printer senses, such as out of paper. The computer also can cause the printer to beep by sending a special byte, which is reserved especially to make the printer beep.

A switch in some dot-matrix printers disables the printer's use of its own speaker but still allows PCs to use the printer's speaker. PC software rarely uses the printer's speaker, so the printer's speaker should rarely make any noise.

Clearing the Buffer

A printer's buffer is similar to a sink with water flowing in faster than it is flowing out. Data can flow in from the PC faster than the printer can print the data (see Chapter 14, "Troubleshooting," for more information).

For example, this situation commonly occurs: you start printing something, see something wrong, and instantly try to stop printing. You press the right buttons for the software in use and then wait for the printer to stop printing. But, the printer does not stop. Software can control only the computer, not the printer. The printer stops receiving information from the computer but still has a buffer full of text to be printed.

The question, then, is how to clear the printer's buffer instantly. The easiest way is to turn the printer off and on. Unfortunately, this option is becoming less attractive. Turning a printer off and then back on takes more and more time as printers download fonts and perform other setup tasks. Some printers have more than 4M of RAM full of fonts and setup information that disappears with the buffer. Therefore, some printers have a mechanism to clear the buffer without turning off the printer (called a soft reset—similar to a warm boot). See the section on resetting, later in this chapter, for methods of clearing the buffer. Some dot-matrix printers have switches that allow the PC to clear the buffer by sending special printer commands.

Controlling Line Feeds and Carriage Returns

Many times during the installation of a printer and micro software, an application will double space or print over and over again on the same line. Although the spacing problem usually is easy to solve, the next program installed on the micro will require a different solution. Eventually, if enough programs are added, a solution satisfactory to all programs can seem impossible. This section reviews the problems, history, and solutions to these problems. It also explains what a confusing set of dip switches does in a dot-matrix printer.

A line feed advances the paper one line. The print head (or laser printer's cursor) does not return to the beginning of the line. If just line feeds are sent<LF>
    the text will print<LF>
                in this "stair-step" pattern.

A carriage return causes the print head (laser printer's cursor) to return to the beginning of the current line. If nothing else happens and more text is sent, the text is printed over the text already there. To stop printers from printing over and over again on the same line, printer manufacturers, cable designers, micro operating systems, and application software have come up with solutions. Unfortunately, you will be left sorting through and coordinating these solutions.

A second source of extra line feeds is unique to parallel cables in the IBM PC world. Connecting pin 14 is a wire that can cause the printer to jump temporarily to option 1, where the printer translates an arriving carriage return to a carriage return and a line feed. If a serial printer is available, set it up and see whether the problems go away. Serial printers do not have a similar wire.

Ideally, parallel printers have a switch or a menu option that instructs them to ignore pin 14. If not, the next step is to attempt configuring DOS so that it does not use the wire attached to pin 14. Unfortunately, this configuration is difficult and unpredictable. The only true way to stop the PC from using pin 14 is to perform surgery. Cut open the parallel cable, find the wire connecting pin 14, and cut it.

Unfortunately, cutting this wire can cause other problems. The operating system software in some IBM PC clones (Old Tandy 1000s, for example) actually uses pin 14 to create single-spacing. Some DOS commands, like PRINT or Shift-PrtSc, may excite pin 14. But, if pin 14 is cut, the printer will never know, and everything will print on one line. Try to reconfigure the PC operating system. Look through CONFIG.SYS options and the DOS MODE command options.

Finally, although you can modify each PC program to trust the operating system to add line feeds to carriage returns, *do not modify programs this way.* Modifying a PC program's line-feed behavior will cause problems later on. PC programs cannot tell the difference between a serial and a parallel port, and they cannot tell which operating system they are running on top of.

Controlling Text Wrap

Dot-matrix printer manuals often list three or more switches that deal with carriage returns and line feeds. From the manual descriptions, the switches all appear to be the same. Two switches are described in the preceding section:

1. Automatically add line feed to carriage return.
2. Pay attention to pin 14 of the parallel port.

The third category where carriage returns and line feeds enter the description deals with how the printer is supposed to respond to the situation of receiving more text then can fit on a line. A switch tells the printer to ignore the extra text or add a carriage return and line feed and put the extra text on the next line. Text that is ignored is essentially deleted, lost, or thrown away. The printer does not keep track of this text.

The trouble with using a switch or front-panel menu selection to instruct the printer to insert a carriage return and line feed in the middle of a too-long line of text is that the PC application program does not know that the carriage return and line feed are being inserted. Suddenly, a page will become longer, and pages suddenly will start creeping down fanfold paper on a long document. A paragraph or word will be split with part on the end of one line and the other part at the beginning of the next line. Or, a line may be short—as if the wordwrap of a PC application stopped working. The worst case is one in which the PC application sends extra spaces at the end of a line, and the extra spaces are put on the next line by the printer. This line looks like a blank line—the same symptom of the carriage-return, line-feed problems mentioned in the preceding section. In short, ask the printer to throw away text that does not fit on the current line.

> **TROUBLE-SHOOTING TIP** — Page creep may be caused by the printer's wrapping long lines of text to the next line. Try turning off the automatic wrap in the printer, but remember that the printer may lose text if the lines are too wide.

> **TROUBLE-SHOOTING TIP** — Blank lines in the middle of a page with no text missing are most likely caused by the software's trying to skip the perforation of fanfold paper. The software has failed. Try turning off the printer, positioning the paper at the top of the form, and turning the printer back on. And, then tell the software that the printer is at the top of a page. With 1-2-3, for example, you use the Align command.

The trouble with asking the printer to throw away text that does not fit is that the printer gives no warnings: no buzzers go off, no lights blink, and the printer gives no error messages indicating that it is throwing away text. If printers are going to throw away instructions or text, the printer should at least let you know. You should not have to proofread each document and guess whether a word is missing at the end of a line. Fortunately, the latest generations of most PC software have stopped sending too-long lines to the printer, and the problem is less prevalent.

The printer should be asked to wrap text to the next line only if the application is error logging or programming. These applications do not try to format pages; therefore, page creep is not possible. If you configure the printer to throw away text, remember that important experimental data or error messages may be missing from the printout.

Testing Front-Panel Menus

The front panels of printers are becoming more complicated, with as many buttons and lights as a TV/VCR/stereo remote control. The trouble with all the buttons is that you need time to learn what they do and where they are located. Today, equipment with many buttons is disappearing. New equipment has an LCD display where menu options appear. Inexpensive dot-matrix printers still have buttons, but most laser printers have menus.

Menus provide more options than manual switches. This section uses the front panel of an HP LaserJet to illustrate how to navigate through these menus. The real question is this: Why not connect a PC to a laser printer as if the PC were a mainframe computer and let the printer menus appear on the PC's screen instead of the printer's LCD screen? The reason this technique is not possible in the IBM PC world is that most printers are character/graphics mode printers. The printers cannot send menu choices to the PC. In other words, these printers cannot talk back.

Object-mode printers can send menu options to the computer's screen; in other words, object-mode printers can talk back. On a Macintosh with a LaserWriter printer, the menus can appear on the Mac's screen. Because the printer can send messages back to the Mac, there is not as much need for printer menus. In the IBM PC world, you have to act as a courier of information between the PC and printer. You interact with the printer through its menus.

> HINT: To manage a printer properly, you need to document standard menu configurations and available options for resetting the printer.

You can press and release rapidly or hold down buttons on printers. Holding down buttons produces results different from just pressing the button rapidly. For example, consider the MENU button on the front panel of an HP LaserJet II. If you press this button quickly, you see a menu from which you can select different fonts. If you hold down the MENU button, a different menu appears. From this menu, you choose which interface to pay attention to, which buffer-management protocol is going to be used, and so on. In addition, buttons can act like Shift keys; one is held down while another button is pressed and released rapidly—like holding the Shift key down while pressing a to create a capital *A*.

Buttons on the front panel do the following:

1. Play with menus
2. Reset and clear errors
3. Self-test the printer

This section deals with front-panel menus. It uses the HP LaserJet's front panel as a specific example. Although not all front panels are the same, they have similar concepts. The goal here is for you to learn how to use a front panel. When you are comfortable with a particular front panel, all printer front panels will seem the same—only the features and options change.

The HP LaserJet's MENU button is on the far right side of the panel (see fig. 8.8). The MENU button and all the other buttons are active only if the light above the ON LINE button is off. To turn off the light, press the ON LINE button.

The HP LaserJet II has two menus, with the following menu options:

PRINTING MENU

00 Ready
Copies (min 1, max 99)
Manual Feed (on or off)
Font Source (Internal, Soft, Left, Right cartridges)
Font Number (min 1, max 99)
Form Length (min 5, max 128)

CONFIGURATION MENU

00 Ready
Symbol Set (a font's character set)
Auto Cont (try and correct errors automatically on, off)
I/O (serial or parallel)
Baud Rate (300,600,1200,4800,9600,19200, see Chapter 13)
Robust Xon (see serial port section of Chapter 13)
Dtr Polarity (see serial port section of Chapter 13)

Fig. 8.8.

HP LaserJet II front panel.

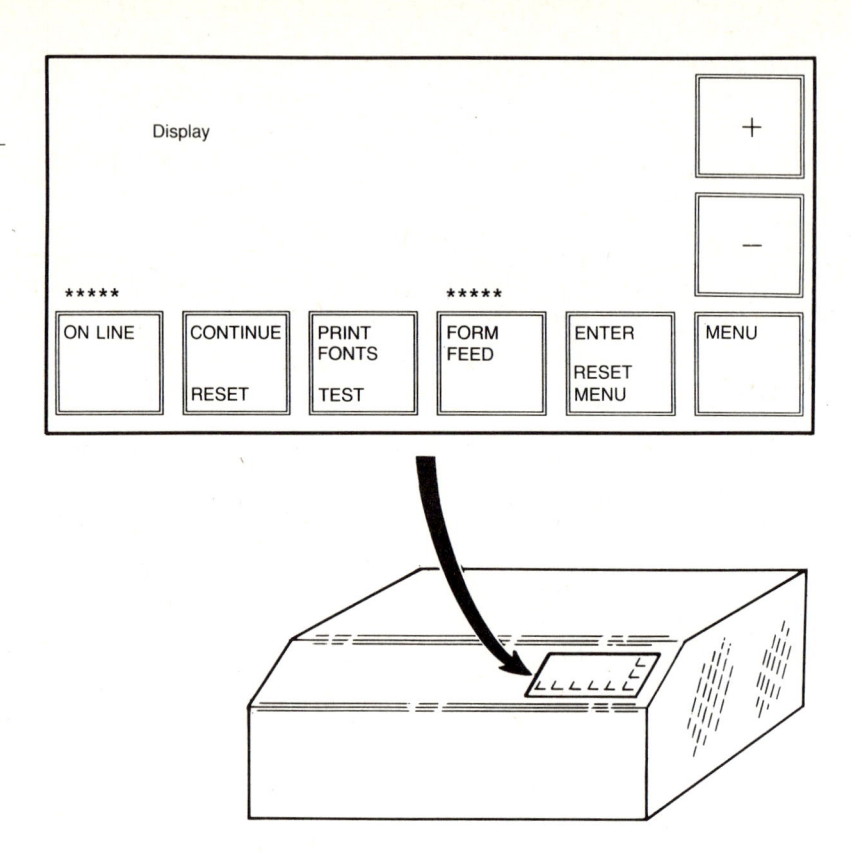

Choosing a Menu

When you first turn on a printer, the front panel says something like Ready to print. Because the front panel has only one line of text, the word Ready has to be replaced with a menu option. To display a menu option, you first must put the printer off-line (press the ON LINE button so that its light goes out); then, press the MENU button. Pressing the MENU button rapidly displays the first option of the PRINTING menu: Copies. Holding the MENU button down displays the first line of the CONFIGURATION menu: Symbol Set.

Scrolling through Menu Options and Parameters

After a menu option appears on the front panel, you press the MENU button rapidly to cycle through all the menu options.

Each menu option has certain values or parameters associated with it. For example, Copies has a number associated with it indicating how many copies of each page should be made. Adjust the number of copies by using the plus (+) and minus (−) buttons. The + and − buttons cycle through all the values or parameters associated with a menu option.

Selecting Menu Option Parameters

The easy part is finding the menus and cycling through all the menu options, values, and parameters. The hard part is telling the printer what to do. You have to choose a value or parameter. The currently chosen parameter or value has an asterisk (*) appearing by it. You choose only one value or parameter at a time. Cycle through all the parameters using the + and − buttons and check. Notice which parameter is chosen.

To select a new value or parameter, use the + and − buttons to display the value on the front panel. Then, press the ENTER button once quickly. The * should now appear by the displayed parameter or value. Check to make sure that the * is associated with the new value or parameter by cycling through some of the possibilities with the + and − buttons.

After you choose all the menu option parameters or values, the next step is to tell the printer to examine all the changes made. First, select the 00 Ready option. Then, you have to hold down the RESET button until 07 RESET appears on-screen. When 07 RESET appears, release the RESET button, and the printer should work.

Resetting the Printer

Back in the days of simple printers, they were either on or off. Today the definitions of *on* and *off* are blurred. Some TV sets remain on even though you turn them off. Computers have internal clocks that keep ticking so that computers can remember the date and time when you turn them back on. Printers remember their front-panel selections. Some laptop computers ask you the question, "Do you really want to power off?" when you turn the power switch to the off position.

Because printers can remember things while off, the whole issue of managing this "remembered" information becomes important. If turning a printer off and then back on does not clear all its memory, what does? Reset.

Learning the methods of resetting printers is just as important as learning what the "bomb" means on a Mac or pressing Ctrl-Alt-Del on a PC. Just as Macs and PCs get locked up, so do printers. Turning the printer on and off cures some problems but creates others.

You need to discover the different methods of resetting a printer before it is attached to the computer. The computer may prevent certain printer resets, or the software itself may reset the printer. For these reasons, you should explore the printer's behavior before attaching it to a PC.

Continue

Continue is the preferred method of resetting whenever you have a problem. Most printers are built like copier machines. They are designed to recover gracefully from paper jams, out-of-paper conditions, and other types of problems. Pressing Continue gives the printer a chance to start over and do its job correctly.

Like their copier machine cousins, laser printers are sensitive to paper jams. Laser printers also are sensitive to memory overflows. To indicate these problems, laser printers beep, flash error messages, or print error messages. The user is supposed to cure the problem and then indicate that the problem is solved by pushing a Continue button.

Press the Continue button (it may be named something like Resume or Clear Error), and notice what happens. (You may have to put the printer off-line first.) Does a page eject, do the lights flicker, or does nothing happen? Your goal is to notice the normal printer response to your pressing Continue. Whatever the printer does, recovering from ideal conditions can be compared to what actually happens when the paper runs out or jams or when the printer's memory has a problem.

In the CONFIGURATION menu of an HP LaserJet II is an option called `Automatic Continue`. Normally, this option should be disabled because you want to know when you have a problem. But, if you change Automatic Continue to Yes, the laser printer will pause for 10 seconds flashing its error message and then continue.

Soft Reset

If Continue does not work or solve the problem, next try to perform a soft reset. In the IBM and Mac worlds, you have quick ways of rebooting. Some information is retained in memory so that the computer returns to life much more quickly. This procedure is sometimes called a *soft boot* or *soft reset*. In the IBM PC world, you perform a soft boot by simultaneously pressing the Ctrl, Alt, and Del keys. In the Mac world, you press Command-S (to save the file) and then open the Special menu and choose the Restart option.

For the LaserJet II printer, you perform a soft reset by holding down the CONTINUE/RESET button until 07 RESET is displayed. This message means that all temporary soft fonts, macros, and stored page data are cleared and all menu option parameters are returned to the front-panel menu values. (The parameters could have been changed by the software). You do not have to download permanent soft fonts again.

Cold Boot

If neither a Continue nor a soft reset works, you have to attempt a *cold reset*. The concept of total death and then rebirth used to be called *cold booting*. Today, the more accurate definition is "resetting to the factory defaults."

Some printers have a button you can push. In some PC laptops, you run a program called COLD as soon as you boot the laptop. There are setup programs, diagnostics disks, setup disks, and reference disks in the IBM PC world. In the older MAC world, you had to remove the battery. In newer MACs, you press Shift, Option, and Command. To cold boot the HP LaserJet II printer, you hold down the RESET MENU button (not to be confused with the CONTINUE/RESET button) until 09 RESET MENU appears on-screen.

Hardware Reset

If a cold boot does not work, the next step is to turn the printer off and on. The same thing is true about official IBM PCs. But, the clone PCs have added another form of reset that still is not available in the printer world. This form of reset simulates turning the power on and off without actually turning the power on and off.

Simulating powering on and off is important for a variety of reasons. Have you noticed that mainframe and minicomputers are never turned off? When a switch is turned on, a tidal wave of electricity hits the light bulb, printer, mainframe, whatever. This stress can damage any of these elements. When a mainframe goes off accidentally, fear and adrenalin flow through the veins of the personnel responsible for turning the mainframe back on.

Ideally, PCs, printers, monitors, and other electrical equipment should not be turned off and on regularly. Thus, many people are hopeful that printers will develop hardware reset buttons similar to PC clones.

Testing the Computer's Capability To Print

After running through all the self-tests and practicing the different resets, hook up the printer cable. The next step is to test the computer's capability to print. This complex topic is discussed in Chapter 9. Here, the goal is to get the computer to print something—enough to check whether the cable is attached to the proper port, the computer's hardware is configured properly, and the switches inside the printer are configured properly. The following sections include the simplest instructions for getting a Mac and a PC to print something.

The following procedures are also useful when you are trying to isolate a problem by determining whether the printer cannot print, the operating system is fouling things up, or the application software has not been properly installed. For example, if the following steps work, but the computer application software cannot print, the computer application software is not properly configured.

Testing the Capability of a PC To Print

PC printers can hook up to so many different places on the back of a PC that connecting the printer cable can be difficult. On the back of a PC are three different connectors where you can attach printers. These connectors are the parallel, 25-pin serial, and 9-pin serial. The parallel connector has 25 holes in it. The 25-pin serial connector has 25 male pins sticking out of it. The 9-pin serial connector has 9 male pins sticking out.

Each connector on the back of the PC has a name that you cannot determine just by looking at the connector. The serial connectors can have names COM1, COM2, COM3, or COM4. The parallel ports can have names LPT1, LPT2, or LPT3.

Look at the PC end of the printer cable and determine whether it is going to hook into a serial port or parallel port. Then, read the appropriate following section.

Testing PC Parallel Ports

After hooking the printer cable to a parallel port, try entering the following commands on the PC keyboard. One of the three should print something. If they don't work, you will get an error message. Otherwise, the printer should print something.

❏ Press PrtSc or Shift-PrtSc

❏ At the DOS prompt, type *DIR > LPT2:*

❏ At the DOS prompt, type *DIR > LPT3:*

If none of the preceding tests works, plug the printer cable into another port on the back of the PC. Keep trying these steps with different PC ports until you run out of ports to test. If none works, check their configuration. Find the manuals for the circuit boards containing the printer ports. Look up how to configure the ports for LPT1 and LPT2. If this method does not solve the problem, recheck the printer configuration. Otherwise, turn to Chapter 13, because you may have a printer cable problem.

Testing PC Serial Ports

PC serial ports come in two styles, 9-pin and 25-pin. Converters between 9-pin and 25-pin ports are readily available. Many serial printers, serial mice, and modems are shipped with these converters. Try attaching the printer cable to a port and then using the following DOS commands to test whether this port will work. All three have to be typed. The last should print something.

❏ Type *MODE COM1:96,N,8,1*

❏ Type *MODE LPT1:=COM1*

❏ Press PrtSc or Shift-PrtSc.

Repeat the preceding commands for each possible serial port by changing *COM1:* to *COM2:*, *COM3:*, and *COM4:*.

If none of these tests works, move the printer cable to another serial port. Keep trying the steps with different serial ports until you run out. If none works, check the ports' configuration. Find the manuals for the circuit boards containing the printer ports. Look up how to configure the ports for COM1:, COM2:, COM3:, COM4:. If this method does not solve the problem, recheck the printer configuration. Otherwise, turn to Chapter 13, because you may have a printer cable problem.

Testing the Capability of a PostScript Printer

PostScript printers are different. They will not work with any of the DOS commands listed in the preceding sections. PostScript printers receive the data coming in and search for commands like SetLineWidth, ShowPage, and so on. By looking at the lights or messages, you can tell whether a PostScript printer is receiving data. But, you cannot tell whether the PostScript printer is understanding the data.

When a PostScript printer does not understand what is sent, it just keeps on blinking its lights as if it were "thinking." After receiving a Shift-PrtSc, the PostScript printer just stops flashing its lights but displays no error messages. In the IBM world, PostScript printers cannot respond to the Shift-PrtSc command. Generally, PostScript printers print what they understand and do nothing if they cannot understand what is sent.

To test a PostScript printer in the IBM PC world, you need PostScript software. This need is why the wise decision is to purchase a printer that has both character and object modes and the capability to switch between them. You can use character mode for testing; then, use object mode after everything is up and running.

Testing a Macintosh Printer

Hook up the Macintosh printer, load the contents of the floppy disk that came with the printer, transfer the printer's icon into the System folder, click the icon, set up the printer, and then try printing the screen. If you have an ImageWriter, press Shift-Caps Lock and Command-4. The simplest way to print on a LaserWriter (a PostScript device) is to save the screen to a disk with Shift-Command-3. This command creates a MacPaint file, which you can then print.

Preparing for Printer Trouble

You should keep a binder with all the printed configuration information, backup disks, repair history, and some printer information beside each PC. Most PC software comes with a test document that exercises the printer. If such a file does not exist, create one. Use boldface, underlining, boldface and underlining, shadow, boldface shadow; do everything possible to each font that exists. Use the document as a tutorial on how to use the printer. Put the document in each binder as a reference.

In addition, print the test document to a file. The electronic form of the printer instructions helps to isolate future problems that may arise. If someone corrupts the PC software, the electronic form of the test document can still be sent to the printer through the operating system and thus determine whether the printer or the PC software is the problem.

If all the PC application programs have had the printer installed (see Chapter 9), print every PC configuration screen (press Shift-PrtSc) and put these printouts in the binder. Now, if the software ever has to be installed from scratch, someone else may be able to do the configuration by matching the printed versions in the binder.

Finally, put copies of the results of the printer's self-tests in the binder. This way, results of future self-tests can be compared with the original results to determine any degradation in quality or changes in printer configuration.

Installing, Testing, and Managing Printers

If you are wasting your time waiting for the printer to finish printing, you may want to add a spooler, queue, print buffer, or more memory. If you are just printing small documents, however, these devices can slow down the printing process.

Queues, spoolers (Simultaneous Print Operations On-Line), and buffers are essentially buckets that catch information intended for the printer and temporarily store the information. The software thinks the spooler's bucket is a very fast printer, and prints it instantly. Later, in the background, the spooler software slowly drains the bucket's data into the printer, freeing the PC to do something else. The PC thinks that it has an infinitely fast cable to the printer and an infinitely fast printer. Sometimes, the PC thinks that the document has finished printing before the printer actually starts. Because the PC finishes much sooner, you can use the PC productively while the printer is churning out sheets of paper at the same time. On some occasions, however, queues, spoolers, and print buffers actually slow down work, do not work at all, and create chaos.

HINT | Don't purchase queues, spoolers, or print buffers for an IBM PC. Most software vendors have added this feature to the application software. Every major word processing vendor includes spoolers with their software. Having multiple queues or spoolers (one you installed and one that came with a program) can create all sorts of problems.

HINT | In the IBM PC world, some application vendors include TSR spoolers and queues that are loaded into memory when the program is executed. These spoolers and queues may stick around in memory after the program is executed and create chaos. If a spooler is already resident, multiple spoolers and queues can climb into PC DOS and fight. Don't purchase software that creates TSRs. To check, print a large document and then quit or exit quickly. If the document continues printing while in DOS, the program has added a TSR to PC DOS. Another way to check is to run the PC DOS program CHKDSK before and after running the application. The amount of free PC RAM memory (not hard disk storage) reported by CHKDSK should be the same.

The major difference among print queues, spoolers, buffers, and printer memory is how much control they enable the PC to have over printer instructions in temporary storage. Print queues offer the most control. Features of a queue include the following: document priority assignments, document routing to different printers if one goes down or is busy, multiple copies, aborting option, whole-page buffering in case the top part of a page is trashed, and so on. Queues are found in local area networks, minicomputer installations, and mainframe installations.

Spoolers are a first-in, first-out system of printing documents in the *bucket*. Spoolers generally have some of the features of a queue. Most spoolers can instantly empty the bucket. Some spoolers can terminate individual files in the bucket. The problem is how to tell the spooler to abort the process. In a MAC, you can add spoolers (as a desk accessory) that are easy to abort. In contrast, PC spoolers are difficult to abort. You have to abort PC spoolers by exiting the application program, customizing the application program, or using a TSR program. None of these ideas are appealing; therefore, this feature is undesirable.

Determining the End of File

Spoolers and queues share a common feature—they receive the entire document before printing. This feature does not cause a problem as long as the PC is printing one document at a time. The spooler or queue can identify the end of a document by a long pause between printer instructions. In a shared environment such as a multitasking, multiuser, or LAN system, the capability to identify the end of a document can become a problem.

PC DOS has not set up a formal *finished printing* protocol. In a shared environment, fragments of pages can be printed the first time, and whole pages can be printed the next time. The random nature of this problem is caused by the activities of other programs or devices trying to share the spooler or the spooler's resources (RAM, hard disk space).

Spoolers and queues have to guess when a document is finished by examining each pause and trying to determine its cause. Sometimes, spoolers and queues guess incorrectly. Suppose that you press the Pause key, forcing the computer to halt, and the spooler also halts. When the spooler wakes up, the spooler sees that some time has passed and closes the print file.

Running PC DOS programs with OS/2 requires that you press Ctrl-Alt-PrtSc when the PC DOS program is finished printing. This key sequence also tells the OS/2 spooler that the print stream is complete and that the data should be printed.

Stopping a Print Job

Because spoolers and queues completely receive a document before printing, the document can be deleted, priorities reorganized, and so on. In contrast, print buffers and printer memory do not receive complete documents before starting to print. Print buffers operate like a shower. When the water is turned on, the water takes a few moments to shoot out of the faucet. When the water is turned off, the faucet drips for a while until the water in the pipes is gone. PC software is like the faucet, and the printer cable is the pipe. Printer buffers make the pipe much longer. If PC software stops printing, many letters in the cable and buffer continue to drip out. Turning off the printer does not help. The letters are still in the pipe. When the printer is turned back on, the printer continues where it stopped. Turning off the PC also does not work, unless the print buffer is inside the PC. If the print buffer is outside the PC and has its own power cord, the PC may have to be turned off to instantly drain all the letters in the pipe.

Finding the Printer Bottleneck

To understand what effect queues, spoolers, and print buffers can have on speed, the highway that data travels must be clear. Bottlenecks can occur anywhere along the way. Ideally, you should have only one print buffer, queue, or spooler. The more queues, spoolers, and buffers you have, the more cooperation is necessary.

When data leaves a PC application, it flows through the operating system (ideally). Additions or modifications to the operating system can redirect this flow into a reserved area of PC RAM, into a file on the hard disk, or both. From there, the data is sent to a printer interface board that contains dedicated print buffer memory. When sent out of the printer interface port, a printer buffer can be attached that also catches printer data. The print buffer then sends the data down the cable into the printer's memory where the data is buffered again.

In most character- and object-mode printer operations, the printer is the bottleneck. In graphics mode, the printer, the cable, or even the PC can be the bottleneck. Methods of speeding up the printing process (queues, spoolers, and buffers) are useful only at certain times.

First, consider the situation in which the PC application software is really slow; for example, when the software is computing each dot's location. The printer receives a horizontal band of graphic information and then prints the band (if dot matrix) or stores the band (if laser) for printing when the page is full. This type of software is not going to benefit from a print buffer.

If the PC is really fast at generating graphics data, the printer cable can be the bottleneck. In this case, the queue, spooler, or buffer has to be located before the slow section of cable. Typical devices used include the PC hard disk, PC RAM, special printer interface board with lots of memory, or a box full of memory and attached to the printer port. If the cable is really fast, the print buffer can be located near the printer or in the middle of the cable.

Spoolers and queues slow down the printing of small files. Suppose that the file takes six seconds to transmit and print without the spooler. Suppose that the spooler takes six seconds to store a page on the PC's hard disk. (Six seconds to open a file, name the file, transmit the page, and close the file—transmitting the amount of data representing a page is negligible.) Then, the spooler takes another six seconds to send the page to the printer. In this case, the PC is again occupied for six seconds, but takes 12 seconds to print the page.

Spoolers are much more useful with large documents. Suppose that a document takes 15 minutes to print. Because the spooler is inside the PC, saving the large document on the hard disk is fast (perhaps 10 seconds). The PC is occupied for 10 seconds, rather than 15 minutes. This frees the user to do other work. The total printing time is 15 minutes, 10 seconds—not much different than 15 minutes.

> HINT | When purchasing a spooler, try to find one that enables you to clear its contents while inside an application and to disable the spooler. Activate the spooler only when printing large documents on a character-mode or graphics-mode printer.

Print buffers and large quantities of print memory do not suffer from this drawback. No files have to be opened, named, and closed. Data flows instantly into the RAM or PC interface circuit boards, printer buffer boxes, and printer memory. The PC is free for you to do other work. Before the first character pops out of the printer interface, buffer box, or memory, is a delay of about 1 second. A file that originally took six seconds to print now takes seven seconds. Unfortunately, PC software has no way to manage the printer buffer. With big files, the buffer offers the same performance improvement as spoolers and queues.

Managing the Buffer

What happens when the file is too large for the spooler, queue, or buffer's bucket? The bucket may be a hard disk, RAM, or other type of memory. Because spoolers and queues are software added to the PC operating system, they might solve the problem or present the problem to the application software or operating system. Or, they might lock up the computer system when there is a problem. A good spooler should be able to solve its problems without involving the user or locking up the computer.

However, printer interfaces with memory, print buffers, dumb printer sharing devices, and dumb printers struggle to report the potential buffer overflow. They yell Xoff (turn yourself off) or EXT (end of transmission) at each other. But, these dumb devices are designed only for data to flow to the printer, not the other direction. Their whole purpose is to baby-sit the printer for the PC, but they don't tell the PC anything when the printer starts "crying." Manufacturers of print buffers don't feel obligated to solve this problem. If the problem occurs, they suggest purchasing more memory. They publish tables matching maximum document sizes with buffer memory quantities required.

> **TROUBLE-SHOOTING TIP** | If pages, paragraphs, lines, or characters are lost when printing, a buffer is overflowing. The easiest solution is to purchase more memory or create a bottleneck between the buffer and the PC—that is, slow the bits per second rate in the cable between the PC and the buffer. See Chapter 14 on troubleshooting for more elegant solutions.

Providing for Two-Way Communication

Object printers can talk to the computer, answering and asking questions. Unfortunately, spoolers, queues, and buffers have not yet evolved to the point of being able to support two-way communication with an object printer. An important feature of object-mode printers, therefore, is lost. This problem is more prevalent in the Macintosh world, where the two-way communication feature of object printers is heavily used. Fonts that were once available will disappear if a queue, spooler, or buffer is inserted.

> **TROUBLE-SHOOTING TIP** | When an object printer does not print a font that is installed as a screen font, try removing spoolers, print queues, buffers, and so on. They may be blocking communication with the operating system.

Using the DOS Print Command

In the PC world, each PC application comes with a spooler that has a different screen and features. If a spooler is added to the PC operating system (DOS includes a spooler called PRINT), the spooler becomes available to all application software. Many additional memory boards sold for PCs include such software as an example of how to use the extra memory. Including this software, however, causes several problems:

- ❏ Many PC programs have their own spoolers; therefore, the PC program's spooler is sending data to the PC operating system's spooler.
- ❏ A PC DOS level spooler (DOS PRINT command, for example) cannot be accessed from within a PC software package. Spooler management is impossible.
- ❏ The PC DOS spooler is memory resident and can cause the keyboard to lock up.
- ❏ If the PC DOS spooler has problems, the spooler cannot interrupt what you are doing and tell you about the problems, which is why most major PC applications have spoolers built into them.

> HINT | Because they cause problems, do not install PC DOS level spoolers. Instead, purchase PC software with spoolers built in.

Using WordPerfect's Spooler

With WordPerfect, you can send multiple print jobs to the printer, and WordPerfect manages printing as you continue to work. Normally, you will not have any problems with the WordPerfect spooler. However, the slightest problem with the spooler operation causes all printing to stop. If WordPerfect will not print anything, press Shift-F7 and then F4. These keystrokes access the screen that enables you to control WordPerfect's spooler to determine what the problem is.

Any problem with printing shows up in WordPerfect's spooler. For example, if you turn off the printer and try to print, the spooler prints this message: `Printer not accepting characters` (see fig. 8.9). Other error messages the spooler can contain range from files that cannot be found to messages to insert paper in the manual paper feed slot and press Go.

```
Print: Control Printer

Current Job

Job Number:  9                                    Page Number:  None
Status:      Initializing                         Current Copy: None
Message:     Printer not accepting characters
Paper:       None
Location:    None
Action:      Check cable, make sure printer is turned ON


Job List

  9    (Screen)           LPT 1              Text=Draft


Additional Jobs Not Shown: 0


1 Cancel Job(s); 2 Rush Job; 3 Display Jobs; 4 Go (start printer); 5 Stop: 0
```

Fig. 8.9.

WordPerfect's spooler.

Possible solutions to the spooler's problem are sometimes suggested next to the action line. For example, attach the printer cable, turn on the printer, and place the printer on-line. If you specified nonexistent pages, subdirectories, or files, cancel the print job. If the printer needs a sheet of paper, put paper in it. Sometimes, the printer can notify the spooler that it is ready to print, and printing starts immediately. Other times, you must select Go.

> HINT If a word processor does not immediately print, check the spooler. The spooler usually displays some information about what is wrong. Usually, the spooler cannot find a file, or the printer is off, out of paper, or off-line. Even if you have cured the problem, the spooler still needs to know that everything is OK again.

Sharing Printers

Sharing an Apple LaserWriter is a dream because the Mac was designed with this feature in mind. In the IBM world sharing printers is a pain. This section is dedicated to the IBM world.

Sharing printers has a few advantages and many disadvantages. Before considering whether to share a printer, consider the cost of sharing versus the cost of a dot-matrix printer (see Chapter 7). Consider the time spent walking back and forth to the shared printer. In this section, the discussion of advantages and disadvantages continues, and then, the various methods are reviewed.

One central printer may be easier to manage. One shared printer is definitely easier to manage than 100 different printer models. If selling management on one big fancy laser printer connected through a network (because the company just came off a minicomputer or dedicated word processing system) is easier, do it. This system demands a more intelligent, higher-paid, systems-analysis person to assume responsibility for keeping the centralized resource up and running. If a batch of cheap dot-matrix printers is purchased, however, the consumable costs are halved, the only maintenance is replacement, and no single vulnerable point exists.

Software expects the printer to be close by. Getting the printout right the first time is almost impossible. This difficulty means that if the printer is more than a few steps away, the path to the printer will quickly become a rut.

Some printer-sharing devices have all the problems of queues, spoolers, buffers, and printer memory discussed in the preceding section. The printer-sharing devices have trouble figuring out when a page ends. These sharing devices have no way to tell the PC application program what is going on. In order to prevent documents of two users from appearing on one sheet, the printer-sharing devices must waste pieces of paper. The PC program starts spacing over what it thinks is a perforation when really no perforation is there.

LAN spooling software is getting as sophisticated as minicomputer spoolers. The network operator can assign priorities, rearrange the printer queue, delay printing to a certain time, and so on. The trouble with this division of tasks is that one person must be in charge of the printer. Requiring everyone to learn the print-spooler management of the network is unreasonable. On the other hand, concentrating spooler-management responsibility in one person's hands usually leads to poor printer use and stifles the creative atmosphere necessary for making unique, personal printouts.

Computer software expects a personal printer attached to a personal computer. This software does not know how to choose different printers on a local area network. Computer software generally expects printer output to leave the first parallel port. Software assumes that the printer is personal and makes educated guesses as to the location of paper and the time needed to eject a sheet of paper. Software can get frustrated by the delays a shared device causes and confused by what a shared device does to perform its function of sharing a printer. In short, sharing a printer today is like going back in time.

The market for devices to share a printer is small. The simplest—and often best—method of sharing is a manual A/B switch box. But, even it can cause problems. The following sections review each of the following methods and give the advantages and disadvantages of each:

- Using a variety of interfaces
- Using a manual switch box
- Using an electronic switch box
- Using local area networks

Using a Variety of Interfaces

The HP LaserJet II comes with two interfaces: one serial and one parallel. If just two people want to use this printer, one computer can be hooked to the serial and the other to the parallel port. The switching can then be accomplished manually by using the front panel of the HP LaserJet. The advantage of this system is that no additional cables or hardware are necessary. The disadvantage is that only two people can use the printer.

A third PC can be hooked through the video port if a PostScript board is purchased. When the PostScript board wants to print, it waits until either the serial or parallel finishes. The PostScript board shares the printer easily. You have to switch between the serial and parallel ports using the front panel. When someone tries to use the disconnected serial or parallel port, the printer acts as if it were dead or turned off. At least when the printer is not connected, the PC has trouble working, and the problem is obvious.

Using a Manual Switch Box

Manual switch boxes are essentially a physical switch. They do not have a power cord, any chips, or circuitry. Manual switch boxes are simple and break only if poorly made or carried around in a suitcase. Manual switch boxes are all the same, whether parallel or serial. They are about two inches high and five inches square. In the front, manual switch boxes have a knob that points to letters. A two-way switch box has just the letters A and B (see fig. 8.10). A four-way switch box has letters A, B, C, and D. Normal printer cables can be used from the switch box to PCs, but sometimes manual switch boxes require a different cable between the switch box and the printer. If you are building your own cables, always purchase the boxes that switch 25 wires and have DB-25 female connectors on the box. That way, you can use the cheaper DB-25 male connectors on the ends of the cables. A more exotic two-way switch involves just pushing a button in and out (also shown in fig. 8.10). The models start at around $15 for the AB manual switch to $50 for the fancy button switch.

Fig. 8.10.

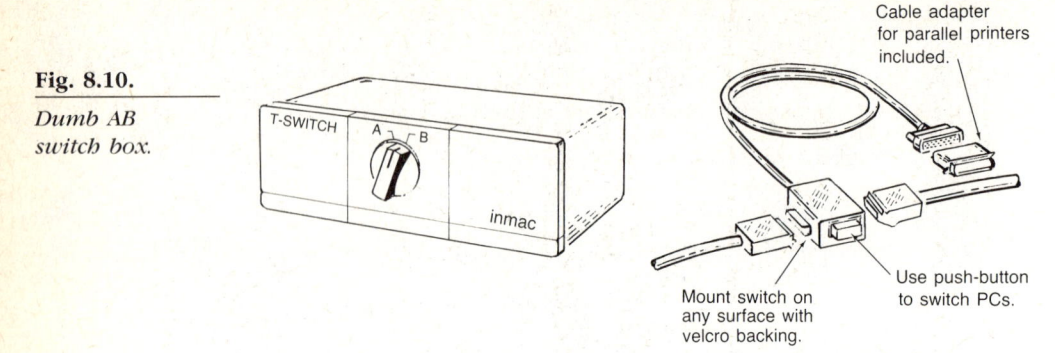

Dumb AB switch box.

Cable T-Switch connects to your existing printer cables.

Manual switch boxes are simple and fairly easy for users to understand. Manual switch boxes have trouble in that they can force a trip to the printer to clear an error message. Usually, the error message is caused by someone's turning off the PC. Because users must make the trip anyway to select their PC, this trip is not a big deal.

What is dangerous about parallel switch boxes is that they can ruin the parallel interface of a laser printer. Most laser printers have special parallel ports that allow the printers to receive data much faster than a dot-matrix printer. But, this capability makes them more sensitive to the surges and spikes that come from a manual switch box. Hewlett-Packard refuses to repair a laser printer (under warranty) if it has ever been attached to a parallel switch box. The other danger with parallel switch boxes is that the cables start to get long. The total cable length between the switch box and the printer should not exceed 15 feet.

Serial switch boxes are fine, but they slow a laser printer. Pulling the wire long distances in a star configuration can cost so much in labor that you can purchase a dot-matrix printer for each micro instead.

Using an Electronic Switch Box

Electronic switch boxes start at around $75. Each has a power cord and circuitry inside. Their major feature is switching automatically between PCs. Instead of one trip to choose your PC and another to pick up the paper, you make just one trip to pick up the paper. Electronic switch boxes come in four kinds: dumb, dumb with buffer, smart, and smart with buffer. Each of these switch boxes is described in the following sections.

Dumb Electronic Switch Box

Dumb switch boxes work by scanning all the PCs, waiting for one that requests to print. Then, the dumb switch box locks onto that PC until it is finished printing. The other PCs are tricked into thinking that the printer is off-line, turned off, or has a full buffer. Unfortunately, the other PCs have to wait longer than normal. These waits increase the natural keyboard lock ups, time outs, and other crazy things that happen to PCs. This situation forces serial cables to be built a specific way. In case the dumb switch does not work well, dumb electronic switch boxes usually have a scan off/on button. When the scan off mode is selected, a single PC can be attached to the printer permanently using a select button (see fig. 8.11).

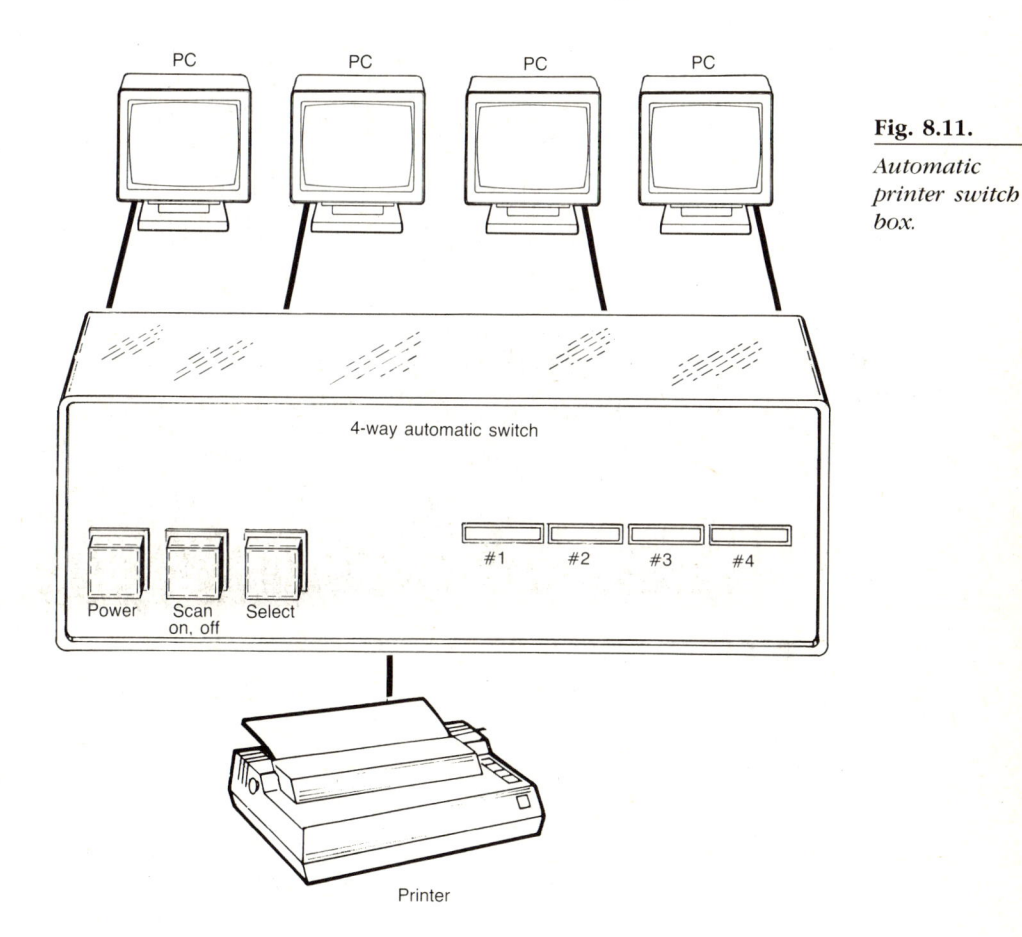

Fig. 8.11.

Automatic printer switch box.

One PC may hog the printer, and the dumb electronic boxes have to guess when the PC is finished printing. Because the switches cannot eject a sheet of paper, two PCs can print on the same sheet of paper. When searching for a PC that is trying to print, the dumb electronic switch box sometimes sees ghosts and starts printing random pages.

Dumb Electronic Switch Box with Buffer

To try to reduce the buffer-overflow, off-line, error-condition, and turned-off error messages that a dumb switch box has to send the printer, some buffers are coming with memory. The cost for these ranges from $50 to $100 per PC. The trouble with adding memory is that memory can be installed without dealing with the serial port problems. The dumb switch box works as long as everyone sharing the dumb switch's buffer prints small documents. But, when you print a long document, paragraphs and even pages disappear. Either you can add more memory or fight a serial port battle.

You can find dumb switches that plug directly into the laser printer itself. Some switches even plug into the video interface input in the back of an HP LaserJet II. Others come with lights that swirl around looking for a printer. The more memory, the more ports and the more these printer-sharing devices cost.

Smart Electronic Switch Box

Smart electronic switch boxes are essentially specialized local area networks. These average from $100 to $200 per PC. Smart electronic switch boxes either require that the PC learn how to talk to them, or they talk a special language among themselves. Rather than requiring an expensive star-wiring topology, these switch boxes daisy-chain PCs together (see fig. 8.12). The point is that you can link smart electronic switch boxes to form networks of boxes that all talk to each other and perhaps talk to the PC.

Smart electronic boxes come with PC software: a device driver and setup program. The setup program allows the PC to set up and program from the remote electronic switch box. The device driver acts like a funnel through which all PC software must send its printer information. Usually, the smart switch attaches itself to the first parallel port. Hopefully, you do not need to configure each PC program.

One disadvantage of the smart electronic switch boxes is that they cost more. Second, the learning curve is higher—they are not as simple to install. A third disadvantage is that the box has more parts that can break.

Chapter 8: Installing and Testing Printers **357**

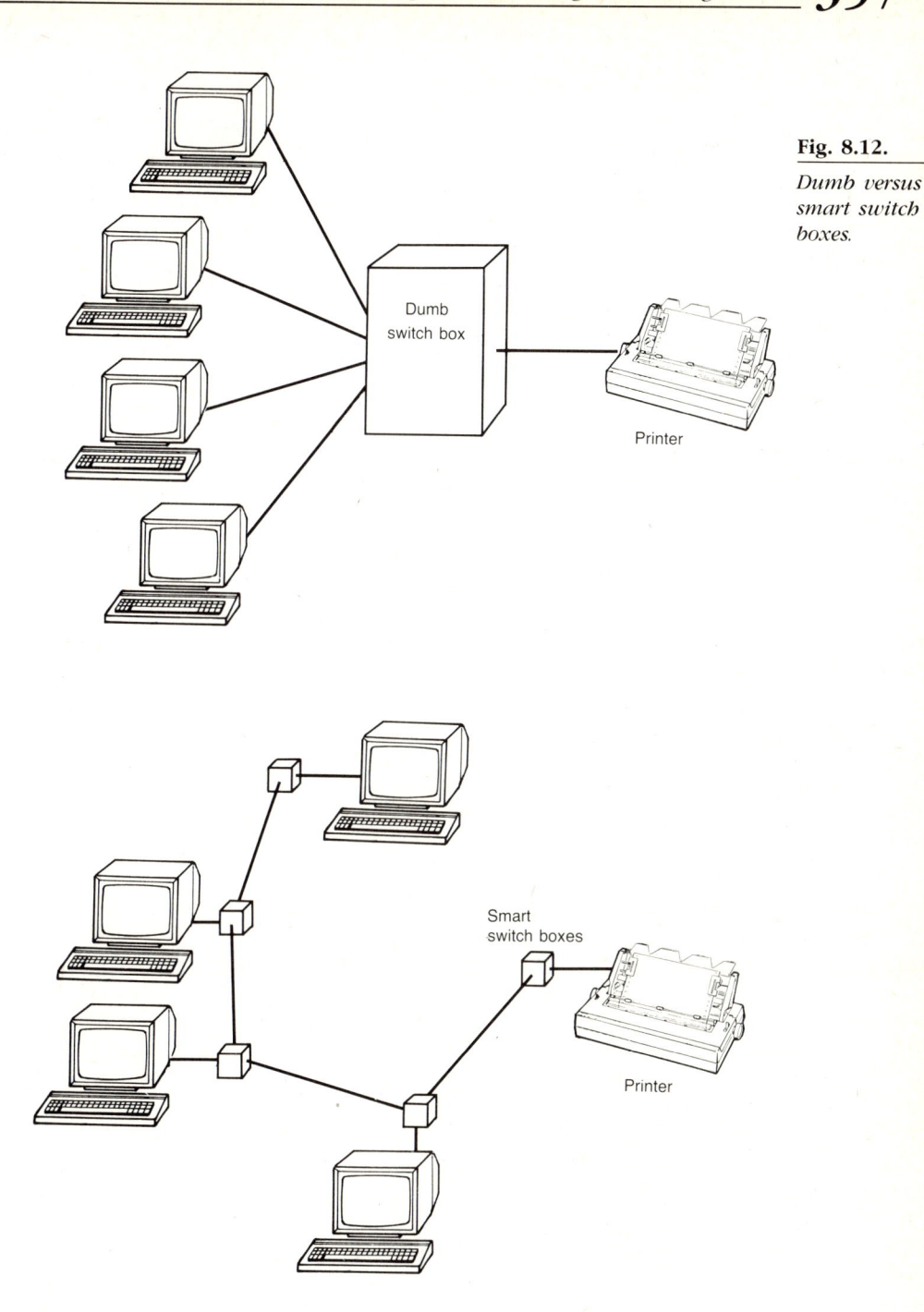

Fig. 8.12.

Dumb versus smart switch boxes.

Smart Electronic Switch Box with Buffer

A fourth type of electronic switch box is essentially a local area network that looks like a printer to the PC. The only disadvantage is expense—about $200 per PC. A box sits next to each PC, like an external modem, and hooks up to the printer's parallel or serial port (usually the parallel port). In the back of the box may be a couple of serial or parallel ports for a local printer or a printer that is being shared. All the boxes are daisy-chained together; therefore, anyone can share someone else's printer. The cable is usually telephone cable already in the walls.

From the PC's point of view, the printing is fast. All data goes out to the box, where a light flashes and then goes on indicating that a document is waiting to be printed (just like a laser printer). After the data to be printed is in the box, you have to push a button on the box to indicate which printer to send the document to. This box is like a manual switch box (your decision is needed) but has these advantages over the manual switch box:

- Switch is located next to your keyboard.
- From the PC's point of view, printing is instantaneous.
- Multiple copies and queuing is possible from the print box.

In many ways, this system is similar to a local area network dedicated to sharing printers. The only disadvantage is that if different printers are being shared, the format of the data sent to the box has to match the printer. This requirement means that you have to make two decisions. First, ask the PC software to create commands specific to a printer of brand X; then push the button on the box that sends the data to a brand X printer. If the brand X document is sent to another type of printer, the document may cause paper to fly out.

Setting Up a Local Area Network

Purchasing an expensive LAN just to share printers does not make sense. The smart switch box with a buffer, described in the preceding section, is a cheaper, better alternative. In the IBM PC world, you can find *Zero Slot LANs* that work in a manner similar to a Local Talk network hooking Macs to the LaserWriter. This is done by hooking PC serial ports up to the PC, with the shared printer in a star fashion. Unfortunately, the IBM PC Zero Slot LAN operates at half the speed of Local Talk and forces one PC to act as a spooler for the printer. This method slows things down even more.

For example, suppose that a file is being transmitted through a cheap LAN that uses serial ports to connect the machines. (MULTILINK is an example.)

The baud rate is 19.2K because the building's computerized phone system is being used for part of the LAN. The 200-page document averages 1,500 characters per page. This document should take only 2 minutes to send, but the entire document has to be received before being printed. And, because printing takes 25 minutes, an extra 2 minutes is no big deal. But, if the document is short, the time required to spool the document to disk and then copy the document to the printer essentially doubles the printing time. The spooling is done on the remote LAN printer server. The analysis does not change except that the time to open a file has been increased by the time required to transmit the file through the LAN.

A spooler PC is needed in the IBM world because a character-mode printer cannot talk back. A PC has to insulate the character printer from the LAN. Because the printer cannot talk to the PC either, the PC ends up guessing what is going on in the printer and what the other PCs are asking the printer to do. Because of this system, the output of most shared printers is simple, with no graphics or font changes. High quality is not a priority. The fancy features of a big laser printer are never used.

The Mac world has object printers directly connected to the Local Talk cables. The Macs can send object data that becomes incredibly detailed drawings. Because the data is in object form, the file size is relatively small—even for desktop publishing documents with graphics. Therefore, the slow speed of a Local Talk network never becomes an issue.

In the IBM world, LANs share printers two ways. Either all the shared printers have to be hooked to a single *printer server box* (usually a PC itself), or any printer on the network can be shared. Obviously, the latter alternative is more attractive. But, the most popular LAN software programs, Novell and 3COM, force the shared printers to be centralized and attached to a printer server. Many add-on utilities allow printers to be shared anywhere in a Novell network. Each of these utilities works differently, but they share common problems.

First, complete support of LPT1 parallel printers is almost impossible. If you press Shift-PrtSc on a workstation in the LAN, the PC hangs because the data is not going to the LAN shared printer but out to a locally attached printer that does not exist. All the problems of multiple printers attached to one PC and spooled printer software exist in the PC LAN world. Each problem is solvable, but the solutions are not timeless and not universal. Writing them down in this book is useless. One hopes that the next generation of PC LAN software will solve these problems once and for all, allowing any printer on a LAN to be shared. Reportedly, Novell Netware 386 and 3COM's 3+Open software solve these printing problems.

Testing the Shared Printers

Testing a shared printer is important because many problems will not occur unless users ask to print many large documents at the same time. And, heavy traffic does not occur unless important documents are being printed. Thus, these problems occur only during the most tense, crisis-prone, emotional situations. Simulating these events first and ironing out the problems is to everyone's best interest. Three good tests exist.

- *Test #1*. Remove all paper from the printer. Then, ask all the PCs simultaneously to print 300-page documents. Wait until the PC reports a printing problem or until the PC thinks that it has printed all the 300-page documents. Then, walk over to the printer and put paper into it. Clear the printer errors if any and clear the PC errors if any. Then, start reading each page as soon as it is printed. You shouldn't have to let all 600 pages print before you find a page with lines, paragraphs, or even missing pages.

- *Test #2*. After the first test is finished, put each PC in a loop printing a page; then, pause different amounts of time between pages. Try several combinations. Examine printouts to see whether documents from two different PCs are placed on the same page.

- *Test #3*. Finally, put each PC in a loop, pausing different amounts of time between lines. Check each page to see whether one page sent was split into two pages by the sharing device.

If any of these tests fail, try reconfiguring the printer sharing device, redesigning the cable (see Chapter 13), living with the problem (avoid printing long documents), or purchasing a nonsharing mechanism.

Managing Fonts

The printing goal is to create electronic documents that look nice on any printer in the organization. If the document can be printed on only one printer, time is wasted during the conversion to a different printer. This printing goal causes uniformity among an organization's documents.

Another printing goal is for individuals to distinguish themselves. Often, this goal is accomplished by using fancy software and unusual fonts. This goal directly conflicts with the first. Corporations want to encourage creativity, yet create a system that is productive and independent of individual personalities and unique PC configurations. This idea makes the challenge of managing PCs a big one. Much time is spent making sure that PC configurations, printers, and software are uniform. PC managers today also need to start managing fonts.

Software has been developed to manage a font library on a network. The software checks fonts, makes sure that they are named and numbered in a consistent fashion, and keeps track of their usage by different object-mode printers. In other words, a PC on the LAN can become a font server to all the printers. All the copy-protection schemes, simultaneous users, and specific machine limitations can be observed and audited. But, this procedure can be automated only with shared printers on a LAN. All other methods are painful manual processes that never work.

If fonts are not managed, documents will not be portable, and much of your organization's time will be wasted copying font files and reformatting documents.

Connecting Multiple Printers to One PC

You can hook up multiple printers to a PC. Officially, PC DOS can support three parallel printers and four serial devices. A total of seven printers can be attached. The following are the DOS names of the seven possible printers:

   LPT1:
   LPT2:
   LPT3:
   COM1:
   COM2:
   COM3:
   COM4:

Multiple printers make sense if you have specific tasks that are unsuitable for certain types of printers. For example, one dot-matrix printer may be dedicated to mailing labels, another for desktop publishing, another for creating stencils, and so on.

The first problem encountered in using several printers is adding inside the PC the extra serial and parallel ports necessary. The additional ports can fight over slots, power, interrupts, and I/O blocks. This problem has been reduced considerably in the IBM PS/2 product line. In the older IBM world, two types of parallel ports exist. One is attached to a videoboard that goes by a variety of names: MDA, HGA, MGA (M = Monochrome, D = Display, H = Hercules, G = Graphics, A = Adapter). This parallel port is the stubborn type; it has to be LPT1. All other parallel ports in the IBM world will change names from LPT1 to LPT2 or LPT2 to LPT3 to make room for this parallel port.

HINT | For IBM PCs (also XTs and ATs), if the printer stops working after the videoboard is replaced, try printing something to LPT2. Maybe, the parallel port changed its name to make room for the port on the videoboard.

The second problem is that PC DOS fully supports only LPT1. Consider the following limitations:

❏ Although many functions can be redirected to LPT2 or COM2, certain functions like Shift-PrtSc and GRAPHICS.COM cannot.

❏ You can redirect output sent to LPT1 to any COM port, but this method disables any printer hooked to LPT1.

❏ Output sent to LPT1 cannot be redirected to LPT2 using the DOS MODE command.

To use multiple printers properly, PC software has to support what the PC DOS MODE command does not. Word processors often support LPT2, COM2, and so on, but most other PC software just assumes that the printer is located at LPT1, and no alternatives are allowed. Therefore, for all practical purposes, you can hook only one printer to a PC unless special software is found to use the second printer.

Chapter Summary

Unpack printers immediately. Install the ribbons and remove all the devices locking the head into position. Check the internal switches and put paper into the printer. Turn on the printer and learn how to use the front panel. Perform all the self-tests and practice resetting the printer in different ways. Hook the printer up to the PC and begin testing, first using the operating system and then using the application software. Then, hook up the printer to a sharing system and test the printer. If more than one printer is available to a PC, set up the system for selecting the various printers and test the system. Finally, establish a system for managing all the various fonts your company uses.

In the Next Chapter

The next chapter reviews how software tries to manage all the different printers. Also reviewed are the potential problems software can cause, the way software organizes itself to talk to all the different types of printers, and ways to manage and modify the printer files.

9

Configuring PC Applications

Instead of covering the whole world of software in this chapter, the following approach is used. An overview of printing features is given, then the principles of printer installation, and finally, step-by-step instructions for installing printers in different environments.

Because so many different application programs exist, computer software is split into the following categories:

- ❑ Macintosh software
- ❑ Windows software (for example, PageMaker and Excel)
- ❑ GEM software (for example, Ventura)
- ❑ Character-oriented software (for example, WordPerfect)
- ❑ Setup string software (for example, 1-2-3)
- ❑ Control-code software (for example, IBM's Personal Editor)
- ❑ Operating systems (for example, DOS)

Programs within each category are similar. Although PageMaker, Excel, PC Paintbrush, Adobe Illustrator, Microsoft Word, CorelDraw, Arts & Letters, and Micrografx Designer are different programs, they are practically identical in the areas of printer installation and printer and screen fonts because all of these programs were developed in the Windows environment. The same is true for Ventura, GEM Draw, and Artline, which share the GEM environment. Character-oriented software packages such as WordPerfect, Multimate, and WordStar support printers in a similar way. Programs like 1-2-3 and Reflex send commands to the printer using setup strings. From each category, a representative package was chosen, but screens and comments from related packages are scattered throughout each section. Macintosh printer support is briefly reviewed. Finally, operating system (DOS and OS/2) support of printers in the PC world is reviewed.

Printer and Font Installation Basics

This section describes the similar features of all software printer support. Although some programs do not support printers, desktop publishing software packages have to know printers intimately. The range of printer support is varied but is implemented uniformly with printer drivers, definition/configuration files, and font files.

Drivers

Programmers cannot write code for one printer because only the people with that printer would purchase the software. Programmers cannot possibly support all printers because they would never finish a program. To support the maximum number of printers with the minimum amount of effort, the software world has developed *printer drivers*.

The primary advantage of printer drivers is that programmers can write software to work with a generic *printer driver*. Programs only have to send data to the printer driver. The printer driver then translates that data into a language that the printer understands.

Typically, printer drivers are shipped on floppy disks along with the software manuals. The installation procedures usually copy these files into a subdirectory automatically. At some point, you are presented with a list of printers on the screen, and you will have to choose one of them. In the WordPerfect world, these files have names like WPRINT1.ALL. In the Windows world, the files are named HPPLC.DRV and PSCRIPT.DRV. In the GEM world, these files are named PD_HPLM5.SYS and PD_POSTS.SYS.

Programs like PageMaker translate the document you created into a language that the operating system or operating environment (Windows, Presentation Manager, QuickDraw) understands. The operating system then sends the information to a printer driver, which in turn translates this information into a language the printer understands.

Printer drivers translate printer data in two basic ways. One method enables users and consultants to modify the printer driver; the other method does not. One method forces users and consultants to purchase new printer driver versions. The other method enables users to upgrade the driver.

Windows and GEM come with specialized programs called printer drivers. These programs have version numbers that increase as their capabilities increase. You must pay for an upgraded version. WordPerfect, Multimate, and some other applications are shipped with separate programs that modify their database-like printer drivers.

WordPerfect-style printer driver editors have become too complicated. When printers had a few simple features, editing these printer driver databases was relatively simple. If a printer was not supported, you had to get out the printer manual and fill in the database's blanks.

Today, WordPerfect's printer driver editor program (PTR) has such a large menu tree that few people successfully edit the WordPerfect printer driver database files. WordPerfect does not even ship documentation on how to use the PTR program; instead, you have to purchase the PTR documentation separately. WordPerfect, Multimate, and WordStar have had to ship databases already filled out for hundreds of printers. Because IBM refused to fill out printer driver databases for non-IBM printers, the DisplayWrite 4 word processor has suffered because users have had to create DisplayWrite printer driver databases for non-IBM printers themselves.

Windows (Microsoft) and Digital Research (GEM) programmers have discovered that writing separate programs for each printer is long, tedious, and expensive. Each new printer requires a separate program. Modifying the printer driver of a similar printer is usually unsuccessful. Furthermore, these drivers frustrate users who have developed a talent for modifying the printer driver databases. Fortunately, both methods are maturing to the point where the creators of printer databases are filling the databases out, and the printer driver programmers are writing a sufficient number of programs to cover many printers.

Font Files

Most new laser printers can store some downloaded fonts, and many software packages have the capability to send these fonts to the printer. The fonts, therefore, have to be stored in a file on the computer's hard disk. Even if the font is permanently stored inside the printer, the software still has to know vital information like the character set, point size, and the width of each character. The dimensions of each character often are called printer font metric files. Windows assigns extension PFM; GEM Ventura assigns WID for width; Multimate assigns CWT for character-width tables.

In addition to the font metric files, there may be separate files containing instructions on how to create each symbol and also a file containing kerning information. GEM and Windows programs use the same file formats and extensions to support HP LaserJet printers: Soft Font Landscape (SFL) and Soft Font Portrait (SFP). These files contain just symbol creation instructions.

A similar file in the WordPerfect world has an extension of PRS as in PRinterS. A PRS file is a subset of an ALL file because fonts are built into the printer driver database. Because the printer driver database gets so large, however, the WordPerfect printer installation procedures create a PRS subset of the ALL file.

Programs such as Windows that place the screen in graphics mode also need screen fonts. These files reside on the hard disk waiting to be loaded into motherboard RAM. Like printer files, they have fairly consistent extensions. For example, in the GEM Ventura world, the screen fonts usually have an extension indicating which videoboard they are designed for—EGA or VGA. Windows screen fonts typically have the extension FON for font. Because WordPerfect operates the screen in character mode, the program has no need for screen fonts.

Almost all PC programs shipped with downloadable fonts are delivering fonts from the same company—BitStream. The fonts that come with GEM Draw, Ventura, WordPerfect, PageMaker, and PostScript clone printers come with BitStream fonts. 1-2-3, Paradox, and dBase, of course, don't need fonts.

A customized BitStream font installation utility is shipped with most application programs. Unfortunately, no universal BitStream font installation or management utilities exist for the PC world. What this means is that if you install both WordPerfect and Ventura, you will have two BitStream installation programs, two copies of the BitStream scalable fonts, and both Ventura and WordPerfect copies of each point size of each font created for character laser printers. This quickly fills up the hard disk with fonts. Occasionally, it is possible to configure programs like Ventura and WordPerfect so that they share fonts. But usually, this is time wasted because when your needs change, a version changes, or you want to add a new font, the tedious process must be repeated. If you value your time, solve the problem by purchasing a larger or additional hard disk.

The BitStream software not only makes character and screen font versions of its shipped scalable fonts but also updates the PFM, WIN.INI, CWT, CNF, and printer description tables associated with each package.

BitStream software is installed in the following subdirectory groups:

Subdirectory	*Contents*
Fontware	BitStream software
Fontware\TDF	Font configuration files
Fontware\DDF	Printer specific information
Fontware\CSD	Character set options
Fontware\BCO	Actual BitStream fontware fonts
Fonts	Printer/application specific font files

Change to the Fontware subdirectory, type *Bits 1*, and follow the menu instructions. When the Bitstream software is executed, it creates a file with a name for each downloadable character. The files are stored in the Fonts subdirectory. The appropriate printer drivers, printer definition tables, and configuration/installation files are updated, making the fonts available within the applications. Packages such as Ventura and WordPerfect have an additional step, explained in the following sections.

Definition/Configuration Files

Copying files to predefined subdirectories and then searching for files with certain extensions works as long as only one printer is supported. When two printers are supported, you need two print drivers, two sets of fonts to download, and perhaps two screen fonts. A third file, the configuration file, is necessary to do the following:

- Know which fonts go with each printer driver
- Match screen fonts to printer fonts
- Change the default screen font subdirectory
- Pass the first eight characters of the font file names to the application
- Tell the driver that more memory has been added to the printer and that more fonts need to be downloaded
- Save the preferred choices as defaults
- Know which fonts are to be downloaded by the program and which are assumed to be previously downloaded
- Know the sizes of paper in each bin and which PC port the printer is connected to

You sometimes have to create the definition/configuration files manually by using a word processor and saving the files in ASCII format. Other applications have built-in menus that edit these files. You typically can print and view files (that look like CONFIG.SYS files) by using the *DOS TYPE* command. However, obtaining a list of exactly what the possible commands are and what they do is next to impossible. In the GEM Ventura world, several of these files have the extension CNF (configuration). In the Windows PageMaker world, one file always has the name WIN.INI. Sometimes WIN.INI can be up to 180 lines long! In the WordPerfect world, this file is called WP{WP}.SET.

The major problem with all these font files, driver files, and configuration files is that old, unused versions start piling up and clog up the hard disks. The other trouble is that your documents do not print right unless all these files are in the right subdirectories. Transferring all the information to a floppy so that you can port the data to another machine becomes an adventure game with the object of finding all the files necessary to print the document. Search through each subdirectory on your hard disk. Learn which files are necessary to print a document, configure the printer, and download the necessary fonts.

Features of Printing

Discussing every application software package screen relating to printing is impossible. The objective of this chapter is to explore different and unusual printing features of application software. The objectives of this review are the following:

- Develop the resources to predict what problems you may encounter when printing
- Be better able to print right the first time
- Know the different printing features for testing purposes
- Assess software packages and learn which features to investigate when purchasing a new package. For example, does the package support multiple forms? binding?

Character Sets

Printers today are developing fonts that differ only in their character sets. Some character sets have small differences—a trademark symbol and the American dollar sign instead of a Japanese yen sign and a copyright symbol.

Ideally, the PC application should not force you to change fonts to access both symbols. PC software should enable you to use all symbols in one document, and the printer driver file should equate all fonts that are identical in all respects except for the character sets. Ideally, the application would be able to support printers and videoboards with very large character sets.

WordPerfect has one of the few printer drivers that provides these features. In fact, WordPerfect 5.1 (and later versions) comes with a graphics version of every symbol in Appendix D. If that symbol is not present in the current character set, WordPerfect places the printer in graphics mode temporarily and prints the symbol. Macintosh, GEM, and Windows systems solve this problem by limiting the number of symbols used in a document.

Document, Font, and Print Driver Relationships

The reasons for saving the document range from archiving to saving time by editing an old document rather than recreating the document. If the document is tied to a specific printer and group of fonts, chances are that such archived documents never see the same combination of printers, software, and fonts again. A tremendous amount of editing work may have to take place just to make the document print as nicely as it printed originally.

Macintosh Documents

Macintosh documents are attached to the screen fonts. Because the Macintosh screen fonts are almost universal, these fonts are a great standard for documents to base themselves on. If a printer does not have a matching font, the Macintosh prints that part of the document in graphics mode or downloads a version of the screen font to the printer temporarily.

The screen fonts, however, are usually not as good looking as the printer fonts. If the printer driver is changed, therefore, the fonts printed may have the *jaggies*—rough edges (the smoothing option works well in this case). The character spacing, however, is proper, and the page formatting should be identical.

Windows Documents

Windows documents attach themselves to the printer driver. Fonts, in turn, are attached to the printer, and screen fonts are attached to the printer's fonts.

If the printer driver is changed, drastic font changes usually occur on-screen because the old fonts associated with the preceding printer driver have to be translated to fonts associated with the new printer driver. The new printer fonts also may associate with the screen fonts in a different way, which makes printing drafts or proofs harder to do on a cheaper printer; many more page formatting errors occur. If the printer driver is changed in Windows, good-looking, but potentially different characters are substituted, and page formatting is messed up.

Ventura Documents

Ventura documents are attached to printer fonts. If the printer driver is changed, the document layout and screen fonts remain the same. If the document is printed on the new printer, the letter spacing is messed up because the new printer's fonts are being printed with the original font's spacing. The result is readable, even though some letters are too close together and others are too far apart.

Despite the letter spacing problems, the document page formatting is like the original. Page breaks and text-flow around graphics are identical. If the printer driver is changed, the characters look nice; page formatting is correct, but character spacing may be messed up.

WordPerfect Documents

To reduce a word processing document's dependence on the printer, WordPerfect 5.0 has developed a *generic* font-changing system that does not use normal font vocabulary. Instead, terms like Extra Large, Very Large, Normal, Small, Fine, Outline, Italics, Shadow, Redline, Underline, Double Underline, Bold, Strikeout, and so on are used. Rather than specifying individual point sizes over and over again in a document, these more generic attributes are changed.

If the entire document needs to made smaller, therefore, you should change the base font. Then, all the "Extra Larges" become smaller, and the "Fines" become smaller—provided that appropriately sized fonts are resident in the printer. For this reason, fonts that can change size, *scalable fonts,* are popular. If the exact size of "Extra Large" is specified, the global shrinking of the entire document would not be possible.

> HINT | Learn to use tags, attributes, and size change commands rather than specifying point size changes or specific font changes. These commands make global enlargement, reduction, and printer changes easier.

WordPerfect limits the fonts available during document editing to those currently present in the printer. If WordPerfect loads a document created with fonts no longer available, the program converts the document to an available font by matching generic font characteristics. Most of the programs already mentioned just match font point size and styles when converting between documents. WordPerfect tries to match an incredible number of font attributes. Although this practice usually produces very good matches, it makes installing new fonts manually almost impossible. WordPerfect keeps track of the following font characteristics:

- ❏ *Style*: casual, connected letters, decorative, formal, futuristic, old style, script, or calligraphic
- ❏ *Attributes*: italic or oblique, outline, shadow, or small caps
- ❏ *Serifs*: cupped, exaggerated, hairline, slab, slanted, transitional, triangular, or ball

- *Shape*: curved, bowed, nonconnecting enclosures, round, or square
- *Stress*: angular, exaggerated, or uniform
- *Weight*: extra light, light, normal, bold, or extra bold
- *Proportions*: capital height, descender height, lowercase x-height, lowercase t-height, or slant adjustment

WordPerfect tries to make sure that document formatting is consistent across all printers by encouraging the use of generic printer fonts. When a different printer is selected, its fonts are compared to the generic printer fonts and good matches result.

Line Spacing Adjustment

Sometimes, after changing a font, the spacing between the lines looks terrible when the document is printed. This section explores the reason behind this problem, the evolution of this problem, and why desktop publishing software and word processors have different solutions.

When the font of a paragraph is changed, PC software has two responsibilities. One task is to recompute the width of each line based on the new character width. Usually, the line is too long, and characters have to be moved to the next line, or the line is too short, and characters from the next line are moved up. As a result, paragraphs can change size.

The other task of PC software is to recompute how many lines are on a page based on the new font's point size. Traditionally, word processing packages have not allowed users to change the line spacing in tiny increments. Today, desktop publishing packages enable you to change the distance between lines. The fine adjustment of line spacing is called *leading*, because typesetters used to place small strips of lead between rows of type, increasing line spacing.

Desktop publishing software adjusts line spacing, or leading, when a font is changed and tries to show the resulting changes of page formatting on-screen. The entire graphics screen has to be redrawn—over 128K worth of screen display memory has to be recomputed and redrawn, which takes a lot of time, but desktop publishing packages are not designed to be word processors.

Just because WordPerfect adjusts line spacing does not change WordPerfect from a word processor to a desktop publishing package. WordPerfect is still quick at redrawing the screen because the screen is in character mode. Only 4K worth of data, therefore, needs to be recomputed and sent to the video-board. WordPerfect does not attempt to change the line spacing on-screen;

instead, the program recomputes where the lines are on the page. The coordinates of each character's location are displayed in the bottom right corner of a WordPerfect screen.

Microsoft Word, on the other hand, runs the screen in graphics mode like a desktop publishing software package. Microsoft Word sends 128K of data to the screen and forces you to wait while the screen is redrawn. Yet, Microsoft Word does not change the line spacing—the worst of both worlds.

Features of Printing Utilities

In the PC DOS world, printer emulation modes, printer setup, and configuration of a printer should not require software to implement them. If a printer comes with such software, the printer should not be purchased because of one major problem: the applications can bypass DOS and talk directly to the printer. These applications are called *ill-behaved* because they do not follow the chain of command (see figure 9.1). When an ill-behaved application bypasses DOS, the application also bypasses the software that comes with these printers. Ill-behaved applications render printer software useless.

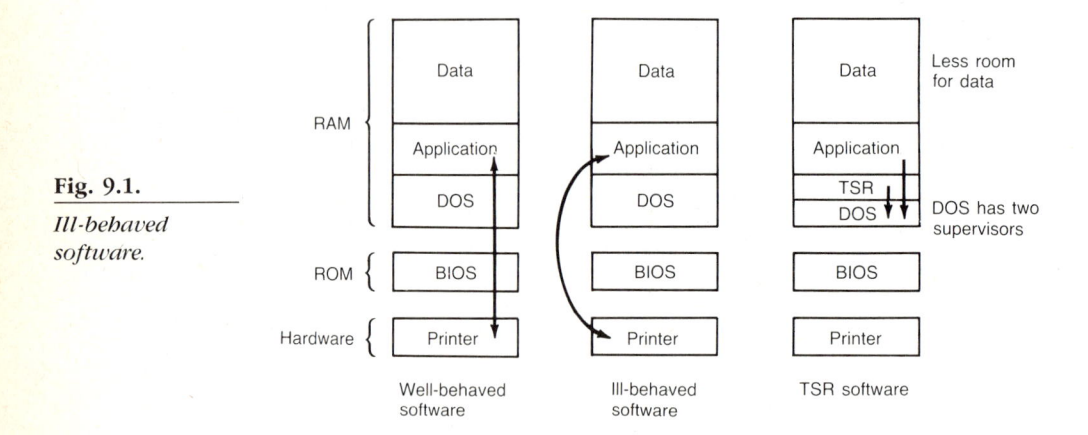

Fig. 9.1.

Ill-behaved software.

Additional printer software also may confuse PC applications, making them run out of memory. Companies throughout the U.S., therefore, are making corporate-level decisions to ban the type of PC software that climbs into memory and never leaves, resulting in intermittent problems. This type of software is called *memory resident software* or *terminate-and-stay-resident* (TSR) software. If a printer needs this software to work, don't purchase the printer.

A harmless type of printer software operates as an application program, turning printing into a two-step process. First, the normal PC DOS application is told to print to a file rather than to the printer. Second, the printer software formats this file for the printer. This type of software, although complex and slow, is better than memory-resident printer software.

> HINT | If application software cannot make the printer do what you want, forget it. Nothing can be added to the operating system that will work consistently. In a static, unchanging world, printer utilities make sense; they will work indefinitely. But, neither PCs or applications are static, and quick fixes eventually cause support and management hassles.

Often, magazines advertise public-domain printer software. Almost always, this software is TSR. Besides the potential TSR problems, you have a fundamental conceptual problem. Suppose that you press Ctrl-Esc to cause a laser printer menu window to pop up in the middle of a PC application. Suppose that the printer menu contains a list of fonts supported by the printer. You pick a font, return to the PC application, and try to print. The printout does not contain the font chosen earlier because the application did not expect other programs to be helping. Because good PC software tries to *clean the slate* before printing, these programs reset the printer, wiping out the benefits of the printer TSR. Adding printer-management software to PC DOS is like adding Don Quixote to a platoon.

Multiple Form Support

Most PC software today needs to know the paper size. Most PC software can instruct printers to print on the different sizes of paper. Even so, the software expects you to place a properly sized sheet of paper in the printer. In a local area network, this procedure can require walking to the printer, removing the letter size tray of paper, inserting the legal size tray, and then walking back to your PC—even if the printer has two trays of paper!

Reasons exist for this glaring deficiency. Early cut-sheet feeders were not reliable. Because they needed a babysitter to operate, you may as well have the babysitter feed paper into them. Multiple bin cut-sheet feeders cost thousands of dollars and had their own microprocessors and programming language. To this day, some PC software is shipped with separate cut-sheet printer driver files.

When paper trays were introduced with the laser printer, an effort was made to point out that the laser printers were an extension of the copy machine technology. To PC software, paper trays were no different than tractor fold paper. Paper trays were an instant success. Copy machine paper was even cheaper than fanfold paper. Just as copy machines have developed multiple bin paper trays and collating equipment to catch the paper, so have laser printers.

Currently, the only popular software package that supports multiple paper tray printers is WordPerfect, starting with Version 5.0. Although this feature can save a lot of time, it increases the complexity of printing and causes additional problems. The rest of this section explores the complexity and problems of supporting multiple paper trays using WordPerfect.

WordPerfect uses the word *form* to describe various paper sizes. Each page of a WordPerfect document has a form associated with it. When asked to print, WordPerfect operates a little differently than most PC software. Most PC software assumes that the proper-sized form is present in the printer. If the wrong form is inserted, the PC software never knows and prints anyway.

WordPerfect, on the other hand, tries to find the location of the form before printing. If WordPerfect cannot find the proper-sized form, the program refuses to print the document. Suppose that you choose the mailing label form, type the names and addresses, insert the mailing labels into the printer, and ask WordPerfect to print. WordPerfect refuses when normal software prints. Perhaps, in the future, WordPerfect will ask the printer to print on mailing labels and only refuse to print if the printer complains. Today, printers cannot complain, even though they are keeping track of different forms to reduce paper-jamming problems. Today, WordPerfect has to be told by you exactly which paper tray or tractor in the printer contains the mailing labels (see fig. 9.2).

> **TROUBLE-SHOOTING TIP** If nothing is printing, check whether the PC software can select different paper trays in the printer. Perhaps the PC software does not think that the proper-sized paper is present in the printer. Also, check the printer indicator lights or front panel for error messages. Certain printers do not print anything unless the paper size is requested by the PC software.

> **HINT** When you want to use a different form type, you must define the form, choose the form, and tell the program the location of the form. If your word processor refuses to print, make sure that you have met these requirements.

```
Select Printer: Forms
                                   Orient Init          Offset
Form type            Size          P L    Pres Location Top   Side

Bond                 8.5i x 11i    Y N    Y    Bin 2    0i    0i
Cardstock            8.5i x 11i    Y N    Y    Bin 1    0i    0i
Envelope             4i x 9.5i     N Y    N    Manual   1.5i  4.5i
Labels               8.5i x 11i    Y N    Y    Bin 3    0i    0i
Letterhead           8.5i x 11i    Y N    Y    Bin 4    0i    0i
Standard             8.5i x 11i    Y Y    Y    Contin   0i    0i
Transparency         8.5i x 11i    Y N    Y    Bin 5    0i    0i
[ALL OTHERS]         Width ≤ 8.5i         N    Manual   0i    0i
```

Fig. 9.2.

WordPerfect Multiple Forms Support file.

```
If the requested form is not available, then printing stops and WordPerfect
waits for a form to be inserted in the ALL OTHERS location.  If the requested
form is larger than the ALL OTHERS form, the width is set to the maximum width.

1 Add; 2 Delete; 3 Edit: 3
```

Binding

Most PC software today supports printing a document that is eventually going to be mass copied onto double-sided paper and bound. To keep text from being hidden, the margins on the edges of the paper bound together have to be larger. Left-hand pages need an extra wide right margin, and right-hand pages need an extra wide left margin. This option is called binding. If activated inadvertently, the margins on a two-page document are different.

> **TROUBLE-SHOOTING TIP** — If the printer is printing different left margins on different sheets of paper, check to see whether binding, double-sided printing, or left/right page printing is turned on.

Preview

Printing drafts over and over again is a terrible waste of resources and time. To reduce the amount of draft printing, most programs have a preview feature. This feature displays a miniature version of the page on-screen. While the letters are too small to read, many page layout features are visible. By looking at the preview pages, you can detect and correct page layout problems before printing a document. Here is a list of typical layout features you can preview:

Headline placement
Page location
Binding appropriate
Paragraph spacing
Balance
Emphasis
Fonts
Page breaks appropriate
Widows (line alone at bottom of page)
Orphans (line alone at top of page)

PageMaker includes a feature that enables you to print the preview. Depending on the page size, around 12 previews can be printed on one page. Because most preview systems can preview only one or two pages on-screen in sufficient detail, the screen has to be redrawn over and over again to preview an entire document. More software should use this feature.

Printing to a File

Almost all PC software has methods of printing to a file rather than printing to the printer. Originally, printing to a file was necessary to provide a method of exchanging data between dissimilar programs. All programs could understand keystrokes, and many programs could understand files full of keystrokes. These keystroke files are typically called DOS, ASCII, or TEXT files. They usually have an extension TXT.

Text files have traditionally had lines of 80 characters or less. They should be printable using any of the following DOS methods. As PC software and printers have become more sophisticated, more than 80 characters per line are being printed. This has created a problem when PC programs print to a file. Are documents with more than 80 characters on a line to be reformatted before printing to a file? Other issues also can cause file-printing problems. For example, are tabs and centering commands supposed to be translated into spaces or stripped? Are columns supposed to be destroyed or left in place? For these reasons, printing to a file is not a good way for exchanging documents between PC applications. Instead, explore the export and import file features of the PC application software.

More often today, printing to a file is done to capture the actual bits that flow to the printer—the mixture of control codes and text. Reasons for wanting files of raw printer codes are as follows:

- Capturing documents to be sent to a typesetter
- Isolating repeatable printing problems
- Capturing screens for documentation purposes
- Capturing fonts stored in encrypted formats
- Capturing clip art stored in an unusual format
- Speeding up printer setup
- Speeding up printing of the same document over and over
- Learning printer programming
- Transferring the features of one page to another
- Showing the raw code for encapsulated PostScript

Typically, file export or import screens create DOS text files. Raw printer code files are created in printer configuration screens where parallel and serial port names can be changed to file names. If printing to a file is not supported directly by the PC application program, you can use utilities like Hijaak and LPT2DSK in conjunction with PC applications.

Other reasons for printing to a file are listed in the following paragraphs. Some have arisen from the expanding capabilities of applications, and some are just sophisticated techniques.

Typesetters and PostScript. Typesetters that cannot understand native Page-Maker or Ventura files usually can print PostScript files. Sending the output intended for a PostScript printer to a file does the trick.

Assessing blame: the printer or the software? If a printer is doing the exact same funny thing, like indenting the first line of a paragraph, print to a file. Look at the mixture of text and printer instructions using your favorite editor or word processor. Find the section where the printer is sending the indented line. See whether extra spaces appear or unusual printer commands are apparent. Figure out whether the PC software is commanding the printer to do the funny thing or whether the printer is acting up on its own.

Documenting programs. Character-oriented screens can be captured using the LPT2DSK program by just using Shift-PrtSc within a software package. Instead of sending the screen to the printer, LPT2DSK sends the screen to a file.

Hunting for fonts. Some programs store their fonts in encrypted formats and supply software that can decode the encrypted files. This practice limits the use of those font files to that particular software program. But, you own them. No law says that you cannot attach that font information and the fonts with another program. Configure the program (the one that encrypted the fonts) for an HP LaserJet printer, even if you don't have a LaserJet. Use a program like LPT2DSK or Hijaak to capture the fonts as the program tries to download the fonts to a LaserJet (that may not even exist). Most of your other programs can import HP LaserJet font files.

Hunting for clip art. Some graphics programs contain large libraries of clip art that are stored in a unique format. The unique format forces you to purchase additional clip art from only them. But, you want to transfer this clip art into a format other drawing or graphics programs can understand. Configure the original graphics program for a PostScript printer or HP plotter, even if you don't have one. Install LPT2DSK or Hijaak and follow the normal steps of printing with the graphics program. The output is routed to a file. Most other drawing programs can import PostScript or HP plotter files.

Speeding up printers. Some printers, especially PostScript clone printers, are shipped with fonts and programs that need to be downloaded every time the computer and printer are turned on. Even though the files of fonts and programs are not encrypted, they are compressed to conserve space. If you have enough room, these files can be captured and sent to one large file. This file can be copied much more quickly to the printer using a regular DOS COPY command (see DOS printing). This command may not work if the printer cannot process data as fast as the DOS command sends the data.

Along the same lines, suppose that you have created a letterhead you want to print occasionally. But, loading the graphics program, retrieving the letter file, printing, and exiting takes too long. Print to a file and then use the DOS COPY command to print the file (see DOS printing).

Programming printers. If you want to brave the world of printer programming, the easiest place to start is by analyzing the programs sent to your printer. Send the printer programs to a disk, get out the printer manual, and start learning printer programming. PostScript programming experience is very valuable to some companies. By programming in PostScript, you can create company logos that are impossible to create with any drawing or graphics program. In fact, PostScript programmers are capable of producing art inexpensively that is prohibitively expensive to create through traditional means.

Transferring program features. If you don't want to learn printer programming but want to duplicate the features of one program in another, try printing to a file with the first and loading the printer file into the second. In the following example the first program is WordPerfect, and the second is IBM's Personal Editor, but almost any two programs will do. Suppose that WordPerfect can fine print using a font. You want IBM's Personal Editor to be able to print using the same font, but an hour of reading the HP LaserJet manual has gotten you nowhere. Get into WordPerfect and create a document that prints a short phrase in the desired font. Surround the phrase with normal text. Print the document to a file. Import the print file into IBM's Personal Editor. Search for the normal text. The escape codes between the normal text and the phrase should be the only ones necessary to switch to that font from within IBM's Personal Editor.

Application Error Messages

PC application programs can experience three kinds of error messages: installation-related, application-specific, and DOS-related. Discovering the category of the error message is the first step in isolating the problem. A fascinating use of Norton Utilities, PC Tools, or Mace Utilities is to search for error messages throughout the files associated with a particular program. Some programs like Ventura have a special file just for printer messages (PRTRERR.STR).

Installation error messages are specific to the application and usually are obvious. They sometimes are phrased in a positive form such as `Enter a printer name in printer option`, which means the program cannot find a printer definition table or printer driver. Installation error messages also can be negative, such as `Invalid Font`, which means a font file cannot be located. To cure these types of error messages, reinstall the package. A quicker way may exist, but you spend more time figuring out what the quick way is than you do reinstalling the application.

Application-specific error messages are related to procedural or internal problems. Procedural problems result in error messages such as `Does not Print`. This message is caused in some word processors by instructions to print pages of a document that does not exist. `Incorrect formatting` could mean that the document needs to be reformatted for the currently selected printer. Internal problems result in error messages like `Out of Memory` because the PC cannot find enough room to compute all the details necessary to print the document. The first type of application error messages are solved by following the correct procedures. The second type are solved by reconfiguring the system so that more memory is available or by making the document less complex.

DOS also can generate error messages. Because application programs cover up DOS when they are running, they receive DOS's error messages and pass them on to the user. Sometimes, application programs translate the DOS error message; other times they just relay the message. Because DOS treats a printer like a file the operating system is writing to, any potential writing error message could be printer-related.

DOS produces four common error messages. The only error message that occurs for printers and for no other reason is `No Paper`. This error message usually has nothing to do with running out of paper. Even an early IBM PC, running the first IBM DOS hooked up by IBM cable to an IBM dot-matrix printer (really an Epson) would say `Out of paper` when the problem had nothing to do with being out of paper. Usually, the problem was caused by the printer being off-line or turned off or by the paper being jammed. The error message should be "Printer Problem." In fact, most application programs translate this error message into something like "Printer needs attention" or "Printer out of paper."

The other two most common DOS error messages are related to DOS treating the printer like a floppy disk drive and the data being sent to the printer like a file. `Error Writing to Device` means that the printer is alive enough to tell DOS that it is having problems. Check to see whether the printer is on-line.

`Abort, Retry, Ignore, Fail` means that an attempt was made to print the document, but nothing happened. Although this error message is most often associated with a missing floppy disk, it could mean that the printer is missing. If the printer is turned on and is on-line, press Retry. Watch the printer lights and the PC application. Search for any clues that the PC is talking and the printer is listening. Turn off everything and try again. Check to see whether the AUTOEXEC.BAT and CONFIG.SYS file are still the same. Self-test the printer. Start swapping. Go to the troubleshooting chapters at the end of this book.

If the printer is off, turn the printer on and try to resume printing. Carefully inspect the first page to see whether the first lines contain the expected text. Sometimes, characters are lost during the process of turning the printer back on. The first page may have to be printed over again.

If the printer is unplugged and serially connected, connecting the PC and printer while the power is on should not harm any hardware. Again, perhaps some characters on the first page are lost. But, if the printer is a parallel printer, always turn off everything before connecting the printer data cable again. Some parallel printers are not designed to handle the stress of connection while power is on.

Macintosh Printing

The Macintosh initially became popular because of its windows, icons, and mouse. The printer interface was largely overlooked. But the Macintosh was not important until January of 1985—the month of the LaserWriter, PostScript, and PageMaker. Since then, the Macintosh has been *one of the prime movers* in the incredible expansion of desktop publishing. While equally powerful programs are available in the PC world and equally powerful PostScript printers are available in the PC world, many features of the Macintosh-LaserWriter relationship are not available (see Chapter 11).

This section examines the features of the Macintosh-LaserWriter connection. The goal here is to review the installation and operation of printers in the Macintosh world. Then, as Windows, Gem, and WordPerfect are reviewed, you can compare these applications with the Macintosh environment.

Installing Printer Drivers

Macintosh printer drivers are easy to install. Each printer sold for a Macintosh comes with a 3 1/2-inch floppy disk containing its Macintosh driver. You insert the disk into the drive, and the printer icon is moved into the Macintosh system folder. In a manner similar to the PC programs, you have to configure the driver. The driver needs to know which port the LaserWriter is hooked up to, whether Local Talk, serial, or SCSI. If more than two printers are attached, you can select one as the default. Nothing could be more simple.

Installing New Screen Fonts

Font means screen font in the Macintosh world. Install a screen font, and the document prints on a LaserWriter or ImageWriter. ImageWriters print in graphics mode and don't need fonts. The ImageWriter turns the best-looking screen font into an object font, so that even screen fonts look nice. The trouble is that printing is slowed down quite a bit. The LaserWriter may have a button called Faster Bit Mapped Printing. Pressing this button causes the Mac to preprocess bit-mapped images before they are sent to the LaserWriter and reduces the load on the LaserWriter, but increases the load on the Mac.

Fonts are added into the system folder of the Macintosh using the Font/DA Mover. After being placed in the system folder, the fonts are available to all other Macintosh applications. These fonts are picked from a list on the distribution font disk. Bit-mapped fonts for use with the graphics screen are selected with System 6 software. System 7 software modifies the Font/DA so that object fonts and bit-mapped screen fonts can be selected. Fonts have to be sent to the printer during startup if they reside on the Mac's hard disk. Printers come with software that sends the fonts to the printer.

Mac graphics fonts are instantly available to all Mac programs. Font disks contain a variety of bit-mapped screen fonts in different sizes. If all the sizes are chosen, the screen has a better chance of matching the printout. Fonts definitely look better on-screen. Unfortunately, the system grows larger;

more RAM is consumed; more hard disk space fills up, and booting takes longer.

Choosing fewer bit-mapped fonts does not limit the point sizes available because the Mac manipulates the closest point sizes to fit. Management of the Mac screen fonts is done with the Font Desk Accessory.

Luckily, most documents need only a few fonts in a couple of sizes. Utilities like SuitCase are added to a Macintosh to help shuffle groups of fonts in and out of memory. Nothing comparable exists in the PC world. WordPerfect's printer definition table has the capability to group fonts. From within WordPerfect, you can manage the groups, but this complex process is applicable only to WordPerfect. A utility like SuitCase is instantly available to all Mac programs.

Adding Printer Fonts

Printer fonts are an afterthought in the Macintosh world. Most users have Imagewriters that just print screen fonts in graphics mode. The font information found in a Macintosh, therefore, is related to screen fonts, not printer fonts. The exact opposite is true in the PC world. PC fonts are almost always printer fonts. Screen fonts are added to better approximate printer fonts. Printer fonts are added in the Macintosh world to better approximate screen fonts. In both worlds, the best font vendors supply identical screen and printer fonts.

> HINT | If a printer is running out of memory for fonts, confirm the problem by changing the entire document to a font in the printer's ROM, turning everything off, and printing. If you get output, the problem is probably too many fonts in the object printer.

Fonts can be automatically downloaded to the LaserWriter immediately after powering on the Mac, starting with System 6, using the equivalent of a PC DOS batch file. Utilities for downloading at any time come with the LaserWriter and other PostScript printers. The object fonts to be downloaded are called *laser fonts* in the Macintosh world. Screen fonts are just called *fonts*.

> HINT | For object or laser fonts to be sent to the printer, the fonts have to be located in the system folder or the startup disk's window. If the object fonts are somewhere else, the Mac cannot find them.

If a LaserWriter is told to print using a font that the printer does not have, the LaserWriter informs QuickCode. QuickCode then searches the system folder or startup disk's window for laser (object) fonts. If none are found, QuickCode assembles the best looking bit-mapped font possible from the screen fonts it has and sends the font to the LaserWriter—even though the laser font may exist somewhere on the Mac hard disk. When finished printing, the LaserWriter immediately forgets the bit-mapped font. Each time the document is reprinted, the font has to be sent again, and the font will not look as good as a scalable version of the font.

Using the Printer Dialog Box

When you choose print in a Mac application, a printer dialog box pops up (see fig. 9.3). This box is not always the same. Some printer dialog boxes have more features than others. This section explores some of the more exotic features of printer dialog boxes.

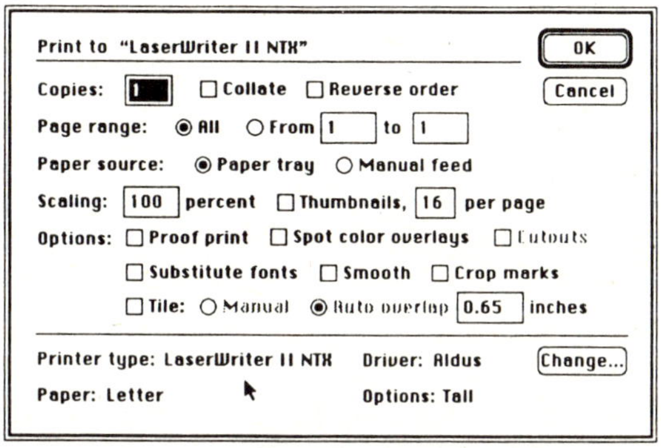

Fig. 9.3.

A Macintosh Print dialog box for PageMaker.

A Macintosh applications program may have a Print dialog box containing a Best Print Quality button. When this button is chosen, a screen font is reduced 50 percent before being sent to the ImageWriter. This reduction produces a higher quality printout but works only if a screen font twice as large as the one requested is installed.

In the Page Setup dialog box of a Mac application printing on a LaserWriter printer is a button called Precision Bitmap Alignment. Using this button adjusts the screen resolution to be a multiple of the printer resolution so that what is seen is closer to what is printed. Precision Bitmap Alignment reduces the entire image on-screen 96 percent before printing, because the screen pixels are 72 dots per inch (a laser printer is 300 dots per inch). 288 divided by 72 equals 4 times, but 72 does not go into 300 evenly. By using only 96 percent of the printable area of a 300-dots-per-inch page, (300×.96=288) an exact match of the screen is possible.

Any screen fonts besides the original four in a Mac are converted to object fonts by a PostScript printer. The original four are controlled by the Font Substitution button in the Page Setup dialog box. Unfortunately, the PostScript printer forgets these fonts after printing the document. The conversion, therefore, has to happen every time the document is printed.

If the character spacing looks terrible on a PostScript printer hooked to a Macintosh, check to see whether the Font Substitution button is on in the Page Setup dialog box. If on, the PostScript printer is converting the original screen fonts that come with a Mac to object printer fonts. Try turning off the Font Substitution.

Comparing System 7 to Adobe TypeManager

At the time this book is being written, the latest release of the Macintosh operating system is System 6. Details about System 7 capabilities are leaking out slowly through the media. Competing with System 7 is Adobe TypeManager, which expands System 6 capabilities to include scalable screen fonts. A battle is brewing over whether the public purchases Adobe TypeManager now or waits for the scalable screen font feature of System 7. Apple has a significant stake in this battle. If Adobe's TypeManager becomes more popular than System 7, Macintosh operating system development could come to a dead halt. This section is about the battle brewing.

In Chapter 4, a description of the font wars pointed out that Apple has sold off all their stock in Adobe and swapped their object font software called Royal for Microsoft's PostScript clone software, because Apple does not want to put any more money in Adobe's pocket. Adobe's TypeManager is threatening Apple's control over the Mac's operating system software. Another threat is a new computer called the NEXT. And NEXT not only has a PostScript printer but also a PostScript display.

The battle between System 7 and TypeManager has two dimensions. The first is the object screen font technology. Adobe has all the wisdom gained from its development of printer object fonts to apply to screen font technologies. Screen object fonts are more difficult than printer object fonts because the on-screen resolution is coarse compared to that of printers. But, Adobe is the acknowledged winner of the very small point-size font quality in the printer world where the resolution is the most coarse.

Apple's Royal technology is just vaporware so far. While the technical details have been released to font creators, no specific products have been released because System 7 has not been released. When released, how the quality stacks up against Adobe's TypeManager remains to be seen. Right now, Adobe's TypeManager has to be given the winning edge. TypeManager is the product of an experienced company; TypeManager is the first product on the market, and it works. Apple is coming to the market late with an unproven technology.

But, the problem is that the playing field is not even. Apple and MicroSoft, two of the biggest computer companies in the country, have ganged up on Adobe. Furthermore, Apple Macintosh users are not used to the freedom of an open technology. Mac users have not learned to purchase non-Apple products because Apple keeps such a tight grip on the market. The trouble is that Apple let an Adobe product—the LaserWriter—slip into the Apple world. Adobe is already a respected, visible presence. Adobe already ships a large selection of ITC fonts.

Apple has said that their font format is open, implying that font competition will come from a number of different font vendors. Does this mean that other vendors' fonts (like Adobe's) will be supported? More likely, Apple plans on being an umpire (defining Royal fonts as the standard) and also a player (selling Royal fonts).

Apple says Adobe's TypeManager is not open. Adobe announced the Type-Manager is being upgraded to translate Apple's Royal fonts to Adobe format when they are finally released. Adobe's fonts come in three formats. One format is for the high-resolution world of typesetters, another for the medium resolution of 300 dpi laser printers, and finally another for the low resolution of very small fonts and screen fonts typically referred to as "hinted" fonts. The font format for high resolution typesetters is not important in the computer world. The medium-resolution 300-dpi object font format is so well known that shareware and public domain laser fonts are available. The major font vendors all support this font format, so that 300-dpi object font format has become the only real standard. Does this sound like a font technology that is not open?

Adobe has been reluctant to publish the details of the third type of font for screens and very small point sizes—the hinted fonts. Adobe has a real advantage when printing small fonts and screen fonts. But, even these fonts are on the verge of being cloned. BitStream claims to have figured out Adobe's hinted font format. Naturally, Adobe is going to hang onto its advantage as long as possible, but even the hinted technology is going to be cloned. How can this environment be described as not open?

The second dimension of the battle between Adobe's TypeManager and System 7 has nothing to do with fonts. This battle is being waged at the programming level, where conceptual ideals and practical realities have a big role. Apple claims that System 7 software makes objects transparent when placed on top of each other. Adobe's TypeManager combines two objects so that the top object totally blocks features of the object underneath. Apple claims that the default mode of TypeManager's overlapping, nontransparent view of objects is a defect. From a programmer's perspective, Typemanager's approach may be harder, but much more is possible.

Besides the preceding skirmish, TypeManager is winning other battles. System 7 does not have the following TypeManager capabilities:

- To produce complicated smooth curves. Individual Mac applications may have this feature, but it is not available to all applications unless you purchase Adobe TypeManager.
- To rotate an object and make maximum use of resolution, gray scale, and color capabilities of a printer.

In summary, Adobe and NEXT have the edge now, but Apple and Microsoft are bigger companies in a war for the typesetting standard—a war that isn't over. For the companies, millions of dollars are at stake. For you and me, an excellent standard (Adobe's) may be replaced by an uncertain one. The details of the battles can be read in magazines like *InfoWorld* and *PC Magazine*.

PageMaker (Windows)

Windows is a Macintosh-like environment that is becoming popular in the DOS world. Many of the most popular applications are written in the Windows environment. Examples include Excel, PC Paintbrush, Adobe Illustrator, Microsoft Word, CorelDraw, Arts & Letters, and Micrografx Designer. Other graphics-, menu-, and mouse-driven application environments exist for PCs, but Windows is dominant. This section describes the printer and font installation methods using PageMaker as an example.

Installing Printer Drivers

Windows printer drivers are files with extensions DRV. These printer driver files are the program variety, not the database variety, meaning that each printer is treated as a unique case. As a result, Windows printer drivers are inconsistent.

The three different printer driver dialog boxes reviewed in the following sections may be completely different in your Windows application. Because these drivers are shipped with PageMaker, they are among the most sophisticated and should apply to many features that your drivers have.

Copying Printer Drivers to Hard Disk

Windows printer drivers are distributed on disks. You can install the driver files into the Windows environment three different ways. The hardest way is to copy the files by hand into the appropriate windows directory. Then, you have to modify a file named WIN.INI using some kind of DOS editor or word processor. WIN.INI keeps track of where all the fonts and printer drivers are located. WIN.INI has its own special syntax and commands that are similar to a DOS CONFIG.SYS file.

Other methods of installing printer drivers modify the WIN.INI file automatically. These include using the SETUP program included with the run-time version of Windows and installing the printer drivers from within PageMaker. Installing printers using the SETUP program is easy—just follow the instructions on the screen. The painful part is that the entire run-time Windows installation procedure has to be repeated for adding each additional printer.

PageMaker, like many other Windows applications, enables you to add printer drivers easily at any time. To install a new printer, find the rectangle box in the upper left corner of the PageMaker startup screen (see fig. 9.4). This box is an entry point into the Microsoft Windows world. The other menus underneath the horizontal names like FILES are often similar across Windows applications. Point to and click on the rectangle. In the box that appears, select `Control panel` to display the Control menu (see fig. 9.5).

Fig. 9.4.

The PageMaker title page.

Installation and Setup menus are on the Windows Control Panel Screen (see fig. 9.6). These two menus are primarily concerned with printer and font installation and setup. The Installation menu has an option called Add New Printer (see fig. 9.7). Select this option to display a screen asking which drive letter to use in search of new *.DRV files. After entering a drive letter, a list of printers pops up (see fig. 9.8).

388 Part II: Printer Setup and Management

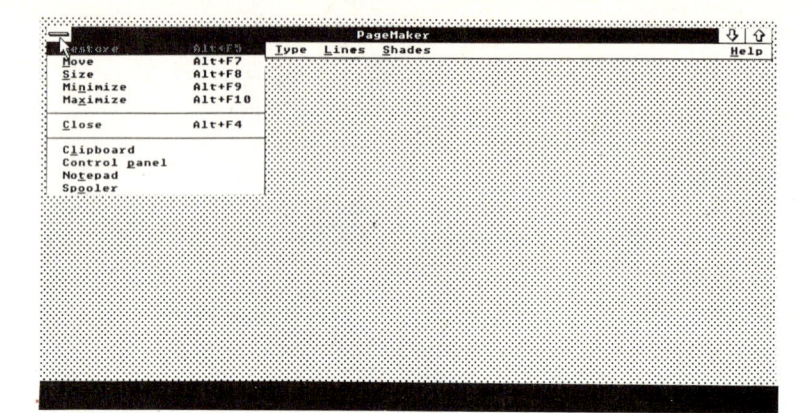

Fig. 9.5.
Rectangle menu.

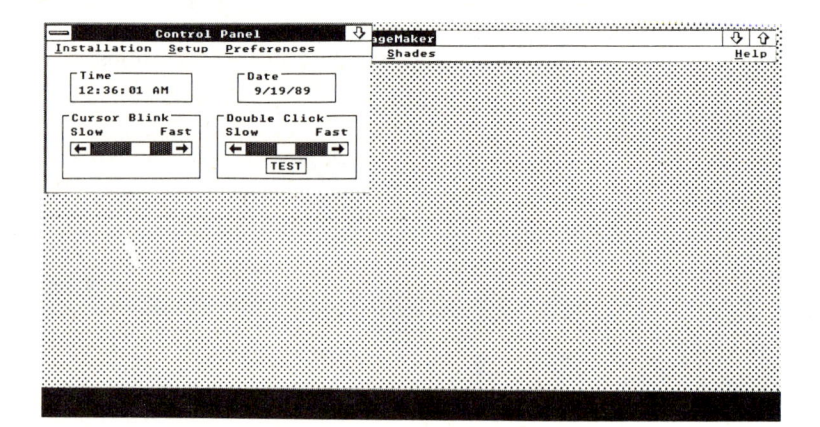

Fig. 9.6.
Control Panel menu.

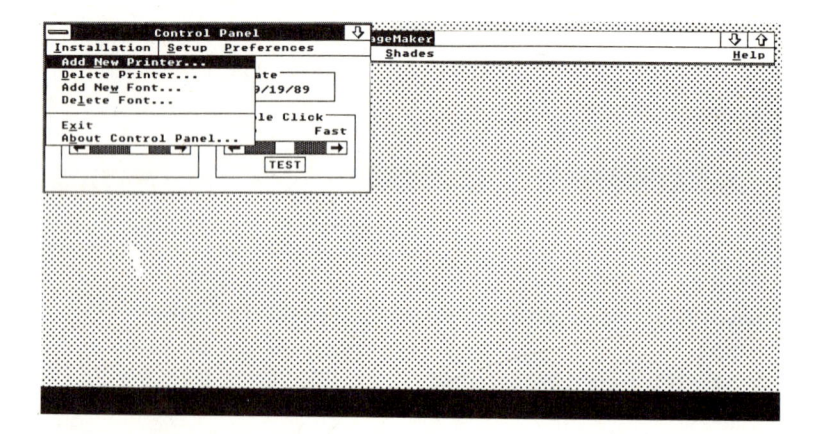

Fig. 9.7.
Installation menu.

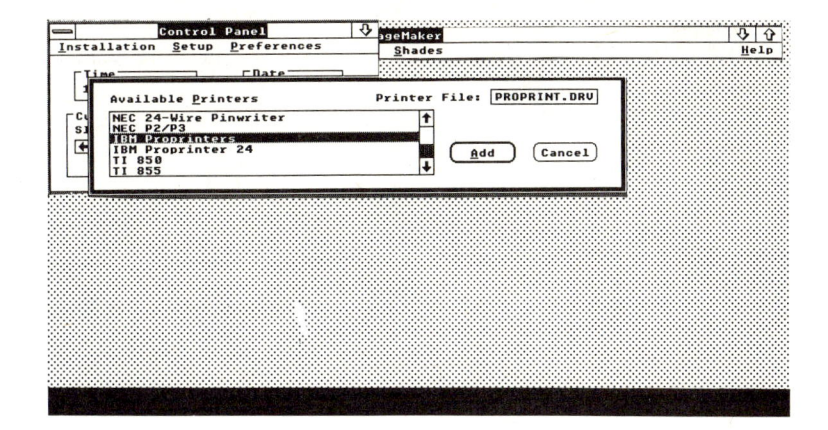

Fig. 9.8.

Add New Printer menu.

Establishing the Printer Port

The Setup menu of the Control Panel bar has three options that have to be done in sequence: Connections, Printer, and Communications (see fig. 9.9). The Connections option lists all the printers and all the ports in two columns (see fig. 9.10). Windows enables two printers to be attached to the same port using an AB switch box. To establish the port, click the printer name, a port name, and the OK button.

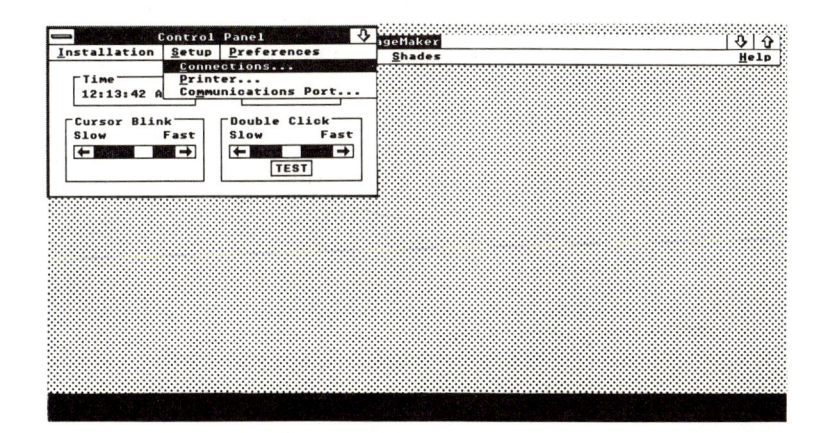

Fig. 9.9.

Setup menu.

Someday, devices will be smart enough that Windows can go out to each port and ask them their names and configure itself accordingly. If devices are turned on after Windows is booted, these devices will be able to notify Windows of who they are. In other words, self-configuration will be possible in the future. An international standards committee is working toward this goal.

Part II: Printer Setup and Management

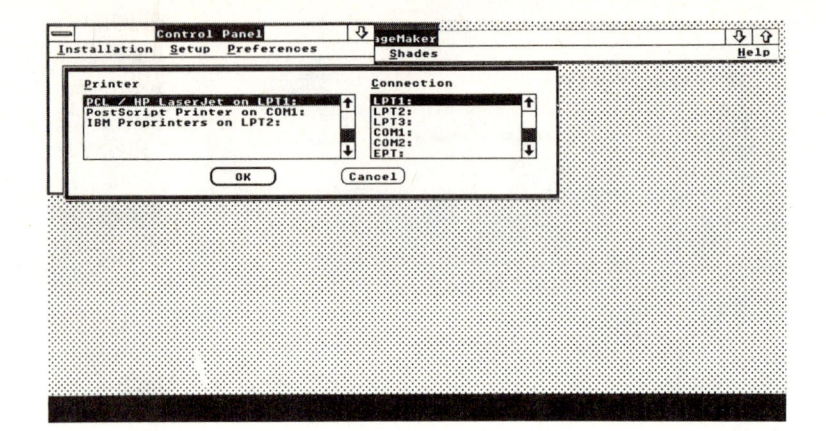

Fig. 9.10.

Connections menu.

Choosing the Default Printer

Windows is an environment that many different programs can share. Some programs may care very much which printer is chosen and which font is used when printing. Other programs may not care too much. These programs could send documents to Windows without explicitly defining which printer or which font to use. In these cases, Windows is responsible for which printer and font are chosen.

Some Windows programs have their own printer defaults. The best programs attach printer information to documents. For example, PageMaker has its own default printer information that the program tracks through the Set Printer option (see fig. 9.11). Each PageMaker document has its own default printer information (see fig. 9.12). Windows keeps track of its printer defaults through the control panel menu.

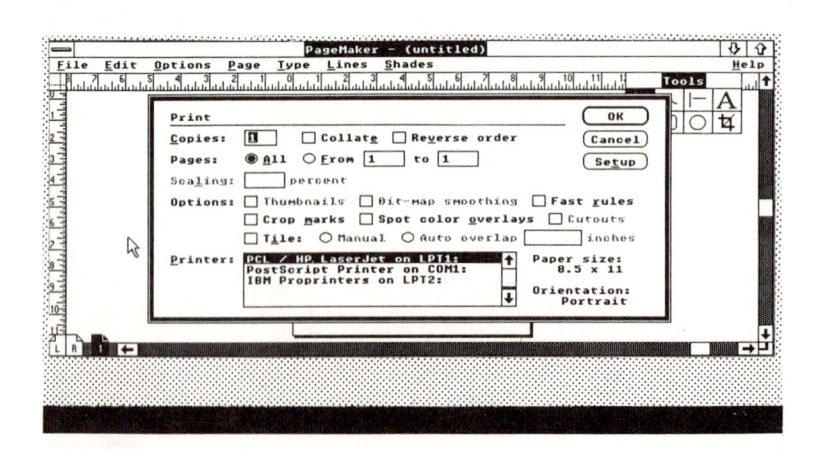

Fig. 9.11.

PageMaker printer defaults.

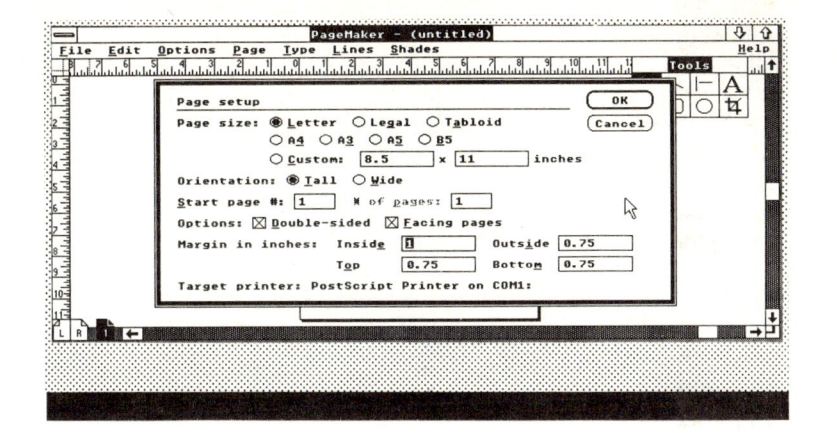

Fig. 9.12.

PageMaker document defaults.

To set Windows' printer default, click on Setup in the Control Panel menu. Then, choose the second option, Printer, to select the default printer if more than one printer exists (see fig. 9.13). If Windows is commanded to print a document without specifically being told which printer to use, the program uses the default printer you specify.

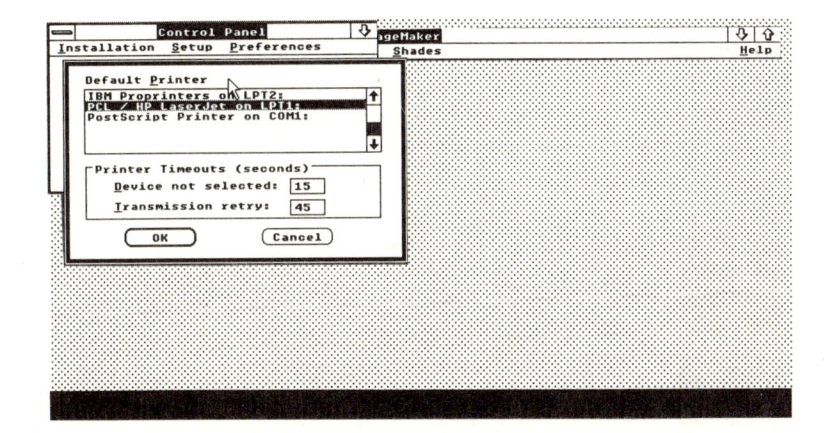

Fig. 9.13.

Default printer.

The Device not Selected value of 15 seconds means that Windows assumes that you have a problem if a printer does not respond within 15 seconds. If a printer starts printing pages and then has trouble, Windows waits 45 seconds before retrying transmission. This value can be changed.

Configuring the Printer Driver

After you choose the default Windows printer, certain information about the options installed in the printer is necessary. For example, which font cartridges have been installed and how much memory has been added. For this reason, another screen pops up after you choose a printer. This screen is different for each type of printer. Three sample screens are reviewed: the dot-matrix printers called ProPrinters made by IBM (see fig. 9.14), the HP LaserJet Series (see fig. 9.15), and PostScript printers (see fig. 9.16).

Fig. 9.14.

Windows ProPrinter driver.

Fig. 9.15.

Windows HP LaserJet driver.

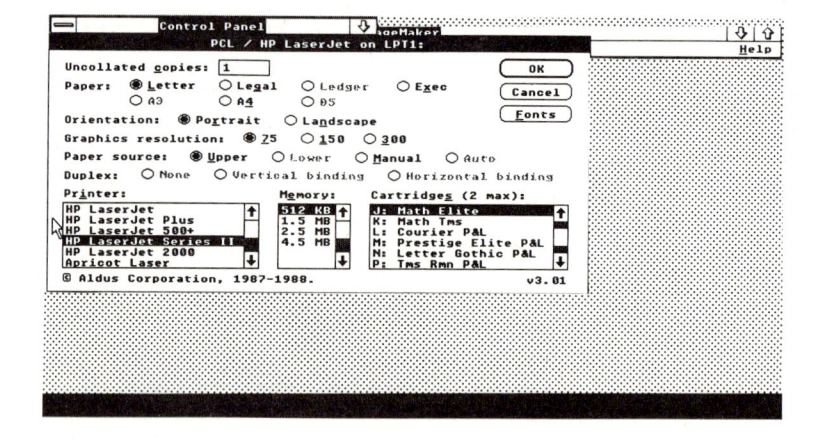

Because each Windows printer driver is an actual program, each printer configuration screen is different. Some screens have additional buttons that can be clicked on and lead to additional screens (see fig. 9.15). For example, the HP LaserJet driver screen has an additional button labeled fonts that leads to menus describing how to download fonts.

The Windows PostScript printer driver has quite a few additional menus attached to it (see fig. 9.16). Clicking on the Options button reveals a screen that has a number of unusual parameters (see fig. 9.17). The first is a job

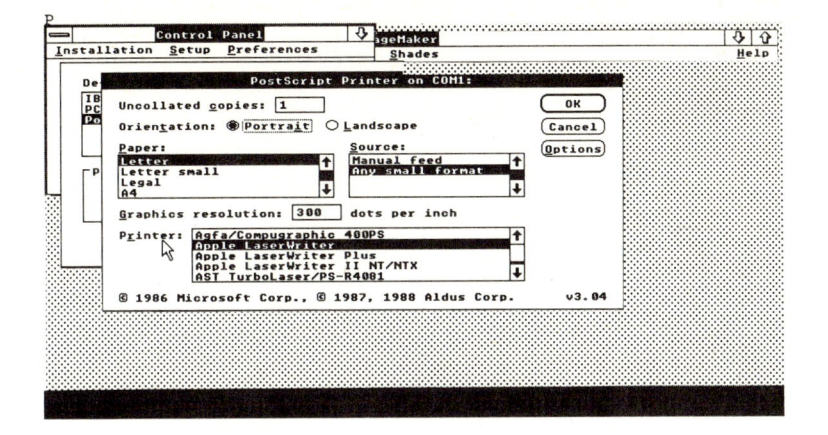

Fig. 9.16.

Windows PostScript printer driver.

time-out. PostScript printers can take 15 minutes or more to figure out how to print a complex page. If the PostScript printer is shared, this use of time can be inconvenient. This parameter gives the PostScript a time limit in which to print the page. If PostScript cannot complete the job within the prescribed time limit, abort the printing. The default value of 0 means that the PostScript printer can think about printing the page forever. Always put some number there; otherwise, you will have to reboot to kill a print job. The time-out value is not to be confused with the Device not Selected and Transmission Retry time outs of figure 9.13. For more speed when printing to a PostScript printer, set transmission retry to 600 and the spooler off.

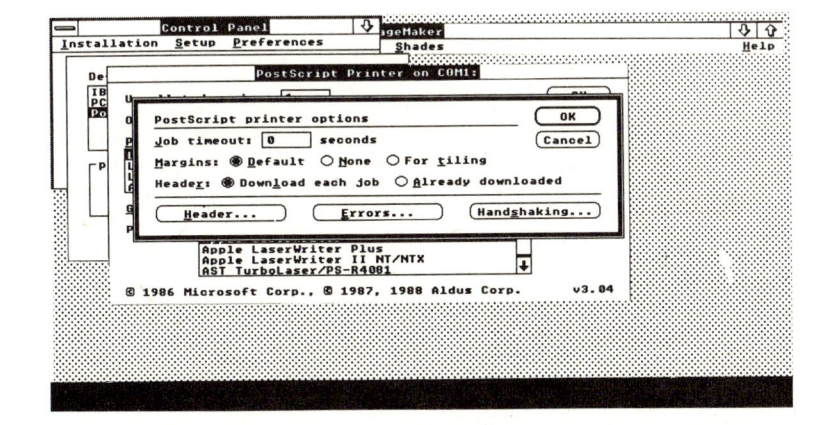

Fig. 9.17.

Windows PostScript printer driver options.

You can use the margins option of the PostScript driver to improve the titling feature of Windows applications. All software packages send a PostScript header to the printer before printing. Transmission of the header can take anywhere from 30 seconds to a couple of minutes. The header is normally transmitted at the beginning of each document, but can be downloaded before entering the Windows application. Then, PostScript printing within the Windows application is faster. This screen can create a file containing the Windows PostScript header for this purpose. Also, the screen can manually transfer the header to the PostScript printer. The header file is like a library of subroutines or programs that are used over and over during PostScript printing.

PostScript printers also generate lots of error messages like compilers and interpreters do when programming. In fact, the PostScript error messages are almost identical to compiler error messages. If any of these types of error messages occur, the problem is a confused printer, an unexpected PostScript version built into the printer, or a bad PostScript printer driver. Turn off and on the PostScript printer just in case some other PostScript document confused the printer.

If clearing out the PostScript printer's memory does not cure the problem, most likely a compatibility problem exists. By manipulating the document to be printed, you may be able to work around the problem, but the potential always lingers. The error feature of the PostScript printer driver of figure 9.17 gives you the option of sending these error messages to the printer or a file. The best idea is to send the PostScript messages to the printer. If the PostScript printer is hooked up through a parallel port, Windows cannot route the messages to a file.

Handshaking normally refers to the printer cable taking care of data sent from the computer to the printer. The printer cable slows the data if the computer sends it too quickly for the printer to keep up. However, PostScript printers have the unusual capability to send data to the computer, and they may transmit data faster than the PC can process it! The handshaking options of figure 9.17 refer to printer-to-computer handshaking. Notice that while figure 9.20 assumes that some printers can keep up with the computers, figure 9.17 assumes that micros can never keep up with printers. If printers are going to be sending data to computers, the handshaking has to be hardware or software.

When you select the hardware option, the hardware handshaking program is actually transmitted to the printer. If the PostScript printer is not on or attached, Windows locks up or generates an error message.

Furthermore, the hardware handshaking program should be sent to the PostScript printer *only once*, at the beginning of the Windows-PostScript relationship. Some PostScript printers are designed to remember this type of program like some printers remember their front-panel settings. If the hardware handshaking program is sent over and over again, the PostScript printers memory could fill up with this information. Just turning the printer off and on again may not cure the problem. You may have to unplug the printer's battery or reset the printer to the factory faults. Macs do not even come with a method of resetting the LaserWriter. Instead, you need a utility like LaserStatus to reset the LaserWriter.

Initializing the Serial Port

If a serial printer is attached to a computer running Windows, the final step of installing the printer driver requires going into the Setup menu of the control panel and choosing Communications Port (see fig. 9.18). The communications port screen contains baud rate, word length, parity, stop bits, and handshaking information about each serial port. This information concerns information transferred from the computer to the printer.

Only hardware handshaking is supported by this version of Windows. Many popular printers today yell X-off at computers when they send data too fast. The current version of Windows is not designed to listen for X-off and the subsequent X-on yelled by the printer when it is ready to receive data again.

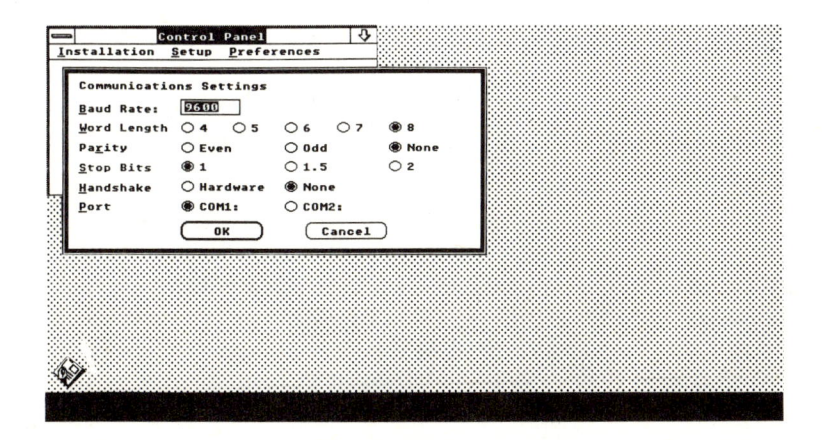

Fig. 9.18.
Windows serial port configuration.

Adding Printer Fonts

You add fonts to a printer in three different ways. Either the printer is upgraded, cartridges are purchased, or fonts are downloaded. Because Windows' printer drivers are programs rather than databases, they are not as flexible. A new Windows printer driver may be needed to download fonts.

Windows can be told that certain font cartridges have been added, but if you purchase a font cartridge that Windows does not know about, the Windows driver has to be rewritten. Suppose that you purchase a font cartridge for an

HP LaserJet that contains all the fonts found in 26 official HP LaserJet font cartridges. The HP LaserJet driver pictured in figure 9.15 enables you to choose only two cartridges because only two physical cartridge slots are in an HP LaserJet printer. The HP LaserJet printer driver prevents all the fonts in the fancy font cartridge from being used at once. Your options are to pray that the all-in-one font cartridge comes with a modified Windows HP LaserJet driver, wait for a new version of the Windows printer driver, or find another software package that can be told they all exist (like WordPerfect's database type printer driver).

Ideally, fonts should be added to a computer's operating system. Then, the fonts would be available instantly to all programs and could be downloaded to any printer. Fonts should not be added to the printer driver. Macs are very close to this ideal. The PC world is very far away. Fonts are not added to Windows, but individual Windows' printer drivers. If the printer or printer driver changes, the older fonts may disappear. But, if fonts are added to Windows, the printer driver or printer could change, and the fonts would still (ideally) be available.

Microsoft considers cartridge fonts part of printers and downloadable fonts part of printer drivers. Therefore, you do not have one universal method of downloading fonts to printers in the Windows environment. Because each printer driver is different, the menus and screens that support downloading fonts are going to be different. Because only the Windows HP LaserJet printer driver can download fonts, the rest of this section revolves around the issue of sending fonts to an HP LaserJet printer using Windows.

The font files that Windows keeps track of are called *printer font metric* or PFM files. PFM files are created two different ways. At first, Windows printer drivers depended on the font vendor. BitStream is shipped with most Windows applications and can create PFM files directly. With current versions of HP LaserJet printer drivers, standard HP font files can be imported. Standard HP font files are expected to end with the extension SFP (Soft Font Portrait) or SFL (Soft Font Landscape). These font files can be found floating around in many different applications. A quick method of checking whether you have found a SFP file is to look at the file using the DOS TYPE command (see fig. 9.19). Typing *TYPE filename.SFP* should display an arrow pointing left and then these symbols)s#W where # is a number larger than 48.

Put all the SFP files in a subdirectory and write down the subdirectory's name. Then, get into the Windows application and find the printer driver screen or dialog box. Click on fonts, and the HP LaserJet Soft Font Installer screen pops up (see fig. 9.20). Select the Add fonts button and type the path of the floppy disk or subdirectory where the SFP files are located. A list of the SFP file names should appear in the right column. Highlighting a font in the right column and then clicking causes this printer driver to place a copy

```
C:\PCLFONTS>dir

 Volume in drive C is DISK1_VOL1
 Directory of  C:\PCLFONTS

.            <DIR>      9-19-89   4:21a
..           <DIR>      9-19-89   4:21a
COUN3010 SFP    18409   9-19-89   4:21a
COPR0100 PFM      246   9-19-89   4:23a
HLVN3006 SFP    12131   9-19-89   4:23a
HLPR0070 PFM      694   9-19-89   4:23a
        6 File(s)  12726272 bytes free

C:\PCLFONTS>type hlvn3006.sfp
+)s75W
C:\PCLFONTS>
```

Fig. 9.19.

Characteristics of an SFP file.

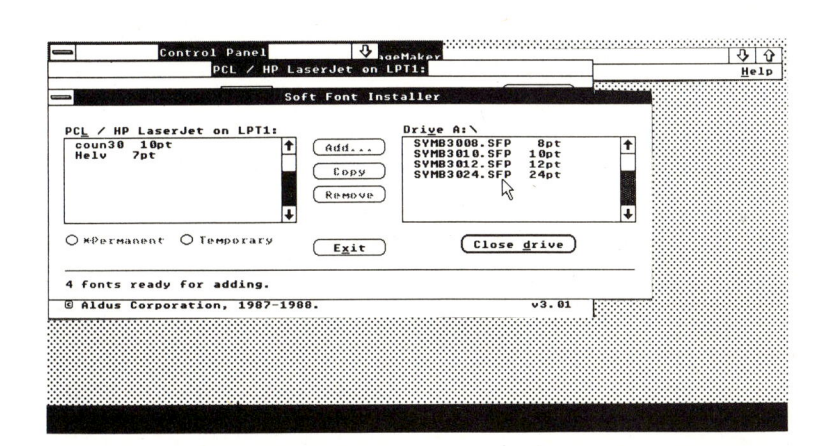

Fig. 9.20.

Windows HP LaserJet Soft Font Installer file.

of the SFP font in a subdirectory where the operating system can keep track of the file (default is \PCLFONTS). After you enter the name of the new font at the prompt, an associated PFM file is created. You end up with a pair of SFP and PFM files for each soft font.

The printer driver also is responsible for keeping track of whether the font is permanent or temporary. Permanent means that the font was present in the printer prior to executing Windows. The permanent font could be in the printer ROM or downloaded permanently by some other program prior to running Windows.

The Windows WIN.INI file keeps track of where these font files are located. The WIN.INI file is like a CONFIG.SYS file to Windows. The words in brackets ([ ]) are categories within the WIN.INI file. Find these category headings, look for similar commands such as Spooler=yes, and modify them.

Be sure to save the WIN.INI file. The file can be 180 lines long or more and all your Windows programs depend on it.

[Windows]	
Spooler=no	Disable Windows' Spooler
[extensions]	
PM3=D:\PM.EXE ^.PM3	Tell Windows that Pagemaker is on a RAM disk, not hard disk (for regular Windows, not Run-time
PT3=D:\PM.EXE ^.PT3	
[ports]	
FILENAME.OUT=	Add the capability to print to a file

Installing New Screen Fonts

Most Windows run-time applications are shipped with the same screen fonts. Each screen font is contained in a separate file with the extension FON. Each printer font references one of the basic six fonts for the purposes of displaying on-screen what is printed. The six screen fonts are as follows:

MODERN.FON
SCRIPT.FON
ROMAN.FON
TMSRB.FON
COURB.FON
HELVB.FON

The first three are bit-mapped fonts in different type styles (Modern, Script, and Roman). The other three are called vector fonts in Windows language (TMSRB, COURB, HELVB); these have been called scalable or object fonts in this book. Fonts are added and deleted using the control panel's Install menu. The Delete Font menu lists the currently installed screen fonts (see fig. 9.21). The different point sizes of the bit-mapped fonts are listed, whereas the vector fonts have no point sizes mentioned. Vector fonts or scalable fonts can be printed in any size.

Because every printer font references one of these six screen fonts, often you do not have a very good screen representation of what prints. Windows, therefore, enables you to modify which screen fonts and printer fonts are to be linked. The better vendors supply Windows fonts installation kits that generate screen fonts at the same time that they generate printer fonts.

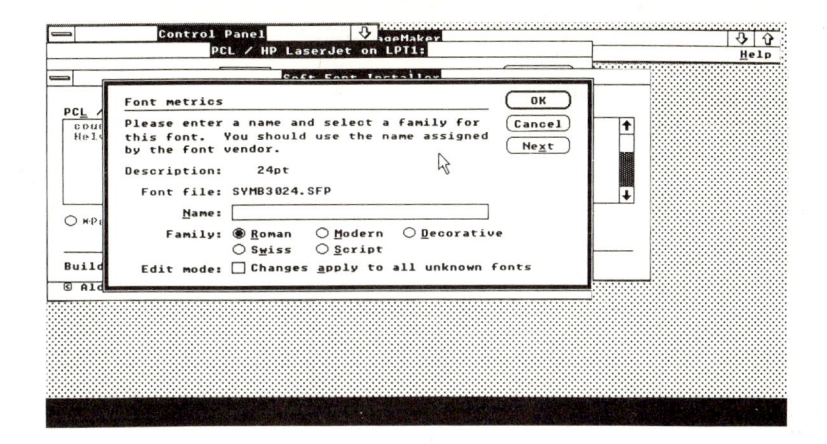

Fig. 9.21.
Windows screen font list.

GEM Ventura

Ventura is one of the top selling desktop publishing software packages for computers. Ventura was written in the GEM graphics environment just like PageMaker is written in the Windows environment. GEM and Windows are development environments that enable programmers to write graphics-mode programs more easily. GEM was developed by Digital Research (the same company that developed CPM). Windows was developed by Microsoft. Both work on top of PC-DOS and try to turn a PC into a Macintosh. This section discusses printing aspects of this program.

Installing Printer Drivers

Although Ventura was written in GEM, the Ventura programmers decided that they needed to rewrite some of the GEM printer drivers. Ventura can use standard GEM printer drivers. For example, GEM/3 has a PaintJet printer driver. Copying this printer driver (files with extension SYS) into the Ventura subdirectory makes the printer available to Ventura. Similarly, copying VENTURA drivers into the GEMAPPS\GEMSYS subdirectory makes the VENTURA drivers available to GEM printing.

The printer driver *.SYS files are copied off the distribution disks onto the hard disk during installation of Ventura and GEM. (Put disk 1 in drive A, type *VPPREP*, and follow the directions on the screen.) They are not modified during the installation process. Whenever printing, GEM applications scan the GEMAPPS\GEMSYS subdirectory for *.SYS files and lists them. INF files keep track of defaults, such as the last printer used.

> HINT Install 150-dpi and 300-dpi laser printer drivers. The difference between the resolutions is seldom obvious because character resolution remains the same. The 150-dpi driver can print more complex documents, but the 300-dpi driver can produce better looking graphics.

Adding Printer Fonts

This section explains how to add fonts to Ventura once the program has been installed. Ventura requires a character width and height information (file with extension WID) about each character that can be printed. If this information does not exist, try the width information associated with another font. For example, a WID table associated with fonts found in a Xerox 4020 printer appears to work well with HP PaintJet fonts.

Ventura enables up to six printers to be installed at one time. The first printer should be the one intended for final printing because the top printer on the list has a printer font width table associated with it. This font width table is used when laying out the document. Page breaks, widows, and orphans are all determined by this font width table. When printing on draft printers, the text may not space correctly. But page breaks, flow around graphic objects, widows, and orphans will match the final draft. The characters are not spaced properly on the draft because they are being spaced using the final output device's width table.

Copying Fonts to a Ventura Subdirectory

Ventura defaults to storing all its fonts in the Ventura subdirectory. Copy your new fonts into the VENTURA subdirectory using the DOS COPY command or installation software from the font vendor.

Ventura requires that printer font files have different extensions for different printer models. When these font files are copied into the Ventura subdirectory, you must rename them according to Ventura conventions. For example, JLaser and Cordata fonts should be renamed with the extension *.B30. AST TurboLaser fonts should be renamed to the extension *.W30. Xerox 4045 fonts should be renamed *.XFN, and PostScript files should be renamed *.PFA. Look up these conventions in the Ventura manual.

> HINT Stick to standard 6 to 24 point fonts and you will have less trouble with running out of memory and Ventura slowing to a crawl. Of course, if you have scalable fonts, you don't have these limitations.

Creating New Width Files

Not all font vendors supply the Ventura-specific width file information needed. Ventura does provide utilities for some printers to create the width information. Ventura provides complete support for the HP LaserJet series printers. For PostScript printers, Ventura provides a width file that supports all the fonts found in an Apple LaserWriter II printer. Additional PostScript fonts need width files supplied by the font vendor for Ventura to use them.

Ventura supplies a program called PORTOLAN that can convert portrait fonts to landscape fonts for character printers if you have just the portrait version. Ventura also contains the programs necessary to build font width tables from the raw font descriptions. This two-step process involves building each font's width table individually using the program HPLTOVFM and then combining them together into a WID table using the program VFMTOWID. These steps are detailed in Appendix K of the Ventura Reference manual.

Selecting New Width Files

Ventura keeps all of its font information in a single WID file. This WID table must contain information on all the fonts used within a document because a single WID table contains all the information necessary to format a document. The first two steps created a new WID table. If the old and the new are desired at the same time, a third WID table needs to be created by merging the old and new together.

The process of merging the WID tables should be done with an empty Ventura screen. If a document is present, the contents may be affected by the process. Therefore, save the document and begin a new chapter. Go to the Options menu and select Set Printer Info (see fig. 9.22). This procedure assigns the new WID table to the new chapter.

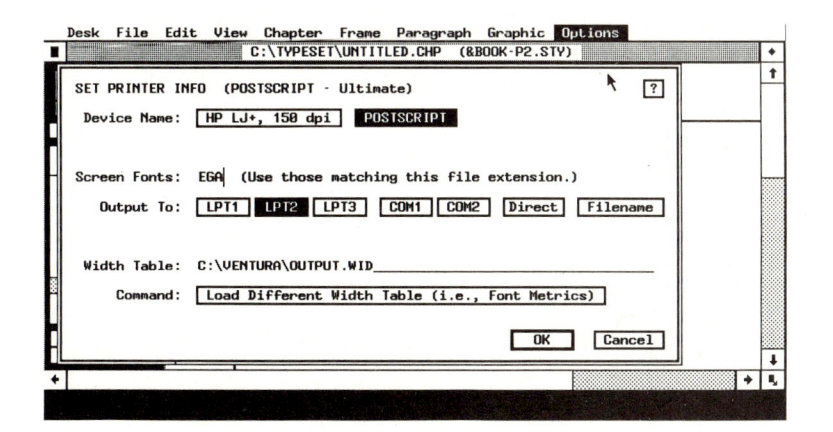

Fig. 9.22.

Ventura's Set Printer Info screen.

HINT | The word Ultimate in the Set Printer Info Box means that the character width table matches the printer chosen. If not, the word Draft appears. This means Ventura cannot do its best at spacing the words and text in the resulting printout. Change printers until the word Ultimate appears for the best results.

Next, go to the Options menu again and select ADD/REMOVE FONTS (see fig. 9.23). Here, you can modify the contents of the WID table assigned to the current document. Before modifying any WID table, you should save a copy of the old one just in case something goes wrong. Ventura provides the option Save With a Different Name just for this purpose.

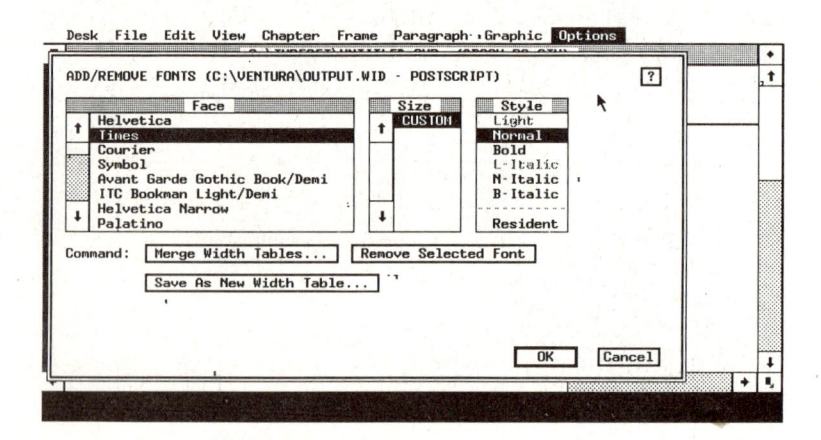

Fig. 9.23.

Ventura's Add/Remove Fonts screen.

Write down the backup WID file name and describe its contents and subdirectory location. When using Ventura, sprinkling files all over the hard disk is easy to do. If you are not careful, the hard disk can become so cluttered that the various files associated with a chapter can be scattered among many subdirectories. In this case, copying a chapter off the hard disk and printing it on another PC becomes difficult.

Next, merge the old and new WID tables together. The results of the combination replace the currently selected WID table. (That is why you should back up the old WID table before this procedure.)

Testing and Cleaning Up Width Files

Create a document that prints the lower- and uppercase alphabet of each font (you may need a couple of pages to accommodate the different fonts). Check to make sure that all the fonts mentioned in the resulting WID table actually do something. If some fonts do not print anything, go to the Add/Remove Fonts screen and remove them. If two names select the same font, remove one of the names. Don't clutter up Ventura's font list with duplicate names or names that don't activate any printer features. Save the resulting test document created for this WID table for troubleshooting purposes in the future.

> HINT If a page is too complex, try building a WID table that just contains descriptions of the fonts used in that document. Removing descriptions of extra, unused fonts frees room in the PC's memory for more complex documents. Always leave 10-point Helvetica (or Swiss) and 10-point Times (or Dutch) for Ventura. Ventura uses these fonts as a reference when modifying screen fonts that the program does not have a copy of.

Downloading Printer Fonts

If the same fonts are going to be used over and over again, printing is much quicker if those fonts are sent to the printer before entering Ventura. If a PostScript printer is used with Ventura, always send the fonts to the printer before using Ventura. Otherwise, Ventura downloads a new PostScript font each time the font changes in a document—even if the font is already in the printer's memory.

> HINT You can use many downloaded fonts without adding memory to a laser printer. Ventura can shuffle fonts in and out of a laser printer's memory. This shuffling takes more time, but saves the cost of adding lots of memory.

Ventura defaults to thinking that all fonts in a width table are to be downloaded over and over again while printing a document. If you have set up the PC system to download the new fonts to the printer prior to executing Ventura, the font's status needs to be changed to Resident. To do so, select Download on the Add/Remove Font screen.

Resident does not mean that the new font is permanent. Turning the printer off and on still erases the new font. But, Ventura cannot tell whether the font has been erased. Ventura is still going to assume that the font is resident and try to print with the nonexistent font. PostScript printers think about the possibility and do nothing. Character printers substitute a font.

If fonts are going to be downloaded by Ventura, the program has to know where they are located. Associated with each width file is a configuration file with the extension CNF (see fig. 9.24). This file configures Ventura like CONFIG.SYS configures DOS and WIN.INI configures Windows. The file contains a lot of commands, including file locations. If a path for file locations is not mentioned in the CNF file, Ventura expects the font files to be located in the Ventura subdirectory.

```
psfonts(C:\PSFONTS\)
eoftype(PC)      : "PC" or "MAC"
imgtype(FAST)    : "FAST" or "COMPACT"
coltype(COLOR)   : "GRAY" or "COLOR"
font(AvantGarde-Book,51,M,TEXT,RES)
font(AvantGarde-BookOblique,51,I,TEXT,RES)
font(AvantGarde-Demi,51,B,TEXT,RES)
font(AvantGarde-DemiOblique,51,BI,TEXT,RES)
font(Bookman-Light,23,M,TEXT,RES)
font(Bookman-LightItalic,23,I,TEXT,RES)
font(Bookman-Demi,23,B,TEXT,RES)
font(Bookman-DemiItalic,23,BI,TEXT,RES)
font(Helvetica-Narrow,50,M,TEXT,RES)
font(Helvetica-Narrow-Oblique,50,I,TEXT,RES)
font(Helvetica-Narrow-Bold,50,B,TEXT,RES)
font(Helvetica-Narrow-BoldOblique,50,BI,TEXT,RES)
font(Palatino-Roman,21,M,TEXT,RES)
font(Palatino-Italic,21,I,TEXT,RES)
font(Palatino-Bold,21,B,TEXT,RES)
font(Palatino-BoldItalic,21,BI,TEXT,RES)
font(NewCenturySchlbk-Roman,20,M,TEXT,RES)
font(NewCenturySchlbk-Italic,20,I,TEXT,RES)
font(NewCenturySchlbk-Bold,20,B,TEXT,RES)
font(NewCenturySchlbk-BoldItalic,20,BI,TEXT,RES)
C:\VENTURA\POSTSCPT.CNF                        Doc 1 Pg 1 Ln 1.5i Pos 2.5i
```

Fig. 9.24.

Ventura PostScript CNF file.

Because character-mode printers seldom come with font-downloading software, Ventura provides font-downloading software for some printers. For example, Ventura provides a program called HPDOWN to download font information to HP LaserJets and compatibles. You can place this program in a batch file that loads these fonts before executing Ventura. HPDOWN uses the information in the HPLJPLU.CNF file to figure out the font file names and locations (see Appendix K of the Ventura Reference manual).

Installing New Screen Fonts

Ventura runs all videoboards in graphics mode. The fonts supported by Ventura, therefore, are graphics fonts, which are completely different from the printer fonts described in the preceding section. Screen fonts are in different files with different names and installation procedures. Sometimes, screen and printer fonts do not exactly match, and seeing what your results will be in advance can be difficult.

Ventura is shipped with 21 different screen font files (two typefaces—serif and sans serif). By stretching and modifying these fonts, Ventura does a decent job of accurately replicating printer fonts on-screen. Ventura looks up a printer font's style and size in the WID table, searches through its list of screen fonts, finds the best match, and stretches to the exact size. The 21 fonts that Ventura is shipped with were designed for EGA and VGA displays. Ventura stretches these fonts to fit HGA and MGA displays and full-page monitor systems.

The screen font installation process is simple. Copy the fonts to the Ventura subdirectory or the Ventura\VPFonts subdirectory. The maximum number of screen fonts is 700, and the maximum size of one screen font file is 35K. Ventura looks in the Ventura subdirectory first and the Ventura\VPFonts subdirectory second. The screen fonts Ventura looks for must all have the extension set in the Set Printer Info screen (see fig. 9.22). But, remember that just like the Mac and Windows environments, many screen fonts can slow down Ventura.

Ventura supports a wide variety of graphics-mode videoboards. Each videoboard has different resolutions and color capabilities. The best-looking graphics fonts are designed specifically for that videoboard, although most any graphics font can be stretched to fit. The trouble is that the screen font file format is not documented in the Ventura manuals.

Ventura provides a utility that extracts screen font information from standard Adobe PostScript file formats (ABFTOFNT) and creates Ventura screen files from them. This utility cannot yet reach out into the printer and grab the information necessary to create a screen font from a font resident in the printer, nor can the utility create screen fonts from regular character fonts. Today, most screen font information has to be purchased in Ventura format.

If no videoboard specific fonts are available, Venture substitutes EGA fonts. If videoboard specific fonts are added later, you can mix EGA and videoboard fonts. Which fonts are used for which purposes are kept track of internally using INF files, one INF file for each videoboard.

> **HINT** If screen fonts take more than a few seconds to load, set BUFFERS = 30 in the CONFIG.SYS file. Also try installing a hard disk cache.

At first, screen font information does not seem related to setting printer information. But, the WYSIWYG ideal demands that screen fonts, printer drivers and printer width tables be intimately related. If a printer is changed, the screen fonts and the character width tables should change. Ventura, therefore, put all these configuration parameters in the same Set Printer Info screen.

Knowing Memory Requirements

Ventura eats up a ton of RAM and scatters files all over the place. Most software forces you to make file organization decisions. Ventura encourages filing chaos. You have to discipline Ventura rather than the usual computers disciplining you. Some may call this freedom a desirable feature of Ventura, but it invites chaos. If you plan ahead, Ventura can be very efficient.

Ventura has trouble living in 640K. After installing Ventura, you may receive an error message saying that certain loadable modules cannot be found. Even if you receive no error message, Ventura may be so cramped for space that the program constantly shuffles files on and off the hard disk, making the system very slow. Even worse, when trying to format a page for the printer, Ventura may just give up. The cursor may freeze. The following hint may help with these problems.

> HINT | Some pages in a Ventura document may cause problems. Separate them from the document and print separately. Reset the printer by turning it off and on before printing.

First, check the CONFIG.SYS and AUTOEXEC.BAT files. Get rid of anything that takes up lots of memory—local area networks, terminate-and-stay resident programs, and so on. If you cannot part with your local area network, the next step is to find more memory.

If you have a 1M AT clone, chances are you have 384K of RAM not being used. Almost all Windows programs (as well as DOS 4.1 and 386 MAX) come with a file called HIMEM.SYS that makes 64K of the 384K available to Ventura. The chance of finding a reliable method to use the rest of the 384K under DOS is slim.

Other methods of freeing up more memory involve fiddling with the batch file that starts Ventura. The batch file that starts up Ventura usually looks something like the following:

```
CD C:\VENTURA
DRVRMRGR VP %1 /D=SD_HERC5.EGA/M=32/A=32
```

The phrase /D=SD_HERC5.EGA means that the videoboard is a Hercules, and the /M=32 means that the mouse is a Microsoft bus mouse. These options configure Ventura each time the PC is booted. Some other options also deal with how Ventura uses memory, and how reliably the program prints. The phrase /A=32 means steal 32K bytes from the videoboard's memory and transfer the stolen memory to text memory. Although this process enables the modules to load and make Ventura run faster, it definitely causes printing problems unless the printer is a Postscript printer. The phrase /A=32 does not cause problems with Postscript printers. If /A=32 does not work, try /A=16.

> HINT | Ventura has a secret memory diagnostic screen. To see how the memory is being used, select the Desk Menu, select Publisher Info, and click on the name Ventura to display the diagnostic menu. Use this screen when playing around with Ventura's memory utilization.

The other option is to purchase additional memory. The type of additional memory that Ventura uses is called EMS 4.0 memory. Purchasing an EMS 4.0 memory board that can be configured in hardware is possible, but Ventura has to be told how much EMS memory you can have by using the /E option.

WordPerfect

WordPerfect has become one of the most important word processors in the PC market. One of the reasons is that WordPerfect has found a method of supporting practically every printer feature in existence. Like most word processors, WordPerfect provides the tools to create your own printer driver. What makes WordPerfect's printer definition tables special is that they have succeeded in organizing the chaos of the printing world. A study of these tables should be mandatory reading for any other word processing or desktop publishing software developer.

The objective of this section is to briefly review the installation and testing of printers in the WordPerfect world.

Reviewing the Printing Menu

When the WordPerfect program is initially copied off the distribution disks onto the hard disk, a simple printer is installed. Specific installation is done from within WordPerfect itself. While inside any document, you can install a new printer. To start the printer installation process, you call the Print screen. This menu provides an entry point into all of WordPerfect's printing options (see fig. 9.25).

The top half of Wordperfect's Print screen contains options for printing parts of documents in PC RAM or out on a disk. Also included are options for downloading permanent fonts to the printer (called initialization), looking at the document in graphics mode (view), and turning the PC into a typewriter (type through).

408 Part II: Printer Setup and Management

```
             Print

                 1 - Full Document
                 2 - Page
                 3 - Document on Disk
                 4 - Control Printer
                 5 - Type Through
                 6 - View Document
                 7 - Initialize Printer

             Options

                 S - Select Printer        Scott's HP LaserJet II
                 B - Binding               0i
                 N - Number of Copies      1
                 G - Graphics Quality      Medium
                 T - Text Quality          Draft




             Selection: 0
```

Fig. 9.25.

WordPerfect Print menu.

The bottom half of the Print screen contains a series of printing options. The options include printing multiple pages, alternating margins for binding purposes, and changing the print quality to speed up draft printing and decrease ribbon or toner use. However, the most important option is Select, which installs, edits, adds, and deletes printer drivers.

Installing Printer Drivers

When you choose Select from WordPerfect's print menu, a list of currently installed printers is displayed (see fig. 9.26). Included in the list are usually two printers called Standard Printer and DOS printer, essentially drivers for the simple printer described in Chapter 1. These are the printers that bold and underline by printing the line twice. Except for PostScript printers, most

```
             Print: Select Printer

                 Apple Laserwriter Plus
               * Scott's HP LaserJet II
                 Standard Printer
```

Fig. 9.26.

WordPerfect's Select Printer screen.

```
         1 Select; 2 Additional Printers; 3 Edit; 4 Copy; 5 Delete; 6 Help; 7 Update: 1
```

printers should be able to work with these drivers minus any font-changing capabilities. Because WordPerfect users could continue printing for years without making full use of their printer's features, WordPerfect reminds you that you have not installed a printer yet when booted.

For each printer listed on the Select Printer screen, an associated file with the extension PRS (printers) is listed in the WordPerfect subdirectory. WordPerfect also maintains a file called WP{WP}.SET that keeps track of printer configuration, including which PRS files have been installed. This file is similar to a Windows WIN.INI or GEM CNF file in terms of its function. The presence of a PRS file in a WordPerfect directory is useless unless WP{WP}.SET knows about the file. However, the WP{WP}.SET file can be edited only from within WordPerfect. The best way to install a printer, therefore, is to follow WordPerfect's instructions.

WordPerfect is shipped with printer disks that contain similar printer information lumped into categories. For example, all the dot-matrix printers are in one file, and all the character lasers are in another file. All object (PostScript) printers are in a third. These files have names like the following:

    WPRINT1.ALL
    WPRINT2.ALL
    WPRINT3.ALL

The process of configuring WordPerfect for a particular printer requires extracting a printer's information from the proper ALL file and creating a second file called a PRS file. You can create this file by using the Add option on the Select Printer screen.

PRS and ALL files are both considered printer definition tables to WordPerfect's printer definition table editor.

Changing the Printer Definitions

When you edit printer drivers, you are editing PRS files, not the original ALL files. Editing ALL files requires leaving WordPerfect and entering the Printer Definition file. The trouble with editing a PRS file is that changes made in this file are vulnerable to being erased, because the ALL file is supposed to be the repository of all standard printer definition tables. Any changes made to the PRS table are considered temporary. There isn't even a method to copy the changes made to a PRS table back into an ALL file.

HINT | If WordPerfect is consistently doing strange things to your document, make sure that the problem is in the printer driver. Print WordPerfect's test file. If it has problems, delete the printer driver and then add the driver back by using the Select Printer screen.

Editing WordPerfect's PRS files is done by selecting the Edit option of the Select Printer screen (see fig. 9.26). The Edit screen has the options displayed in figure 9.27.

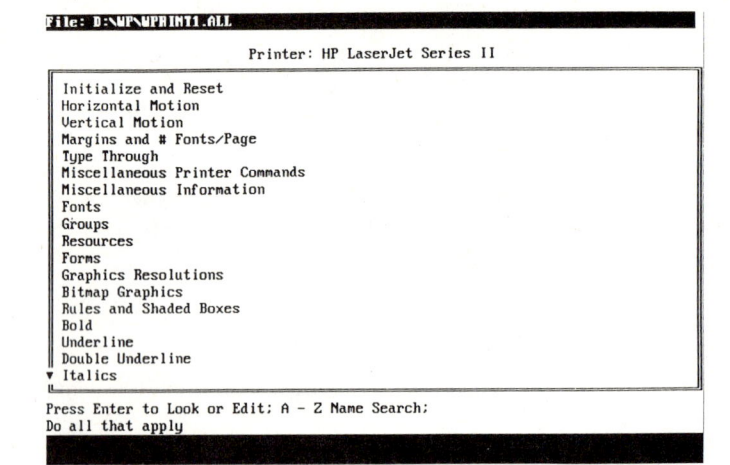

Fig. 9.27.

Editing WordPerfect's printer driver.

```
File: D:\WP\WPRINT1.ALL
                    Printer: HP LaserJet Series II
   Initialize and Reset
   Horizontal Motion
   Vertical Motion
   Margins and # Fonts/Page
   Type Through
   Miscellaneous Printer Commands
   Miscellaneous Information
   Fonts
   Groups
   Resources
   Forms
   Graphics Resolutions
   Bitmap Graphics
   Rules and Shaded Boxes
   Bold
   Underline
   Double Underline
▼  Italics

Press Enter to Look or Edit; A - Z Name Search;
Do all that apply
```

The Port location lists the standard LPT1 and COM1 options and a file name in case you want to print to a file. Someday, you will be able to type the name of a printer on a local area network. The Sheet Feeder option is for the old cut-sheet feeders found on daisywheel printers. The paper trays of laser printers do not need any special installation. The Forms option is described earlier in this chapter. The last three options deal with WordPerfect's Font Management. The next section covers adding printer fonts.

TROUBLE-SHOOTING TIP | If a printer does not print and another serial or parallel port is available, move the printer to the other port. Then, tell WordPerfect where you moved the printer and try printing. This process can isolate whether the problem is in the printer or the PC interface.

Adding Printer Fonts

WordPerfect wants an incredible amount of information about fonts. WordPerfect has its own universal character set and universal fonts. The known world has to be mapped into the WordPerfect universe. Because WordPerfect demands this information, the program can support larger character sets than any other package. In addition, WordPerfect can do a better job of font substitution than any other software package. You pay for these features in the time spent installing the fonts, or you can purchase your fonts from a vendor who already has installed the fonts for you. WordPerfect, like every other PC software package, is shipped with BitStream software that installs fonts for you. Other font vendors are starting to support the WordPerfect font installation.

Font vendors install their fonts in the ALL files, not the PRS files. After installing new fonts, therefore, the old PRS file has to be deleted and a new one built using the Add command of the Select Printer screen. Actually, the Delete command does not delete the PRS file but removes the file from the WP{WP}.SET file. When adding, you receive a message Replace HPLJPLUS.PRS (Y/N) No. Choose Yes to overwrite the old PRS file.

After the new PRS file has been created, the next step is to edit the new printer driver. Select the new driver's name and choose Edit. Tell WordPerfect the location of the new font files. Then, choose the option Cartridges & Fonts. This option asks you whether you are adding cartridges or downloadable fonts. If you have added more memory to the laser printer, then the quantity can be increased. If you are using a font cartridge that is 24 cartridges in 1, WordPerfect enables you to change the number of cartridges from 2 to 24 (see fig. 9.28). Because WordPerfect comes with support for

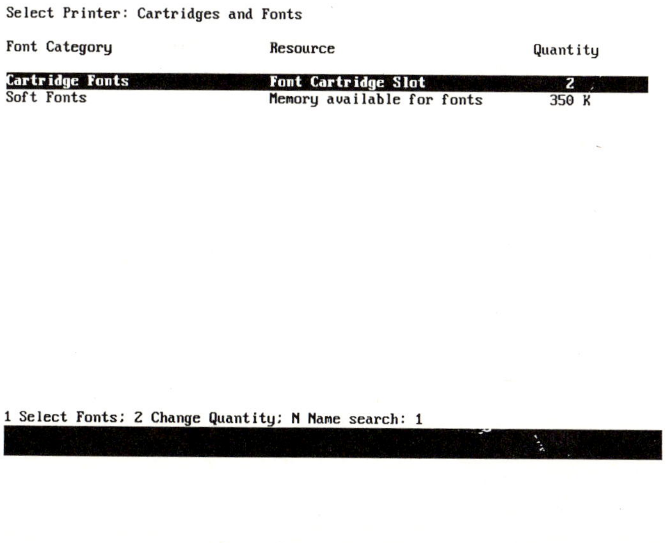

```
Select Printer: Cartridges and Fonts

Font Category                Resource                      Quantity

Cartridge Fonts              Font Cartridge Slot              2
Soft Fonts                   Memory available for fonts     350 K
```

Fig. 9.28.

Cartridges and Fonts screen.

```
1 Select Fonts; 2 Change Quantity; N Name search: 1
```

many of the font cartridges made by printer manufacturers for their printers, this section is as easy as picking out the font cartridge's name from a list.

If fonts are to be downloaded or are soft fonts, select Soft Font. All the new fonts added with BitStream or another vendor's package should appear on-screen (see fig. 9.29). Go through and put a * by all the fonts that you want to permanently download. Watch the amount of free memory slowly decrease. Keep in mind that about 1M of memory may be required to print graphics that are included in the WordPerfect document. While most graphics are smaller, the amount of printer memory required is significant. If you fill the printer memory up with fonts, don't plan on printing graphics.

Fig. 9.29.

Soft font management.

```
Select Printer: Cartridges and Fonts
                                         Total Quantity:    350 K
                                         Available Quantity:  37 K

Soft Fonts                                         Quantity Used

  (FW) Dutch Roman 10pt (ASCII) (Land)                  10 K
* (FW) Dutch Roman 10pt (ASCII) (Port)                  11 K
+ (FW) Dutch Roman 12pt (ASCII) (Land)                  13 K
* (FW) Dutch Roman 12pt (ASCII) (Port)                  13 K
+ (FW) Dutch Roman 15pt (ASCII) (Land)                  19 K
* (FW) Dutch Roman 15pt (ASCII) (Port)                  19 K
+ (FW) Dutch Roman 20pt (ASCII) (Land)                  30 K
  (FW) Dutch Roman 20pt (ASCII) (Port)                  30 K
+ (FW) Swiss Bold 10pt (ASCII) (Land)                   10 K
  (FW) Swiss Bold 10pt (ASCII) (Port)                   11 K
+ (FW) Swiss Bold 12pt (ASCII) (Land)                   14 K
* (FW) Swiss Bold 12pt (ASCII) (Port)                   14 K
+ (FW) Swiss Bold 15pt (ASCII) (Land)                   19 K
* (FW) Swiss Bold 15pt (ASCII) (Port)                   19 K
  (FW) Swiss Bold 20pt (ASCII) (Land)                   30 K

Mark Fonts: * Present when print job begins        Press Exit to save
            + Can be loaded during print job       Press Cancel to cancel
```

The asterisk by each font means that the font is permanently downloaded, and the overall amount of printer memory required decreases. Alternatively, putting a plus by each font causes that font to be downloaded only if needed for the page being printed. After printing that page, the font is forgotten and needs to be re-sent to the printer before printing the next page. This process does not require as much memory in the printer but slows the printer. If the printer is hooked up over a local area network, re-sending a font also can slow down the local area network.

When all the fonts have been selected, press F7 for exit. At the Cartridges and Fonts screen pick your default font—the font that is used if no specific font is specified in a document. Then, exit out all the way to the WordPerfect screen. Now, the names of the fonts that were added should be available when pressing Ctrl-F8 or Font (see fig. 9.30).

```
Base Font
    Courier 10 pitch (PC-8)
    Courier 10 pitch (Roman-8/ECMA)
    Courier Bold 10 pitch (PC-8)
    Courier Bold 10 pitch (Roman-8/ECMA)
    Dutch Bold 10pt (ASCII) (Port) (FW)
    Dutch Bold 12pt (ASCII) (Port) (FW)
    Dutch Bold 15pt (ASCII) (Port) (FW)
    Dutch Bold 20pt (ASCII) (Port) (FW)
    Dutch Bold Italic 10pt (ASCII) (Port) (FW)
    Dutch Bold Italic 12pt (ASCII) (Port) (FW)
    Dutch Bold Italic 15pt (ASCII) (Port) (FW)
    Dutch Italic 10pt (ASCII) (Port) (FW)
    Dutch Roman 10pt (ASCII) (Port) (FW)
    Dutch Roman 12pt (ASCII) (Port) (FW)
  * Dutch Roman 15pt (ASCII) (Port) (FW)
    Line Draw 10 pitch
    Line Printer 16.66 pitch (PC-8)
    Line Printer 16.66 pitch (Roman-8/ECMA)
    Solid Line Draw 10 pitch
    Swiss Bold 12pt (ASCII) (Port) (FW)
    Swiss Bold 15pt (ASCII) (Port) (FW)

1 Select; N Name search: 1
```

Fig. 9.30.

WordPerfect base font screen.

Even if fonts can be selected on the Base Font screen, they still may not appear when a document is printed because all the fonts marked with a + in figure 9.29 have to be downloaded. You can download a font by using an AUTOEXEC.BAT file or the Initialize Printer option on the WordPerfect Print menu.

Editing Printer Definition Tables

Most word processors come with a separate program you use to edit printer definition files. To use this program, you have to exit the word processor and then enter the printer definition editing program. Early programs were simple. They asked, what is the printer command for bold? You opened the printer manual and entered the command for boldfacing. As printers grew more complex, so did the editing programs.

> HINT | If modifying a printer driver file, make a copy of the original one. Leave the name of the first printer driver file the same and modify the new name. This way, all previous documents continue to print as they have before.

> HINT | When modifying the printer driver file, make one change at a time (makes testing the change easier).

The organization of the printer definition table reflects the design philosophy of the actual program the table is supporting. When unannounced PC software version changes are made, what often changes is the printer definition file. Often the printer definition files change so much that the work you put into the older version cannot be transferred. Conversion utilities usually don't exist.

> HINT | WordPerfect 5.0 went through a number of unannounced version changes. If an updated version of WordPerfect 5.0 has been received, but new ALL files are not available, the old ALL files can be reformatted in the new format by entering the PTR program and selecting and saving the ALL file.

Printer definition tables are not meant to be user friendly. In fact, they are purposely designed to intimidate and frustrate all but the most reclusive techies. Most companies do not bother documenting them. WordPerfect sells a separate book that attempts to describe what is going on in its printer definition files.

> HINT | If a clone printer can download more fonts and put more fonts on a page than an HP LaserJet that it is emulating, you probably have to modify the printer definition file to exercise this feature of the printer (see Appendix A).

1-2-3 Printing

1-2-3 is rapidly undergoing changes. Add-on utilities abound that make spreadsheets more attractive and easier to print. Releases 3 and 2.2 are out, and OS/2 versions are coming. But, so far, the printer and font support still appears cumbersome. What is covered here is just the plain, simple, standard 1-2-3 Version 2.01 that is so popular. The most important contribution to printer usage was 1-2-3's popularization of printer setup strings.

This section covers 1-2-3 installation and typical printing problems. The discussion assumes that you can navigate through the 1-2-3 menus. The goal is to cover the most common problems—but not all of them. *Using 1-2-3 Special Edition* contains a much more thorough description of 1-2-3 printing.

Installing the Printer

1-2-3 was developed back in 1982 when the world consisted of character-mode printers and some graphics-mode printers. All these printers had fixed fonts. 1-2-3 has not changed much since those early days, and neither has 1-2-3's printer driver. Support of proportional fonts and PostScript printers is nonexistent. You should not try to install 1-2-3 to print to a PostScript printer.

1-2-3 printer installation is very simple. Run the INSTALL program and select First Time install. Answer the questions, and eventually you are asked which text printer you want (see fig. 9.31). Choose four possible printers that you may ultimately want to use.

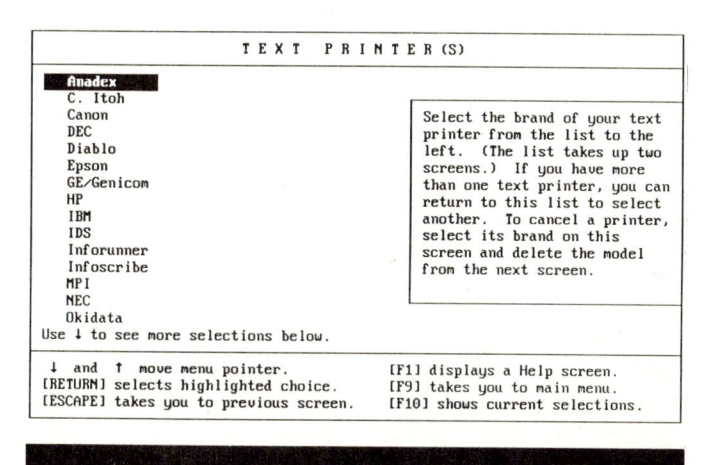

Fig. 9.31.

1-2-3 text printer installation.

If your printer is not on the lists, guess which one listed is most similar to yours or call your dealer and ask whether any more INSTALL.LBR files may have your printer defined.

The installation process creates a PR.DRV file that contains a description of your printer's character set, resolution, and some commands to place your printer into graphics mode. When this process is completed, use /Worksheet Global Default Printer Name to select a default printer. The port that the printer is hooked to can be defined with the /Worksheet Global Default Printer Interface command. Similarly, you need to configure the PrintGraph Utility (see fig. 9.32).

```
Copyright 1986 Lotus Development Corp.  All Rights Reserved. Release 2.01  MENU
Set type of graphics printer
Graphs-Directory  Fonts-Directory  Interface  Printer  Size-Paper  Quit

GRAPH       IMAGE OPTIONS                        HARDWARE SETUP
  IMAGES      Size              Range Colors       Graphs Directory:
  SELECTED    Top        .395   X Black              A:\
              Left       .750   A Black            Fonts Directory:
              Width     6.500   B Black              A:\
              Height    4.691   C Black            Interface:
              Rotate     .000   D Black              Parallel 1
                                E Black            Printer Type:
              Font              F Black              HP LaserJet+/lo
               1  BLOCK1                           Paper Size
               2  BLOCK1                             Width      8.500
                                                    Length     11.000

                                                  ACTION OPTIONS
                                                    Pause: No    Eject: No

                                                                    NUM
```

Fig. 9.32.

1-2-3 graphic printer installation.

Using Setup Strings

A setup string is a powerful concept that revolutionized spreadsheet printing when 1-2-3 was released. 1-2-3's early competition was Visicalc. But Visicalc had to be told to print the next document in a compressed font—each time the document was printed. Visicalc actually reset the printer each time a document was printed, wiping out the previous compressed printing setting.

1-2-3 improved on this process by enabling users to send a sequence of printer commands at the beginning of each page. Default printer setup strings can be defined through the /Worksheet Global Default Printer Options Setup Strings path. Setup Strings attached to a document when it is saved are entered with /Print Printer Options Setup String (see fig. 9.33).

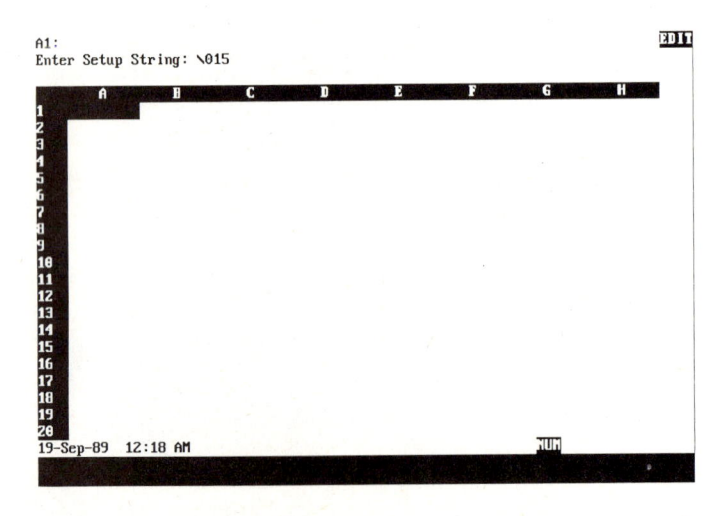

```
A1:                                                              EDIT
Enter Setup String: \015
      A       B       C       D       E       F       G       H
 1
 2
 3
 4
 5
 6
 7
 8
 9
10
11
12
13
14
15
16
17
18
19
20
19-Sep-89  12:18 AM                                              NUM
```

Fig. 9.33.

1-2-3 setup string.

In both of these setup strings, you can enter decimal values of printer commands or ASCII text. For example, if the letter A needs to be sent to the printer, press A. If an ESC needs to be sent, enter its decimal equivalent as follows: /027. Enter decimal values by preceding them with a slash and then a three-digit number from 000 to 255. This same format for entering printer codes has been copied by a number of programs.

Setup string usage has largely been replaced by the front panel of printers. Because most printers allow all their fonts to be selected from the front panel, the need to learn the printer codes is not necessary anymore. In some cases, the printer codes to send the printer into compressed print are so long that you should always try to use the front panel.

> HINT | The last setup string used influences the next document printed. Practice using /Print Printer Clear All.

Solving Common Problems

1-2-3 has some frustrating problems. The problems of character sets are discussed in Chapter 3. A weird problem is that the | in the left most cell of a row does not print that row. But, most problems can be summarized into the categories of page creep, large spreadsheets, alignment, and PrintGraph problems.

Page Creep

Page creep has two variations: the pages are too short, and text creeps closer and closer to the top of the page; or the pages are too long and text creeps closer and closer to the bottom of the page. Many solutions exist, but none are easy or elegant.

First, diagnose the problem. Turn page formatting off (/Print Printer Options Other Unformatted) and turn the printer off and on. Create a spreadsheet that is at least three pages long, with no blank lines. Number each row with the /Data Fill command. Now, print the page. Look carefully at the printout. Were all the rows printed? Were some blank rows added by the printer? Carefully note which lines were added by the printer. Then, turn page formatting back on and print the same document again.

Hold the formatted pages under good light and look for page creep. If the creep looks to be exactly the height of a row, the problem is a software problem. If the creep is very tiny, the problem is a mechanical one with the printer. The mechanical problem is usually solved by adjusting the paper feeding mechanism. If the problem is software, follow these instructions.

Lotus adds blank rows for three different reasons:

- ❏ 1-2-3 adds a top and bottom margin of three rows. These margins cannot be adjusted if page formatting is turned on.
- ❏ The top and bottom margins in the menus add to these original margins.
- ❏ The top and bottom margins also can be increased using borders of blank rows.

Together, all these margins have to be subtracted from the number of rows that can fit on a page.

First, compute the number of rows that can fit on a page. Start with the number of rows printed on the unformatted printout. For example, most 11-inch-long pages are printed at 6 lines per inch. The page can have 66 lines printed on it. But, suppose that the printer is an HP LaserJet that cannot print anything on the top three and the bottom three rows. The number of printable lines is reduced to 60. The correct number should be entered with the /WorkSheet Global Default Printer Pg-Length command.

Ideally, these steps cure page creep on new spreadsheets. Because old spreadsheets have the wrong page length attached to them, you need to change each to the new value.

Large Spreadsheets

1-2-3 really falls apart when trying to print large spreadsheets. If the spreadsheet is going to require many pages, you must specify the page ranges each time the spreadsheet is printed or write a macro. These solutions are detailed in Que's *Using 1-2-3 Special Edition*.

In 1-2-3, if the print range width is larger than the right margin, the program prints the first vertical half of the print range first and the second vertical half next. You can paste the two halves together if needed.

Extra Blank Rows

Mysterious extra blank rows can come from two sources: the printer or 1-2-3. The printer adds blank rows to skip over the perforation or the unprintable regions. Unfortunately, dot-matrix printers may lose track of where the perforation is, and the blank rows appear in the middle of the page. This problem is solved by turning the printer off, adjusting the perforation so that the line is just above the print head, and then turning the printer back on again.

1-2-3 loses track of where the bottom of a page is even if the document is printing on a laser printer. This practice is almost unheard of with more modern spreadsheet software. 1-2-3 adds its margins just about anywhere on a page. To prevent random-looking margins, make a habit of pressing Align before printing a new page. Align tells 1-2-3 that the print head is at the top of the page. Lasers are at the top of the page when the light indicating whether a partial page's data has been received is out.

Compressed Print

A compressed font needs to be selected in the printer. Selecting a font is most easily done by using the front panel of modern printers. Older printers may require sending a setup string. Most printers go into compressed print if a /015 is entered as the setup string. Only the printers that require a long, complicated setup string are going to be hard to get into compressed print mode. All the old HP LaserJets (prior to HP LaserJet series II) require a long escape code string to get into compressed print:

Regular compressed print
   Page-Length = 60
   Right Margin = 132
   Setup = \027E\027(s16.66H

Landscape, compressed print (requires font cartridge if not series II)
   Page-Length = 45
   Right Margin = 176
   Setup = \027E\027&l1O\027(s16.66H

A common problem with compressed print is that the document prints in a compressed font, but the right margin is not reset. If compressed print is to be used often, enter the preceding information with the /WorkSheet Global Default Printer command so that all new spreadsheets have this information attached to them.

PrintGraph Problems

1-2-3 has notorious problems printing graphs. What is seen on-screen is rarely what is printed. The scaling changes and the labels move or disappear. If the PrintGraph utility produces graphs that you can live with, fine. If it doesn't, give up. The cure to PrintGraph printing problems is to purchase another package. Almost all can edit Lotus PrintGraph PIC files.

DOS Printing

Printing from the DOS command prompt is usually not very desirable. Page formatting is impossible. Printing files usually does not work; therefore, most of the printing involves recording the command line conversation or printing a previously formatted document. This section explores these options. The examples assume that the printer is attached to LPT1. Instead of LPT1, LPT2, or COM1, any other parallel or serial port can be substituted.

Initializing the Port

Serial ports need to be initialized. Port initialization is done with the DOS MODE command in a way identical to that of OS/2. See the section on OS/2 for more information on what the following means:

    MODE COM1:9600,N,8,1
    MODE LPT1:=COM1:

This is explained more thoroughly in Chapter 14.

Using Typewriter Mode

DOS has a typewriter mode. Although very clumsy, this mode enables you to type one entire 80-character line before sending the information to the printer. From the DOS point of view, this feature should be called copying a file from the keyboard to the printer. Start off by typing *COPY* from the keyboard (DOS name of a keyboard is CON, for CONSOLE) to LPT1 or the printer. End by pressing Ctrl-Z or F6 and then pressing Enter to indicate that the file from the keyboard has ended. The following example prints the message This is a test. on the printer:

    COPY CON: LPT1:
    This is a test.
    ^Z

Printing a Directory

Printed directories or lists of files are nice to store in floppy jackets. Floppies are always piling up around desks and hours are spent sorting them. If the floppy disks have pieces of paper in them listing their files, they are much easier to sort. You can print directories easily by *piping*: sending the output of a program (in this case DIR) to a printer instead of the screen. The piping symbol ">" can be used to send the output of any program to printers or files.

    C:\>DIR > LPT1:

Printing a File

You can print files only if they contain a simple printer's instructions. Checking a file to see whether it can be printed is simple. Use the TYPE command to display the file on-screen. Look at the screen and search for any strange looking characters. If the document looks correct on-screen, it prints correctly. Any strange characters (other than the sex symbols) mean that the document prints using the DOS COPY command:

```
TYPE file.TXT
COPY file.TXT LPT1:
```

Recording DOS Conversation

When you type at the C:› prompt, you are conversing with DOS. Sometimes you may want to record the conversations. You can do this by pressing Ctrl-P or Ctrl-PrtSc. When you want to stop recording DOS conversations, press Ctrl-P again.

Spooling a File

The DOS PRINT command is supposed to spool files that also can be copied to the printer. The PRINT command was designed for large documents that take a long time to print. Most documents printed from DOS are short; therefore, the utility of this program is limited.

Using Shift-PrtSc To Print Graphics

If you press Shift-PrtSc and don't like what you see on-screen, exit the program, return to the DOS subdirectory, type GRAPHICS, return to the program, and press Shift-PrtSc again to solve the problem. The trouble is that the Graphics command only works with some videoboards. Color graphics adapters always work.

> HINT | Never purchase a software package that prints only using the PrintScreen command. This works with only an old videoboard that most people don't buy anymore.

OS/2 Printing

OS/2 eventually will replace PC DOS. Although announced in 1985 and first released on April 2, 1987, OS/2 is not yet popular. OS/2 initially was buggy and complex. The latest versions have a Macintosh-like interface and offer much better hard disk performance.

OS/2 supports PC programs like the Macintosh operating system supports Mac application programs. This support makes installing printers under the OS/2 environment as easy as installing printers in the Macintosh environment. The first step is configuring the parallel or serial port; the second step is installing the printer driver and fonts. Currently, the most recent version of OS/2 can install only parallel and serial ports. OS/2 applications are still individually responsible for including their own printer drivers and fonts.

The part of OS/2 that eventually will support printer drivers and fonts is called Presentation Manager. This section therefore, is divided into two parts: printer port installation and Presentation Manager configuration. The final section describes how to configure OS/2 so that a DOS program (running on top of OS/2) can print to a serial printer.

Installing Printer Ports

Like PC DOS, OS/2 printer port installation is easy if the printer uses a parallel port. If the printer is going to be attached serially, the process becomes messy. You complete three major steps to printer port installation under OS/2: port definition, port initialization, and spooler installation.

Port Definition

Ports under OS/2 have the same names as ports under DOS: LPT1, COM1, and so on. The default printer port is LPT1. The serial or COM ports operate differently. Under DOS, a serial port can have anything attached to it. The individual program was responsible for figuring out what was attached and communicating with the device properly. Because only one program tried to use the device at a time, DOS did not need to get involved managing the serial port. A serial port, therefore, can have a mouse, a modem, and a printer attached simultaneously through an ABC switch box. When a program needed the mouse, you could activate the mouse by pointing the switch to A. When another program needed the modem, you could activate the modem by pointing the switch to B. When a third program wanted to talk to a serial printer, you could point the switch to C.

OS/2 enables multiple programs to run simultaneously. Obviously, the mouse, modem, and serial printer programs cannot simultaneously try to access the same serial port. You would have no way of knowing when to move the ABC switch. To allow a serial printer to be shared by multiple programs, the multiple programs have to cooperate. OS/2 has to make sure that they cooperate, preventing mouse and modem software from accessing the serial port a printer is attached to. OS/2 has to know what device is attached to the serial port.

OS/2 is configured through a CONFIG.SYS file just like DOS. Some DOS CONFIG.SYS commands no longer apply, and many new CONFIG.SYS commands were added with OS/2. Among them is the capability to tell OS/2 which device is attached to the serial port.

The following are OS/2 CONFIG.SYS commands for a serial mouse attached to COM1:

    Device = Pointdd.sys
    Device = Mousa02.sys

The following is an OS/2 CONFIG.SYS command for a printer attached to COM1:

    Device = COM02.SYS

The COM02.SYS program is shipped with OS/2. The Pointdd.sys and Mousa02.sys are shipped with some versions of OS/2.

> **TROUBLE-SHOOTING TIP** OS/2 works only with a serial port built around a UART with the part number 16540 stamped on it. Look at the circuit board containing the serial port. One big rectangular CPU size chip has the number 8250 or 16540 stamped on it.

Port Initialization

IBM serial ports always have been flexible and complex. They also have to be told how to communicate with the serial device attached. The serial port does not know how to communicate with a serial printer. Like DOS, OS/2 serial ports are initialized with the MODE command. Unlike DOS, OS/2 does support primitive handshaking with serial printers. If a serial printer is sent data faster than it can print the data, a DOS serial printer starts losing characters. OS/2 can be configured to slow down at the serial printer's request.

Like DOS, parallel printers can be configured using the mode commands in the following format:

MODE LPTx: right margin, lines per inch, retry

x = the parallel printer port number
right margin = the number of characters per line
retry = P stands for continuous retry

Here is one example of a mode command:

MODE LPT1: 132, 8, P

Like DOS, serial printers have to be told the data transfer rate and a few other parameters. In addition, OS/2 can be told to continuously monitor the serial port in case the printer requests that transmission be temporarily halted. Chapter 13 is dedicated to the technical details of this process because DOS fails to listen to printers and PC applications may or may not. OS/2 promises to drastically reduce the problems of printers losing characters because the computer is transmitting them too fast.

MODE COMx:baud,parity,databits,stopbits,TO=?,XON=?,IDSR=?,DTR=?, RTS=?

Baud	110, 150, 300, 600, 120, 2400, 4800, 9600, 19200 bits per second
Parity	Odd, Even, None, Mark, Space
Databits	5, 6, 7 or 8
Stopbits	1, 1.5, or 2
TO=	ON or OFF (timeout)
XON=	ON or OFF (Xon, Xoff handshaking originating, does not force OS/2 to listen to printer's Xoff, sends Xoff itself)
IDSR=	ON or OFF (On means send data only if Data Set Ready [pin 6] is pulled high by the printer)
DTR=	ON, OFF, or HS (Data Terminal Ready: Force High, Force Low, or drop low if receiver buffer overflows, only applies when PostScript printers are transmitting data to the PC)
RTS=	ON, OFF, TOG, HS (Request To Send, Force High, Force Low, Toggle, or wait for CLS to come back before transmitting, a method of asking the printer for permission to transmit)

The following is an example:

MODE COM1:9600,N,8,1.TO=ON,XON=ON,ISDR=ON,DTR=ON,RTS=HS

Despite all the new features of the MODE command, it is disappointing that the simplest method of all, Xoff/Xon is not supported. The XON=ON command does not force OS/2 to *listen* for Xoff/Xon to be sent by the printer, but rather activates OS/2's capability to *send* Xoff/Xon to the printer. The only possible reason OS/2 may need to send Xoff to the printer is that the operating system cannot process data the printer is sending fast enough. Currently, printers do not send anything to the computer. This feature, therefore, is useless. Someday, printers will send screen fonts to OS/2. Then, the current Xon/Xoff feature may be used.

The MODE command is normally part of the OS/2 equivalent of DOS's AUTOEXEC.BAT called STARTUP.CMD. OS/2 calls these files command files rather than batch files. OS/2 has two different command files. The STARTUP command file is executed whenever an OS/2 computer is turned on. Because multiple programs can be executed at the same time in OS/2, another command file is executed whenever a new program is started up. The second command file is called OS2INIT.CMD. Do not put the MODE command in this file.

Spooler Initialization

OS/2's spooler sends all printing requests to a disk file. After the application has completed transmitting the document to OS/2's spooler, the document is printed. OS/2's spooler is not a printer queue. The spooler cannot rearrange priorities, assign the output to a different printer, temporarily stop printing, or permanently kill a print job. OS/2's spooler is needed whenever two application programs are trying to print on the same printer at the same time. OS/2's spooler makes sure that the applications take turns, in the following format:

Spool spooldrive:\spooldir /d:input-virtual-device /O:output-real-device

Here is an example:

```
Spool C:\printext /d:LPT1: /o:COM1:
```

The example command would create its temporary spool files on drive C, in the Printext subdirectory. The operating system would listen to programs sending pages to the parallel port (LPT1:) and redirect the pages to the serial port (COM1:). When a OS/2 program has finished printing the last page, the program should send OS/2 an explicit "spool-release" command. OS/2 programs printing simultaneously are given a file in the C:\printext directory. When receiving the explicit "spool-release" command, the file is closed down and queued for printing.

Unfortunately, DOS programs running under OS/2 do not send the explicit "spool-release" command. When you are finished printing using a DOS program, therefore, you have to tell OS/2 that printing is completed by pressing Ctrl-Alt-PrtSc.

You can install OS/2's spooler four different ways. The first is in the OS/2 equivalent of DOS's AUTOEXEC.BAT called STARTUP.CMD. Enter this command:

```
Spool C:\printext /d:LPT1: /o:COM1:
```

You also can place the spooler command in OS/2's CONFIG.SYS file using the RUN command:

```
RUN = Spool.exe C:\printext /d:lpt1: /o:com1:
```

The default OS/2 prompt is [C:\]. At one of these prompts, you can type the spool command:

```
Spool C:\printext /d:LPT1: /o:COM1:
```

The problem with this method is that the spool program now consumes one of the 12 "screen groups". Under OS/2, the concept of a traditional program has been split into four parts: code, threads, processes, and screen groups. Screen groups are similar to a program. Typically, 12 screen groups or programs can be executed simultaneously. Each screen group contains a prompt. Because the spool program does not display anything on-screen, the program does not need to use up one of the 12 screen groups. OS/2 starts off with 16 screen groups and assigns 4 for special functions. One of the special functions is called the Detached screen group. This screen group does not have a prompt and never displays anything on the screen. Multiple programs that do not display anything on the screen (for example a database sort or duplicate check) can be executed at the same time in this screen group. To send a spooler into the special Detached screen group, use the DETACH command:

```
DETACH Spool C:\printext /d:LPT1: /o:COM1:
```

The OS/2 spooler program is not rich in features. The program probably was included in the OS/2 package as an example of a detached program for users and a blueprint for how to write a detached program for programmers. Someone will write a much better printer spooler someday.

Installing Printer Drivers (Presentation Manager)

Presentation Manager was not included in the original versions of OS/2. Early versions of OS/2 were completely command driven like current DOS versions. Windows with menus pulled down by mice were not available. Presentation Manager was added to provide a Macintosh-like interface to OS/2, but the combination is a closer cousin of Microsoft Windows. Currently, Presentation Manager does not support any printers or fonts and is primarily used to replace the command line prompt. One goal of Presentation Manager is to provide a virtual printer interface for application programmers and a device driver interface for printer manufacturers. Printers will come with OS/2 drivers, just like printers for the Mac have to be shipped with software.

Presentation Manager's other goal is to provide font resources to programs. Ideally, font vendors could provide fonts independent of printers and screens, users could purchase different character sets without limitations, and the font file format would be public domain, to encourage font vendors to support the format with no worries about royalties to Microsoft or Apple. Reality will probably mean none of the above. Microsoft is promising to give other vendors the right to create their own font formats, their own encryption scheme, and their own character and object font support and character set limitations.

Two font environments probably will not be capable of complementing each other under OS/2. At the time of this writing, Microsoft has traded PostScript clone printer software for the right to incorporate Apple's Royal fonts into OS/2. For more information on that, see the Macintosh section earlier in this chapter.

DOS Emulation Printing

DOS programs can be executed in a special OS/2 screen group. DOS programs that normally print directly to the serial port will not work. OS/2 defaults to preventing DOS printing on serial printers because a DOS program may mess up an OS/2 program, confuse the serial port, or mix documents on pages coming out of the printer.

If only the DOS program is going to be printing to the serial printer, then DOS programs can be given permission to print on an OS/2 serial printer. The following example enables DOS programs to print on serial printers attached to serial port COM1; type this command line at the OS/2 prompt of the special DOS screen group.

```
SetCom40 COM1=ON
```

The DOS EMULATION PRINT command operates differently under OS/2. Instead of spooling like the DOS PRINT command, the emulated DOS PRINT command merely sends data to OS/2's spooler. If the OS/2 spooler is not installed, the emulated DOS PRINT command does no spooling at all.

Chapter Summary

The details of installing printer drivers, definition tables, printer fonts, and screen fonts were examined in this chapter. Each software package splits up these features in different ways. The specifics of Windows applications like PageMaker, GEM applications like Ventura, a word processor, and a spreadsheet were reviewed. Similar processes in the Macintosh world were discussed also. Database programs like dBASE actually program the printer directly; see Appendix B for more help with databases. Finally, the printer support of DOS and OS/2 was reviewed.

In the Next Chapter

Chapter 10 introduces printing in the desktop publishing world. Laser printers are starting to do some of the tasks that normally could only be done by typesetters. What PC printers are good at and what they will never be good at also are discussed.

III

The Publishing Challenge

Includes

Typesetting
PostScript Printers

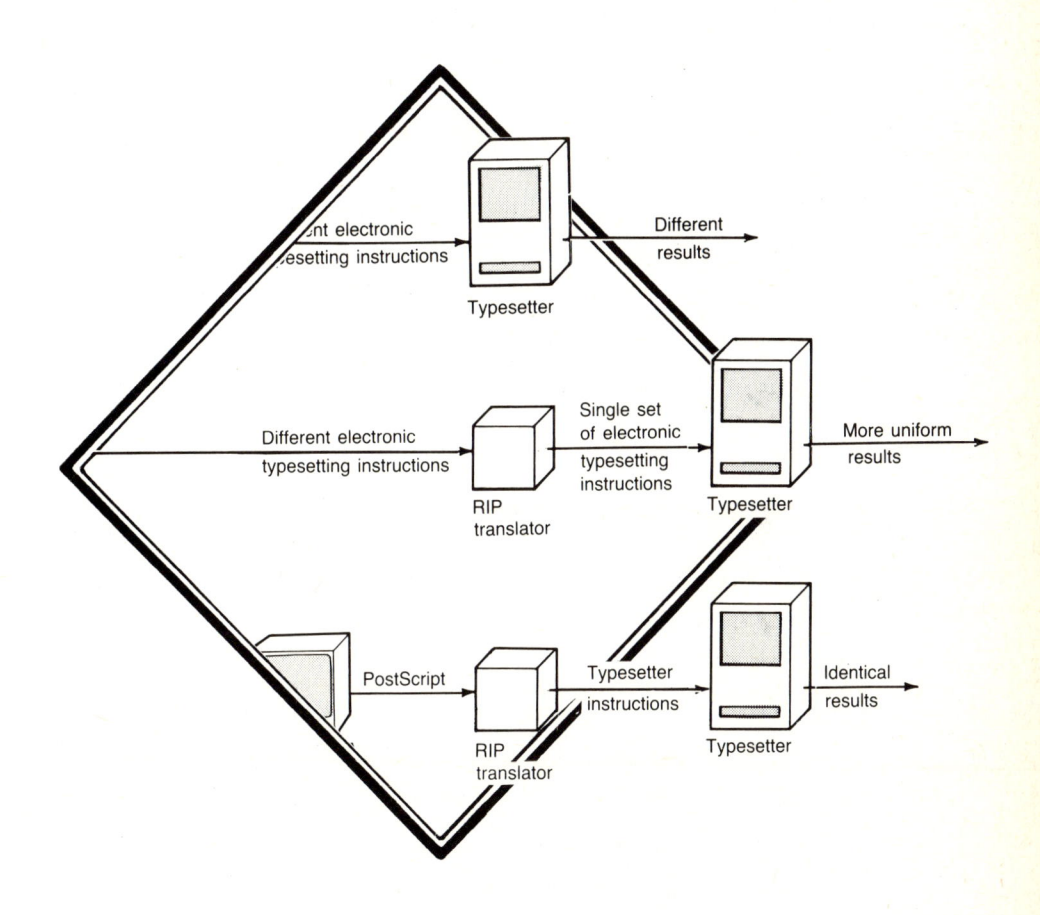

Different electronic
typesetting instructions → Typesetter → Different results

Different electronic
typesetting instructions → RIP translator → Single set of electronic typesetting instructions → Typesetter → More uniform results

PostScript → RIP translator → Typesetter instructions → Typesetter → Identical results

10

Typesetting

Typesetting involves the production of documents that attract attention, improve communication, and give format and structure to a document. PCs are great for printing company memos, mimeographs, and stencils. This chapter is about producing documents that impress.

Those in the PC world usually refer to the entire process of producing a book or magazine as *typesetting*. The term *typography* is probably more accurate, but I use the word *typesetting* to refer to the current process of producing books, magazines, brochures, and newspapers. *Desktop publishing* refers to producing documents from PC printers that look as good as typeset documents.

This chapter is organized into three parts. The first part describes how PCs are used in the typesetting world. It is important to separate how PCs are used in the typesetting world from how they are used for desktop publishing.

The second part of this chapter describes how PCs are used in desktop publishing, answering these questions: If just PCs and PC printers are used, is typeset quality possible? What are the prospects; what are the possibilities? What equipment do you need? Are the capabilities going to meet your needs?

The third part of this chapter describes how to combine desktop publishing and typesetting to build better-looking documents quicker and for less money.

Defining the Typesetting Process

Today, as in the past, there are two different methods of producing documents. The old method of using a typewriter, stencil, and mimeograph machine has been replaced by computers. The other method of producing documents is to send them to the publishing industry. Today, these two methods are beginning to merge and cooperate.

Even if you never use a typesetting service or print shop, the information in this chapter is important because desktop publishing faces the same problems and issues the typesetting industry has already mastered. If, for example, you are interested in scanning black and white photographs for desktop publishing purposes, read the section on gray scales.

If you are going to send your desktop published output to the typesetting industry, it is important to understand how the industry works, what its language is, and how to work with typesetters.

Creating Text

Authors put words on paper, sketch illustration ideas, and suggest photographs. Authors are the creative people behind a document. Editors receive the document and provide the accountability authors need to be motivated writers. Some editors examine content and manage the review process. Other editors check spelling and grammar. Still other editors read the book from a marketing point of view. A publisher is the company that finds the authors, hires the editors, prints the copies, and sells them.

Authors write on PCs using PC spelling checkers, thesauruses, grammar checkers, and so on. Authors occasionally try to influence which font is chosen and how the pages are laid out, but mostly authors concentrate on content. The files they create usually have no special underlining, boldface, or page formatting information.

Authors hand over their electronic files to editors. Editors know the different font names, document layout techniques, and so on that their publishing company uses. Editors add this type of information to the author's text while correcting spelling and grammar. Editors can add this information to the electronic file, print the file out and write the information in by hand, or use a page formatting language.

Page formatting languages are essentially word processors that have a built-in standard page formatting language that can be translated into other formatting languages that typesetting equipment understands. These page formatting languages are difficult to learn. They require much time, experience, and practice, and they are expensive.

The exciting news is that page formatting languages are evolving in a different form in the desktop publishing world. One of the most popular features of WordPerfect is that it hides the page formatting commands. But if you want to see them, WordPerfect has a mode to reveal them. You can then delete or add formatting commands. Unfortunately, you cannot edit WordPerfect's page formatting instructions themselves. WordPerfect's Reveal codes are a primitive version of the page formatting languages that editors use.

Most page-formatting software now is available in PC form. The package many consider the best is called Magnatype, with a list price starting at $7,500. Most competitor's prices are in the $2,000 to $4,000 range. Today, the page formatting languages are being challenged by PC desktop software that is WYSIWYG—what you see is what you get. But command-driven typesetting programs will always have a place in society.

Page-formatting languages have all the features of a PC word processor. Most WYSIWYG desktop publishing software is designed to make a document more attractive, not to edit. Methods of jumping from word to word, sentence to sentence, paragraph to paragraph, or screen to screen are usually not as quick in a desktop publishing software package.

Desktop publishing software may come with a 2M file describing where words can be hyphenated, but not with a spelling checker. Desktop publishing software comes with a large amount of kerning information, but not a thesaurus. Page formatting languages can do search and replaces that involve "if clauses" like a programming language. A page formatting language will usually have the best of both worlds: a thesaurus, spelling checker, and hyphenation file, as well as large kerning tables.

WYSIWYG desktop publishing software creates files using a page-formatting language. In fact, Ventura (a popular desktop publishing package) leaves page-formatting instructions that can be seen and edited using the word processor in which the document was originally created. In figure 10.1, note the commands enclosed in angle brackets at the beginning of a line. Ventura can be thought of as a graphical front end to the page formatting language. Instead of using a mouse, you can create the Ventura documents using a word processor to type Ventura page formatting commands. Then, you can view the document on-screen with Ventura, make last minute changes, and print through Ventura.

Besides entering Ventura page formatting instructions from within a word processor, you can create a database reporting program that produces Ventura page-formatting instructions. You could print a typeset catalog of the database information using Ventura.

Fig. 10.1.

Ventura page-formatting commands in a document.

```
@CHAPTER HEAD = USER INTERFACE<><$IUser interface><>

@MAJOR HEADING = <><$&WYSIWYG[u]><>WYSIWYG

<><$IProblem;Can't print what's on screen><><><$IWYSIWYG;Defined><>Ventura
Publisher is designed to provide What You See (on the screen) Is What
You Get printed (WYSIWYG).  This means that the computer display should
match as closely as possible, at all times, what you will see on the
final printed page.  ....  Several thin ruling lines, with
little space between, may show on the screen as one thick line.

@MINOR HEADING = Keyboard Keys

Various keys on the keyboard perform special functions:

@BULLET = The keyboard Cursor <><$ICursor keys><><><$IText editing;Cursor
keys><>keys control the Text Cursor (The text cursor is displayed
as a thin vertical line.)

@BULLET = The Home <><$IHome key><><><$IText editing;Home key><>key
goes to the first page of the document.

@BULLET = The End <><$IEnd key><><><$IText editing;End key><>key goes
to the last page of the document.
C:\TYPESET\MANUAL.TXT                         Doc 1 Pg 1 Ln 1i Pos 3.09i
```

Page formatting languages allow greater precision than mouse-driven drawing packages. Suppose that you want to draw a vertical line every inch. With a page formatting language, this can be done with one command. With DTP software, you would have to use the mouse to click the one-inch boundaries, and you would be responsible for the spacing. In the page formatting language, the spacing will be more precise because it is explicitly defined. Page formatting languages make it easier to specify conditional page breaks and to keep tagged paragraphs and figures together. You can type explicit instructions describing what needs to be done. You can create forms and tables with a few commands. The drawback is that you have to learn the commands.

Creating Drawings

Artists are employed by publishers to draw figures, diagrams, and illustrations. Many times, artists use the same drawings over and over again. Often times artists purchase illustrations from an outside source. These illustrations are called *clip art*. Clip art has become so prevalent that many artists no longer spend much time drawing original art. Instead, the artists cut and paste different clip art drawings together, sizing and arranging them in unique ways.

Electronic clip art has many advantages over traditional clip art. First, electronic clip art never gets old or dirty, and it can be used over and over again. Cutting and pasting is never messy and is much more accurate. Special effects such as shadows, fill patterns, and distortions are possible. Although a good artist can draw a human hand quickly, consider what is possible with an electronic human hand. Fingers could be moved, or the hand enlarged and duplicated. The right hand could be copied from the left so that the two are exactly the same.

See the "Creating and Adding Drawings" section later in this chapter for a complete discussion of how clip art is used, created, stored, modified, and imported.

Adding Color

Incredible special effects are possible with photography. But the publishing process that photographs must go through rarely makes a picture look better.

The first step in processing color film in the typesetting world is called separation. If the finished output is to be black and white, separation is not necessary. However, printing in color is a complicated, messy process. To understand it, you need to learn something about color fundamentals.

Color Fundamentals

Color printing is complicated. Back in grade school, you may have used red, yellow, and blue pieces of plastic to make different colors of light. You may have mixed different paint colors together. You learned that from three primary colors, you could create any other colors.

The color printing process uses the primary colors cyan, magenta, and yellow (CMY). When you mix these colors, they create black. Unfortunately, the black created is not a perfect black. Thus, most color printing requires a fourth color—black (CMYK). Together, these four colors can be combined in a color printing process to create any possible color. This is how color photographs are printed. Four-color printing is often called CMYK.

Four-Color or CMYK Color Printing

Four-color printing or CMYK printing does not mean that the document is limited to four colors. All colors are possible because the four can be mixed during the printing process. Mixing the four colors requires that a document be printed four different times, once with each color.

If a document is printed four different times, this means that the inks mix together on the paper. Different temperatures, humidities, paper chemistry, and a host of other things influence how the ink mixes. Four-color printing is difficult and does not always guarantee perfect color.

Quite often, a specific color needs to be consistent throughout the magazine. If the magazine name is in red letters on the front of each issue, for example, the publisher may require that the red be exactly the same on each issue. This is hard to guarantee with CMYK printing. Instead, a specially colored ink is created before the printing process.

One-, Two-, Three-, and Five-Color Printing

A one-color document contains one color of ink. Two-color printing involves the mixing of CMY colors before printing to form a special color of ink. The process is similar to the process of adding color to cans of paint at the hardware store and then shaking the can. Two-color printing usually means printing black and one other premixed color.

In the typesetting industry, the Pantone company has developed a system of mixing colors of ink so that the color is guaranteed to be the same each time. The specially colored ink is called *spot color* or *flat color*. The Pantone company produces ink swatch books that show a range of color hues on both coated and uncoated paper. Pantone colors are expensive because the ink has to be mixed before the printing process. The Pantone color-matching system has become so popular that it is the color standard for the printing industry.

The disadvantage of Pantone colors is that the correct amounts of CMY ink have to be mixed before the printing process, which increases the setup time, which increases the cost of the project. Because of the cost, Pantone colors usually are used only in small-run publications like limited-run brochures that use only a few colors or use the Pantone color on the front cover only.

Because they are the industry standard, the Pantone color numbers can be used for color specification. Choose a Pantone color and tell your printing company to approximate that color as closely as possible with the four-color CMYK process. If you have purchased a PostScript color printer, you can tell your desktop publishing software which Pantone color to use and the software will instruct the printer to mix the CMYK colors as accurately as possible to generate that Pantone color.

If black and two Pantone colors are used during the printing process, it is called three-color printing. (CMY printing is sometimes called three-color printing, but is rarely used. Without the fourth black color, the original cannot adequately be re-created. The image often appears flat and lifeless. To correct this, black is added to provide the needed grays, shadows, and contrast.)

If CMYK and one Pantone color are specified, the page is printed in a 5-color process. Five-color printing can print color photographs, black, and one Pantone color.

Separation

The first step in printing a color photograph or image is to produce *separations*. To do this, a printing or separation company uses high-resolution equipment from companies like Scitex, Hell, and Corsfield to scan slides or film through filters that break the slide's colors into the four CMYK components. The photograph is shot through a screen that breaks up the image into hundreds of dots, creating a *halftone image*. The color original is turned into four single-color halftone images (one for each of the CMY colors plus black). The result of the separation process is called film or *film master*.

Next, the printing or separation company will send you a proof of the photograph as it will appear when printed. The most popular color printout is called a *Cromalin proof*. Cromalin is a special process developed by DuPont that uses the four film masters to create a single-color photo rapidly. The process is not cheap. Cromalin proofs cost about $50 each. 3M has a similar system called Matchprint. 3M also has a cheaper system that involves colored acetate sheets that are placed on top of each other, called a *color key*.

To produce the separations, the scanning process can be either a photographic process or a digital process. Digital slide-based PC scanners are available for about $10,000. The resulting quality is sufficient for many color applications. The PC is used as a tool for generating and storing the results of the scanner's data. The quality of PC separation will never match that of special photographic equipment costing over $300,000, but PCs are worth considering for many applications, such as newsletters, newspapers, brochures, single-color publications, and so on. Glossy, good-looking color photographs need to be done by specialists.

Color Adjustment

Different manufacturer's scanners are more sensitive to different colors. When the CMYK printing is done, adjusting the color is a constant battle. When separation companies feel that their equipment is adjusted properly, they separate the colors.

Most of the computer-based color adjustment systems require high-resolution videoboards and monitors. Specialized hardware and software are available for PCs to do the color adjustment. Very high-resolution color monitors are necessary, and the monitor's colors have to be absolutely perfect. Perfect color is practically impossible to maintain because different lighting conditions and temperature variations can affect the monitor's color. Some of the fanciest systems have a device that attaches to the glass of the monitor and cable that feeds back color information into a circuit board in the Macintosh. Software in the Mac then automatically adjusts the colors until the monitored color is perfect. Radius Precision Color Calibrator, from Radius Inc., is an automatic color adjustment system like those on a TV set, except that this adjustment looks at light coming out of the monitor. Color monitors without this device have to be adjusted by hand. Of course, this equipment is useful only to those color adjustment specialists that are interested in making sure that a photograph's colors look as realistic as possible.

After the screen has been calibrated and the scanned CMYK image data files are located, color needs to be adjusted. With color adjustment software, the range of highlight to shadow can be magnified or reduced, and the maximum and minimum shading allowed and individual CMY colors all can be adjusted.

Scanners typically wash out corners and sharp contrasts. The blacks necessary are not usually created properly through CMY combinations. Thus, most good color adjusting systems have a software process called *global unsharp masking* or just plain *sharping*. This involves making a decision on how much black is to be added and how the black is going to be distributed around the sharp contrasts in the scanned image. Then the color adjusting software searches for areas of high contrast and adds some black.

Typesetting

The typesetting procedure involves a machine called a typesetter. This is confusing, because the word *typesetter* could refer to a person, a company, a task, or a machine. To avoid this confusion, the word *phototypesetter* will be used to describe the machine throughout the rest of this book. Brand names of phototypesetters include Compugraphic, Linotype, and Varityper. These machines receive electronic text and perhaps some instructions, and they print on special photographic paper. The resolution is much higher than that of a standard PC printer.

Laying Out the Pages

The next step is to take the galley and measure how long each article is in inches. Then the galley is cut into columns and pasted onto paste-up boards. These boards are called *mechanicals*. The process of fitting the text, photographs, and advertisements on a page is called *layout*. Once the mechanicals are finished, they are photographed, resulting in a film of the page.

If the editor has been using a page formatting language, the phototypesetter output may be a complete page rather than strips of text—actual layout is not necessary. Phototypesetters can produce film ready for the next step, which is stripping.

Typesetting environments that support printing instructions contain a box called Raster Image Processor (RIP) that receives the data. The page-formatting program has to be able to speak a language that the RIP understands. One of the most common RIP languages today is PostScript. Hewlett-Packard is working with Compugraphic to develop a RIP capable of understanding HP Printer Control Language (HPCL). But unless HPCL undergoes major revisions and develops more PostScript features, do not expect much support in the typesetting world.

Stripping

Stripping is the process of combining film from the separation process with film from the layout process. Stripping combines the four halftone (CMYK) film masters with the black and white film master from the typesetting and layout process. First, all the black and white film masters of a page are gathered together. Then the cyan, magenta, and yellow film masters are sorted. Stripping is the process of creating one composite black and white film master and one composite cyan film master, and so on. With great precision, each film master color must be assembled with photographs and text in the exact spot. The four film masters must have all the colored objects in exactly the same place on the page so that the colors will combine properly during the printing process.

To print all four copies of the same page on top of each other, the film masters are marked with squares. Square brackets are placed on the photographs at the beginning of the separation process. These are called *crop marks* and *crosshairs*. The separation process places special symbols on the masters so that they can be aligned. This alignment is called *registration*.

If the precision is not exact, the color portions of the printed page can look terrible—colored shadows will appear, and the picture is said to be out of registration.

Trap is the term used to describe how successful the stripping of various film pieces was. If the background surrounding a photograph is supposed to be blue, blue ink cannot be deposited behind the photograph without disturbing the photograph; thus a white square for the photograph has to be cut out of the surrounding blue background. If the photograph does not exactly fit into the white square, an unwanted white border on two sides may appear. The other two edges will be dark from the mixture of the photograph, and the blue overlaps. This is called bad trapping. Good stripping involves overlapping the photograph and the blue background slightly everywhere. Black boarders around photos will reduce the impact of the planned overlap. Other names for trap are *shrink, spread, skinny, fatty, choke,* and *butt*.

Printing

The result of the stripping process are four sheets (if in color) of what is called *composite film* or *final film*. The composite film is used to make the printing plates. A phototypesetter also can produce final plastic film plates good for 50K impressions.

The printing plates are put in the printing machine; the printing machine is loaded with ink, and the pages are printed. Although PC printers can produce multiple copies of pages, they are much more expensive per page than copy machines, mimeograph machines, stencil machines, and other printing mechanisms.

When printing on a big printing press, ideally, ink should deposit on paper like jelly on peanut butter—the jelly does not spread out nor does the jelly mix with the peanut butter. When ink flows like syrup on top of a pancake, it mixes or absorbs unevenly. This causes the color to splotch. This is called bad ink trapping. Ink trapping problems indicate paper and ink chemistry problems.

Summarizing the Typesetting Process

Text is created by authors and editors who send electronic files to typesetters. The typesetters produce galleys that are pasted onto cardboard along with black and white photographs and artwork. The result is called a mechanical. Single-color Pantone drawings and the mechanicals are taken to a photographer who creates Pantone film masters and black and white film masters.

Color drawings and photographs follow a different path. They are sent to a separator who separates color documents into the primary CMYK film masters. The next step is to combine all the film masters into one set of masters in a process called stripping. The resulting combined film masters or composite masters then are turned into plates for the printing process (see fig. 10.2).

Fig. 10.2.

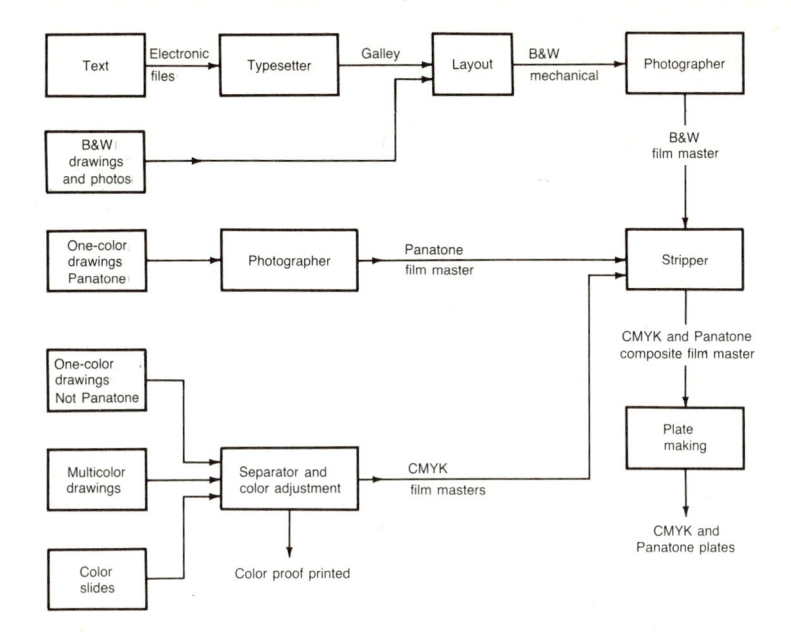

Traditional typesetting.

PCs and PC printers are used in many different ways. PCs are used by authors and editors to create the electronic files sent to the typesetter. Editors can use a PC-based page formatting language and PC printer to produce drafts. You can equip PCs with hardware and software to do low-quality color separation and adjustment. PC color laser printers are close to being able to provide reliable color proofs.

PCs cannot produce color documents with the quality you are used to seeing on book covers and in advertisements. The scanners and printers available cannot handle the job. Even printing of black and white photographs is difficult. The high-resolution text expected in books is impossible to achieve with PC printers. The next section explores what is possible with a PC-based system.

Desktop Publishing

Desktop publishing attempts to do everything outlined in figure 10.2. Desktop publishing software is challenging the traditional typesetting world. At its best, PC desktop publishing can reduce use of expensive typesetting equipment, speed up the time it takes to produce a document, and allow more flexibility.

At its worst, desktop publishing is as technically demanding as typesetting. The lingo, procedures, and problems do not change. To use top-of-the-line desktop publishing software, you must learn the same typesetting concepts. Desktop publishing also can increase development time, require the same specialized typesetting equipment, and produce ugly documents. The trick is to identify what desktop publishing is good at and what it is not good at.

Setting Up Your Desktop Publishing System

Desktop publishing software for the PC can be divided into three categories: low-end desktop publishing programs, high-end word processing programs, and high-end desktop publishing programs. This section explores the equipment needed and makes recommendations. To perform desktop publishing, the following are necessary:

Page Layout Software
Drawing Software
Electronic Clip Art Files
Scanners
Printer

The middle three items are optional if digital art is desired.

Using a Low-End Desktop Publishing Program

When you begin desktop publishing, you may want to make a small initial investment. The Macintosh comes with simple desktop publishing software, and public domain fonts and clip art are available from user groups and other sources. The PC starting point is less clear. You can use a word processor with desktop capabilities—Microsoft Word or WordPerfect, for example—or you can purchase a low-end desktop publishing software package. One of the more popular low-end packages, PFS: First Publisher, is easy to use, has many fonts, and is shipped with the largest clip art collection of any PC product.

All these packages are designed to work with dot-matrix printers. You can add PostScript printers, but the output does not look much better. A cheap low-end dot-matrix printer will produce an output that looks great. For the Mac world, purchase an ImageWriter.

For a drawing package, purchase a mouse—most mice come with a drawing package, usually either PC PaintBrush or Dr. Halo. Macs come with a simple drawing package called MacPaint. Also, you may want to add a scanner. Excellent hand-held scanners are available for under $200. The HS-3000 from Diamond Flower Electrical Instrument Company is a great model.

Low-end desktop publishing is not much different than a drawing package with word wrap. Low-end desktop publishing packages lack the capability to produce CMYK or Pantone separations, although they exercise the color printing capabilities of a dot-matrix printer. In summary, low-end desktop publishing packages are easy to use, work well with hand scanners, and come with much low-resolution clip art.

Using a High-End Word Processing Program

Word processors capable of mixing graphics and text are available in both the Mac and PC world. The top two word processing packages for the PC, WordPerfect and Word, also are available for the Mac. Certain features, like adjusting the spacing between individual letters, are difficult, but in terms of laying out pages quickly and uniformly, the word processors are very quick. They also include spelling checkers and thesauruses that most of the desktop publishing packages don't. Seeing a graphic representation or preview of what is going to be printed is possible, but is not as useful as true WYSIWYG.

If you have run into the limitations of the graphics packages supplied with the system (Mac) or the mouse (PC), you should purchase a new graphics package. GEM Draw is an excellent, low-end package, but creates graphics files that are hard to import into word processing programs. (See the section on Converted Images for more information.)

For better quality output, purchase one of the low-end laser printers available for under $1,000. Most of the word processors can produce good looking output on these printers. In the Mac world, the low-end lasers are going to be clones of the LaserWriter II SC. However, be careful when purchasing LaserWriter II SC clones. They should be upgradeable to full PostScript printers. Otherwise, purchase the Hewlett-Packard LaserJet IIp and purchase HP LaserJet driver software for it.

Using a High-End Desktop Publishing Program

If you need more capabilities than those offered by high-end word processors or low-end desktop systems, you should consider a high-end desktop publishing program. You can choose from two packages—PageMaker and Ventura Publisher. Depending on your needs, one package may be more appropriate than the other.

The layout software of choice for short brochures and documents is PageMaker from Aldus. PageMaker is easier to learn than Ventura Publisher. PageMaker is available in both PC and MAC versions. Because it is written in the Windows environment, you will want a high-end drawing package to go along with it like Micrografx Designer or CorelDraw. In the Mac world, Canvas is a good package. A large, high-resolution clip art library is an add-on that may be more cost effective than purchasing the drawing packages. Perhaps even purchasing a CD ROM and CD ROM versions of the clip art will be cost effective. Clip art can take up so much space that a CD ROM becomes a viable alternative. Again, a hand-held scanner is probably all that is needed.

Using fixed fonts is painful. The scaled fonts of a PostScript printer are absolutely necessary. Many of the new PostScript printers make these scalable fonts available in HP emulation mode.

If you write long books, split them into chapters, and manage many files, you should choose Ventura. Ventura also has other unique aspects. You can, for example, write a dBASE report that specifies font changes, graphic file names, and formatting information, which Ventura understands. The dBASE report could create a mail-order catalog automatically. Then you could use Ventura to check the page layout and print the catalog.

Ventura is harder to use than PageMaker and is built to work with a word processor. So if you purchase Ventura, buy a good word processor like WordPerfect or Word. Because Ventura was written in the GEM environment, you should purchase a drawing package like GEM's Artline written in the GEM environment. Although Ventura can convert other drawing types, it will operate faster if it doesn't have to translate from one graphic file type to another.

You may want to add a scanner capable of scanning large photographs. As with Aldus's PageMaker, a PostScript printer is the preferred output device.

Laying Out Your Pages

When you lay out a page, you decide where words and figures are going to appear on a page, decide which fonts to use, where the page numbers are going to be located, what the headers and footers are going to be, and how much you want to indent the chapter titles and subheadings.

Using Desktop Publishing Software for Page Layout

Packages like PageMaker and Ventura concentrate on performing the layout function. Their goal is to do the layout before sending anything to the phototypesetter or PostScript printer. Editors have been doing this for years using page formatting languages. Desktop publishing software seems like a step backward—it slows you down and offers fewer features and less flexibility. But desktop publishing saves much time if the documents required are simple or repetitive in nature.

The challenge of creating a layout is calculating where the page elements (articles, advertisements, drawings, photos, and so on) are going to go. Meanwhile, authors are submitting revised versions, editors are demanding that a particular advertisement be next to a certain article, and so on. The pressure to change things is constant. Desktop publishing allows you to rearrange text and graphics electronically. Instead of working with codes and trying to visualize what is going to be printed, you can see the changes on the screen. This not only makes the changes easier, but also allows you to do your job quicker with fewer mistakes and with better quality. Desktop publishing software is to the layout process what a word processor is to a typewriter.

During the process of planning the layout, you can use your printer to print rough drafts. In fact, some people feel that the printer layout drafts are good enough to bypass the typesetting step altogether. If a print quality of 300-600 dpi is sufficient, the printer's output can be used as the galley and be sent directly to a photographer. If the laser printer has printed the entire layout and no pasting or cutting of drawings or photos is required, the laser printout is called *camera ready* copy. The painful, time-consuming manual layout process can be skipped entirely (see fig. 10.3).

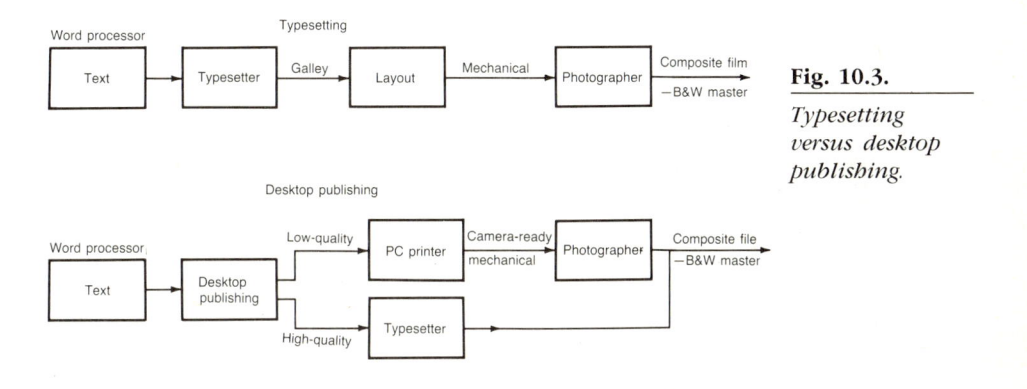

Fig. 10.3.

Typesetting versus desktop publishing.

If the output of the laser printer is not good enough, a phototypesetter must be used. But even then, you can bypass the layout process. Most phototypesetters can understand PostScript instructions, and many phototypesetters can produce finished film. If layout can be avoided, galleys can be avoided—thus there is no need for mechanicals.

Creating Galleys with a Laser Printer

Typesetting can be done with any PC software package. You send text to the typesetting machine and out comes the galley. Many small weekly newspapers are beginning to use PC typesetting because the 300 to 600 dpi output of a PC laser printer is adequate for their needs. A word processor that can support multiple proportionally spaced fonts and right margin justification on the PC laser printer may be adequate.

Galleys created on laser printers can save much money. Normal typesetting equipment prints on a special photographic paper that costs more than plain paper. The capital cost of the PC laser printer, while less than a phototypesetter, is not the selling point. The tremendous savings are in the paper costs. The small weekly newspapers can afford to purchase high-resolution 600 dpi PC laser printers.

Creating and Adding Drawings

The trouble with drawings is that they easily can force desktop publishing into the manual layout process. PCs can print good looking text, but printing good drawings is much more difficult. This section explores how desktop publishing influences drawings used during publication. Because desktop publishing has to perform the artist's functions of creating drawings and managing clip art files, this section also describes the sources of drawings.

Types of Drawings

Drawings come in three forms—graphic, character, and object. Graphic drawings are usually designed for dot-matrix printers. They don't look better and in some cases look worse when printed on high-resolution laser printers. They look even worse when sent to phototypesetters. Low-resolution drawings come with packages like PFS: First Publisher. These drawings look best on dot-matrix printers. They are advertised in large quantities for little money, but don't purchase these drawings unless you are just interested in low-quality, dot-matrix output.

High-resolution drawings, designed for 300 dpi graphics-mode laser printers, are available. These are slightly more expensive than the low-resolution forms intended for dot-matrix printers.

Character drawings should be discouraged (see the discussion of character graphics in Chapter 3 on character sets). Character drawings are supported on only some PC printers and are not supported by desktop publishing or the typesetting industry. No drawing packages try to import them or trace them, so the effort of drawing them is completely wasted. No PostScript printer can print them.

Object drawings are the only type of drawings that look good on PC printers and look even better coming from phototypesetters. You can tell which type of drawing that you have by printing it enlarged and reduced. If the curves of the drawing look smooth at both resolutions, you have an object drawing. Most object drawings have an extension such as EPS (Encapsulated PostScript).

Object and graphic drawings each have their advantages. Graphic drawings are much better at shadows and shading. Graphic drawings can look bad on one printer and good on another. When stretched, graphic drawings do not look as good. When printed, a circle may turn into an oval. Object drawings have none of these problems. In addition, you can enlarge or reduce object drawings without much observed effect on quality.

You can convert graphic drawings to object drawings automatically using PC software. PC software traces the graphic drawing, but tracing shadows and reproducing shading is difficult. The traced drawing is usually a good starting point, but you have to put in many hours to make the object drawing look good. This means that object drawings are much more expensive than graphic drawings.

> HINT | To convert character graphic drawings, display the drawing on-screen and translate the screen into a graphics drawing using a program like Hijaak. Then use a program like Adobe Illustrator to convert the graphics drawing to an object drawing using the autotrace function. Finally, expect to clean the new object drawing up manually. This process could be so time-consuming that it would be quicker to start over from scratch.

Drawing Software

Drawings are called art work or clip art. Art work generally implies that you or someone in your company created it from scratch with PC software packages or by hand and then transferred it into electronic form using a scanner. Clip art implies that it was purchased. Other sources of drawings are other PC software packages.

Desktop publishing software usually has little drawing capability. At most, you can draw lines, boxes, and circles. Top-of-the-line packages like Ventura cannot edit individual pixels. You will want to purchase a high-end drawing package like GEM's Artline or CorelDraw if you purchase Ventura or PageMaker.

Low-end products like PFS: First Publisher are more like drawing packages than desktop publishing software. With PFS: First Publisher, you can edit the pixels of the text just as if it was a paint program. However, PFS: First Publisher does not support object drawing modes like the Micrografx Designer and other high-end drawing programs, nor can it automatically trace a scanned image and turn it into an object drawing.

Before purchasing a drawing program, remember that drawing takes time. Even scanned and traced images must be cleaned up. It may be a better investment of your time and money to purchase a CD ROM player and clip art rather than spending time drawing.

Scanned Drawings

You can convert physical drawings on paper, figures cut out of magazines, and books into electronic form using a scanner. Scanners come in three varieties: roller, flatbed, and hand held. The roller scanners use facsimile machine technology and look like a facsimile machine. A company named DEST made some of the first scanners of this variety. The roller scanners have been replaced by flat-bed scanners. These scanners look similar to a small copy machine. The original sits on a glass plate, a plastic lid covers it, and a beam of light sweeps by underneath. Flat-bed scanners cost about $1,000. Hewlett-Packard's ScanJet is one of the more popular models.

Roller and flat-bed scanners are designed for large drawings. However, most drawings are less than 4 inches square. The extra capacity only makes the scanner more complicated, the scanning software more complicated, and the files that are created larger. Small hand-held units are available for under $200.

The hand-held units have no moving parts except a button. You hold the scanner over the image to be scanned and press a button. Then you slowly move the scanner over the image. As your hand moves, the scanned image appears on-screen. These scanners can accommodate images up to 4 by 10 inches.

Hand-held scanners can scan anything. They are not limited to copy machine output. They can scan real objects. The best can scan body parts like hands, faces, ears, and so on. An example is the DFI HS-3000 hand scanner.

The best hand-held scanners scan at 400 dpi and 32 levels of gray. Even though all this information can never be displayed or printed in the PC world, you can send this scanned image to the typesetter along with your document.

Scanners come with the necessary software. Normally, the scanner software is run outside of the desktop publishing software to create a file containing the scanned image. Then, you run the desktop publishing software and import the scanned file. Sometimes, the scanner software can be executed while inside the desktop publishing package, and the image scanned can be placed directly into the document file.

Purchased Drawings

Clip art is added to a document just like the electronically scanned files. Currently, volumes of graphic clip art are available. This clip art is often organized along certain themes like holidays, nature, religious, sporting, and so on. Each theme or category may have hundreds of drawings in it. If the clip art does not come with a printed copy, you could spend hours either printing out all the drawings or scanning through the different drawings on-screen.

There is not a standard file format for clip art or scanned images. Thus, most desktop publishing software packages support a variety of file formats. But there are so many formats that a good clip art file format conversion utility is needed. This issue is explored in the section entitled "Converted Images."

> HINT | When purchasing clip art, purchase only clip art that comes with a binder illustrating all the drawings available. This will save you time. Searching through the art in electronic form or printing it out takes time.

Clip art does not have to be artistic. Visa cards and stop signs, headlines and borders, trash cans, and beds all make good clip art. Clip art can come in very low-resolution form that doesn't size well or look good when printed on laser printers or sent to a phototypesetter.

Computer Screen Images

IBM PC videoboards can contain very low-resolution graphic images. Software exists that captures these drawings, but they look nice only when shrunk to a much smaller size than they were originally. For the PC DOS machines, you need good public domain software like Optiks or purchased software like Hijaak. The Mac supports the capture of any screen image using the operating system.

> HINT | You can turn anything appearing on a PC or MAC screen into a graphic drawing. PCs will require the purchase of a program like Hijaak. The Mac method is built into the operating system. Pressing Shift, Caps Lock, Option-4 sends the screen to the printer (like PrtSc in the PC world). Pressing Shift-Option-3 saves the screen in MacPaint file format.

Converted Images

In the IBM world, there is no single dominant drawing file standard. A fairly comprehensive list of different file formats follows. The most common file type supported is a graphics (sometimes called raster) file type. Other file types are character (sometimes called library), object (sometimes called language), and a primitive object file type called vector.

Because of the different file types, file conversion software is available that can convert from one format to another. Hijaak is a commercial conversion product, and Optiks is a public domain product. PageMaker, Ventura (desktop publishing software), WordPerfect (word processing with graphics), Hijaak, and Optiks are all compared in table 10.1. All five support the following file types:

> PCX Zsoft PC
> PIC PC Paint
> MAC MacPaint file format (no standard extension in the IBM world)
> EPS Encapsulated Postscript (raw PostScript program)
> HPG Hewlett Packard Plotter Language file (no standard extension)
> TIF Tag and Image Format Files TIFF (created by Aldus and Microsoft for use in the Windows environment)

The MAC and EPS file formats dominate the Macintosh world. The original Mac came with software that created drawing files. Later, PostScript files have formed a standard. Most of the more expensive software packages either directly support different file types or include a translation utility. If they can print to a file while configured for a HP plotter or PostScript printer, you can convert that file to clip art for just about any program. Otherwise, you need conversion software like Optiks or Hijaak.

Public domain clip art is available on CompuServe. You can download this clip art using a modem. You also can purchase public domain on CD ROMs.

Color Drawings

You may want the letters of your chapter title to be filled with the color blue. Perhaps the drawing of a tree needs to be filled with green. You can specify these colors with drawing software or from within top-of-the-line desktop publishing software. Or you can specify the color by using Pantone's system or some other percentage system. In either case, the desktop publishing software or drawing software is told which colors to use.

The desktop publishing software cannot guess the colors of a photograph or colored piece of paper. Desktop publishing software today does not attempt to scan a document four times and do the separation. The four different halftones from a separation service cannot be used by desktop publishing software.

Color support in desktop publishing software is intended only for output to phototypesetters. PC printers cannot print grays and blacks evenly enough to be photographed and turned into film masters. This means that the CMYK color separations generated by desktop publishing software are useful only when sent to a phototypesetter. Once at the phototypesetter, the color becomes the typesetter's and print shop's responsibility (see fig. 10.4). The desktop publishing software saves much money over the traditional typesetting system, however. No layout, no separation, and no stripping are required; only electronically added color is used. The savings can be seen by comparing figures 10.2 and 10.4.

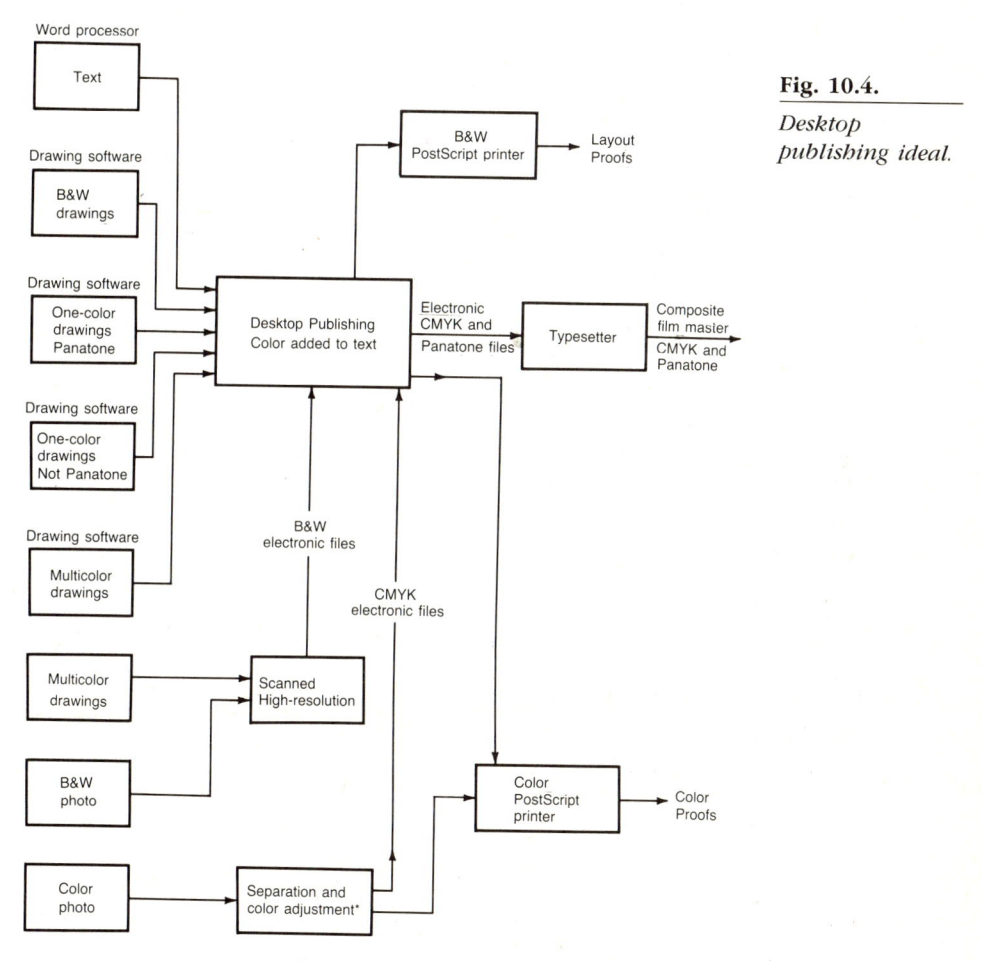

Fig. 10.4.

Desktop publishing ideal.

*Not yet possible to send CMYK color-adjusted files to desktop publishing software.

Table 10.1
Converting Images

File Ext	Page-Maker	Optiks	Ventura	Hijaak	Word-Perfect	Description
ART		Yes				PFS: First Publisher Clip Art
ART						Ashton-Tate Byline Clipart
BAS		Yes				Basic Bload/Bsave
BSG		Yes				Fontasy (same as RAW)
CA		Yes				NewsRoom Pro
CGM	Yes		Yes		Yes	Computer Graphics Metafile
CPF				Yes		The complete PC
CPS				Yes		Color PostScript
CTF				Yes		TIFF compressed
CUT		Yes				Dr. Halo, Cut Files
DAT		Yes				PrintShop
DCX		Yes				Panasonic Fax PCX files
DD						CBM Doodle
DHP					Yes	Dr. Halo
DRW						Freelance
DRW						MicroGrafx
DRW						NBI Legend
DXF					Yes	AutoCad
EPS	Yes	Yes	Yes	Yes	Yes	Encapsulated PostScript
EV						NCN Execuvision
FAX				Yes		CCITT Group 3 fax files
FG						Slidewrite Plus
GAL						HP Gallery
GEM			Yes			GEM Draw
GMF						Computer Graphics Metafile
GIF		Yes		Yes		Compuserve Graphics Interchange
GX1						PC PaintBrush
HPC		Yes		Yes	Yes	HP LaserJet Graphics
HPG	Yes	Yes	Yes	Yes	Yes	HP Plotter Language
IFF	Yes					Amiga Interchange Format File
IMA		Yes				Zenographics' Mirage
IMG		Yes	Yes	Yes	Yes	DataCopy Wips
IMG		Yes		Yes		GEM Paint
IMG		Yes				IBM Image Support Facility
JTF				Yes		Boeing Graph
MAC	Yes	Yes	Yes	Yes	Yes	JT Fax
						Apple Macintosh MacPaint

Chapter 10: Typesetting 455

File Ext	Page-Maker	Optiks	Ventura	Hijaak	Word-Perfect	Description
MAK		Yes				Apple Macintosh MacPaint—no header
MCX				Yes		Intel Connection
MH				Yes		TeliFax "500"
MP1				Yes		Microsoft Windows Paint
MSP	Yes			Yes	Yes	Microsoft Windows Paint
P						Ashton-Tate Draw Applause
PCR		Yes				OPTIKS/PCRGB
PCC		Yes				Zsoft PC PaintBrush
PCL				Yes		HP LaserJet
PCX	Yes	Yes	Yes	Yes	Yes	Zsoft PC PaintBrush
PDA		Yes				Palantir Scanner Graphics Files
PGA						IBM PGA image file
PI1		Yes				Atari Degas uncompressed images
PI2		Yes				Atari Degas uncompressed images
PIC		Yes	Yes	Yes	Yes	Lotus
PIC	Yes	Yes	Yes	Yes	Yes	Mouse systems PC Paint
PIG		Yes				Ricoh Pixel Image Generator File
PIX				Yes		Hijaak
PIX				Yes		InSet
PM				Yes		PrintMaster
PRN		Yes				PostScript, any Image file
RAS		Yes				Show file RAS format
RAW		Yes				Basica Array format
RIC				Yes		Ricoh Fax File format, 1-D compression
RLE		Yes				CompuServe, Run Length Encoded
SLD		Yes	Yes			AutoCad Slide
SFL		Yes		Yes		Soft Font single letter
SHP		Yes		Yes		Printmaster, Newsmaster
TXT			Yes	Yes		Text
TIF	Yes	Yes	Yes	Yes	Yes	Aldus/Microsoft Tag Image Format Files
WPG		Yes		Yes	Yes	WordPerfect Graphics 5.0
WFX				Yes		WorldPort
XFX				Yes		Fax Manager, JetFax, EFax

Adding Photographs

Black and white photographs can be scanned with $200 hand-held scanners at 400 dpi and 32 shades of gray. If the shades of gray are translated into bits, the effective resolution is 2000 dpi—from a hand scanner! Black and white photographs printed on laser printers are limited to an effective resolution of 300 dpi. You must struggle to get them to look nice. But, when printed on a phototypesetter at 400 dpi with 32 shades of gray, they can look nice. What this means is that black and white photos can be incorporated into the desktop publishing system with a sacrifice in quality limited only by the phototypesetter and scanner. Hand-held scanner resolutions are rapidly increasing. Black and white photograph desktop publishing can only get better.

Color photographs are the only piece of the puzzle that desktop publishing software has not attempted. Color photograph printing is very demanding. Slide scanners, not hand-held scanners, are required. Slide scanners have four different colored filters; you must scan the same color photograph four times. Although the resolution of the cheap $10,000 scanners is about 2000 dpi—the same as the hand-held black and white scanners—the resolution is not nearly the same as the $300,000 laser scanners that separation companies use. Besides a scanner, expensive videoboards and monitors are required for color separation. Together with the cost of the slide scanner, color adjustment software, and high-resolution monitors, you must have $23,000 to $30,000 worth of equipment plus a $7,000 PC or Mac.

Suppose that you just want to print black and white photographs on your 300 dpi laser printer. How is it done? The secret is in scanning at the right resolution, choosing the right number of grays, and using good-looking photographs. The rest of this section explores the terminology and concepts behind this.

Lines Per Inch versus Dots Per Inch

Laser printing, photocopying, offset printing, and almost any other kind of printing do not produce true continuous tone grays. Instead these processes create the impression of gray through a process called half-toning.

Suppose that you have taken a photograph. The photograph was developed in a process that produces continuous tone grays. Your goal is to reproduce this photograph in a brochure. First, you must scan the photograph. In essence, the scanner puts a piece of graph paper over the photograph. Tiny square cells are formed by the intersecting lines of the graph paper. In each cell, the scanner determines which shade of gray is present. The result is a half-tone version of the photograph.

In the typesetting world, the graph paper is known as a *screen*. The size of the screen's tiny square cells is determined by the number of lines per inch (lpi). The word *frequency* rather than line density or line spacing generally is used to describe this feature of a screen. If, for example, you are asked, "What is the frequency of your scanner?" the most accurate reply would be, "400 lpi." Technically, there is a difference between lpi and dpi. Because the concepts are so similar, they are often used interchangeably. How can a laser printer print 300 dpi and then 60 dpi? How can a typesetting machine be capable of 2,540 dpi and then only 127 dpi? The answer is that the smaller dpi figure is really lpi.

But there also is another reason for the confusion. Laser printers and even typesetters can only turn the laser on and off. There is no gray in between—no way they can make the dot bigger or smaller. Laser printers can place dots in a cell; however a typesetter can put so many dots in a cell that they can form circles with the dots. Thus, the cell holds a variable-size dot made up of much smaller fixed-size dots. The spacing of the larger, variable-size dot will be the smaller dpi density. Thus, 2,540 dpi refers to the smaller fixed-size dots a typesetting machine can create, and 127 dpi refers to the larger variable-size dot spacing.

Dot Shapes and Sizes

The shapes of dots formed in cells dramatically influence how a document looks. Back when fax machines were being designed, different dot shapes were experimented with. Consider the 2,540 dpi, 127 lpi typesetting machine. It would have available in a cell $2,540/127 \times 2,540/127 = 400$ dots to play with. Suppose that a 20 percent gray was requested. This means that 80 dots (400 multiplied by 20 percent) could be turned on in the cell. The question is how should the dots be arranged? Should they fill the cell uniformly, randomly, or lump all the dots together in the middle of the cell?

Randomly distributing the dots produces streak marks in the output. Uniformly distributing dots produces quilt-like patterns called *moiré* patterns. Because the goal is to produce continuous grays, this is not acceptable. Lumping all the dots in the middle produces the best results. More precisely, dots are best looking at almost white gray levels, and black squares with white holes are the best looking at almost black gray levels. Early PostScript printers (Versions 25 through 37) used dots exclusively. Starting with PostScript Version 38, the dot patterns change depending on the different gray levels requested. Dark grays are black squares with white holes in them. Light grays are white squares with black holes in them. Exactly 50 percent gray is a checkerboard of squares.

Although lumping dots together in the middle of a cell produces the best looking results on a typesetter, a regular 300 dpi laser printer does not have that many dots. If a 150-lpi screen is applied, there could be only four dots per cell ($300/150 \times 300/150$). This produces an output that has fine detail, but the contrasts between light and dark are too great, making the reproduction very dark.

If the screen size of 50 lpi is used, there are more dots available per cell and more grays can be made, but the coarse cell structure is visible. The optimal screen size for a 300 dpi laser printer is about 60 lpi, which generates the optimal number of grays and frequency. According to pure math, the number of gray levels should be $(300/60) \times (300/60) = 25$, but in reality, 33 gray levels are available.

Angle

Back in the days when screens were placed in front of camera lenses, it was discovered that rotating the screen sometimes produced better-looking halftones.

There also is an electronic form of rotating the screen. Imagine a grid of 300 dots per inch. If 60 lines per inch are drawn so that they don't intersect any dots, boxes of 25 dots would be formed. But when the screen is rotated, the screen lines intersect dots. Because fractions of dots are not available, the computer that is doing the scanning has to adjust both the requested frequency (lines per inch) and angle in order to create cells that do not intersect dots.

> HINT: Try scanning a photograph at different angles and compare results. Look at the edges where there is a sharp contrast between black and white. The different angles should make the high contrast edges appear more or less uniform throughout the document. Later the photograph can be digitally rotated and cropped by a drawing package.

Most 300 dpi laser printers (including PostScript printers) default to 60 lines per inch at an angle of 45 degrees when asked to make shades of gray, which makes a scanned photo look best. Otherwise, some areas of high contrast will seem in focus and other areas out of focus. At 60 lines per inch and an angle of 45 degrees, many of the dots will be split. Thus, the 60 lines per inch is reduced to 53 lines per inch, and the number of dots in the cell are $(300/53 \times 300/53) = 32$. If pure white is considered a gray, the total number of grays available is $32 + 1 = 33$.

The Optimal Scanner Resolution

The optimal scanner resolution is related to the screen frequency chosen by the printer, not to the pixel resolution of the printer. Because the screen frequency can be determined by the printer (character and object modes) or by software running in the computer (graphics mode), the optimal scanner resolution could vary. But because the optimal frequency is 60 lpi and optimal angle is 45 degrees for a 300 dpi printer, assume that the printer will be using 60 lpi when printing gray scales.

Scanning at a higher resolution than the screen applied by the printer produces the better results. Again, the goal is to avoid a situation in which the frequency of high contrast areas in the photo being scanned match the frequency of the scanner, the frequency of the screen applied by the printer, and the dots per inch resolution of the printer. The more these differ, the more uniform the grays produced.

You should scan at least a resolution 1.25 times more than the screen applied by the printer. If the printer is going to print using a 60 lpi screen, the scanner should scan at $60 \times 1.25 = 75$ dots per inch minimum. If the typesetter is going to print at 133 lpi, the scanner should scan at 167 lpi or more. Fax research has shown that there is only marginal improvement when increasing the scanning frequency from 1.25 to 2.5 times the screen applied by the printer. After a 2.5 increase, there is no improvement. Thus, the maximum scanning rate for a 60 lpi gray scale should be 210 dpi. For a 133 lpi typesetting machine, 333 lpi is the maximum.

The resolution of hand-held scanners is currently at 400 dpi. Do not expect improvement in this resolution because there is no need to. If scanning for printing on laser printers, 75 dpi will do—300 to 400 dpi is necessary only if the image is going to be sent to a typesetter. Even then, the difference between 300 dpi and 400 dpi in the typesetting proof is going to be marginal.

| HINT | The difference between scanning at 75 dpi and 400 dpi for most laser printers is minimal. But the file sizes created are much different. A 75 dpi file will be almost 300 percent smaller. Most of the time, you should scan at 75 dpi for output to be printed on a typical 300 dpi laser printer. |

Optimal Number of Scanner Grays

The next issue is how many grays the scanner should be asked to resolve. If the angle of 45 degrees is assumed, 32 grays are possible in the typical laser printer. Because most scanners specify the number of grays to scan in bits, five bits are needed to create 32 grays.

| HINT | If a normal laser printer is asked to print grays, it can place only 32 different values in a cell. Thus, no benefit is achieved by asking a scanner to scan more at more than five bits unless the scanned image is being sent to a typesetter. |

How many grays can the human eye distinguish? Suppose that you were asked to sort 1,000 cards with different shades of gray. Chances are that you would sort the cards into approximately 250 categories. For this reason, no typesetting machines and even PostScript printers can keep track of more than 256 dots in a cell. This means that the maximum number of grays a scanner needs to scan for are 256, or eight bits.

Probably the most powerful effect of gray scaling is the reduction in data needed to image a document. If information about every dot in a 300 dpi laser was tracked by the gray-adjusting software, almost 1M of gray information per page would have to be processed. Yet a 75-dpi five-bit scan takes up 320K—just one third the size! Although this does make file sizes smaller and transmission quicker, some information is lost.

Scanning Uniform Grays

Scanners apply screens to images. Ideally the scanned image has uniform grays. If the image came from a newspaper, magazine, or photocopying machine, the image has already been scanned and printed. The information lost during the first scan is still lost. The second scan loses even more information in an ugly pattern that is visible to the eye—the dreaded moiré patterns. Only under ideal circumstances can the second scan pick up all the information of the first scan.

> HINT: Try to scan the original item or photograph, not a photocopy or magazine clipping. Otherwise, the scan will not look good.

Scanning the original is always going to be more beneficial than scanning a photocopy. Most scanners are a little color blind. Thus, a variety of scanners, sensitive to different colors, would be the ideal. Some scanners are available that can directly scan your fingertips and skin colors. Hand-held scanners make it easier to scan the real thing.

Print Engine Influence on Grays

A printer uses the scanner's information, translates it to a smaller rotated screen, and then figures out how to provide the gray levels scanned. The trouble is that, although the correct number and position of the dots can be computed, paper chemistry influences the practical results.

When paper with toner on it rolls over the fusion bar, the toner melts into the paper. As a dot of toner melts, it spreads a little. This is called *dot gain*. The result is that grays between 0 and 20 percent are impossible as are grays between 90 and 100 percent. Of course, completely black and completely white are possible.

HINT | Photos without medium grays scan and print the best. Areas that shade to complete white or complete black will contain the most obvious defects.

The actual gray levels printed and available depend on two things under your control. First, special white laser paper reduces dot gain, which increases the number of grays available. In addition, the write-white engines, like the Ricoh engine used in the AST TurboLaser and Texas Instruments OmniLaser, can produce a wider range of grays.

HINT | Purchase special laser paper for printing scanned images. The difference can be significant. The printed image will not be so dark, and there will be smoother transitions between black and dark.

Printing in Color

Since the days of black and red typewriter ribbons, the possibility of color printing has existed. IDS Paper Tiger dot-matrix printers attached to Apple IIs were printing in color long before the IBM PC and Macintosh existed. Many of the dot-matrix printers currently on the market can be upgraded to color printers at costs ranging from the price of a color ribbon to a $70 kit that includes a color ribbon and a ROM chip. The ROM chip contains color printing instructions for the printer. You open the printer's lid and insert the new ROM. Probably the most inexpensive, fully functional color dot-matrix printer on the market today is C.Itoh's C-610 with a list price of $799.

Despite the apparent ease, few people print in color. There are three reasons why. First, printing in color usually takes three to four times longer. Second, the colored document does not look anything like newspaper or magazine color. It looks terrible. Third, the color document cannot be reproduced easily. How are you going to reproduce it? Take it to a color copy machine? The cost is about $1 per page. It may be cheaper to take a color photo of it and print multiple copies.

The only type of color printing done on a regular basis is with plotters. Because plotters use pens, brightly colored inks can be used. Plotters can create much better looking colored documents than dot-matrix printers. But plotter output quality is still not sufficient to aid the desktop publishing process. Colored documents from typewriters, plotters, and dot-matrix printers are rare.

Efforts to bring color printing to the masses have failed. The only commercial application of a color printer is that of proofing the results of the separation and color adjustment process. Each color proof costs around $50.

Alternatives to this process have recently surfaced that can color pages for around $1 to $2 dollars each. The printer prices have dropped to under $10,000. The recommended model is QMS's ColorScript 100 model 10. However, the largest the color document can be is 5 by 7 inches. It also takes a long time for the printer to print. A 5- by 7-inch, 300 dpi, 256 color document requires the computation of 3M worth of data—a large process for a simple microprocessor.

The new color printers use a process called dye diffusion thermal transfer. Digital images are sent to a thermal head, which transfers ink from a ribbon to paper with heat. The ribbon is 5 inches wide, and each of the four colors is 7 inches long. The paper rolls underneath each colored section of the ribbon. The paper makes four revolutions while the circular ribbon makes one revolution. A thermal head melts dye from the ribbon onto the special paper. The amount of dye transferred is controlled through the thermal head, rather than having color shading controlled at the pixel level. This is called continuous tone color technology.

The only people who get excited about high-quality $10,000 color printers are those paying $50 per photo to make sure that the color separation and color adjustment has been done properly. In this application, the printer would pay for itself after printing just 225 color prints. All color printers advertised come with PostScript. The output looks unique and is attractive, but the paper is shiny, and moiré patterns are obvious. Reproduction is still a problem. The shiny gloss, the special paper, and the moiré patterns can all be tolerated for proofing purposes. Advertisements of one color laser company claim:

> Pantone, Inc., has certified that our printer is Pantone Color Capable. QMS and Pantone developed process color combinations for the ColorScript 100 very closely simulate all colors in the Pantone Matching System 747XR except for metallics and fluorescents... commercial printing proofs and in-house color separations can be produced with this color printer.

However, the fine print at the bottom of the ad reads:

> Process color reproduction may not match Pantone-identified solid color standards.

Summarizing Desktop Publishing

Desktop printing has not completely replaced typesetting. Only when the desired output is low-resolution text can the entire typesetting industry be bypassed. If higher resolutions are needed, desktop publishing software can send the electronic files to a typesetter.

Object drawings mixed with text from a desktop publishing system can look passable on a 300 dpi laser printer. Graphic drawings don't look better when sent to a phototypesetter. If you want just text and black and white object drawings, you can bypass the typesetting process.

You can add color to text and drawings using software. Desktop software can produce the CMYK separations needed to print this type of color. However, laser printers cannot produce camera-ready CMYK separations. The toner is too uneven, and the gray scale is too small, or the lines per inch are too coarse. The CMYK separations produced by desktop publishing software must be sent to a phototypesetter.

Scanned black and white photographs rarely look good when produced with a 300 dpi laser printer. If scanned at 400 dpi at 32 gray levels, the photographs can look passable when produced with a phototypesetter. In this case, you can use the PC printer to proof the desktop publishing layout and the final file generated from a phototypesetter. However, the black and white photograph quality is not going to look nearly as good as black and white photos that go through the galley, paste-up, mechanical, and photography processes.

Color slides, photographs, paintings, and so on cannot yet be processed through desktop publishing software. You can purchase special software, special slide scanners, and special high-resolution monitors for $25,000 to $30,000 for a PC that produce good results.

Whether done with a PC-based system or service, the CMYK file generated still must be stripped. Desktop publishing can help speed the stripping process. This is done by scanning the color document with a black and white scanner, and then processing the information as if it were a graphics drawing. The 300 dpi laser printer proofs generated can accurately describe exactly where the CMYK film generated is to be stripped into place.

Improving Your Document's Appearance

Now that you know what is possible with typesetters and desktop publishing systems, you know when you need an outside service to help produce the document you need.

Printing Large and Reducing or Printing Small

If printing a document smaller makes the document look better, usually you are in graphics mode. This is the only way to make a graphics file look better.

However, if the document looks about the same or even better looking when printed larger, try printing twice the size. Then using a camera, the typesetter can reduce the original and improve the quality. Laser printers can print on only 8-inch wide paper. Thus, the reduced documents have to be smaller than 8 inches wide to have any improvement in document quality. Otherwise, find a slow inkjet printer that can print at laser resolution on big paper.

Renting Time on a PostScript Printer

If you have only a dot-matrix printer, don't despair. A laser printer for rent may be around the corner. Next time you visit a copier store, check whether they have a desktop publishing system. Usually, such stores charge by the hour and by the page. An expert is usually available to help with your questions. The best rates you will find are probably $5 per hour and 15 cents per page.

These stores try to set up systems so that you can walk in and print. But this rarely works. If you come in with a document already written and laid out using desktop publishing software, the process of printing can change the entire document's layout. Even in the Mac world, there is enough chaos that LaserWriter printing may force you to spend hours redoing the desktop publishing you already did.

The easiest way to approach renting time on a desktop publishing system is to type a document, but don't try to format it on your machine. Take the document to the rental system and then explore how they have their system set up. Then go back to work or home and configure your system to be as close to theirs as possible. You should try to match desktop publishing software and fonts as closely as possible. Install your software as if you had the same brand of printer as the rental company.

If you have different desktop publishing software or different fonts, you will have to make floppy disk backups of all your software and reinstall it on the rental. Reinstalling on the rental can be a nightmare or very easy. In the Mac world, this usually is a simple step. The PC world is so chaotic that anything could happen. The only way to find out is to try.

Sending Files to a TypeSetter

Desktop publishing files can be very large. A 4-by-4-inch black and white photo scanned at 400 dpi with a five-bit gray scale will create a 1.5M file. Because the files can be so large, transporting them to the typesetter can be a real challenge. Following are some strategies for transporting the results of your desktop publishing efforts to the typesetter.

Transferring Files through LAN Cables

The ideal method of transferring files to a typesetter is through LAN cables, but the PC that originally created the file must be on the LAN. Phototypesetters can be attached directly into Apple's slower Local Talk network. Maybe this will change someday.

Exchanging Floppy Disks

Floppy disks are probably the simplest, cheapest, and most reliable way to send data to a typesetter. The drawbacks are that they don't transfer instantly, and they could become damaged or lost in the mail. But more likely the files are too large to fit on a floppy. Software exists that shrinks files and chops them into floppy-sized chucks, but the typesetter needs the same software to expand and piece together the file. The 3 1/2-inch disks survive mail travel much better than 5 1/4-inch disks, and they store more data. The 3 1/2-inch disks hold 800K in the Mac world and 1.44M in the IBM world. Both PCs and MACs can be designed that read both of them. Check to make sure that the phototypesetter can read the 3 1/2-inch disks.

Exchanging Tapes and Removable Hard Disks

The advantages of tapes and removable hard disk systems is that all the files are in one place and the files can be huge. The disadvantage is that tapes and removable hard disks are harder to send through the mail. They also are more expensive and more prone to problems. If the typesetter and you can agree on a system, this method can work. If you are starting from scratch, probably the best solution is a Bernoulli Box from Iomega. These removable floppies can store up to 44M. A 5 1/4-inch drive costs about $995, and cartridges cost $84 each.

Transferring Files through Modems

Sometimes the files are so large that they cannot fit onto a floppy. This means they have to be transferred using modems. Transferring files to typesetters can be fairly straightforward if the typesetter has a PC to receive the file. PostScript files are very easy to transfer using modems—too easy. The transfer can work for months and then one little error creeps in that does not show until you receive the film. The important concept is to transfer files from the desktop publishing system using a file transfer protocol. Following is a list of the typical PC file transfer protocols:

XModem
YModem
ZModem

Hayes
Crosstalk
Kermit
Carbon Copy
PC Anywhere

Read this list of protocols to the remote typesetter. If the typesetter doesn't understand what you are describing, find another typesetter. You should avoid modems whenever possible. The problems can be very frustrating.

Typesetters expect either raw text files or PostScript files. The raw text files are used to generate galleys for the paste-up process. Film versions of the PostScript files are usually created. Both files contain bit patterns that represent text characters in the ASCII table. The bad news is that this makes the files so easy to transfer through modems that normal precautions are not taken. The good news is the software can shrink these files tremendously. Public domain programs like ARC or ZIP can reduce file sizes by 30 percent or more.

Avoiding Potential Typesetting and Printing Problems

Setting up the method of transferring files can be so painful that typesetting companies have started to charge a $50 first time fee. After that, the charge is between $5 and $15 per page or separation. The actual output could be either galleys or film, but usually is film. Sometimes problems can be corrected by the typesetter before mistakes are made. The following sections describe precautions to take and things to watch for when the results are received from the printer.

Sending Desktop Publishing Drafts

Desktop publishing is much easier when drafts can be printed. It is important that the drafts look identical to the typeset output. Because the phototypesetter (or RIP in front of it) is a PostScript device, the best draft will be produced by a PostScript printer. The draft should differ from the final copy only in quality, not page breaks, hyphenation changes, and so on. Typesetters love it when draft printouts are good enough to judge the output of their phototypesetters. With good drafts, they have a better chance of doing their job right the first time and a better chance of correcting mistakes and making adjustments without harassing you.

Sending a Copy of the Fonts Used

Traditionally, typesetters have provided fonts for the printing process. Adobe sells fonts designed for the increased resolution of phototypesetters. Trouble occurs when the typesetter's fonts do not match the fonts the draft was printed with and which the PostScript files call for. This is such a problem that many typesetters request that the fonts used for producing the draft be included with the electronic PostScript files sent. Even though the PC fonts are less quality and the legality of this is questionable in some cases, the practice is becoming more and more common.

Sticking with Standard Font Names

Font problems arise from two sources. First, the font names could be different in the desktop publishing system. Even though Adobe names their fonts consistently when they are shipped, there is the opportunity to rename or renumber fonts in most PostScript systems during installation. Often a font specified by the desktop publishing software exists in the phototypesetter RIP under a different name.

Sticking with Adobe Fonts

The second part of the font problem is that of clone fonts. If HP scalable fonts or Apple Royal fonts are used during the desktop publishing process and the draft is printed using these fonts, will the typesetter necessarily have a matching font? Most typesetters support only fonts from Adobe. If the fonts are going to be understandable by a phototypesetter RIP at all, they have to be in PostScript format. Right now, clone PostScript printers with BitStream fonts are at a disadvantage because many BitStream fonts are in a unique form that cannot be understood by the PostScript RIPs. Chances are that BitStream has made a PostScript version of the font you want to use, but it will have to be purchased and sent to the typesetter. If any other font vendor is chosen, the chances of an exact match decrease, special typesetter versions don't exist, and the possibilities of matching errors increase.

Staying Away from Bit-Mapped Fonts

In the MAC world, if a LaserWriter cannot find a font, it will ask for a bit-mapped version of the screen font in the MAC. The LaserWriter will then use the bit-mapped font when printing. Often the output does not look bad. The bit-mapped fonts can even be rotated and still not look that bad. The Mac has smoothing functions that make the curves as smooth as possible, even at the 300-dpi resolution of the LaserWriter.

If bit-mapped fonts are used during desktop publishing, they have to be sent to the typesetters. Bit-mapped fonts look worse when fed through a typesetter. The rotating does not look as nice. Smoothing functions, which are done by the MAC, are not going to be done by the phototypesetter RIP.

Capturing PostScript Header Files

Some PC software can send a PostScript smoothing program to the printer. Other programs send their own header files to the PostScript printer before printing the file. These header files customize the PostScript printer in unique ways that make their PostScript documents print with unique features. These header files need to be included with the normal PostScript files sent to a typesetter.

Most PC and MAC software can redirect output to a file, but perhaps not header files. Programs like Hijaak, Optiks, and LPT2DSK can capture these files. But some micro systems may be set up to download these header files automatically when the PC is turned on—before Hijaak, Optiks, and LPT2DSK have a chance to do their job. This means that some careful detective work, searching for header files, needs to be done before sending PostScript files to a typesetter.

Standardizing Margins

Normal PC lasers need a border of least .25 inch all the way around a piece of paper. But phototypesetters can print anywhere on the page. This can cause problems when using PC laser printers to print drafts of the phototypesetter output. The best practice is to keep the margins consistent throughout the desktop publishing process. If the wider margins of the phototypesetter are desired, set the margins that way at the beginning of the desktop publishing process—you will have to tolerate characters that disappear on the edges of the drafts. Changing the margins at the last minute can cause all sorts of formatting problems. A draft with characters missing in the margins is better than risking this problem.

Critiquing Typesetting and Printing Problems

The finished product received from typesetters is not always perfect. The next few pages review some of the problems and mistakes that can be made. As micro printers get better, they too will develop these problems.

Moiré Patterns

When registration is perfect, defects of the gray scaling mechanism should be visible. Gray scales ideally are created with dots of different diameters. Dots of different diameter are easy to create with a photographic process. The finest and best quality photographs today are separated using a photographic process. The color adjustment is done by hand, not with computers. Color adjustment involves changing the gray levels. The gray levels are adjusted by placing screens over the plates created. The screens block ink from reaching the paper. If the screen is not fine enough, moiré patterns appear.

Gray scales can be created by computer using different dot densities, which also can cause moiré patterns. Computerized separation, color adjustment, and stripping save much time and are more precise. The difference between a PC laser printer and a typesetting machine is their resolution—the number of dots per inch they can create. Typesetting machines increase their resolution by slowing down and working directly with film. See the gray scale discussion in Chapter 5. Although it may be possible to change the exposure of the photosensitive drum in a laser printer, this would increase the complexity of the printer tremendously. Currently, it is more cost effective to design PC laser printers and typesetting machines with higher resolution.

Dark Photos

A problem unique to computerized separation and color adjustment occurs when the number of grays available is too small. For example, assume that the PC laser prints at 300 dpi. If the separations are color adjusted at 300 lines per inch, only three gray levels are available. If 150 lines per inch are used, then 9 gray levels are available (see Chapter 5 for more details.) As the number of lines per inch decreases, the number of gray levels increases. A photograph looks best at 60 to 75 lines per inch.

If the number of lines per inch is increased (a function of graphics mode software in the PC), the increased resolution allows more detail to be presented. In addition, because of fewer grays available, the contrast increases. This may sound good, but the photograph becomes too dark—a shadow is either black or white. So detail is sacrificed in order to create more grays and thus make the photo more natural looking.

> HINT Printing scanned black and white photographs on a 300 dpi printer is a time-consuming process that requires optimal conditions. At best, the 300 dpi printer produces a low-quality reproduction; 300 dpi printers are best at printing line drawings.

Washed-Out Photos

Washed out photographs occur when, instead of stripping to four colors, only three colors are used. The color left out is black. Theoretically, the three colors cyan, magenta, and yellow can be combined to form black, but it is difficult. The result is that none of sharp contrast edges in a photo look nice. Sometimes to save money, a three-color process is specified instead of a four-color printing process.

Chapter Summary

Desktop publishing is challenging the typesetting world. PC printers are challenging phototypesetters in lower quality text applications like newspapers and newsletters. Using camera-ready laser printer output, you can skip the typesetting process altogether. When photographs are required, however, most applications require typesetting services. PC printers do not have the resolution or gray scales necessary to print good looking photographs.

PCs now can understand PostScript. This means that they can program phototypesetter RIPs. This means that anyone with PC desktop publishing software has the same opportunity as professional typesetters. They can even send instructions that originate color printing.

When printing color photographs, desktop publishing software falls short of typesetting. Although PC software and hardware is available to process color photographs, the combination is very expensive ($30,000), and the information generated cannot be integrated with desktop publishing software.

The future can only get better. Scanners and monitors are increasing their resolutions. Typesetting machines are developing LAN interfaces, and the costs of color proofs are dropping. Quality color printing is becoming more available to the masses.

In the Next Chapter

Now that you know all about desktop publishing, the next step is to explore the inner world of desktop publishing—that of a PostScript printer. The next chapter is dedicated to PostScript printers, the object printers.

11

PostScript Printers

The golden age of printers will arrive when every printer is a PostScript printer. Maybe someday even the slowest laser printer will be a PostScript printer (dot matrixes will be obsolete). Ten years from now, the majority of books and articles will be written about the various PostScript commands, how they are implemented in different printers, and the various features of the implementations. If LANs take off, even the printer's processing power and hard disk could become a shared network resource.

The goal of this chapter is to introduce you to PostScript printers and their characteristics. Most important, the objective of this chapter is to prove to you that PostScript is the universal solution—the language for all output devices. The goal also is to show you that it is not one company's product (Adobe), but the fertile ground on which companies are already competing. Furthermore, PostScript has broad implications for videoboards and perhaps even the operating system development of computers.

This chapter is split into the following sections. The first section is a brief introduction to PostScript: its origin, development, and current status. Then a description of PostScript's importance to you is included (such as why you should invest your time and money in such a printer). The third section reviews current PostScript printers on the market. Finally, the last section reviews some futuristic PostScript possibilities.

History of PostScript Printers

PostScript is the brain child of John Warnock. After working on various similar languages, he and Chuck Geschke formed Adobe Systems in 1982 and developed PostScript. Adobe's PostScript language has become an integral part of all printing. Every printer company and every computer company is committed to supporting the PostScript language. If you were to place bets on the dominant printer language of the future, PostScript is practically the only choice. In fact, PostScript is so dominant that it has an excellent chance of becoming the first software product to be uniformly implemented in all computer environments: from micro to mini to mainframe. This section first explores how PostScript invaded the typesetting industry, and then describes how PostScript is affecting the printer industry.

PostScript's Influence on Typesetting

The concept of electronically planned layouts evolved out of the typesetting industry almost accidentally. Features were added to typesetters that aimed at reducing the layout headaches. These features included the capability to kern letter pairs, justify right margins, switch fonts automatically, change the line spacing, draw lines, and so on. As the list of features grew, the commands necessary to activate the features in the typesetter became longer and longer. Unfortunately, typesetter manufacturers developed these features in a haphazard, chaotic way. Sending a document to different typesetters produced different results.

Adobe was one of the first companies to see the opportunity of making money from this chaos. Adobe designed a box that intercepted the electronic typesetting instructions intended for the typesetter. The box then translated the commands so that more uniform results were possible (see fig. 11.1). The electronic typesetting instructions grew into the page-formatting languages described in Chapter 10. Page-formatting language companies discovered that if they translate their instructions to the native or generic instructions of Adobe's box, no translation is necessary, and typesetting speeds up tremendously. The native or generic language of Adobe's box is PostScript.

The typesetting companies also have been evolving their equipment to give the Adobe box more control over what occurs in the phototypesetter. The incentive for companies making phototypesetters is to produce more consistent, uniform results with fewer software problems.

Today, the box sitting between the computer world and the phototypesetter is called a raster image processor (RIP). Adobe does not sell RIPs; Adobe sells the software that goes in the RIPs. The RIPs are sold by the typesetting companies. Manufacturers of phototypesetters license Adobe software, put it in their RIPs, and sell the RIPs. A RIP is the brain of the typesetter. It contains a computer with more RAM and hard disk storage than most PCs. RIPs crank out images at resolutions of 2540 dpi. Special scalable fonts, designed especially for the high resolutions, are loaded before printing the documents.

Fig. 11.1.
RIP and PostScript evolution.

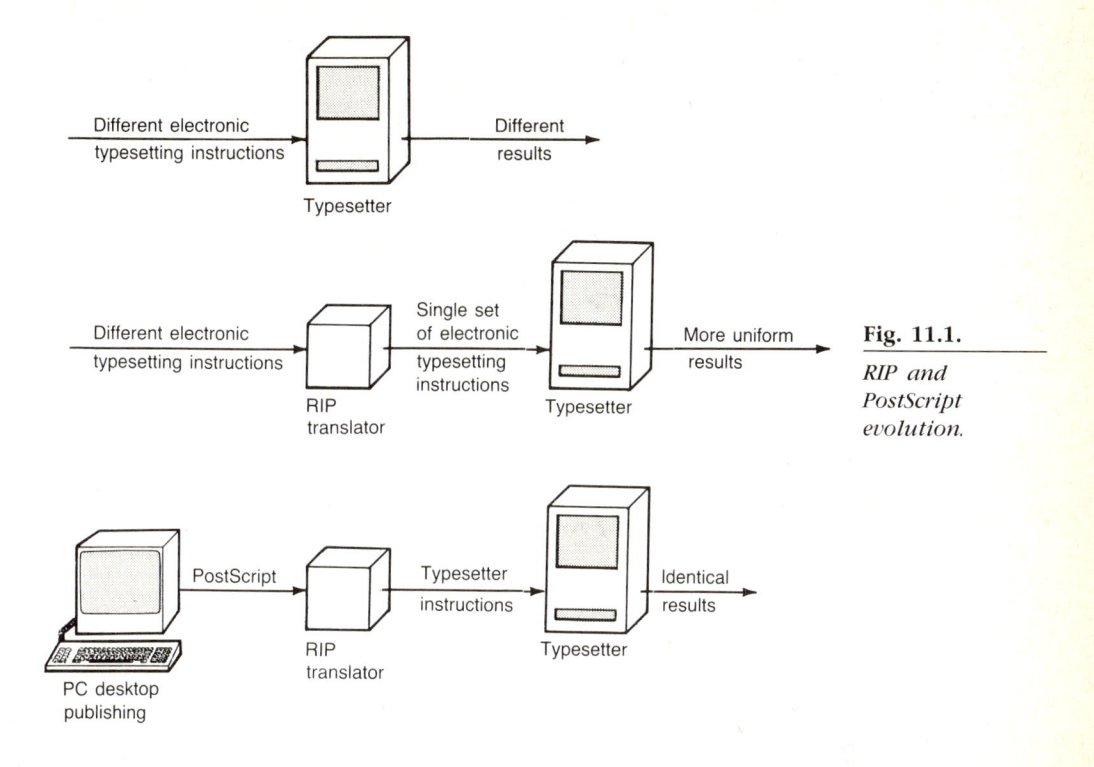

PostScript software from Adobe and Adobe-licensed fonts dominate the phototypesetting market. Because PostScript is sold actively by most phototypesetting vendors, print shops have become more efficient and more competitive. Now, rather than having to learn a specific vendor's phototypesetting commands, just PostScript compatibility is required. Features of the phototypesetter become the issue, not software compatibility. Print shops can switch phototypesetter vendors without upsetting the client base. Print shops are not at the mercy of the phototypesetting vendors, locked into their hardware and software.

If the typesetting world were a game with the vendors of the phototypesetting equipment the players, PostScript would be the referee. Because of the competition, print shops, and ultimately users, win. PostScript already is starting to exercise a referee-type influence in the micro, mini, and mainframe worlds.

PostScript in the Microcomputer World

The history of PostScript in the microcomputer world starts with the history of the Macintosh. At the same time that Steve Jobs was leading the design team of the Macintosh, John Warnock was forming Adobe and working out the details of PostScript. While John Warnock's goal was to provide a uniform imaging model for typesetters, Steve Jobs' goal for the Macintosh was to provide a uniform imaging and printing model for a microcomputer. These goals led both men to the same design objectives.

After the Macintosh was released in January of 1983, Steve Jobs discovered PostScript. Immediately, he saw that PostScript was the ultimate solution to the improvements planned for the Macintosh. He motivated Apple to form a relationship with Adobe, contracting to put Adobe's software in a new printer—a laser printer. In January of 1985, the first PostScript printer was announced—the LaserWriter. By the end of 1987, Steve Jobs had left Apple, formed a new company, and built a computer that put PostScript in the videoboard and printer. The new computer, called NeXT, was first sold in 1989.

Although the jury is still out on the NeXT computer, the excitement is high. Watching NeXT is going to be a major activity of most computer vendors in the early 1990s. NeXT has all the major innovations; the real question is whether NeXT is a computer before its time.

Even if NeXT fails, PostScript already has won the battle of the printer languages. The Macintosh has ridden the coattails of the LaserWriter to grab a large chunk of the microcomputer market and compete directly with PCs. Without the LaserWriter, the Macintosh would be just another graphics machine. In the midst of the current font wars, PostScript is solidifying its position as the premier printer language.

As of this writing, Apple and Microsoft have ganged up on Adobe and NeXT and are trying to develop an alternative font technology. What is not widely reported is that Microsoft traded PostScript clone software (that it purchased) to Apple in return for the rights to Apple's font technology. This means that Microsoft and Apple see PostScript as a pivotal part of printer technology. When asked about their printer driver or printer language plans, Apple and Microsoft will say only that it will be PostScript-compatible—that current PostScript programs will run on future printers containing their software. But at the same time, Apple and Microsoft are implying that future software they create (including operating system software) will not run on current PostScript printers.

Apple and Microsoft are big enough that they may pull this off. If they do, Apple will control printer sales in the Macintosh world with an even tighter grip than it does now. In the PC world, Microsoft will open up a whole new market (for itself) by selling software to printer manufacturers so that its printers will work with DOS and OS/2. Microsoft may even start selling its own printers.

If Apple and Microsoft win, they will claim that anybody can write a printer driver program to bridge the gap between Apple and Microsoft's operating systems and the printer. But reality will be different. Writing a printer driver will require five years of programming time, and one year for digging information out of Microsoft and Apple.

Here are the specific details of the Microsoft and Apple game plan. PMScript (Presentation Manager) is Microsoft's PostScript clone that Apple may put in new versions of the LaserWriter. Currently, Microsoft and Apple have other printer language products. Apple has a printer version of QuickCode that it currently sells in the LaserWriter II SC. (SC stands for the SCSI interface it uses to connect to a Macintosh.) Microsoft has a printer language called GPI (Graphics Programming Interface) that a printer company called QMS is putting in a printer. QuickCode and GPI are sold as cheaper, faster alternatives to PostScript. Unfortunately, because both were designed for graphics-mode videoboards, they are low-resolution devices, which means that their output on a high-resolution laser printer may not look good. Furthermore, improvements to QuickCode and GPI hinge on Apple's Royal fonts and Microsoft's ability to sell OS/2. Currently, Apple's improvements to QuickCode are threatened by Adobe's TypeManager, and Microsoft's OS/2 is not selling.

Ideally, Microsoft and Apple want to phase out Adobe and HP-PCL. They want to position their printer language products as cheaper and faster, but with less resolution. This elevates PostScript into a Cadillac-type of role. Microsoft and Apple want to offer compatibility to PostScript, while improving their printer language products until they squeeze PostScript out of existence.

Fortunately, Apple and Microsoft are not going to win for three reasons:

1. HP-PCL has a strong presence in the low-end laser printer language market. Both companies are going to need to compete with HP on the low end. Neither has successfully competed in the low-end printer market. Furthermore, the long-term health of Apple and Microsoft demands that they avoid competing in the low-end markets.

2. Apple and Microsoft have never successfully put software in printers and sold them. Look at the figures for 1989, for example. Of the 35 new laser printers released in 1989, 16 were PostScript or PostScript clone printers. All of the color lasers released in 1989 were PostScript printers. All of the lasers targeted at the Macintosh market contained PostScript. All the laser printers sold by Apple contained PostScript. All the others were HP-PCL printers. In other words, Adobe and Hewlett-Packard are dominating the current printer

software. A majority of the laser printers installed understand HP-PCL or PostScript. Can Apple and Microsoft muscle their way into Hewlett-Packard's and Adobe's world? You just have to wait and see.

3. PostScript competition has risen. A number of different companies have cloned PostScript and are successfully competing with Adobe. Already PostScript prices are dropping. At the time of this writing, a $450 PostScript cartridge is available that turns an HP LaserJet into a PostScript printer.

Currently, there is a little competition between Adobe and Hewlett-Packard. HP has teamed up with Agfa Compugraphic (a phototypesetter manufacturer) to compete with Adobe. Agfa Compugraphic has released an HP-PCL RIP. Official, scalable fonts for HP LaserJets have been developed. Currently, HP-PCL is fighting an uphill battle. The strength of HP-PCL is its installed base of microcomputer printers. Its weakness is that the language is character-oriented. A logical move on HP's part would be to combine HP-PCL with HP's plotter graphics language, HP-GL, and create a new product compatible with both. However, if a winner had to be announced, PostScript would win easily. For example, Microsoft already has shipped a primitive PostScript driver for OS/2's Presentation Manager, but a HP-PCL driver is just rumored for April of 1990.

PostScript as a Translator

PostScript exists for practically any printer—even dot-matrix printers. Just as PostScript helped print shops develop a uniform interface to their wide variety of phototypesetting equipment, PostScript is giving programmers a uniform interface to all output devices in the microcomputer world. When programmers want to position text at a certain location, they tell PostScript the symbol names, fill patterns, and location in a generic fashion, independent of the output device. In fact, the programmer does not need to know what the output device is. In this respect, PostScript is acting like a global, common language.

When Steve Jobs (founder of Apple and NeXT) discovered PostScript in the typesetting world, he realized how much better it was than anything in the Macintosh world. Apple then risked the Macintosh WYSIWYG software by putting PostScript in the LaserWriter. PostScript is not an Apple product. If many Mac programmers learn PostScript, they may begin to demand it as the primary programming interface. Then PostScript would influence a Mac's behavior just as DOS influences a PC. In fact, this has happened. Macintosh programmers realized the enormous capabilities of PostScript. To give their software an edge, Macintosh programmers send PostScript commands to the

LaserWriter and QuickDraw commands to the Macintosh. By doing this, programmers can get the LaserWriter to spin and deform objects or characters in ways a pure Quickcode interface does not allow.

Today, programmers struggle with QuickDraw to get it to perform like PostScript. Similarly, in the DOS world, programmers struggle with Windows. In the OS/2 world, programmers must battle to get the Presentation Manager to perform like PostScript. Developers would be much happier with a uniform video and printer interface across all machines.

PostScript's advantage is that it is output-device independent and resolution independent. It does not matter whether the output device is a printer, screen, slide-creation system, or fax machine. From the programmer's view, PostScript looks the same. Because PostScript puts out graphics data, the output device needs only a simple graphics interface.

Already PostScript is translating. QuickCode now talks to PostScript printers. Adobe's Type Font Manager has taken the first step of translating between QuickDraw and the screen. Whether Microsoft and Apple can wrestle responsibility of PostScript's evolution from Adobe remains to be seen. Even if neither company wins, PostScript still wins. PostScript, in its present form, has enough features to last the rest of history.

PostScript as the Standard

PostScript sells so well because it can print a document that looks the same, no matter where it is printed. Even more important, PostScript devices listen to the same language. Thus, the same PostScript software can drive all output devices without modification, making PostScript a standard printer programming language.

PostScript will never be out-of-date. PostScript is a language like COBOL or FORTRAN or C. Just like FORTRAN is revised every now and then, PostScript will be revised every now and then. Ultimately, however, PostScript is a collection of tools rather than a repository of printer features. PostScript is a method of building printer features, not the printer features themselves. PostScript contains the capability to modify, replace, or add output device-imaging tools. If some of the tools are modified, replaced, or added, PostScript does not change. The only effect is that the quality of the documents printed are enhanced.

PostScript became a standard in 1985, the year the Apple LaserWriter was released. Also, in that same year Adobe authored a series of books (published by Addison-Wesley, 1985) that defined the language, good programming practices, and so on:

PostScript Language, Reference Manual (red book)
PostScript Language, Program Design (green book)
PostScript Language, Tutorial and Cookbook (blue book)

These books form the basis of the PostScript standard. PostScript clones ensure that their printers operate as described in these books. Several independent companies offer testing services to ensure that this is true. These books, along with the behavior of the ImageWriter, have become the PostScript standards to which everyone adheres strictly.

Beside Microsoft's PMScript PostScript product, Destiny and Phoenix are selling PostScript software. Unfortunately, the names of these products cannot include the word "PostScript" because it is trademarked by Adobe. Instead, names like PMScript, PageStyler, PhoenixPage, PacificScript, ImageScript, UltraScript, and so on are being used. If Adobe would put the name of *PostScript* in the public domain, PostScript's dominance would be much clearer.

Long-Term Benefits of PostScript Printers

PostScript is a novel concept that really needs to be repeated in many other areas of computer technology and society. PostScript climbed into the typesetting world and became successful; it is doing the same in the PC world. The reasons are not obvious, but the long-term benefits are. The following is a short list of these benefits:

❏ If the printer breaks and you need to use one down the hall, the document will print correctly.

❏ If your company purchases a new printer, existing files will print correctly.

❏ If you switch application software packages, the files transfer without losing a single formatting, font change, or special effect.

❏ Your company can purchase a phototypesetter and hook it up to the LAN, and you can begin using it immediately.

❏ You can make such things as your logo a little smaller, without any loss in quality.

These benefits sound like the benefits of uniformity. You may associate uniformity with mediocrity and lack of creative stimulus. PostScript promotes the preceding benefits without sacrificing the creative stimulus. In fact, PostScript provides the tools to be more creative than ever before. This section explains why all this is true.

Fonts

What needs to be made clear is that PostScript is a printer language, not a font library. PostScript is the language with which fonts are created. Exactly which fonts are created and the qualities and features of these fonts have nothing to do with PostScript itself. Scalable fonts are actually PostScript programs. At the precise moment a character is printed, the character's PostScript program is typically in total control of a 68000 microprocessor (or better) with 2M to 4M of memory. Anything can happen. The program can use any PostScript command and produce any PostScript error message. This gives the font designer a tremendous amount of power in terms of what can be done with the font—and a lot of responsibility. An inefficient or poorly written character can severely reduce the speed of the PostScript.

Fonts written in the PostScript language can be poorly written, take up huge amounts of space, slow the printer to a crawl, and look ugly. PostScript fonts can be be well written, take up small amounts of space, make the printer look very fast, and look great. These fonts can be purchased from a variety of companies, and the competition is becoming more healthy every day.

Adobe, the company that designed the PostScript language, also sells fonts. These are called "PostScript fonts," which merely means that each character is a PostScript program. Anybody with the correct documentation and training can write a PostScript program that draws characters. Ideally, PostScript would be just the language that font vendors use to compete against each other. Although this is becoming more and more true, there are many Adobe PostScript printers and clone PostScript printers that can accept fonts only from certain vendors.

Companies like International Typeface Corporation (ITC) were supplying fonts to the typesetting industry well before anyone ever thought of computers. These companies have their own trade associations and methods of doing business. Because the fonts they create are not protected by copyrights, trademarks, and patents, they have to protect their font investments through other means. Many of these companies felt that making fonts available in electronic form was inviting people to steal the fonts.

On the other side of the fence are the printer manufacturers. They want to make money on the fonts that are put in their printers. Many try to design their printers so that you have to purchase fonts from them. Take, for example, the HP LaserJet IIp (the laser under $1000). It has a new font cartridge; font cartridges from the older HP LaserJet II and IId cannot be used. Instead, you have to purchase new font cartridges from HP.

When Adobe tried contacting the traditional font vendors, asking whether it could create electronic versions of its fonts, the font vendors were interested in encrypting the electronic files so that no one could steal the work done in creating the fonts. The printer manufacturers that were going to be purchasing Adobe's PostScript software also were interested in encrypting the electronic files. Adobe encrypted the font files because of customer demand.

Adobe encrypted the electronic versions of the fonts it sells. This required unencrypting the fonts when downloading to the printer. Thus, special programs are required to download official Adobe fonts to PostScript printers. In the PC world, these programs are called PSDOWN (for serial interfaces) and PCSEND (for parallel interfaces). The font vendors were happy because no one could steal the electronic form of the fonts, duplicate the fonts, and sell them under a different name.

Printer vendors had a different concern. They wanted to make sure that the printers they sold could use fonts sold by the vendors only. They did not want just any fonts from other companies made available for downloading into the printer. This conflicted, however, with Adobe's goal of providing language independent of the output device, so a compromise was reached. Adobe would add some special secrets to PostScript that only official Adobe fonts could access. These special secrets would enable official Adobe fonts to run quicker and look better in small font sizes, but other font companies could still add fonts.

This cozy relationship was copied by the PostScript clone manufacturers. Clone manufacturers use BitStream fonts. To load specially encrypted BitStream fonts, PostScript clone vendors supply special programs similar to PSDOWN and PCSEND. For example, PSFONT is the name of a program shipped with Destiny's PostScript clone called PageStyler. The PostScript clones also have their own special secrets that enable official BitStream fonts to run quicker and look better in small font sizes.

The cozy relationship between PostScript and font vendors started to break down when Apple wanted exclusives on Adobe's fonts and software. Adobe said no and started supplying printer companies with the software identical to that in the LaserWriter. This enabled printer manufactures to create 100-percent clones of Apple's LaserWriter. Apple retaliated by selling its Adobe stock, developing its own fonts, and trading for PostScript clone software.

Users suddenly found that PostScript clone printers with BitStream fonts were much cheaper than official Adobe PostScript printers. However, then they discovered that the good-looking Adobe fonts used by Apples and typesetters would not work in the clones.

In the fall of 1989, Apple and Microsoft swapped PostScript clone technology for scalable font technology. By this time, two printers (RIPS' Image 4000 and Princeton Publishing Labs' PS-388) had figured out Adobe's encryption and hinting methods. PostScript clones were coming out and getting good reviews. Adobe immediately responded by releasing its encryption secrets to the public. However, hinting is still proprietary. In addition, Adobe lowered its PostScript printer software prices to be competitive with the clone competition.

It remains to be seen whether encryption and hinting will still be considered proprietary secrets. Currently, you can add fonts on your PostScript printer in two ways. You can purchase the fonts from the company where you purchased your printer, or you can purchase generic PostScript compatible fonts from anybody. Expect the generic PostScript-compatible fonts to run slower, to look less attractive, and to not be supported by print shops. If Apple's Royal fonts do become reality, the resulting competition could free the information that would allow very good quality fonts from everyone.

Character Set

The character set used in the Apple LaserWriter has become a standard by default. Officially, PostScript has no character set limitations. To PostScript, a character set is a dictionary object. Each element in the dictionary is character. When told to print a certain character, PostScript looks up the character's name in the dictionary and reads the definition (or PostScript program). The name of a character is like the name of a file. A symbol's name in PostScript is not limited to the 256 patterns of 8 bits, but rather to 128 characters arranged in any fashion. This means that there really are no limitations on a PostScript character set inherent in the PostScript standard.

If a PostScript printer does not have the character set mentioned, you can program the printer to ask the PC for the character set. Thus, character sets can be downloaded automatically.

Emulation of Other Printers

Suppose that your company has 2,000 documents that were designed to print on a specific printer that is no longer available or no longer economical to use. Your company needs to pick another printer. Picking another printer most likely is going to require manually reformatting each of the 2,000 documents. But picking a PostScript printer offers another solution. You can hire someone to write a PostScript program that will emulate the older printer. This program can be sent to the PostScript printer whenever one of the 2,000 older documents needs to be printed. For example, suppose that you want pressing Shift-PrtSc to work with a PostScript printer. A PostScript program for turning a PostScript printer into a simple printer is available in the green book, (PostScript Language, Program Design). Even the escape codes of Appendix A can be emulated with a PostScript program. PostScript is not only easily cloned—it can be used easily to emulate other printers.

Printer Independence

The design goal of the Adobe language has never been speed, but device independence. Consider the role of PC DOS. PC DOS is merely a disk operating system—a collection of subroutines to help make the life of the programmer easier. The goal of PC DOS is to relieve programmers of the need to know all the intimate details of different floppy and hard disk drives that their software may be using. The software talks to DOS in a standard, planned way, and DOS handles all the different types of floppy and hard disks (see fig. 11.2). Similarly, PostScript is designed to insulate programmers from needing to know the details of output devices. Output devices include videoboards, printers, and slide-producing equipment.

Fig. 11.2.

PostScript as a printer operating system.

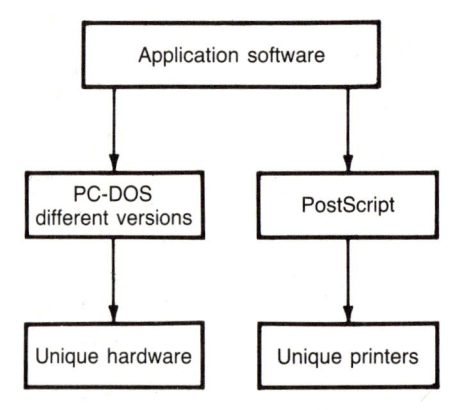

PostScript printers can rotate letters around a circle, stretch the letters, fill them in, or shadow and deform them in ways that are limited only by a programmer's imagination.

Therefore, the first printer supported by any operating system is going to be a PostScript printer. PostScript is supported by Windows, QuickDraw, and Presentation Manager. Although more printer languages may be supported in the future, PostScript is one of the easiest printers to support.

Objectivity

PostScript has been called an object program, in an effort to distinguish it from character and graphic types of programs. Apple's QuickDraw, Microsoft's Windows, and Presentation Manager turn the screen and the printer into graphic devices. These programs try to do the entire imaging job themselves. Even their predefined libraries of subroutines and functions manipulate individual pixels that are displayed.

In PostScript, everything is an object with a name that can be changed and features that can be modified. The drawing act is a two-step process. First, the surface to be drawn on is defined (it can be warped, wrinkled, and so on) and then it is drawn on. This means that the library of PostScript subroutines and functions places pixels on a device-independent surface. Then the pixels are mapped to the real, previously-defined surface. Distortions, rotations, and other special effects can be computed within the printer—and not tie up the computer. Even more important, any GKS function can be translated into a PostScript function.

Standard File Format

PostScript EPS files (encapsulated PostScript) are becoming standard files for everything. Fonts, clip art, documents, and backups have all benefited by being stored in an EPS file. What is difficult to understand is how such a multipurpose file structure can store such an incredible diversity of special effects.

An EPS file does not have a strict file structure like a database's data dictionary. Nor does EPS have special meanings attached to specific control codes. In fact, only letters of the alphabet and normal punctuation are present in an EPS file, even if it contains bit-mapped graphics images. The file can be imported by any word processor that can import standard ASCII text files.

EPS files can be sent to the printer using the regular DOS COPY command—for example, *COPY CALIF.EPS LPT2:*, but EPS files will not print unless a little modification is done to the last two lines of the file. Instead, the PostScript printer will think about printing the file and then at the last moment stop. To force it to print the file, load the EPS file into your word processor, move to the bottom of the document, and switch the position of the last two commands (SHOWPAGE and GRESTORE). Make sure that the last character is a Ctrl-D (the only control code in the whole file). Then the file will print with the DOS COPY command.

> **TROUBLE-SHOOTING TIP** Because EPS files are created in text form, they are huge. Fortunately, you can compress these files easily by using public domain utilities like ARC or ZIP.

Many Macintosh programs are storing temporary copies of files in EPS formats. If a file is corrupted, you can try looking for the backup EPS files with a program that can convert EPS files to more traditional MacPaint files. If you are trying to transfer a drawing or document with the maximum detail present, try creating an EPS file by printing to a file rather than printing to the LaserWriter. Then the EPS file can be loaded onto another application with much more clarity and information than the Macintosh's clipboard.

| TROUBLE-SHOOTING TIP | To print to a file rather than the LaserWriter and thus create an EPS file, choose the Print command and click OK as you would normally on the Macintosh. Then immediately press and hold down the Option key and press F. The file created will be named PostScript. |

Two-Way Communication

One of the biggest features of object printers is that they can talk back to PCs. They even can initiate conversations with the PC or multiple PCs on a LAN. Following are some comments or questions that a PC could send to the printer:

- ❏ Is the paper at the top of the form?
- ❏ Has the letterhead been installed yet?
- ❏ How much memory do you have free?
- ❏ Which fonts have been downloaded?
- ❏ How many pages have you printed in your lifetime?
- ❏ Please recompute these cells of this spreadsheet.
- ❏ Please display your front panel on my screen.
- ❏ Here are some changes to how you are to compute gray scales from now on.
- ❏ Please run this memory diagnostic program and tell me how you are feeling.

Here are some possible comments or questions the printer could send to the PC:

- ❏ Which bin has the letterhead?
- ❏ No legal-size paper present; insert the tray.
- ❏ Do you have the fonts PC #4 on the LAN?
- ❏ Do you have the fonts PostScript laser #2 on the LAN?

❏ I'm finished computing spreadsheet cells; here are the results.

❏ I'm having problems with...

❏ I'm busy printing a huge document for somebody else.

A PostScript printer is intelligent. It can answer a computer's questions. It can initiate conversations with a computer, and it even can hook directly to a local area network.

Basic PostScript Features

You need to ask six basic questions about any PostScript product:

❏ How compatible is it?

❏ How fast is it?

❏ How much memory is available for your PostScript programs?

❏ Does the PostScript product attempt to communicate with the computer?

❏ Can you use the printer on a local area network?

❏ Which manufacturers' fonts does it accept?

Compatibility, Clones, Upgrades, and Version Differences

In the worst case scenario, clone PostScript printers fill boxes with solid black instead of displaying text on a gray background. Some come with fonts that look positively ugly. Some seem to substitute bold characters for regular characters every now and then. Others ignore the BitStream hints. Some clones even generate random patterns of gibberish where characters should appear. More obvious are clones that intermittently refuse to print graphics. But all these problems are present in the pre-release 1.0 versions of the clones. Most clones that have been on the market for more than a year are very compatible. They do create printouts that look exactly like the output of an Apple LaserWriter.

The larger issue is who controls the definition of PostScript, and what are the prospects of its evolution. The first point that needs to be made clear is that PostScript version numbers are more like serial or model numbers than software version numbers. If a PostScript version number is higher than another version, it does not necessarily mean that it has more features and less bugs. In fact, Adobe assigns each new version of the PostScript software it customizes for a company a new version number. This enables Adobe to pinpoint exactly which manufacturer and printer model is being used by someone who has called Adobe with a question or problem.

Since Version 25, Adobe has been careful not to change the PostScript programming language in any way. For certain printer manufacturers, Adobe has added new commands that were specially requested, but these commands are never present in the software Adobe designs for the next manufacturer's printer. The core PostScript commands have not changed since sometime in 1984. This means that the PostScript clone companies are not chasing a moving target like they are in the HP and Epson worlds. Hewlett-Packard improves HP-PCL each time it releases a new HP LaserJet. Epson has published a book describing all the differences between its different printer lines. The PostScript clone makers have a nice stable product to emulate, and they can do so successfully.

Adobe has not been sitting still, however. Although Adobe has not added commands or changed the syntax of commands, it has improved command performance. Adobe has made commands execute quicker, and in some cases, Adobe has improved the quality of its output. For example, the PostScript SPOT command is used to compute which dots in a cell are to be made black to simulate a certain percentage of gray. PostScript has modified what the SPOT command does so that the grays look better on 300 dpi laser printers. Older PostScript printers are not going to produce grays that look as good (see Chapter 10).

Another exciting, innovative feature of PostScript is that old versions can be upgraded through software downloaded to the printer. An old printer that needs a new SPOT function can be upgraded by downloading a new version of the SPOT function, for example. This upgrade will work on the clones as well as the real Adobe product. In fact, there is an opportunity for PostScript utility programs that will update and add features to old PostScript printers.

Utility programs are already in existence. Font companies can trademark the names that they give to fonts. As a result, Adobe's fonts will have different names than clone fonts. A clone PostScript printer, in order to be compatible with software that uses Adobe font names, would need a utility program downloaded to the PostScript clone. This utility would translate Adobe font names to the similar clone font names.

In summary, PostScript clones are compatible. Although the PostScript language is not changing, performance and features are changing. You can upgrade old PostScript printers using software. You need to avoid only the original versions of a PostScript clone printer.

Speed

Probably the biggest difference between PostScript printers is how fast they can print pages. The fastest black-and-white PostScript printers (at a cost of about $10,000) do not give you an increase in speed proportionate to the increase in cost. Probably the most cost-effective printer from the price/speed point of view is the $7,000 Apple LaserWriter IINTX. Table 11.1 was complied from various reviews of PostScript printers. Different test documents cause wide fluctuations within certain categories of printers. Don't look at the actual numbers as being accurate for the specific 72-page document or 8-page newsletter you produce. What is important is the relative times of the different PostScript Printers.

Table 11.1
Time To Print Test Documents

Printer	72-page manual	8-page newsletter
$10,000 B&W PostScript	5 minutes	4 minutes
$7,000 LaserWriter IINTX	10 minutes	4 minutes
$3,500 PostScript Clones	14-24 minutes	29-44 minutes
Slowest Clone	2 hours	1.5 hours
Software Emulation	2.5 hours	2.5 hours

Don't purchase a printer unless you see its speed compared to an Apple LaserWriter IINTX for a variety of documents.

Virtual Memory

Virtual memory, or VM, is the memory that fonts and PostScript programs are stored in. Other memory is reserved for storing the pixels of the image before it is printed, as well as for the PostScript interpreter. *Virtual memory* is the amount of memory free after reserving an imaging area and loading the PostScript interpreter. The total amount of memory advertised in a PostScript printer may be the same, but the amount of VM free can vary depending on how small the PostScript interpreter is and what additional features may have been added. Many times the startup page that is printed when a PostScript printer is turned on lists the amount of VM free.

For example, in a PostScript clone with 2.5M of RAM, 312,444 VM bytes were free. After upgrading the clone to 4.5M, 1,769,748 bytes of VM were free. These numbers are typical of PostScript printers. VM sizes available should be compared with equal numbers of fonts loaded. Here are some typical uses of VM:

Fonts	30,000 bytes × number of fonts
Dictionaries	20 bytes × number of reserved spaces (not used spaces)
Arrays	8 bytes × number of elements
Names	40 bytes × number of names

For example, if you have 1,200,000 bytes of VM memory, you could download 39 fonts (39×30,000 = 1,170,000) a few dictionaries, arrays, and names. More VM is always better. The cost of memory ranges from $100 to $200 per megabyte. More available memory enables you to download more fonts, to have bigger bit-mapped graphic files, and to build larger font caches. Whether you implement PostScript using microcomputer system memory or printer memory, you will need a great deal of memory; a minimum of 3M is a good idea.

Two-Way Communication

When purchasing a PostScript printer, an important issue is whether the printer comes with software that supports two-way communication. Although this is described as optional in the red book (Adobe's PostScript Reference Manual), it is absolutely necessary if you want to write PostScript programs or use the utility programs that involve two-way communication. If the two-way feature is not present, the PostScript printer will not be fully functional in the Macintosh environment. Many of the new Macintosh utilities (such as those that ask the printer to generate a screen font) cannot be used.

The PostScript implementation and the interface cables must support two-way communication in order to support some of the features mentioned in the previous sections. Official PostScript printers and the clones should come with software that turns the PC into a terminal and the PostScript printer into a host. Ask the salesperson or look through the documentation associated with the printer for a program called PSTALK or something of a similar nature. According to official Adobe publications, the talking back feature of a PostScript printer is called the interactive mode. It is an optional feature, according to the Adobe documents, but it is necessary if the PostScript printer is going to communicate error messages to the computer.

LAN Connection

Another important feature that has not been developed yet in the PC world is PostScript support on a local area network. Only Apple LaserWriters connect directly to LANs. In the PC world, network printers are attached to PCs, and the PCs are called printer servers. The PC must be on for printing to occur. If the PC locks up, the shared resource is gone.

To date, the major PC LAN software vendors have not provided software support for laser printers directly attached to LANs. Furthermore, printer vendors have not attempted yet to put local area network interfaces into laser printers and attach them directly to a network. The pieces all exist to hook PostScript printers to PC LANs; someone just has to put these pieces together. Perhaps someday PostScript RIPs will attach typesetters to PC LANs as well as Macintosh LANs.

Fonts

You should not purchase a PostScript printer unless it is advertised as coming with the same 35 fonts that the Apple LaserWriter IINT and LaserWriter IINTX are shipped with. These 35 fonts can be clones of the fonts in the LaserWriter, but there should be a one-to-one correspondence. In the PC world, all software that can talk to a PostScript printer expects these fonts to exist. If you purchase a PostScript printer with less fonts, the software will not work quite right. If you purchase a PostScript printer with more fonts, you may not be able to use the extra fonts.

Before purchasing a PostScript printer, compile a list of font products that will work with that printer. Ask vendors which font products have been tested. Ask which will not work. Determine whether the fonts available in the pages of magazines will work on the PostScript device you are considering. If vendors tell you that their fonts are PostScript fonts, ask them if they have licensed any Adobe software. If they have, assume that their fonts will not work on the PostScript clones. If the font vendors have not licensed any Adobe software, ask them whether their fonts will work only on certain manufacturers' printers. If they tell you that the fonts will work on any PostScript printer, chances are that the fonts will work on a PostScript clone. Remember that the only printer all fonts work on is an official Adobe PostScript printer.

HP LaserJet versus PostScript

In the Macintosh world, the immediate benefits of owning a LaserWriter are obvious. The increased resolution, the more even blacks, the better-looking fonts are all obvious; these are the benefits of a laser printer—any laser printer. The decision is much more difficult in the PC world, where alternative laser printer technologies and software are more prevalent.

In the IBM world, the real choice is between an HP LaserJet printer, which is approximately $2,500 cheaper, and a PostScript printer. You can buy an HP LaserJet for about $1,000 to $1,600, complete with 512K of RAM and some fixed-spaced character fonts. Although these printers are good replacements of typewriters, their output still looks like that of a typewriter. True 300 dpi graphics are not possible with only 512K of RAM. There is 384K available for downloading fonts, but then no room is left if a graphic needs to be printed. In effect, spending $1,000 to $1,600 for a laser printer gets you a good typewriter.

Spending another $1,700 to $2,500 will get you a PostScript printer. PostScript printers need at least 2M of RAM and typically come with 3M or 4M. But 4M of RAM can be added to an HP LaserJet, at a cost of $750, as can a Pacific Page PostScript clone cartridge, at a cost of $450, to give you most of the same features. To decide which is right for you, examine your software. If your software turns the PostScript printer into a typewriter, then you can save yourself money by purchasing an HP LaserJet. If your software tries to rotate fonts or draws high-resolution drawings with different shades of gray, you need a PostScript printer.

So what can a PostScript printer do that an HP printer with the same amount of memory and the same scalable fonts cannot do? Probably the number one feature is that the PostScript can generate accurate proofs of what is going to come out of a phototypesetter. But what if you never plan on using the services of a typesetter?

More and more software is coming out that becomes fully functional only when programming a PostScript printer. With any other printer, the software suddenly becomes crippled and cannot print white letters on a black background, put letters at different angles on the paper, stretch or deform the letters, outline objects, or fill them with different colors or patterns. When only simple commands are needed to activate these features in a PostScript printer, why go to all the effort of forcing the PC to compute each dot's location and send those locations to an HP LaserJet? In the future, expect many of the features that software companies add to their products to be available on only PostScript printers.

The HP LaserJet made the idea of laser printing popular. PostScript is going to make laser printing universal.

Who Should Use a PostScript Printer?

You need a PostScript printer if you plan to output text to a Linotype or other typesetter with a PostScript RIP. You need a PostScript printer if you are interested in creating any unusual graphics or special effects. You also need a PostScript printer if you plan on doing serious desktop publishing.

Don't purchase a PostScript printer to print mailing labels, accounting reports, or database dumps. Many programs in the PC world do not know how to talk to a PostScript printer. Do purchase a PostScript printer to generate attractive brochures, seminar or course workbooks, and other documents that you want to give a professional look.

Purchasing or Upgrading to a PostScript Printer

More than 50 percent of the new laser printer models released in 1989 were PostScript or PostScript clone printers. Circuit boards are available to convert older printers to PostScript printers. Software exists to translate from PostScript to languages the older printer understands. But all these products are not the same, however.

The most popular PostScript laser printers are those sold by Apple. The original LaserWriter comes with four fonts. The LaserWriter Plus comes with 35 fonts; the LaserWriter IINT comes with 11 fonts; the LaserWriter IINTX comes with 35 fonts. Most manufacturers of clones today think that they have to supply all 35 fonts to be competitive. The list price of the LaserWriter IINT is $4,999, and the list price of the LaserWriter II NTX is $6,999.

Currently, the demand for pure PostScript printers is not large enough to drive the price down. Although most of the major printer vendors are coming out with PostScript products, the pricing has not become competitive. The competitive pricing is seen only in printer controller and cartridge markets where most of the clone PostScript software is showing up.

In summary, purchase a LaserWriter for the Macintosh world. For the PC world, you also may want to consider a LaserWriter. The LaserWriter is the safe choice. If you want a pure Adobe PostScript printer, try finding someone that will sell you a QMS PS 810 for between $3,800 and $4,000. For a fully functional clone printer with dual HP-PCL and PostScript personalities, purchase an HP LaserJet II and a Destiny printer controller for a price of $3,200. If you want the cheapest clone PostScript, purchase an HP LaserJet II, add 2M of RAM and the Pacific Page PostScript cartridge for a total cost of $2,400 (street prices).

Adding PostScript to Your Computer System

PostScript printer page description languages can be divided into five categories:

- ❏ Software
- ❏ A card added to an AT
- ❏ A font cartridge added to laser
- ❏ An upgraded printer logic board
- ❏ A new purchase printer

Practically all these methods are identical in price, because they all require massive amounts of memory. For a discussion about whether to purchase a clone PostScript printer, read the "Compatibility, Clones, Upgrades and Version Differences" section as well as the font section earlier in this chapter.

PostScript for Dot-Matrix Printers

Three major programs on the market have the capability of turning a dot-matrix printer into a PostScript printer using software that runs on a PC:

- ❏ Freedom of Press
- ❏ Ultrascript PC
- ❏ Go Script Plus

All require at least 640K of conventional memory and 1M to 2M of expanded memory in the PC. The most reliable of these programs, Freedom of Press, requires that you print to a file, exit your program, and then print that file using the utilities sold by the manufacturer of that program. These utilities average about seven times longer to print than an Apple LaserWriter IINT. Because these three programs are running on the PC's motherboard, the PC's CPU, clock speed, and presence of numeric coprocessor are all going to affect performance.

Freedom of Press, Ultrascript PC, and Go Script Plus are your only choices if you want PostScript printouts on your dot-matrix printer. They cost between $400 and $500 for the software, plus another $200 to $400 for the additional expanded memory if you don't already have it. Purchase the versions that contain at least 35 fonts, because your PC software is going to expect 35 fonts. Some companies have cheaper versions that don't include all the fonts. Similar products are coming out to turn the ImageWriter into a LaserWriter. Freedom of Press and Postprint have announced Macintosh products.

Do not expect to have two-way communication or to incorporate your new dot-matrix PostScript printer in a PC LAN with these software versions of PostScript. Fonts can be added to the programs, but expect more problems trying to manage all this in expanded memory. Expect the cursor to lock up more, to have more incompatibility problems with certain programs and LANs, and to get out-of-memory error messages. Watch this category of PostScript implementation though; some really exciting products could come out in the future.

A similar product in this category uses software to turn dot-matrix printers into HP LaserJet II clones. This product takes advantage of all the fonts available for HP LaserJet printers that will not be available for dot-matrix printers. This package, called LaserTwin, from Metro Software costs $179, uses 29K of RAM, and comes with all the fonts built into a standard HP Series II LaserJet. Fonts from HP, Agfa Compugraphic, BitStream, and others can be downloaded to this software package.

Purchasing a Printer Controller

PostScript controllers are essentially hardware versions of the PostScript software described in the preceding section. Most circuit boards that are purchased contain a 68000 family CPU, 2M to 4.5M of RAM, and cables that connect to most of the popular laser printer engines. In essence, a specialized computer is purchased that is dedicated to a current laser printer. These boards offer the following advantages:

- ❑ Uploading and downloading of fonts at PC slot speeds

- ❑ Bidirectional communication with specialized software; when writing PostScript programs, you can view error messages the PostScript interpreter generates.

- ❑ Fast (because of the dedicated hardware) compared to the software versions of PostScript already mentioned.

- ❑ Capability to use the local PC's hard disk as if it were the built-in hard disk of the fancier $10,000 PostScript printers.

Manufacturers of these boards also are developing serial ports for the purpose of enabling other PCs to share the PostScript controller without any additional software. Just run a cable from another PC (or LAN printer server) to the PC containing the PostScript controller. For a discussion of this subject, read "The Future of PostScript Printers," later in this chapter.

The recommended board in this category is called the PageStyler II, made by Destiny Technology—one of the first PostScript clone vendors. This board is in its second generation and ranks at the top of most clone speed tests. Its speed is about the same as that of the slower, lower-priced Apple LaserWriter IINT. The board's list price is $1,690. Competitors in this category of PostScript hardware add-ons are IBM's PostScript printer (Personal PagePrinter II), Conographic's Conodesk 6000, Eicon Technology's Eiconscript, Imagen's PC Publish Kit, Abaton's PostCard, and RIPS Image 4000.

There are many other non-PostScript, proprietary products in this category of hardware add-ons to give your old printer PostScript-like capabilities. Most of these products are much faster than PostScript and provide all the features of PostScript except one: the dedication to output device independence. These products do not have the bidirectional capabilities of PostScript, nor the books and magazines dedicated to exploring their possibilities. All information about these boards is proprietary. If your immediate needs cannot be met with PostScript products, consider the video controllers and printer controllers sold by LaserMaster Corporation.

Adding a PostScript Cartridge

One of the hottest PostScript products on the market today is a product that looks, feels, and acts like a traditional font cartridge. No add-ins, software, or cables are required. Just plug into one of the two font cartridge slots on an HP LaserJet II and instantly, the printer is turned into a PostScript printer—if the HP LaserJet has 2.5M of RAM. Most HP LaserJets are shipped with only 512K of RAM, so you would need to add 2M at a cost of $400.

Currently, Pacific Data Products is selling a clone PostScript cartridge called PacificPage. The PacificPage PostScript cartridge already has been discounted to around $450. Hewlett-Packard is selling an official Adobe PostScript cartridge for the IID that lists for $995. IBM has announced, but not released, a $2,000 Adobe PostScript cartridge for its LaserPrinter that competes directly with HP's LaserJet II.

The PostScript clone software inside the Pacific Data Products cartridge was developed by Phoenix Technologies—the same company that wrote the first ROMs that enabled clones of IBM PCs and XTs to be built. It is being sold as a scalable font cartridge. Early reports show that it is slow, at about the same speeds of the software used to change dot-matrix printers into PostScript printers. Because it comes with no software, this means the following:

❏ You will have to add good-looking fonts by purchasing another font cartridge from Pacific Data Products.

- ❏ Bidirectional communication is not possible.
- ❏ Although it can accept downloading of generic PostScript fonts, it really needs to be treated as a scalable font cartridge for an HP LaserJet printer.

Upgrading Laser Printers

For first-generation laser printers such as the original 128K HP LaserJet and its competitors, upgrading to a laser printer is the only realistic option for adding PostScript capabilities. You can upgrade by taking the printer apart, throwing away the current printer logic board, and substituting a PostScript logic board.

This type of upgrade was popular in late 1987 and early 1988, but today is not popular because most of the modern HP LaserJets have an Optional I/O port that enables a printer controller to take over the printer engine temporarily. When finished, the PostScript controller can release control back to the printer's original logic board. This enables the original printer logic board and the new printer controller to function with the same printer engine. If you rip out the old printer logic board and substitute the PostScript controller, your original printer is gone. It is an advantage to have both PostScript and the original printer controller because many older software packages can talk only to the older printer logic boards.

Currently, Apple is the only printer manufacturer that is promoting this expensive upgrade path of replacing printer logic boards. Apple's $2,800-LaserWriter II SC (not a PostScript printer) can be upgraded to a LaserWriter IINT ($4,999) or IINTX ($6,999) just by purchasing a new printer logic board. The prices mentioned are the list prices of the machines.

PostScript Language

This section is a short introduction to the PostScript language. There are four reasons that you may want to program in PostScript:

- ❏ You may want to add a special text manipulation feature to Ventura or PageMaker by redefining the PostScript header files.
- ❏ You may want to create a special company logo that cannot be produced with any drawing package.
- ❏ Your PostScript printer is not working, and you want to watch the commands going to the printer and read the error messages that the printer sends the computer.

❑ You may be interested in a new career—programming in PostScript.

The PostScript language is similar to an HP calculator in that stacks of data are processed. Data comes before the command. For example, to add numbers on an HP calculator, you press these keys:

3 Enter
3 +

Then 6 is displayed.

In PostScript, you enter the data as follows:

3 3 add

To see the result, press the equal (=) sign.

Like modern object-oriented programs, the objects created have certain types. After you create the objects, they can be used by other objects. In this sense, PostScript is similar to programming languages such as FORTH or SMALLTALK.

PostScript is an interpreter; error messages are generated immediately when problems are encountered. In this sense, programs can be debugged like the interpretive Basic programs. To see and correct these errors, however, requires a printer interface that provides two-way communication. Furthermore, PC software has to be available that activates this feature.

These are some of the features of the PostScript language mentioned in earlier chapters:

❑ Documents can become too complex with too many font changes or too much detail in drawings.

❑ PostScript is more easily confused then regular graphic and character printers.

❑ Switching out of PostScript into another printer emulation mode is difficult.

❑ You can create special effects that are impossible to create by using an air brush, pen, or PC drawing package.

When these features are coupled with the interactive mode, PostScript actually starts looking like an operating system. It has a DOS or UNIX-like prompt. Commands are typed in and error messages are received. Printer memory is managed; passwords are requested, and hard disk files are managed. PostScript could be called an output device operating system.

Future of PostScript Printers

PostScript printers demand a great deal of memory, a fast CPU, and a hard disk. Computers already have all these features. Why have two CPUs, one in the printer and one in the computer? Why have 4 or 5M of RAM in the printer and 4 or 5M of RAM in the computer? Steve Jobs designed NeXT precisely to save us money by removing the duplication. The ideal PostScript solution for the current IBM world would be for someone to combine the features of the dedicated PostScript printer controller with the flexibility of the software that turns dot-matrix printers into PostScript printers. Ideally, the CPU and the hard disk used would be those found in current PCs, whether they are older PC, XT, or AT models, clones, or the PS/2s.

Imagine taking an old AT, adding a cheap video interface to the old HP LaserJet II, and a video interface card to the AT. You would boot the DOS operating system, add the LAN software, and then dedicate the whole computer to a PostScript program. Now the LAN has a PostScript printer that everyone can share. The PC support personnel have a standard old PC they know and love to support and fix. Even a Macintosh on a LAN cannot distinguish between this printer and a LaserWriter. Look for this solution in future.

In the meantime, expect PostScript videoboards to appear in the Macintosh and PC worlds. Expect EPS (encapsulated PostScript files) to become the standard file format for document interchange. Expect to see PostScript invading the world of X-Windows and becoming the premier language of all output devices.

Chapter Summary

PC Magazine predicts that 100 percent of the magazine will be produced using PostScript sometime in 1990. The momentum toward PostScript is incredible. The capability of the PostScript printer to off-load the pixel generation and its capability to operate like a smart node on a network promise exciting features in the printer.

The safe PostScript printer to purchase is an Apple LaserWriter (even if you live in an IBM or clone world). Clones of PostScript products are going to play a significant role in driving the cost of PostScript down in the near future. Currently, in the IBM world, PostScript built into circuit boards that fit into a slot inside of an AT-class machine and hook up to a standard HP LaserJet II-class laser printer is the most functional, cost-effective route to go, but you risk font problems with typesetters. The only safe purchase is an Apple LaserWriter.

In the Next Chapter

Chapter 12 explores general troubleshooting principles and applies them specifically to printers. When you are frustrated with a printing problem, or when Chapter 14's symptoms and solutions don't help, turn to Chapter 12. Ideally, you will learn to anticipate printing problems, and have fun fixing them after reading Chapter 12.

IV

Maintenance and Troubleshooting

Includes

Isolating Problems and Finding Solutions
Solving Serial and Parallel Interface Problems
Troubleshooting

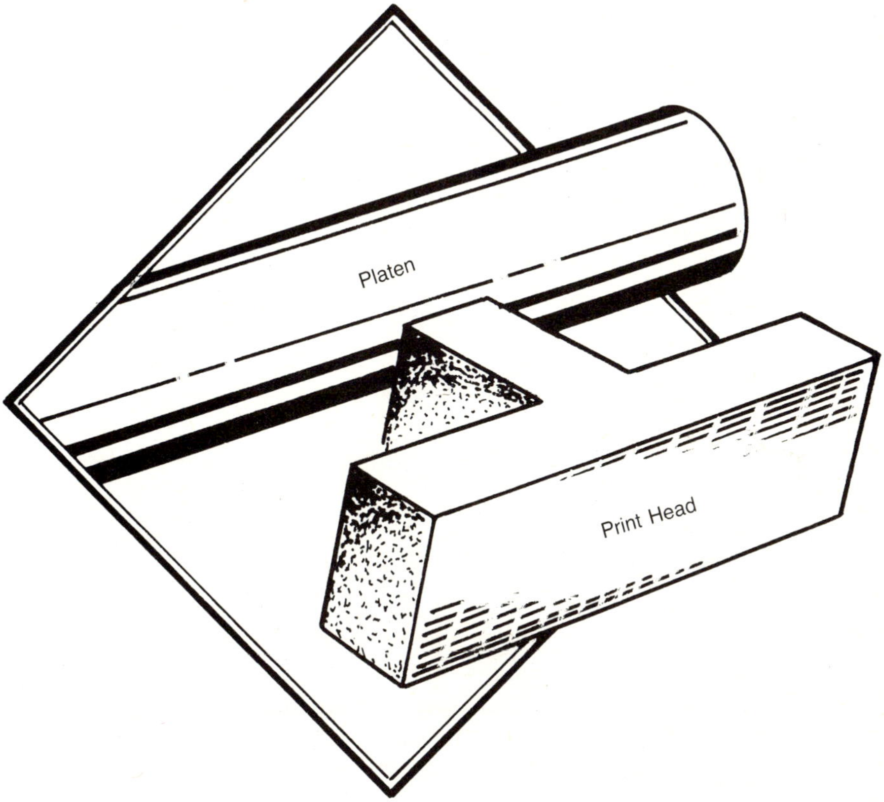
Platen
Print Head

12

Isolating Problems and Finding Solutions

Printing problems take all shapes and forms. The computer may not send the data, or the keys (or mouse buttons) pressed to start the printing process may not work. Perhaps you are trying to print a bar chart for the first time, and the software is looking for the printer's fonts on a floppy disk in drive B. Maybe the printer's ribbon is not properly inserted, or the toner cartridge is bad. These specific printing problems do have specific solutions.

But this chapter does not address specific printing problems. Instead, all printing problems are lumped into one category: something is wrong. And the focus of this chapter is on teaching you how to organize yourself, what tools you need, what mental attitude you should have, and what preparation and training you need in order to solve problems.

The first part of this chapter could be applied to troubleshooting anything—printers, microcomputer systems, elevators, or automobiles. Later in the chapter, printer-specific troubleshooting hints, tricks, and techniques are reviewed. When you are frustrated with a problem, read this chapter. It may help convert the tension of troubleshooting into productive activity and build your confidence. And remember that becoming a good troubleshooter takes practice, just as sports, foreign language, and music do.

Developing the Magic

Have you ever met someone who seemed to work computer magic—someone who could just talk to a computer system to get it to work, someone who could merely walk by or touch the computer system and fix it? These people exist. And so does the magic. You can develop it. You merely need to have a positive attitude, learn from your experiences, and document your troubleshooting experiences.

Gaining a Positive Attitude

Remember that because the equipment was built by human hands, it *can* be fixed. The first step is to set aside a chunk of time, free from other pressures of life. If your true objective is to fix things so that you can print the report that was due yesterday, then you will never learn to troubleshoot. You must be able to walk up to your poor computer system, accept the worst-case scenario, and then say to yourself, "If I fix it, I am going to feel great." Remove from your mind the objective of printing the report. The goal has to be fixing the computer system. Reward yourself for that accomplishment, not for printing the report.

After you are relaxed, have dedicated a chunk of time to the problem, and have accepted the losses, start fiddling. Search for what is working; don't look for something broken. Turn on the printer, turn on the computer, and check whether the lights flash and the print head moves normally. Time how long the laser printer takes to warm up. Inventory what parts of the computer system are working. Build your confidence in the system.

Someone looking over your shoulder may think that you're playing with the computer system—wasting time playing your favorite games, printing in your favorite font, playing with some strange software, or writing programs that no one will ever use. That's OK. Learn to play and have fun with the computer system. Do whatever you feel like doing.

When you stumble across something that does not work, don't try to figure out why it is not working. Instead, study the symptoms. If an error code is present, don't try to decipher it. Instead, try to figure out where it came from, because the software that generated the error message is working, and the device that stored the error code is functioning. If the printer beeps, don't immediately think that you're getting an error message indicating that the printer is on the verge of death. Instead, read the manual and assume that the printer is trying to tell you something, such as "insert a sheet of paper in the manual feed slot." Start by assuming that everything is a naturally occurring event that you have never seen before.

Finally, learn to ask yourself lots of questions. Every bit of information you dig up should ideally stimulate 10 other questions. Struggle to ask the computer system or the manuals each question in different ways. The computer system was designed by regular people, so try climbing into their heads and imagining what they were thinking when they designed this part of the system. The physical world, whether electrical or mechanical, fluidic or optic, chemical or magnetic, is understandable. Convince yourself of this fact.

Learning from Experience

Troubleshooting is not a special skill that only a few can learn. Anyone who has dealt with frustration, guilt, and the unknown knows how to troubleshoot. Anyone who has listened to a two-year-old tearfully describe a problem knows what troubleshooting is. The brain is a marvelous tool. If you relax, it will draw parallels and analogies with previous stressful situations. Your brain will start suggesting solutions that seem to come from nowhere.

Don't avoid troubleshooting problems. One of the most fascinating parts of life is solving troublesome situations. When you meet someone, chances are they have a computer also (one-third of households in the United States have one). Ask others how their computers are behaving. People love to talk about their problems. Use every opportunity to accumulate troubleshooting experiences.

Hovering over the shoulder of an experienced problem-solver is a great way to learn. When you are just beginning, troubleshooting is frustrating. You have too many unknowns, too many observations, and too many events that don't make sense. For every answered question, another unanswered one pops up. What is neat about troubleshooting, however, is that, somewhere, someone else has already figured out the answer—if only you can ask the right question. Through practice, you learn the most important questions and answers.

Try asking *lots* of questions, perhaps unrelated ones. Whenever you read a manual or converse with a troubleshooter, ask many "What if" and "Why" questions. Clear up the fog. Live for the special moment when a manual or conversation supplies the answer. When you're alone, puzzle over unanswered questions—even if your equipment is working. Reserve some time each day, such as when you are driving home from work, for this kind of activity.

All this thinking serves a purpose. Those with the most knowledge and experience can discover problems more easily. Problems are never identified; they are discovered. Don't form hypotheses and look for evidence to support them. "Hunches" have a nasty habit of blinding the truth. Instead, look for clues and learn which clues are more important than others. After gathering enough evidence, the exact problem should be clear—and the solution easy. The section on "Using Evidence-Gathering Tools" is full of tips for gathering evidence about printer problems.

But experiences with problems are not the only experiences necessary. You need to have many *successful* experiences operating and using the equipment. A fine line exists between problem behavior and correct behavior. Trying to distinguish between the two after some problems have developed is frustrating and difficult. *Before* the equipment breaks, learn what every button does; test every combination and feature that you can, even if you never plan on using that feature. Later, when the features that you or your client normally use fail, you can check the other features to see whether they are still working, and thus narrow down where the problem is located.

But be careful. Successfully solving a problem is exhilarating and addicting. You can carry your troubleshooting too far and turn into a computer whiz. The phone will start ringing, and you will end up solving other users' problems and not doing your real job. These are some symptoms of troubleshooting fanatics:

- They can hear printer and computer noises that nobody else hears.
- They can see lights flickering that nobody else sees.
- They smell and feel components while power is on.
- They gossip about microcomputer equipment.
- They secretly collect manuals.
- They read the manual at night in bed.
- They never read manuals in front of clients.
- They insult each other with dumb questions.
- They honor each other with extremely technical questions.

Documenting Your Troubleshooting

Documentation is an important part of troubleshooting. Even if you are troubleshooting full-time, remembering every detail of every piece of equipment that you run across is impossible. Just as important are details about the users and companies involved. Repair tickets and return authorizations are necessary for large repair organizations that involve more than one person in the repair process.

The documentation suggested here, however, is more of a personal journal, which is not used to build a corporate artificial intelligence database but rather to help build confidence. A troubleshooting journal should not be considered corporate property, but corporations should encourage this type of documentation.

The first entry in your troubleshooting log should be a description of your first experience (or your client's experience) with the problem. What symptoms did you notice first? Usually users report concise descriptions of the problem, including specific error messages. For example, suppose that you turn on the PC and see the error code 901 flash on-screen. Because you have been to a troubleshooting course, you happen to have a manual describing what all the IBM error codes mean. 901 is described as "printer error." Later, suppose that you hear another printer problem described as "901." If you have recorded or sorted your previous troubleshooting experiences by reported symptoms, you can look up how you last solved the 901 problem.

After writing down the reported symptom, include a description of all clues—evidence that you gathered to solve the problem. For the 901 problem, for example, your entry may look something like this:

This job was an install.

The printer was an old used one, formerly attached to another computer system.

They tried to use the old printer cable.

Printer turned out to be a serial printer. Discovered this fact by looking at the printer's connector and by reading description of switches found inside printer. Old serial printer cable was plugged into the PC's parallel port.

901 occurred during power on the PC, and only occurred when the printer was attached to PC.

Solution was to build serial cable.

Although you may never run across this particular 901 problem again, reading the entry in the future will build your confidence, focus your mind in reality, and start the creative juices flowing. And if the 901 problem does occur again, you will be able to isolate the problem more quickly because of your previous experience.

Solving Paradoxes

A *paradox* is a situation in which the symptoms presented are contradictory—they seemingly rule each other out. Solving these paradoxes can seem magical because paradoxes do not really exist in the troubleshooting world. Whenever you sense a paradox surfacing, do not give in to it. A paradox can blind like an assumption or a hypothesis can. Instead, consider a developing paradox a warning sign. A paradox indicates that a false assumption has been made; a bit of evidence has been overlooked, or a troubleshooting procedure has been sloppily performed.

For example, suppose that printer X does not work with computer A but does work with computer B. You therefore take printer Y (formerly attached to computer B) and attach it to computer A. Printer Y works with that computer also. You say to yourself, "Great. Everything is working." But the next day someone calls and says that printer Y is not working with computer A. So you take printer Y back to computer B, and it does not work there either. But now printer X works with computer A.

This problem is a typical paradox. You have to read the discussion 15 times plus draw pictures on napkins just to figure out what is going on. But the problem probably has nothing to do with the printers that are being moved around. Probably the printer cable or font cartridge is causing the problem. A solution always exists.

Common troubleshooting sense often seems to be innate. It is usually accompanied by a stubborn, tunnel-vision, independent streak that irritates others. But where most would give up trying to fix something, troubleshooters don't. At first this trait is called stupidity. After enough practice, the stupidity turns into common sense and later into magic. Experience builds common sense. Experience, for example, tells you that hardware develops problems one at a time, that multiple symptoms point to a single problem, and that a serial printer setup expecting a faster baud rate than the PC is transmitting prints extra characters.

Using Evidence-Gathering Tools

When troubleshooting, the most important step is gathering evidence about what is wrong. Think of the following ideas as tools rather than procedures. Use them to troubleshoot printer problems.

Checking the Simple Things

When your printer develops a problem, first check the simple things. See whether the power cords are all plugged in, the data cable to the printer is attached, the printer is on-line, the printer's power is turned on, and the printer is plugged into the power strip. Check the computer's configuration to make sure that no one has messed with the CONFIG.SYS or AUTOEXEC.BAT files in the PC world, and the system folder in the Mac world.

Unfortunately, the exact contents of CONFIG.SYS files are almost always different, no matter how hard you try to configure all machines the same way. AUTOEXEC.BAT files work with the CONFIG.SYS files and often contain commands that influence the behavior of printers associated with the particular computer. You have no way to tell by looking what should be in the CONFIG.SYS file or the AUTOEXEC.BAT file. You should store backups of these files on a floppy and in a subdirectory hidden somewhere on the hard disk, where a simple batch file can resurrect them if they are accidentally trashed.

Isolating the Problem

This section is intended for those of you who have no idea where the printer problem is. This material also is intended to help you isolate random, intermittent problems.

Before isolating a problem, you first need to determine whether the printer has *ever* worked. An indirect question that approaches this issue is "How frequently has the printer been used?" "Trouble" calls are often the result of installation problems or inexperienced operators. When the problem is due to poor software installation or lack of training, the following steps do not work as well. Review Chapter 8 for installation and configuration help.

Printing problems could be anywhere. Perhaps you are attempting to print something that the printer or the computer is not capable of printing. Or perhaps staples were dropped into the keyboard and are intermittently disabling the keys you use to control the printing process. The first step is to isolate the problem to one of the components. In a printer subsystem, the major components are

- ❏ Operator experience
- ❏ Application software
- ❏ Operating system
- ❏ Computer printer port
- ❏ Printer cable
- ❏ Printer

Check these components in the order that they are listed.

Operator Experience

The first time you have problems printing something, try printing an older document that you have successfully printed before. If that document again prints successfully, perhaps you are doing something wrong while trying to print the problem document. Perhaps you are asking the application software to do something that the manual implies is possible but is really not. Or maybe the problem document is unusual—for example, the largest ever attempted. Perhaps you are using a new printer or a new feature of the software program. Merge the old and the new documents, cut the new document into sections, and print each section. Search for anything in the new document that may be different from the old document. Keep repeating the problem, print pages again and again, while trying to analyze what you are doing differently.

Ask other users whether they have experienced the same sort of problems. Usually, most users share the same frustrating experiences when learning a new microcomputer software package.

Application Software

Even if the application software is working, check the application program's configuration. Ideally, before a problem occurred, the person who installed the printer created a folder or document describing exactly how the software package was configured, and also printed each configuration screen. Using this information, you can compare the original configuration with the current configuration. Rather than have a separate printer configuration program that can be hidden away, some software programs enable users to modify the printer configuration within the application program. This feature creates the possibility that users may accidentally ruin the printer configuration while exploring the application program.

If the current configuration is identical to the original, next determine whether the problem is in the application itself. First try printing the document that is causing the trouble. Print the document over and over again, turning on and off the printer and the PC each time. If the problem occurs in the same spot every time, save the document. Try inserting text at the beginning of the document and then printing. Try inserting text at the end and then printing. See whether the problem moves or stays at the same spot on the page.

If the problem moves with the text, the problem is most likely in the application software. If the problem stays at a certain spot on the page, no matter what is printed, the problem is probably in the printer. In either case, find a similar program with the same capabilities. Set the similar program up to print the same document if possible and then test the printer. For example, if one program has trouble making the top line double height, try another program that can make the top line of a page double height. If both programs fail, the problem is not in either program. If just one program fails, that program is the problem.

If the application software is the source of the problem, report the problem to the technical support staff of the company that wrote the application software. The support people may have already heard of the problem and may have a solution. Otherwise you must convince them that a problem exists. They may ask you to send a disk containing the problem file. They may try to point the finger at something else. In this case, you can try convincing them that you have indeed properly isolated the problem. (Perhaps you will need to read them this chapter over the phone.) Your other alternative is to contact your local users group. Usually someone else there will be willing to duplicate the problem on another machine and help you convince the application software company that a problem exists.

Operating System

In both the Macintosh and PC worlds, the operating system in many cases is responsible for some printer information. If the operating system configuration is messed up, the printer can stop working. In the PC world, the CONFIG.SYS and AUTOEXEC.BAT files are sometimes used to configure the printer. You should make a printout of the original contents of these files. (See this chapter's section on "Checking the Simple Things.") The first screen you see when turning on a computer should have options that check system configuration information or at least print the configuration so that it can be compared to a backup paper copy of the configuration information.

In the PC world, you are most likely to have operating system problems if you use serial printers. Very little parallel printer information is maintained by PC DOS anymore. PC DOS in serial mode abuses printers and does not listen to a printer's cries of "stop, stop, you are sending data too fast." And, because parallel printers are the default configuration, if the PC reverts to the default conditions, serial printers are dead. Other problems with the operating system are described in Chapter 13.

In the Mac world, printer drivers may cause the problem. Different manufacturers require their own special driver software. If the software is provided by a third party or the alternative printer company, the software is going to be suspect. Even in the Apple printer world, version problems are possible. The same is true of Windows and GEM environments.

To check the operating system configuration, remove any print buffers and spoolers and see whether the printer works. Move the printer off the LAN to a stand-alone machine and see whether the printer works better. Try reproducing the problem with older operating system versions. If none of these methods changes the printer's behavior, move on to checking the computer's printer ports. If only one of these methods works, you have enough information to identify the problem.

In the PC world, try using the operating system to print. Use the COPY command to copy a text file to the printer. Pressing Shift-PrtSc should always print something. Sometimes the application software can print, but PC DOS cannot. In the IBM PC world, you have to check each application software separately to see whether it can print after installation. Merely checking the operating system's printing capability and extrapolating to application software is impossible.

Computer Printer Port

The computer printer port is the circuit board containing the printer circuitry inside the computer. In the old IBM world of PCs, XTs, and ATs and the old Apple world of Apple IIs, the printer port circuitry was on an expansion circuit board. This design made the board easier to throw away. In the PS/2 world and the Macintosh world, the computer printer port is built into the machine. The printer port circuitry is harder to remove.

Some printers, as well as the PC, have both serial and parallel ports. Purchase or build both and test both if possible. This approach provides excellent backup and is a troubleshooting aid. Testing both parts help isolate the cable and interface problems.

> HINT | If a printer contains both parallel and serial ports, purchase parallel and serial ports and parallel and serial cables. Set up both and make sure that both work. In the future, troubleshooting should be much easier.

You can upgrade many PC laser printers by adding printer memory and PostScript printer controllers inside the PC. These controllers often attach to the printer through video cables or through cables directly into the printer's bus. In many cases, the original cables and ports are only temporarily disabled and can still be activated. If the original port worked, yet the add-on PostScript board or JLaser card does not, you have isolated the problem.

> TROUBLE-SHOOTING TIP | Laser parallel ports are particular and don't often work with PC parallel ports. Although slower, the serial ports seem to work over a broader range of PCs.

The final option to try before giving up on the parallel ports is to reduce the operating speed of the PC. Most XT and AT clones sold today can operate at different speeds. The front panel of AT clones sometimes contains a button that changes the operation speed. You can toggle many clone XTs between slow and "turbo" modes by holding down the Ctrl and Alt keys and pressing the plus (+) or minus (-) key on the numeric keypad. Both clone ATs and XTs often have a jumper on the motherboard that activates turbo speeds. By changing the speed of a computer, you can identify which boards have arthritis.

If the optional ports are not available or if both parallel and serial ports exhibit the same failure symptoms, the next step is to change printer cables.

Printer Cables

Printer cables all have maximum lengths, depending on the type of circuitry driving the cable (such as SCSI, HPIB, parallel, or serial). Special-order cables can be too long, causing letters to be lost. Standard cables ordered out of catalogs follow the industry's collective cable-length wisdom. Often, however, the industry standards don't seem to apply because they assume "standard wire" but do not directly specify the characteristics of such "standard wire."

Cables can be made out of paper clips, paper, tape, string, and aluminum foil in a pinch. Ribbon cables contain Y-shaped connectors that are smashed onto the ends and are notorious for causing connection problems. For this reason, you should always purchase a perfectly built cable to keep on hand for testing purposes. This way you can replace your cheap cable temporarily with an expensive one to see whether the cheaper cable is causing the problems. If changing the cables does not make the printer behave itself, your next step is to check the printer.

The Printer

Printers are rarely the problem. If they do act up, they are usually consistent. They mess up during self-tests as well as while printing PC data. A situation in which the circuitry that receives data fails but the rest of the printer passes the self-test is extremely uncommon. But in the rare instance where the problem is not detected by the printer's self-test, the following isolation procedure can prove whether the problem is in the printer.

Swap the suspect printer with a printer in another system (leave the cable attached to the PC). If the problem stays in the computer system, the port or cable in the computer is suspect. If the problem moves with the printer, you have isolated the problem to the printer. If the problem is in the computer, try swapping the printer interface within the computer. In Macs and PS/2s, this task will be impossible. But you can do it in the older Apple IIs and PCs, XTs, and ATs.

Repeating the Problem

The most important information-gathering method for troubleshooting purposes is to repeat the problem event over and over again. Once you can repeat the problem on demand, play Sherlock Holmes. Design experiments that repeat the problem in different ways. For example, if the problem was originally associated with printing, try printing with a software package that uses different keys on the keyboard for printing. If the problem has something to do with the printer, the keys used should not make a difference. If the problem has something to do with the keyboard, however, the printer should start working.

If the problem occurs intermittently, determine the frequency of the problem. Write down how many times the problem occurs during a week, a day, or an hour. Write down exactly what software packages were being used and which documents were being printed. Look for a pattern. Computer memory problems as well as printer memory problems can cause intermittent random glitches that make printers look sick.

Repeat problems in search of clues, but deciding which clue to pursue next should not always be determined by logic. Instead, pursue clues that are new and interesting; pursue clues in foreign territory where you have never been. Lifting the fog of ignorance and unanswered questions is the goal of all troubleshooting. Consciously relax and play with the broken equipment. Poke at it. Design new ways to torture it. Don't let the stress of a troubleshooting challenge ruin your life. Instead, use the stress to generate new insights. Then solutions usually appear before you are aware of them.

Configuring the Printer to the Minimum

When a printer is having trouble, remove all optional font cartridges, extra memory, special cut-sheet feeder trays, specialized interfaces, and add-on products. This stripped-down printer is called a *minimal printer*. Do the same in the PC. A minimal PC has just a motherboard, a videoboard, a hard disk, floppy disk drives, and a printer port. Test this system. If the problem is still present, go through the previously outlined isolation steps (see "Isolating the Problem").

Otherwise, add the options one at a time until the entire system is reassembled, or until the problem reappears. By adding the options one at a time, you can identify exactly what is working and not working. If everything is added and then the printer works, try cleaning all metal surfaces, blowing out the dust, pushing all socketed chips back into their sockets, and pushing all the boards back into their slots. If the problem reappears when you add an option, find the manuals associated with that option, and read through its configuration. Try reconfiguring the option all the different possible ways. If none of the reconfigurations work, then try reconfiguring the board to which the printer is attached. If you cannot find a solution, call the manufacturer and explain your difficulties.

Swapping Printers

How many programmers does it take to change a light bulb? None—it is a hardware problem. How can a programmer be distinguished from a troubleshooter when fixing a flat tire? The troubleshooter is swapping tires to figure out which one is broken.

These jokes illustrate the weaknesses of both programmers and engineers or techies. Although programmers don't want to touch hardware, troubleshooters have a tendency to swap hardware whenever a problem occurs. Swapping can be dangerous and must be approached with caution.

Suppose that printer A does not work at all when attached to system 1. Printer B is working fine with system 2. The idea is to determine whether the problem is in printer A or system 1. Thus printers A and B are swapped. Printer A is attached to system 2 and does not work. Printer B is attached to system 1, and it does not work either. Printer A and B are switched back. Again, printer A does not work with system 1. But now printer B does not work with system 2. It seems as if system 1 is destroying printers.

In summary, swapping can allow one device to destroy many others. The option or component that is destroying other components is sometimes called a "devil." Suppose that the devil is located in the printer controller inside the case of the computer. Whenever a printer is attached, the devil destroys the printer. Because devils are hard to identify, you should make every effort to identify a problem without swapping. Only when you have tried everything else and have not found the problem, should you attempt swapping.

Most devils kill permanently. If the problem is intermittent, a devil or disease usually is not present. Swapping is fine in this circumstance. But if equipment completely dies, smokes, or explodes, your chances of having a devil increase dramatically.

Fortunately, devils are rare in mature equipment. Engineers are designing better devices. As revisions are made to an old product line, engineers eliminate devils from the circuit board or module level. Inside a module, however, one chip may blow up another. For engineers and most corporations, this situation is OK as long as the devil's activity is confined to the circuit board or module. This is alright because module replacement has proven to be much more cost-effective than component replacement.

TROUBLE-SHOOTING TIP	If you are troubleshooting a one-of-a-kind or original production model of any piece of equipment, expect devils to be more prevalent.

Changing One Thing at a Time

Any time system components are changed, the dangers mentioned previously are present. Changing system components, whether entire devices like monitors or pieces of a printer, requires patience and discipline. Usually, an amateur is interested in solving the problem as quickly as possible. In the rush to solve one problem, most of the time more problems are created.

For example, suppose that you are changing one part. If the swapped part does not produce any changes, you swap another part but don't replace the original first part you swapped. The mixture of swapped good parts and original parts can sometimes create new problems or change the symptoms of the old. Furthermore, if the phone rings or the sun goes down, you may not remember the exact combination, forgetting which parts were swapped and which were original. Parts all look the same. Panic sets in, and you have to try to create the original problem. Instead, a different problem appears. You have no way to tell whether this problem is the original problem changing disguises, a second old problem revealed, or a new problem creeping up. What was one problem can explode into multiple problems.

When troubleshooting, label the original parts of each machine. Write down the initial settings. After swapping unsuccessfully, swap back. Always try to keep the swap and trouble machine parts together. Perhaps the trouble machine has a unique combination of parts that fight each other. Losing the ability to duplicate the problem can ruin a troubleshooting effort and hang a black cloud of suspicion over both the swap and the formerly broken printer—even if both are working.

The final bit of advice is to start always in the broken system and try to find a part that breaks the working system. After the working system has been broken, a part should be left over that will make the broken system work. In the troubleshooting world, this tactic is called "moving the problem."

If a part from the broken system does not break the functioning system, put the part back into the broken system. Then check to see whether the broken system is still broken. Often the trip to a functioning system somehow heals the broken part. The reason is that most problems are dirty connectors, chips climbing out of their sockets, and so on.

The alternative is to find a part in the working system that makes the broken system function. But finding a broken part and using it to break a functioning system is better for the following reasons.

A broken part inserted into a functioning machine is less likely to contain a devil because most devils take up residence in parts that are not easy to swap. In fact, most devils are located in the power supply. This device is usually the last one you move out of a broken system into a functioning system. First change the easiest parts to remove, then progress to the heavier parts like motors and power supplies.

If parts are moved out of a functioning system into a broken one, the devil or disease is being fed with nice functioning boards to break. If parts are moved out of the functioning system, those parts receive the benefit of your attention, not the parts that are broken. Boards in the broken machine are the ones that need fixing. The boards in the broken printer need their chips pushed down and their connectors cleaned. Cables in the broken system need to be abused. If parts are moved from the functioning system to fix the broken one, the broken system's parts do not receive enough attention.

A second and more important reason for trying to break a working system rather than fixing a broken one is this: Once a formerly broken system is working, the natural response is to leave it alone—don't fix it if it isn't broken. This approach is bad for two reasons. First, the devil or disease normally takes time to inflict its damage. If the good part is left in the formerly broken machine, the devil can surface and break the good part. Then you are left with two broken machines. Second, in this situation you will probably throw away the left-over bad part. But suppose that the bad part is not really bad. Perhaps it just needs its chips pushed down and connectors cleaned. How many times does a "bad" part have to wait years in a troubleshooter's junk heap or travel around flea markets before the part gets a fair trial?

In summary, try to break working machines and thoroughly test suspect parts before throwing them away. If you're a good troubleshooter, you will gather all broken parts and take them home.

Resetting the Printer

Before turning off and on a printer, try resetting it. Many different reset options are described in Chapter 8. Explore all of them. Learn the methods for your printer. Resetting the printer rather than turning it off and on is usually quicker, is just as effective, and reduces wear and tear.

Turning off and on any computer equipment stresses every chip. Think back to the last time one of your light bulbs burned out—probably when you turned it on. The reason is that when you flick on the wall switch, a tidal wave of energy rushes at almost the speed of light toward the light bulb. When the light bulb is hit, it has two choices: live or die. The same is true of computer equipment. Ever wonder why mainframe computer centers are always left on? Ever wonder why computer center directors are always paranoid about the mainframe being turned off? The reason is that whenever the mainframe is turned back on, something usually breaks.

Supposedly, printers and microcomputers are built to withstand more abuse, but why take a chance? Leave them on. Learn to reset them. Keep in mind, however, that leaving computers and printers on all night and all weekend is risky unless the air is clean, air conditioning is guaranteed, and the wall outlets are supplying good, clean, surge-free, and spike-free power. You have to balance the risks.

> HINT: Learn to set a printer's top of form without turning the printer on and off. This procedure is explained in your printer's manual. Usually the process involves putting the printer off-line, adjusting the location of the perforation between sheets so that it is just above the print head, and then pressing a button or combination of buttons.

Turning the Printer Off and On

Turning a printer off and on is just as effective as turning a computer off and on. Turning a printer off and on helps clear memory. Leave a printer off for at least 20 seconds before turning it back on—many models must wait for their power supply to lose all residual energy.

Often the software is what makes a printer sick. Perhaps the printer is choking to death over too many fonts per page. Intermittent printer memory problems also can cause printer illness. In these cases, turning the printer off and on is just a temporary cure.

Performing Self-Tests

Performing printer self-tests is an excellent way of isolating problems. Self-tests can provide information about what is going on within the printer. For example, the HP LaserJet sometimes does not make contact with the font cartridge. In this case, the font self-test does not list the fonts in the cartridge. Turn the printer off, push the font cartridge back in, turn the printer back on, and try the self-test again. The fonts should print.

If fonts are being downloaded into the printer, the self-test can tell you whether this procedure was done successfully. Sometime PC software can download the fonts correctly but cannot select, position, and print them correctly. The self-test helps determine whether the PC software was at least successful at downloading the fonts. If downloading is done, then the problem is in the PC software's capability to use the fonts.

Printer self-tests are getting more exotic every day. See Chapter 8 for a thorough review of HP self-tests.

Printing a Test Page

Most of the better software packages can print test pages, illustrating the software's and the printer's capabilities. These test pages serve as a useful test of the printer. They test the application software's capability to exercise the printer just as a printer's self-test exercises itself. If the printer's self-test works, but the application software's test page does not print properly, the problem is most likely in the configuration of the application software.

The problem also can be in DOS. DOS can be influencing the data transmitted to the printer. Try using the application software package to print to a file rather than to the printer. Or capture the contents of the test pages to a file, using a program like Hijaak or LPT2DSK. Once the contents are stored on a disk, you don't need the original program to print the file. This way you can test DOS's capability to print the file independent of the application software package. Take the file to another PC and see if the DOS located there can print the file. (See Chapter 9 for instructions.) Test the DOS on the suspect machine. If DOS can print the file, but the application software cannot, then something is wrong with the application software. If one DOS can print the file, but another DOS cannot, then something is wrong with DOS.

These techniques are not always going to work with printers put in graphics mode or with PostScript printers. DOS will interpret a Ctrl-Z, present in the graphics data being sent to the printer, as the end of the print file and thus will not print the entire graphic. And some PostScript printers need a Ctrl-D at the end of the print job.

Moving the Printer to a Different Location

A surprising number of printer- and microcomputer-related problems are related to electromagnetic (E&M) waves traveling through the air, or magnetic fields emanating from electrical equipment. The printer, computer, keyboard, monitor, and other peripherals can mess each other up if they radiate and collect E&M energy. The United States Federal Communication Commission (FCC) tries to regulate computer system designs to eliminate the potential of E&M problems. Unfortunately, the FCC does not have police force hovering over production lines or design labs.

E&M waves can travel long distances. The sources of these E&M fields can be anywhere—radar dishes on ships, ham radio stations, dimmer switches, ballast in fluorescent lamps, air conditioners underneath the floor, copy machines on the other side of the wall, race car engines out in the street, and so on. You can pinpoint these environmental influences by trying to correlate problem occurrence with on/off cycles of nearby equipment or by moving the printer to a different location.

Sometimes an AM radio can help you find E&M waves. Tune the radio to a quiet station and then start waving the radio around the room, looking for the sources of static.

Installing Software That Shares the Printer

Printers are normally told to do things in a sequence. Ideally, the order in which documents are printed does not matter. As printers become more complex, however, the order in which programs are executed can make a difference. Certain computer programs are written as if they "own" the printer, as if no other software is ever going to print on the printer in the future. This type of program fills the printer with its header files and its macros, making its software print more quickly and its program run more efficiently. Download times are reduced, and font flexibility is increased. The printer works great until another program tries printing. All of a sudden, the printer does not have enough room for the second program's fonts.

Unfortunately, a standard printer does not exist. Each software package can have total control over the printer and create such a mess that no other software can print. What is needed is some type of printer operating system that is designed to prevent this problem. PostScript fulfills this role, and essentially reboots the printer after every print job. If PostScript is not available, then you must teach your software to cooperate.

Teaching software to cooperate involves installing the application over and over again in different ways and coordinating when fonts are downloaded and who downloads them. AUTOEXEC.BAT files and occasionally CONFIG.SYS files must be used to set up printers in a prenegotiated standard way. Setting up a computer in this manner requires much work, and success is not guaranteed. Success achieved may be fleeting because the next version of any software participating in the shared system could violate all agreements, forcing you to fight the installation battle again.

Resigning Yourself to Wasted Paper

Most dot-matrix printers force you to waste a page for each document printed. Plan on this waste. Don't fight it. Don't remove all the plastic and wire that a printer comes with so that you can waste less paper. Set up the printer so that it prints as it was designed to print. If mailing labels are used, never try to pull them out the back of the printer. They will peel off inside. Instead, waste mailing labels. In the long run, your time and the reduced wear and tear on the printer offer more savings.

Printing to a File

Sometimes the isolation methods described in the previous sections do not work. The printer may operate, but strange things may keep happening. Sending the printer's text and instructions to a file can help isolate the problem. Try printing the file through the operating system, and printing on different printers. If the problem still persists, it is in the application that generated the file.

Often the data being sent to the printer provides the clues necessary to solve the problem. To examine this data, you must be familiar with the printer's programming language. (See Chapter 6 and Appendix A for more information.) Fortunately, the programming language of printers is not much more difficult than Excel or Lotus spreadsheet macros.

> HINT: Before diving into the details of the printer commands, try browsing through the printer driver file to see whether it is set up properly. The printer driver files also are a good introduction to printer programming.

Many programs have a built-in feature that enables them to print to a file. The information sent to the file, however, is not the same information that would have normally been sent to the printer. Therefore some generic tools, such as Hijaak and LPT2DSK, are necessary in order to capture the data.

Inserting Paper in Manual Feed

Sometimes software asks the laser printer to grab paper from the manual paper feed slot rather than the paper tray. When this situation occurs, the laser can appear broken; the display flashes some weird letters that look like an error message. Put a piece of paper in the manual feed slot and see whether the printer grabs it.

Preventing Problems

You have four different ways to prevent problems. The first is to do everything right the first time—install the printer correctly. The second is to check the environment. The third is to follow proper operation procedures, and the fourth is to perform some regular preventive maintenance.

Installing the Printer Correctly

Most of Chapter 8 is devoted to installing printers. The major emphasis is on trying to discover problems and iron out quirks. Just unpacking a printer and turning it on is probably going to damage it. You must follow the unpacking instructions explicitly. Note evidence of prior tampering with the printer. Compare a list of what you found in the box with what the documentation says should have been shipped.

Installing the ribbons and toner cartridges the first time is difficult. Go slowly. Expect problems and quirks. Don't expect new equipment to function beautifully. Don't just give up and return the printer in a fit of frustration, but try to figure out what is wrong. Perhaps the printer's cables are being tripped over, and the cables or connectors are being damaged. Perhaps the printer is in the sun, and the heat is causing it to flake out. Perhaps the paper, ribbons, and cartridges are not appropriately matched to the printer. All these things can affect printer reliability.

Checking the Environment

The environment in which the printer operates can have a dramatic effect on its performance. Environmental factors can be classified into these categories: heat, dust, E&M (described in this chapter's section on "Moving the Printer to a Different Location"), and power problems. Electronic devices work best at around 70 degrees Fahrenheit. Heat damages printers and computers and reduces their life spans. Dust creates a blanket that causes the printer's electronics to heat up. The heat created by dust is much less obvious than a hot room.

The rest of this section deals with power problems associated with all electronic digital devices: surges and spikes. To address these problems, take the following steps, which are listed in order of importance and cost effectiveness:

1. Check wall outlets.
2. Check for shared circuits.
3. Check the grounds.
4. Purchase surge and spike protectors.

Notice that surge and spike protectors are low on the list. Properly wired wall outlets, properly isolated circuits, and properly grounded circuits are necessary before surge and spike protectors can be effective.

Checking Wall Outlets

Power problems can be frustrating but are often easy to fix. Many problems are created because your wall outlets are not wired properly. As long as the printer, computer, and monitor are plugged into the same wall outlet, everything will work just fine—even if the wall outlet is wired improperly. But when the printer is plugged into a different wall outlet from the computer, all sorts of strange things can happen. The printer may start spitting paper when the computer is turned off. The printer may sporadically develop error messages that just need to be cleared. The PC may think printer problems exist when nothing is wrong with the printer.

If the circuit is wired improperly, the printer or computer can explode like a grenade. If the printer and computer are attached to a local area network, the entire network can explode, or the LAN cables can melt in the wall. The worst-case scenario is that you die. You accidentally kick the metal leg of a desk and lean on the case of your PC at the same time.

Checking for properly wired wall outlets is easy. You can purchase "circuit testers" at most hardware stores and electronic parts stores for under $6. The circuit testers have three colored lights that turn on in different patterns to indicate different problems.

Checking for Shared Circuits

Ideally, computer equipment should not share a circuit breaker with any other electronic device. The electronic heating element of coffee pots and baseboard heaters can lock up a printer or computer—the same with air conditioners, microwave ovens, copy machines, refrigerators, ovens, dishwashers, washing machines, dryers, and so on. Anything big with a motor in it can cause intermittent problems.

The worst-case scenario can develop if you hook the microcomputer and printer to the same circuit to which an old furnace is attached. New motors should not create as many problems as old motors. New motors contain electronics that absorb the "momentum" of a moving motor when it is turned off. Old motors lose the capability to absorb the momentum and thus pump the energy of the momentum back into the circuit. Large old motors—such as furnace motors—are the most dangerous. The surge generated from stopping these motors can be so large that the printer or computer can explode, just as if the circuit was not wired properly.

You can easily create a special circuit for just the computer. Turn off all computers and unplug them. Plug a lamp into the wall outlet where the computer was attached. Find the circuit breakers and turn them off and on until the light bulb goes off. Every day turn off this circuit breaker. Eventually, all electronic equipment migrates off the outlets because the outlets are consistently dead. After a month of following this procedure, walk around with a can of orange spray paint, a screwdriver, and a lamp. Test the wall outlets with the light bulb. If a wall outlet is dead, unscrew the face plate, spray paint it orange, and reattach it. You can then generate a memo indicating that only microcomputer equipment is to be plugged into the orange wall outlets.

Checking the Grounds

Some people claim that a laser printer draws so much current that the printer also should have its own separate circuit. This claim is wrong for three reasons. First, the laser printer does not have moving motors with momentum that generates dangerous surges and spikes. Second, the current drawn during start-up is not where the damage is done. The damage occurs when big motors are turned off. Third, the heating element in the laser printer is on continuously. A laser printer thus should not cause problems for other microcomputer equipment on the same circuit.

If the laser printer does cause problems for other microcomputer equipment, usually the problem is in how the building or the house is grounded. Grounding is accomplished with the third prong or round prong of a three-prong outlet. If the third prong is not hooked up or is broken off an extension cord, then many more surge and spike problems will occur.

For example, one company suffered because all their computers and printers stopped working at approximately 5:30 p.m. Much investigation revealed that the problem first began on the day the washrooms backed up. While repairing the washrooms, the plumber removed a section of cast-iron sewer pipe, replaced it with plastic PVC pipe, and jumpered the PVC pipe with a metal braid or wire. Evidently, during the day when people were flushing the toilets, a ground path was formed through the septic water. After people went home, the flushing stopped, and the computer system stopped working.

Homes and businesses are usually grounded through the public water pipes. Unfortunately, other grounds typically exist in buildings. All these grounds may need to be tied together or watered to make them reliable. The water keeps the ground wet around them and improves the ground.

Purchasing Surge and Spike Protectors

Surge and spike protectors are excellent at siphoning harmful power surges and spikes away from the printer and computer. The protector absorbs the energy itself. The big problem about surge and spike protectors is knowing whether they are working. Unfortunately, the cheaper surge and spike protectors (those under $50) have a tendency to die. When they do, the device in which they are housed continues to work, and the attached printer and computer continue to work. The next surge or spike thus goes through the printer or computer.

Unfortunately, you cannot easily test surge and spike protectors by using normal voltage and ohm current-measuring devices. To compensate for this limitation, most surge and spike protector manufacturers include a circuit-breaker button that pops out when a surge or spike hits, usually indicating that the surge- and spike-protecting devices have died. If you push the circuit-breaker button back in, the printer and computer hook back to the wall outlet, but the next surge and spike will go through your printer and computer. Most surge and spike protectors have a light that flickers or goes on if the protector is dead.

Following Proper Operation Procedures

If you own a laser printer, you need to be trained in the proper operation of laser printers. You should be familiar with obvious rules like not putting cardboard, floppy disks, acetate overheads, mailing labels, or other pieces of plastic in the printer. If special laser-proof acetate and laser-proof mailing labels are available, make sure that you know the differences between the two. You need to know how to clear paper jams, how to rip out the toner sealing strip on toner cartridges, and how to install the cartridges. Remember not to force anything.

For dot-matrix printers, you need to know how to feed paper properly so that it does not jam when you leave the room. You need to know the difference between tractor feed activation and friction feed activation. And you need to listen to a printer's healthy noises and be alert if they change dramatically. Remember not to turn the printer's knobs while the printer is on and to turn off the printer if either the paper cannot advance or the print head cannot move. A motor that cannot do its job heats up and destroys itself. These self-destructing motors have a nasty habit of turning into devils.

Performing Preventive Maintenance

You should regularly perform some preventive maintenance. Dot-matrix printers are covered first, then lasers. In either case, start by disconnecting the printer's power cord. Then you can remove the lid of the dot-matrix printer. Four screws are usually holding it on. In some machines the screws are located underneath the print head; in others they are in the corners of the lid. Carefully put the screws in a cup so that you don't lose them. Printer screws can be in weird shapes designed to slide down tapered plastic tunnels and into the holes just perfectly. If you lose the original screws, you may never find replacements that slide into the starting position properly.

Once the lid is off, clean out all the paper. Move all the motors by hand and make sure that they are moving smoothly. Moving the motors manually should be silent and should feel smooth and easy. According to preventive maintenance manuals, practically every moving or vibrating part needs lubrication every six months—even if the printer is doing nothing. The bars or rails on which the print head travels need to be lubricated. The dot-matrix print head needs to be cleaned. This maintenance is rarely done and thus becomes the primary cause of printer death. The same is true of lawn mowers, cars, and most other devices with moving parts. Try moving the motors on a new printer to see what a good printer feels like. Maybe then you will be motivated to lubricate your printers as often as you lubricate your lawn mower and car.

The lubricant used for a printer is much different from most lubricants because the moving parts of a printer do not normally heat up. Thus the lubricant's cold-temperature performance is important. (Mail-order catalogs such as Inmac carry special printer lubricants.) Although WD-40 can clean anything, you should use it only on metal surfaces. Some general-purpose cleaners practically melt plastic. Printer cleaning kits that cost $150 can be worth the price if they prevent just one printer from death at an early age. Such a kit includes all the strippers, sprays, oils, and cleaners needed to lubricate and clean the print heads.

Circuit board components are attached in one of two ways. One attachment method involves soldering or welding the component into place. This method is permanent, because removing the component without damage takes skill, practice, and patience—and requires that you purchase and learn how to use soldering equipment. Usually only manufacturers attempt this removal.

Other chips are attached so that you can remove them by hand or with a screwdriver. These chips are placed in "sockets." (A few socketed chips require a special tool to remove them.) As a printer heats up and cools down, the metal inside the sockets, as well as the component leads, swells and contracts. This motion eventually causes chips to climb out of their sockets. One of the most important preventive maintenance steps is pushing the chips back into their sockets.

The only way to push chips into their sockets is to remove the circuit board from the printer and push as hard as possible equally from both sides of the board. Removing the board is necessary because when the board is mounted in the printer you cannot press hard enough without the board warping. And, if the board is warped, the board or traces (wires glued or etched onto boards, which carry electrical power or information) could crack. Finally, with the board in the printer, the chips you push may go down, but every other chip is being flexed and is climbing out of its socket. You need to take the board out and push so hard that the blood leaves your fingers. You cannot push too hard as long as you are squeezing from both sides.

Another important preventive maintenance step is to disconnect circuit boards and cables one at a time and clean the connections. Most of the time the act of plugging and unplugging is enough to clean the connection. If the connection is made by placing the edge of a circuit board into a slot, you need to clean it. Traditionally, pink erasers were used to clean the edge connectors. Pink erasers are effective but have unpleasant side effects—the erasers rub off some of the protective plating and leave behind pink flakes containing acid. The acid eats grooves in the edge connectors, providing protected areas for microscopic plants to thrive. The plants disconnect boards and cables, the printer develops problems more rapidly, and you have to reuse the eraser soon. Instead, clean the edge connectors with rubbing alcohol and a rag.

Laser printers need to have the toner periodically cleaned out, the corona wire cleaned, and the fuse bar assembly cleaned. Pictures with instructions in five different languages are included with most toner cartridges, describing how to clean the corona wire and fuse bar assembly. The new HP LaserJet IIp (costing under $1,000) has simplified this process by including a special sheet of paper that cleans everything as the printer attempts to print on it. All laser printers produce ozone during operation and have filters to absorb the ozone. In most laser models, the filters are supposed to last a lifetime. But when the filters are old, the laser is in heavy use, and the air smells of the ozone, you need to order a new ozone filter.

In summary, to minimize printer problems, you should clean out the dust, lubricate the moving parts, push the chips down, and clean the connectors.

Chapter Summary

This chapter summarized the philosophies and attitudes necessary for troubleshooting successfully—for developing the magic. Troubleshooting requires that you begin solving a problem by repeating the problem in different ways and trying to isolate it. Methods and tricks were suggested in this chapter. This chapter also explained counter-intuitive ideas, such as breaking the working printer rather than fixing the broken one. The dangers of swapping were explored, and proper swapping methods suggested. Finally, this chapter covered general troubleshooting techniques and preventive maintenance issues.

In the Next Chapter

The next chapter lists common symptoms and solutions. The goal of the chapter is to help you develop your own troubleshooting abilities and to help you identify the problem and discover the solution. Use this chapter to build the foundation of experience from which to tackle any printing problem.

The next chapter is dedicated to the problem of getting a new printer to print its first letter. While this is easy in most cases, serial printers can drive a person crazy. This chapter describes how to design and build or order a serial cable. Then it goes through how to test the cable. Along the way, several problems unique to serial printers are reviewed.

13

Solving Serial and Parallel Interface Problems

This chapter shows you how to specify or build printer cables. You then learn the step-by-step procedures for hooking parallel and serial cables to printers and testing the cables. This chapter reviews the potential problems that can arise during this process. Read this chapter if you are trying to hook an Apple LaserWriter or an old Digital Equipment Corporation dot matrix to a PC.

When possible, purchase the printer cables. Parallel printer cables are almost universal; the differences among them are minor. Most of this chapter, therefore, deals with serial printers.

After a discussion of parallel printer cables, this chapter focuses on what you need to do to hook a serial printer to a computer. First, you learn about building or purchasing a cable. The rest of the chapter is about configuring the printer and computer interface cards and software and about testing the printer.

Working with Parallel Interfaces

The first dot-matrix printer that became popular was made by an American company called Centronics. The company developed a simple one-way parallel communication system and released all the technical details about the system to the public. This strategy made Centronics popular until Epson came along with a better printer. Epson's printer used the Centronics parallel interface but was more reliable.

Table 13.1 describes a typical modern "Centronics" parallel interface. (Actually, everyone calls the printer a Centronics, but it is really an Epson.) In table 13.1, the computer is on the left side, and the printer is on the right side. The numbers refer to the pins to which wires are connected. An asterisk by a wire means that the printer can operate without this wire; not all wires are necessary.

The pin numbers refer to holes or numbered locations in the connectors. Pin 1, for example, is usually in a corner of the connector. Wires are attached to these pins in one of two ways: crimped or soldered. The crimped method is becoming more common but is less reliable. Soldered connectors are much more expensive. Usually, you cannot tell whether the cable you purchase is crimped or soldered without tearing it apart. If you do take the connector cover off, look at how the wires are attached to the connector. Wires that are soldered look welded. Wires that are crimped have a circular piece of metal smashed onto the ends of them.

Table 13.1
Centronics Parallel Port

Computer Pin			Printer Pin	
1	strobe	----->	1	tells printer to latch onto data
2	data bit 0	----->	2	data
3	data bit 1	----->	3	data
4	data bit 2	----->	4	data
5	data bit 3	----->	5	data
6	data bit 4	----->	6	data
7	data bit 5	----->	7	data
8	data bit 6	----->	8	data
9	data bit 7	----->	9	data
10	ack.	<-----	10	printer tells computer received
11	busy	<-----	11	printer tells computer buffer full
12	paper out	<-----	*12	not necessary
13	select	<-----	*13	not necessary
14	auto feed	----->	*14	not necessary
15	error	<-----	*15	not necessary
16	initialize	----->	*16	not necessary
17	select	<-----	*17	not necessary
18-25	ground	------	18-30	

When you purchase a cable, the wires are connected already (see table 13.1). Even labeled wires are not necessarily connected. You should have to modify this cable only when faced with once-in-a-lifetime printing problems.

When troubleshooting parallel interfaces, you should have two cables: one cable that has all the wires listed in table 13.1 hooked up and another with the wires marked by asterisks removed. The cable with the smaller number of wires often works in situations where the larger cable does not. The following section gives descriptions of the wires that are left out of the smaller cable so that you know why you can disconnect them.

Optional Wires

The original IBM PC tried to distinguish between the printer's being out of paper and other error conditions, but this feature never worked well. The operating system always thought that the printer was out of paper when it wasn't. A general error condition is much safer, so connecting pin 12 (on the printer side) is not worth the trouble.

The select line means that the printer is on-line and ready to receive input. The two select lines accommodate two types of printers and have opposite voltages. If one select line is positive, the other is 0 volts. Both can be ignored. Most software does not pay attention to these select lines.

The definition of the auto-feed line and the rationale for not connecting it are given in Chapter 8. This input into the printer forces the printer to add a carriage return to every line feed received. Cutting this wire helps some of the Radio Shack PCs talk to normal PC dot-matrix parallel printers.

The error line is another line on which most printers never put any information. The printer either works or doesn't work. Although probably some DOS error message is triggered by this wire, printers rarely use the error line. DOS programs will not miss it.

Initialization

When your printer will not self-test, the reason is that the printer is being turned off by the PC through the initialization wire in the parallel printer cable. When this wire is released, the parallel printer is forced to reinitialize. This wire is like a remote printer-reset button that PC software can push. Actually, the PC's power-on software is the only software package that regularly uses this line. Most contemporary PC software tries to send reset instructions (like PC DOS Ctrl-Alt-Del) to reset the printer.

You can tell when this wire is being used. Turn on the printer and then turn on the PC. You will see and hear the dot-matrix printer "hiccup." Every "hiccup" occurs when this line is accessed. It is probably accessed just once during the power-on phase of the PC. Deactivating this line gives you one less thing to worry about.

Buffer Management

Most of the time, the computer can send data faster than the printer can print. Although the printer is printing as fast as it can, it cannot keep up with the computer. Imagine filling up a sink with water. If the water flows into the sink faster than the sink drains, the sink overflows. The printer *buffer* is similar to the sink. If the computer is turned off, the printer often continues to print while it empties its buffer—just like the sink continues to drain water.

Parallel interfaces indicate that their buffers are getting full by pulling *busy* (the wire connecting pin 11) *high*. Pulling the busy line high is the equivalent of the printer turning one light bulb labeled "busy" in the PC. The computer pays attention to this wire and refuses to send any more data until this wire goes low again. The printer turns the "busy" light in the PC off. If this wire does not go low in a reasonable length of time, the computer generates an error message. Technically, this condition is described as a *time-out* by the operating system.

Some modern software programs expect printers that are much faster than the older ones. If modern software ejects a page and the printer takes too long ejecting that page, the software thinks that something is wrong with the printer. After you press any key, the first thing the software does is try again to eject the page. Another page is ejected—this time a blank page—and again the software times out, just because the printer cannot get rid of the paper fast enough. Another blank page is ejected. The only solution is to try to adjust the time-out length. You can make this adjustment with the DOS MODE command.

When the printer is signaling busy to the computer, the printer should be printing as fast as it can. No pauses should occur between changes in the direction of the print head. If pauses occur, the printer is printing faster than the computer is sending data. This situation usually happens because of the following reasons: the computer is computing graphics data for the printer; the wrong printer driver is installed, or the software is poorly written. Some modern printers actually compute the pixels of more exotic fonts internally and slow themselves. The NEC Pinwriter is an example of this type of printer.

Constructing a Serial Printer Cable

Getting serial printers to work is a challenge. So many different serial printer cables exist that ordering one that works is almost impossible. After the cable is built, you must configure the serial interface hardware in both the printer and the computer. Then, you have to install the PC software properly. Finally, extensive testing is necessary because serial ports can work well with small documents but lose information when printing large documents.

In the Macintosh world, serial printers come configured; so you need to read this section only if you are trying to hook an old non-Apple, third-party serial printer to a Macintosh. And in this case, you will have major problems unless you can write printer-driver software for the Macintosh. Macs require software in order to talk to printers.

The PC world is designed to work with character printers. Many older, smaller printers hooked to old mainframes and minicomputer systems are character oriented and use serial interfaces. An IBM computer is designed to work with character parallel printers. To talk to character serial printers, the PC has to be reconfigured each time it is turned on. But, you can connect PCs to Apple printers as well as to other old serial printers.

Even if you never build a serial cable, you still need to know this information because you may have to special-order your printer's serial port cable. Cables consist of three parts: the connectors on either end, the wires, and a diagram showing how to connect the wires to the connectors on either end.

Identifying the Connectors

The connectors on the ends of cables are split into two categories: plug and socket, or male and female. Males, or plugs, are fragile. They have pins that stick out. The pins can be bent, pushed back into the body of the connector, or broken off. Female, or socket, connectors consist of holes into which the pins fit. On the printer end of the cable, usually 25-pin males are required to fit into the 25-hole females built into the printers. This condition is not universally true, however. Look at the serial printer you are attempting to hook up. Draw a picture of the connector mounted in the printer. Then, determine which type of connector you need on the printer end of the serial printer cable.

Look in the printer manual if you are not sure. Some printers come with multiple interfaces. Make sure that you can identify the serial connector coming out of the back of the printer and describe the connector needed on the printer end of the serial printer cable.

The computer end of the serial printer cable may require one of four connectors:

Serial printer cable connector	Computer to attach to
25-hole female	IBM PC, XT, PS/2, clones
9-hole female	IBM AT, clones, PS/2s
9-pin male	Apple Macintosh original
8-pin Din male	Most Apple Macintoshes

Converters exist in both the PC and Macintosh worlds. Converters from 9-pin male to 25-pin male are shipped regularly with 9-pin male connectors. Converters from the original 9-pin male to the 8-pin Din male in the Mac World are common. In fact, many Mac users convert to a wiring system using telephone-like cables. Converters make re-using old serial printer cables easier.

If you are planning to build the cable yourself, you must know Radio Shack's (and most of the rest of the world's) names for these connectors:

Connector	Common name
25-hole female	DB 25 female
9-hole female	DB 9 female
9-pin male	DB 9 male
8-pin Din male	8-pin Din male

Connectors come in two styles; the style you choose is determined by how you plan to attach wires to the connectors. Wires can be attached by soldering or crimping. Soldering is much better but requires so much skill that a novice can usually make a better cable through crimping. Correct soldering takes a great deal of practice. If you are purchasing a cable, ask for a soldered cable. If building the cable yourself, you probably are better off crimping. Purchase crimp-style connectors (they have holes in the back rather than solder posts), a crimping tool, and approximately two dozen tips that are to be crimped on the ends of the wires.

Connector covers also are important. The best are made of or are lined with metal. Plastic connectors painted with a metallic type of paint are more common. These connectors are labeled *metal-like or metallic* connector covers. Solid metal connector covers add about $15 to $25 to the price of a serial cable; but they add reliability and last much longer. When you are building your own cable, purchasing metal connector covers is difficult. Usually, you are building the printer cable yourself to save money, and so the plastic connector covers are attractive because they are $3 each instead of $8 to $15 each.

Purchasing Serial Cable Wire

The cables used to build a serial cable vary in four ways. First, the diameter of the wire can change. Wire size is measured using gauge numbers, as are regular extension cords. The typical gauge size used in serial cables is around 24 gauge. The smaller the gauge number, the thicker the wire. A 22 gauge is a thicker wire and is almost too large if you are soldering cables together. A 26 gauge is a thinner wire and will not work as well when the printer cable needs to be more than 50 feet long. Ribbon cables have wires that are about 30 or 32 gauge and make terrible printer cables.

The second issue when purchasing serial printer cable wire is whether to purchase stranded or solid wire. Solid wire tends to break and is stiffer and thus less reliable. Stranded wire is preferable, but solid wire is more noise-free. Noise in a wire causes the data in the wire to be corrupted, and false data may be created. The symptoms are usually garbled characters and occasional random ejection of sheets of paper. Noise is caused by the printer cable acting like an antenna. Most often, this is caused by not hooking the third round prong up in the power cord to the wall. Serial cables that are not built properly also may turn into antennas.

The third consideration for purchasing wire is how well shielded it is. Longer serial cables are going to require more expensive wire. The best serial cables pair up wires, wrapping each pair in foil together with a bare wire. The foil has electrical insulation on the outside and is conductive on the inside. The bare wire makes electrical contact with the foil and siphons away any noise or antenna effects the foil picks up. This type of wire can be used to create serial printer cables more than 300 feet long. You can purchase cheaper wire with just a metal sock around the entire bundle of wires. Together, the metal socks, foil, and wires without insulation form a *shield* that protects the wires carrying data from receiving false signals generated from noise and treating them as data. The cheapest wire has no such shielding. The maximum length of a serial cable built without shielding is around 50 feet.

The last criterion is the number of individual wires in the cable. A few slow printers can be hooked up using only two wires. Today, most serial printers require at least four wires. Purchase cables that have four wires or conductors.

Drawing a Cable Pinout Diagram

Every connector mentioned has its holes or pins numbered in a universal way. A *pinout diagram* shows exactly which pin or hole has a wire leaving it and exactly which pin or hole the wire arrives at on the other end. Because of all the different computer connectors and all the different types of printers, the number of combinations is so large that manufacturers or stores cannot possibly stock all the possible cables.

The other problem is that given all the technical details about a printer's and a computer's serial interface, still one "right" way to wire up a printer cable does not exist. One software program can demand one cable, and another software package can force you to use a different cable. This problem arises because PC programs control the serial port hardware. Ideally, DOS would manage the serial port uniformly, but DOS doesn't. This factor forces PC software to speak directly to the serial port hardware. And, different PC software programs can require that different wires be hooked up to the printer.

> TROUBLE-SHOOTING TIP: If a printer works fine with one software package and not at all with another, check the PC software configuration. But, keep in mind that the serial printer cable can be used differently by different PC software packages causing the same symptom.

In the following diagrams, the assumption is that a 25-pin or 25-hole connector is required on either end of the serial printer cable. Translate to the 9-pin connectors of the IBM world by using this diagram:

9-pin	25-pin	Description
1	8	Data carrier detect
2	3	Receive data
3	2	Transmit data
4	20	Data terminal ready
5	7	Ground
6	6	Data set ready
7	4	Request to send
8	5	Clear to send
9	22	Ring indicator

One of the following two serial printer cables will print something. If you are building cables yourself, you have the luxury of building a cable, testing it, rebuilding it, testing it, and so. The trouble with purchasing a cable is that you do not have these experiences to help build the cable properly. If you are reading this section in order to draw a diagram of how you want a cable custom built, continue reading. Don't just assume that one of the two following cables will solve your printing problems.

The following two cables are called *computer-happy cables*, because the computer is fooled into thinking that a serial printer is ready and "happy" to print data—even when the printer is off.

Computer-Happy Cable #1

```
Computer          Printer

2 ---------------------> 3
3 <--------------------- 2
7 ---------------------  7
4 --|
5 --|

6 --|
8 --|
20 -|
```

Computer-Happy Cable #2

```
Computer          Printer

2 ---------------------> 2
3 <--------------------- 3
7 ---------------------  7
4 --|
5 --|

6 --|
8 --|
20 -|
```

If you can find your printer's manual, you may be able to determine which of the two cables to start with. The printer manual should have a page describing the serial port. Look for the acronym DCE or DTE. If the printer is a DTE, try the first cable. If the printer is described as a DCE, try the second cable. Some printers have inside switches or jumpers, to be configured either way. So even if the manual says one kind, the printer may be configured for the other.

If the printer manual shows a picture of the serial port connector with wires attached, look at the drawing for an indication of whether the printer is listening or talking on pin 2. If the printer is talking on pin 2, use the first cable. If the printer is listening on pin 2, choose the second cable. If you guess wrong, nothing will burn up or smoke. No hardware damage can be done, so build both cables and try them out.

Configuring the Printer's and PC's Serial Interfaces

Because a PC can have multiple serial ports (up to four standard with PC DOS 3.3), these serial ports must be configured properly. Otherwise, they fight with each other. Ideally, you should test the serial port on the PC before you try to connect the serial port to the printer. Unfortunately, no similar method of testing the printer's serial port exists. After the PC serial port is configured, you must configure the printer serial port. This section explains these two procedures.

Configuring the PC Serial Interface

Configuring the PC serial interface consists of two steps. A PC can have up to four officially supported serial ports. These serial ports must be installed so that to DOS they become COM1, COM2, COM3, and COM4. If two serial ports are configured as COM1, they may work, but the PC will lock up, and the printer will print strange things and lose data. So, the first step is to make sure that the serial ports within a PC are all configured properly. The second step is to test the serial ports. Some may not be functioning. This section explains how to configure and test the ports.

Configuring the COM1, COM2, COM3, and COM4 Ports

A PC can have up to seven interfaces through which to communicate with a printer. All seven interfaces must cooperate and share the same PC, or else the devices hooked up to the interfaces don't work correctly. For example, if both serial interfaces inside a PC think that they are COM1, the PC's keyboard may seem to lock up intermittently when you try to print.

In the older world of PCs, XTs, and ATs, serial ports can be found on many of the boards added to a machine. Many of these serial ports are never used. They may have been disabled so that they don't fight with any other boards. Therefore, just because the serial port connector exists, it is not necessarily active. Furthermore, the physical location of the serial port has nothing to do with its configuration. The serial port may exist without a connector coming out the back of the computer, or a serial port may exist, and yet coming out the back is the connector to a telephone or mainframe cable.

The point is that a serial port connector, even though it is visible on the back of a PC, may not necessarily be working. Find the manual for the circuit board on which the serial interface circuitry resides. Take the board out of the PC and look at its switches, jumpers, and/or jumper blocks. See whether the manual describes what all the switches, jumpers, and/or jumper blocks do. The on/off, COM1, COM2, COM3, and COM4 status of a serial interface is created by manipulating two different switches, jumpers, and/or jumper blocks.

COM ports need two limited resources that have to be allocated to the expansion boards in a PC, XT, or AT. These limited resources are called *interrupts* (IRQ lines) and *I/O ports* (I/O blocks).

Interrupts, or IRQ lines, are wires that a serial interface can "yank on" (put some voltage on or turn on a light bulb in the PC) to get the PC's attention. The PC has to stop what it is doing and pay attention to the serial interface. But, a serial interface issues an interrupt only in response to the serial printer talking. Because character-mode serial printers cannot talk back, this feature is not often activated.

In a PC, COM1 is supposed to use IRQ 4; COM2 is supposed to use IRQ 3; COM3 is supposed to use IRQ 3, and COM4 is supposed to use IRQ 4. In other words, COM1 and COM4 are supposed to share an interrupt. Although the hardware of a PC is usually designed to support two serial devices sharing an IRQ line, the software in the PC rarely can figure out which serial port needs attention. Because a character or graphics mode serial printer just listens and never talks, it will never yank an IRQ line. Therefore, asking the serial printer to share an interrupt with another serial device (like a modem or mouse) that does need an interrupt line is not a good idea. For example, if the modem is using COM3, set the serial printer to use COM2.

Serial interfaces also need an address where the PC can send information or read information. Serial interfaces are assigned I/O addresses, or I/O blocks, for this purpose. In the PC world, the following are the assignments as determined by IBM and Microsoft:

Port	*I/O Block*	*Interrupt*
COM1	$3F8-$3FF	4
COM2	$2F8-$2FF	3
COM3	$3E8-$3EF	3
COM4	$2E8-$2EF	4

After you have located and properly configured the serial interface to which the printer is to be attached, the next step is to test the serial port.

Testing the Serial Port Hardware

You must test the serial port hardware for a variety of reasons. The port may not be configured properly, or the serial port circuitry may be broken. Serial interfaces in the older PCs are built around a chip with the part number of

8250 or 16540. Serial interfaces built around the 8250 chip are notorious for allowing some pins to work but not allowing others. This failure is so prevalent that some experts estimate that more than 50 percent of the serial ports built around this chip have some pin that is not working.

Testing the serial port requires diagnostic software. You can use any diagnostic disk. All diagnostic programs can test the serial port. In the older PCs, XTs, and ATs, the diagnostic disk was supposed to be stored in the *Guide to Operations Manual*. In the PS/2s, the diagnostics program is on the Reference or Startup Disk. A great public domain program called DIAGS, written by Joan Riff, can test the serial ports. All these programs test the serial port by having it send data to itself. The idea is that if the serial port can hear itself talk, it is working.

The serial port cannot send data to itself automatically. You have to connect pins 2 and 3 with a wire. If you are building a serial cable yourself, build a special cable that just has pins 2 and 3 connected. If not, search for a *loopback plug*. Loop-back plugs are connectors built with pins 2 and 3 connected. In a pinch, you can use a tiny screw driver with a plastic handle. Simultaneously touch pins 2 and 3 of the male connector coming out the back of the PC. A paper clip also works, but you will feel the current flowing in and out of your body as the paper clip is charged to +12 volts and −12 volts over and over again. This condition is not good. If you accidentally touch the metal case of the PC or the grounded leg of a table or a metal filing cabinet at the same time, you could go to the hospital in an ambulance. Try to find or make a loopback plug; then run the diagnostic software.

Configuring the Printer's Serial Interface

The first step in interfacing a serial printer is to scan the manual and figure out how the printer is configured.

Some printers come with multiple interfaces. You need to choose the serial interface by using switches, jumpers, or the front panel. After you choose the serial port, you need to answer some other questions about how to use the serial port. Four configuration parameters have to match on the printer and the computer ends. You don't have to understand these four bits of information; they just have to match. The computer is told the serial information through software, and the printer is told serial information through switches or menus on the front panel. The four items are as follows:

- *Baud rate*: Number of bits per second. 10 bits per letter. Typical values include 300, 1200, 2400, 4800, 9600, and 19200. Guess 9600 if no information is available.

- *Data bits*: Either 7 or 8. Guess 8 if no information is available.

- *Parity*: Odd, even, mark, space, or none. Guess none if no information is available.
- *Stop bits*: 1 or 2. Guess 1 if no information is available.

If any guesses are incorrect, the printer prints garbage—but consistent garbage. Sometimes the printer seems to work except for a couple of letters. Other letters seem to be translated by the printer in some strange way.

In the Macintosh world, all Imagewriters and many LaserWriters are hooked up serially. Apple designs and sells the printer driver software and the printers. Because of this factor, Apple can assume responsibility for these values and make sure that the Macintosh software matches the Apple printer. This information does not need to be published, and users or technicians working on Macs do not need to know this information.

Printing on a Serial Printer through DOS

If followed successfully, the instructions in this section cause a serial printer to put the first characters on paper. Because PC DOS does have some primitive serial port support, the way to use PC DOS to test the serial printer is described here. Many other methods in existence improve on PC DOS's support. They are described elsewhere in this chapter.

Type the following DOS commands at the DOS prompt, pressing Enter after each line:

    MODE COM1:9600,N,8,1
    MODE LPT1:=COM1:

The first command initializes the serial port; the second redirects out of the serial port to the parallel port all information the software sends.

Now, press Shift-PrtSc. Watch the lights of the printer. If the lights flicker, the printer is receiving data. If the baud rate, parity, data bits, and stop bits don't match, the printer may do nothing or may spit out paper. If nothing works, start guessing. Instead of COM1, guess COM2, COM3, or COM4. Instead of 9600, guess 19600, 4800, 2400, 1200, or 300. Instead of N for no parity, guess E for even parity or O for odd parity. Instead of 8 data bits, guess 7. Instead of 1 stop bit, guess 2.

If none of these guesses works, switch pins 2 and 3. If this change doesn't work, try guessing again. You probably skipped a combination. If all this effort seems too long and tedious, find the printer manual. Look up how to use the switches or front panel to configure the printer's serial port. Look at the current setup and try to predict what the printer is expecting. Look up the DOS MODE command in the DOS manual, and check to see whether the command is being used properly. Get the printer working somehow.

Remember that PostScript printers will not actually print something when you press Shift-PrtSc. These printers should flash their lights indicating that data is received. If you want to print something, get into a program that supports PostScript.

Otherwise, follow these instructions to create a simple PostScript program and send it to the printer. The first step is to copy a file from the console (Con:) or keyboard to a file called TEST. After typing the first line, you will see just a cursor. Make sure that you follow uppercase and lowercase exactly. The ^D and ^Z mean press and hold the Ctrl key and press D; then press and hold the Ctrl key and press Z. ^D and ^Z should appear on-screen as a result. As soon as ^Z appears and you press Enter, the prompt comes back.

```
Copy Con:test
/Helvetica findfont
12 scalefont setfont
288 720 moveto
(Hello) showpage
^D^Z
```

Typing the preceding creates a PostScript file called TEST, which prints the word *Hello* on the page and ejects the page. The file is stored on a disk.

The next step is to send this file out the serial port. At the DOS prompt, type the following:

Copy Test COM1:

If a different COM port is used, make the substitution in the preceding line. This command should print the word *Hello* in the middle of the page on the top line.

Testing the Serial Printer with an Application

After you get the DOS Shift-PrtSc command to work and actually print something, your next step is to configure the application programs to print on the serial printer. Then, you must test the capability of the application software to listen to a printer asking the PC software to slow down (buffer-management protocols). This test may require rebuilding the serial printer cable or asking that another printer cable be built.

Configuring the PC Application Software

The preceding section describes how to configure DOS to print on a serial printer by using the MODE COM1:9600,N,8,1 command. The MODE LPT1:=COM1: command, which followed, told the computer to forward to the serial port all printer instructions normally meant for the parallel port. Because most PC application software is designed to print on parallel, LPT1, printers, you can use DOS to redirect this printer information to serial printers.

Although this method does have some drawbacks, start configuring your serial printer by typing the MODE commands given previously. Then, configure your application software to "think" that you have a parallel printer —even if you really don't have a parallel printer. The MODE LPT1:=COM1: command instructs DOS to pretend that it has a parallel printer when the application software requests one and then to send the printer information to a serial printer instead.

Understanding the Buffer-Management Protocols

Most serial printers receive data much faster than they can print it. Typical baud rates going into the printer are 9600 baud, approximately 9,600 bits per second. Because there are approximately 10 bits (8 data bits plus stop and start) per letter of the alphabet, this rate works out to around 960 characters per second (cps). Typical printing rates are around 200 cps to 400 cps.

One way of avoiding the speed mismatch is to slow the computer until it is slower than the printer. This method, described in the next section, works but usually cripples printers.

Printers that receive data faster than they can print have buffers that fill up with the excess data to be printed. When the buffers are about full, the printer has two choices:

   Yank a wire (hardware handshaking)

   Signal XOFF (software handshaking)

To get maximum performance from a printer, however, you must tell the printer what to do when its buffer overflows. The serial printer cable has to be wired to transfer this information to the PC, and the PC software has to be told which type of buffer management is necessary. If any of these three elements fails, the symptom will be lost characters, words, lines, even entire paragraphs. The following sections describe the different buffer-management methods commonly in use. A comparison and the specific details on how to implement these methods follow.

Making the Computer Slower than the Printer

A simple method that always works is to slow the transfer of data (baud rate) through the serial printer cable. When the baud rate is slower than the printing speed, the printer never accumulates characters in its buffer. This option is not usually implemented because all printers would print at the same slow speed. If you must use this option, you can do some risky things to allow the computer to send faster than the printer receives. See the following implementation details for more information.

Using Hardware Handshaking

Hardware handshaking requires that the printer turn on a light bulb inside the PC using a special wire dedicated to this purpose (the printer "yanks" a wire in the PC). The serial printer cable must connect this wire to the PC, and the PC software must pay attention to this wire. The problem with this method is that the pin or wire the printers grab varies among different manufacturers. Another complicating element is that the wire the PC software expects to be yanked may vary among different PC software programs.

Ideally, you can look at the PC software manuals and figure out which pin numbers each PC software program expects to be yanked. Then, you can read the printer manual, figure out which pin numbers the printer can yank, and run wires between these pins in the cable. But, finding this information is difficult.

Typical pins yanked by printers when their buffers fill up are 20, 19, 11, 8, and 6. Printer manuals usually document which pin is yanked in small print in an appendix.

The next question is, "To which pin is the wire connected on the computer side?" This question is even harder to answer. Because most computer software talks straight to the chip that controls the serial port, each PC software package can decide to pay attention to a different pin. As a result, the same cable can work with some software and not with others. PC software typically expects pin 5, 6, or 8 to be yanked by the printer when its buffer overflows.

Using Software Handshaking

Software handshaking is a buzz word describing the most popular method of configuring printers and PCs so that the printer's buffer does not overflow. Software handshaking is the most desired method because no additional wires have to be added to the serial printer cable. And, this method directly emulates a procedure many users of minicomputers and mainframes are already familiar with: pressing Ctrl-S and then Ctrl-Q to stop temporarily and then restart the host. In addition, because software handshaking can co-exist with hardware handshaking, old PC software that expects hardware handshaking also can be supported.

Software handshaking requires that printers send stop and start commands to the PC. (Even Macintosh serial printers are meeting this requirement.) The industry has pretty much standardized the specific bit patterns printers are to send. When the printer wants to stop the PC, the printer sends 00010011. This pattern also is known as DC3, Ctrl-S, or XOFF. When the printer wants the host to start sending data again, the printer sends 00010001. This pattern is known as DC1, Ctrl-Q, or XON. Most DEC printers support this type of handshaking. HP started supporting this handshaking in the HP LaserJet II models. HP calls this type of handshaking *ROBUST ON*.

The following is the conversation between the computer and printer:

Computer   *Printer*

sending data ------------------>
printer's buffer gets too full
<---------------printer sends XOFF
computer stops sending data
printer's buffer becomes empty
<---------------printer sends XON
sending data ------------------>

Older printers used more primitive, error-prone, complicated systems that usually involved bytes known as ETX and ACK. If a printer is advertised as supporting ETX and ACK, don't buy that printer. Supporting complicated, error-prone ancient history is an indication that the printer company is not in touch with the market place.

Implementing and Testing a Buffer-Management Protocol

After the printer prints the first few words, most users tend to stop and pronounce the printer and PC married. However, the ceremony is not over. Even though a few words or characters are printed, what happens if 400 pages are sent to the printer?

The next step is to select and test the buffer-management protocol. You can use one of the following three possible ways of testing:

Slowing the PC
Using hardware
Using software (the most desired)

Slowing the PC

If you chose this method, read the printer manual to find the rated speed of the printer. Look through all the options for the slowest printing rate. (Usually, this rate is in letter-quality mode.) Suppose that this printer's slowest rate is 16 characters per second. Then, you must use a baud rate slower than 160 baud. Most printers cannot even be configured for a baud rate this slow. Hopefully, the printer's slowest mode is faster than 30 cps. Then, you can choose a baud rate of 300. Keep in mind that the printer then always will print at this rate of 30 cps, even in the so-called "fast," draft print mode. The printer may print a line at 200 cps, wait, and then print another line at 200 cps. The effective throughput, however, will be 30 cps.

The baud rate can be increased if the printer has a large buffer, and the buffer is never entirely full. Suppose that the printer's buffer is 65,536 characters (64K bytes) and the printer can print at 30 cps. If the baud rate is increased to 9600 baud (960 cps), the printer will receive data 32 times faster than the printer can print the data. In 70 seconds, the computer will have sent $70 \times 960 = 67,200$ bytes. The printer, however, will have printed only $70 \times 30 = 2,100$ bytes. In the buffer are $67,200 - 2,100 = 65,100$ bytes; the buffer is almost full when 67,200 bytes have been sent. The average page of text contains 1,500 bytes (assuming trailing spaces are not sent). This statement means that $67,200/1500 = 45$ pages (approximately) can be sent before the buffer is filled. If fewer than 45 pages in a row are to be printed, the buffer will never fill up. Remember that these computations are based on the assumption that no graphics are going to be printed and that the average page contains 1,500 characters. Therefore, even if you never send more than 45 pages, someday, someone may try to, and the printer you set up will appear to be broken.

Doing these kinds of calculations for the HP LaserJet is a little more difficult. In the LaserJet, the speed of printing is limited by the motors that move the paper, not by the speed with which the laser can draw characters. The LaserJet prints 8 pages per minute. The stock Laserjet 500+ and the LaserJet II come with 512K of memory. Of this 512K, 395K is available for use as a buffer. (This memory can be used for other things also.) Assume again that the average number of characters per page is 1,500. This assumption means that the LaserJet can print at $1500 \times 8 = 12,000$ characters per minute or $12,000/60 = 200$ characters per second. If data is sent for 500 seconds, the computer transmits 480,000 characters. The laser printer prints 100,000 characters (assuming 1,500 characters per page again), and the buffer holds

380,000 characters—almost full. This amount means that more than 480,000/1500 = 320 consecutive pages would have to be sent to the HP LaserJet before its buffer would overflow. Of course, if fonts are downloaded or the page includes graphic drawings, this number decreases significantly.

Testing with Hardware

The hardware method requires reading the printer's manual to determine whether the printer will yank a wire when the printer's buffer gets full. This table shows the diversity of wires different printer manufacturers yank:

HP	pin 20
NEC	pin 19
Diablo	pin 11
EPSON	pin 8

After you know this pin number, you need to modify the computer-happy cable in the following manner:

Computer-Happy Cable (modified)

```
Computer            Printer
2 ---------------->  3
3 <---------------- 2
7 ------------------ 7
5,6,8 <------------ wire yanked
```

Testing this cable is difficult. The responsibility for knowing whether the wires 5, 6, and 8 are yanked is definitely not in the DOS operating system. If the DOS MODE command MODE LPT1:=COM1: is used (as recommended in most printer-installation manuals), PC DOS ignores wires the printer yanks.

Different PC application programs that are configured to send data directly to the printer port rarely document which wire they observe. By hooking the printer up to all the inputs into the PC, every micro light bulb possible will go on when the printer's buffer is full. Try printing huge documents in each program that is configured to send data to a serial port. Look for missing pages, paragraphs, and lines.

The other fact to remember is that more than half the PC serial ports in existence have a pin (like 5, 6, or 8) that is not working. The PC may think that the wire attached is permanently yanked or never yanked. In either case, the PC software may ignore the wire. If the printer does yank the wire, the PC side does not feel the yank. Sometimes, the printer yanks the wire, and the PC stops sending data and never starts sending data again. Only one page prints. If everything is turned off, the printer will print one page again and then stop. These kinds of problems result from the serial port chip's living in the twilight zone of half dead and half alive. The transmit and receive pins work, but the wires may not. In fact, count on the wires not working.

To test the wires, you need a special serial-port diagnostic software package. In the PC world, an excellent public domain program called DIAGS is available. DIAGS tests pins 6 and 8, which are the primary pins software examines. DIAGS is a menu-driven program. At the first screen, you select serial ports. On the second screen, you choose parameters. On the parameters screen, you open the serial port. At the top of the screen underneath DSR (data set ready pin 6) you should see the word No. Underneath CR (carrier detect pin 8) you should see the word No. By touching pins 8 and 20 with a paper clip, you should be able to see CR flicker between Yes and No. By touching pins 6 and 20, you should be able to flicker DSR between Yes and No. If the word Yes appears and does not go away, you have a problem. If the word No does not change to Yes, press a character on the keyboard and then try again. If nothing happens, search for another serial port inside the PC. Maybe you are not testing the right one.

Testing with Software

Although printers automatically yank a wire, whether or not a wire connects that wire to the PC, printers do not automatically signal XON and XOFF. You must configure the printer for this purpose by using the front panel. PostScript printers are the only exception. They default to using XON and XOFF. HP LaserJet II printers have a menu option in the front panel called ROBUST ON or ROBUST OFF. This option activates or deactivates XON and XOFF.

The hard part, as with the hardware method, is testing whether the PC application software is going to listen for XON and XOFF coming from the printer. Normally, no information ever flows into pin 3 from the printer. If XON and XOFF handshaking is never used, pin 3 into the PC does not need a wire attached. Only recently have PC application programs started to listen for XON and XOFF coming from the printer. If XON and XOFF is mentioned in the application installation instructions, feel blessed. Many programs and printers do not support XON and XOFF. Thorough testing by sending large documents is absolutely necessary even if XON and XOFF are supported by both the application and the printer.

Implementing a Software-Management Scheme

In the crazy, chaotic world of PC serial printers, you need a configuration strategy in order to operate efficiently. Decide whether to install PC application software so that all output goes directly to the serial port or to force all printer data to flow through the operating system. Your options are as follows:

- ❏ Let each PC software program talk to the serial port.
- ❏ Use DOS to redirect from parallel to serial.
- ❏ Use third-party software to redirect parallel to serial.

Letting Each PC Application Talk to the Serial Port

In a PC, the serial-interface hardware consists of a few chips, the biggest of which usually has a part number of 8250 or 16540 stamped on it somewhere. This chip has to be initialized; it must be told how to configure itself before it will transmit data to a serial printer. This chip must be told the baud rate, stop bits, parity, and data bits. The chip is initialized two ways: through DOS or through the application software program. The MODE 9600,N,8,1 command of DOS initializes this chip.

Some PC application programs require DOS to initialize the chip; others initialize the chip themselves. If the PC program mentions the names COM1, COM2, COM3, or COM4 but does not give the baud rate, parity, data bits, and stop bits, the program is depending on DOS to configure, or initialize, the serial port. PFS: First Publisher, for example, shows only the names of the COM ports. Be careful to search all screens and installation programs for questions about baud rates, parity, data bits, and stop bits. If you cannot find these questions, you need to use the DOS MODE command to initialize the serial port.

Some programs mention baud rate but not all the other necessary configuration details: parity, data bits, and stop bits. These programs are frustrating. Because they ask the baud rate, you know that they are going to initialize the serial port. But you do not know what type of parity or how many data bits and stops bits the PC program is going to configure the PC's serial interface for. The printer's serial interface must be configured identically. How can you configure the printer's serial interface identically when you do not know how the PC application program is going to configure the PC's serial interface? 1-2-3 falls into this category. You just hook up the serial printer and start configuring the serial printer's interface in different ways, guessing which parity, data bits, and stop bits 1-2-3 is forcing the PC's serial port to send. When the printer seems to start working, you should test the configuration by printing very long documents.

Some PC programs ask about baud rates, parity, data bits, and stop bits, but these programs never ask questions about printer-buffer management. You have no idea whether the PC application is going to monitor pins 5, 6, or 8 coming into the PC serial interface or listen for XOFF and XON arriving on pin 3. The PC application program could do both or neither. These PC programs are frustrating because they give you clues but never the whole picture. WordPerfect falls into this category.

Finally, some programs give you the option of software handshaking or hardware handshaking. Although this choice is comforting in that the PC software has been designed to deal with the serial printer buffer management, the trouble is that these programs still do not give you enough information to configure the printer. For example, look at the typical Windows printer serial interface configuration screen. Two handshaking options are labeled software or hardware. However, the hardware option does not specify whether the Windows printer driver is observing pin 5 or pin 6 being yanked. The software option does not specify whether the XON/XOFF protocol is being used or some earlier ancient protocol like ETX or ACK, found on early Diablo daisywheel printers. Again, guessing and testing is the only solution.

In summary, the PC application market is in sad shape in regard to configuring serial printers. Ideally, companies that sell PC software that is designed to work with serial printers should include this information somewhere in their manuals so that users can connect printers and PCs without wasting time guessing and testing. Specifically, every single PC program that can be configured to use a serial port should include the following information:

- Baud rate
- Parity
- Data bits
- Stop bits
- Hardware protocol: pin numbers being monitored
- Software protocol: which technique?
- Protocol activation: both, hardware, software, none

This inclusion is not going to happen until users start complaining. Otherwise, the world of hooking up serial printers will remain mysterious and complicated, just because of the lack of published information.

Using DOS To Redirect from Parallel to Serial

All IBM PC software defaults to the parallel port because the only PC printers IBM has put its name on have been parallel printers. Thus, serial printers have always gone against IBM. But, if you must use serial printers, the common recommendation is to use the DOS MODE command to redirect printer output from the parallel port (LPT1:) to the serial port (COM1:). This change is done through the following commands:

    MODE COM1:9600,N,8,1
    MODE LPT1:=COM1:

You can type these commands at the DOS prompt or put them in an AUTO-EXEC.BAT file. The trouble with these commands is that they cause all applications to trust DOS to listen for wires being yanked or XOFF being sent. Unfortunately, no version of DOS listens to either of these commands (yet). Some clone manufacturers have added XON and XOFF capabilities to the specific DOS for their machines.

The trouble with DOS's implementing a buffer-management protocol is that DOS does not have a method of communicating this information to the application software. DOS can be designed to translate XON/XOFF or wires being yanked to the equivalent of the parallel port busy line, but Microsoft has not seen fit to add this design yet. Instead, third-party software packages have added this feature to DOS.

Using Third-Party Software To Redirect Data

Each PC software program can initialize the serial port in a different way, feeling different wires being tugged by the printer and expecting different buffer-management protocols from the printer. Solving this problem by fooling all PC programs into thinking that the printer is a parallel printer and then using DOS to route all the data to the printer does not work either because DOS does not listen to printers at all. The only alternative that completely solves this problem is third-party software.

With third-party software, you can set up PC applications to print to what they think is the parallel port. The third-party software can then take the data and send it anywhere—out a serial port or into a local area network. If problems occur, the third-party software simply has to inform DOS that the fictitious parallel printer is having problems. The PC software and DOS then cannot tell the difference between a real parallel port and a simulated parallel port.

A company called AST ships with every serial port the software necessary to make this distinction. The program, called SuperSpool, is essentially a print spooler that uses RAM and attaches itself to DOS. The manual for AST Super-Spool clearly explains how to force SuperSpool to pay attention to wires being yanked on pins 5, 6, and 8. The manual also clearly describes how to force SuperSpool to pay attention to XOFF and XON. Consider, for example, this command:

SUPERSPL LPT1:=COM1:/RATE=9600,N,8,1/ON=DCD,DSR,CTS,XON

This AST SuperSpool command asks that a simulated parallel printer be created and that the serial printer be initialized at 9600 baud, no parity, 8 data bits, and 1 stop bit. In addition, this command asks SuperSpool to pay attention to the wires named DCD (Data Carrier Detect—pin 8), DSR (Data Set Ready—pin 6), and CTS (Clear To Send—pin 5). The command also asks SuperSpool to monitor data coming in on pin 3 for the printer's sending XOFF and XON. All this action happens simultaneously. This program adds the missing part to DOS. AST SuperSpool is an excellent product. Its only drawback is that it also includes a spooler. Try making the spooler as small as possible.

Chapter Summary

Parallel ports are consistently used in the IBM PC world with few problems. You can isolate most problems quickly by building two parallel cables: a minimum one and a maximum one. The minimum cable runs just the minimum number of wires. The maximum cable runs all the wires possible between the printer and the PC. Occasionally, the maximum cable carries so much information that the PC becomes confused or double-spaces. The minimum cable seems to work better.

Serial interfaces, on the other hand, are a pain. There are no easy answers. The IBM PC world has never officially supported serial printers, so you find complete chaos trying to get a serial printer working consistently. The cable, the pins to which wires are soldered, the baud rates, and buffer-management possibilities were reviewed in this chapter. Step-by-step procedures were outlined for getting the serial printer to work.

In the Next Chapter

The last chapter of this book lists in alphabetical order symptoms of printing problems, as well as solutions. Scan through this list. Look for the symptom similar to your unique problem. The goal of the upcoming chapter is to stimulate your creative thought when dealing with printer problems.

14

Troubleshooting

The first part of this chapter describes general troubleshooting symptoms, which are organized alphabetically by printer problem. The last two sections cover a typical laser printer's (the HP LaserJet) error messages and problems and a typical dot-matrix printer's (Epson) problems. These two brands are the most popular in their respective categories—problems and solutions for them apply to many other printers. Many of the problems have already been mentioned in previous chapters, but here the purpose is to give you some ideas when you are troubleshooting and to provide you with possible solutions.

Browse this chapter for ideas when you're confronted with a printer problem. If the solutions described do not solve your problem, you have several options. Look through the index to see whether your problem is mentioned elsewhere in this book. The books that came with your printer, computer, and software should contain troubleshooting tips. Read through these. Reread Chapter 12 for help in narrowing down where the problem is located. If you think the problem is with software configuration, reread Chapter 9. If you think the problem is with printer installation, reread Chapter 8.

General Problem Areas

This section is organized alphabetically by symptom and covers a wide range of printing-related problems, from blank lines in the middle of the page, through left margins jumping around, to white letters not printing. Scan this chapter's table of contents for a description that most closely matches your problem.

Black Lines

If, when printed, all the letters typed have a solid black line going through them, the problem is in the circuitry that tells the print head when to fire its wires. In some printer models, the circuitry is on its own little circuit board, which you can replace for approximately $80. On other printer models, this circuitry is built onto the main printer logic board. Replacing this board usually costs as much as a printer.

If blank lines appear in the middle of a page, either the printer or the software put them there. Dot-matrix printers themselves can add the blank lines in the middle of the page. Laser printers cannot. Try using DOS or another software package to print, and check whether the blank lines remain in the same place. If the blank lines disappear, the problem is in the original PC software package—check its configuration. If you're using Lotus 1-2-3, learn to use the Align command. If the blank lines remain while printing with DOS, the printer is adding them. For background information, refer to Chapter 6's sections on the perforation skip and the unprintable region.

The possible solutions to this problem involve doing one of the following:

- ❏ Using the front panel or switches, configure the printer so that it does not add the blank lines. Configure the printer to disable perforation skip, unprintable region protection, and LF translation to LF+CR.

- ❏ Learn to turn on the printer only when the horizontal perforation is just above the print head.

- ❏ Configure the application to disable temporarily the capability of the printer to add the blank lines while it is printing. Disable perforation skip in the application, unprintable region protection, and LF tranlation to LF+CR.

Boldface Type

When a word processor has been commanded to boldface certain words, and the printer does not print them in bold, you first need to ask whether the same combination of software and printer has ever boldfaced before. If the pair has never worked together, the problem could be that the software is sending bold commands that the printer does not understand. You can test for this possibility by configuring the software for a simple printer. Most simple printers can boldface by printing a line twice.

Next check the default font used in the document. If the default font is bold to begin with, finding a bolder font may be difficult. Character laser printers will have this trouble. Because dot-matrix printers boldface characters by printing them twice, the shape of the characters does not matter. Character lasers print in bold by selecting different fonts. Try selecting a normal font and boldfacing it instead of trying to boldface the bold.

If the computer and printer previously worked with boldface type and the printer driver supports the use of boldface, the problem has to be in the printer. If the printer is a dot matrix and the type is very light or very dark, maybe the contrast is not great enough. If the type is too dark, run the self-test a few times and break in the ribbon. If too light, replace the ribbon. Check to see whether the ribbon is advancing properly.

If you're using a laser printer, check the print density knob. You usually can find this knob under the cover. Lift the lid as if the paper were jammed and then search for a round knob about an inch in diameter. If this knob is in the extreme light or extreme dark position, the bold may not be distinguishable from the regular text. If adjusting the knob does not solve the problem, try replacing the toner cartridge.

Centering

If you have trouble centering, remember that dot-matrix printers have no idea where the paper edges are. You control where the paper edges are, and thus you control the exact position of the centering. Turn on the dot-matrix printer and watch the head movement. It always moves to where it thinks the left edge of the paper is going to be. Try to align the left edge of the paper with the print head.

If the centering is uneven, remember that two types of character centering exist. If you're centering on a character-mode printer, characters are placed into boxes, and only sentences or words with an odd number of characters are exactly centered. Those with an even number of characters are always one character off. Nothing can be done about these types of centering problems, other than rewording the phrase so that it contains an odd number of characters.

Most printers today have a *microcentering* capability built in. If the proper commands are sent before the text to be centered, the printer has responsibility for centering exactly, whether an odd or even number of characters is involved. Read through the application software manual to see whether your software supports this type of centering.

Columns Are Misaligned

If the left-hand columns do not align, and they are on the extreme left side of the page with only a white left margin between the left column and the left edge of the paper, first suspect a hardware problem. Most likely the head positioning system needs to be cleaned or is faulty; the paper is not installed properly; or a cut-sheet feeder, printer, and software are fighting over responsibility for controlling print head movement.

If the right margin is lined up and the left margin is ragged, you accidentally may have selected this mode of operation. Printing ragged left margins is a feature of some word processors.

If the first column on the left side of the paper is lined up but the second column is not, try changing to a fixed-width font, such as Courier. Otherwise, try using the column-definition features of the software or the Tab key. You can usually find spaces instead of tabs between columns when they do not line up.

Decimals Are Misaligned

Back in the era of typewriters and fixed-width characters, columns of numbers all lined up properly. You could align decimal places underneath each other. Both the left and the right margins could be ragged. This layout was easy to do manually, but proportional spacing has made it difficult. Because the number symbols have different widths, lining up the decimal places is tricky. The easy solution is to pick a fixed-spaced font, such as Courier. Otherwise, software concepts like decimal tabs have to be available. See Chapter 9 for more discussion on this issue.

Dead Printers

If a printer is dead, listen to see *how* dead. Even if none of the lights come on, watch for print head movement when power is first applied. Any little sign of movement indicates that something is alive inside the printer and also indicates that the printer has major problems. If the printer is totally dead, perhaps a fuse has blown. Unplug the printer from the wall before removing the lid and checking the fuse. Live wires are exposed inside printers (even with the power off). Remember that the hood usually has to be put back on for the printer to work.

Printer power supplies are not usually in one tidy box that is easily replaced. The power supply itself is typically a traditional linear that is easy to fix, but when the power supply dies, it usually destroys other parts of the printer. Thus, repairing the power supply only exposes some other problem.

Devils or Shorts

The devil is most often called a "short" by engineers and technicians because most devils take the form of an electrical short. Devils have a nasty tendency to take up residence in a circuit component and then blow up other parts of the circuitry. Devils are hard to find. Because they are usually shorts, they often heat up much more than normal. The additional heat can be felt or measured with heat-sensitive plastic that changes color at different temperatures or grease pencils that melt at different temperatures. You also can use your finger, but chips can be hotter than an iron. See Chapter 12 for more information about devils.

Disappearing/Reappearing Characters

Software or the printer can be given conflicting instructions. Suppose that the software and printer are told to print a line of text and, in addition, center a word on the same line. To print, the word processor or printer has to make some decisions. Either the letters have to be printed on top of each other, or certain characters have to be skipped. If letters are skipped, they disappear. But if the line is edited, they may reappear.

Solve this problem by typing the line over again within the application program without adding any instructions for centering, tabbing, or justifying right margins.

Display Does Not Match Printout

In the PC world, four different character sets can mess things up. You can press a key on the keyboard, but a different symbol appears on-screen. A symbol that appears on-screen may not be exactly the same character that is printed. The possible sources of problems are numerous, but they can all be summarized as "character set problems."

For you to be able to print every character that can be displayed, the character set of the printer must match the character set of the videoboard if both are in character mode of operation. If both are in graphics mode, a single software package supplies the same character set information for both, and less problems occur. Most PC word processors have the capability to translate the screen character set to the printer character set. More sophisticated word processors have a universal character set to which the keyboard, videoboard, and printer character sets are matched. Because the videoboards and printers are starting to support multiple character sets, software is beginning to incorporate the capability to find symbols in different character sets. Thus, the capability exists to tell word processors in which font to look first for a symbol, in which font to look second, and so on.

In the PC world, two solutions to this type of problem are available. The easiest method is to select within the printer a similar font with a different character set. This tactic is usually possible by using the front panel or the dip switches. But it may not work. Ultimately, character sets are the responsibility of each individual software package. Probably WordPerfect offers the most character set support today. Look through your application software manuals for discussions relating to symbol set or character set.

In the Mac world, the font selected determines the character set assignment. Only when printing on a LaserWriter can this problem occur. And it will occur when the screen font does not match an existing laser font. The solution in this case is to delete the laser font version and force the LaserWriter to use the screen fonts when printing.

Divide Overflow, Divide by Zero, and Fatal Stack Error Messages

Divide overflow, divide by zero, and the fatal stack error messages are peculiar to PC DOS microcomputers. The origin is in the Intel-designed microcomputer CPU chip. A CPU chip can be told to act like a detective, searching for ill-behaved software that violates rules by which various programs cooperate with each other inside a computer. Usually the CPU cannot perform the operation requested. The CPU's only alternative is to ask PC DOS for help. PC DOS offers no help but instead generates one of these cryptic, terror-inspiring error messages that cause you to panic. A better error message would be `I'm DOS and I'm lost`. Macintoshes display a little bomb as if the system is going to explode.

Printers can cause these error messages when they are off-line while software is trying to print. Usually some other event, such as users pounding on the keyboard, is associated with one of these error messages. If the problem occurs more and more frequently within a machine that has worked fine in the past, the problem is more likely in the computer's memory or RAM chips. In most cases, the error message is no cause for alarm. Just turn the computer off and on.

Double-Height Characters on First Line

Most character printers determine where characters are to be located on the paper. If the character printer receives an instruction for double-height characters while on the first line, conceptually this command causes a problem. If the character is double height, where is the extra part of the character to be printed? The character is already on the first line of the page. A character printer does not know whether a top margin exists. Is the printer a laser printer with an unprintable region at the top, or a 24-pin dot-matrix printer with a perforation skip region at the top? The character printer has a choice. It can either ignore the double height, move the line down the page, and risk messing up the page format, or it can print only the bottom half of the character.

In keeping with most character printer personalities, the character printer would prefer to print something legible rather than an obvious error. Thus, most character printers do not print double-height characters on the first line. No solution is available; the problem cannot be fixed.

Downloading Fonts

Font downloading problems are unique to PCs. First figure out the font subdirectory in the PC. Then determine when the font should have been downloaded. The font-download process should be an observable event associated with a noticeable amount of time passing. The process can occur when the PC is turned on, through some chosen menu option, or automatically when a document is printed. Once you see that the computer is trying to download a font, check to see whether the font arrived at the printer. Usually, the printer has a self-test that displays a sample character set of the font that was downloaded. Finally, the PC software has to be able to access and use the new font properly. Because this feature is such a new one in PC software, many PC programs cannot properly use the new fonts. For example, if the wrong version of WordPerfect is used, the character spacing is all messed up. The only solution is to call WordPerfect and ask for the latest version.

Duplicated Characters

Duplicated characters are rare today. Early printers and software had coordination problems. The typewriter/printer/terminal device can duplicate characters for two reasons. If hooked up using parallel cables, the printer may think that it received two characters when the PC sent only one. This problem comes and goes. For example, the first two characters of each cell of a spreadsheet may be printed twice—even if the cells are on the same row. The problem is in the printer itself and is caused by differences between a true Centronics parallel port and the more common Epson parallel port of today.

If the typewriter/printer/terminal is duplicating characters when hooked up serially, it is being used as a terminal. What is happening is that a letter pressed on the keyboard is printed and also sent to the host computer system. On reception, the host computer system sends a copy of the letter back to the terminal, where the letter is printed a second time. Look on the terminal for configuration switches called full or half duplex. If you're getting duplicate characters, change the switch from half to full duplex.

If any other parallel printer starts duplicating characters, the problem could be in either the PC's parallel transmitting port or the printer's receiving parallel port. Swap printers and PC printer ports until the problem is isolated. Then replace the broken piece of hardware. If the printer is a serial printer, the problem is usually in the software configuration, either in the printer or the PC.

Errors Caused by Current Document Version

If the current document causes a printer error, but the earlier version did not, check to see whether the current document is more complex. Check to see whether more fonts are used or more objects are drawn. If the document is more complex, try removing a font or an object. You may have reached a software/hardware limitation of the printer. Solutions are either to purchase better written software or purchase more memory for the printer. But these solutions may not work. Ultimately, this limitation is something you will have to live with. For more information, see the "Document Is Too Complex" discussion in Chapter 6.

Extra Characters

Extra characters are different from duplicate characters or garbled characters. Extra characters increase line lengths and may be normal or garbled. If the extra characters are normal, usually the problem is due to radio frequency interference (the E&M waves described in Chapter 12). These problems are caused by cables being too long, too close to RF or E&M sources, or not properly grounded or designed.

If every character sent by the computer results in two or more characters printed, usually the printer is a serial printer, and the problem is that the baud rates do not match. Specifically, the printer is set to receive data much faster than the computer is sending it; thus the printer thinks that the computer is sending more than one character when only one character is sent. In these cases, the characters printed do not change, even if the text sent is changed. Make sure that the baud rate configuration information in both the PC and printers is the same. For more information on this topic, see Chapter 13.

Font Chosen Doesn't Print

If the font you have chosen doesn't print, the problem is one of character- and object-mode printers. If told to print with a font that does not exist, these printers choose another font instead. The process of selecting fonts is confusing (see Chapter 4). When a font does not exist, the selection process is even more perplexing. Sometimes you stumble across a method of selecting fonts, and it works great until you add new fonts.

Check to make sure that the chosen font exists in the printer. Many printers have a self-test that prints all resident and downloaded fonts. Turn off the printer and pull out all the font cartridges. Clean the connections and then reinsert them firmly. If the font can be displayed on-screen in the Mac world, the printer should be able to print the font. In the PC world, usually only one font can be displayed on-screen. The printer has to be sent explicit instructions about which font to use when printing. Look in your PC software's manual for instructions on how to install and select different fonts. Chapter 9 of this book can give you more ideas.

In addition, check all spoolers and queues to see whether they are blocking the downloading of fonts needed.

Front Panel Does Not Work

The most common problem with front panel operation is conceptual. Users expect front panels to operate a certain way, and they don't. Remember, the front panel can be overridden by software. In most printers, you cannot change fonts in midstream by using the front panel. Front panel changes do not take effect unless the printer is turned on and off or reset (similar to rebooting the computer). In addition, because many front panels display only one line at a time, scrolling through the options is different from choosing an option. All these concepts are explored in Chapter 8.

Garbled Characters

Garbled characters stem from many different causes. First, determine whether you're getting extra characters or whether you can find a one-to-one correspondence between the character sent and the garbled character printed. If extra characters exist, refer to the section on "Extra Characters."

The next step is to make a list of the character sent and the character printed. See whether you can find any consistency. For example, does the letter *A* always change to a *B*? Secondly, determine whether all letter *A*s change to *B*s, or just some of them.

If you can note no consistency, and the garbled values occur randomly, check the printer cable. Maybe it is too long; maybe a connection is dirty; maybe the cable is acting like an antenna. If you're using a serial printer, check to make sure that the printer and computer are configured for the same number of start, data, parity, and stop bits (see Chapter 13 for methods).

If the pattern of garbled characters is consistent, find the ASCII table in Chapter 3 and write out the bit patterns of both the character sent and the character printed. Look at the differences between the bit patterns. Usually one bit is consistently a 0 or a 1. This situation indicates a memory problem within the printer. Take the printer apart, push the chips back into their sockets, and clean the connectors. Perhaps the problem will go away. Otherwise, if the memory chips are soldered in, you have to replace the printer's logic board. In laser printers, the memory chips are often socketed and can be replaced. Each chip holds a bit, so look for a row of eight chips. Replace groups of eight chips at a time until the problem is solved.

Ghosts of Previously Printed Characters Appear

With laser printers, sometimes ghosts of previously printed characters appear. This problem indicates that the printer has a problem either in a power supply or in erasing lamp connection. First try replacing the toner cartridge. If the new toner cartridge develops the same symptoms within a short period of time, send the laser printer in for service. You probably don't have the manuals, time, or spare parts needed to fix this problem. Furthermore, putting yourself through the learning curve as well as ordering the proper manuals and spare parts will not be cost effective.

Initializing

Most dot-matrix printers initialize by sending the print head to the left margin. If the printer is turned on and the print head doesn't move, first check to see whether the power cords are attached. Then make sure that the PC is turned on. A PC turned off or a sick PC can prevent the printer from initializing. If a printer is physically disconnected from the PC, the printer should still initialize. (Check to make sure that the cable is firmly connected at both ends.)

Look at the lights on the front panel. Check for any signs of life. If the printer looks totally dead, disconnect the printer from the wall and take off the lid. Look for fuses that may need replacing. Otherwise, send the printer in for repair. If it is an old, cheap dot matrix, throwing the printer in the junk heap and purchasing a new printer is probably cheaper than paying for repairs.

Later, when the junk heap is full of enough similar printer models, you may have enough spare parts to get an old version of the printer working.

If the print head makes any movement when power is applied, the printer's logic board is probably functioning. If the printer initializes but does not print, the problem is either in the print head or the print head driver board. If the paper does not advance but everything else works, take the printer apart and find the motor that advances the paper. The motor and the circuitry that drives it are probably bad. The same may be true of the motor that pulls the print head across the page. Usually this problem indicates that something major is wrong within the printer. Most of the time you should send the printer in for repair.

Intermittent Operation

Printers can work intermittently for a variety of reasons. First try to notice some sort of a pattern. Does the problem occur only at a certain time during the day? Does it occur only when the printer is hooked into a certain wall outlet? Does it occur only when the printer is in a certain location? Gather all the clues you can and then try figuring out what the problem is.

If the printer works for the first 20 minutes and then starts becoming erratic, the problem is usually in the printer, and the printer needs to be taken in for servicing. But first, take the printer apart and check for loose and dirty connections.

Otherwise, the problem is usually outside, somewhere in the environment. Either the power coming out of the wall is dirty; some other device with a big motor is on the same circuit; or a high-speed, external tape backup system or scanner has its cable running right next to the printer cable, and both cannot be in use at the same time. Maybe the ballast in the fluorescent lamp in the ceiling is releasing radio waves that are messing up the printer cable. Race cars in a nearby street can cause a similar problem. Every time the intermittent event occurs, try changing something in the environment. See Chapter 12 for more thoughts on this matter.

Justifying Last Line of Paragraph

If you have turned on both left- and right-margin justification so that text prints in nice even blocks, the printer has a problem with what to do with the last line of text. The line could either be long enough to stretch out to the right margin or too short to warrant stretching. If the PC software tries to activate the right-margin justification software within a printer, then the printer's software could be causing the problem. Normally PC software assumes responsibility for this function. Try turning right-margin justification off before the last line of the paragraph if reconfiguring the software does not help.

Left Margin

You should be able to control the left margin easily. In a typewriter, the left margin is determined by where paper is inserted and where you start typing. You also have control over where you put paper in a dot-matrix printer, but only indirect control over where the printer starts printing. Most printers can have left margin instructions sent to them. In addition, PC software can add its own left margin, and you can use the space bar or Tab keys to create left margins manually. Some software has a special concept called "indent" that temporarily creates a new left margin for the current paragraph. All these margins can add up. Deleting them all is like going on a scavenger hunt. See Chapter 6 for more information on this problem.

If a left margin is jumping around, the cause is probably a mechanical failures. Software problems are consistent. Try removing the cut-sheet feeder if one exists. Try cleaning the left margin micro switch or LED and sensor. If this tactic doesn't work, look for the circular piece of metal under the sheet metal hood near the motor that turns the circular piece of metal and moves the print head. Clean the circular piece of metal. If a cut-sheet feeder is present, you may have a printer software problem.

Legal-Size Paper

All printers need to know how long the paper is in order to respond to what is known as a form feed. A form feed tells the printer to eject the current sheet of paper, load the next page, and position the page at the beginning of the first line. The form feed can be generated from the front panel of all printers or can be sent to the printer by software.

Unfortunately, the printer has no way of knowing where the end of the current page is and where a new page begins. This fact is true of all printers regardless of whether the printer is installed with tractor or cut-sheet feeders. Even the laser printer thinks a long sheet of legal-size paper is a paper jam unless the laser is told to expect legal-size paper. Even if told how long the paper is, most tractor feed printers still have to guess where one page stops and another starts.

Some of the fancier laser printers have paper trays that hold only legal-size paper. When the legal-size paper tray is inserted, the printer automatically knows (through switches that detect holes or cutouts in the paper trays) that the paper is legal size. Cheaper laser printers have a switch on the front panel that has to be put in legal- or letter-size mode much like some copy machines.

In summary, for every paper feed path, a mechanism must exist to tell the printer how long the paper is. This mechanism can either be a switch or button on the front panel of the printer, a menu option on the front panel, or a special command that must be sent to the printer, using software.

Some printers have to be told where the perforation is so that they can skip over it and go to the top of a new page when receiving a form feed. You can usually send this message by positioning the paper at the top of a page before turning on a printer. (See "Setting the Top of the Page" in this chapter.)

In addition to telling the printer how long the paper is, the software has to be told how long the paper is. Even if the laser printer is ejecting the legal sheet properly, the software still may be using only the letter-size portion of it. Most software packages have a mechanism to tell them how long the paper is. The software may ask how many printed lines on a page, how many inches long, or the generic legal or letter size. For example, HP LaserJet II has two paper feed paths: the tray and a manual slot on top of the tray. The tray path is told the size of the paper by the tray itself. Certain switches inside the HP LaserJet II are activated when the tray is pushed in. Different trays activate different combinations of these switches. Thus, the HP LaserJet II knows what size of paper is in the tray. When you use the manual feed slot, you have to tell the HP LaserJet II the size of the paper. This message is sent through software only. The same is true if you feed envelopes or letter-size paper manually. You cannot handle this task by using the front panel.

Letters Are Not Fully Formed

If the top half or bottom half of a letter is missing, two possibilities exist. Either the ribbon is the problem, or the platen is not square with the print head. Fixing this problem requires making some trial-and-error mechanical adjustments, which are described in Chapter 2.

Letters Misaligned

Creating newspaper-style columns of text was easy with a typewriter and with a word processor. But proportional fonts make properly lining up the left margin of the second column a difficult task. For this reason, most word processors today have developed a column-creation capability.

If your goal is to align text in columns, your options are to purchase software packages that support this feature or to select only fixed fonts—not proportional fonts.

Letter Spacing

Irregular spacing sometimes occurs with the printing of proportional fonts. The problem is usually improper configuration of the software. If you have a daisywheel printer, maybe the software and daisywheel don't match. All software has a problem with spacing proportional fonts because each font is a different width. Furthermore, if a *V* and an *A* are to be printed next to each other, they will look too far apart if the same spacing is used to separate a *V* from an *M*. This problem is one of kerning. See Chapters 4 and 9 for more information.

Lost Characters

Lost characters are rare today. Lost characters, like lost paragraphs and lines, used to be a symptom of a buffer problem. Today the lost characters are probably more likely caused by the printer interpreting the characters as commands to respond to rather than data to be printed. If this problem occurs with a parallel printer, look for multiple spoolers in the computer's configuration. If the problem occurs with a serial printer, an easy solution is to slow down the baud rate. The better solutions involve activating hardware or software handshaking (see Chapter 13).

If characters look as if they were sliced in half at the beginning or end of a line, the software is sending text into the unprintable region of the laser printer. Adjust the margins of the software.

Another cause of this symptom occurs in character printers that are supposed to have proportional fonts downloaded to them. If the proportional font is requested but does not exist, then the character-mode printer has to suggest a fixed-width font. The software, thinking that the printer is in proportional mode, asks the printer to print more characters on a line than can fit in character mode. Then the character-mode printer starts losing characters at the end of the line. The solution is to make sure that all the proportional fonts are properly downloaded.

Lost Paragraphs and Lines

Lost paragraphs and lines are hard to find unless the output is carefully proofread. Although you should not have to proofread the printer's output just to make sure that the printer is working, many serial printers are set up in a way that makes lost paragraphs or lines possible. Solutions to these problems are described in Chapter 13.

If you are using a laser printer in character mode, most of the printer's memory is used to hold page data. If the laser printer has 512K, 300K is free for text. If the average page is 1.5K, then 200 pages of text can be stored in the laser printer before it runs out of memory. Because most documents are under 200 pages, normally memory is not a problem. If the printer is hooked up serially and has only a few pages of buffer memory, however, lack of memory could be a significant worry. See Chapter 13 for more details on this problem.

LPT1/LPT2 Switch

In the IBM PC world, DOS names the parallel ports LPT1, LPT2, and LPT3. (LPT stands for Line PrinTer). Almost all software expects the printer to be attached to LPT1. When multiple parallel ports are put in a system, each parallel port has to be configured as LPT1 or LPT2. A parallel port becomes LPT3 when a special, high-priority parallel port (on the monochrome videoboards) takes over the LPT1 spot and bumps all the other LPTs up a spot. If a printer is attached to the "old" LPT1, the printer then does not work because that LPT1 has changed to LPT2. The solution is to try attaching the printer to every parallel port. Hopefully, you will find one that works.

Noise Produced when Head Moves

If the printer makes a lot of noise when the head moves, turn off the printer. Clean off the old lubricant and reapply special printer lubricant to the threads or rails on which the head slides. Slide the head up and down by hand until it moves easily and without noise. If the printer is allowed to continue working while making all that noise, motors burn out and can start acting like shorts, blowing up the circuitry that controls them.

Nothing Prints

If the software indicates that it printed successfully, yet nothing is printed, check first to see whether the printer is turned on, on-line, and ready to receive data. If the lights flashed while data was being transmitted, the problem is inside the printer. Typically, PostScript printers flash their lights and do nothing when they do not understand what was sent. In this situation, the PC application software has not been configured to talk PostScript.

If motor noises are evident and paper moves, but no paper comes out, check to see whether paper is being ejected from the back of the printer.

If the printer is healthy and no data appears to be arriving at the printer, try checking the computer's spooler. Spoolers in the PC world are contained in the application software package. Spoolers in the Mac world are purchased for all applications. Neither environment uses a single, standard spooler. In the PC world, however, you should assume that a spooler exists and try to figure out how to access the spooler control of the current application. In the Mac world, check to see whether the spooler is installed by checking the desk accessories. Once in the spooler control screen, check to see whether the spooler is clogged—perhaps it is receiving data to print but cannot print because of a printer problem. Keep in mind that the printer problem could have occurred hours ago and may need to be cleared manually.

Old Documents Do Not Print Correctly

If old documents do not print like they used to, you need to ask what changed. If the software changed, try finding an older version of the software. If the printer changed, you have to reformat the document. Changing printers or software, even today, forces you to reformat all your documents. Plan for it. Be surprised when the day comes that old documents do *not* have to be reformatted.

Out of Memory

If a printer runs out of memory, turn the printer off and on. Downloaded fonts, macros, and bits and pieces of other documents may have accumulated in the printer's memory. Turning off and on the printer gets rid of all this clutter. Character-mode printers collect the most clutter.

Reduce the complexity of the document. If you're printing a drawing, remove some objects in the drawing. If you're printing a document, turn off all the graphics being printed or reduce the font changes. If the printer works with the less complex document, find the printer manual and try to reconfigure the memory. Otherwise, purchase more memory for the printer.

Outbound Paper Feeding into the Inbound

In a dot-matrix printer that does not have a straight-through paper path, the paper curls around the platen. Humidity can curl the paper permanently. Then, when printed, the paper may curl into the inbound paper path, and the platen starts rolling the paper up like kite string. This situation is dangerous because the motors work harder, and the delicate alignment between the print head and platen is ruined.

To reduce the possibility of paper curling, always eject the first sheet of paper already in the printer before printing. Reduce the relative humidity to around 50 percent by running a dehumidifier during the summer.

Output Is Faint and Uneven

The output can be faint and uneven in a variety of printers. In dot-matrix printers, the ribbon may not be advancing properly. Each printer manufacturer has a different method for advancing the ribbon. Usually the ribbon-advancement mechanism feeds off the print head motor. The tricky part is that the ribbon has to advance in the same direction regardless of which direction the print head is traveling. Therefore, the gear assembly that moves the ribbon can get complicated.

Check to see whether the ribbon is installed correctly. Check the mechanical assembly to make sure that the ribbon is advancing properly. If the ribbon has to change directions, make sure that the direction-change mechanism is working. Perhaps you just need to change the ribbon.

With laser printers, the cause for faint and uneven output can be wrinkled paper or a lack of toner. Check paper alignment and toner cartridge.

Page Creep

Page creep is caused by a variety of reasons. None of the solutions work unless you are trained to behave consistently. To train yourself, learn to set consistent top and bottom margins, choose fonts consistently, enable or disable the perforation skip or the unprintable regions consistently, leave the page length alone, and so on. Most problems are with the Lotus spreadsheet program, which does a miserable job at page layout. See Chapter 9 for Lotus printing strategies.

Page creep also can be caused by the printer wrapping lines of text that are too long to the next line. Try turning off the automatic wrap within the printer, and tell users that the printer could lose text if the lines are too wide.

Paper Advancement

Your printer may not be able to move the paper. The motors that pull paper will heat up and kill themselves if you do not make sure that the paper is easy to pull. Most printers should be able to pull paper fairly hard, but once a motor is weak, you may have to baby it by putting the box of paper right in back of the printer or just underneath. The most trouble-free method is to feed the paper from directly underneath the printer. But this method requires that you cut a hole in the counter supporting the printer.

If the paper does not advance, make sure that the tractor or friction feed is engaged. Carefully look at the platen to see whether it is moving. If it is not moving, feel the case near where the motor responsible for moving the platen is located. Often the motor is hot—dead. Grab the paper and feel the strength of the motor. Motors become weak as they die. The primary causes of motor death are friction and users grabbing printer knobs, preventing the motor from doing its job.

Another common reason that paper does not advance properly is that a mailing label has peeled off in the paper path, causing friction with the fanfold paper. In this case, remove the label.

Paper Is Spewed

If a printer starts spewing paper, the most likely problem is that the software is configured for a different printer. If the software is configured properly, make sure that the printer's emulation mode matches the software configuration. You usually control the printer's emulation mode through the front panel or switches inside the printer (see Chapter 8). The computer's software is configured for the printer in a variety of different ways (see Chapter 9). If paper still spews forth and the printer is attached serially, check the serial port configuration (see Chapter 13). If problems persist, start the isolation procedure described in Chapter 12.

Paper Out

When PC DOS experiences a printer problem, the system almost always thinks the printer is out of paper. All DOS manuals have documented an error message that DOS can float up to application programs. Good application programs translate this error message into a generic "printer problem" error message. The poorer programs put the words Paper Out on-screen. This fictitious error message is normally associated with parallel ports only.

When a printer runs out of paper, it tells you. The printer beeps or flashes a warning sign. But DOS has no way of knowing that this sequence of events is happening unless it pays attention to the paper-out wire running from a parallel printer to the parallel port of the PC.

If DOS gives you a `Paper Out` message, the solution is to check to see whether the cable is hooked up, the printer is on-line, paper is inserted, and so on. The solution probably has nothing to do with paper problems. If the message is coming from the printer, insert paper.

Parity-Check Error Message

In some situations, whenever a PC is asked to print, the whole computer locks up. The cursor just sits there blinking. Other times, the screen clears, and a parity-check error message or a `201` error message appears in the upper left corner. The printer is not causing the problem; the software you are using is not causing the problem. Instead, all these symptoms indicate that the PC's memory is causing the problem. The reason the PC memory acts up only when you try to print is that the PC memory is not checked until the software tries to use it. Printing takes up a lot of PC memory. Thus whenever you print, you are uncovering a chunk of PC memory not normally used. And if that memory has a bad spot, the PC locks up. Usually this memory is one of the middle banks in a PC. *Upgrading and Repairing PCs*, published by Que Corp., offers information on how to locate the bad memory chip in a PC.

Power-Up 901 Error Message

Official IBM computers are all designed to display the printer error message 901 when turned on if a printer problem exists. This problem is rare and is usually caused when a serial printer is attached to the parallel port. You may encounter this problem during installation of an old serial printer.

Try turning on the IBM computer without attaching a printer. If the error message goes away, the problem is in the printer. If the message remains, try removing the printer cable. If the error message disappears, the problem is in the printer cable. If the 901 error message continues to display even when the printer and its cable are not attached, the problem has to be in the PC. If the PC is an old one, open it and remove the parallel port. If the error message is still present, or the printer port is built onto the PC motherboard, take the PC in for repair.

Printer Error Messages

Printer error messages can be broken into three basic categories: problems with printer hardware, problems with the reception of data from the PC, and problems with software internal to the printer. Most hardware and data-transfer error messages are obvious (for example, the paper jams, or the printer goes off-line by itself). Problems that are less obvious (and generally not explained clearly in the printer manuals) are usually related to the software asking the printer to use too much memory or to print too complex a document. See Chapter 8 for a discussion of documents that are too complex.

Print Head

If the print head hammers away on the far right side of the page, the motor that pulls or screws the print head back and forth is not working. Possibly a belt has slipped off, broken, or come loose. Try mounting the belt properly and reattaching the print head to the belt.

If the print head is going back and forth but the wires are not firing, most likely something has gone wrong in the print head driver circuitry inside the printer. Sometimes you can easily replace the separate circuit board independent of all other printer parts. The trick is finding a good, functioning driver board at a reasonable price. Unfortunately, the driver board also has a tendency to destroy the print head. For this reason, purchasing a new printer is often cheaper. Throw the old printer in a junk heap; maybe someday you will have enough working parts to assemble a functioning printer.

If the print head moves when the printer is turned on but the printer does not print, the logic board in the printer is working, and the motors are working. The problem is either the print head driver circuitry or the print head. Swap print heads to isolate the problem. Don't leave a good print head in the broken printer for more than a couple of seconds when the printer doesn't work. The print head driver circuitry can destroy print heads in some failure modes—whether all the wires or just one wire of the print head fails.

If a motor cannot do its job, isolate the problem by removing two motors: one from a functioning printer and one from the broken printer. Compare the winding resistance. If the winding resistances are not within 10 percent of each other, the motor from the broken printer is bad. Otherwise the motor's drive circuitry or logic board is bad. If the motors have the same resistance, swap them and prove that the problem is not in the motor before you replace the motor drive circuitry or logic board. But don't swap motors that appear to be bad. They can damage the driver circuitry themselves.

If a print head bangs against the left side of the printer repeatedly, try cleaning the left margin micro switch or removing the rubber inserts used to hold the print head in place during shipment.

Printer-Specific Instructions

Learning printer-specific commands or instructions is dangerous. The document created with them can be printed only on the specific printer model currently attached. Programmers usually make this mistake when writing customized programs. Consultants do not have the time to create a printer definition file; thus the software created works with only one printer. The freedom to purchase any printer is lost.

Solve this problem by purchasing and using only software that has printer drivers or printer definition tables.

Printing Stops before the End of the Page

Beeping and stopping the printing before the end of the page is a problem of the first generation of dot-matrix printers. They were designed for tractor feed operation. The friction feed necessary to pull a single sheet of paper was an extra. Unfortunately, the paper-out switch in these printers is about three inches before the print head. Thus, the printer stops printing when three inches remain at the bottom of the paper.

To solve this problem, you can disable the paper-out switch. Use one of the following methods (they are listed in order of preference):

1. Use the software. Some printers can ignore the paper-out switch if the software sends the proper command. Refer to the printer's manual for the exact instruction needed to disable the printer's paper-out switch. Then enter this information in the PC software package's printer definition table and setup strings. If this method is impossible, pursue the next alternative.

2. Use the dip switch inside the printer (see the printer's manual).

3. Locate the paper-out switch by pulling strips of paper through the paper feed path. Then put a piece of tape over the switch. Paper-out switches are usually mechanical types of switches that can be held in the ON position with a piece of tape.

4. Electronically short the switch. Take the printer apart, cut the switch out of the circuit, strip the ends of two wires, and twist the wires together (recommended only for techies).

The first option *temporarily* disables the paper-out switch through software and then turns the paper-out switch back on. Using any of the last three options is somewhat dangerous. If you continue printing with no paper, the platen gets dirty and can become pitted, and the print head itself can become damaged. Most print heads today are made from pot metal; thus the pot metal holding the individual print head wires wears out before the wires bend or break or stop firing. Printing without paper causes the pot metal to wear out.

Right Margin

The right margin is controlled by three potential sources:

- ❏ Application software
- ❏ DOS
- ❏ Printer

Most application software has to be told where the right margin is located. In Lotus, if the print-range width is larger than the right margin, Lotus prints the first vertical half of the print range first, and the second vertical half next. Thus, you can paste the two halves together if necessary. Even if the printer is sent into compressed mode and can print more characters per line, you still need to increase the right margin.

Right margins are a problem only when too many characters are sent to fit on one line. The printer has to be told what to do with them. Printers can make text disappear or wrap to the next line. Ragged left margins can be too ragged if a conversion is made from fixed-spaced characters to proportionally spaced characters without reformatting the document. The letters of the last line of a paragraph may be stretched until the line fills up, but the characters are too far apart. All these problems are associated with software, not the printer.

Rotated Text

Even though some applications claim the capability to rotate text 90 degrees, your printer may not be capable of doing so. This problem cannot be fixed.

Some printers can print text rotated 90 degrees and upside down with respect to other characters on the same page. Other printers allow text to flow in only one direction across a page. Still other printers force the text to appear across only one dimension of the page. These are features of the printer that cannot be changed.

Setting the Top of the Page

Most dot-matrix printers assume that the paper crease is just above the print head and that the printer is positioned to print on the first line of the page. If the paper is tractor fed and the tractor is after the print head, then an extra sheet of paper has to be wasted to reach the tractor and to put a crease on top of the print head.

Many software packages guess the location of the end of the page through a mechanism that involves ejecting the current sheet and inserting a new one. This way the new page is at the top of what the printer thinks is the top of form.

Programs such as 1-2-3 also like to keep track of where the top of form is. 1-2-3 has no way to query the printer, however, so the program must guess where the top of the page is, assuming that the first print job begins at the top of the page. But the printer also is guessing. Only *you* know where the top of the page is. No wonder page creep is a problem. No wonder top and bottom margins appear in the middle of pages. A long discussion about the page creep problem and solutions to it appears in Chapter 9.

Setup Instructions Are Not Remembered

Printers should be able to remember instructions fed to them from the front panel. If not, look through the manuals for mention of a battery. Most printers do not use batteries, and thus if they lose their configuration while off, a hardware problem has occurred. Often the printer still can be used; you may have to reconfigure it every time you turn it on.

Shared Printers

Sharing a character printer with downloaded fonts requires that everyone agree on a couple of fonts in a few sizes. Otherwise, every user has to download fonts each time the user wants to print a document. Sharing a parallel printer through a manual AB switch is dangerous because the Centronics or Epson parallel interface is not an official standard like the serial port standard. The official RS-232C standard states that every pin should be capable of shorting to another pin without harming any hardware. No such statement has ever been made about the Centronics or Epson parallel interface. Many other shared printer problems are described in Chapter 8.

Shift-PrtSc Key Combination Does Not Work

The PrtSc key on an IBM keyboard is designed to work only when the videoboard is in character mode and a character printer is attached to LPT1. GRAPHICS.COM, shipped with PC DOS, enables certain graphics videoboards to send data to an Epson-compatible dot-matrix printer. Don't expect Shift-PrtSc to work with all software and all printers.

Single-Spacing

Printers that cannot single space are usually having trouble because the printer formerly printed double-spaced text. Reconfiguring the line feed setting may succeed in forcing the printer to single space rather than double space, but this also causes other programs to print the same thing repeatedly on the same line. The problem is a classic called the CR and LF problem and is discussed in more detail in Chapter 8.

Slow Operation under PC DOS

A slow computer in PC DOS is a particular problem connected with the original Tandy 1000 PC clone keyboard. In that keyboard, the Ctrl key is located where the Shift key normally is. If you try to press a capital P while at the DOS prompt, you accidentally may press Ctrl-P. In PC DOS (as well as CPM), pressing Ctrl-P means that you send everything appearing on-screen to the printer. If the printer is off, however, PC DOS still tries to copy each new line to the printer in addition to the screen. The printing attempt takes about a second or two to fail. But no error messages are displayed on-screen. You just notice DOS slowing down all of a sudden. The solution is to press Ctrl-P again to tell DOS to stop sending everything to the printer.

Small Fonts

When PostScript printers are asked to make small fonts (6 points and smaller), the fonts look ugly. The fonts look even worse on-screen. This problem is not the fault of the printer or PostScript but a problem of rounding errors. See Chapter 3 for more details.

Spaces Print instead of Symbols

If a printer displays spaces rather than the symbols that appeared on-screen, the fault is not with the printer. Instead, the software has determined that the symbol does not exist in the printer's character set and has decided to send a space instead. You can do nothing about this problem other than purchase a font for the printer that contains all the symbols that appeared on-screen.

Start-Up Page Prints

PostScript printers print a start-up page after they have successfully powered on. If they experience problems while printing, they reboot themselves and print a start-up page again. For example, some programs use PostScript in incompatible ways, causing PostScript to reboot when switching from one program to another. You can fix this problem only by calling the vendors of the software and asking for versions that don't have this feature.

Underlining

Underlining problems fall into a number of categories. First, you have the problem of underlining spaces, tabs, and margins—sometimes called "white space." Some users want white space underlined; others don't. White-space underlining decisions have always been the responsibility of the software. Thus, the solution to this problem is going to be in the software's manual. Sometimes software makes all the different underlining options available, and other times it does not.

On the other hand, the vertical position and the thickness of the underline is the responsibility of the font design—wherever it is located. Because fonts are in different sizes and styles, the vertical position and thickness of the underline can change from font to font. This situation poses a conceptual problem of what to do when underlining two different fonts on the same line. If your underline position jumps up and down and changes thickness, you may have to use a pen and ruler after printing. Many word processing packages are supporting the capability to put "rules," or lines, in documents. You can use rules to create uniform underlines of different fonts on the same line.

White Letters

White letters are printed on a black background. Because paper is white, the printer has to print the black background in such a manner that it leaves a white hole in the shape of a character.

Many dot-matrix printers do not have this feature because it would cause their print heads to heat up too much. Laser printers usually don't try this feature because it doesn't look good. Solid, even blacks are difficult for laser printers to print consistently.

You have two ways to print in white. First, try using a program that prints in graphics mode. These programs can usually print white letters. Otherwise, select a printer, such as a PostScript printer, that has this capability.

White Lines

A white line appearing through the text of a dot-matrix printer indicates that a wire is not firing. Immediately stop printing, take the print head out, and look at the wires. If the wiring is missing or bent, or the hole it lives in is not tight any more, you probably need a new print head. Otherwise, you can clean the print head. The chemistry of the print head materials is going to determine the type of cleaner you need. Many cleaners are hard on plastic surfaces and etch-metal surfaces. You need to avoid these types of cleaners. Call Inmac or another mail-order catalog, and purchase the special cleaner for print heads.

If you don't clean the print head, its capability to fire the wire will disappear rapidly. Then even cleaning the print head will not solve the problem, and replacing the print head will be your only alternative.

Wrapping Text

When a character printer receives more characters than can fit on a line, the extras are either discarded or moved to the next line. The decision is left up to the printer. If characters are discarded, some of the document is not printed. If the extra characters are moved to the next line, the page length is messed up.

The solution to this problem is to reformat the paragraph that contains the lengthy line. If reformatting is unacceptable, then change to a smaller font, switch to a software package that will not make these kinds of mistakes, or purchase a wide-carriage dot-matrix printer.

Wrinkled or Jammed Paper

If the paper wrinkles or jams when you leave the room, numerous causes are possible. First, check to make sure that both friction feed and tractor feed are not on simultaneously. Second, remove the paper and make sure that it slides freely through the printer, not binding unequally on one side, not grabbed or pinched anywhere. Third, make sure that the paper is pulled squarely out of the box below the printer. Fourth, check the output path. If the printer has to push paper at all, problems may eventually develop. Ideally, a printer stacks paper on the floor. The weight of the hanging paper on the output path helps pull the paper out of the printer. Try stacking the printed copies on the floor and not tearing them off until the entire print job is complete.

Laser Printer Error Codes and Symptoms

The first part of this section lists some of the error codes that appear on the front panel of the HP LaserJet. You can use this information to determine printer status and solve any printer problem. The sections that follow describe other kinds of errors that don't generate an error code, with some helpful hints included.

00 Printer ready means that the printer is ready to receive data.

The following temporary codes mean that the printer is working. After a while, the printer should display 00.

```
02  Wait
05  Self-test (nonprinting)
06  Self-test (printing staggered characters—barber pole)
07  Reset
15  Test print (alignment)
```

The following operational codes mean that the printer or the computer has messed up. If the suggested action doesn't solve the problem, warm boot the printer or bring it back to normal by pressing the RESET button.

```
11  Out of paper
12  Lid open
13  Paper jam
14  No EP cartridge installed
20  Memory overflow (This code means that too much data has been
    sent to the printer.)
```

21 Print overrun error means that the information being sent is too complex. If you press CONTINUE, the printer prints only what has been received. For example, you may be asking for too many fonts or drawing too many different objects, using the laser's macro language.

40 Line error is a problem that typically occurs if the computer was rebooted while the laser was left on, and occurs with manual switch boxes when you switch while the printer is on. Press RESET to clear the error.

41 Print check error means that while drawing a page, the printer was messed up. Press CONTINUE, and the printer redraws the page on a new sheet of paper. If this message persists, you have a problem.

PC means that you should insert a different paper cassette size.

PF means that you should insert paper in the manual feed slot.

`PE` means that you should insert an envelope in the manual feed slot.

`FC` means that you should check the font cartridge.

The `FE Font cartridge removed` error message can be cleared by turning the printer on and off.

The following codes indicate that the printer may be broken. Try turning the printer off and on. If it starts working again, blame the error message on the cosmic rays. Otherwise, try the suggestions that follow each message.

`FF Memory buffer overflow`
Reduce the complexity of the document being sent, and try again.

`22 Receiving buffer overflow`
Handshaking protocol not working (see "Getting Serial Ports To Work" in Chapter 13).

`42,43 Expansion interface error`
Problem has occurred between circuit board in expansion slot and the LaserJet. Take out the circuit board and clean the connectors.

`50 Fusing assembly malfunction`
This error code is the only one that seems to be misleading. The problem is hard to track down. Check to see whether the fusing assembly is correctly installed and seated. Then check to see whether the circuit breaker on the right back corner (as you stand in front looking at the control panel) is pushed down. Look at the gears on the fusing assembly. They can be stripped if two sheets of paper become melted together into one long sheet, and both the paper-grabber motor and the fusing motor start fighting over the long sheet of paper. Otherwise, the thermistor, fuser bulb, thermoprotector, or power supplies may be defective.

`51 Beam detect malfunction`
A tab is protruding out of the toner cartridge's flap that lets the laser's light into the cartridge. If this tab is broken, the flap cannot be opened. Or the mechanism in the laser that opens the flap may be broken. The fiber-optic cable coming from the top circuit board may be pulled loose. Otherwise, the DC power supply or the laser generator could be defective.

`52 Scanner malfunction`
The scanner motor makes a variable-pitch whirling noise. If you see this error message but don't hear the scanner motor, check the scanner motor electrical connections. Otherwise, the scanner motor or the DC supply may be defective.

`53 Laser temp. control circuit malfunction`
See error 50.

54 Main motor malfunction

The main motor also can strip gears if two sheets of paper become glued together and the paper-grabbing motor and the fusing motor start fighting over the long sheet of paper.

55 Printer command error

Run the Cannon Engine Self-Test. If this test passes and the error persists, the HP part of the laser printer (that is, the motherboard) needs to be replaced. If this adjustment does not work, then replace the motherboard's power supply.

60 Bus error
See errors 42 and 43.

For the following errors, 61 through 68, you cannot do much except remove the HP's motherboard, clean off the dust, and push down all the socketed chips. If those tactics don't work, you have to replace the HP motherboard.

    61 Program ROM checksum error
    62 Internal font ROM checksum error
    63 D-RAM error
    64 Scan buffer error
    65 D-RAM controller error
    67 Miscellaneous hardware error
    68 Memory that remembers with power-off error

When 69 Expansion interface time-out error appears, you have a problem with an expansion card. Consult the expansion card's manual for what to do next.

Black Pages

A high-voltage wire in the toner cartridge has broken, or power to this wire is not connected. The circuitry that produces the laser on the HP's motherboard can fail and cause this problem. Try replacing the cartridge. If this approach does not work, look carefully at the electrical connection the cartridge makes with the printer. Look for broken pins. If you cannot find anything, replace the printer's motherboard.

Faint Print

Faint print can be caused by an empty cartridge, a dirty transfer corona wire, or a bad electrical connection to the cartridge. Or maybe your kids have been playing with the darkness adjustment (inside of LaserJet IIs).

The erase lamps in the hood of the printer shine through a flap and erase the drum within the cartridge. These lamps shine through a red filter. If the flaps start to fail or wear out, slightly faint spots appear. Also, a flap has to open to allow the erase lamp light into the cartridge. This flap may be stuck or not all the way open.

The drum within the cartridge is sensitive to light. If either the erase flap or the laser draw flap is opened while the cartridge is outside the printer, the drum is exposed to light. This exposure causes faint print also. Replacing the cartridge solves the problem.

Each cartridge triggers two micro switches in the lid of the printer. These micro switches tell the motherboard how sensitive the drum is to the laser light. The motherboard can vary three different laser light intensities. If these micro switches are malfunctioning and the laser is too dim, faint print can result.

Horizontal Streaks

Horizontal streaks are caused by the printer motherboard turning on the laser full blast in an effort to detect the laser. This problem indicates that the detect mechanism or the laser itself is malfunctioning. See error 51 in the section on "Error Codes."

Right Side of Paper Is Missing or Distorted

If the right side of the paper is missing or distorted, the mirror off of which the laser bounces is at the wrong angle. Check to see that the mirror is mounted properly. Otherwise, try replacing the toner cartridge.

Smeared Print

Smeared print can be caused by one of the following problems:

- ❏ The fusing assembly is not heating up enough. Send the printer in for servicing.
- ❏ The fuser cleaning pads are dirty. Replace the cleaning pads.
- ❏ You are using the wrong kind of paper. Purchase copy paper.
- ❏ The static teeth (parallel to the transfer corona wire in the bottom of the printer) are not working and are pulling paper off the drum. Send the printer in for servicing.

Repetitive Defects

Repetitive defects (splotches) repeat themselves at precise distances along the direction of paper feed. By knowing the diameter of the different rollers and measuring the distance between splotches, you can identify the particular roller causing the splotch. You can then clean or replace the bad roller.

Inches	Roller causing the problem
0.5	Registration assembly transfer
1.5	Upper registration
1.75	Lower registration
2.0	EP cartridge development
2.56	Lower fusing assembly
3.16	Upper fusing assembly
3.75	EP cartridge photoconductive drum

White Pages

A totally white page can be caused by one of the following problems:

- ❏ The sealing tape has not been removed from the cartridge. Remove tape.
- ❏ The transfer corona wire (thin wire that is cleaned in printer) is broken. Replace the wire.
- ❏ The flap that lets the laser's light into the cartridge cannot be opened. Check for broken pieces of plastic.
- ❏ The electrical connection to the cartridge (broken pins again) is not made. Try replacing the cartridge.
- ❏ The drum in the cartridge is not rotating. Replace the cartridge or look at the motor that spins the cartridge.

White Streaks (Vertical)

Vertical white streaks can appear for one of two reasons. Either the mirror in the lid of the printer (off of which the laser bounces) is dirty, or the transfer corona wire is dirty.

Other Laser Printer Problems

Splotches are caused by bad cartridges. Replace the cartridge.

If random, tiny, white streaks appear on a black background, you have an intermittent laser problem caused by laser circuitry or the motherboard. Take the laser in for repair.

Distorted print is caused by motor speed problems. Again, take the laser in for repair.

If you have paper-jamming problems, a resistor that drains the static off the paper feed path may be broken. Replace the resistor with one of a similar size.

Dot-Matrix Printer Problems

Epson printers have dominated the dot-matrix printer market since 1981. The history of their problems is representative of most other dot-matrix printers. What follows are some problems that you may experience with Epsons and dot-matrix printers in general.

Excessive Component Lead Length

In most older and even some newer dot-matrix printers, many components are soldered onto circuit boards. The circuit boards have holes where the component's leads are inserted. These leads pass all the way through the circuit board, creating a sharp point on the other side of the board.

Usually an insulating material is located underneath the circuit board in printers, keyboards, and laptop computers to prevent the sharp points from touching metal below. In the early Epsons, the insulating material was a thin piece of cardboard. The sharp points would poke holes through the cardboard, touch the metal underneath, and cause all the electronics in the printer to act crazy. Sometimes the printer would go off-line by itself. Other times it would print bits and pieces of what was being sent. And other times the PC would think the printer was sick when the printer seemed perfectly healthy.

The solution is to cut off the sharp points. An easy way of determining whether you have this problem is to remove the top cover, turn on the printer, and apply downward pressure with your finger on the motherboard. Observe the Ready and On lights. If they go out when pressure is applied, some leads are too long.

Ribbon Problems

Dot-matrix ribbon problems fall into three categories: the ribbon does not advance; the ribbon never worked, or the ribbon jams. Most ribbon problems are caused during initial installation. Every printer model has its own trick to ribbon insertion, although ribbons have become easier to insert in recent years.

Inserting a ribbon has two parts. First, some mechanism always exists for advancing the ribbon. This mechanism attaches to the ribbon cartridge. Some pole or shaft sticks out of the printer and into the ribbon cartridge, turning and advancing the ribbon in the cartridge. This pole or shaft has to be attached to the ribbon cartridge properly; otherwise, the ribbon does not advance and in some cases may damage a new cartridge.

The second problem is placing the ribbon over the print head. Seeing what you're doing is difficult, even if the room has good lighting. A bright light is almost always needed in order to see exactly where the ribbon is supposed to go. Once you have tackled that problem, insertion is usually quick and easy.

Replacing ribbons is always a problem. When you're not using official replacement ribbons, you may have these types of things to worry about:

- Damage because of ribbon drive gears and carriage drive motor not aligning with cartridge drive opening.
- Re-inking devices causing damage to print head wires and other metal and plastic parts because of chemicals used in the ink. Some inks contain acidic, caustic chemicals that have pitted metal parts and completely deteriorated the plastic parts.

Dot-matrix ribbons have a shelf life of one year. The ribbon life is three million characters or one year.

Serial Interface Problems

In 1981, dot-matrix printers came with parallel ports, and daisywheel printers came with serial ports. Putting a serial interface in a dot-matrix printer was a difficult experience, and most interfaces had to go through about four revisions before they worked reliably. The only serial interfaces on dot-matrix printers that seemed to work reliably were those found on high-speed, expensive printers like the Texas Instruments 810 line. You should view serial interfaces on cheaper, low-end dot-matrix printers with extreme suspicion. In summary, if you have trouble with an old, small, low-end dot-matrix printer that is configured serially, repairing it is probably going to cost more than purchasing a new one.

Possible Adjustments

Within dot-matrix printers, many adjustments are possible, just as when you're working on a car. The following chart lists the adjustments for a typical dot-matrix printer. These adjustments normally are already properly set for the printer and should last the printer's entire life. But as a printer starts to die, the components age, and fiddling with these adjustments can prolong the life of the printer. The trouble is in locating the adjustment knobs and screws. You should not attempt the adjustments just from reading this list. They are listed here so that you can look them up in your printer manuals—or, in the more likely case, order the technical manuals that contain this information. Information regarding what features are affected by the adjustments are listed in the second column of the chart.

Adjustment	*Affected feature*
Head driving pulse width	Printing energy
Time pulse generating position	Coordination with the computer
Phase relationship between timing and reset signals	Coordination with the computer
Adjust position of home position sensor	Left margin location
Squareness of platen	Formation of characters
Gap between print head and platen	The number of carbons
Paper feed stepper motor play	Even line spacing

In addition, the sprocket wheels for the tractor feed must be aligned so that the paper is pulled without jamming. The carriage tension belt should get taut about halfway into the other side of the belt. Otherwise, vertical columns will not line up. Another factor that affects alignment of vertical columns is the play between the metal gear on the carriage motor and the plastic belt driving the print head. Making an adjustment can also affect the life of the motor.

At some point, you may need to replace your print head. Dot-matrix print heads were created to be disposable. On January 8, 1981, an Epson MX-80 print head with a 100-million character life cost $36. Epson reduced the price to emphasize the throwaway nature of the print head, and encouraged users to buy spare print heads. Today the print heads cost $80 but are much more reliable. Consider purchasing a spare print head along with a new printer if you are buying them in quantity for a company. Finding spare print heads later may be difficult.

Chapter Summary

This chapter reviewed general printer trouble symptoms. Much of the material appeared as troubleshooting tips or hints in other parts of this book. In addition, specific printer error messages of the HP LaserJet printer line of printers were detailed along with typical laser printer and dot-matrix printer problems.

A

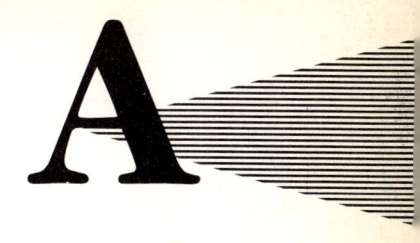

Programming Command Language Reference

In this appendix, you learn how to customize or configure a printer. Many times you know your printer has features such as a small half-sized font, but you cannot get the feature to work. This chapter will show you how to access the special features of your printer.

This appendix reviews graphic and character printer commands. Most printer commands begin with a control code. In Chapter 3, control codes are briefly mentioned in the discussion of character sets. In Chapter 6, there is a short introduction to printer programming.

Introducing Printer Programming

Printers can be instructed to change fonts, eject paper, switch to graphics mode, and many other things besides just printing symbols found on keyboards. These instructions or commands to the printer can be called programs. Unfortunately, as printers change and add features, their programming languages change. So even printers from the same manufacturer all have their little quirks and programming language differences.

Usually, printers are programmed by word processors and other application software so that users are insulated from printer programming just as they are insulated from computer programming. Unfortunately, this is not always the case. Printers always have some hidden, new feature that most application software cannot take advantage of it. Users who read their printer manuals often find examples of output that they have not been able to create.

Begin by exploring the many different fonts and special effects an application software program can produce on a printer. Print these special effects. Each application has different methods of customization, and often it is impossible to figure out what the application software is doing versus what the printer is doing. So play with more than one software package. One may be able to print a symbol because it puts the printer in graphics mode. Another may print only the symbol because it is in the printer's character set.

There are two potential sources of information for the special effects that a printer displays: the printer itself and the application software. By testing the printer using known software packages, you can learn which features have been added by the software and which are features of the printer. Features that are available in only one program but not in the rest are features of that program. Features that appear no matter which program is printing indicate a printer feature. This exercise is also useful in isolating where printer problems are located.

One of the software packages you use to test the printer should be BASIC. The reason for this is almost all computers come with some version of BASIC, and most printer manufacturers give examples of sending their printers commands using BASIC. The known software consists of one BASIC command, **LPRINT**, and one BASIC function, **CHR$**.

Revisiting ASCII

As described in Chapter 3, ASCII is a method of communicating commands and text to the printer. The symbols of the ASCII character set represent byte patterns that cause the printer to print that symbol in the current font. However, if the same character is preceded by another special ASCII character, instead of printing a symbol, it may change the line spacing. The printer may respond by assuming that the character was part of the instruction, not text to be printed.

ASCII is a method of assigning 95 symbols and 33 specific instructions to patterns of 1s and 0s (see fig. A.1). Another 128 characters are interpreted differently by different computers. Characters with decimal values 0 through 31 and value 127 are specific commands or instructions. The values from 32 to 126 are for printers to fill in any way they want.

In figure A.1, the top row and first column contain 0, 1, 2, 3, 4, 5, 6, 7, 8, 9, A, B, C, D, E, and F. These characters are the digits of the hexadecimal numbering system. For a more complete definition, see Chapter 3. Together, the row and column hex values can enable you to compute the bit pattern for any box listed below. The codes in the first two columns are called control codes. The next six columns contain the primary character set. The characters in double boxes can be changed to other characters when selecting foreign character sets.

Appendix A: Programming Command Language Reference 591

	0	16	32	48	64	80	96	112	128	144	160	176	192	208	224	240
R\C	0	1	2	3	4	5	6	7	8	9	A	B	C	D	E	F
0	NUL	DLE*	SP*	0	@	P		p*								
1	SOH	DC1*	!	1	A	Q	a	q*								
2	STX	DC2*	"	2	B	R	b	r*								
3	ETX	DC3	#	3	C	S	c	s*								
4	EOT	DC4	$	4	D	T	d	t*								
5	ENQ	NAK*	%	5	E	U	e	u*								
6	ACK	SYN*	&	6	F	V	f	v*								
7	BEL	ETB*	'	7	G	W	g	w*								
8	BS	CAN*	(	8	H	X	h	x*								
9	HT	EM *	)	9	I	Y	i	y*								
A	LF	SUB*	*	:	J	Z	j	z*								
B	VT	ESC*	+	;	K	[	k	{								
C	FF	FS *	,	<	L	\	l										
D	CR	GS *	-	=	M	]	m	}								
E	SO	RS *	.	>	N	^	n	~								
F	SI	US *	/	?	O	_	o	DEL*								
	15	31	47	63	79	95	111	127	142	159	175	191	207	223	239	255

Fig. A.1.

Generic ASCII table.

The empty boxes are called the secondary character set. Different printers use these boxes different ways (see Chapter 3). The numbers at the top and bottom of each column are helpful in counting the boxes consecutively. These numbers are called decimal numbers.

The control codes are the most important from the printer programming point of view. Some of these printer commands or control codes are used consistently by all printers; for example, FF means form feed, and CR advances the carriage. Other control codes are used differently by different printers; SI (Shift In), for example, means go into compressed print when sent to an Epson printer, but means select the current primary font when sent to an HP printer.

Sending Instructions to a Printer

From the printer's point of view, the 1s and 0s it receives can have two meanings. The codes can be either text that is to be printed, or they can be instructions to the printer. When the printer receives a bit pattern from the Control Code column, an instruction is expected. Otherwise, the printer tries to print whatever is sent.

Testing printers is a three-step process. The first is to print some text, then send an instruction, and then print more text and see what is different. If the control code works, something should be different—perhaps the font or the character spacing.

Using BASIC

Sending instructions can be accomplished by using a BASIC command and function. You type the LPRINT command followed by the text to be printed enclosed in quotation marks. When you press Enter, the text enclosed in quotation marks is sent to the printer. For example, the following instruction sends the message *This is a test of this printer* to the printer:

LPRINT "This is a test of this printer"

The quotation marks do not appear on the printed page.

Because the printer commands are not letters of the alphabet, they cannot be enclosed in quotation marks. Thus, a special mechanism is used to send control codes or printer commands. This special mechanism is the function CHR$($x$), where x is a number between 0 and 255. All control codes have to be changed to a number before they can be sent using the CHR$($x$) function. Suppose that you want to send a CR or carriage return to return the carriage without advancing the paper. Find CR in figure A.1. Figure out which number it is by finding which column CR is in and then counting down from the top starting with 0. NUL is 0, SOH is 1, STX is 2, and so on until you reach CR, which is 13. To send the CR to the printer, you type the following:

LPRINT CHR$(13);

If you want to send and underline text using the CR method, you could do it using the following instruction:

LPRINT "This will be underlined";CHR$(13);"__ __ __"

Suppose that you want to put the printer into compressed print mode. On most dot-matrix printers, this is done by sending the printer the command

Shift In or SI. It is the last entry in the column, so it is number 15. The BASIC command to print the word *Test* in compressed print is:

LPRINT "This will be compressed";CHR$(15);"test"

The quotation marks in the preceding example contain text that the printer is supposed to print. The semicolon at the end of the line tells BASIC not to send the printer to the next line. The semicolon between quotation marks and CHR instructs BASIC to send the eight-bit pattern representing SI immediately after the lowercase *d* at the end of the word compressed.

Using Utility Programs

Using BASIC has many flaws. BASIC can add its own commands to the printer and refuse to send yours. Most utility programs such as PC Tools, Norton Utilities, and Mace Utilities have an editor that enables you to create files of random patterns of bytes. These files can then be sent to the printer using the DOS COPY command.

Generating Codes from the Keyboard

The IBM PC and the PC DOS operating system were designed so that all of the 256 possible patterns of eight bits could be generated from the keyboard. Almost all PC DOS software, especially the utility programs mentioned, expect you to know how to generate any pattern of eight bits using the keyboard. There are three basic methods of generating these eight-bit patterns. None of these methods works all the time with all the PC software, generating all the 256 eight-bit patterns possible. So you need to know all three of the methods.

You can type the eight-bit patterns of ASCII in the following three ways:

1. Press the appropriate key.
2. Use the Ctrl key and alphabet to type 32 control codes.
3. Use the Alt key to type the decimal value.

In the IBM PC world, these methods are available to all programs.

Keys on the Keyboard

Certain keys on the keyboard generate ASCII codes. For example, the Esc and Backspace keys generate an eight-bit pattern. Other keys, such as Alt and Ctrl, do not generate eight-bit patterns. Still other keys generate 16-bit patterns.

The Ctrl Key

Control codes don't normally have associated keys on the keyboard. Thus, to generate these codes, you have to use the Ctrl key. It functions like a Shift key, and you can use it to generate 32 different eight-bit patterns. In figure A.1, find a capital letter and move four columns to the left to discover the control code created by pressing Ctrl and that letter. For example, you press Ctrl-M to generate CR and Ctrl-] to generate GS.

Remember that control codes can be either a command or data to the printer. When displayed on-screen or typed on the keyboard, they are the same. Thus, the method of generating the eight-bit pattern is independent of how the printer interprets the pattern. Typing a control code on the keyboard does not mean the printer will interpret it as a control code.

If the control code (number) is part of a graphics picture, the printer may interpret the number as a mole on the face of somebody's picture or as the font to use.

If the control code is sent by itself, the printer usually assumes that it is a command. If two control codes follow each other, the second may be data. This will be apparent when the printer command languages are reviewed. The effort now is to understand how to generate them from the keyboard.

The Alt Key

The Alt key is used primarily to generate the graphics characters that don't have their own special key. After you figure out the decimal value of the graphics character of interest, you can use most utility programs to generate the character by pressing and holding down the Alt key and then, on the numeric key pad, typing the decimal value of the graphics character.

Using Printer Commands

Printer commands always begin with a special command that is not a letter of the alphabet, punctuation symbol, or a number. This special command is called a control code. Figure A.1 shows 32 control codes. Normally these are the potential control codes used as the first byte of a printer command. Figure A.2 shows the possible bytes that can begin a printer command. All the empty boxes of figure A.1 can contain symbols of the printer's character set.

In some printers, the 32 control codes are repeated. This reduces the printer's character set. The repetition usually occurs in serial printers that have a limited character set (Apple's ImageWriter falls into this category).

Control Key Possibilities

CTRL	MEANING	CTRL	MEANING	CTRL	MEANING	CTRL	MEANING
@	NUL,0	H	BS,8	P	DLE,16	X	CAN,24
A	SOH,1	I	HT,9	Q	DC1,17	Y	EM,25
B	STX,2	J	LF,10	R	DC2,18	Z	SUB,26
C	ETX,3	K	VT,11	S	DC3,19	[	ESC,27
D	EOT,4	L	FF,12	T	DC4,20	\	FS,28
E	ENQ,5	M	CR,13	U	NAK,21	]	GS,29
F	ACK,6	N	SO,14	V	SYN,22	^	RS,30
G	BEL,7	O	SI,15	W	ETB,23	_	US,31

Fig. A.2.

Simple ASCII control code structure.

Other printers use more than 32 control codes. Rather than duplicating the 32, an additional 32 have been created. Of the additional 32 control codes created, the ones normally used by a printer are listed in figure A.3. The additional control codes must be accessed using the Alt key rather than the Ctrl Key. Some printers have the capability to switch between the character sets. They use the Extended ASCII standard that specifies how to switch between the three modes (ANSI X3.42-1974).

Creating Files of Printer Commands

The reasons for creating a file of printer commands are many. Suppose that you want 1-2-3 to print in compressed mode every time you use the program. You can build a batch file that sends printer commands before running 1-2-3.

The reason for creating files of printer commands is to learn how they work—so that you can customize PC application software and use the exotic features of your printer. The best way to create a file of printer commands is to find a PC program that is already printing correctly, capture this file to a disk, and then start decoding it. LPT2DSK is a shareware product written by George G. Bouche. This program sends what normally goes to the printer to a file. Thus, if one application seems to make the printer work, yet another does not, you can use LPT2DSK to create two files and compare the exact printer commands.

When troubleshooting software problems, the first step is to isolate whether the application is sending garbage, or the printer is malfunctioning. You can use a PC utility program, such as Norton's, to examine the file, and the printer manual to help you figure out what the problem is. It is possible to figure out exactly what the application software is doing and what the printer is supposed to do. By comparing what the printer is supposed to do with a printout, printer software problems become clear.

R\C	0	1	2	3	4	5	6	7	8	9	A	B	C	D	E	F
0	NUL	DLE														
1	SOH	DC1														
2	STX	DC2														
3	ETX	DC3														
4	EOT	DC4														
5	ENQ	NAK						NEL								
6	ACK	SYN														
7	BEL	ETB														
8	BS	CAN						HTS								
9	HT	EM														
A	LF	SUB						VTS								
B	VT	ESC						PLD	CSI							
C	FF	FS						PLU								
D	CR	GS						RI								
E	SO	RS														
F	SI	US														

Column headers top: 0 16 32 48 64 80 96 112 128 144 160 176 192 208 224 240
Column footers bottom: 15 31 47 63 79 95 111 127 142 159 175 191 207 223 239 255

Fig. A.3.

Extended ASCII control codes.

HPCL, Epson, ISO, and Diablo Command Reference

The following command reference is meant for those who are staring at a screen of printer commands that were sent to a file rather than a disk. This reference also is meant for those who are reading the printer manual and have no idea what it is is talking about when it says "Job Control."

Many dot-matrix printers are sold that emulate Epsons. How do you know which Epson your printer is emulating? Although this Command Reference cannot answer the question directly, it can at least tell you the differences among the Epson models. If you need a more thorough Command Reference, call the printer manufacturer. Cardinal Point, Inc., publishes the *Programmers' Handbook of Computer Printer Commands*. New volumes are released as different printer models come out.

HP, Epson, ISO, and Diablo printer commands can be divided into the following categories: Job Control, Page Control, Cursor Positioning, Font Manipulation, Font Selection, Font Management, Word Processing, and Graphics. All variables or options within printer commands are represented with the symbol #. The following sections list the different printer commands and the possible value meanings of the symbol #.

Job Control

Whenever a document is printed, a job is completed. Prior to printing, the printer has to be told something about the pages it will receive. Sometimes, as in the case of PostScript printers, the printer may ask for a password before it prints. But most job control commands are more mundane. The following lists apply to certain popular printers and printers that emulate them.

HP Job Control

ESC E	Reset printer
ESC &l#X	Print # number of copies of each page
ESC &p#X	# number of bytes of transparent data
ESC &f#Y	Create macro with number #, make current
ESC &f#X #	Define, invoke, delete, stop definition of current macro

Epson Job Control

BEL	Cause the printer's speaker to beep (not HS)
ESC @	Reset or initialize the printer
DC1	Activate printer
DC3	Turn off printer
CAN	Clear print buffers (not MX)
ESC U 1	Set unidirectional mode (not HS)
ESC U 0	Cancel unidirectional mode (not HS)
ESC <	Unidirectional one line only (not HS)
ESC >	Set most significant bit on (not HS, CX, RX)
ESC =	Set most significant bit off (not HS, CX, RX)

ESC #	Accept most significant bit as sent (not HS, CX, RX)
ESC s 1	Set low speed mode (not CR, HS, MX)
ESC s 0	Cancel low speed mode (not CR, HS, MX)
DC1	Select printer (not CR, MX, RX)
DC3	Deselect printer (not CR, MX, RX)
ESC 9	Enable paper out sensor (not CR-420, HS, only LQ-1500, SX)
ESC 8	Disable paper out sensor (not CR-420, HS, only LQ-1500, SX
ESC V # data	Repeat data # times (no 9 pin, only LQ-1500,SX)
ESC V Nul	Cancel repeat data (no 9 pin, only LQ-1500,SX)
ESC i 1	Turn on immediate mode (only FX, JX, EX, no 24 pin)
ESC i 0	Turn off immediate mode (only FX, JX, EX, no 24 pin)
ESC 6	Assign control codes at 80h-9Fh (not CR, LX, MX, RX, SQ, LQ-1500)
ESC 7	Assign characters at 80h-9Fh (not CR, LX, MX, RX, SQ, LQ-1500)
ESC I 1	Redefine control codes (not CR, LX, MX, RX, no 24 pin)
ESC I 0	Restore control codes (not CR, LX, MX, RX, no 24 pin)

ISO Job Control

ESC #	In ISO models, the eighth and ninth columns (see ASCII table) as well as the zero and first columns contain control codes. Using the ASCII table as a reference, pressing Ctrl and the letter of the alphabet four columns to the right (in the same row) will generate the control codes in the zero and first columns. Pressing Esc and then a letter of the alphabet four columns to the left (in the same row) of the eighth or ninth column will select the additional control codes.
ESC c	Hard reset, to initial power-on status
ESC <	Soft reset, delete temporary data in printer
ESC =	Initialize print parameter
CSI #.z	# stands for the number of bytes following in the startup macro, which is executed during any hard or soft reset
CSI #/z	Same as CSI #.z except data following is in HEX
CSI #q	# is either manual or cassette paper-feed mode
CSI #v	# is number of copies to be made
CSI z	Eject all pages in printer memory
CSI #n	Ask printer status, printer will send CSI #n back # could be READY, BUSY, or ERROR
ESC ?#	Ask printer to respond with the character width of the proportional character of the current font with a bit pattern #

so that word processors could compute how many characters to put on a line
CSI #&y   Put number # on the printer display
BELL   Ring printer bell

DIABLO Job Control

ESC /   Automatic backward printing
ESC \   No backward printing
ESC ?   If line is too long, add carriage return and wrap to next line
ESC !   If line is too long, forget the rest
ESC 6   Print backward for this line only
ESC 5   No backward printing (same as ESC \ )
ESC CR P   Reset printer
ESC SUB # # is number to reset printer, reset from error, request status, ask printer to do memory test

Page Control

After the job has been set up, the process of printing each page begins. The printer must know where the page comes from, it's size and the margins. A character printer needs to be given some general instructions about where to put characters on the paper. Below are some specific examples.

HP Page Control

ESC &l#H   # is number indicating paper source
ESC &l#A   # is number indicating paper size
ESC &l#P   # is number of lines per logical page
ESC &a#L   # is column number of left margin
ESC &a#M   # is column number of right margin
ESC 9   Resets left and right margins to maximum width
ESC &l#E   # is number of lines of the top margin
ESC &l#F   # is number of text lines on a page
ESC &l#L   # enables or disables perforation skip
ESC &K#H   # is the horizontal motion index in 1/120th of inch
ESC &l#C   # is the vertical motion index in 1/48th of inch
ESC &l#D   # is line spacing in lines per inch

Epson Page Control

ESC C Nul #   Set page length to # inches
ESC C #   Set page length to # lines
ESC N #   Skip over perforation, # lines to be skipped

ESC O	Skip over perforation, cancel
ESC l #	Set left margin (not MX)
ESC Q #	Set right margin
ESC 0	8 lines per inch
ESC 1	10 lines per inch
ESC 2	6 lines per inch
ESC 3 #	#/180 or #/216 line spacing
ESC A #	#/60 or #/72 line spacing
ESC EM #	Cut sheet feeder Control (some FX,HS,EX,RX)
0	Disable
1	Bin 1
2	Bin 2
4	Enable
R	Eject

ISO Page Control

CSI #;#;#p	Select page format
	# paper source and orientation to print (landscape/portrait)
	# length perpendicular to paper motion path
	# width parallel to paper motion path
CSI #%r	# indicates whether to rotate image placed on page or to return to standard page layout (similar to landscape/portrait)
CSI #;#;#&s	Page registration
	# means start or end sending data to page
	# which page
	# make current page permanent (survives soft reset)
CSI #;#&w	Page overlay
	# start/end page overlay operation
	# page registration number
CSI #t	Set current cursor position as a margin #
CSI #u	Clear margin #

DIABLO Page Control

ESC T	Set top of page at current position
ESC L	Set bottom of page at current position
ESC C	Clear top and bottom margins
ESC 9	Set left margin at current position
ESC 0	Set right margin at current position
ESC FF #	Set number of lines per page to #

Appendix A: Programming Command Language Reference — 601

ESC HT # Move to position # character spaces over
ESC EM # # controls which paper tray, hopper, or tractor to get paper from

Cursor Positioning

After the job has been set up and some general information about the paper or page has been defined, the printer needs to know exactly where to put a symbol. In character printers, the printer itself can decide where to put the symbol, or the micro can explicitly tell the printer where the character is to go. To tell the printer where to place the character, the micro first moves the printer's "cursor" to the location where the next character will be printed. The following are some printer cursor-positioning commands that software can send to the printer. The term *relative* means relative to the previous cursor's position.

HP Cursor Positioning

ESC &a#C   # column to move to
ESC &a#H   # number 1/720 inch move to, if signed is relative
ESC *p#X   # number 1/300 inch move to, if signed is relative
CR   Move cursor to beginning of current line
SP   Move cursor one position right, space
BS   Move printer cursor back one character, backspace
HT   Horizontal tab to next printer tab set, tabs fixed every eighth column
ESC &a#R   # number of rows to move to, can have decimal places if signed is relative
ESC &a#V   Row to move to in 1/720 inch, if signed relative
ESC *p#Y   Row to move to in 1/300 inch, if signed relative
ESC =   Move cursor down paper half row
LF   Move cursor down one line
FF   Move cursor to beginning of next page, eject current page
ESC &k#G   # selects various options translating CR, LF, and FF
ESC &f#S   # indicates whether to save or recall a cursor position off a stack

Epson Cursor Positioning

BS   Move printer cursor back one character, backspace
LF   Move cursor down one line
FF   Move cursor to beginning of next page, eject current page

CR	Move cursor to beginning of current line
SP	Moves cursor one position right, space
HT	Horizontal tab to next printer tab set with ESC D
VT	Vertical tab to next printer tab set with ESC B
ESC D #,#	Horizontal tab positions, set at #, #, #, #,..
ESC e Nul #	Horizontal tab increment set (LX, RX only, no 24 pin)
ESC f Nul #	Horizontal skip (LX, RX only, no 24 pin)
ESC S 0	Superscript
ESC S 1	Subscript
ESC T	Cancel super and subscript
ESC B #,#, Nul	Vertical tab positions (not MX) set at #, #, #, #
ESC e 1 #	Vertical tab increment set (LX, RX only, no 24 pin)
ESC f 1 #	Vertical skip (LX, RX only, no 24 pin)
DEL	Delete last character in buffer (not HS)
ESC $ # #	Set absolute print position (FX86, FX85, EX only)
ESC \ # #	Set relative print position (FX86, FX85, EX only)
ESC J #	Forward paper feed #/180 or #/216 inch
ESC j #	Reverse paper feed #/216 inch (only FX, JX, EX, no 24 pin)

ISO Cursor Positioning

CSI #h	# selects various CR, LF translation options, character spacing
CSI #l	# deselects various CR, LF translation options, proportional spacing
ESC # 1	# selects movement units of printer; # must be followed by a space, then lowercase L.
HTS	# horizontal tab set at current cursor position
VTS	# vertical tab set at current cursor position
CSI #g	# clear either all horizontal or all vertical
HT	Execute horizontal tab
VT	Execute vertical tab
CR	Move cursor to beginning of current line
BS	Move printer cursor back one character, backspace
LF	Move cursor down one line
NEL	New line, equivalent of CR and LF
PLD	Subscript (partial line down)
PLU	Superscript (partial line up)
RI	Specify a reverse index (tab backwards)
FF	Move cursor to beginning of next page, eject current page
CSI #d	Move to absolute vertical position #
CSI #`	Move to absolute horizontal position #

CSI #k	Move relative backwards vertically #
CSI #e	Move relative forwards vertically #
CSI #a	Move relative to the right #
CSI #j	Move relative to the left #
CSI #;##x	Save, recall, move to stored cursor positions
	# memorize current or jump
	# number to store under or jump to
	# jump to different row or column, keeping current row or column the same

Diablo Cursor Positioning

ESC 1	Set horizontal tab stop at current position
ESC 8	Clear horizontal tab stop at current position
ESC -	Set vertical tab stop at current position
ESC 2	Clear all vertical and horizontal tab stops
ESC RS #	Specify how far apart rows are on a page
ESC VT #	Move to the # line vertically
ESC U	Move half a line down, subscript
ESC D	Move half a line up, superscript
ESC LF	Move up a line
ESC BS	Backspace 1/120 of an inch
HT	Horizontal tab to next stop
VT	Vertical tab to next stop
CR	Move to beginning of current line
BS	Type over the previous character
LF	Move down to the next line
FF	Eject sheet of paper, get another

Font Manipulation

Some printers can manipulate font information stored within the printer. This section explores the capabilities of several character printers to manipulate the information about a font.

HP Font Manipulation

The HP LaserJet does not manipulate stored fonts like most dot-matrix printers. Instead of slanting a font to make italics, for example, the HP requires a special customized italic font. Even bold is a special font, because a specially designed bold looks much better than other methods such as typing over, moving over 1/2 dot, and so on.

ESC &d#D	# describes type of underlining

Epson Font Manipulation

SO	Expand everything on current line only
ESC SO	Expand everything on current line only
DC4	Expanded, cancel
ESC W 1	Expanded, on
ESC W 0	Expanded, cancel
SI	Condensed set
ESC SI	Condensed set
DC2	Condensed, cancel
ESC DC2	Condensed, cancel
ESC w 1	Double height, on (FX-86s, some LQs only)
ESC w 0	Double height, off (FX-86s, some LQs only)
ESC E	Emphasized on
ESC F	Emphasized off
ESC G	Doublestrike on (not SX)
ESC H	Doublestrike off (not SX)
ESC - 1	Underline on
ESC - 0	Underline off
ESC 4	Italic on
ESC 5	Italic off
ESC q #	Character style (no 9 pins)
	0 normal characters (no 24 pins)
	1 Outline (except LQ-500)
	2 Shadow
	3 Outline and Shadow
ESC ! #	Master select (not CR-420, MX, RX)
	0 Pica
	1 Elite
	2 Proportional
	4 Condensed
	8 Emphasized
	16 Double-Strike
	32 Double-Width
	64 Italic
	128 Underline

ISO Font Manipulation

The ISO standard is similar to the HP in font manipulation. The ISO standard does have two commands that do modify fonts. These commands do not select any stored data in the printer memory but modify data in the printer memory. In the ISO standard, each font has attached to it specific instructions on how it is to be underlined. Thus, the underline command in the ISO model has to be smarter than just blindly underlining everything like most other printers do. The ISO underline command has to look for underlining instructions in the character set description of the ISO font.

The ISO standard can do a few things the HP standard can't: create inverse video and do shading. To get an HP to do shading, the computer must draw the text, compute where a box should go, and then use the HP graphics commands to place a box on top of the text. The box never quite matches because the computations are inherently inaccurate. The HP cannot create inverse video. In the HP world, inverse video would require a completely different font.

CSI #m Select graphic rendition
is a number between 0 and 28. Most of these numbers select different fonts, but some actually manipulate fonts already in memory:
4 Underline
5 Some kind of background shading
6 Inverse video printing mode
7 Print all spaces (for password protection)

CSI #;# B Double height, width, or both of characters
is how much to enlarge in vertical direction
is how much to enlarge in horizontal direction
Two numbers are followed by space and B

Diablo Font Manipulation

ESC E   Underline, on
ESC R   Underline, off
ESC O   Bold, on
ESC W   Bold, on
ESC &   Bold, off

Font Selection

Some printers have multiple fonts stored within them. The computer must send commands to select among these different fonts. Such commands are explored in this section.

HP Font Selection

ESC &l#O   # used to select either landscape or portrait orientation
ESC (##   Set the primary symbol set to ##
ESC)##   set the secondary symbol set to ##

ESC (s#P	# chooses fixed or proportional primary spacing
ESC)s#P	# chooses fixed or proportional secondary spacing
ESC (s#H	# if fixed, characters per inch primary
ESC)s#H	# if fixed, characters per inch secondary. Note: if pitch selected is not available as a predesigned font, then closest predesigned font is used with characters spaced in the pitch desired.
ESC (s#V	# primary height in 1/72 inch
ESC)s#V	# secondary height in 1/72 inch
ESC (s#S	# primary italics or upright
ESC)s#S	# secondary italics or upright
ESC (s#B	# primary stroke weight (thin, light, bold, black)
ESC)s#B	# secondary stroke weight
ESC (s#T	# lettering style of primary
ESC)s#T	# lettering style of secondary
ESC (3@	Default primary font characteristics
ESC)3@	Default secondary font characteristics

Epson Font Selection

ESC k #	Choose typeface or font (no 9 pins; 24 pin may require cartridge)

    0 Roman
    1 Sans Serif
    2 Courier
    3 Prestige
    4 Script
    5 Optical Character Reader

ESC x 0	Draft
ESC x 1	Near letter quality
ESC P	10 characters per inch (not MX)
ESC M	12 characters per inch (not MX)
ESC g	15 characters per inch (no 9 pin, not LQ-1500, SQ)
ESC p 1	Proportional spacing, set (not HS, LX, MX, RX)
ESC p 0	Proportional spacing, cancel (not HS, LX, MX, RX)
ESC Sp #	Set intercharacter spacing (only EX, FX-85s, FX-86s); adds # dots to each character
ESC r #	Color to print with (only JX, EX, and LQ-2500)

    0 Black
    1 Red
    2 Blue
    3 Violet
    4 Yellow
    5 Orange

	6 Green
ESC t 0	Italic character set (only FX86, EX, LX, no LQ-1500, SX)
ESC t 1	Epson graphic character set (only FX86, EX, LX, no LQ-1500, SX)
ESC t 2	Remap user-defined symbols to 80h-FFh (no 9 pin, only LQ 500, 850, 1050, 2500)
ESC R #	International character sets
	0 USA
	1 France
	2 Germany
	3 UK
	4 Denmark I
	5 Sweden
	6 Italy
	7 Spain
	8 Japan
	9 Norway
	10 Denmark II
	11 Spain II
	12 Latin America
ESC m 4	Select HX-20 graphic symbols (only LX, RX, no 24 pin)
ESC m 0	Deselect HX-20 graphic symbols (only LX, RX, no 24 pin)

ISO Font Selection

ISO has landscape or portrait fonts and can place them on the same page; the HP Laserjet cannot. The ISO also can rotate the entire page 90 degrees. When the page is rotated, this becomes a page formatting issue rather than a font selection question.

CSI #;# G	Spacing increment
	# how wide a space is
	# represents how much to advance paper if line is blank; must be followed by space and then a G
CSI # L	# represents how many lines per inch for text, followed by space
CSI #;#w	Select proportional character offset
	# amount of offset
	# whether to add or subtract the offset
ESC (##	Designate graphic set ## as primary
ESC)##	Designate graphic set ## as secondary
CSI # K	# is number of characters per inch followed by space and K

CSI #m	Using #, specify character attributes such as bold, italic, and up to 10 other character set design alternatives
CSI # C	Select point size or height of character set; the units of # are determined by the ESC # 1 command
CSI #y	Specify line, pica, elite, courier, etc., typefaces

Diablo Font Selection

These proportional spacing commands really should not be included because the DIABLO will proportionally space anything—even if the font was not designed to be proportionally spaced. These proportional commands should be up in the font manipulation section, but are here for comparison with other printers.

ESC A	Lift ribbon to change color
ESC B	Return to the primary color
ESC US #	Specify different number of characters per inch
ESC S	Return to original pitch of current character set
ESC P	Turn on proportional space printing
ESC Q	Stop proportional spacing
ESC DC1 #	Offset proportional spacing by #
GS	Choose character set one on the print wheel
EM	Choose second character set on the print wheel.
ESC Y	Switch to printwheel type 0
ESC Z	Switch to printwheel type 95

Font Management

Some printers can receive font information from the computer. Commands that name, describe, transmit, and delete fonts are described in this section.

HP Font Management

ESC *c#D	Create font file with number #; makes current
ESC *c#F	# is code; can delete or change status of current font
ESC (#X	Assign # font as primary
ESC)#X	Assign # font as secondary
ESC)s#W	# describes characteristics of font to be downloaded
ESC *c#E	# bit pattern referencing character data coming next
ESC (s#W	# number of bytes of character data (maximum 32,767)

Epson Font Management

ESC & Nul
    # # # data   Downloaded characters (not CR,HS,MX,RX)
                          # character box width in dots
                          # actual character width in dots
                          # right margin in dots (for centering in character box)

ESC : Nul
    # Nul   Copy ROM-RAM (not CR, HS, MX, RX)
                          # font selection numbers of ESC k

ESC % 0   Select ROM character set or font (not CR, HS, MX, RX)

ESC % 1   Select download character set or font (not CR, HS, MX, RX)

ISO Font Management

CSI #;.p binary data
CSI #;./p hex data

This one command completely describes and downloads a font:

\# total number of bytes
\# number of characters
\# how to respond to hard, soft and parameter reset
\# portrait or landscape font
\# graphic set number
\# proportional or even spacing
\# pitch
\# size
\# upright or italic
\# bold, light, regular
\# typeface (elite, pica)
\# cell width
\# cell height
\# base line position
\# how to underline
\# 7- or 8-bit character set
\# make font permanent or temporary
\# whether base line number above is positive or negative, binary or hex data is a 7- or 8-bit pattern of character, followed by graphics data

Diablo Font Management

Diablos have only one font available at a time. Some software can pause in mid-print so that you can change print wheels. This is not exactly sophisticated font management.

Word Processing Support

Several typewriter formatting features used to be implemented in printers as word processing support, but today, software controls most formatting. This section examines some of these support features that are still found.

HP and ISO Word Processing Support

ISO and HP really have no word processing support commands. This is the trend of most new printers. Older printers had the capability to control the right margin justification for the word processor. But now most word processors control right margin justification. A word processor controls justification by telling the printer where to put each character using horizontal cursor positioning commands. In fact, today's word processors do not even let the printer compute where to put characters in fixed-spacing modes. Some word processors allow the printer to compute where to put characters in proportional-spacing mode, although word processors are starting to develop character-spacing tables.

Epson Word Processing Support

ESC a #   Justification (FX85,FX86,EX,LX)
           0   Flush Left (not LQ-1500 1.8)
           1   Centering
           2   Flush Right
           3   Justified

Diablo Word Processing Support

Diablo documentation has a category called word processing modes. According to Diablo, these modes are underline, bold, changing pitch, and proportional spacing using character width tables for print wheels stored in ROMs in the printer. All these features are documented elsewhere in this appendix because they are not true word processing features.

In the old days when underlining and bold was accomplished using carriage returns and typing over the previously printed line, these commands were an improvement. Now all printers perform them; word processors expect them, and they are not special word processing mode commands any more.

ESC X   Cancel all word processing modes except for proportional spacing

Graphics

Most character printers have a *graphics mode*, which makes it easier for them to print drawings. The computer can send commands to put the printer in graphics mode and specify the location for the dots. This section explains many of these commands.

HP Graphics

ESC *t#R	# specifies resolution of graphics data coming next
ESC *r#A	# indicates upper left corner of graphics data
ESC *b#W	# number of bytes in row of graphics data coming
ESC *rB	End of transfer of graphics data

The following are rectangle shading and drawing commands similar to a plotter's language:

ESC *c#H	Width of rectangle in 1/720th inch
ESC *c#A	Width of rectangle in 1/300th inch
ESC *c#V	Height of rectangle in 1/720th inch
ESC *c#B	Height of rectangle in 1/300th inch
ESC *c#G	# indicates how dense the shading pattern is to be
ESC *c#P	# which shading pattern to fill rectangle with

Epson Graphics

ESC * # # #
   data   Graphics mode (not CR-420, HS, MX)
                                   # resolution

0	60 dpi
1	120 dpi
2	120 dpi high speed
3	240 dpi
4	80 dpi
5	72 dpi
6	90 dpi
7	144 dpi
32	60 dpi (not 9 pin)
33	120 dpi (not 9 pin)
38	90 dpi (not 9 pin)
39	180 dpi (not 9 pin)
40	360 dpi (not 9 pin, LQ1500, SX)

                # # 16-bit counter of number of graphic bytes

ESC K # #
   data   Graphics 60 dpi
ESC L # #
   data   Graphics 120 dpi

ESC Y # #
    data   Graphics 120 dpi high speed (not CR-420, JX, MX)

ESC Z # #
    data   Graphics 240 dpi (not CR-420,JX,MX)

ESC ^ 0 # #
    data   Graphics 60 dpi (not CR,MX)

ESC ^ 1 # #
    data   Graphics 120 dpi (not CR,MX)
                              # # 16-bit counter of number of graphic bytes

ESC ? # #   Reassign graphics mode (not CR, old FX, HS, MX, RX)
                              # K,L,Y,Z commands above reassigned to
                              # one of the numbers under ESC *

ISO Graphics

CSI #&z   # resolution of graphics data, how much memory to use

CSI #&}   # enter vector mode, whether to use current cursor position or not to begin drawing

CSI #;#;#{   Start of a line position

CSI #;#;#}   End of a line position
                     # line width
                     # solid or dotted lines
                     # top, bottom, left, right, center, current start, or end position

CSI #;#s   Shading start position

CSI #;#r   Shading end position
                     # shading density
                     # top, bottom, left, right center, or current position

CSI #;#;#.r   Binary data

CSI #;#;#/r   HEX data

The previous two commands are for filling boxes with patterns and commanding that the boxes be printed

data quantity

width

resolution

Diablo Graphics

ESC 3   Go into graphics image mode (prints using the period)

ESC 4   Disable graphics mode

Printer Vendor List

You can write to any of the printer manufacturers in the following list for printer specifications. If you already own a printer, use this list to write to the manufacturer of your printer for service, programming, and technical reference manuals.

AEG Olympia Corp.
3140 Route 22
Somerville, NJ 08876
(201) 231-8300

Advanced Matrix Technology, Inc.
765 Flynn Rd
Camarillo, CA 93010
(805) 388-5799

AGFA Corp.
AGFA Compugraphic Division
200 Ballardvale
Wilmington, MA 01887
(800) 343-1237
(508) 658-5600

ALPS
(800) 825-ALPS

Apple Computer, Inc.
20525 Mariani Ave.
Cupertino, CA 95014
(408) 996-1010

Amstrad
1915 Westridge Dr.
Irving, TX 75038
(214) 518-0668

AT&T Information Systems
100 Southgate Parkway
Morristown, NJ 07960
(800) 247-1212

Axonix Corp.
2257 South 1100 East Suite 2C
Salt Lake City, UT 84106
(801) 466-9797

Blue Chip International
P.O. Box 40910
Mesa, AZ 85274
(602) 731-6980

Brother International Corp.
8 Corporate Pl.
Piscataway, NJ 08855-0159
(800) 284-2844 ext. 5337
(201) 465-6969

Caminton Corp.
2332A McGaw Ave.
Irvine, CA 92714-4992
(714) 553-0247

Canon USA, Printer Division
One Canon Plaza
Lake Success, NY 11042
(516) 488-6700

Citizen America Corp.
2401 Colorado Ave. #190
Santa Monica, CA 90404
(800) 556-1234
(213) 453-0614

C. Itoh Electronics Co.
2505 McCabe Way
Irvine, CA 92714-6297
(800) 347-2484
(714) 660-1421

DataProducts Corp.
6200 Canoga Ave.
Woodland Hills, CA 91365
(818) 887-8000

Desktop Systems, Inc.
48431 Milmont Dr.
Fremont, CA 94538
(800) 444-5321
(415) 683-2727

Eastman Kodak Co.
Personal Printer Products
901 Elm Grove Rd.
Rochester, NY 14653-6201
(800) 255-3434

Epson America, Inc.
2780 Lomita Blvd.
Torrance, CA 90505
(800) 922-8911

Facit, Inc.
400 Commercial St.
P.O. Box 9540
Manchester, NH 03108-9540
(603) 647-2700

Fortis Information Systems, Inc.
6070 Rickenbacker Rd.
Commerce, CA 90040
(213) 727-1227

Fujitsu America, Inc.
3055 Orchard Dr.
San Jose, CA 95134
(800) 626-4686
(408) 432-1300

GCC Technologies
580 Winter St.
Waltham, MA 02154
(617) 890-0880

Genicom Corp.
Genicom Dr.
Waynesboro, VA 22980
(800) 535-4364
(703) 949-1000

Hewlett-Packard Co.
19310 Pruneridge Ave.
Cupertino, CA 95014
(800) 752-0900 ext. 277J

Howtek, Inc.
21 Park Ave.
Hudson, NH 03051
(603) 882-5200

Hyundai Electronics America
166 Baypointe Parkway
San Jose, CA 95134
(408) 473-9200

Appendix B: Printer Vendor List

IBM Corp.
101 Paragan Dr. Dept. 122
Montvale, NJ 07645
(800) IBM-7257 ext. 122
(800) IBM-2468 ext. 130

IBM Corp.
Old Orchard Road
Armonk, NY 10504
(800) 426-2468

Laser Computer, Inc.
550 E. Main St.
Lake Zurich, Il 60047-2576
(312) 540-8335

Mannesmann Tally Corp.
8301 S. 180th St.
Kent, WA 98032
(800) 843-1347
(206) 251-5524
(800) 426-4813
(206) 251-5580

NCR Corp.
3718 N. Rock Rd.
Wichita, KS 67226
(316) 636-8570

NEC Information Systems, Inc.
1414 Massachusetts Ave.
Boxborough, MA 01719
(508) 264-8000
(617) 264-8000

Okidata
532 Fellowship Rd.
Mount Laurel, NJ 08054
(800) OKI-DATA
(609) 235-2600

Output Technology Corp.
9922 E. Montgomery #6
Spokane, WA 99206
(800) 422-4850
(509) 926-3855

Panasonic Industrial Co.
Computer Products Division
2 Panasonic Way
Secaucus, NJ 07094
(800) PIC-8086
(201) 348-7000

Printronix
17500 Cartwright Rd.
P.O. Box 19559
Irvine, CA 92713
(800) 826-3874
(714) 863-1900

Professional LaserMaster Corp.
7156 Shady Oak Rd.
Eden Prairie, MN 55344
(612) 944-6069

QMS, Inc.
One Magnum Pass
Mobile, AL 36618
(800) 631-2692
(205) 633-4300

Qume Corp.
500 Yosemite Dr.
Milpitas, CA 95035
(408) 942-4000
(800) 223-2479

Raster Devices Direct
P.O. Box 5629
Hopkins, MN 55343
(800) 468-1732
(612) 941-4919

Ricoh Corp.
3001 Orchard Parkway
San Jose, CA 95134
(408) 432-8800
(800) 447-4264

Seiko Instruments
1130 Ringwood Ct.
San Jose, CA 95131
(408) 922-5800

Sekiosha America, Inc.
1111 Macarthur Blvd.
Mahwah, NJ 07430
(800) 338-2609

Siemens Information Systems
20 Olney Ave.
P.O. Box 5040
Cherry Hill, NJ 08034
(609) 751-6958

Spear Technology
710A Landwehr Rd
Northbrook, IL 60062
(800) 282-1212
(312) 480-7300

Star Micronics America, Inc.
420 Lexington Ave. #2710
New York, NY 10170
(212) 986-6770

Talaris
6059 Cornerstone Court West
P.O. Box 261580
San Diego, CA 92126
(619) 587-0787

Tandy Corp.
1800 One Tandy Dr.
Fort Worth, TX 76102
(817) 390-3700

Tektronix, Inc.
P.O. Box 1000 Mail Sta. 63-447
Wilsonville, OR 97070
(800) 835-6100

Texas Instruments
(800) 527-3500

Toshiba America, Inc.
Information Systems Divison
9740 Irvine Blvd.
Irvine, CA 92718
(800) 457-7777

Unisys Corp.
Box 500
Bluebell, PA 19424
(215) 542-2240

Varityper, Inc.
11 Mt. Pleasant Ave.
East Hanover, NJ 07936
(800) 631-8134
(201) 887-8000

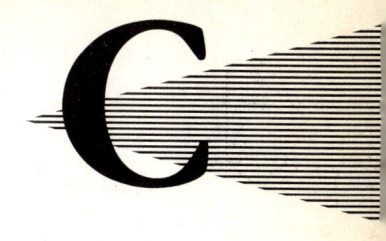

Font Vendor List

The following is a list of the companies that sell fonts for PC and Macintosh printers. Write to each of them for free samples and literature.

Acorn Plus, Inc.
4219 W. Olive Ave.
Suite 2011
Burbank, CA 91505
(213) 876-5237

Adobe Systems, Inc.
1585 Charleston Rd.
P.O. Box 7900
Mountain View, CA 94039-7900
(415) 961-4400
(800) 344-8335

Agfa Compugraphic Corp.
200 Ballardvale
St. Wilmington, MA 01887
(800) 622-8973
(508) 658-5600

Alphabets, Inc.
P.O. Box 5448
Evanston, Il 60204
(800) 326-4083

Allotype Typographics
1600 Packard Rd. #5
Ann Arbor, MI 48104
(313) 663-1989

Altsys Corp.
720 Ave. F #109
Plano, TX 75074
(214) 424-4888

Architext
121 Interpark Blvd. #208
San Antonio, TX 78216
(800) 346-9873
(800) 343-0211
(512) 490-2240

Atech Software
629 S. Rancho Santa Fe Rd. #367
San Marcos, CA 92069
(619) 438-6883

Beyond Words
1 Saunders Ave.
San Anselmo, CA 94960
(800) YES-TYPE
(415) 721-1000

BitStream, Inc.
215 First St.
Cambridge, Mass 02142
(617) 497-6222
(800) 522-FONT

Budgetbytes
1647 SW 41st St.
Topeka, KS 66609
(800) 356-3551
(913) 266-2200

Casady & Greene, Inc.
P.O. Box 223779
26080 Carmel Rancho Blvd. #202
Carmel, CA 93922
(800) 331-4321
(800) 851-1986
(408) 624-8716

Casey's Page Mill
6528 S. Oneida Ct.
Englewood, CO 80111
(303) 220-1463

Computer Peripherals, Inc.
667 Rancho Conejo Blvd.
Newbury Park, CA 91320
(800) 854-7600
(805) 499-5751

Conographic Corp.
16802 Aston St.
Irvine, CA 92714
(714) 474-1188

Data Transformations, Inc.
616 Washington St.
Denver Colo. 80203
(303) 832-1501

Devonian Int'l Software
P.O. Box 2351
Montclair, CA 91763
(714) 621-0973

D.H. Systems, Inc.
1940 Cotner Ave.,
Los Angeles, CA 90025
(213) 479-4477

Digifonts, Inc.
3000 Youngfield St. #285
Lakewood, CO 80215
(800) 242-5665
(303) 233-8113

Dubl-Click Software
9316 Deering Ave.
Chatsworth, CA 91311
(818) 700-9525

Eagle Systems
P.O. Box 502
Moorpark, CA 93021
(805) 529-6992

Ecological Linguistics
P.O. Box 15156
Washington, DC 20003
(202) 546-5862

Elfring Soft Fonts
P.O. Box 61
Wasco, IL 60183
(312) 377-3520

Appendix C: Font Vendor List

Emdash
P.O. Box 8256
Northfield, IL 60093
(312) 441-6699

Everex
48431 Milmont Dr.
Fremont, CA 94538
(800) 821-0806
(415) 683-2382

Express Data Lane, Inc.
2900 Wilcrest Suite H25
Houston, TX 77042
(713) 787-0481

First Class Graphics
2005 Perkings Lane
Redondo Beach, CA 90278
(213) 371-6669

The Font Company
12629 N. Tatum Blvd. #210
Phoenix, AZ 85032
(602) 996-6606

The Font Factory
2400 A Central Parkway
Houston, TX 77092
(713) 682-8973
(800) 44-FONTS

FontCenter
P.O. Box 6007
Lynnwood, WA 98036
(206) 771-8366

George Monagle/Graphic Partners
120 Walton St.
Syracuse, NY 13202
(315) 426-0513

Glyph Systems, Inc.
P.O. Box 134
Andover, MA 01810
(508) 470-1317

Hewlett Packard Co., Boise Division
1131 Chinden Blvd.
Boise, ID 83714
(203) 323-2551
(800) 752-0900

Hewlett-Packard Co.
19310 Pruneridge Ave.
Cupertino, CA 95014
(800) 752-0900

Image Club Graphics, Inc.
1902 11 St. SE #5
Calgary, Alberta T2G 3G2 Canada
(800) 661-9410

Image Processing Software, Inc.
6409 Appalachian Way
P.O. Box 5016
Madison, WI 53705
(608) 233-5033

Innovative Type, Inc.
13 Fairview Cr.
Groveland, MA 01834
(508) 372-7046

ISC Int'l
4025 N. Keystone Ave.
Chicago, IL 60641
(312) 286-5600

ISS, Inc.
3463 State St. #283
Santa Barbara, CA 93105
(805) 964-9671

Kingsley/AFT Type Corp.
Software Division
2559-2 E. Broadway
Tucson, AZ 85716
(602) 325-5884
(800) 289-TYPE

Laser Connection
7852 Schillinger Park W.
Mobile, AL 36608
(800) 233-6687
(205) 633-7223

Laser Technologies Int'l
14742 Beach Blvd. #440
La Mirada, CA 90638
(714) 739-1453

Letraset USA
40 Eisenhower Dr.
Paramus, NJ 07653
(800) 343-TYPE
(201) 845-6100

Linguist's Software, Inc.
925 Hindley Lane
Edmonds, WA 98020
(206) 775-1130

Linotype Co.
425 Oser Ave.
Hauppauge, NY 11788
(516) 434-2000
(800) 645-5764

LTI Softfonts International
14742 Beach Blvd. Suite 440
La Mirada, CA 90638
(714) 739-1453

Mactography
326-D N. Stonestreet Ave.
Rockville, MD 20850
(301) 424-3942

Merlin Publishing Group
2182 Kinridge Rd.
Marietta, GA 60032
(800) 637-5460
(404) 973-0741

Micrologic Software
6400 Hollis St. #9
Emeryville, CA 94608
(800) 888-9078
(415) 652-5464

Miles Computing
5115 Douglas Fir Rd. Suite 1
Calabasas, CA 91302
(818) 340-6300

Mcgathcrium Enterprises
P.O. Box 7000-417
Redondo Beach, CA 90277
(213) 545-5913

Mephistopheles Systems
3629 Lankershim Blvd.
Hollywood, CA 90068
(818) 762-8150

Monotype, Inc.
2500 Brickvale Dr.
Elk Grove, IL 60007
(800) MONOTYPE
(312) 350-5600

Olduvai Corp.
7520 Red Rd. Suite A
South Miami, FL 33143
(800) 822-0772
(305) 665-4665

Page Planners, Inc.
10607 Howerton Ave.
Fairfax, VA 22030
(703) 273-4870

Appendix C: Font Vendor List

Page Studio Graphics
3175 N. Price Rd. #1050
Chandler, AZ 85224
(602) 839-2763

Palantir, Inc.
17314 Tomball Parkway #101
Houston, TX 77064-1108
(800) 368-3979
(713) 955-8787

Paperback Software
2830 9th St.
Berkeley, CA 94710
(415) 644-2116

PC-Sig, Inc.
1030 E. Duane Ave. Suite D
Sunnyvale, CA 94086
(800) 245-6717
(408) 730-9291

Plotter Supplies, Inc.
10475 Irma Dr. #2
Denver, CO 80233
(303) 450-2900

S. Anthony Studios
889 De Haro St.
San Francisco, CA 94107
(415) 826-6193

Showker Graphic Arts
15 Southgate
Harrisonburg, VA 22801
(703) 433-1527

SMK
5760 S. Blackstone
Chicago, IL 60637
(312) 947-9157

SoftCraft, Inc.
16 N. Carroll St. Suite 500
Madison, WI 53703
(608) 257-3300
(800) 351-0500

Software Complement
8 Pennsylvania Ave.
Matamoras, PA 18336
(717) 491-2492

Software Publishing Corp.
1901 Landings Dr.
Mountain View, CA 94039-7201
(415) 962-8910

Springboard Software, Inc.
7808 Creekridge Circle
Minneapolis, MN 55435
(800) 445-4780
(612) 944-3915

Studio 231
231 Bedford Ave.
Bellmore, NY 11710
(516) 785-4422

SWFTE International Ltd.
128D Senatorial Drive
Greenville, DE 19807
(302) 429-8434
(800) 237-9383

T/Maker Co.
1390 Villa St.
Mountian View, CA 94041
(415) 962-0195

Treacyfaces, Inc.
111 Sibley Ave. 2nd floor
Ardmore, PA 19003
(215) 896-0860

Vinh Software
214 W. Main St.
Alhambra, CA 91801
(818) 576-0488

VN Labs/The Diplomat
4320 Campus Drive
Newport Beach, CA 92660
(714) 474-6968

VS Software
P.O. Box 165920
209 W. 2nd St.
Little Rock, AR 72216
(501) 376-2083

Weaver Graphics
Fox Pavilion
Box 113
Jenkintown, PA 19046
(215) 884-9286

Wendt
1325 Chestnut St.
Henderson, NV 89015
(702) 564-3265

Wilkes Publishing Corp.
25251 Paseo de Alicia,
Laguna Hills, CA 92653
(714) 855-0730

World Research Institute for Science & Technology, Inc.
8-33 40th Ave.
Long Island City, NY 11101
(718) 937-7955

Worthington Data Solutions
417A Ingalls St.
Santa Cruz, CA 95060
(800) 345-4220
(408) 458-9993

Xiphias
13646 Washington Blvd.
Marina Del Rey, CA 90292
(213) 821-6074

D

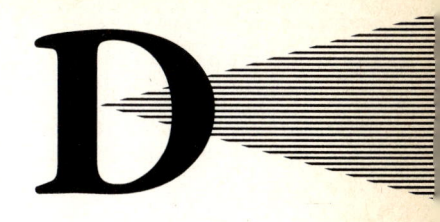

Symbol Names of Characters

The purpose of this appendix is to expand your alphabets. You learned how to pronounce the 26 letters of the English alphabet in school, but today over 1,500 symbols are in use. This appendix is organized alphabetically by symbol name. In object or PostScript printers, the names of the symbols are increasing in importance. The traditional method of defining 256 symbols by using 8 bits becomes increasingly restrictive as the world economy develops. Probably, the most important way to use this appendix is to scan the symbols and start using the additional ones that you need in your daily work.

0	0	7/8	⅞
1	1	8	8
1/3	⅓	9	9
1/8	⅛	a	a
2	2	A	A
2/3	⅔	a Acute	á
3	3	A Acute	Á
3/8	⅜	a Breve	ă
4	4	A Breve	Ă
5	5	a Circumflex	â
5/8	⅝	A Circumflex	Â
6	6	a Diaeresis (Umlaut)	ä
7	7	A Diaeresis (Umlaut)	Ä

a grave	à	alpha Circumflex	ᾶ
A grave	À	alpha Circumflex w/Iota	ᾷ
a Macron	ā	alpha Grave	ὰ
A Macron	Ā	alpha Rough	ἁ
a Ogonek	č	alpha Rough Acute	ἅ
A Ogonek	Ą	alpha Rough Acute w/Iota	ᾅ
a ring	å	alpha Rough Circumflex	ἇ
A ring	Å	alpha Rough Circumflex w/Iota	ᾇ
a tilde	ã	alpha Rough Grave	ἃ
A tilde	Ã	alpha Rough w/Iota	ᾁ
Absolute Value (Divides)	|	alpha Smooth	ἀ
Absolute Value [1.5x High]	|	alpha Smooth Acute	ἄ
Absolute Value [2x High]	|	alpha Smooth Acute w/Iota	ᾄ
Absolute Value [3x High]	|	alpha Smooth Circumflex	ἆ
Absolute Value [4x High]	|	alpha Smooth Circumflex w/Iota	ᾆ
Absolute Value [Top/Bottom/Extension]	|	alpha Smooth Grave	ἂ
acute	´	alpha Smooth w/Iota	ᾀ
Acute (Greek)	´	alpha w/Iota	ᾳ
Acute Diaeresis	̈́	Ampersand	&
Acute w/Iota Subscript	ͅ	angle	∠
ae Digraph	æ	angle left	⟨
AE Digraph	Æ	angle right	⟩
Alif/Hamzah	ʾ	Angstrom	Å
alpha	α	Apostrophe Accent Above	ʼ
Alpha	A	Apostrophe Accent Above Off Center	ʼ
alpha Acute	ά	Apostrophe Accent After and Above	ʼ
alpha Acute w/Iota	ᾴ		

Appendix D: Symbol Names of Characters 625

Apostrophe Accent Before and Above	'	Bar Overmark [2x Wide]	—
Apostrophe Accent Below	,	Bar Overmark [3x Wide]	—
Apostrophe Accent Beside	'	Base Asterisk	*
Approximately equal	≈	Base Double Quote	"
Arc Overmark	⌒	Base Single Quote	,
Arc Overmark [1.5x Wide]	⌒	Because	∵
Arc Overmark [2x Wide]	⌒	Beginning of Line	⌐
arrow both	↔	Bent Radical	√
arrow double both	⇔	beta	B
arrow double down	⇓	Beta	β
arrow double left	⇐	beta (Medial or Terminal)	ϐ
arrow double right	⇒	Beta (Medial or Terminal)	B
arrow double up	⇑	Between (Quantic)	|
arrow down	↓	Big Circle	○
arrow left	←	Big Triangle Down	▽
arrow right	→	Big Triangle Up	△
arrow up	↑	Bottom	⊥
Assertion	⊢	Bowtie	⋈
Asterisk	*	Box [Bottom Shade]	■
Asymptotically Equivalent	≍	Box [bottom]	-
At	@	Box [Bottom]	=
Ayn	'	Box [LEFT BOTTOM]	⌐
b	b	Box [left BOTTOM]	⌐
B	B	Box [left bottom]	⌐
Backslash	\	Box [LEFT bottom]	⌐
Bar Overmark [1.5x Wide]	—	Box [left RIGHT bottom]	⊥
		Box [LEFT RIGHT BOTTOM]	⊥

Box [LEFT RIGHT bottom]	╫	Box [LEFT top RIGHT BOTTOM]	╪
Box [LEFT right bottom]	╥	Box [left TOP RIGHT bottom]	╫
Box [LEFT right BOTTOM]	┯	Box [left TOP right BOTTOM]	┻
Box [left right BOTTOM]	┝	Box [LEFT TOP RIGHT BOTTOM]	╩
Box [left RIGHT BOTTOM]	┰	Box [left TOP right bottom]	┿
Box [left right bottom]	┝	Box [left top RIGHT bottom]	╫
Box [LEFT right]	╾	Box [LEFT top right bottom]	╂
Box [left RIGHT]	═	Box [left TOP RIGHT BOTTOM]	╨
Box [left right]	─	Box [LEFT top right]	┻
Box [LEFT RIGHT]	╪	Box [left top RIGHT]	┙
Box [Left Shade]	▌	Box [LEFT top RIGHT]	╢
Box [left TOP bottom]	╁	Box [LEFT TOP right]	┸
Box [left top bottom]	┬	Box [LEFT TOP RIGHT]	╣
Box [LEFT top bottom]	╥	Box [left top right]	┤
Box [LEFT top BOTTOM]	╇	Box [left TOP RIGHT]	┷
Box [LEFT TOP bottom]	╅	Box [left TOP right]	┥
Box [left top BOTTOM]	╤	Box [left top]	┐
Box [LEFT TOP BOTTOM]	╦	Box [LEFT top]	┑
Box [left TOP BOTTOM]	╤	Box [left TOP]	┒
Box [LEFT TOP right BOTTOM]	╩	Box [LEFT TOP]	┓
Box [left top right BOTTOM]	┻	Box [left]	┼
Box [left top RIGHT BOTTOM]	╫	Box [LEFT]	│
Box [LEFT TOP right bottom]	╬	Box [right bottom]	│
Box [left top right bottom]	┻	Box [right BOTTOM]	└
Box [LEFT top RIGHT bottom]	╫	Box [RIGHT bottom]	╬
Box [LEFT TOP RIGHT bottom]	╬	Box [RIGHT BOTTOM]	║
Box [LEFT top right BOTTOM]	┿	Box [Right Shade]	▐

Box [right]	│	Byelorussian short u	ў
Box [RIGHT]	║	Byelorussian SHORT U	Ў
Box [Shade 1]	▒	c	c
Box [Shade 2]	▒	C	C
Box [Shade 3]	▒	c Acute	ć
Box [Shade 4]	▊	C Acute	Ć
Box [TOP bottom]	╫	c Caron (Hachek)	č
Box [top BOTTOM]	╼	C Caron (Hachek)	Č
Box [TOP BOTTOM]	═	c Cedilla	ç
Box [TOP right bottom]	╠	C Cedilla	Ç
Box [TOP RIGHT bottom]	╫	c Circumflex	ĉ
Box [top right bottom]	└	C Circumflex	Ĉ
Box [TOP RIGHT BOTTOM]	╚	c Dot Above	ċ
Box [top RIGHT BOTTOM]	╟	C Dot Above	Ċ
Box [TOP right BOTTOM]	╩	C fraktur	ℭ
Box [top RIGHT bottom]	╚	Cadauna	‰
Box [top right BOTTOM]	╧	Candrabindu	̐
Box [TOP right]	╜	Care of	℅
Box [top right]	┘	Caret	^
Box [top RIGHT]	┘	Caron (Hachek)	ˇ
Box [TOP RIGHT]	╝	Cedilla	¸
Box [Top Shade]	▬	Cent	¢
Box [top]	─	Centered Dot	·
Box [TOP]	═	Centered Ring	•
Breve	˘	Check Mark	✓
Broken Vertical Bar	¦	CHI	Χ
Bullet	•	chi	χ

628 The Printer Bible

Circle (Empty, For Operator)	○	Circumflex Overmark [2x Wide]	∧
Circle Asterisk	⊛	Circumflex Overmark [3x Wide]	∧
Circle Circle	⊚	Circumflex w/Iota Subscript	ᾶ
Circle Dash	⊖	Clock	⊕
Circle Divide	⊘	Club	♣
Circle Divide [1.5x High]	⊘	Colon	:
Circle Divide [2x High]	⊘	Comma	,
Circle Dot	⊙	Compass	✼
Circle Dot [1.5x High]	⊙	Complex Number (Hollow C)	ℂ
Circle Dot [2x High]	⊙	Congruent	≅
Circle M	●	Contour Integral	∮
Circle Minus	⊖	Contour Integral [1.5x High]	∮
Circle Minus [1.5x High]	⊖	Contour Integral [2x High]	∮
Circle Minus [2x High]	⊖	Contour Integral [Middle]	∮
Circle Multiply	⊗	Coproduct	∐
Circle Multiply [1.5x High]	⊗	Coproduct [1.5x High]	∐
Circle Multiply [2x High]	⊗	Coproduct [2x High]	∐
Circle P	ⓟ	Copyright	©
Circle Plus	⊕	Corresponds To	≙
Circle Plus [1.5x High]	⊕	Cruzeiro	₢
Circle Plus [2x High]	⊕	Curly Right Arrow	→
Circle U	⊍	d	d
Circumflex	ˆ	D	D
Circumflex (Greek)	˜	d Apostrophe Beside	d'
Circumflex Below	ˆ	D Apostrophe Beside	D'
Circumflex Overmark [1.5x Wide]	∧	d Caron (Hachek)	ď

Appendix D: Symbol Names of Characters

D Caron (Hachek)	Ď	Dotless j	ȷ
d Cross Bar	đ	Double Acute (Hungarian Umlaut)	˝
D Cross Bar	Đ	Double Arrow Down	⇓
d Macron	d̄	Double Arrow Left (Implied By)	⇒
D Macron	D̄	Double Arrow Left and Right (Iff)	⇔
Dagger	†		
dagger dbl	‡	Double Arrow Right (Implies)	⇒
Daku-ten	ˋ		
Dark Happy Face	●	Double Arrow Up	⇑
Defined As	△	Double Arrow Up and Down	⇕
Degree	°	Double Bar [1.5x High]	‖
delta	δ	Double Bar [2x High]	‖
Delta	Δ	Double Bar [3x High]	‖
Diaeresis (Greek)	¨		
Diaeresis (Umlaut)	¨	Double Bar [4x High]	‖
Diamond	♦	Double Bar [Top/Bottom/Extension]	‖
Diamond (Hollow)	◇		
Digamma	Ϝ	Double Dagger	‡
Direct Sum (Dot Plus)	∔	Double Dot Below	̤
Ditto	˝	Double Exclamation Mark	‼
Division	÷	Double Intersection	⋒
Does Not Divide	∤	Double Prime	″
Does Not Follow	⊁	Double Subset	⋐
Does Not Precede	⊀	Double Superset	⋑
Dollar	$	Double Underline	=
Dot Above	˙	Double Union	⋓
Dot Below	̣	Down Arrow	↓
Dotless i	ı		

Down Harpoon Left	⇃	En Dash	–
Down Harpoon Right	⇂	epsilon	ε
e	e	Epsilon	E
E	E	epsilon Acute	έ
e Acute	é	epsilon Grave	ὲ
E Acute	É	epsilon Rough	ἑ
e Caron (Hachek)	ě	epsilon Rough Acute	ἕ
E Caron (Hachek)	Ě	epsilon Rough Grave	ἓ
e Circumflex	ê	epsilon Smooth	ἐ
E Circumflex	Ê	epsilon Smooth Acute	ἔ
e Diaeresis (Umlaut)	ë	epsilon Smooth Grave	ἒ
E Diaeresis (Umlaut)	Ë	epsilon Variant	ε
e Dot Above	ė	Equal	=
E Dot Above	Ė	Equal by Definition	≐
e Grave	è	Equivalent	≡
E Grave	È	Error (Script e)	e
e Macron	ē	eta	η
E Macron	Ē	Eta	H
e Ogonek	ę	eta Acute	ή
E Ogonek	Ę	eta Acute w/Iota	ῄ
Eighth Note	♪	eta Circumflex	ῆ
element	∈	eta Circumflex w/Iota	ῇ
ellipsis	…	eta Grave	ὴ
Em Dash	—	eta Grave w/Iota	ῂ
EMF (Script E)	ℰ	eta Rough	ἡ
Empty Ballot Box	☐	eta Rough Acute	ἥ
Empty Set	∅	eta Rough Acute w/Iota	ᾕ

Appendix D: Symbol Names of Characters

eta Rough Circumflex	ἦ	Figure Slash (Fraction)	/
eta Rough Circumflex w/Iota	ᾖ	Figure Slash [1.5x High]	/
eta Rough Grave	ἢ	Figure Slash [2x High]	/
eta Rough w/Iota	ᾑ	Figure Slash [3x High]	/
eta Smooth	ἠ	Figure Slash [4x High]	/
eta Smooth Acute	ἤ	fl	fl
eta Smooth Acute w/Iota	ᾔ	Flat	♭
eta Smooth Circumflex	ἦ	Florin/Guilder	ƒ
eta Smooth Circumflex w/Iota	ᾖ	Follows	≻
eta Smooth Grave	ἢ	Follows or Equals	≽
eta Smooth w/Iota	ᾐ	For All	∀
eta w/Iota	ῃ	Forward Slash	/
European Currency Symbol	₠	Fourier Transform (Script F)	ℱ
exclamation down	¡	fraction	/
Exclamation Point	!	Francs	₣
existential	∃	Frown	⌢
f	f	g	g
F	F	G	G
Female	♀	g Acute	ǵ
Feminine Spanish Ordinal	ª	G Acute	Ǵ
fi	fi	g Breve	ğ
Figure Backslash (Set Minus)	\	G Breve	Ğ
Figure Backslash [1.5x High]	\	g Caron (Hachek)	ǧ
Figure Backslash [2x High]	\	G Caron (Hachek)	Ǧ
Figure Backslash [3x High]	\	g Cedilla (Apostrophe Above)	ģ
Figure Backslash [4x High]	\	G Cedilla	Ģ
Figure Dash	–	g Circumflex	ĝ

G Circumflex	Ĝ	Hebrew Aleph	א
g Dot Above	ġ	Hebrew Ayin	ע
G Dot Above	Ġ	Hebrew Beth	ב
gamma	γ	Hebrew Chaph	כ
Gamma	Γ	Hebrew Chaph (end of words)	ך
General Currency Symbol	¤	Hebrew Cheth	ח
German Double s	ß	Hebrew comma	,
gradient	∇	Hebrew Daleth	ד
Graphic Space		Hebrew Feh	פ
Grave	`	Hebrew Feh (end of words)	ף
Grave (Greek)	`	Hebrew Gimel	ג
Grave Diaeresis	̀	Hebrew Heh	ה
Grave w/Iota Subscript	̀	Hebrew Kaph	כ
Greater Than	>	Hebrew Koph	ק
Greater Than Or Equal	≥	Hebrew Lamed	ל
Greek Question Mark	;	Hebrew Mem	מ
Greek Semicolon	·	Hebrew Mem (end of words)	ם
h	h	Hebrew Nun	נ
H	H	Hebrew Nun (end of words)	ן
h Circumflex	ĥ	Hebrew Peh	פ
H Circumflex	Ĥ	Hebrew Resh	ר
h Cross Bar	ħ	Hebrew Samekh	ס
H Cross Bar	Ħ	Hebrew Shin	שׁ
Half Circle Below	̮	Hebrew Sin	שׂ
Handaku-ten	゚	Hebrew Teth	ט
Happy Face	☺	Hebrew Thav	ת
Heart	♥	Hebrew Tsadi	צ

Hebrew Tsadi (end of words)	ץ	Horiz Arrow [Right]	→
Hebrew Vav	ו	Horiz Arrow [Terminal Bar]	⊢
Hebrew Veth	ב	Horiz Arrow [Terminal Left Hook]	↶
Hebrew vowel digraph Holem (superscript)		Horiz Arrow [Terminal Right Hook]	↪
Hebrew vowel digraph Pathah	ֽ	Horiz Bottom Brace [Extension]	‒
Hebrew vowel digraph Qamas	ֽ	Horiz Bottom Brace [Left End]	⌣
Hebrew vowel digraph Segol	ֽ	Horiz Bottom Brace [Middle]	⌣
Hebrew vowel digraph Shureq (middle)		Horiz Bottom Brace [Right End]	⌣
Hebrew vowel sign Hireq	ִ	Horiz Dbl Arrow [Extension]	=
Hebrew vowel sign Pathah	ַ	Horiz Dbl Arrow [Left]	⇐
Hebrew vowel sign Qamas	ָ	Horiz Dbl Arrow [Right]	⇒
Hebrew vowel sign Qubbus	ֻ	Horiz Harpoon [Extension]	‒
Hebrew vowel sign Segol	ֶ	Horiz Harpoon [Left Harpoon Down]	↽
Hebrew vowel sign Sereh	ֵ	Horiz Harpoon [Left Harpoon Up]	↼
Hebrew vowel sign Shewa	ְ	Horiz Harpoon [Right Harpoon Down]	⇁
Hebrew Yod	י	Horiz Harpoon [Right Harpoon Up]	⇀
Hebrew Zayin	ז	Horiz Top Brace [Extension]	‒
High Prime	′	Horiz Top Brace [Left End]	⌢
Hollow Bullet	○	Horiz Top Brace [Middle]	⌢
Hollow Square Bullet	□	Horiz Top Brace [Right End]	⌢
Hook (Tail) to the Left	↵	Horizontal Bar	―
Hook (Tail) to the Right	↳		
Hook Left Arrow	↩		
Hook Right Arrow	↪		
Horiz Arrow [Extension]	‒		
Horiz Arrow [Left]	←		

Horizontal Baseline Bar [Extension]	—	Image (Falling Dots Equals)	⌐
Horizontal Rectangle	▬	Infinity	∞
Horn	ˏ	Integer (Hollow I)	𝕀
Hourglass	⧖	Integral	∫
Hyphen	-	Integral [1.5x High]	∫
i	i	Integral [2x High]	∮
I	I	Integral [Bottom]	⌡
i Acute	í	Integral [Extension]	│
I Acute	Í	Integral [Top]	⌠
i Circumflex	î	Intersection	∩
I Circumflex	Î	Intersection [1.5x High]	∩
i Diaeresis (Umlaut)	ï	Intersection [2x High]	∩
I Diaeresis (Umlaut)	Ï	Inverse Bullet	◘
i Dot Above	i	Inverse Hollow Bullet	■
I Dot Above	İ	Inverted Apostrophe Accent Above	`
I fraktur	ℑ	Inverted Beginning of Line	⌐
i Grave	ì	Inverted Double Quote	"
I Grave	Ì	Inverted Exclamation Point	¡
i Macron	ī	Inverted Mirrored Apostrophe Accent Above	'
I Macron	Ī	Inverted Question Mark	¿
i Ogonek	į	Inverted Single Quote	'
I Ogonek	Į	iota	ι
i Tilde	ĩ	Iota	Ι
I Tilde	Ĩ	iota Acute	ί
Identical (Four Dots)	∷	iota Acute Diaeresis	ΐ
ij Digraph	ĳ	iota Circumflex	ι̂
IJ Digraph	Ĳ		

634 The Printer Bible

Appendix D: Symbol Names of Characters

iota Diaeresis	ϊ	Japanese Phonetic du (zu)	づ
iota Grave	ὶ	Japanese Phonetic e	え
iota Grave Diaeresis	ῒ	Japanese Phonetic ga	が
iota Rough	ἱ	Japanese Phonetic ge	げ
iota Rough Acute	ἵ	Japanese Phonetic gi	ぎ
iota Rough Circumflex	ἷ	Japanese Phonetic go	ご
iota Rough Grave	ἳ	Japanese Phonetic gu	ぐ
iota Smooth	ἰ	Japanese Phonetic ha	は
iota Smooth Acute	ἴ	Japanese Phonetic he	へ
iota Smooth Circumflex	ἶ	Japanese Phonetic hi	ひ
iota Smooth Grave	ἲ	Japanese Phonetic ho	ほ
Iota Subscript	ͺ	Japanese Phonetic hu (fu)	ふ
Isomorphic	≎	Japanese Phonetic i	い
j	j	Japanese Phonetic ka	か
J	J	Japanese Phonetic ke	け
j Circumflex	ĵ	Japanese Phonetic ki	き
J Circumflex	Ĵ	Japanese Phonetic ko	こ
Japanese Phonetic a	あ	Japanese Phonetic ku	く
Japanese Phonetic ba	ば	Japanese Phonetic ma	ま
Japanese Phonetic be	べ	Japanese Phonetic me	め
Japanese Phonetic bi	び	Japanese Phonetic mi	み
Japanese Phonetic bo	ぼ	Japanese Phonetic mo	も
Japanese Phonetic bu	ぶ	Japanese Phonetic mu	む
Japanese Phonetic da	だ	Japanese Phonetic n	ん
Japanese Phonetic de	で	Japanese Phonetic na	な
Japanese Phonetic di (ji)	ぢ	Japanese Phonetic ne	ね
Japanese Phonetic do	ど	Japanese Phonetic ni	に

Japanese Phonetic no	の	Japanese Phonetic small yu	ゅ
Japanese Phonetic nu	ぬ	Japanese Phonetic so	そ
Japanese Phonetic o	お	Japanese Phonetic su	す
Japanese Phonetic pa	ば	Japanese Phonetic ta	た
Japanese Phonetic pe	ぺ	Japanese Phonetic te	て
Japanese Phonetic pi	ぴ	Japanese Phonetic ti (chi)	ち
Japanese Phonetic po	ぽ	Japanese Phonetic to	と
Japanese Phonetic pu	ぷ	Japanese Phonetic tu (tsu)	つ
Japanese Phonetic ra	ら	Japanese Phonetic u	う
Japanese Phonetic re	れ	Japanese Phonetic wa	わ
Japanese Phonetic ri	り	Japanese Phonetic wo	を
Japanese Phonetic ro	ろ	Japanese Phonetic ya	や
Japanese Phonetic ru	る	Japanese Phonetic yo	よ
Japanese Phonetic sa	さ	Japanese Phonetic yu	ゆ
Japanese Phonetic se	せ	Japanese Phonetic za	ざ
Japanese Phonetic si (shi)	し	Japanese Phonetic ze	ぜ
Japanese Phonetic small a	ぁ	Japanese Phonetic zi (ji)	じ
Japanese Phonetic small e	ぇ	Japanese Phonetic zo	ぞ
Japanese Phonetic small i	ぃ	Japanese Phonetic zu	ず
Japanese Phonetic small ka	ゕ	k	k
Japanese Phonetic small ke	ゖ	K	K
Japanese Phonetic small o	ぉ	k Cedilla	ķ
Japanese Phonetic small tu	っ	K Cedilla	Ķ
Japanese Phonetic small u	ぅ	Kana Comma	、
Japanese Phonetic small vu	ゔ	Kana Period	。
Japanese Phonetic small ya	ゃ	Kana White Period	・
Japanese Phonetic small yo	ょ	kappa	κ

Appendix D: Symbol Names of Characters

Kappa	K	Left and Right Harpoons	⇌
kappa (Variant)	ϰ	Left Angle Bracket	⟨
Koppa	ϙ	Left Angle Bracket [1.5x High]	⟨
l	l	Left Angle Bracket [2x High]	⟨
L	L	Left Angle Bracket [3x High]	⟨
l Acute	ĺ	Left Angle Bracket [4x High]	⟨
L Acute	Ĺ	Left Arrow	←
l Caron (Hachek)	ľ	Left Brace	{
L Caron (Hachek)	Ľ	Left Brace [1.5x High]	{
l Cedilla	ļ	Left Brace [2x High]	{
L Cedilla	Ļ	Left Brace [3x High]	{
l Center Dot	l·	Left Brace [4x High]	{
L Center Dot	Ŀ	Left Brace [Bottom]	⎩
l Macron	ī	Left Brace [Extension]	⎪
L Macron	Ḹ	Left Brace [Middle]	⎨
l Stroke	ł	Left Brace [Top]	⎧
L Stroke	Ł	Left Bracket	[
lambda	λ	Left Bracket [1.5x High]	[
Lambda	Λ	Left Bracket [2x High]	[
Laplace Transform (Script L)	ℒ	Left Bracket [3x High]	[
Large Bullet	●	Left Bracket [4x High]	[
Large Hollow Bullet	○	Left Bracket [Bottom]	⎣
Large Hollow Square Bullet	□	Left Bracket [Extension]	⎢
Large Solid Star	★	Left Bracket [Top]	⎡
Large Square Bullet	■	Left Broken Bracket	⌊
Left and Right Arrow	↔	Left Ceiling	⌈
Left and Right Arrows	⇄		

Left Ceiling [1.5x High]	⌈
Left Ceiling [2x High]	⌈
Left Ceiling [3x High]	⌈
Left Ceiling [4x High]	⌈
Left Ceiling [Bottom/Extension]	|
Left Ceiling [Top]	⌈
Left Double Bracket	⟦
Left Double Bracket [1.5x High]	⟦
Left Double Bracket [2x High]	⟦
Left Double Bracket [3x High]	⟦
Left Double Bracket [4x High]	⟦
Left Double Bracket [Bottom]	⟦
Left Double Bracket [Extension]	‖
Left Double Bracket [Top]	⟦
Left Double Guillemet	«
Left Double Quote	"
Left Floor	⌊
Left Floor [1.5x High]	⌊
Left Floor [2x High]	⌊
Left Floor [3x High]	⌊
Left Floor [4x High]	|
Left Floor [Bottom]	|
Left Floor [Top/Extension]	|
Left Harpoon Down	↽
Left Harpoon Up	↼
Left Lenticular Bracket	〔
Left Parenthesis	(
Left Parenthesis [1.5x High]	(
Left Parenthesis [2x High]	(
Left Parenthesis [3x High]	(
Left Parenthesis [4x High]	(
Left Parenthesis [Bottom]	⎝
Left Parenthesis [Extension]	|
Left Parenthesis [Top]	⎛
Left Pointing Index	☜
Left Single Guillemet	‹
Left Single Quote	'
Less Than	<
Less Than Or Equal	≤
Ligature ff	ff
Ligature ffi	ffi
Ligature ffl	ffl
Ligature fi	fi
Ligature fl	fl
Lire	£
Liter (Script l)	ℓ
Logical And	∧
Logical And [1.5x High]	∧
Logical And [2x High]	∧
Logical Exclusive Or	⊻
Logical Not	¬

Appendix D: Symbol Names of Characters

Logical Or	∨	Micro	μ
Logical Or [1.5x High]	∨	Milreis/Escudo	$
Logical Or [2x High]	∨	Minus	−
Long Vowel	‐	Minus or Plus	∓
Low Prime	‚	Mirrored Apsotrophe Accent Below	˴
Low Rising Tone Mark	‚	Mirrored Assertion	⊣
Lowercase Eng	ŋ	Mixed Horiz Arrows [Extension]	=
Lowercase Eth		Mixed Horiz Arrows [Left Bottom]	⇋
Lowercase Greenlandic k	ĸ	Mixed Horiz Arrows [Left Top]	⇌
Lowercase Thorn			
Lozenge	◊	Mixed Horiz Arrows [Right Bottom]	⇉
m	m		
M	M	Mixed Horiz Arrows [Right Top]	⇄
Macedonian SOFT DJ	Ѓ	Mjagkij Znak	´
Macedonian soft dj	ѓ	mu	μ
Macedonian SOFT K	Ќ	MU	M
Macedonian soft k	ќ	Much Greater	≫
Macedonian ZELO	Ѕ	Much Less	≪
Macedonian zelo	ѕ	Much Much Greater	⋙
Macron	¯	Much Much Less	⋘
Male	♂	Multiply (x)	×
Maps To	↦	Multiset Union (U Plus)	⊎
Marked Ballot Box	☒	Multiset Union [1.5x High]	⊎
Masculine Spanish Ordinal	º	Multiset Union [2x High]	⊎
Measured Angle	∡	n	n
Member (Element)	∈	N	N
Mho	℧		

n Acute	ń	Not a Member (Not an Element)	∉
N Acute	Ń	Not Approximately Equal	≄
n Apostrophe	ŉ	Not Asymptotically Equivalent	≭
N Apostrophe	Ṅ	Not Congruent	≇
n Caron (Hachek)	ň	Not Equal	≠
N Caron (Hachek)	Ň	Not Equivalent	≢
n Cedilla	ņ	Not Greater Than	≯
N Cedilla	Ņ	Not Isomorphic	≆
n Macron	ñ	Not Less Than	≮
N Macron	Ñ	Not Parallel	∦
n Tilde	ñ	Not Reflex Subset	⊄
N Tilde	Ñ	Not Reflex Superset	⊅
Nabla (Gradient)	∇	Not Similar	≁
Natural	♮	Not Similar or Equal	≄
Natural Number (Hollow N)	ℕ	Not Subset	⊄
Neither Follows Nor Equals	⋡	Not Superset	⊅
Neither Greater Than Nor Equal	⋡	nu	ν
Neither Less Than Nor Equal	⋠	NU	N
Neither Precedes Nor Equals	⋠	Number (No.)	№
Neutral Double Quote	"	Number/Pound	#
Neutral Single Quote	'	o	o
Newline	↵	O	O
Nonconnecting Cedilla (Mirrored Ogonek)	˛	o Acute	ó
Northeast Arrow	↗	O Acute	Ó
Northwest Arrow	↖	o Apostrophe Beside	ȯ
Not (Slash)	/	O Apostrophe Beside	Ȯ

o Circumflex	ô	omega (Variant)	ϖ
O Circumflex	Ô	omega Acute	ώ
o Diaeresis (Umlaut)	ö	omega Acute w/Iota	ῴ
O Diaeresis (Umlaut)	Ö	omega Circumflex	ῶ
o Double Acute	ő	omega Circumflex w/Iota	ῷ
O Double Acute	Ő	omega Grave	ὼ
o Grave	ò	omega Grave w/Iota	ῲ
O Grave	Ò	omega Rough	ὡ
o Macron	ō	omega Rough Acute	ὥ
O Macron	Ō	omega Rough Acute w/Iota	ᾥ
o Slash	ø	omega Rough Circumflex	ὧ
O Slash	Ø	omega Rough Circumflex w/Iota	ᾧ
o Tilde	õ	omega Rough Grave	ὣ
O Tilde	Õ	omega Rough w/Iota	ᾡ
oe Digraph	œ	omega Smooth	ὠ
OE Digraph	Œ	omega Smooth Acute	ὤ
Ogonek (Polish Hook)	˛	omega Smooth Acute w/Iota	ᾤ
Old Bulgarian YUS	Ѫ	omega Smooth Circumflex	ὦ
Old Bulgarian yus	ѫ	omega Smooth Circumflex w/Iota	ᾦ
Old Russian FITA	Ѳ	omega Smooth Grave	ὢ
Old Russian fita	ѳ	omega Smooth w/Iota	ᾠ
Old Russian izhitsa	ѵ	omega w/Iota	ῳ
Old Russian IZHITSA	Ѵ	omicron	o
Old Russian yat	ѣ	Omicron	O
Old Russian YAT	Ѣ	omicron Acute	ό
omega	ω	omicron Grave	ὸ
OMEGA	Ω		

omicron Rough	ὀ	Pound/Sterling	£
omicron Rough Acute	ὄ	Power of 1	¹
omicron Rough Grave	ὂ	Power of n	ⁿ
omicron Smooth	ὀ	Precedes	≺
omicron Smooth Acute	ὄ	Precedes or Equals	≼
omicron Smooth Grave	ὂ	Prescription (Rx)	℞
Open Script P	℘	Prime	′
Overline (Long Mark)	‾	Product	∏
p	p	Product [1.5x High]	∏
P	P	Product [2x High]	∏
Paragraph Sign	¶	Proper Subset	⊂
Parallel	∥	Proper Superset	⊃
Partial Derivative	∂	Proportional	∝
Per Thousand	‰	psi	ψ
Percent	%	PSI	Ψ
Period	.	q	q
Perpendicular Double Right (Models)	⊢	Q	Q
		Question mark	?
Peseta	₧	Questioned Equality	≟
phi	φ	quote dbl	"
Phi	Φ	quote dbl left	"
phi (Variant)	ϕ	quote dbl right	"
pi	π	quote left	'
PI	Π	quote right	'
pi (Variant)	ϖ	quote single	'
Planck's Constant	ℏ	r	r
Plus	+	R	R
Plus or Minus	±		

Appendix D: Symbol Names of Characters

r Acute	ŕ	Right Angle Bracket [2x High]	⟩
R Acute	Ŕ	Right Angle Bracket [3x High]	⟩
r Caron (Hachek)	ř	Right Angle Bracket [4x High]	⟩
R Caron (Hachek)	Ř	Right Arrow	→
r Cedilla	ŗ	Right Brace	}
R Cedilla	Ŗ	Right Brace [1.5x High]	}
R fraktur	ℜ	Right Brace [2x High]	}
r Grave	r̀	Right Brace [3x High]	}
R Grave	R̀	Right Brace [4x High]	}
Raised Negative Sign	⁻	Right Brace [Bottom]	⎭
Real Number (Hollow R)	ℝ	Right Brace [Extension]	⎪
Reflex Subset (Contained In or Equals)	⊆	Right Brace [Middle]	⎬
Reflex Superset (Contains or Equals)	⊇	Right Brace [Top]	⎫
Registered Trademark	®	Right Bracket	]
Repeat Kana	ヽ	Right Bracket [1.5x High]	]
Repeat Kana w/Daku-on	ヾ	Right Bracket [2x High]	]
Reverse Image (Rising Dots Equals)	≓	Right Bracket [3x High]	]
rho	ρ	Right Bracket [4x High]	]
RHO	Ρ	Right Bracket [Bottom]	⎦
rho (Variant)	ϱ	Right Bracket [Extension]	⎥
Right and Left Arrows	⇄	Right Bracket [Top]	⎤
Right and Left Harpoons	⇌	Right Broken Bracket	⟩
Right Angle	∟	Right Cedilla	¸
Right Angle Bracket (Ket)	⟩	Right Ceiling	⌉
Right Angle Bracket [1.5x High]	⟩	Right Ceiling [1.5x High]	⌉

Right Ceiling [2x High]	]	Right Harpoon Up	→
Right Ceiling [3x High]	]	Right Lenticular Bracket	]
Right Ceiling [4x High]	⎤	Right Parenthesis	)
Right Ceiling [Bottom/Extension]	⎥	Right Parenthesis [1.5x High]	)
Right Ceiling [Top]	⎤	Right Parenthesis [2x High]	)
Right Double Bracket	⟧	Right Parenthesis [3x High]	)
Right Double Bracket [1.5x High]	⟧	Right Parenthesis [4x High]	)
Right Double Bracket [2x High]	⟧	Right Parenthesis [Bottom]	)
Right Double Bracket [3x High]	⟧	Right Parenthesis [Extension]	⎟
Right Double Bracket [4x High]	⟧	Right Parenthesis [Top]	⎞
Right Double Bracket [Bottom]	⟧	Right Pointing Index	☞
Right Double Bracket [Extension]	‖	Right Quote	'
Right Double Bracket [Top]	⟧	Right Single Guillemet	›
Right Double Guillemet	»	Right Single Quote (Like 9)	'
Right Double Quote	"	Ring	°
Right Double Quote (Like 99)	"	Ring Below	.
Right Floor	⌋	Root [1.5x High]	√
Right Floor [1.5x High]	⌋	Root [1x High]	√
Right Floor [2x High]	⌋	Root [2x High]	√
Right Floor [3x High]	⌋	Root [3x High]	√
Right Floor [4x High]	⌋	Root [4x High]	√
Right Floor [Bottom]	⌋	Root [Bottom]	√
Right Floor [Top/Extension]	⎢	Root [Top Corner]	⌐
Right Harpoon Down	→	Root [Vert Extension]	⎢
		Rough Breathing	ʽ
		Rough Breathing Acute	ʽ́

Appendix D: Symbol Names of Characters

Rough Breathing Acute w/Iota Subscript	ᾅ	Russian er	р
Rough Breathing Circumflex	ἇ	Russian ER (HARD SIGN)	Ъ
Rough Breathing Circumflex w/Iota Sub	ᾇ	Russian er (hard sign)	ъ
Rough Breathing Grave	ἃ	Russian ery	ы
Rough Breathing Grave w/Iota Subscript	ᾃ	Russian ERY	Ы
		Russian es	с
Rough Breathing w/Iota Subscript	ᾁ	Russian ES	С
		Russian GHE	Г
Rude	ˏ	Russian ghe	г
Russian A	А	Russian ha	х
Russian a	а	Russian HA	Х
Russian be	б	Russian i	и
Russian BE	Б	Russian I	И
Russian che	ч	Russian KA	К
Russian CHE	Ч	Russian ka	к
Russian DE	Д	Russian O	О
Russian de	д	Russian o	о
Russian e	е	Russian PE	П
Russian E	Е	Russian pe	п
Russian EF	Ф	Russian REVERSE E	Э
Russian ef	ф	Russian reverse e	э
Russian el	л	Russian SHA	Ш
Russian EL	Л	Russian sha	ш
Russian em	м	Russian SHCHA	Щ
Russian EM	М	Russian shcha	щ
Russian EN	Н	Russian SHORT I	Й
Russian en	н	Russian short i	й
Russian ER	Р		

Russian soft sign	ь	S Cedilla	Ş
Russian SOFT SIGN	Ь	s Circumflex	ŝ
Russian te	т	S Circumflex	Ŝ
Russian TE	Т	s Macron	s̄
Russian TSE	Ц	S Macron	S̄
Russian tse	ц	Sad Face	☹
Russian u	у	Sampi	ϡ
Russian U	У	Section Sign	§
Russian VE	В	Semicolon	;
Russian ve	в	Serbian HARD DJ	Џ
Russian YA	Я	Serbian hard dj	џ
Russian ya	я	Serbian, Macedonian je	j
Russian yo	ё	Serbian, Macedonian JE	J
Russian YO	Ё	Serbian, Macedonian SOFT L	Љ
Russian YU	Ю	Serbian, Macedonian soft l	љ
Russian yu	ю	Serbian, Macedonian SOFT N	Њ
Russian ze	з	Serbian, Macedonian soft n	њ
Russian ZE	З	Serbian SOFT DJ	Ђ
Russian ZHE	Ж	Serbian soft dj	ђ
Russian zhe	ж	Serbian soft t	ћ
s	s	Serbian SOFT T	Ћ
S	S	Servicemark	℠
s Acute	ś	Sharp	♯
S Acute	Ś	sigma	σ
s Caron (Hachek)	š	SIGMA	Σ
S Caron (Hachek)	Š	sigma (Terminal)	ς
s Cedilla	ş	SIGMA (Terminal)	Σ

Appendix D: Symbol Names of Characters

Similar	∼	Solid Triangle Down	▼
Similar or Equal	≃	Solid Triangle Left	◀
Sixteenth Notes	♬	Solid Triangle Right	▶
Small Bullet	.	Solid Triangle Up	▲
Small Center Dot	·	Southeast Arrow	↘
Small Circle	∘	Southwest Arrow	↙
Small Hollow Bullet	○	Space	
Small Hollow Square Bullet	▫	Spade	♠
Small House	⌂	Spherical Angle	⦦
Small Solid Circle	•	Square	□
Small Square Bullet	■	Square Bullet	■
Small Triangle Left	◂	Square Intersection	⊓
Small Triangle Right	▸	Square Intersection [1.5x High]	⊓
Smile	⌣	Square Intersection [2x High]	⊓
Smooth Breathing	᾿	Square Not Reflex Subset	⊄
Smooth Breathing Acute	῎	Square Not Reflex Superset	⊅
Smooth Breathing Acute w/Iota Subscript	ῌ	Square Not Subset	⊄
Smooth Breathing Circumflex	῏	Square Not Superset	⊅
Smooth Breathing Circumflex w/Iota Sub	ῌ	Square Proper Subset	⊏
Smooth Breathing Grave	῍	Square Proper Superset	⊐
Smooth Breathing Grave w/Iota Subscript	ῌ	Square Reflex Subset	⊑
Smooth Breathing w/Iota Subscript	ῌ	Square Reflex Superset	⊒
Solid Lozenge	♦	Square Subset But Does Not Equal	⊊
Solid Square	■	Square Superset But Does Not Equal	⊋
Solid Star	★	Square Union	⊔

Square Union [1.5x High]	⊔
Square Union [2x High]	⊔
Stigma	ς
Stroke	´
Subset But Does Not Equal	⊊
Such That (Contains as a Member)	∍
Summation	Σ
Summation [1.5x High]	Σ
Summation [2x High]	∑
Summation [Bottom Angle Extension]	/
Summation [Bottom Angle]	∠
Summation [Bottom Extension]	—
Summation [Bottom Right]	⌟
Summation [Center Angle]	〉
Summation [Top Angle Extension]	\
Summation [Top Angle]	⌜
Summation [Top Extension]	–
Summation [Top Right]	¬
Superset But Does Not Equal	⊋
t	t
T	T
t Caron (Hachek)	ť
T Caron (Hachek)	Ť
t Cedilla	ţ
T Cedilla	Ţ
t Cross Bar	ŧ

T Cross Bar	Ŧ
t Macron	t̄
T Macron	T̄
tau	τ
TAU	Τ
Telephone	☎
There Exists	∃
There Never Exists	∄
Therefore	∴
theta	θ
THETA	Θ
theta (Variant)	ϑ
Three Fourths Em Dash	–
Tilde	˜
Tilde Overmark [1.5x Wide]	~
Tilde Overmark [2x Wide]	∼
Tilde Overmark [3x Wide]	⁓
Top	⊤
Trademark	™
Triangle Down	▿
Triangle Left	◃
Triangle Right	▹
Triangle Up	▵
Triple Prime	‴
Tverdyj Znak	″
Two Horiz Arrows [Extension]	=
Two Horiz Arrows [Left]	⇇

… Appendix D: Symbol Names of Characters

Two Horiz Arrows [Right]	⇉	U Macron	Ū
Two Horiz Harpoons [Extension]	—	u Ogonek	ų
		U Ogonek	Ų
Two Horiz Harpoons [Left Bottom]	↽	u Ring	ů
Two Horiz Harpoons [Left Top]	↼	U Ring	Ů
Two Horiz Harpoons [Right Bottom]	⇁	u Tilde	ũ
		U Tilde	Ũ
Two Horiz Harpoons [Right Top]	⇀	Ukrainian HARD G	Ґ
Two Left Arrows	⇇	Ukrainian hard g	ґ
Two Right Arrows	⇉	Ukrainian I	І
u	u	Ukrainian i	і
U	U	Ukrainian I WITH TWO DOTS	Ї
u Acute	ú	Ukrainian i with two dots	ї
U Acute	Ú	Ukrainian ye	є
u Apostrophe Beside	ư	Ukrainian YE	Є
U Apostrophe Beside	Ư	Underscore	_
u Breve	ŭ	Underscored Up and Down Arrow	↨
U Breve	Ŭ	Union	∪
u Circumflex	û	Union [1.5x High]	∪
U Circumflex	Û	Union [2x High]	∪
u Diaeresis (Umlaut)	ü	Up and Down Arrow	↕
U Diaeresis (Umlaut)	Ü	Up Arrow	↑
u Double Acute	ű	Up Harpoon Left	↿
U Double Acute	Ű	Up Harpoon Right (Restriction)	↾
u Grave	ù	Upadhmaniya	ᳰ
U Grave	Ù	Uppercase Eng	Ŋ
u Macron	ū		

upsilon	υ	Vert Harpoon [Down Harpoon Right]	⇁
UPSILON	Y	Vert Harpoon [Extension]	│
UPSILON (Variant)	ϒ	Vert Harpoon [Up Harpoon Left]	↿
upsilon Acute	ύ	Vert Harpoon [Up Harpoon Right]	↾
upsilon Acute Diaeresis	ΰ	Vertical Mark	'
upsilon Circumflex	ῦ	Vertical Tilde	˜
upsilon Diaeresis	ϋ	w	w
upsilon Grave	ὺ	W	W
upsilon Grave Diaeresis	ῢ	w Circumflex	ŵ
upsilon Rough	ὑ	W Circumflex	Ŵ
upsilon Rough Acute	ὕ	Weierstrass	℘
upsilon Rough Circumflex	ὗ	Wreath Product	≀
upsilon Rough Grave	ὓ	x	x
upsilon Smooth	ὐ	X	X
upsilon Smooth Acute	ὔ	XI	Ξ
upsilon Smooth Circumflex	ὖ	xi	ξ
upsilon Smooth Grave	ὒ	y	y
v	v	Y	Y
V	V	y Breve	y̆
Vector Overmark	→	Y Breve	Y̆
Vert Arrow [Down]	↓	y Circumflex	ŷ
Vert Arrow [Extension]	│	Y Circumflex	Ŷ
Vert Arrow [Up]	↑	y Diaeresis (Umlaut)	ÿ
Vert Dbl Arrow [Down]	⇓	Y Diaeresis (Umlaut)	Ÿ
Vert Dbl Arrow [Extension]	‖	y Grave	ỳ
Vert Dbl Arrow [Up]	⇑	Y Grave	Ỳ
Vert Harpoon [Down Harpoon Left]	⇃		

Yen	¥
z	z
Z	Z
z Acute	ź
Z Acute	Ź
z Caron (Hachek)	ž
Z Caron (Hachek)	Ž
z Dot Above	ż
Z Dot Above	Ż
Z fraktur	ℨ
zero	0
zeta	ζ
ZETA	Z

Glossary

AC (alternating current). Electric current that reverses direction at regular intervals—the kind that goes into a power supply.

Analog device. A device that physically moves or processes information by amplifying or attenuating it. Audio cassettes and TVs are analog devices. See also *Digital devices*.

Application software. Software purchased or written that makes a person's job more efficient and the data involved more reliable.

Ascent line. The maximum height of a font.

ASCII file (American Standard Code for Information Interchange file). A standard file that contains characters found on a keyboard and a few printer commands. ASCII files can be read by many types of devices. See *Text file* and *Binary file*.

Attribute. A feature that describes a font.

Baseline. The lowermost point of letters, not including descenders. For example, the baseline of a line of text would be the lowermost point of letters such as a and x, excluding the tails of p and q.

Baud. The number of bits per second transferred through a serial printer cable.

Bidirectional. A print head that can print left to right and right to left.

Binary. Combinations of 1s and 0s that are used to represent computer bits on paper. See also *Hexadecimal*.

Binary file. A file can contain any pattern of bits. A binary file is usually created by a spooler, queue, or print buffer that is printing graphic data. See also *ASCII file* and *Text file*.

Binding. The additional space added to the side of a page to allow for binding pages.

Bit. A voltage pattern that could be either of value one or zero. Eight bits make a byte. And one byte is the equivalent of a character or symbol printed in the PC world.

Bit map. A method of describing what is to be printed by specifying the value of each pixel or dot that is to be printed. Graphics-mode printers are sent bit map information by computers. Character and object printers develop their own bit maps from instructions given by the PC.

Bleed. A graphic that extends to the edge of the paper. Also refers to capability of printer to add two bit-mapped images to each other so that all the features of both are printed. Some printers choose to overlay objects instead of bleeding them together.

Boot. The process of loading the software that is necessary to operate a PC.

Buffer. The part of a printer that stores the characters not yet printed. When the PC or Mac sends data to the printer faster than it can print the information, the printer stores the extra characters in this buffer. When the buffer overflows, the characters are lost.

Built-in fonts. Fonts that a printer comes with, located in ROM chips on the logic board of a printer.

Bullet. A circle, square, or other symbol before an indented paragraph or line that is used to highlight items in a list.

Byte. A group of 8 bits that a computer stores in one location. Each letter pressed on the keyboard generates a byte that the computer tracks.

Callout. The text used to point out and identify parts of an illustration. Also, headings that appear in a narrow margin next to the body copy.

Caption. Descriptive text accompanying a figure or drawing.

Cartridge. A plastic box containing fonts or printer emulation software. Cartridges slide into a special slot in the printer.

Character graphics. The characters sent to the videoboard and printer that represent symbols not found on a typewriter keyboard. These symbols are lines used in drawing boxes, foreign letters, math symbols, etc. See also *Object graphics*.

Character mode. When software sends characters and instructions to videoboards and printers. This is the most common method of communication with printers. See also *Graphics mode*, *Character graphics*, and *WYSIWYG*.

Character set. A collection of symbols. For example, the alphabet is a character set. If some foreign characters are added, the character set changes. Different countries have different character sets. Each oriental language has a character set of around 13,000 symbols. The non-oriental world has a character set of approximately 1,500 characters. Of these 1,500 characters, only about 223 are available to us at one time. See also *Symbol set*.

Chooser. A Macintosh desk accessory that enables applications to print to any printer with a driver installed in the system folder.

Cicero. A unit of measurement—common in Europe—that is similar to a point. It is equivalent to 44.5 millimeters.

Collated. Copies stacked in the order that they are printed. Multiple copies are separated under this option.

Color separations. The films needed to create plates for multicolor offset printing. In four-color printing, separate black and white films are created for magenta, cyan, yellow and black inks.

Comp. Abbreviation of comprehensive—used to describe the preproduction trial printout that shows exactly how the finished product will look.

Composite. Output of a color printing process that refers to colors mixed together during the printing process.

Configuration files. Each program in the PC world is responsible for talking to the attached printer. DOS offers no support. Thus, each PC program is associated with configuration files that contain information on printers.

Control codes. A specific group of 32 binary patterns defined by ASCII that are created when the Control key is pressed, followed by a letter or other symbol. Control codes are used to program printers.

CPU (central processing unit). This is the boss of the printer. The CPU tells all the other chips what to do. Another name for a CPU is microprocessor.

Cps (characters per second). A measure of the speed at which printers print. To convert from pages per minute (ppm) to cps, multiply ppm by 40 for a conservative estimate.

Crop. To trim the edges from a graph; to make it fit a given space or remove unnecessary parts of the image.

CRT (cathode ray tube). The name for the big tube most of us watch TV on and look at when working on a computer. See also *TTY*.

Cut-sheet feeder. A paper tray that holds single sheets of paper like a copy machine. Cut-sheet feeders often cause paper jams.

CR (carriage return). A command that means move the printhead from the current position to the beginning of the current line. This command does not mean advance to the next line. See also *LF*.

Daisywheel. A printer with one hammer that strikes letters from a spinning wheel. Daisywheel printers haven't been produced since 1987.

DB-25. The name of a connector used on the ends of cables to connect PCs and printers.

DC (direct current). A constant electric current that flows in one direction. See also *AC*.

Default. What a computer assumes when it is not given all necessary information. The initial setting of a value or option. Defaults can be changed.

Descender. The portion of a lowercase letter that hangs below the the baseline. Five lowercase letters of the alphabet have descenders: g, j, p, q and y.

Desktop publishing. Running a program that performs more exacting page layout than a word processor.

Desk accessories. Macintosh programs that can be switched to without kicking the current Mac program out of memory. Similar to TSR programs in the IBM PC world.

Device driver. A program that accepts input from an application program and translates that information into a form that the printer can understand. The input information in the PC world is not standardized, forcing each PC program to have its own printer driver (except for Windows or GEM programs). See *Configuration files*, and *Printer definition table*.

Device redirection. Changes the flow of information; for redirecting printer information to a file, getting information from a file rather than the keyboard, redirecting a file to a remote hard disk through a LAN rather than the local hard disk. A Unix concept appearing in most modern operating systems.

Dialog box. An options window that appears in response to a command.

Digital device. A circuit board or circuitry that processes information by examining and propagating discreet, square pulses. Examples of digital devices are computers and compact disks. See also *Analog device*.

Digitize. To convert an image to a system of dots that can be stored in the computer. See *Bit map*.

Dingbats. Traditionally, ornamental characters such as bullets, stars, and flowers. The laser font Zapf Dingbats includes many of these traditional symbols.

DIP switches. The 4 to 16 switches in a printer that are used to select which interface, default fonts, and other information used to configure the printer when it is powered on.

Dots per inch (dpi). The larger the number and the smaller the dots, the better looking the characters, the smoother the curves, and the more precision the printer has when placing dots on paper.

Download. A term used to refer to the transmission of information from a PC to a printer. Usually this term is used to refer to font information that is remembered by the printer and used when printing future documents.

Dot matrix. A printer that uses tiny wires firing at a ribbon to create dots on paper. By controlling which dots in the matrix are created, different characters can be formed.

Drop cap. Capital letter at the beginning of a chapter that is in a larger font and drops down into the paragraph one or more lines of text.

Dumb terminal. A terminal that sends keystrokes to the host, while expecting the host to echo each letter back. Thus, this type of terminal does not store keystrokes and send them all at once. It will not display what is typed unless the host computer sends the letter pressed back to the terminal.

Em. Traditionally, a unit of measure equal to the width of the letter M in the current point size.

En. One half the width of an em. Identifies the width of an en dash or an en space.

Face up. When the paper coming out of a laser printer is stacked so that the printed side is face up, a multipage document is sorted in the wrong order. But, printers that stack paper face up can usually feed envelopes better. Thus, most printers have at least two optional paper feeding paths, face up and face down.

Fanfold. The type of paper that is folded into a box and has holes on the sides.

Feathering. Adding an even amount of space between all lines on a page or column to force vertical justification.

FF (Form feed). Eject the current sheet of paper. Usually also means load in the next sheet of paper, although this is a separate command on some printers that feed sheets of paper in one at a time.

Finder. Name for the part of the Mac operating system that manages files and folders.

Firmware. Program or data that is stored in a ROM chip or hardware rather than on a floppy or hard disk. Font cartridges are an example of firmware.

Fixing rollers. The rust-colored rollers in a laser printer that melt toner onto the paper.

Flush. Aligned with something, usually one side of a page.

Font. One style of a character set. A change in the style, other than size or underlining, creates a different font.

Font/DA mover. A program that manages fonts in a Mac. DA stands for Desk Accessory.

Font metric. The width and height information for each character in each font. This information is stored in a width table.

Formatting. The process of arranging where words and paragraphs are physically located on a page.

Frequency. Another way of describing the number of lines per inch. The term is used for cells with gray scale values (shades of gray).

Fully formed. Refers to a printing mechanism that uses a hammer to print a letter molded into a piece of metal. Examples are daisywheel, thimble, and band printers.

Generic printer. Features common to all printers. Specific features found in one printer but not another would not be included in a generic printer.

Graphics mode. When dot or pixel information is sent to the printer or videoboard. This is usually associated with WYSIWYG software. See *WYSIWYG*, *Character mode*, *Character graphics*, and *Object graphics*.

Gray scale. Term used to describe the method of changing the grays the camera creates into numbers describing the gray value numerically within a certain region of the camera's photograph.

Greeking. The conversion of text to symbolic bars or lines that show the position of the text on-screen.

Gutter. *Binding*, except that the space is on the inside margins rather than the outside margins.

Handshaking. The negotiation between a printer and a computer over how data is sent.

Hanging indent. The first line of a paragraph that extends to the left of the rest of the lines in the same paragraph. This glossary has hanging indents.

Head driver circuitry. Circuitry that controls the firing of the wires in a dot-matrix print head or the firing of the hammer in a daisywheel.

Head-movement circuitry. The circuitry that moves print heads back and forth in dot-matrix and daisywheel printers.

Hexadecimal. Method of describing the contents of a byte using the symbols 0, 1, 2, 3, 4, 5, 6, 7, 8, 9, A, B, C, D, E, and F.

I-beam. The shape of the pointer locating text insertion or deletion when proportional characters are displayed on-screen.

Image data. Data created in the memory of a printer that is directly related to dots to be printed.

Impact printer. A printer that smashes a ribbon against the paper with such violence that carbons, stencils, and mimeographs can be created. Dot-matrix and daisywheel printers are examples of impact printers.

Interface. The circuitry inside a computer or printer that puts information into a cable or takes information out of a cable.

Interlock. A switch that detects whether the printer's lid is on. If the printer's lid is not on, the switch prevents the printer from powering on.

Inverse. Normally, the piece of paper is white, and the letters are black. Inverse is the opposite.

Inkjet. A type of printer that squirts drops of ink at paper. Inkjet printers function like dot matrixes but can produce laser-quality output. Unfortunately, they have a limited life span and are expensive to operate.

Justified text. Text that is flush at both the left and right edges.

Kerning. The amount of spacing between letters, especially certain combinations of letters that must be moved close together to create visually consistent spacing.

Landscaping. The rotation of a page design to print text and graphics across the longer axis of the page.

LAN (local area network). A method of allowing two computers to share a printer.

Leaders. Dotted or dashed lines that fill the space between tab settings.

Leading. The adjustment of vertical spacing between two individual text baselines.

LF (Line feed). A command that means move the carriage down a line from the current position, not necessarily to the left hand margin. See also *CR*.

Line art. Object drawings consisting of lines, with no gray scale shading.

Line spacing. A method of determining the spacing between lines by specifying the number of lines per inch.

Logic board. The main circuit board inside a printer.

Masthead. Section of a newsletter or magazine giving the title and details of the ownership, advertising, subscription dates, and so on. Sometimes used to describe the banner on the front of a magazine.

Mbps (mega bits per second). A measure of how fast data is transferred between the PC and the printer.

Mode. Printers are in various states or modes. On-line, off-line, text, and graphics are examples.

Moiré pattern. An undesirable grid pattern. Caused by gray scaling methods with too few grays, low resolution, scanning a document already scanned, and so on.

Monospaced font. Font that contains symbols with the same width. Most typewriter and monitor characters are monospaced fonts.

MTBF (mean time between failure). A statistical figure indicating that half of the machines built will fail before and half after the indicated amount of time.

Near-letter quality. Used by dot-matrix printer manufacturers to describe their best-looking font.

Network. A system in which a number of independent computers are linked together to share data and peripherals.

Object graphics. When software sends formulas describing how to draw an object. After this initial setup, object-oriented software then can tell the printer where to copy the object, what size, color, and line type to use. See *Character graphics*.

OCR (optical character read). A type of font that usually appears on checks, designed to be read by scanning equipment.

Offset printing. The type of printing done using a printing press to reproduce many copies of the original. The press lays ink on a page based on the raised image on a plate created by photographing the camera-ready masters.

Off-line. When a printer stops listening to the computer.

Operating system. Collection of programs necessary to manage files, memory, and peripherals of a computer.

Orphan. When the first line of a paragraph appears all by itself at the bottom of a page. See *Widow*.

OS/2. IBM and Microsoft's new multitasking operating system.

On-line. When a printer is expecting printable characters or instructions to arrive from a computer.

Peripheral. A component of a computer system besides the computer itself—hard disks, monitors, printers, and so on.

Pica. A unit of measure equal approximately to 1/6 inch, or 12 points.

Pitch. The number of characters per inch when fixed-spaced or monospaced fonts are used. For example, 10 pitch means 10 characters per inch.

Pixel. The smallest unit on a computer screen or printer (a dot).

Platen. The rubber cylinder that paper wraps around in a dot-matrix printer and typewriter.

Point. A standard unit of measurement—72 points per inch.

Port. The connector that a cable plugs into.

Portrait printing. The normal printing orientation for a page.

POST (power on self test). The first program run when a printer is turned on. This program is stored in ROM chips located on the logic board of a printer.

PostScript. A page-description language developed by Adobe Systems.

Printer database. A database relating generic printer commands to printer commands for a specific computer. There is usually one database for each printer model of a manufacturer.

Printer definition table. A file used by a PC software program that defines which commands it will send the printer. It is an alternative to a printer driver that gives consultants and users an opportunity to influence the features of a printer the PC software exercises.

Printer driver. A software program that translates from application software printer to commands the specific printer model can understand. This translation is done with a *printer database*.

Print head. The device that moves back and forth in front of a sheet of paper and actually draws the characters on the paper.

Print to a file. An option of some software programs that allows the printout to be sent to a file rather than to a printer. Sometimes, printing to a file is a the method of transferring data to another program or troubleshooting printer problems.

Proportional spacing. When spacing varies between characters.

Pull-out. Quotation extracted from a newsletter or magazine article and printed in larger type in the column, often blocked off with ruled lines.

Queue. The list of files a spooler creates that are waiting to be printed.

RAM (Random Access Memory). Used to execute programs, store downloaded fonts, and store image of what is to be printed.

Rules. Horizontal or vertical black lines added to a page.

Scanned image files. The electronic form of a photograph. Created by a scanner which turns the photograph into a series of dots, each with a different level of gray.

Self-test. A diagnostic of a printer initiated by the user. Usually involves holding a button down while turning the printer on.

Simple printer. A printer that only understands three commands, CR, LF and FF. This printer usually has only one font, and underlines and boldfaces using the CR command. See also *Generic printer*.

Soft fonts. Fonts within a printer that disappear when the printer is turned off. These fonts are sent to the printer by the PC.

Spike. An almost instantaneous increase in voltage that stresses hardware.

Spooler. A software program or feature of the operating system that sends all application program's printer data to a file before printing. Once the file is complete, it is printed as soon as the printer is free.

Test page. A page, document, spreadsheet, or test database that is used to exercise a printer for a particular application.

Text file. A file containing characters that can be found on a keyboard, plus commands to eject the current sheet of paper and get a new page, commands to go to the beginning of the current line, and a command to move down a line. See also *Binary file* and *ASCII file*.

Thin space. A space the width of a period.

Tile. The portion of the page in an oversize publication that is printed on a single sheet of paper. To make a complete page, you must assemble and paste together the tiles.

Tracking. Decreasing or increasing the amount of space between letters in a word.

Tractor feed. Method of pulling fanfold paper using spokes that grab the paper and pull it.

TSR (terminate and stay resident program). Programs in the DOS world that climb into memory and stay there until the PC is turned off. They often cause problems.

TTY (teletype terminal). An early computer terminal that did not have a CRT—all information was printed. They were essentially an automated manual typewriter.

Typeface. A single type family of one design in all sizes and styles. Each typeface has many fonts. Sometimes the terms typeface and font are used interchangeably.

Typesetter. A printer that prints on film rather than paper. Also the person or operator of the machine.

Videoboard. A circuit board inside the computer that the monitor's data cable hooks up to. In some clones and IBM PS/2s, the videoboard is part of the motherboard.

White space. Empty space on a page.

Widow. When the last line of a paragraph appears at the top of a page all by itself. See also Orphan.

WYSIWYG (what you see is what you get). A term describing the ideal situation, when what you see on-screen is what is printed.

X-height. A distinguishing characteristic of a font. The height of lowercase letters (not including descenders).

INDEX

1-2-3, 118
   Align command, 35
   installing printers, 415
   printing, 414
      common problems, 417-419
         page creep, 417
   using setup strings, 416
8-pin Din male connector, 534

A

Abort, Retry, Ignore, Fail message, 380
AC (alternating current), 653
accounting applications, purchasing
   printers, 300
acknowledge wire, 43
Adobe *see also* PostScript printers
   PostScript, 242-243, 441, 661
      character sets, 481
      clones, 485-487
      dot-matrix printers, 493
      font cartridge, 494
      fonts, 479-481
      microcomputer environment, 473-496
      printer
         driver, 392-395
         emulation, 481
         interface, 353
         language, 272-276, 278, 478-480,
            495, 496
      software, 472-496
      typesetting environment, 472-473
   Systems, 471-472
   TypeManager, 384-386
Alt key, 116-117, 120, 594
American Standard Codes for Information
   Interchange (ASCII), 86
Analog device, 653
analog plotters, 229-230
ANSI (American National Standards
   Institute), 99
   SCSI printer interface, 174
appearance, improving document, 463-469
Apple II computers, 4
application software, 653
applications
   1-2-3, 118
   configuring, 29-32
   WordPerfect 5.0, 119-121

ascent line, 653
ASCII
   character set, 99-101, 103-106, 109, 168, 590-596, 598
   file, 653
      characteristics, 26-28
   keyboard codes, 593-595
   notation, 83, 86-87
   printing to a file, 376-378
attribute, 653
AUTOEXEC.BAT file, 380

B

back-to-top paper path, 197
backspace method for creating special characters, 109-111
band printers, 65-66, 266
banners, 294
barber-pole test, 322-323
baseline, 653
BASIC language, 590-594
   printer instruction, 117-118
baud, 653
Baudot character set, 98-99
BCD see binary coded decimal
Beam detect malfunction message, 580
Bezier curves, 92-93
bi-directional, 653
   tractor, 53
   printers, 61
binary, 653
   characteristics, 26-28
   language, 83-87
binary coded decimal character set, 98-99
binding, 654
bit, 82-83, 654
bit map, 654
Bitstream FontWare, 150, 366
black letter family of fonts, 126-127
bleed, 654
bold fonts, 138-139
boot, 654

bottlenecks, printing, 190-195, 347-349
bottom-to-top paper path, 197
bps (bits per second), 169, 174
BS (backspace), 260
buffering, 28
buffers, 33-35, 49, 345-350, 654
   clearing, 333
   managing, 532, 543-546
built-in fonts, 654
bullet, 654
Bus error message, 581
buttons
   clear, 181
   continue, 181
   FF (form feed), 178
   front panel, 178-182
   LF (line feed), 178
   on-line/off-line, 42, 178, 181
   printer scan at power on, 42
bytes, 82-83, 654
   generating from the keyboard, 115-120, 122

C

cables
   parallel, 529-532
   printer, troubleshooting, 512-513
   serial, 529, 533-538
   dot-matrix printers, 206
callout, 654
camera ready, 295, 447-448
caption, 654
carriage return, 16
   see also CR (carriage return) command
cartridge, 654
   fonts, 223, 264, 494
   toner, 67-68, 70-71, 219-222, 319
centering text, 135-136
Centronics printer interface, 170, 172-173, 529-532
character
   centering, 135-136
   drawings, 448-449

Index 667

file type, 452, 454-455
graphics, 654
mode, 33-35, 245, 257-264, 654
    printer, 164, 191-192, 227-229
print mode, 87-88
spacing, 259
width, 131-132
character set, 3, 96-111, 368, 655
    ASCII, 99-101, 103-106, 109, 590-596, 598
    Baudot, 98-99
    binary coded decimal, 98-99
    dingbat, 106
    EBCDIC, 101-102
    ECMA-94 Latin 1, 101, 118
    IBM-Denmark/Norway (PC-8D/N), 101
    IBM-US (PC-8), 101
    PC-8, 87, 101, 103-105, 109
    PostScript, 481
    problems, 112-116
    ROMAN-8, 101, 109
    standards, 97
    symbol, 106, 109
    symbol names, 623-651
characters
    dingbat, 105-106
    foreign language, 106-109
    international, 107-108
    line-draw, 102-105
chooser, 655
CHR$ (BASIC) function, 590, 592-593
cicero, 655
circuitry
    head driver, 659
    head-movement, 659
    laser-movement, 60-61
    paper-movement, 52
    print head, 41, 60-61
clear button, 181
CMYK printing, 437-439, 441-442
cold boot, 341
collated, 655
color
    drawings, 452
    key, 439

printing, 437-438, 461-462
    adjustments, 439-440
    separations, 439, 453, 655
command language, printer, 589-612
commands
    LPRINT (BASIC), 590, 592-593
    PRINT (DOS), 350
    printer, 594-612
    syntax, 267-274
composite, 655
    film, 442
compressed print, 72-74, 146
computers
    Apple II, 4
    IBM, 4
    Macintosh, 4
condensed print, 146
CONFIG.SYS file, 380
configuration
    files, 367, 655
    test, 325
configuring
    applications, 29-32
    printer driver, PageMaker
        (Windows), 391-395
    serial ports, 538-540
    serial printer interface, 541-542
connectors, serial cables, 533-534
continue button, 181, 340-341
control codes, 101, 116-117, 267-269, 655
costs, printer life-cycle, 290-293
cps (characters per second), 169, 191-195, 655
CPU (central processing unit), 655
CR (carriage return) command, 26, 34, 248,
    333-334, 591-592, 656
Cromalin proof, 439
crop, 655
crop marks, 441
cross hairs, 441
CRT (cathode ray tube), 14, 655
Ctrl key, 116, 117, 120, 594
cursor positioning, 257-258
    printer commands, 601-603
cut-sheet feeders, 52, 56-58, 204-205, 656

D

D-RAM controller error message, 581
D-RAM error message, 581
daisywheel, 656
    printing mechanisms, 75-76
data image, 50-51
database applications, purchasing
    printers, 298-299
DB-9, 301, 534
DB-25, 46, 534, 656
dBASE language, 117-118
DC (direct current), 656
DCE cable, 536
decimal notation, 83-84, 87
default, 656
    printer, 332, 390-391
defining the printer to software, 29-32
definition files, 367
descender, 144, 656
desk accessories, 656
desktop publishing, 433, 435, 437,
    443-445, 656
    applications, purchasing printers, 299
    color printing, 453, 462
    drawings, 448-452, 454-455
    layout, 446-448
    photographs, 456-461
device
    driver, 656
    redirection, 27, 656
Diablo printers
    cursor positioning, 603
    font
        management, 609
        manipulation, 605
        selection, 608
    graphics, 612
    job control commands, 599
    page control commands, 600-601
    printer languages, 269-270
    word processing support, 610
diagnostic tests, power on, 41

dialog box, 656
    Macintosh, 383-384
digital
    device, 656
    plotters, 229-230
digitize, 657
DIN serial port connector, 301
dingbat, 657
    character set, 105-106
dip switches, 180-181, 206, 657
directories, printing with DOS, 420
Divide by zero error message, 558
Divide overflow error message, 558
document appearance, improving, 463-469
Does not print message, 379
DOS
    command, PRINT, 350
    end of file, 346
    printer languages, 275-279
    printing, 419-421
    testing serial printer, 541
    typewriter mode, 420
dot-matrix printers, 73-74, 202-207, 657
    adjustments, 586-587
    cables/cords, 206
    changing ribbons, 205-206
    cleaning, 205
    fonts, 148-149, 206, 264
    friction feed, 204-205
    hand feed, 202-204
    mailing labels, 165, 196
    paper size, 164
    PostScript, 493
    purchasing, 303-305, 310-311
    stencils, 196
    tractor feed, 197-205
dots per inch (dpi), 163, 657
double-height characters on first line, 558-559
downloading, 657
    fonts, 152, 155-159, 169, 403-404
dpi *see* dots per inch
drawings, 436-437
    character, 448-449

Index

color, 452
graphic, 448-449
object, 448-449
purchased, 450-452
scanned, 450
screen images, 451-452
software, 449-450
drivers, printer, 17-18, 364-365, 662
drop cap, 657
drum plotter, 231
DTE cable, 536
dumb terminal, 657
duty cycle, 211-212

E

EBCDIC character set, 101-102
ECMA-94 Latin 1 character set, 101, 118
educational applications, purchasing printers, 301
em (—), 657
emulation,
    mode, 242-243
    printer, 481
    software, 242-243
en (–), 657
encrypted fonts, 479-481
end of file protocol, 346
engines, 176
    interface, 176
    laser printer, 210-212
Enter a printer name in printer option message, 379
envelope feeder, 216-218
envelopes, printing, 165
EPS (encapsulated PostScript) files, 483-484
Epson printers, 44-45
    cursor positioning, 601-602
    font
        management, 609
        manipulation, 604
        selection, 606-607
    graphics, 611-612

job control commands, 597-598
page control commands, 599-600
printer languages, 270-271
word processing support, 610
Epson/IBM printer interface, 170-174
error messages, 571-572
    Abort, Retry, Ignore, Fail, 380
    Beam detect malfunction, 580
    Bus error, 581
    D-RAM controller error, 581
    D-RAM error, 581
    Does not print, 379
    Enter a printer name in printer option, 379
    Error Writing to Device, 380
    Expansion interface error, 580
    Expansion interface time-out error, 581
    FE Font cartridge removed, 580
    FF Memory buffer overflow, 580
    Fusing assembly malfunction, 580
    Incorrect formatting, 379
    Internal font ROM checksum error, 581
    Invalid Font, 379
    Laser temp. control circuit malfunction, 580
    Lid open, 579
    Line error, 579
    Main motor malfunction, 581
    Memory overflow, 579
    Memory that remembers with power off error, 581
    Miscellaneous hardware error, 581
    No EP cartridge installed, 579
    No Paper, 380
    Out of Memory, 379
    Out of Paper, 380, 579
    Paper jam, 579
    PC, 579
    PE, 580
    PF, 579
    Print check error, 579
    Print overrun error, 579
    Printer command error, 581
    Printer ready, 579

Program ROM checksum error, 581
Receiving buffer overflow, 580
Reset, 579
Scan buffer error, 581
Scanner malfunction, 580
Self-test, 579
Wait, 579
errors
    codes, 245-247
        Laser printer, 579-581
    current document version, 560
expanded print, 72-74, 146
Expansion interface error message, 580
Expansion Interface slot, 176-177
Expansion interface time-out error message, 581

F

face up, 657
failures, mean time between, 184-185, 211
fanfold, 657
Fatal stack error message, 558
FE Font cartridge removed message, 580
feathering, 657
FF (form feed), 16, 26, 35, 178, 248, 658
FF Memory buffer overflow message, 580
file types
    character, 452, 454-455
    converting, 452, 454-455
    graphics (raster), 452, 454-455
    object (language), 452, 454-455
    vector, 452, 454-455
files
    ASCII, 26-28
    AUTOEXEC.BAT, 380
    binary, 26-28
    CONFIG.SYS, 380
    configuration, 367
    definition, 367
    EPS (encapsulated PostScript), 483-484
    fonts, 365-367
    PFM (printer fonts metric), 396-398

printer, characteristics, 25-28
printing with DOS, 419-421
SFM (soft font landscape), 396-398
text, 26-28
film
    composite (final), 442
    master, 439
finder, 658
firmware, 658
fixed fonts, 146-147, 151-152, 155
fixed-space
    fonts, 131-132
    mode, 259
fixing rollers, 658
flat-bed
    scanner, 450
    plotter, 231
flush, 658
font/DA mover, 658
fonts, 97, 125-127, 658
    adding printer, 382-383, 395-398, 400-404, 411-413
    attributes, 137
        bold, 138-139
        italic, 138
    cartridge, 264
        PostScript, 494
        laser printer, 223
    characteristics, 3
    creation, 152-153
    dot-matrix printers, 148-149
    downloading, 152, 155-159, 169, 403-404
    encrypted, 479-481
    enhancing, 260-261
    families
        black letter, 126-127
        Roman, 126
        san serif, 126
        script, 126
    files, 365-367
    fixed, 146-147, 151-152, 155
    fixed-space, 131-132
    front panel selection, 179-182
    generation software, 150

Index

hard, 95-96
height, 128-131
high-resolution, 152
internal, 264
landscape, 147, 327
laser, 148-149, 218, 223, 307, 308
low-resolution, 152
managing, 361, 608-609
manipulation, 260-261, 603-605
medium-resolution, 152
metric (PFM), 396-398, 658
numbering, 159
object, 92
outline, 142-143
portrait, 147, 326
PostScript, 479-481, 489-492
proportional, 132-135
purchasing, 145, 150
scalable, 146, 148-152, 155, 480-481
screen, 369-371, 381-382, 398, 404-405
selection, 262-266, 605-608
soft, 264
sources, 152-153
storing, 152, 154
test, 325-327
upgrading, 166-168
vendor list, 617-622
foreign language characters, 106-109
form feed, 15-16
forms, printing, 290, 295, 373-374
frequency, 658
friction feed, 52-56, 204-205
front panel, 15-16, 178-182
    laser printer, 224
    testing, 336-340
    fonts, 179-182
    resetting, 180-182
fully formed, 658
fuse, printer, 40
Fusing assembly malfunction message, 580
fusion assembly, 71

G

galleys, 440, 447-448
GEM Ventura
    character sets, 368
    fonts, adding, 400-404
    installing screen fonts, 404-405
    memory requirements, 406-407
    printer driver, 364-365, 399-401
    screen fonts, 369
generic printer, 658
    commands, 23-25
global unsharp masking, 440
GPIB (General Purpose Interface Bus), 175-176
graphics
    applications, purchasing printers, 300
    drawings, 448-449
    mode, 33-35, 87-92, 245, 265-266, 658
    printer commands, 610-612
    printing, 265-266, 421
    raster file type, 452-455
    screen, 25
graphics-mode printer
    hardware, 227-229
    speed, 192-195
gray scale, 658
gray-scale test, 327-329
Greeking, 658
ground wire, 43
gutter, 658

H

hand feed
    laser printer, 217-218
    paper, 202-204
hand-held scanners, 450
handshaking, 659
    hardware, 544
    software, 544-545
hanging indent, 659

hard
    fonts, 95-96
    space, 136
hardware
    handshaking, 544
    Macintosh, 121-122
    requirements, 161-163, 301-303
    reset, 341
    testing, 546-548
head driver circuitry, 659
head-movement circuitry, 659
headers, 246-247
Hewlett-Packard printers
    cursor positioning, 601
    font
        management, 608
        manipulation, 603
        selection, 605-606
    graphics, 611
    job control commands, 597
    page control commands, 599
    printer languages, 271
    word processing support, 610
hexadecimal, 659
    notation, 83, 85-87
hidden treasure syndrome, 18
high-resolution fonts, 152
HPCL (Hewlett-Packard Control Language), 271-272
HPIB (Hewlett-Packard Interface Bus), 43, 47-48, 169-170, 175-176

I

I-beam, 659
IBM
    fonts, 166, 167
    computers, 4
IBM-Denmark/Norway (PC-8D/N) character set, 101
IBM-US (PC-8) character set, 101
IEEE (Institute of Electrical and Electronic Engineers), 175-176

ill-behaved printer software, 372-373
image data, 50-51, 659
    transfer, 47
images, converting file types, 451-452, 454-455
imaging software, 50-51
impact printer, 659
Incorrect formatting message, 379
initializing
    ports, 395, 420, 423-425
    spoolers, OS/2, 425, 426
ink trapping, 442
inkjet, 659
    printers, 207-209
        maintenance, 208-209
        purchasing, 305-306, 311
        resolution, 208
    printing mechanisms, 74-75
installing
    ports, 422-423
    printer drivers
        GEM Ventura, 399-401
        Macintosh, 381
        OS/2, 426-427
        PageMaker (Windows), 386-388
        WordPerfect, 408-409
    printers, 317, 330-335, 363-427
        1-2-3, 415
        loading paper, 319-320
        power-on, 320-321
        ribbons, 319
        self-test, 321-329
        toner cartridges, 319
        unpacking, 318
    screen fonts
        GEM Ventura, 404-405
        PageMaker (Windows), 398
interactive mode, 275
interface, 659
    speed, 169
interlock, 659
    switch, 40
intermittent operation, 563
Internal font ROM checksum error message, 581

Index

internal fonts, 264
international characters, 107-108
International Typeface Corporation (ITC), 479
interpretive programs, 238-240
`Invalid Font` message, 379
inverse, 659
ISO (International Standards Organization)
    printer languages, 272
    printers
        cursor positioning, 602-603
        management, 609
        manipulation, 604-605
        selection, 607-608
    graphics, 612
    job control commands, 598-599
    page control commands, 600
    word processing support, 610
italic fonts, 138

J

jams, paper, 215
job control printer commands, 597-599
jumper blocks, 331
justification, 659
    last line of paragraph, 563-564
    right, 136-137

K

kerning, 137, 258-259, 659
keyboard codes, 593-595
keys
    Alt, 116-117, 120, 594
    Ctrl, 116-117, 120, 594
    PrtSc (print screen), 35-168
    Shift, 116-117

L

LAN (local area network), 659
    PostScript printers, 488-489
    printer interface technology, 48
    setting up, 358-359
    spooling, 352
landscape
    fonts, 147
    orientation, 257, 327
landscaping, 659
languages
    BASIC, 117-118, 590-594
    binary, 83-87
    dBASE, printer instruction, 117-118
    page-formatting, 435-436, 472
    Pascal, 117-118
    plotters, 274-275
    printer, 241-245, 269-271, 273-274
        operating systems, 275-279
        PostScript, 478-480, 495-496
        standards, 272
    programming, 243-245
        command, 589-612
laser printers, 210-224
    engines, 210-212
    error codes, 579-581
    fonts, 223, 264, 148-149
    front panel, 224
    hand feed, 217-218
    memory, 222
    object-oriented, 93-94
    paper
        chemistry, 216
        jams, 215
        quality, 214
        size, 163-164
        trays, 216

ports, 225
purchasing, 306-309, 311-312
resolution, 212
speed, 212-214
stacking paper, 213-214
supplies, 219-222
toner cartridge, 219-222
laser printing mechanisms, 67-68
Laser temp. control circuit malfunction message, 580
laser-movement circuitry, 60-61
LaserJet, 353
driver, 396, 397
fonts, 479
printers, 271, 489-490
LaserWriter, 380
fonts
screen, 381-382
print, 382-383
printers, 130-131, 474-475, 489-490
sharing, 351
layout, 440
desktop publishing, 446-448
LCS (liquid crystal shutter) printing mechanisms, 69-71, 210-211
leaders, 660
leading, 660
LED (light emitting diode) printing mechanisms, 69-71, 210-211
letter-quality print, 146
LF (line feed), 16, 26, 34, 178, 248, 333-334, 591-592, 660
Lid open message, 579
ligatures, 144
line
art, 660
feed, 15-16
printers, 65-66
spacing, 660
adjusting, 371-372
Line error message, 579
line-draw characters, 102-105
linear power supply, 40
loading paper, 319-320

Local Talk printer interface, 170, 172, 225
logic board, 660
loop-back plug, 540
low-resolution fonts, 152
LPRINT (BASIC) command, 590-593

M

Macintosh computers, 4
character sets, 368
fonts, 166-168
screens, 369, 381-382
printing, 380
adding print fonts, 382-383
dialog box, 383-384
drivers, 381
System 7, 384-386
symbols, 121-122
System 7, printer languages, 276-279
testing print capability, 344
macros, printer, 238-239, 245-247
Magnatype, 435
mailing labels, 294
dot-matrix printers, 196
printing, 165
Main motor malfunction message, 581
managing
buffers, 532, 543-546
printers, 345-362
software, 547-552
margins, printer page control, 254
masthead, 660
Matchprint, 439
mathematic symbols, 111
mbps (mega bits per second), 660
mean time between failures, 184-185, 211
mechanicals, 440
medium-resolution fonts, 152
memory
laser printer, 222
printer, 49
required for resolution, 188
Memory overflow messages, 579

Index 675

memory resident software, 372-373
Memory that remembers with power off error message, 581
menu pad, 15-16
micro centering, 135-136
mimeographs printing, 290
minimal printer, 514-515
Miscellaneous hardware error message, 581
mode, 660
modes, printer
   character, 87-88, 95-96
   graphics, 87-92
   object, 87-88, 92-95
modes of operation
   character, 33-35, 164, 191-192, 227-229
      printer feedback, 245, 257-264
   graphics, 33-35, 192-195, 227-229, 265-266
      printer feedback, 245
   object, 194-195, 226-230, 309
      printer feedback, 245, 257-264
moir pattern, 457, 468-469, 660
monospaced font, 660
MTBF (mean time between failure), 660
Multimate, printer driver, 364-365
multiple forms printing support, 373-374

N

near-letter quality, 660
network, 660
NeXT printer, 474, 476-477
No EP cartridge installed message, 579
No Paper message, 380
notation
   ASCII, 83-87
   decimal, 83-87
   hexadecimal, 83, 85-87
numbering fonts, 159

O

object (language) file type, 452, 454, 455
object
   drawings, 448-449

   fonts, 92
   graphics, 660
   mode, 87-88, 92-95, 245, 257-264, 309
      devices, 151
      printer, 194-195, 226-230
   plotter, 93-94
   printer, 94-95
object-oriented laser printer, 93-94
OCR (optical character read), 660
off-line, 661
offset printing, 661
on-line, 661
on-line/off-line buttons, 15-16, 42, 178, 181
operating system, 661
   troubleshooting printer problems, 511-512
   printer languages, 275-279
optimization, 61
Optional I/O, 176-177
orientation, 257
orphan, 661
OS/2, 661
   end of file, 346
   printer languages, 276-279
   ports, 423-426
   printer drivers, 426
   spoolers, 425-426
Out of Memory message, 379
Out of Paper message, 380, 579
out-of-paper switch, 202-204
outline fonts, 142-143
output types, 293-295

P

page control
   layout, 252-253
   margins, 253-254
   new page, 251
   number of copies, 252
   paper source, 250
   printer commands, 599-601
   skipping perforations, 254-255
   unprintable regions, 255-256
page
   creep, 417

length, 257
printers, 266
page-formatting languages, 435-436, 472
PageMaker
   default printer, 390-391
   fonts
      printer, adding, 395-398
      screen, 398
   ports
      establishing, 389
      initializing serial ports, 395
   printer driver, 364-365
      configuring, 391-395
      installing, 386-388
paper
   caliper, 214
   chemistry, laser printer, 216
   jams, 215, 578
   loading, 319-320
   movement, 52-59
      cut-sheet feeders, 52, 56-88, 204-205
      friction feed, 52, 54-56, 204-205
      hand feed, 202-204, 217-218
      paper trays, 52, 58-59, 204-205, 217-218, 223
      tractor feed, 52-53, 197-205
   path, 197
   plotter, 232-233
   quality, laser printer, 214-215
   size, 163-165, 290
   source, 251
   stacking, laser printer, 213-214
   trays, 52, 58-59, 204-205, 216-218, 223
   wax pick measurement, 215
   weight, 214
Paper jam messages, 579
paper-movement circuitry, 52
parallel
   ports, testing, 342-343
   printer interface, 43-45, 169-174, 225, 301-302, 353-359, 529-532
Parity-check error message, 571
Pascal language printer instruction, 117-118

PC DOS
   end of file, 346
   PRINT command, 350
   printer languages, 275-279
PC Magazine, 288-290
PC message, 579
PC-8 character set, 87, 101, 103-105, 109
PCSEND program, 480
PE message, 580
pen movement, plotters, 231
perforations, skipping, 254-255
peripheral, 661
personality module, 170-172
PF message, 579
photographs, 456-461
phototypesetter, 440-441, 447-448
pica, 131-132, 661
pinout diagram, 535-536
pitch, 661
pixel, 661
platen, 661
plotters, 231
   analog, 229-230
   digital, 229-230
   object, 93-94
   pen movement, 231
   printer languages, 274-275
   purchasing, 309-310
   resolution, 230
   styles
      drum, 231
      flatbed, 231
      rollerbed, 231
   supplies, 232-233
points, 130-131, 661
port, 661
   connector, serial, 301
   laser printer, 225
   troubleshooting, 512-513
portability, 289-290
portrait
   orientation, 257
      fonts, 147, 326
   printing, 661

Index

POST (power on self test), 41-42, 661
PostScript printers, 309, 471-472, 489-491
    fonts, 489-492
    improving document appearance, 464-469
    LAN (local area network), 488-489
    LaserWriter printer, 474-475
    NeXT printer, 474
    purchase or upgrade, 312, 492
    speed, 487
    testing print capability, 343-344
PostScript software, 472-496
power on
    printer, 39
    memory diagnostic test, 41
power supply, 39-40
    linear, 40
    switching, 40
power switch, 39-40
power-on printer, 320-321
Power-up 901 error message, 571
Presentation Manager (OS/2) printer driver, 426-427
preventive maintenance, 521-527
preview
    mode, 375-376
    screen, 25
Print check error message, 579
print
    engine, 460-461
    head, 41, 662
        alignment, 77-79
        circuitry, 60-61
        driver circuitry, 41
        movement, 60-65
            pulley system, 61-62
            screw system, 61-62
        position, 63-65
    queue, 28
Print overrun error message, 579
print to a file, 662
printer
    commands, 267-274, 594-596
        cursor positioning, 601-603

font
    management, 608-609
    manipulation, 603-605
    selection, 605-608
generic, 23-25
graphics, 610-612
job control, 597-599
page control, 599-601
word processing support, 610
database, 661
definitions
    changing, WordPerfect, 409-410
    table, 17-18, 661
    editing, 413, 414
file characteristics, 25-28
interface, 170-177, 225
    Centronics, 170, 172-173
    characteristics, 169
    Epson/IBM, 170-174
    HPIB, 43, 47-48, 169-170, 175-176
    Local Talk, 170, 172, 225
    multiple interface options, 178
    parallel, 43-45, 169-174, 225, 301-302, 353-359, 529-532
    RE-232 Serial, 170-172, 176
    SCSI, 43, 48, 169-170, 174-176, 225
    serial, 43, 45-46, 169-174, 176, 225, 301-302, 353-359, 533-549, 585
    standard, 175-176
    video, 43, 46-47, 169-170, 176-177, 225, 353
modes
    character, 87-88, 95-96
    graphics, 87-92
    object, 87-88, 92-95
ports, troubleshooting, 512-513
querying, 248-249
recovery from disaster, 296
resetting, 180-182, 339-341, 517-518
server box, 359
sharing, 295-296
speed, 487
utilities, 237, 279-281, 372-373

Printer command error message, 581
Printer ready message, 579
printing
    bottlenecks, 190-195
    color, 438-440, 461-462
    envelopes, 165
    four-color, 437
    graphics, 265-266
    mailing labels, 165
    mechanisms, 66-77, 210-211
        daisywheel, 75-76
        dot-matrix, 72-74
        inkjet, 74-75
        laser, 67-68
        LCS, 69-71, 210-211
        LED, 69-71, 210-211
        thermal, 76-77
    problems
        identifying, 469, 553-558
        preventing, 521-527
    speed, 189-190
        character mode, 191-192
        graphics mode, 192-195
        object mode, 194-195
    utilities, 372-373
printing to a file, 376-379
Program ROM checksum error message, 581
programming
    applications, purchasing printers, 300-301
    printers, 267-274, 589-612
programs
    PCSEND, 480
    PSDOWN, 480
    PSFONT, 480
proportional
    fonts, 132-135
        decimal tabs, 135
        lining up columns, 134-135
    spacing, 259, 662
PrtSc (print screen) key, 35, 168
PSDOWN program, 480
PSFONT program, 480
public domain fonts, 152, 153
pull-out, 662

pulley system, print head movement, 61-62
purchasing
    drawings, 450-452
    plotters, 309-310
    printers, 287-296
        accounting applications, 300
        checklist, 314-316
        database applications, 298-299
        desktop publishing applications, 299
        dot-matrix, 303-305, 310-311
        educational applications, 301
        graphics applications, 300
        hardware requirements, 301-303
        inkjet, 305-306, 311
        laser, 306-309, 311-312
        programming applications, 300-301
        spreadsheet applications, 297-298
        vendors, 313-314
        word processing applications, 299

Q

querying the printer, 248-249
queues, 345-349, 662
QuickCode, 475-477

R

RAM (random access memory), 41-42, 662
    chips, 42
    diagnostic test, 41-42
    printer, 49, 152, 155
read-only memory
    chips, 41, 237-240
    printer, 50-51
Receiving buffer overflow message, 580
recovering from printer problems, 296
redirecting data, parallel to serial, 550-552
redline, 142
registration, 441
    test, 327-329
Reset message, 579

resetting the printer, 180-182, 339-341, 517-518
resolution
   inkjet printers, 208
   laser printer, 212
   memory requirements, 188
   plotters, 230
   printer, 302, 307
   scanner, 186-188
   scanners, 458-461
   text, 185-186
response time, 184
ribbons
   dot-matrix printer, 305
   installing, 205-206, 319
   problems, 585
right margin justification, 136-137
RIP (raster image processor), 441, 472
rocker switch, 330
roller scanner, 450
rollerbed plotter, 231
ROM *see* read only memory
Roman family of fonts, 126
ROMAN-8 character set, 101, 109
RS-232 Serial printer interface, 170-172, 176
rules, 662

S

sans serif family of fonts, 126
scalable fonts, 146, 148-152, 155, 480-481
Scan buffer error message, 581
scanned
    drawings, 450
    image files, 662
Scanner malfunction message, 580
scanners, 186-188, 450
    resolution, 458-461
scientific symbols, 111
screens
   displaying printer instructions, 20-25
   fonts, 369-371
   graphics, 25
   preview, 25

screw system print head movement, 61-62
script family of fonts, 126
SCSI printer interface, 43, 48, 169-170, 174-176, 225
self-test, 518-519, 662
   printer, 321-329
   programs, power on, 41-42
   user initiated, 41
Self-test message, 579
separations, 439, 655
   color printing-desktop, 453
serial ports
   initializing, 395
   testing, 343
serial printer interface, 43, 45-46, 169-176, 225, 301-302, 353-359, 533-537, 543-549
   configuring, 538-542
   problems, 585
   standard EIA-232D, 46
serial printer testing, 541-542
serifs, 126, 143, 144
shareware fonts, 152-153
sharing printers, 295-296, 351-362
sharping, 440
Sheffield scale, 214
Shift key, 116-117
SI (shift in), 591-592
simple printer, 662
slide switch, 330
slowing the PC, 545-546
soft
   boot (resetting the printer), 340
   fonts, 152, 155, 264, 662
   reset, 340-341
   space, 136
soft font landscape (SFM), 396-398
software
   defining the printer, 29-32
   drawing, 449-450
   emulation, 242-243
   font generation, 150
   handshaking, 544, 545
   ill-behaved, 372-373
   imaging, 50-51

    management scheme, 547-552
    memory resident, 372-373
    PostScript, 472-496
    printer, 237-281
    support for print instructions, 20-25
    terminate-and-stay-resident (TSR), 372-373
    testing, 547-548
solenoid, 51
speed
    laser printer, 212-214
    printing, 189-195
    testing printer, 303
spike, 662
spike protectors, 525
spoolers (Simultaneous Print Operations On-Line), 28, 345-346, 348-349, 662
    DOS, 421
    initializing with OS/2, 425
    LAN software, 352
    PC DOS, 350
    WordPerfect, 350-352
spreadsheets, 295, 418-419
    applications, purchasing printers, 297-298
stacking paper, laser printer, 213-214
standards
    character sets, 97-111
    PostScript printer language, 478-480
    printer interfaces, 175-176
    printer languages, ISO (International Standards Organization), 272
stencils, 196, 290
stepper motor, 185-186
storing fonts, 152, 154
strikeout, 142
stripping, 441-442
strobe wire, 43
supplies
    laser printers, 219-222
    plotters, 232-233
surge protectors, 525
swapping printers, 514-515

switches
    boxes
        electronic, 354-359
        manual, 353-354
    dip, 180-181, 206
    out-of-paper, 202-204
    interlock, 40
    power, 39-40
    printer, 329-332
    printer scan at power on, 42
switching power supply, 40
symbol set *see* character set
symbols
    character set, 106-109
    names of characters, 623-651
    printing from document, 119, 121-122
    scientific/mathematic, 111
System 7, 384-386

T

T-resistor, 175
tab stops, 259
Teletype, 14-15, 99
test
    page, 662
    programs, 41-42
testing
    ports, 342-343
    print capability, 342-344
    printers, 317, 319, 336-340, 345-346
        hardware, 546-548
        self-test, 321-329
        software, 547-548
        speed, 303
    shared printers, 360
text underlining, 260-261
text file, 662
    characteristics, 26-28
    printing to, 376-378
text resolution, 185-186

text wrap, 334-341
thermal printing mechanisms, 76-77
thimble printers, 270
thin space, 663
tile, 663
toner cartridges, 319
    laser printer, 67-68, 219-222
    LED/LCS printer, 70-71
tracking, 663
tractor feed, 52-53, 197-205, 663
transparencies, 290
trap, 441-442
trays, paper, 216
troubleshooting, 2, 4, 503-506, 516-528, 553-587
    evidence gathering, 508-513
    paradoxes, 507-508
    swapping printers, 514-515
TSR (terminate and stay resident)
    program, 663
    software, 372-373
TTY (teletype terminal), 99, 663
typeface, 125-127, 143-144, 663
    characteristics, 127
    families, 126, 127
types of printer output, 293-295
typesetter, 663
typesetting, 433-443
    PostScript, 472
    problem identification, 469
    terms, 3
    to improve document appearance, 464-469
typewriter mode
    DOS, 420
typewriters, 14
typography, 433

U

underlining text, 139-140, 260-261
unpacking printers, 318
unprintable regions, 255-256
upgrading fonts, 166-168
utilities, 237, 279-281, 372-373

V

vector file type, 452, 454-455
vendors
    fonts, 617-622
    printers, 613-616
Ventura, 435-436
vertical-line test, 323-324
video interface, 46, 176
    slot, 177
video printer interface, 43, 47, 169-170, 176-177, 225, 353
videoboard, 663
viewing documents before printing, 375-376
virtual memory, PostScript printers, 487-489

W

Wait message, 579
warranty, printer, 183-184, 302
wax pick paper measurement, 215
white space, 663
widow, 663
width, character, 131-132
Windows
    character sets, 368
    printer driver, 364-365
    screen fonts, 369
wires
    acknowledge, 43
    ground, 43
    strobe, 43
word processing
    applications, purchasing printers, 299
    support, 610
WordPerfect
    5.0 application, 119-121
    character sets, 368
    fonts,
        printer, adding, 411-413
        screen, 370-371
    printer definitions
        changing, 409-410
        editing, 413-414

printer driver, 364-365
    installing, 408-409
printing, 407-410, 412-414
spooler, 350-352
WordStar printer driver, 365
WYSIWYG (What You See Is What You Get), 19-20, 25, 663

X

x-height, 144, 663

Computer Books From Que Mean PC Performance!

Spreadsheets

1-2-3 Database Techniques	$29.95
1-2-3 Graphics Techniques	$24.95
1-2-3 Macro Library, 3rd Edition	$39.95
1-2-3 Release 2.2 Business Applications	$39.95
1-2-3 Release 2.2 Quick Reference	$ 7.95
1-2-3 Release 2.2 QuickStart	$19.95
1-2-3 Release 2.2 Workbook and Disk	$29.95
1-2-3 Release 3 Business Applications	$39.95
1-2-3 Release 3 Quick Reference	$ 7.95
1-2-3 Release 3 QuickStart	$19.95
1-2-3 Release 3 Workbook and Disk	$29.95
1-2-3 Tips, Tricks, and Traps, 3rd Edition	$24.95
Excel Business Applications: IBM Version	$39.95
Excel Quick Reference	$ 7.95
Excel QuickStart	$19.95
Excel Tips, Tricks, and Traps	$22.95
Using 1-2-3, Special Edition	$26.95
Using 1-2-3 Release 2.2, Special Edition	$26.95
Using 1-2-3 Release 3	$27.95
Using Excel: IBM Version	$29.95
Using Lotus Spreadsheet for DeskMate	$19.95
Using Quattro Pro	$24.95
Using SuperCalc5, 2nd Edition	$29.95

Databases

dBASE III Plus Handbook, 2nd Edition	$24.95
dBASE III Plus Tips, Tricks, and Traps	$24.95
dBASE III Plus Workbook and Disk	$29.95
dBASE IV Applications Library, 2nd Edition	$39.95
dBASE IV Programming Techniques	$24.95
dBASE IV QueCards	$21.95
dBASE IV Quick Reference	$ 7.95
dBASE IV QuickStart	$19.95
dBASE IV Tips, Tricks,and Traps, 2nd Ed.	$24.95
dBASE IV Workbook and Disk	$29.95
R:BASE User's Guide, 3rd Edition	$22.95
Using Clipper	$24.95
Using DataEase	$24.95
Using dBASE IV	$27.95
Using FoxPro	$26.95
Using Paradox 3	$24.95
Using Reflex, 2nd Edition	$22.95
Using SQL	$24.95

Business Applications

Introduction to Business Software	$14.95
Introduction to Personal Computers	$19.95
Lotus Add-in Toolkit Guide	$29.95
Norton Utilities Quick Reference	$ 7.95
PC Tools Quick Reference, 2nd Edition	$ 7.95
Q&A Quick Reference	$ 7.95
Que's Computer User's Dictionary	$ 9.95
Que's Wizard Book	$ 9.95
Smart Tips, Tricks, and Traps	$24.95
Using Computers in Business	$22.95
Using DacEasy, 2nd Edition	$24.95
Using Dollars and Sense: IBM Version, 2nd Edition	$19.95
Using Enable/OA	$29.95
Using Harvard Project Manager	$24.95
Using Lotus Magellan	$21.95
Using Managing Your Money, 2nd Edition	$19.95
Using Microsoft Works: IBM Version	$22.95
Using Norton Utilities	$24.95
Using PC Tools Deluxe	$24.95
Using Peachtree	$22.95
Using PFS: First Choice	$22.95
Using PROCOMM PLUS	$19.95
Using Q&A, 2nd Edition	$23.95
Using Quicken	$19.95
Using Smart	$22.95
Using SmartWare II	$29.95
Using Symphony, Special Edition	$29.95

CAD

AutoCAD Advanced Techniques	$34.95
AutoCAD Quick Reference	$ 7.95
AutoCAD Sourcebook	$24.95
Using AutoCAD, 2nd Edition	$24.95
Using Generic CADD	$24.95

Word Processing

DisplayWrite QuickStart	$19.95
Microsoft Word 5 Quick Reference	$ 7.95
Microsoft Word 5 Tips, Tricks, and Traps: IBM Version	$22.95
Using DisplayWrite 4, 2nd Edition	$24.95
Using Microsoft Word 5: IBM Version	$22.95
Using MultiMate	$22.95
Using Professional Write	$22.95
Using Word for Windows	$22.95
Using WordPerfect, 3rd Edition	$21.95
Using WordPerfect 5	$24.95
Using WordPerfect 5.1, Special Edition	$24.95
Using WordStar, 2nd Edition	$21.95
WordPerfect QueCards	$21.95
WordPerfect Quick Reference	$ 7.95
WordPerfect QuickStart	$19.95
WordPerfect Tips, Tricks, and Traps, 2nd Edition	$22.95
WordPerfect 5 Workbook and Disk	$29.95
WordPerfect 5.1 Quick Reference	$ 7.95
WordPerfect 5.1 QuickStart	$19.95
WordPerfect 5.1 Tips, Tricks, and Traps	$22.95
WordPerfect 5.1 Workbook and Disk	$29.95

Hardware/Systems

DOS Power Techniques	$29.95
DOS Tips, Tricks, and Traps	$24.95
DOS Workbook and Disk, 2nd Edition	$29.95
Hard Disk Quick Reference	$ 7.95
MS-DOS Quick Reference	$ 7.95
MS-DOS QuickStart	$21.95
MS-DOS User's Guide, Special Edition	$29.95
Networking Personal Computers, 3rd Edition	$24.95
The Printer Bible	$29.95
Que's Guide to Data Recovery	$24.95
Understanding UNIX, 2nd Edition	$21.95
Upgrading and Repairing PCs	$29.95
Using DOS	$22.95
Using Microsoft Windows 3, 2nd Edition	$22.95
Using Novell NetWare	$29.95
Using OS/2	$29.95
Using PC DOS, 3rd Edition	$24.95
Using UNIX	$24.95
Using Your Hard Disk	$29.95
Windows 3 Quick Reference	$ 7.95

Desktop Publishing/Graphics

Harvard Graphics Quick Reference	$ 7.95
Using Animator	$24.95
Using Harvard Graphics	$24.95
Using Freelance Plus	$24.95
Using PageMaker: IBM Version, 2nd Edition	$24.95
Using PFS: First Publisher	$22.95
Using Ventura Publisher, 2nd Edition	$24.95
Ventura Publisher Tips, Tricks, and Traps	$24.95

Macintosh/Apple II

AppleWorks QuickStart	$19.95
The Big Mac Book	$27.95
Excel QuickStart	$19.95
Excel Tips, Tricks, and Traps	$22.95
Que's Macintosh Multimedia Handbook	$22.95
Using AppleWorks, 3rd Edition	$21.95
Using AppleWorks GS	$21.95
Using Dollars and Sense: Macintosh Version	$19.95
Using Excel: Macintosh Version	$24.95
Using FileMaker	$24.95
Using MacroMind Director	$29.95
Using MacWrite	$22.95
Using Microsoft Word 4: Macintosh Version	$24.95
Using Microsoft Works: Macintosh Version, 2nd Edition	$24.95
Using PageMaker: Macintosh Version	$24.95

Programming/Technical

Assembly Language Quick Reference	$ 7.95
C Programmer's Toolkit	$39.95
C Programming Guide, 3rd Edition	$24.95
C Quick Reference	$ 7.95
DOS and BIOS Functions Quick Reference	$ 7.95
DOS Programmer's Reference, 2nd Edition	$29.95
Oracle Programmer's Guide	$24.95
Power Graphics Programming	$24.95
QuickBASIC Advanced Techniques	$22.95
QuickBASIC Programmer's Toolkit	$39.95
QuickBASIC Quick Reference	$ 7.95
QuickPascal Programming	$22.95
SQL Programmer's Guide	$29.95
Turbo C Programming	$22.95
Turbo Pascal Advanced Techniques	$22.95
Turbo Pascal Programmer's Toolkit	$39.95
Turbo Pascal Quick Reference	$ 7.95
UNIX Programmer's Quick Reference	$ 7.95
Using Assembly Language, 2nd Edition	$29.95
Using BASIC	$19.95
Using C	$27.95
Using QuickBASIC 4	$24.95
Using Turbo Pascal	$29.95

For More Information, Call Toll Free!
1-800-428-5331

All prices and titles subject to change without notice. Non-U.S. prices may be higher. Printed in the U.S.A.

Upgrading and Repairing PCs
by Scott Mueller

The ultimate resource for personal computer upgrade, repair, maintenance, and troubleshooting! This comprehensive text covers all types of IBM computers and compatibles—from the original PC to the new PS/2 models. Defines your system components and provides solutions to common PC problems.

Order #882
$29.95 USA
0-88022-395-2, 750 pp.

Using Computers in Business
by Joel Shore

This text covers all aspects of business computerization, including a thorough analysis of benefits, costs, alternatives, and common problems. Also discusses how to budget for computerization, how to shop for the right hardware and software, and how to allow for expansions and upgrades.

Order #1020
$22.95 USA
0-88022-470-3, 450 pp.

Using DOS
Developed by Que Corporation

The most helpful DOS book available! Que's *Using DOS* teaches the essential commands and functions of DOS Versions 3 and 4—in an easy-to-understand format that helps users manage and organize their files effectively. Includes a handy **Command Reference**.

Order #1035
$22.95 USA
0-88022-497-5, 550 pp.

Introduction to Business Software
Developed by Que Corporation

A useful introduction to the best-selling IBM-compatible software programs. Discusses the basics and benefits of each application.

Order #1034
$14.95 USA
0-88022-496-7, 400 pp.

Que Order Line: **1-800-428-5331**

All prices subject to change without notice. Prices
and charges are for domestic orders only.
Non-U.S. prices might be higher.

1-2-3 Release 2.2 QuickStart
Developed by Que Corporation

Que's award-winning graphics approach makes it easy for you to get up and running with 1-2-3 Release 2.2! More than 200 pages of illustrations explaining the program's worksheets, reports, graphs, databases, and macros. Also covers Release 2.01.

Order #1041
$19.95 USA
0-88022-502-5, 450 pp.

MS-DOS QuickStart
Developed by Que Corporation

The visual approach to learning MS-DOS! Illustrations help readers become familiar with their operating systems. Perfect for all beginning users of DOS—through Version 4.0!

Order #872
$21.95 USA
0-88022-388-X, 350 pp.

dBASE IV QuickStart
Developed by Que Corporation

The fast way to teach yourself dBASE IV! Follows Que's award-winning, visual approach to learning. Two-page illustrations show you how to create common dBASE applications, including address lists and mailing labels.

Order #873
$19.95 USA
0-88022-389-8, 400 pp.

WordPerfect QuickStart
Developed by Que Corporation

WordPerfect QuickStart **shows** how to produce common documents and leads users step-by-step through the most essential features of WordPerfect 5.

Order #871
$19.95 USA
0-88022-387-1, 350 pp.

Que Order Line: **1-800-428-5331**
All prices subject to change without notice. Prices and charges are for domestic orders only.
Non-U.S. prices might be higher.

Using Excel: IBM Version

by Ron Person and Mary Campbell

Que's *Using Excel: IBM Version* helps users master Excel. Includes **Quick Start** tutorials plus tips and tricks to help improve efficiency and troubleshoot problems. Also includes a special section for 1-2-3 users making the switch to Excel.

Order #87
$29.95 USA
0-88022-284-0, 804 pp.

MS-DOS User's Guide, Special Edition

Developed by Que Corporation

A special edition of Que's best-selling book on MS-DOS, updated to provide the most comprehensive DOS coverage available. Includes expanded EDLIN coverage, plus **Quick Start** tutorials and a complete **Command Reference** for DOS Versions 3 and 4. A **must** for MS-DOS users at all levels!

Order #1048
$29.95 USA
0-88022-505-X, 900 pp.

Using Professional Write

by Katherine Murray

Quick Start tutorials introduce word processing basics and helps you progress to advanced skills with this top-selling executive word processing program. Also contains a section on macros, easy-to-follow examples and printing tips. Using Professional Write with other programs also is discussed.

Order #1027
$22.95 USA
0-88022-490-8, 400 pp.

Using SmartWare II

by Andrew N. Schwartz

A new book for the new version of this popular integrated program! All of the program's modules are covered in depth, as are Smart's advanced integrated applications and Project Processing.

Order #939
$29.95 USA
0-88022-405-3, 650 pp.

Que Order Line: **1-800-428-5331**

All prices subject to change without notice. Prices and charges are for domestic orders only. Non-U.S. prices might be higher.

Using 1-2-3 Release 2.2, Special Edition
Developed by Que Corporation

Learn professional spreadsheet techniques from the world's leading 1-2-3 books! This comprehensive text leads you from worksheet basics to advanced 1-2-3 operations. Includes Allways coverage, a Troubleshooting section, a Command Reference, and a tear-out 1-2-3 Menu Map. The most complete resource available for Release 2.01 and Release 2.2!

Order #1040
$27.95 USA
0-88022-501-7, 850 pp.

Using Harvard Graphics
by Steve Sagman and Jane Graver Sandlar

An excellent introduction to presentation graphics! This well-written text presents both program basics and presentation fundamentals to create bar, pie, line, and other types of informative graphs. Includes hundreds of samples!

Order #941
$24.95 USA
0-88022-407-X, 550 pp.

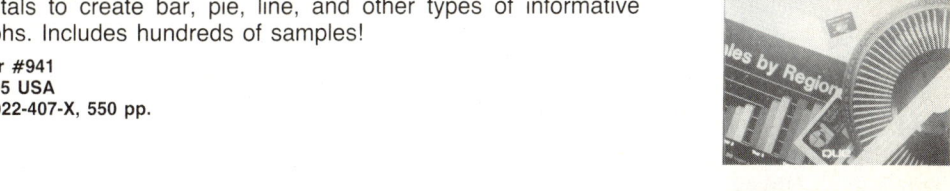

dBASE IV Handbook, 3rd Edition
by George T. Chou, Ph.D.

A complete introduction to dBASE IV functions! Beginning users will progress systematically from basic database concepts to advanced dBASE features, and experienced dBASE users will appreciate the information on the new features of dBASE IV. Includes Quick Start tutorials.

Order #852
$23.95 USA
0-88022-380-4, 785 pp.

Using WordPerfect 5
by Charles O. Stewart III, et al.

The #1 best-selling word processing book! Introduces WordPerfect basics and helps readers learn to use macros, styles, and other advanced features. Also includes **Quick Start** tutorials, a tear-out command reference card, and an introduction to WordPerfect 5 for 4.2 users.

Order #843
$27.95 USA
0-88022-351-0, 867 pp.

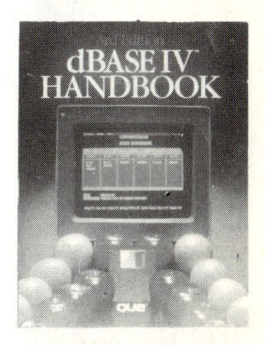

Que Order Line: **1-800-428-5331**

All prices subject to change without notice. Prices and charges are for domestic orders only. Non-U.S. prices might be higher.

Using Microsoft Word 5: IBM Version
by Bryan Pfaffenberger

The definitive guide to new Microsoft Word 5! A series of examples and applications takes readers step-by-step from Word basics to the advanced features of Word 5.

Order #943
$22.95 USA
0-88022-409-6, 550 pp.

Using Ventura Publisher, 2nd Edition
by Diane Burns, S. Venit & Linda Mercer

Highlights the features of Ventura Publisher 2.0—including the Professional Extension. Provides numerous successful design concepts.

Order #940
$24.95 USA
0-88022-406-1, 621 pp.

Using PageMaker: IBM Version, 2nd Edition
by S. Venit and Diane Burns

Updated for the IBM-compatible version of PageMaker 3.0, this popular text now covers the cover separations capabilities of the program. An ideal introductory text, *Using PageMaker* presents both program basics and basic design concepts. Soon you'll be producing professional publications—just like the dozens of detailed examples presented in this book!

Order #953
$24.95 USA
0-88022-415-0

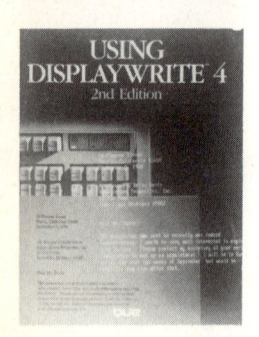

Using DisplayWrite 4, 2nd Edition
by David Busch

Features **Quick Start** lessons and timesaving shortcuts. Also discusses how to use DisplayWrite 4 in the OS/2 environment.

Order #975
$24.95 USA
0-88022-445-2, 438 pp.

Que Order Line: **1-800-428-5331**

All prices subject to change without notice. Prices and charges are for domestic orders only. Non-U.S. prices might be higher.